Cases and Materials on Federal Constitutional Law

Volume VI

The First Amendment

CAROLINA ACADEMIC PRESS
MODULAR CASEBOOK SERIES

FEDERAL CONSTITUTIONAL LAW, VOLUME I
Introduction to Interpretive Methods and the
Federal Judicial Power, Third Edition
Scott W. Gaylord, Christopher R. Green, and Lee J. Strang

FEDERAL CONSTITUTIONAL LAW, VOLUME II
Federal Executive Power and the Separation of Powers, Third Edition
Scott W. Gaylord, Christopher R. Green, and Lee J. Strang

FEDERAL CONSTITUTIONAL LAW, VOLUME III
Introduction to the Federal Legislative Power, Third Edition (forthcoming)
Scott W. Gaylord, Christopher R. Green, and Lee J. Strang

FEDERAL CONSTITUTIONAL LAW, VOLUME IV
Federalism Limitations on State and Federal Power, Second Edition
Scott W. Gaylord, Christopher R. Green, and Lee J. Strang

FEDERAL CONSTITUTIONAL LAW, VOLUME V
The Fourteenth Amendment, Second Edition
Scott W. Gaylord, Christopher R. Green, and Lee J. Strang

FEDERAL CONSTITUTIONAL LAW, VOLUME VI
The First Amendment, Second Edition
Scott W. Gaylord, Christopher R. Green, and Lee J. Strang

Cases and Materials on Federal Constitutional Law

Volume VI

The First Amendment

SECOND EDITION

Scott W. Gaylord

Christopher R. Green

Lee J. Strang

CAROLINA ACADEMIC PRESS

Durham, North Carolina

ISBN   978-1-5310-1677-7
eISBN   978-1-5310-1678-4
LCCN   2020947463

Carolina Academic Press
700 Kent Street
Durham, North Carolina 27701
Telephone (919) 489-7486
Fax (919) 493-5668
www.cap-press.com

Printed in the United States of America

To Pamela and our family and to all the families who serve and sacrifice to protect the Constitution.
S.W.G.

To Bonnie and Justice John Marshall Harlan I.
C.R.G.

To Elizabeth and Saint Thomas Aquinas.
L.J.S.

Contents

Introduction to the Modular Casebook Series

By now you have realized that the course materials assigned by your instructor have a very different form than traditional casebooks. The *Modular Casebook Series* is intentionally designed to break the mold. Course materials consist of one or more separate volumes selected from among a larger set of volumes. Each volume is relatively short so that an instructor may "mix and match" a suitable number of volumes for a course of varying length and focus.

Each volume is also designed to serve an instructional purpose rather than as a treatise; as a result, the *Modular Casebook Series* is published in soft cover. Publication of the separate volumes in soft cover also permits course materials to be revised more easily so that they will incorporate recent developments. Moreover, by purchasing only the assigned volumes for a given course, students are likely to recognize significant savings over the cost of a traditional casebook.

Traditional casebooks are often massive tomes, frequently exceeding 1,000 or even 1,500 pages. Traditional casebooks are lengthy because they attempt to cover the entire breadth of material that *might* be useful to an instructor for a two-semester course of five or six credits. Even with six credits, different instructors will cover different portions of a traditional casebook within the time available. As a consequence, traditional casebooks include a range of materials that may leave hundreds of unexplored pages in any particular six-credit class. Especially for a student in a three- or four credit-course, such a book is hardly an efficient means of delivering the needed materials. Students purchase much more book than they need, at great expense. And students carry large, heavy books for months at a time.

Traditional casebooks are usually hard cover publications. It seems as though they are constructed to last as a reference work throughout decades of practice. In fact, as the presence of annual supplements to casebooks makes clear, portions of casebooks become obsolete shortly after publication. Treatises and hornbooks are designed to serve as reference works; casebooks serve a different purpose. Once again, the traditional format of casebooks seems to impose significant added costs on students for little reason.

The form of traditional casebooks increases the probability that the content will become obsolete shortly after publication. The publication of lengthy texts in hardcover produces substantial delay between the time the author completes the final draft and the time the book reaches the hands of students. In addition, the broader scope of material addressed in a 1,600 page text means that portions of the text are more likely to be superseded by later developments than any particular narrowly-tailored volume in the *Modular Casebook Series*. Because individual volumes in the *Modular Casebook Series* may be revised without requiring revision of other volumes, the materials for any particular course will be less likely to require supplementation.

Most importantly, the cases and accompanying exercises in the *Modular Casebook Series* provide students with the opportunity to learn and deploy the standard arguments in the various subject matters of constitutional law. Each case is edited to emphasize the key arguments made by the Court and justices. For instance, in many older cases, headings were added to note a new or related argument. Furthermore, the exercises following each case focus on identifying and critiquing the Court's and justices' arguments. The exercises also form the basis for rich class discussion. All of this introduces students to the most important facet of constitutional law: the deployment of standard arguments in each doctrinal context and across constitutional law doctrines.

We hope you enjoy this innovative approach to course materials.

Acknowledgments

We thank Tom Odom for proposing and initiating the Modular Casebook Series, and for inviting us to participate in the Series, and, for research leave and support, to the Elon University School of Law, the Jamie Lloyd Whitten Chair of Law and Government Endowment at the University of Mississippi School of Law, and the University of Toledo College of Law. Without our wives' and children's loving support, this project would not have been completed.

Preface to the Second Edition

Technological improvements permit the compilation of resources in a manner unthinkable when we were law students. Materials that permit further examination of assigned reading can be delivered in a cost-effective manner and in a format more likely to be useful in practice than reams of photocopies.

With regard to assigned reading, there is no good reason to burden students with stacks of hand-outs or expensive annual supplements. Publication through the *Modular Casebook Series* ensures that even very recent developments may be incorporated prior to publication. Moreover, if important cases are decided after publication of the latest edition of a volume, they will be included on the series website www.federalconstitutionallaw.com. Cases and materials that shed additional light on matter in the hard-copy casebook are also included on the website.

We welcome comments from readers so that we may make further improvements in the next edition of this publication.

Scott W. Gaylord
Christopher R. Green
Lee J. Strang

Technical Note from the Editors

The cases and other materials excerpted in this Volume have been edited in an effort to enhance readability. Citations of multiple cases for a single proposition have been shortened in many places to reference only one or two prominent authorities. In some places, archaic language or spelling has been revised. Headings were added to some of the longer decisions to permit ease of reference to various parts of the opinion. Such headings may also assist the reader in identifying a transition from one point to another.

Cases have been edited to a suitable length. In order to achieve that result, many interesting but tangential points have been omitted. The length of some opinions also hindered the inclusion of excerpts from concurring or dissenting opinions. Where such opinions have been omitted, it is noted in the text.

In editing these cases, we have not indicated the portions of cases we deleted unless such deletion with the absence of ellipses would have been misleading. However, any time we inserted material into a case, we indicated the insertion with the use of brackets.

Scott W. Gaylord
Christopher R. Green
Lee J. Strang

Introduction to Volume 6

The First Amendment was ratified in 1791 as part of what we know today as the Bill of Rights. This Volume addresses constitutional limitations imposed upon the federal government (and states) by the Free Speech, Free Exercise, and Establishment Clauses.

A. The Free Speech Clause

The "freedom of speech" clause is one of the most well-known and prized provisions of the United States Constitution. In the nearly century of modern treatment of the Free Speech Clause, the Supreme Court has generated one of, if not the most complex set of constitutional law doctrines you will cover in your introductory constitutional law courses. This area of law has numerous tests, doctrines, exceptions, and doctrinal categories. At the same time, the Supreme has successfully kept its free speech case law coherent. This complex body of law is the subject of **Chapter 1**.

B. The Religion Clause(s)

1. Free Exercise

The Free Exercise Clause, by contrast, has not generated significant complexity. Instead, this area of the law is defined by the Supreme Court's important, and controversial, decision, *Employment Division v. Smith*, 494 U.S. 873 (1990). There, the Supreme Court ruled that the Free Exercise Clause provided relatively modest protection to the free exercise of religion. The Free Exercise Clause is the subject of **Chapter 2**.

2. Establishment

The Establishment Clause has created one of the most contentious areas of American constitutional law and, partly as a consequence, the case law that you will review in **Chapter 3** is unclear, to put it charitably. Like the Free Exercise Clause, this area of law also has a seminal case, *Everson v. Board of Education*, 330 U.S. 1 (1947).

The Constitution of the United States

We the People of the United States, in Order to form a more perfect Union, establish Justice, insure domestic Tranquility, provide for the common defence, promote the general Welfare, and secure the Blessings of Liberty to ourselves and our Posterity, do ordain and establish this Constitution for the United States of America.

Article I

Section 1. All legislative Powers herein granted shall be vested in a Congress of the United States, which shall consist of a Senate and House of Representatives.

Section 2. The House of Representatives shall be composed of Members chosen every second Year by the People of the several States, and the Electors in each State shall have the Qualifications requisite for Electors of the most numerous Branch of the State Legislature.

No person shall be a Representative who shall not have attained to the Age of twenty five Years, and been seven Years a Citizen of the United States, and who shall not, when elected, be an Inhabitant of that State in which he shall be chosen.

Representatives and direct Taxes shall be apportioned among the several States which may be included within this Union, according to their respective Numbers, which shall be determined by adding to the whole Number of free Persons, including those bound to Service for a Term of Years, and excluding Indians not taxed, three fifths of all other Persons. The actual Enumeration shall be made within three Years after the first Meeting of the Congress of the United States, and within every subsequent Term of ten Years, in such Manner as they shall by Law direct. The Number of Representatives shall not exceed one for every thirty Thousand, but each State shall have at Least one Representative; and until such enumeration shall be made, the State of New Hampshire shall be entitled to chuse three, Massachusetts eight, Rhode-Island and Providence Plantations one, Connecticut five, New-York six, New Jersey four, Pennsylvania eight, Delaware one, Maryland six, Virginia ten, North Carolina five, South Carolina five, and Georgia three.

When vacancies happen in the Representation from any State, the Executive Authority thereof shall issue Writs of Election to fill such Vacancies.

The House of Representatives shall chuse their Speaker and other Officers; and shall have the sole Power of Impeachment.

Section 3. The Senate of the United States shall be composed of two Senators from each State, chosen by the Legislature thereof, for six Years; and each Senator shall have one Vote.

Immediately after they shall be assembled in Consequence of the first Election, they shall be divided as equally as may be into three Classes. The Seats of the Senators of the first Class shall be vacated at the Expiration of the second Year, of the second Class at the Expiration of the fourth Year, and of the third Class at the Expiration of the sixth Year, so that one third may be chosen every second Year; and if Vacancies happen by Resignation, or otherwise, during the Recess of the Legislature of any

State, the Executive thereof may make temporary Appointments until the next Meeting of the Legislature, which shall then fill such Vacancies.

No Person shall be a Senator who shall not have attained to the Age of thirty Years, and been nine Years a Citizen of the United States, and who shall not, when elected, be an Inhabitant of that State for which he shall be chosen.

The Vice President of the United States shall be President of the Senate, but shall have no Vote, unless they be equally divided.

The Senate shall chuse their other Officers, and also a President pro tempore, in the Absence of the Vice President, or when he shall exercise the Office of President of the United States.

The Senate shall have the sole Power to try all Impeachments. When sitting for that Purpose, they shall be on Oath or Affirmation. When the President of the United States is tried, the Chief Justice shall preside: and no Person shall be convicted without the Concurrence of two thirds of the Members present.

Judgment in Cases of Impeachment shall not extend further than to removal from Office, and disqualification to hold and enjoy any Office of honor, Trust or Profit under the United States: but the Party convicted shall nevertheless be liable and subject to Indictment, Trial, Judgment and Punishment, according to Law.

Section 4. The Times, Places and Manner of holding Elections for Senators and Representatives, shall be prescribed in each State by the Legislature thereof; but the Congress may at any time by Law make or alter such Regulations, except as to the Places of chusing Senators.

The Congress shall assemble at least once in every Year, and such Meeting shall be on the first Monday in December, unless they shall by Law appoint a different Day.

Section 5. Each House shall be the Judge of the Elections, Returns and Qualifications of its own Members, and a Majority of each shall constitute a Quorum to do Business; but a smaller Number may adjourn from day to day, and may be authorized to compel the Attendance of absent Members, in such Manner, and under such Penalties as each House may provide.

Each House may determine the Rules of its Proceedings, punish its Members for disorderly Behaviour, and, with the Concurrence of two thirds, expel a Member.

Each House shall keep a Journal of its Proceedings, and from time to time publish the same, excepting such Parts as may in their Judgment require Secrecy; and the Yeas and Nays of the Members of either House on any question shall, at the Desire of one fifth of those Present, be entered on the Journal.

Section 6. The Senators and Representatives shall receive a Compensation for their Services, to be ascertained by Law, and paid out of the Treasury of the United States. They shall in all Cases, except Treason, Felony and Breach of the Peace, be privileged from Arrest during their Attendance at the Session of their respective Houses, and in going to and returning from the same; and for any Speech or Debate in either House, they shall not be questioned in any other Place.

No Senator or Representative shall, during the Time for which he was elected, be appointed to any civil Office under the Authority of the United States, which shall have been created, or the Emoluments whereof shall have been encreased during such time; and no Person holding any Office under the United States, shall be a Member of either House during his Continuance in Office.

Section 7. All Bills for raising Revenue shall originate in the House of Representatives; but the Senate may propose or concur with Amendments as on other Bills.

Every Bill which shall have passed the House of Representatives and the Senate, shall, before it become a Law, be presented to the President of the United States; If he approve he shall sign it, but if not he shall return it, with his Objections to that House in which it shall have originated, who shall enter the Objections at large on their Journal, and proceed to reconsider it. If after such Reconsideration two thirds of that House shall agree to pass the Bill, it shall be sent, together with the Objections, to the other House, by which it shall likewise be reconsidered, and if approved by two thirds of that House, it shall become a Law. But in all such Cases the Votes of both Houses shall be determined by yeas and Nays, and the Names of the Persons voting for and against the Bill shall be entered on the Journal of each House respectively. If any Bill shall not be returned by the President within ten days (Sundays excepted) after it shall have been presented to him, the Same shall be a Law, in like Manner as if he had signed it, unless the Congress by their Adjournment prevent its Return in which Case it shall not be a Law.

Every Order, Resolution, or Vote to which the Concurrence of the Senate and House of Representatives may be necessary (except on a question of Adjournment) shall be presented to the President of the United States; and before the Same shall take Effect, shall be approved by him, or being disapproved by him, shall be repassed by two thirds of the Senate and House of Representatives, according to the Rules and Limitations prescribed in the Case of a Bill.

Section 8. The Congress shall have Power To lay and collect Taxes, Duties, Imposts and Excises, to pay the Debts and provide for the common Defence and general Welfare of the United States; but all Duties, Imposts and Excises shall be uniform throughout the United States;

To borrow Money on the credit of the United States;

To regulate Commerce with foreign Nations, and among the several States, and with the Indian Tribes;

To establish an uniform Rule of Naturalization, and uniform Laws on the subject of Bankruptcies throughout the United States;

To coin Money, regulate the Value thereof, and foreign Coin, and fix the Standard of Weights and Measures;

To provide for the Punishment of counterfeiting the Securities and current Coin of the United States;

To establish Post Offices and post Roads;

To promote the Progress of Science and useful Arts, by securing for limited Times to Authors and Inventors the exclusive Right to their respective Writings and Discoveries;

To constitute Tribunals inferior to the supreme Court;

To define and punish Piracies and Felonies committed on the high Seas, and Offences against the Law of Nations;

To declare War, grant Letters of Marque and Reprisal, and make Rules concerning Captures on Land and Water;

To raise and support Armies, but no Appropriation of Money to that Use shall be for a longer Term than two Years;

To provide and maintain a Navy;

To make Rules for the Government and Regulation of the land and naval Forces;

To provide for calling forth the Militia to execute the Laws of the Union, suppress Insurrections and repel Invasions;

To provide for organizing, arming, and disciplining, the Militia, and for governing such Part of them as may be employed in the Service of the United States, reserving to the States respectively, the Appointment of the Officers, and the Authority of training the Militia according to the discipline prescribed by Congress;

To exercise exclusive Legislation in all Cases whatsoever, over such District (not exceeding ten Miles square) as may, by Cession of particular States, and the Acceptance of Congress, become the Seat of the Government of the United States, and to exercise like Authority over all Places purchased by the Consent of the Legislature of the State in which the Same shall be, for the Erection of Forts, Magazines, Arsenals, dock-Yards, and other needful Buildings;—And

To make all Laws which shall be necessary and proper for carrying into Execution the foregoing Powers, and all other Powers vested by this Constitution in the Government of the United States, or in any Department or Officer thereof.

Section 9. The Migration or Importation of such Persons as any of the States now existing shall think proper to admit, shall not be prohibited by the Congress prior to the Year one thousand eight hundred and eight, but a Tax or duty may be imposed on such Importation, not exceeding ten dollars for each Person.

The Privilege of the Writ of Habeas Corpus shall not be suspended, unless when in Cases of Rebellion or Invasion the public Safety may require it.

No Bill of Attainder or ex post facto Law shall be passed.

No Capitation, or other direct, Tax shall be laid, unless in Proportion to the Census or Enumeration herein before directed to be taken.

No Tax or Duty shall be laid on Articles exported from any State.

No Preference shall be given by any Regulation of Commerce or Revenue to the Ports of one State over those of another; nor shall Vessels bound to, or from, one State, be obliged to enter, clear, or pay Duties in another.

No Money shall be drawn from the Treasury, but in Consequence of Appropriations made by Law; and a regular Statement and Account of the Receipts and Expenditures of all public Money shall be published from time to time.

No Title of Nobility shall be granted by the United States: And no Person holding any Office of Profit or Trust under them, shall, without the Consent of the Congress, accept of any present, Emolument, Office, or Title, of any kind whatever, from any King, Prince, or foreign State.

Section 10. No State shall enter into any Treaty, Alliance, or Confederation; grant Letters of Marque and Reprisal; coin Money; emit Bills of Credit; make any Thing but gold and silver Coin a Tender in Payment of Debts; pass any Bill of Attainder, ex post facto Law, or Law impairing the Obligation of Contracts, or grant any Title of Nobility.

No State shall, without the Consent of the Congress, lay any Imposts or Duties on Imports or Exports, except what may be absolutely necessary for executing it's inspection Laws: and the net Produce of all Duties and Imposts, laid by any State on Imports or Exports, shall be for the Use of the Treasury of the United States; and all such Laws shall be subject to the Revision and Control of the Congress.

No State shall, without the Consent of Congress, lay any Duty of Tonnage, keep Troops, or Ships of War in time of Peace, enter into any Agreement or Compact with another State, or with a foreign Power, or engage in War, unless actually invaded, or in such imminent Danger as will not admit of delay.

Article II

Section 1. The executive Power shall be vested in a President of the United States of America. He shall hold his Office during the Term of four Years, and, together with the Vice President, chosen for the same Term, be elected as follows

Each State shall appoint, in such Manner as the Legislature thereof may direct, a Number of Electors, equal to the whole Number of Senators and Representatives to which the State may be entitled in the Congress: but no Senator or Representative, or Person holding an Office of Trust or Profit under the United States, shall be appointed an Elector.

The Electors shall meet in their respective States, and vote by Ballot for two Persons, of whom one at least shall not be an Inhabitant of the same State with themselves. And they shall make a List of all the Persons voted for, and of the Number of Votes for each; which List they shall sign and certify, and transmit sealed to the Seat of the Government of the United States, directed to the President of the Senate. The President of the Senate shall, in the Presence of the Senate and House of Representatives, open all the Certificates, and the Votes shall then be counted. The Person having the greatest Number of Votes shall be the President, if such Number be a Majority of the whole Number of Electors appointed; and if there be more than one who have such Majority, and have an equal Number of Votes, then the House of Representatives shall immediately chuse by Ballot one of them for President; and if no Person have a Majority, then from the five highest on the List the said House shall in like Manner chuse the

President. But in chusing the President, the Votes shall be taken by States, the Representation from each State having one Vote; A quorum for this Purpose shall consist of a Member or Members from two thirds of the States, and a Majority of all the States shall be necessary to a Choice. In every Case, after the Choice of the President, the Person having the greatest Number of Votes of the Electors shall be the Vice President. But if there should remain two or more who have equal Votes, the Senate shall chuse from them by Ballot the Vice President.

The Congress may determine the Time of chusing the Electors, and the Day on which they shall give their Votes; which Day shall be the same throughout the United States.

No Person except a natural born Citizen, or a Citizen of the United States, at the time of the Adoption of this Constitution, shall be eligible to the Office of President; neither shall any Person be eligible to that Office who shall not have attained to the Age of thirty five Years, and been fourteen Years a Resident within the United States.

In the Case of the Removal of the President from Office, or of his Death, Resignation, or Inability to discharge the Powers and Duties of the said Office, the Same shall devolve on the Vice President, and the Congress may by Law provide for the Case of Removal, Death, Resignation or Inability, both of the President and Vice President, declaring what Officer shall then act as President, and such Officer shall act accordingly, until the Disability be removed, or a President shall be elected.

The President shall, at stated Times, receive for his Services, a Compensation, which shall neither be encreased nor diminished during the Period for which he shall have been elected, and he shall not receive within that Period any other Emolument from the United States, or any of them.

Before he enter on the Execution of his Office, he shall take the following Oath or Affirmation:—"I do solemnly swear (or affirm) that I will faithfully execute the Office of the President of the United States, and will to the best of my Ability, preserve, protect and defend the Constitution of the United States."

Section 2. The President shall be the Commander in Chief of the Army and Navy of the United States, and of the Militia of the several States, when called into the actual service of the United States; he may require the Opinion, in writing, of the principal Officer in each of the executive Departments, upon any Subject relating to the Duties of their respective Offices, and he shall have Power to grant Reprieves and Pardons for Offenses against the United States, except in Cases of Impeachment.

He shall have Power, by and with the Advice and Consent of the Senate, to make Treaties, provided two thirds of the Senators present concur; and he shall nominate, and by and with the Advice and Consent of the Senate, shall appoint Ambassadors, other public Ministers and Consuls, Judges of the supreme Court, and all other Officers of the United States, whose Appointments are not herein otherwise provided for, and which shall be established by Law but the Congress may by Law vest the Appointment of such inferior Officers, as they think proper, in the President alone, in the Courts of Law, or in the Heads of Departments.

The President shall have Power to fill up all Vacancies that may happen during the Recess of the Senate, by granting Commissions which shall expire at the End of their next Session.

Section 3. He shall from time to time give to the Congress Information of the State of the Union, and recommend to their Consideration such Measures as he shall judge necessary and expedient; he may, on extraordinary Occasions, convene both Houses, or either of them, and in Case of Disagreement between them, with Respect to the Time of Adjournment, he may adjourn them to such Time as he shall think proper; he shall receive Ambassadors and other public Ministers; he shall take Care that the Laws be faithfully executed, and shall Commission all the Officers of the United States.

Section 4. The President, Vice President and all civil Officers of the United States, shall be removed from Office on Impeachment for, and Conviction of, Treason, Bribery, or other high Crimes and Misdemeanors.

Article III

Section 1. The judicial Power of the United States, shall be vested in one supreme Court, and in such inferior Courts as the Congress may from time to time ordain and establish. The Judges, both of the supreme and inferior Courts, shall hold their Offices during good Behaviour, and shall, at stated Times, receive for their Services, a Compensation, which shall not be diminished during their Continuance in Office.

Section 2. The judicial Power shall extend to all Cases, in Law and Equity, arising under this Constitution, the Laws of the United States, and Treaties made, or which shall be made, under their Authority;—to all Cases affecting Ambassadors, other public Ministers and Consuls;—to all Cases of admiralty and maritime Jurisdiction;—to Controversies to which the United States shall be a Party;—to Controversies between two or more States;—between a State and Citizens of another State;—between Citizens of different States;—between Citizens of the same State claiming Lands under Grants of different States, and between a State, or the Citizens thereof, and foreign States, Citizens or Subjects.

In all cases affecting Ambassadors, other public Ministers and Consuls, and those in which a State shall be a Party, the supreme Court shall have original Jurisdiction. In all the other Cases before mentioned, the supreme Court shall have appellate Jurisdiction, both as to Law and Fact, with such Exceptions, and under such Regulations as the Congress shall make.

The Trial of all Crimes, except in Cases of Impeachment, shall be by Jury; and such Trial shall be held in the State where the said Crimes shall have been committed; but when not committed within any State, the Trial shall be at such Place or Places as the Congress may by Law have directed.

Section 3. Treason against the United States, shall consist only in levying War against them, or in adhering to their Enemies, giving them Aid or Comfort. No Person shall be convicted of Treason unless on the Testimony of two Witnesses to the same overt Act, or on Confession in open Court.

The Congress shall have Power to declare the Punishment of Treason, but no Attainder of Treason shall work Corruption of Blood, or Forfeiture except during the Life of the Person attainted.

Article IV

Section 1. Full Faith and Credit shall be given in each State to the public Acts, Records, and judicial Proceedings of every other State. And the Congress may by general Laws prescribe the Manner in which such Acts, Records and Proceedings shall be proved, and the Effect thereof.

Section 2. The Citizens of each State shall be entitled to all Privileges and Immunities of Citizens in the several States.

A Person charged in any State with Treason, Felony, or other Crime, who shall flee from Justice, and be found in another State, shall on Demand of the executive Authority of the State from which he fled, be delivered up, to be removed to the State having Jurisdiction of the Crime.

No Person held to Service or Labour in one State, under the Laws thereof, escaping into another, shall, in Consequence of any Law or Regulation therein, be discharged from such Service or Labour, but shall be delivered up on Claim of the Party to whom such Service or Labour may be due.

Section 3. New States may be admitted by the Congress into this Union; but no new State shall be formed or erected within the Jurisdiction of any other State; nor any State be formed by the Junction of two or more States, or Parts of States, without the Consent of the Legislatures of the States concerned as well as of the Congress.

The Congress shall have Power to dispose of and make all needful Rules and Regulations respecting the Territory or other Property belonging to the United States; and nothing in this Constitution shall be so construed to Prejudice any Claims of the United States, or of any particular State.

Section 4. The United States shall guarantee to every State in this Union a Republican Form of Government, and shall protect each of them against Invasion; and on Application of the Legislature, or of the Executive (when the Legislature cannot be convened) against domestic Violence.

Article V

The Congress, whenever two thirds of both Houses shall deem it necessary, shall propose Amendments to this Constitution, or, on the Application of the Legislatures of two thirds of the several States, shall call a Convention for proposing Amendments, which, in either Case, shall be valid to all Intents and Purposes, as Part of this Constitution, when ratified by the Legislatures of three fourths of the several States, or by Conventions in three fourths thereof, as the one or the other Mode of Ratification may be proposed by the Congress; provided that no Amendment which may be made prior to the Year One thousand eight hundred and eight shall in any Manner affect the first and fourth Clauses in the Ninth Section of the first Article; and that no State, without its Consent, shall be deprived of its equal Suffrage in the Senate.

Article VI

All Debts contracted and Engagements entered into, before the adoption of this Constitution, shall be as valid against the United States under this Constitution, as under the Confederation.

This Constitution, and the Laws of the United States which shall be made in Pursuance thereof; and all Treaties made, or which shall be made, under the Authority of the United States, shall be the supreme Law of the Land; and the Judges in every State shall be bound thereby, any Thing in the Constitution or Laws of any State to the Contrary notwithstanding.

The Senators and Representatives before mentioned, and the members of the several State Legislatures, and all executive and judicial Officers, both of the United States and of the several States, shall be bound by Oath or Affirmation, to support this Constitution; but no religious Test shall ever be required as a Qualification to any Office or public Trust under the United States.

Article VII

The Ratification of the Conventions of nine States, shall be sufficient for the Establishment of this Constitution between the States so ratifying the Same.

Go. Washington — Presidt.
And deputy from Virginia

Delaware
Geo: Read
Cunning Bedford jun
John Dickinson
Richard Bassett
Jaco: Broom

Maryland
James McHenry
Dan of St. Thos. Jenifer
Danl. Carroll
Virginia
John Blair —
James Madison Jr.

North Carolina
Wm: Blount
Richd. Dobbs Spaight.
Hu Williamson

New Hampshire
John Langdon
Nicholas Gilman
Massachusetts
Nathaniel Gorham
Rufus King

Connecticut
Wm. Saml. Johnson
Roger Sherman

New York
Alexander Hamilton

New Jersey
Wil: Livingston
David Brearley
Wm. Paterson
Jona: Dayton

South Carolina
J. Rutledge
Charles Cotesworth Pinckney
Pierce Butler.

Georgia
William Few
Abr Baldwin

Pennsylvania
B Franklin
Thomas Mifflin
Robt. Morris
Geo. Clymer
Thos. Fitzsimons
Jared Ingersoll
James Wilson
Gouv Morris

The Bill of Rights

(1791)

Amendment I

Congress shall make no law respecting an establishment of religion, or prohibiting the free exercise thereof; or abridging the freedom of speech, or of the press; or the right of the people peaceably to assemble, and to petition the government for a redress of grievances.

Amendment II

A well regulated militia, being necessary to the security of a free state, the right of the people to keep and bear arms, shall not be infringed.

Amendment III

No soldier shall, in time of peace be quartered in any house, without the consent of the owner, nor in time of war, but in a manner to be prescribed by law.

Amendment IV

The right of the people to be secure in their persons, houses, papers, and effects, against unreasonable searches and seizures, shall not be violated, and no warrants shall issue, but upon probable cause, supported by oath or affirmation, and particularly describing the place to be searched, and the persons or things to be seized.

Amendment V

No person shall be held to answer for a capital, or otherwise infamous crime, unless on a presentment or indictment of a grand jury, except in cases arising in the land or naval forces, or in the militia, when in actual service in time of war or public danger; nor shall any person be subject for the same offense to be twice put in jeopardy of life or limb; nor shall be compelled in any criminal case to be a witness against himself, nor be deprived of life, liberty, or property, without due process of law; nor shall private property be taken for public use, without just compensation.

Amendment VI

In all criminal prosecutions, the accused shall enjoy the right to a speedy and public trial, by an impartial jury of the state and district wherein the crime shall have been committed, which district shall have been previously ascertained by law, and to be informed of the nature and cause of the accusation; to be confronted with the witnesses against him; to have compulsory process for obtaining witnesses in his favor, and to have the assistance of counsel for his defense.

Amendment VII

In suits at common law, where the value in controversy shall exceed twenty dollars, the right of trial by jury shall be preserved, and no fact tried by a jury, shall be otherwise reexamined in any court of the United States, then according to the rules of the common law.

Amendment VIII

Excessive bail shall not be required, nor excessive fines imposed, nor cruel and unusual punishments inflicted.

Amendment IX

The enumeration in the Constitution, of certain rights, shall not be construed to deny or disparage others retained by the people.

Amendment X

The powers not delegated to the United States by the Constitution, nor prohibited by it to the states, are reserved to the states respectively, or to the people.

Later Amendments

Amendment XI

(1795)

The judicial power of the United States shall not be construed to extend to any suit in law or equity, commenced or prosecuted against one of the United States by Citizens of another State, or by Citizens or Subjects of any Foreign State.

Amendment XII

(1804)

The Electors shall meet in their respective states and vote by ballot for President and Vice-President, one of whom, at least, shall not be an inhabitant of the same state with themselves; they shall name in their ballots the person voted for as President, and in distinct ballots the person voted for as Vice-President, and they shall make distinct lists of all persons voted for as President, and of all persons voted for as Vice-President, and of the number of votes for each, which lists they shall sign and certify, and transmit sealed to the seat of the government of the United States, directed to the President of the Senate;—The President of the Senate shall, in the presence of the Senate and House of Representatives, open all the certificates and the votes shall then be counted;—the person having the greatest number of votes for President, shall be the President, if such number be a majority of the whole number of Electors appointed; and if no person have such majority, then from the persons having the highest numbers not exceeding three on the list of those voted for as President, the House of Representatives shall choose immediately, by ballot, the President. But in choosing the President, the votes shall be taken by states, the representation from each state having one vote; a quorum for this purpose shall consist of a member or members from two-thirds of the states, and a majority of all the states shall be necessary to a choice. And if the House of Representatives shall not choose a President whenever the right of choice shall devolve upon them, before the fourth day of March next following, then the Vice-President shall act as President, as in the case of the death or other constitutional disability of the President. The person having the greatest number of votes as Vice-President, shall be the Vice-President, if such number be a majority of the whole number of Electors appointed, and if no person have a majority, then from the two highest numbers on the list, the Senate shall choose the Vice-President; a quorum for the purpose shall consist of two-thirds of the whole number of Senators, and a majority of the whole number shall be necessary to a choice. But no person constitutionally ineligible to the office of President shall be eligible to that of Vice-President of the United States.

Amendment XIII

(1865)

Section 1. Neither slavery nor involuntary servitude, except as a punishment for crime whereof the party shall have been duly convicted, shall exist within the United States, or any place subject to their jurisdiction.

Section 2. Congress shall have power to enforce this article by appropriate legislation.

Amendment XIV

(1868)

Section 1. All persons born or naturalized in the United States, and subject to the jurisdiction thereof, are citizens of the United States and of the State wherein they reside. No State shall make or enforce any law which shall abridge the privileges or immunities of citizens of the United States; nor shall any State deprive any person of life, liberty, or property, without due process of law; nor deny to any person within its jurisdiction the equal protection of the laws.

Section 2. Representatives shall be apportioned among the several States according to their respective numbers, counting the whole number of persons in each State, excluding Indians not taxed. But when the right to vote at any election for the choice of electors for President and Vice President of the United States, Representatives in Congress, the Executive and Judicial officers of a State, or the members of the Legislature thereof, is denied to any of the male inhabitants of such State, being twenty-one years of age, and citizens of the United States, or in any way abridged, except for participation in rebellion, or other crime, the basis of representation therein shall be reduced in the proportion which the number of such male citizens shall bear to the whole number of male citizens twenty-one years of age in such State.

Section 3. No person shall be a Senator or Representative in Congress, or elector of President and Vice President, or hold any office, civil or military, under the United States, or under any State, who, having previously taken an oath, as a member of

Congress, or as an officer of the United States, or as a member of any State legislature, or as an executive or judicial officer of any State, to support the Constitution of the United States, shall have engaged in insurrection or rebellion against the same, or given aid or comfort to the enemies thereof. But Congress may by a vote of two-thirds of each House, remove such disability.

Section 4. The validity of the public debt of the United States, authorized by law, including debts incurred for payment of pensions and bounties for services in suppressing insurrection or rebellion, shall not be questioned. But neither the United States nor any State shall assume or pay any debt or obligation incurred in aid of insurrection or rebellion against the United States, or any claim for the loss or emancipation of any slave; but all such debts, obligations and claims shall be held illegal and void.

Section 5. The Congress shall have power to enforce, by appropriate legislation, the provisions of this article.

Amendment XV

(1870)

Section 1. The right of citizens of the United States to vote shall not be denied or abridged by the United States or by any State on account of race, color, or previous condition of servitude.

Section 2. The Congress shall have power to enforce this article by appropriate legislation.

Amendment XVI

(1913)

The Congress shall have power to lay and collect taxes on incomes, from whatever source derived, without apportionment among the several States, and without regard to any census or enumeration.

Amendment XVII

(1913)

The Senate of the United States shall be composed of two Senators from each State, elected by the people thereof, for six years; and each Senator shall have one vote. The electors in each State shall have the qualifications requisite for electors of the most numerous branch of the State legislature.

When vacancies happen in the representation of any State in the Senate, the executive authority of such State shall issue writs of election to fill such vacancies: *Provided*, That the legislature of any State may empower the executive thereof to make temporary appointments until the people fill the vacancies by election as the legislature may direct.

This amendment shall not be so construed as to effect the election or term of any Senator chosen before it becomes valid as part of the Constitution.

Amendment XVIII

(1919)

Section 1. After one year from the ratification of this article the manufacture, sale, or transportation of intoxicating liquors within, the importation thereof into, or the exportation thereof from the United States and all territory subject to the jurisdiction thereof for beverage purposes is hereby prohibited.

Section 2. The Congress and the several States shall have concurrent power to enforce this article by appropriate legislation.

Section 3. This article shall be inoperative unless it shall have been ratified as an amendment to the Constitution by the legislatures of the several States, as provided in the Constitution, within seven years from the date of the submission hereof to the States by the Congress.

Amendment XIX

(1920)

The right of citizens of the United States to vote shall not be denied or abridged by the United States or by any State on account of sex.

Congress shall have power to enforce this article by appropriate legislation.

Amendment XX

(1933)

Section 1. The terms of the President and Vice President shall end at noon on the 20th day of January, and the terms of Senators and Representatives at noon on the 3d day of January, of the years in which such terms would have ended if this article had not been ratified; and the terms of their successors shall then begin.

Section 2. The Congress shall assemble at least once in every year, and such meeting shall begin at noon on the 3d day of January, unless they shall by law appoint a different day.

Section 3. If, at the time fixed for the beginning of the term of the President, the President elect shall have died, the Vice President elect shall become President. If a President shall not have been chosen before the time fixed for the beginning of his term, or if the President elect shall have failed to qualify, then the Vice President elect shall act as President until a President shall have qualified; and the Congress may by law provide for the case wherein neither a President elect nor a Vice President elect shall have qualified, declaring who shall then act as President, or the manner in which one who is to act shall be selected, and such person shall act accordingly until a President or Vice President shall have qualified.

Section 4. The Congress may by law provide for the case of the death of any of the persons from whom the House of Representatives may choose a President whenever the right of choice shall have devolved upon them, and for the case of the death of any of the persons from whom the Senate may choose a Vice President whenever the right of choice shall have devolved upon them.

Section 5. Sections 1 and 2 shall take effect on the 15th day of October following the ratification of this article.

Section 6. This article shall be inoperative unless it shall have been ratified as an amendment to the Constitution by the legislatures of three-fourths of the several States within seven years from the date of its submission.

Amendment XXI

(1933)

Section 1. The eighteenth article of amendment to the Constitution of the United States is hereby repealed.

Section 2. The transportation or importation into any State, territory, or possession of the United States for delivery or use therein of intoxicating liquors, in violation of the laws thereof, is hereby prohibited.

Section 3. This article shall be inoperative unless it shall have been ratified as an amendment to the Constitution by conventions in the several States, as provided in the Constitution, within seven years from the date of the submission hereof to the States by the Congress.

Amendment XXII

(1951)

Section 1. No person shall be elected to the office of the President more than twice, and no person who has held the office of President, or acted as President, for more than two years of a term to which some other person was elected President shall be elected to the office of the President more than once. But this article shall not apply to any person holding the office of President when this article was proposed by the Congress, and shall not prevent any person who may be holding the office of President, or acting as President, during the term within which this article becomes operative from holding the office of President or acting as President during the remainder of such term.

Section 2. This article shall be inoperative unless it shall have been ratified as an amendment to the Constitution by the legislatures of three-fourths of the several States within seven years from the date of its submission to the States by the Congress.

Amendment XXIII

(1961)

Section 1. The District constituting the seat of government of the United States shall appoint in such manner as the Congress may direct:

A number of electors of President and Vice President equal to the whole number of Senators and Representatives in Congress to which the District would be entitled if it were a State, but in no event more than the least populous State; they shall be in addition to those appointed by the States, but they shall be considered, for the purposes of the election of the President and Vice President, to be electors appointed by a State; and they shall meet in the District and perform such duties as provided by the twelfth article of amendment.

Section 2. The Congress shall have power to enforce this article by appropriate legislation.

Amendment XXIV

(1964)

Section 1. The right of citizens of the United States to vote in any primary or other election for President or Vice President, for electors for President or Vice President, or for Senator or Representative in Congress, shall not be denied or abridged by the United States or any State by reason of failure to pay any poll tax or other tax.

Section 2. The Congress shall have the power to enforce this article by appropriate legislation.

Amendment XXV

(1967)

Section 1. In case of the removal of the President from office or his death or resignation, the Vice President shall become President.

Section 2. Whenever there is a vacancy in the office of the Vice President, the President shall nominate a Vice President who shall take office upon confirmation by a majority vote of both Houses of Congress.

Section 3. Whenever the President transmits to the President pro tempore of the Senate and the Speaker of the House of Representatives his written declaration that he is unable to discharge the powers and duties of his office, and until he transmits to them a written declaration to the contrary, such powers and duties shall be discharged by the Vice President as Acting President.

Section 4. Whenever the Vice President and a majority of either the principal officers of the executive departments or such other body as Congress may by law provide, transmit to the President pro tempore of the Senate and the Speaker of the House of Representatives their written declaration that the President is unable to discharge the powers and duties of his office, the Vice President shall immediately assume the powers and duties of the office as Acting President.

Thereafter, when the President transmits to the President pro tempore of the Senate and the Speaker of the House of Representatives his written declaration that no inability exists, he shall resume the powers and duties of his office unless the Vice President and a majority of either the principal officers of the executive department or of such other body as Congress may by law provide, transmit within four days to the President pro tempore of the Senate and the Speaker of the House of Representatives their written declaration that the President is unable to discharge the powers and duties of his office. Thereupon Congress shall decide the issue, assembling within forty-eight hours for that purpose if not in session. If the Congress, within twenty-one days after receipt of the latter written declaration, or, if Congress is not in session, within twenty-one days after Congress is required to assemble, determine by two-thirds vote of both Houses that the President is unable to discharge the powers and duties of his office, the Vice President shall continue to discharge the same as Acting President; otherwise, the President shall resume the powers and duties of his office.

Amendment XXVI

(1971)

Section 1. The right of citizens of the United States, who are 18 years of age or older, to vote, shall not be denied or abridged by the United States or any State on account of age.

Section 2. The Congress shall have the power to enforce this article by appropriate legislation.

Amendment XXVII

(1992)

No law varying the compensation for the services of the Senators and Representatives shall take effect until an election of Representatives shall have intervened.

Cases and Materials on Federal Constitutional Law

Volume VI

The First Amendment

Chapter 1

The Free Speech Clause

A. Introduction

Today, after nearly a century of jurisprudence, the Supreme Court has articulated a set of complex, comprehensive, and generally well-ordered, free speech doctrines. In fact, this is likely the most complex area of constitutional law that you will encounter in your introductory constitutional law courses. Some of the Court's current doctrine is best explained in light of the history and original meaning of the Free Speech Clause. Many portions are justified by the Clause's (original and otherwise) purposes. Still other facets of the doctrine are best explained as reflecting the justices' best conception of the role of free speech in American society.

Exercise 1:

Apply the first four forms of argument to the Free Speech Clause.

1. Looking at the Constitution's text, what information do you gather regarding free speech?

2. Looking at the Constitution's structure, what do you learn about free speech?

3. Reviewing evidence of the Constitution's original meaning, what does it tell you about free speech?

4. Do the materials following adoption of the Constitution offer any insight into free speech?

———————

There are three foundational aspects to the Supreme Court's modern case law: (1) the distinction between content-based and content-neutral regulations of speech; (2) the categorical approach to speech that designates speech as fully protected, less protected, and unprotected; and (3) public forum doctrine.

As you read the materials below, some of the issues to consider include:

What are the reasons for or purposes of free speech doctrine?

What speech is protected?

What is expressive conduct?

Why does expressive conduct receive different treatment from pure speech?

What is the origin of expressive conduct doctrine?

What purposes does the classification of activity as expressive conduct serve?

What is the distinction between content-based and content-neutral regulations of speech?

What is the origin of this distinction?

What purposes does the distinction serve?

What speech is unprotected and less protected?

From what source(s) do these categories of protected and unprotected speech arise?

Are the categories of unprotected and less protected speech appropriately articulated by the Supreme Court? Should one or both be broader or narrower? Why?

What are the types of public fora articulated by the Supreme Court?

From what sources is public forum doctrine drawn?

What roles does public forum serve?

B. Original Meaning of the Free Speech Clause

1. Introduction

The scholarly treatment and debate on the original meaning of "abridging the freedom of speech" is decades old.[1] This brief Introduction surveys some of the major historical periods and influences on the Free Speech Clause. It begins by describing English law governing the freedom of speech, and then turns to the American expe-

---

1. The major works in the area are by the respected legal historian Leonard Levy. LEONARD W. LEVY, EMERGENCE OF A FREE PRESS (1985); LEONARD W. LEVY, FREEDOM OF SPEECH AND PRESS IN EARLY AMERICAN HISTORY: LEGACY OF SUPPRESSION (1960). Levy's later book somewhat modified his earlier conclusions. For critical reviews of Levy's revisions, because they were not substantial enough, see David M. Rabban, *The Ahistorical Historian: Leonard Levy on Freedom of Expression in Early American History*, 37 STAN. L. REV. 795 (1985); David A. Anderson, *Levy v. Levy*, 84 MICH. L. REV. 777 (1986). Other works on the Clause's original meaning and background history include: MICHAEL KENT CURTIS, FREE SPEECH, "THE PEOPLE'S DARLING PRIVILEGE": STRUGGLES FOR FREEDOM OF EXPRESSION IN AMERICAN HISTORY (2000); Stanley C. Brubaker, *Original Intent and Freedom of Speech and Press*, in EUGENE W. HICKOK, THE BILL OF RIGHTS: ORIGINAL MEANING AND CURRENT UNDERSTANDING 82 (1991); David M. Rabban, *The Original Meaning of the Free Speech Clause of the First Amendment*, in 6 THE UNITED STATES CONSTITUTION: THE FIRST 200 YEARS (R.C. Simmons ed. 1989); ZECHARIAH CHAFEE, JR., FREE SPEECH IN THE UNITED STATES (1941); Lawrence Rosenthal, *First Amendment Investigations and the Inescapable Pragmatism of the Common Law of Free Speech*, 86 IND. L.J. 1 (2011); Eugene Volokh, *Tort Liability and the Original Meaning of the Freedom of Speech, Press, and Petition*, 96 IOWA L. REV. 249 (2010); Eugene Volokh, *Symbolic Expression and the Original Meaning of the First Amendment*, 97 GEO. L.J. 1057 (2009); David Jenkins, *The Sedition Act of 1798 and the Incorporation of Seditious Libel into First Amendment Jurisprudence*, 45 AM. J. LEGAL HIST. 154 (2001); William T. Mayton, *Seditious Libel and the Lost Guarantee of a Freedom of Expression*, 84 COLUM. L. REV. 91 (1984); David A. Anderson, *The Origins of the Press Clause*, 30 UCLA L. REV. 455 (1983); Thomas F. Carroll, *Freedom of Speech and of the Press in the Federalist Period; The Sedition Act*, 18 MICH. L. REV. 615 (1919–20).

rience, covering the colonial period, the revolutionary period, and the Framing and Ratification of the Free Speech Clause, along with some post-Ratification evidence.

The narrative below suggests that the freedom of speech expanded somewhat over time, though, by 1791, most evidence suggests that it remained relatively limited (at least by today's standards). This evidence indicates that "the freedom of speech" (at least) prohibited prior restraints on speech, and limited seditious libel by making truth a defense and giving the question of sedition to a jury. However, there is also evidence suggesting that "the freedom of speech" had expanded further, including, most importantly, a revised conception of sovereignty that located sovereignty in the American People which, in turn, gave the freedom of speech the important function of helping the People control government. This evidence is bolstered by the widespread practice of Americans, in the late-eighteenth century, to robustly criticize the government.

2. English Background

The early-English understanding of freedom of speech was limited, and it evolved modestly over time. There were two key components to English speech regulations: libel and licensing. Both were aimed at protecting the crown's and established Church's authority, and reflected the prevalent conception of sovereignty.

Libel became criminally punishable as early as 1275, when Parliament outlawed "any false news or tales whereby discord or occasion of discord or slander may grow between the king and his people or the great men of the realm...."[2] Henry VIII applied the Anglican Church's system of censorship of heretical manuscripts to writings on all subjects.[3] Under this system, a would-be publisher had to receive permission—a license—to publish.[4] "Anything published without official imprimatur was criminal."[5] Elizabeth I developed this into a complex licensing system for publishing.[6] After the Stuart Restoration in 1661, the licensing system was based upon an act of Parliament, and continued until 1694, but this was not the end of restraint upon the press because the press remained subject to common law restrictions.[7]

Later English legal authorities pointed to the licensing system as the epitome of what "the freedom of speech" prevented. Sir William Blackstone, one of the most influential English authorities for Americans at the time of the Framing and Ratification of the First Amendment, stated that "to subject the press to the restrictive power of the licenser [is] to subject all freedom of sentiment to the prejudices of one man,

---

2. Van Vechten Veeder, *History of the Law of Defamation, in* 3 SELECTED ESSAYS IN ANGLO-AMERICAN LEGAL HISTORY 452–54 (1909); LEVY, *supra* note 1, at 7. In 1379, the statute was reenacted for the prevention of "subversion and destruction of the said realm" by false speech. *Id. See* LEVY, *supra* note 1, at 8 (finding that, together, laws against heresy and libel began a "long history of suppression of opinions deemed pernicious").

3. LEVY, *supra* note 1, at 8.

4. *Id.*

5. *Id.*

6. *Id.*

7. *Id.* at 8–9.

and make him the arbitrary and infallible judge of all controverted points in learning, religion, and government."[8] Prominent and well known English writers also criticized the licensing system.[9]

The switch from the licensing system to the common law meant that a license was no longer required to publish — there was no longer a prior restraint — but one still risked libel, both private and seditious.[10] Libel against a government official — seditious libel — was a great offense because, as described in Sir Edward Coke's *Reports*, "it concerns not only the breach of the peace, but also the scandal of government."[11] Seditious libel was broadly defined to include a statement's truth *or* falsity.[12]

By the time of the Revolution, Blackstone summarized the English conception of the freedom of speech as: "[the liberty of the press] consists in laying no previous restraints upon publication, and not in freedom from censure for criminal matter when published."[13] The freedom of speech permitted punishment for seditious libel: "if he publishes what is improper, mischievous, or illegal, he must take the consequence of his own temerity. To ... punish (as the law does at present) any dangerous or offensive writings, which, when published, shall on a fair and impartial trial be adjudged of a pernicious tendency, is necessary for the preservation of peace and good order, of government and religion, the only solid foundations of civil liberty."[14]

3. American Colonies

In colonial America, as in England, the common law of seditious libel limited discussion, but by the eighteenth century, America was, in practice, more speech protective than England. For example, during the seventeenth and eighteenth centuries, England held hundreds of trials for seditious libel, while in America before the Revolution, there were very few.[15]

Many of the popularly elected colonial assemblies suppressed speech.[16] Colonial assemblies, following the House of Commons' practice, needed no grand jury to indict and no jury to convict, allowing for greater suppressive power.[17] This form of suppression of speech began as early as 1620, when the Virginia House of Burgesses found Captain Henry Spellman guilty of "treasonable words."[18] Many state assemblies

---

8. 4 SIR WILLIAM BLACKSTONE, COMMENTARIES ON THE LAWS OF ENGLAND *151–52 (1769).

9. *E.g.*, JOHN MILTON, AREOPAGITICA — A SPEECH FOR THE LIBERTY OF UNLICENSED PRINTING (1664).

10. LEVY, *supra* note 1, at 9.

11. *Id.*

12. *Id.* at 9–10.

13. BLACKSTONE, *supra* note 8, at *152.

14. *Id.*

15. LEVY, *supra* note 1, at 19–20. The *John Peter Zenger* trial, discussed below, was famous, in part, because it was rare. *Id.* at 19.

16. *Id.* at 20.

17. *Id.*

18. MARY PATTERSON CLARKE, PARLIAMENTARY PRIVILEGE IN THE AMERICAN COLONIES 117 (New Haven, 1943); LEVY, *supra* note 1, at 21.

utilized the same practices to restrict speech.[19] For example, "the Protestant Association, led by John Coode, who had earlier been tried for seditious speech…, revolted against Lord Baltimore's proprietary government" as early as 1689.[20] The group's declaration of reasons for the revolt cited harsh laws limiting the freedom of speech that had been severely enforced in Maryland.[21] The punishments handed out under this law included whipping, branding, boring through the tongue, fine, imprisonment, banishment, or death.[22]

In 1686, Pennsylvania censored its first printer, William Bradford, and his first publication, an almanac, and warned Bradford "not to print anything but what shall have Lycence from ye Council."[23] Bradford later printed, *An Appeal from the twenty-eight Judges to the Spirit of Truth*, which criticized the colony's leadership.[24] Bradford's press was seized; he was jailed and charged with seditious libel.[25] Bradford was convicted "without All Hearing or Tryal" by some of the same magistrates he had criticized in the publication.[26]

Bradford managed to obtain a trial by appeal to the Magna Carta's promise of a trial by jury.[27] At his trial, Bradford argued that the jury should decide whether the publication was seditious.[28] The judge's instruction to the jury surprisingly accepted Bradford's argument.[29] The jury deadlocked and, while awaiting a new trial, Bradford was released.[30]

The most famous pre-Revolution legal event was the 1735 *Zenger Trial*.[31] Zenger published the *New York Weekly Journal*. Zenger criticized New York's colonial governor, and Zenger was then charged with seditious libel. Zenger's attorney, Andrew Hamilton,

---

19. *See* Levy, *supra* note 1, at 23–87 (describing colonial assembly speech restrictions, along with other forms of restriction).

20. *Id.* at 23.

21. *The Declaration of the Reasons and Motives for the Present Appearing in Arms of Their Majesties Protestant Subjects In the Province of Maryland*, 1689, at 309, *in*, Narratives of the Insurrections, 1675–1690 (Charles M. Andrews, ed., New York, 1915); Levy, *supra* note 1, at 23.

22. Levy, *supra* note 1, at 23.

23. 3 David Paul Brown, The Forum: Or, Forty Years Full Practice at the Philadelphia Bar 375 (Philadelphia, 1856–1887); Levy, *supra* note 1, at 24.

24. Levy, *supra* note 1, at 26.

25. *Id.* at 25–26.

26. *Id.* at 26.

27. New England's Spirit of Persecution Transmitted to Pennsylvania, And the Pretended Quaker Found Persecuting the True Christian-Quaker, in the Tryal of Peter Boss, George Keith, Thomas Budd and William Bradford … 1693. Giving an Account of the Most Arbitrary Procedure of that Court 10 (Philadelphia, 1693, printed by William Bradford); Levy, *supra* note 1, at 26–27.

28. New England's Spirit of Persecution Transmitted to Pennsylvania, And the Pretended Quaker Found Persecuting the True Christian-Quaker, in the Tryal of Peter Boss, George Keith, Thomas Budd and William Bradford … 1693. Giving an account of the most Arbitrary Procedure of that Court 33–34 (Philadelphia, 1693, printed by William Bradford); Levy, *supra* note 1, at 27–28.

29. Levy, *supra* note 1, at 28.

30. *Id.* at 28–29.

31. *Id.* at 126–34.

constructed a rationale for freedom of speech that built on prior writings, especially the radical English Whig writer Cato.[32] Hamilton argued that freedom of speech helped expose villainy in the government. He suggested two modifications to the common law of sedition: (1) truth was a defense to seditious libel; and (2) the jury should decide the law as well as the facts.[33] The court rejected Hamilton's first argument, but the jury disregarded the judge's instructions and returned a "not guilty" verdict,[34] which was widely taken by Americans as a limit on seditious libel.

James Alexander, Zenger's newspaper editor, wrote *A brief Narrative of the Case and Tryal of John Peter Zenger*, published by Zenger in 1736, which was one of the most widely known sources of libertarian thought in England and America during the eighteenth century.[35] Alexander also wrote an essay on the freedom of speech that was published in the *Pennsylvania Gazette*.[36] Alexander articulated the reasons for freedom of speech:

> Freedom of speech is a principal Pillar in a free Government: When this Support is taken away, the Constitution is dissolved, and Tyranny is erected on its ruins. Republics and limited monarchies derive their strength and vigour from a Popular Examination into the Actions of the Magistrates.[37]

Alexander suggested modifying, but not eliminating, seditious libel, through truth-as-a-defense.[38] This was, like the *Zenger Trial*, a modest liberalization of the common law.[39]

4. Revolutionary Period

The Revolution did not appear to significantly alter American legal conceptions of the freedom of speech and possibly—though likely temporarily—moved Americans toward more rigorous use of legal mechanisms, such as seditious libel, to regulate speech in order to advance the Revolution. "Speech and press were not free anywhere during the Revolution."[40] However, the dramatic move toward popular sovereignty away from parliamentary sovereignty also influenced some Americans to rethink and expand their conception of freedom of speech.[41]

The Continental Congress, in presenting its case before the inhabitants of Quebec, connected the function of free press with popular sovereignty:

---

32. *Id.* at 129–30.
33. Rutherfurd Livingston, Trial of Zenger 206, 223 (1904); Levy, *supra* note 1, at 130–31.
34. Levy, *supra* note 1, at 133.
35. *Id.* at 133–34.
36. *Id.* at 134.
37. Pennsylvania Gazette, Nov. 17, 1737; Levy, *supra* note 1, at 135.
38. Levy, *supra* note 1, at 136.
39. *Id.*
40. *Id.* at 176.
41. It is unclear how this theoretical alteration impacted the law and widespread conceptions of the freedom of speech.

The last right we shall mention regards the freedom of the press. The importance of this consists, besides the advancement of truth, science, morality and arts in general, in its diffusion of liberal sentiments on the administration of government, its ready communication of thoughts between subjects, and its consequential promotion of union among them, whereby oppressive officials are shamed or intimated into more honorable and just modes of conducting affairs.[42]

This statement, however, was a relatively rare American declaration of a broad conception of open discussion.[43]

The writings of John Adams display the manner in which Americans still embraced the common law.[44] In 1774, Adams argued that abuse of the press was not a part of the liberty of the press.[45] Adams argued for adherence to the Revolution as the test so that "the presses will produce no more seditious or traitorous speculations. Slanders upon public men and measures will be lessened."[46]

Francis Hopkinson, a member of the Continental Congress and a signer of the Declaration of Independence, published a similar view.[47] He argued that the liberty of press was important to free government because it enabled the channels of information to remain open,

[b]ut when this privilege is manifestly abused, and the press becomes an engine for sowing the most dangerous dissensions, for spreading false alarms, and undermining the very foundations of government, out not that government upon the plain principles of self-preservation to silence by its own authority, such a daring violator of its peace, and tear from its bosom the serpent that would sting it to death? ... [The council would be justified in] silencing the press, whose weekly productions insult the feelings of the people, and are so openly inimical to the American cause.[48]

During the Revolution, most states created their first state constitutions, some of which protected the freedom of speech. Pennsylvania's constitution of 1776 was the first to protect the freedom of speech.[49] It stated:

---

42. *Letter to the Inhabitants of the Province of Quebec, in* 1 Journals of the Continental Congress, 1774–1789, at 239 (Oct. 24, 1774); Levy, *supra* note 1, at 176–77.

43. Levy, *supra* note 1, at 177.

44. *Id.* at 179.

45. *Id.* at 179–80.

46. *Letter to John Winthrop*, June 23, 1776, *in* 9 The Works of John Adams 409 (Charles Francis Adams ed. 1856); Levy, *supra* note 1, at 180.

47. Levy, *supra* note 1, at 180.

48. Arthur M. Schlesinger, Prelude to Independence: The Newspaper War on Britain 1764–1776, at 298 (1958) (quoting Hopkinson's article in the *Pennsylvania Evening Post*, Nov. 16, 1776); Levy, *supra* note 1, at 180.

49. Levy, *supra* note 1, at 183.

That the people have a right to freedom of speech, and of writing, and publishing their sentiments; therefore the freedom of the press ought not to be
restrained.[50]

There is no clear evidence of what was meant by "freedom of speech," though the
suppression of loyalist speech during the Revolution suggests that speech remained
restricted by seditious libel.[51]

Vermont, admitted to the Union in 1791, copied the Pennsylvania free speech provision.[52] Most other states, however, did not grant freedom of speech the same constitutional protection. For example, Massachusetts in 1780 adopted a constitution
that protected only the "liberty of the press."[53] And other states did not protect either
speech or press.[54] Many have argued that the states that did not protect the freedom
of speech, as well as the states that only protected freedom of press, meant that they
preserved the common law.[55]

Another source of evidence, the Cushing-Adams correspondence of 1789, also indicates an expanding conception of the freedom of speech, but one that did not abandon of the concept of seditious libel.[56] William Cushing was chief justice of the
Massachusetts Supreme Judicial Court when he wrote to John Adams giving his interpretation of the state's free press clause, originally drafted by Adams.[57] The clause
stated that: "The liberty of the press is essential to the security of freedom in a state;
it ought not, therefore, to be restrained in this commonwealth."[58] Cushing believed
that it did not protect criminal libel "injuring the public or individuals by propagating
falsehoods."[59]

Cushing wrote:

But the words of our article understood according to plain English, make
no such distinction, and must exclude *subsequent restraints,* as much as *previous
restraints.* In other words, if all men are restrained by the fear of jails, scourges
and loss of ears from examining the conduct of persons in administration
and where their conduct is illegal, tyrannical and tending to overthrow the
Constitution and introduce slavery, are so restrained from declaring it to the
public *that* will be as effectual a restraint as any *previous* restraint whatever.

---

50. Pennsylvania Constitution of 1776, Declaration of Rights, Article XII, *in* 5 The Federal and
State Constitutions, Colonial Characters, and Other Organic Laws 3083 (Francis Newton
Thorpe, ed., Washington, 1909).

51. Levy, *supra* note 1, at 183. For example, Quaker meetings were disrupted and members either
imprisoned or exiled from the state. *Id.*; *see also* Claude Halstead Van Tyne, The Loyalists in
the American Revolution 60–86 (1902) (describing the suppression of loyalist speech).

52. Levy, *supra* note 1, at 184.

53. Mass. Const. art. xvi (1780).

54. Levy, *supra* note 1, at 185.

55. *Id.*

56. *Id.* at 192.

57. *Id.* at 193.

58. Mass. Const. art. xvi (1780).

59. Levy, *supra* note 1, at 193.

The question upon this article, is this—What is that liberty of the press, which is essential to the security of freedom? The propagating literature and knowledge by printing or otherwise tends to illuminate men's minds and to establish them in principles of freedom. But it cannot be denied also, that a free scanning of the conduct of administration and showing the tendency of it, and where truth will warrant, making it manifest that it is subversive of all law, liberty and the Constitution; it can't be denied. I think that the liberty tends to the *security of freedom in a State*; even more directly and essentially than the liberty of printing upon literary and speculative subjects in general. Without this liberty of the press could we have supported our liberties against british administration? or could our revolution have taken place? Pretty certainly it could not, at the time it did. Under a sense and impression of this sort, I conceive, this article was adopted. This liberty of publishing truth can never effectually injure a good government, or honest administrators; but it may save a state from the necessity of a revolution, as well as bring one about, when it is necessary. It may be objected that a public prosecution is that safe and regular course, in case of malfeasance. But what single person would venture himself upon so invidious and dangerous a task against a man high in interest, influence and power?

But this liberty of the press having truth for its basis who can stand before it? Besides it may facilitate a legal prosecution, which might not, otherwise, have been dared to be attempted. When the press is made the vehicle of falsehood and scandal, let the authors be punished with becoming rigour.

But why need any honest man be afraid of the truth? The guilty only fear it; and I am inclined to think with Gordon [Vol. 3 No. 20 of Cato's Letters] that truth sacredly adhered to, can never upon the whole prejudice, right religion, equal government or a government founded upon proper balances and checks, or the happiness of society, in any respect, but must be favorable to them all.

Suppressing this liberty by penal laws will it not more endanger freedom than do good to governments? The weight of government is sufficient to prevent any very dangerous consequences occasioned by *provocations* resulting from charges founded in truth; whether such charges are made in *a legal course of otherwise*. In either case, the *provocation* (which Judge Blackstone says is the sole foundation of the law against libels) being much the same.

But not to trouble you with a multiplying of words; If I am wrong I should be glad to be set right, &c., &c.[60]

---

60. *Id.* at 193–95.

Adams replied:

> The difficult and important question is whether the truth of words can be
> admitted by the court to be given evidence to the jury, upon a plea of not
> guilty? In England I suppose it is settled. But it is a serious Question whether
> our Constitution is not at present so different as to render the innovation
> necessary? Our chief magistrates and Senators &c are annually eligible by
> the people. How are their characters and conduct to be known to their con-
> stituents but by the press? If the press is stopped and the people kept in Ig-
> norance we had much better have the first magistrate and Senators hereditary.
> I therefore, am very clear that under the Articles of our Constitution which
> you have quoted, it would be safest to admit evidence to the jury of the Truth
> of accusations, and if the jury found them true and that they were published
> for the Public good, they would readily be acquit.[61]

The Cushing-Adams correspondence evinces the belief that the freedom of speech
is consistent with seditious libel, so long as truth is a defense and the jury determines
whether libel had occurred.[62]

In the Cushing-Adams correspondence, one can also see Americans wrestling
with the implications of America's move from parliamentary or legislative sovereignty to popular sovereignty.[63] One of the key justifications for seditious libel had
been that it protected the common good by protecting the sovereign — the government — from disrepute. Once the sovereign became the People, however, the People's criticism of the government was the sovereign's criticism of its agents' misdeeds.
Such criticism was not harmful to the public good; it was essential to maintain the
public good.

James Wilson, the most influential framer of the United States Constitution after
James Madison, stated, at the 1787 Pennsylvania ratification convention, that "there
is given to the general government no power whatsoever concerning [freedom of
speech]: and no law, in pursuance of the constitution, can possibly be enacted, to
destroy that liberty."[64] Wilson's argument was the standard Federalist argument against
a bill of rights: the federal government did not have an enumerated power to restrict
the freedom of speech. However, when answering a claim that federal judges might
proceed under federal statutes punishing libels he said:

> I presume it was not in the view of the honorable gentleman to say that
> there is no such thing as a libel, or that the writers of such ought not to be

---

61. *Id.* at 195–96.

62. *Id.* at 196–197. This line was also drawn during John Adams' presidency in the Sedition Act
of 1798. *Id.* at 197–200.

63. *See* Rabban, *supra* note 1, at 821–54 (arguing that Americans' embrace of popular sovereignty
broadened their conception of freedom of speech).

64. Levy, *supra* note 1, at 201.

punished. The idea of the liberty of the press is not carried so far as this in any country—*what is meant by the liberty of the press is that there should be no antecedent restraint upon it*; but that every author is responsible when he attacks the security or welfare of the government, or the safety, character and property of the individual.

> With regard to attacks upon the public, the mode of proceeding is by prosecution.... Now, Sir, if this libel is to be tried, it must be tried where the offence was committed ... the trial must be held in the State; therefore on this occasion it must be tried where it was published, if the indictment is for publishing; and it must be tried likewise by a jury of that state.[65]

Wilson's statement shows that, in his view, seditious libel was consistent with the freedom of speech.[66] Wilson's description of the freedom of speech went unchallenged.[67]

Respublica v. Oswald, a Pennsylvania case from 1788, shows a similar view of the freedom of speech.[68] Oswald was indicted for gross libel against a private person. Chief Justice McKean stated that "there is nothing in the constitution of this state, respecting the liberty of the press, that has not been authorized by the constitution of that kingdom [England] for near a century past."[69]

Pennsylvania adopted a second constitution in 1790, which was drafted by James Wilson and, like the earlier one, protected the freedom of speech:[70]

> That the printing presses shall be free to every person who undertakes to examine the proceedings of the legislature, or any branch of government: And no law shall ever be made to restrain the right thereof. The free communication of thoughts and opinions is one of the invaluable rights of man; and every citizen may freely speak, write and print on any subject, being responsible for the abuse of that liberty. In prosecutions for the publication of papers, investigating the official conduct of officers, or men in a public capacity, or where the matter published is proper for public information, the truth thereof may be given in evidence: And, in all indictments for libels, the jury shall have a right to determine the law and the facts, under the direction of the court, as in other cases.[71]

Note how the clause's text itself acknowledged that libel remained a limit on the freedom of speech, though it incorporated the changes of truth-as-a-defense and jury determinations of law and fact.[72]

---

65. *Id.* at 201–02.
66. *Id.* at 202.
67. *Id.*
68. *Respublica v. Oswald*, 1 U.S. 319 (Pa. 1788).
69. *Id.* at 322.
70. *Id.*
71. Penn. Const., art. IX, §vii (1790).
72. Levy, *supra* note 1, at 203.

Even after the 1790 Constitution, Chief Justice McKean remained of the view that the freedom of speech was declaratory of common law.[73] McKean gave an instruction to the jury of William Cobbett, charged of criminal libel in 1797, stating:

> The liberty of the press is, indeed, essential to the nature of a free state, but this consists in laying no previous restraints upon public actions, and not in freedom from censure for criminal matter, when published. Every freeman has an undoubted right to lay what sentiments he pleases before the public; to forbid this, is to destroy the freedom of the press; but if he publishes what is improper, mischievous or illegal, he must take the consequences of his temerity. To punish dangerous or offensive writings, which when published, shall, on a fair and impartial trial, be adjudged of a pernicious tendency, is necessary for the preservation of peace and good order, of government and religion, the only solid foundation of civil liberty. Thus the will of individuals is still left free; the abuse of that free will is the object of punishment. Our presses in Pennsylvania are thus free. The common law, with respect to this, is confirmed and established by the Constitution.[74]

Thus, while Pennsylvania's constitutional provisions of 1776 and 1790 possessed potentially the broadest protections for the freedom of speech at the time, they appear to have only modified the common law of sedition, not eliminated it.[75]

5. Drafting and Ratification of the Constitution and the First Amendment

The drafting and ratification of the Constitution and the First Amendment does not suggest significant change to the public's conception of freedom of speech.[76] For instance, at the Philadelphia Convention, a motion to insert a declaration "that the liberty of the Press should be inviolably preserved" in the original Constitution, was defeated because, as Roger Sherman of Connecticut stated, "[i]t is unnecessary. The power of Congress does not extend to the Press."[77] The primary evidence for this lack of change is the relative lack of discussion, debate, or disagreement over the freedom of speech, which suggests that any protection for the freedom of speech was consistent with widely-held views.[78]

---

73. *Id.* at 206.

74. *Trial of Cobbett for Libel*, Nov. 1797, *in* State Trials of the United States During the Administrations of Washington and Adams 323–24 (Francis Wharton ed., 1849); Levy, *supra* note 1, at 206–07.

75. Levy, *supra* note 1, at 207.

76. *Id.* at 214.

77. *Id.*

78. *Id.* at 215.

One of the exceptions to this lack of specific discussion of the freedom of speech was Benjamin Franklin.[79] Franklin favored as much discussion as possible of "public measures and political opinions," but also supported punishment for anyone harming the government's reputation.[80]

Hugh Williamson, a delegate from North Carolina, stated in his essay "Remarks in the New Plan of Government" in 1788, that:

> [t]here was a time in England when neither book, pamphlet, nor paper could be published without a license from government. That restraint was finally removed in the year 1694; and, by such removal, the press became perfectly free, for it is not under the restraint of any license. Certainly the new government can have no power to impose restraints.[81]

Williamson's understanding of freedom of speech was consistent with the common law.[82] George Nicholas, a member of the Virginia ratifying convention, expressed a similar view: "The liberty of the press is secured.... In the time of King William, there passed an act for licensing to press. That was repealed. Since that time it has been looked upon as safe."[83]

Only three states that ratified the Constitution suggested amendments to protect the freedom of speech: Virginia, North Carolina, and New York.[84] Their suggested amendments were modeled on Pennsylvania's 1776 provision, discussed above, which did not suggest an expansive conception of the freedom of speech. Furthermore, given the strong Anti-Federalist sentiment that prompted many amendment proposals, one explanation for the proposed protections for the freedom of speech is a fear of federal power, not a solicitousness for speech.[85]

This last point is worth emphasizing, because it influenced the First Congress' discussion of what became the First Amendment. The major concern of the Anti-Federalists was too much federal power, and the major claim made by the Federalists in response was that the federal government was one of limited and enumerated powers. Therefore, the principle of limited and enumerated powers was a foundational assumption of all parties to the debate. This assumption pushes toward a relatively broader conception of the freedom of speech.

The debates by the First Congress, during the framing of the First Amendment, are also relatively unilluminating.[86] In the course of the discussion on the First Amend-

---

79. *Id.*
80. *Id.*
81. *Id.* at 216.
82. *Id.*
83. *Id.* at 217.
84. *Id.* at 217–218.
85. *Id.* at 218–19.
86. *Id.* at 221.

ment, Congress spent most of its time debating the Free Exercise Clause.[87] James Madison, who drafted and introduced the Bill of Rights, made the only significant statement about the freedom of speech.[88] In the context of debates over the right to assembly, Madison stated that, if by peaceably assemble:

> we mean nothing more than this, that the people have a right to express and communicate their sentiments and wishes, we have provided for it already. Their right of freedom of speech is secured; the liberty of the press is expressly declared to be beyond the reach of this Government....[89]

Madison's statement stated that the federal government is disabled from regulating the "freedom of speech," but he did not explain how broad or narrow that freedom was. As discussed above, Madison's key concern may have been the principle of limited and enumerated powers, which translated into a capacious interpretation of the freedom of speech, but there is no direct evidence of that.[90]

The states' ratification debates over the First Amendment provide little additional evidence on the freedom of speech's meaning for two reasons. First, the records of these debates are notoriously spare. Second, there does not appear to have been much debate, which could suggest that the freedom of speech was not a significant change from the status quo.[91]

6. Post-Ratification Evidence

One of the key events bearing on the Free Speech Clause's meaning is the Sedition Act of 1798.[92] The Act proscribed "false, scandalous and malicious writing or writings against the government of the United States, or either House of the Congress of the United States, or the President of the United States, with intent to defame the said government, or either House of the said Congress, or the said President, or to bring them, or either of them, into contempt or disrepute; or to excite against them, or either or any of them, the hatred of the good people of the United States...."[93] The Act was passed by the Federalist Congress which believed that the baleful influence of France was leading Americans to criticize the government and thereby undermine the necessary popular respect for it. The Act made truth a defense and required a jury trial, as Zenger had argued.

The Sedition Act was enforced against and strongly criticized by Jeffersonian Republicans. For example, Thomas Jefferson and James Madison respectively drafted the Kentucky and Virginia Resolutions, which argued that the federal government

---

87. *Id.*
88. *Id.*
89. *Id.*
90. *Id.* at 221–23.
91. *Id.* at 233.
92. The Sedition Act, 1 Stat. 596–97 (July 14, 1798).
93. *Id.*

lacked the power to pass the Act and that the Act violated the First Amendment.[94] The Act later lapsed and President Jefferson pardoned those convicted under the Act.

It is difficult to know which way this evidence cuts. On the one hand, many have argued that the Sedition Act shows that the First Amendment enacted the common law status quo, which made truth a defense and gave the question to the jury. On the other hand, many have argued that the strong negative reaction against the Act showed that the freedom of speech was more capacious than the common law permitted.[95]

Exercise 2:

1. What does this history tell us about the Free Speech Clause's meaning and scope, along with any potential exceptions? What is protected? What is not protected? Does some speech have a "preferred" position?

2. Assume, as many justices and scholars do, that the Free Speech Clause's original meaning is narrow in scope, relative to what most Americans today would find appropriate. How, if at all, should that tension cause you to modify your interpretation of the Clause?

Below, in Part C, we first review the purposes of the freedom of speech. Then, we cover what counts as protected "speech" in Part D. Third, in Parts E and F, we examine what government actions "infringe" the freedom of speech and the doctrines of vagueness and overbreadth, respectively. Part G covers the architectonic distinction between content-based and content-neutral regulations, and Part H covers the Supreme Court's categorization of speech into protected, less protected, and unprotected speech. Lastly, Part I studies public forum doctrine. This is a large quantity of intricately related doctrines, the most you have covered in your introductory constitutional law course.

C. Contested Purpose(s) of Free Speech Protection

Both the Supreme Court in its case law and scholarly commentary frequently connects the scope and content of free speech doctrine to the purpose(s) for protecting free speech. For example, one of the most famous statements by a Supreme Court Justice of the reasons free speech is protected, is found in a concurrence by Justice Brandeis. The case, *Whitney v. California*, 274 U.S. 357 (1927), *overruled by Brandenburg v. Ohio*, 395 U.S. 444 (1969), involved criminal prosecution of the defendant for active membership in the Communist Labor Party of America, which advocated revolution. Justice Brandeis stated:

---

94. *The Kentucky and Virginia Resolutions of 1798, in* Documents of American History 178–83 (Henry Steele Commager ed. 1958).

95. This Introduction did not discuss what impact, if any, adoption of the Fourteenth Amendment had on the freedom of speech.

Those who won our independence believed that the final end of the state was to make men free to develop their faculties; and that in its government the deliberative forces should prevail over the arbitrary. They valued liberty both as an end and as a means. They believed liberty to be the secret of happiness and courage to be the secret of liberty. They believed that freedom to think as you will and to speak as you think are means indispensable to the discovery and spread of political truth; that without free speech and assembly discussion would be futile; that with them, discussion affords ordinarily adequate protection against the dissemination of noxious doctrine; that the greatest menace to freedom is an inert people; that public discussion is a political duty; and that this should be a fundamental principle of the American government. They recognized the risks to which all human institutions are subject. But they knew that order cannot be secured merely through fear of punishment for its infraction; that it is hazardous to discourage thought, hope and imagination; that fear breeds repression; that repression breeds hate; that hate menaces stable government; that the path of safety lies in the opportunity to discuss freely supposed grievances and proposed remedies; and that the fitting remedy for evil counsels is good ones. Believing in the power of reason as applied through public discussion, they eschewed silence coerced by law — the argument of force in its worst form. Re[c]ognizing the occasional tyrannies of governing majorities, they amended the Constitution so that free speech and assembly should be guaranteed.

274 U.S. at 375–76.

Over the years, four primary purposes have been identified by the Court and scholars. This listing roughly represents the ordering of weight and frequency with which these purposes are identified, though the first two purposes appear substantially more frequently and are given greater weight than the others.

First, protection of free speech facilitates democracy and self-government. "The maintenance of the opportunity for free political discussion to the end that government may be responsive to the will of the people and that changes may be obtained by lawful means, an opportunity essential to the security of the Republic, is a fundamental principle of our constitutional system." *Stromberg v. California*, 283 U.S. 359, 369 (1931). Free speech is necessary for an effective democratic republic, like the United States, because it enables citizens to learn the information necessary to effectively participate in the political process. Free speech also enables citizens to persuade other citizens to their views on sound public policy. Lastly, free speech provides citizens with a means to check government officials through public criticism. The foundational scholarly presentations of this view are ZECHARIAH CHAFEE, JR., FREEDOM OF SPEECH IN WAR TIME (1919); ALEXANDER MEIKLEJOHN, FREE SPEECH AND ITS RELATION TO SELF-GOVERNMENT (1948).

Relatedly, free speech provides a "safety valve" to disgruntled citizens. Without the ability to voice criticisms of the government or current public policy, merely-dissatisfied citizens could become so frustrated that they become threats to public order.

On the other hand, with an outlet for robust criticism, such citizens not only may be able to initiate the change they seek, but the simple ability to articulate their criticism may reduce the likelihood of destabilizing action.

Second, protection of free speech creates a "marketplace of ideas" out of which the truth arises. This conception of free speech is most strongly associated, in the law, with Justice Holmes, who articulated it in an early dissent. *Abrams v. United States*, 250 U.S. 616, 630 (1919) (Holmes, J., dissenting). As Justice Holmes explained:

> Persecution for the expression of opinions seems to me perfectly logical. If you have no doubt of your premises or your power and want a certain result with all your heart you naturally express your wishes in law and sweep away all opposition. To allow opposition by speech seems to indicate that you think the speech impotent, as when a man says that he has squared the circle, or that you do not care whole heartedly for the result, or that you doubt either your power or your premises. But when men have realized that time has upset many fighting faiths, they may come to believe even more than they believe the very foundations of their own conduct that the ultimate good desired is better reached by free trade in ideas — that the best test of truth is the power of the thought to get itself accepted in the competition of the market, and that truth is the only ground upon which their wishes safely can be carried out. That at any rate is the theory of our Constitution. It is an experiment, as all life is an experiment. Every year if not every day we have to wager our salvation upon some prophecy based upon imperfect knowledge. While that experiment is part of our system I think that we should be eternally vigilant against attempts to check the expression of opinions that we loathe and believe to be fraught with death, unless they so imminently threaten immediate interference with the lawful and pressing purposes of the law that an immediate check is required to save the country.

Id. See also United States v. Associated Press, 52 F. Supp. 362, 372 (S.D.N.Y. 1943) (Learned Hand, J.) (stating that free speech "presupposes that right conclusions are more likely to be gathered out of a multitude of tongues, than through any kind of authoritative selection.").

Third, some argue that free speech protection is a precondition for full human flourishing. Human flourishing is when humans live rich, happy lives. The idea of human flourishing stretches back to the Greeks. For example, Aristotle tied together citizenship, happiness, and free speech. He argued that a citizen is "[h]e who has the power to take part in the deliberative or judicial administration of any state … and … a state is a body of citizens sufficing for the purposes of life." Aristotle, Politics 1275b18-21. The key insight in this line of thinking is that humans need to be able to speak freely in order to engage in those activities that make life worth living: From political life, to family life, to professional life, speech is a necessary mechanism. *See* Robert P. George, Making Men Moral: Civil Liberties and Public Morality 192–208 (1993) (explaining how free speech doctrine can advance human flourishing). The Supreme Court expressed this connection in *Paris Adult Theatre I v. Slaton*, 413

U.S. 49, 63 (1973), where it argued that its holding that obscene material is outside of First Amendment protection because "commerce in obscene books, or public exhibitions focused on obscene conduct, have a tendency to exert a corrupting and debasing impact leading to antisocial behavior."

Relatedly, proponents of free speech argue that free speech is an expression of individual autonomy. Erwin Chemerinsky, Constitutional Law: Principles and Policies 957–58 (4th ed., 2011). Without the ability to freely express oneself, one's autonomy is stunted. *See Hurley v. Irish-American Gay, Lesbian and Bisexual Group of Boston, Inc.*, 515 U.S. 557, 573 (1995) ("[T]he fundamental rule of protection under the First Amendment [is] that a speaker has the autonomy to choose the content of his own message.").

Fourth, free speech is said to be necessary to inculcate the virtue of tolerance, which is itself important to life in a modern pluralistic society, such as the United States. Proponents of this view suggest that a viable pluralistic society requires tolerance of different people and different policy perspectives. Lee Bollinger, The Tolerant Society: Freedom of Speech and Extremist Speech in America (1986). Free speech facilitates acquisition of tolerance because people are exposed to distasteful — and sometimes extremely offensive — speech, and through those experiences, acquire a "thick skin." *See Terminiello v. City of Chicago*, 337 U.S. 1, 4 (1949) (stating that speech "may indeed best serve its high purpose when it induces a condition of unrest, creates dissatisfaction with conditions as they are, or even stirs people to anger").

Of course, each of these purposes is contestable on many grounds. One may contest the purposes substantively. For example, critics have argued that the marketplace of ideas does not, in fact, lead to truth. Stanley Ingber, *The Marketplace of Ideas: A Legitimizing Myth*, 1984 Duke L.J. 1. For instance, critics point to how Nazi anti-Semitic views survived and even thrived in the marketplace of ideas in Weimar Germany. Max Lerner, The Mind and Faith of Justice Holmes 290 (1943).

One may also contest whether one or more of these purposes is actually a purpose of the Free Speech Clause. For instance, critics have claimed that the only purpose that the Free Speech Clause possessed in 1791, when it was ratified, was facilitating democratic self-government. Following this perspective, Robert Bork famously argued that the Clause protected only political speech, because that type of speech facilitated the Clause's purpose of promoting self-governance. Robert Bork, *Neutral Principles and Some First Amendment Problems*, 47 Ind. L.J. 1 (1971).

Lastly, if, as many on and off the Supreme Court contend, more than one purpose animates free speech law, how should the Supreme Court decide a case when those purposes conflict? For example, as we will see below, the Supreme Court has ruled that obscenity is not protected by the Free Speech Clause. One of the arguments relied on by the Court to reach that result was that obscene speech did not facilitate the search for truth. *Roth v. United States*, 354 U.S. 476, 485 (1957). On the other hand, the Justices who disagreed with that ruling argued that protecting obscenity would facilitate individual self-expression. *Paris Adult Theatre I v. Slaton*, 413 U.S. 49, 70–73 (1973) (Douglas, J., dissenting). Or, how much weight should a Justice give each of the purposes when they conflict; are the purposes subject to lexical ordering, where one purpose is always more weighty than another?

Which purpose or purposes animate Free Speech Clause jurisprudence can have a major impact on the resultant doctrine, because the purposes, in some cases, may lead to different results. For instance, your view of whether and, to what extent, restrictions on campaign financing are consistent with freedom of speech may be influenced by which purposes you believe animate the Free Speech Clause. If you believe that free speech is primarily justified by individual autonomy, then you will be suspicious of campaign finance restrictions. If, however, you believe that free speech is primarily a vehicle to facilitate democratic self-government, then you (may) believe that campaign finance restrictions are acceptable because they limit imperfections in elections caused by monetary inequality.

What purposes do you believe animate the freedom of speech? Upon what bases do you base your view?

D. What Counts as Protected "Speech"

1. Introduction

The Free Speech Clause protects "the freedom of *speech*." U.S. Const. amend. I (emphasis added).[96] If the government is regulating something else — something other than "speech" — then the Free Speech Clause is inapplicable.

Speech includes those activities that you likely assume constitute speech, but it also includes a number of other activities as well that, at first blush, you may not think are "speech." As we will see, below, the Free Speech Clause protects both "pure speech," and "expressive conduct," and it does not protect nonexpressive conduct. Both pure speech and expressive conduct receive protection from government regulation by the Free Speech Clause.

2. "Pure Speech"

"Pure speech" is probably what you normally think of when you think of free speech. When you communicate with another person orally or in writing — in a personal conversation or in a letter, for example — that constitutes speech. In many cases involving pure speech, it is clear that the regulated activity is constitutionally protected, so the issue of constitutional protection is not raised. A classic example is:

---

96. If you studied the Incorporation Doctrine, covered in Volume 5, you will recall that the Supreme Court ruled that the Fourteenth Amendment's Due Process Clause "incorporated" the Free Speech Clause against the states. *See Gitlow v. New York*, 268 U.S. 652, 666 (1925) ("For present purposes we may and do assume that freedom of speech and of the press — which are protected by the First Amendment from abridgment by Congress — are among the fundamental personal rights and 'liberties' protected by the due process clause of the Fourteenth Amendment from impairment by the States.").

Cantwell v. Connecticut

310 U.S. 296 (1940)

MR. JUSTICE ROBERTS delivered the opinion of the Court.

Newton Cantwell and his two sons, Jesse and Russell, members of a group known as Jehovah's witnesses, and claiming to be ordained ministers, were arrested in New Haven, Connecticut, and each was charged with statutory and common law offenses. After trial in the Court of Common Pleas of New Haven County each of them was convicted on the third count, which charged a violation of s 6294 of the General Statutes of Connecticut, and on the fifth count, which charged commission of the common law offense of inciting a breach of the peace.

[T]he appellants press[] the contention that the statute under which the third count was drawn was offensive to the due process clause of the Fourteenth Amendment because it denied them freedom of speech and prohibited their free exercise of religion. In like manner they made the point that they could not be found guilty on the fifth count, without violation of the Amendment.

The facts follow. On the day of their arrest the appellants were engaged in going singly from house to house on Cassius Street in New Haven. They were individually equipped with a bag containing books and pamphlets on religious subjects, a portable phonograph and a set of records, each of which, when played, introduced, and was a description of, one of the books. Each appellant asked the person who responded to his call for permission to play one of the records. If permission was granted he asked the person to buy the book described and, upon refusal, he solicited such contribution towards the publication of the pamphlets as the listener was willing to make. If a contribution was received a pamphlet was delivered upon condition that it would be read.

Cassius Street is in a thickly populated neighborhood, where about ninety per cent of the residents are Roman Catholics. A phonograph record, describing a book entitled 'Enemies', included an attack on the Catholic religion.

The statute under which the appellants were charged provides:

> "No person shall solicit money, services, subscriptions or any valuable thing for any alleged religious, charitable or philanthropic cause, from other than a member of the organization for whose benefit such person is soliciting or within the county in which such person or organization is located unless such cause shall have been approved by the secretary of the public welfare council...."

The facts which were held to support the conviction of Jesse Cantwell on the fifth count were that he stopped two men in the street, asked, and received, permission to play a phonograph record, and played the record 'Enemies', which attacked the religion and church of the two men, who were Catholics. Both were incensed by the contents of the record and were tempted to strike Cantwell unless he went away. On being told to be on his way he left their presence. There was no evidence that he was personally offensive or entered into any argument with those he interviewed.

First. We hold that the statute, as construed and applied to the appellants, deprives them of their liberty without due process of law in contravention of the Fourteenth Amendment. The fundamental concept of liberty embodied in that Amendment embraces the liberties guaranteed by the First Amendment. The First Amendment declares that Congress shall make no law respecting an establishment of religion or prohibiting the free exercise thereof. The Fourteenth Amendment has rendered the legislatures of the states as incompetent as Congress to enact such laws. The constitutional inhibition of legislation on the subject of religion has a double aspect. On the one hand, it forestalls compulsion by law of the acceptance of any creed or the practice of any form of worship. On the other hand, it safeguards the free exercise of the chosen form of religion. Thus the Amendment embraces two concepts, freedom to believe and freedom to act. The first is absolute but, in the nature of things, the second cannot be. Conduct remains subject to regulation for the protection of society. The freedom to act must have appropriate definition to preserve the enforcement of that protection. In every case the power to regulate must be so exercised as not, in attaining a permissible end, unduly to infringe the protected freedom. No one would contest the proposition that a state may not, by statute, wholly deny the right to preach or to disseminate religious views. Plainly such a previous and absolute restraint would violate the terms of the guarantee.[5] It is equally clear that a state may by general and non-discriminatory legislation regulate the times, the places, and the manner of soliciting upon its streets, and of holding meetings thereon; and may in other respects safeguard the peace, good order and comfort of the community, without unconstitutionally invading the liberties protected by the Fourteenth Amendment. The appellants are right in their insistence that the Act in question is not such a regulation. If a certificate is procured, solicitation is permitted without restraint but, in the absence of a certificate, solicitation is altogether prohibited.

The appellants urge that to require them to obtain a certificate as a condition of soliciting support for their views amounts to a prior restraint on the exercise of their religion.... The State insists that the Act ... merely safeguards against the perpetration of frauds under the cloak of religion. Conceding that this is so, the question remains whether the method adopted by Connecticut to that end transgresses the liberty safeguarded by the Constitution.

The general regulation, in the public interest, of solicitation, which does not involve any religious test and does not unreasonably obstruct or delay the collection of funds, is not open to any constitutional objection, even though the collection be for a religious purpose. Such regulation would not constitute a prohibited previous restraint on the free exercise of religion or interpose an inadmissible obstacle to its exercise.

It will be noted, however, that the Act requires an application to the secretary of the public welfare council of the State; that he is empowered to determine whether the cause is a religious one, and that the issue of a certificate depends upon his affirmative action. If he finds that the cause is not that of religion, to solicit for it be-

---

5. Compare *Near v. Minnesota*, 283 U.S. 697, 713 [(1931)].

comes a crime. He is not to issue a certificate as a matter of course. His decision to issue or refuse it involves appraisal of facts, the exercise of judgment, and the formation of an opinion. He is authorized to withhold his approval if he determines that the cause is not a religious one. Such a censorship of religion as the means of determining its right to survive is a denial of liberty protected by the First Amendment and included in the liberty which is within the protection of the Fourteenth.

Nothing we have said is intended even remotely to imply that, under the cloak of religion, persons may, with impunity, commit frauds upon the public. Certainly penal laws are available to punish such conduct. Without doubt a state may protect its citizens from fraudulent solicitation by requiring a stranger in the community, before permitting him publicly to solicit funds for any purpose, to establish his identity and his authority to act for the cause which he purports to represent. The state is likewise free to regulate the time and manner of solicitation generally, in the interest of public safety, peace, comfort or convenience. But to condition the solicitation of aid for the perpetuation of religious views or systems upon a license, the grant of which rests in the exercise of a determination by state authority as to what is a religious cause, is to lay a forbidden burden upon the exercise of liberty protected by the Constitution.

Second. We hold that, in the circumstances disclosed, the conviction of Jesse Cantwell on the fifth count must be set aside. Decision as to the lawfulness of the conviction demands the weighing of two conflicting interests. The fundamental law declares the interest of the United States that the free exercise of religion be not prohibited and that freedom to communicate information and opinion be not abridged. The state of Connecticut has an obvious interest in the preservation and protection of peace and good order within her borders. We must determine whether the alleged protection of the State's interest, means to which end would, in the absence of limitation by the federal Constitution, lie wholly within the State's discretion, has been pressed, in this instance, to a point where it has come into fatal collision with the overriding interest protected by the federal compact.

Conviction on the fifth count ... is based on a common law concept of the most general and undefined nature. The offense known as breach of the peace embraces a great variety of conduct destroying or menacing public order and tranquility. Here we have a situation analogous to a conviction under a statute sweeping in a great variety of conduct under a general and indefinite characterization, and leaving to the executive and judicial branches too wide a discretion in its application.

Having these considerations in mind, we note that Jesse Cantwell was upon a public street, where he had a right to be, and where he had a right peacefully to impart his views to others. There is no showing that his deportment was noisy, truculent, overbearing or offensive. He requested of two pedestrians permission to play to them a phonograph record. The permission was granted. It is not claimed that he intended to insult or affront the hearers by playing the record. It is plain that he wished only to interest them in his propaganda. The sound of the phonograph is not shown to have disturbed residents of the street, to have drawn a crowd, or to have impeded traffic. Thus far he had invaded no right or interest of the public or of the men accosted.

The record played by Cantwell embodies a general attack on all organized religious systems as instruments of Satan and injurious to man; it then singles out the Roman Catholic Church for strictures couched in terms which naturally would offend not only persons of that persuasion, but all others who respect the honestly held religious faith of their fellows. The hearers were in fact highly offended. One of them said he felt like hitting Cantwell and the other that he was tempted to throw Cantwell off the street. The one who testified he felt like hitting Cantwell said, in answer to the question "Did you do anything else or have any other reaction?" "No, sir, because he said he would take the victrola and he went." The other witness testified that he told Cantwell he had better get off the street before something happened to him and that was the end of the matter as Cantwell picked up his books and walked up the street.

Cantwell's conduct, in the view of the court below, did not amount to a breach of the peace. We find in the instant case no assault or threatening of bodily harm, no truculent bearing, no intentional discourtesy, no personal abuse. On the contrary, we find only an effort to persuade a willing listener to buy a book or to contribute money in the interest of what Cantwell, however misguided others may think him, conceived to be true religion.

In the realm of religious faith, and in that of political belief, sharp differences arise. In both fields the tenets of one man may seem the rankest error to his neighbor. To persuade others to his own point of view, the pleader, as we know, at times, resorts to exaggeration, to vilification of men who have been, or are, prominent in church or state, and even to false statement. But the people of this nation have ordained in the light of history, that, in spite of the probability of excesses and abuses, these liberties are, in the long view, essential to enlightened opinion and right conduct on the part of the citizens of a democracy.

The essential characteristic of these liberties is, that under their shield many types of life, character, opinion and belief can develop unmolested and unobstructed. Nowhere is this shield more necessary than in our own country for a people composed of many races and of many creeds. There are limits to the exercise of these liberties. The danger in these times from the coercive activities of those who in the delusion of racial or religious conceit would incite violence and breaches of the peace in order to deprive others of their equal right to the exercise of their liberties, is emphasized by events familiar to all. These and other transgressions of those limits the states appropriately may punish.

Although the contents of the record not unnaturally aroused animosity, we think that, in the absence of a statute narrowly drawn to define and punish specific conduct as constituting a clear and present danger to a substantial interest of the State, the petitioner's communication, considered in the light of the constitutional guarantees, raised no such clear and present menace to public peace and order as to render him liable to conviction of the common law offense in question.[10]

The judgment affirming the convictions on the third and fifth counts is reversed and the cause is remanded for further proceedings not inconsistent with this opinion. So ordered.

Reversed and remanded.

Exercise 3:

1. In what "speech" did the Cantwells engage? What criteria did you use to identify that "speech"? Keep those criteria in mind when we cover expressive conduct, below, and see whether the Supreme Court utilized the same or similar criteria in its Spence Test.

2. In what ways did Connecticut limit the Cantwells' speech?

3. What interests did Connecticut argue its prosecution of the Cantwells advanced?

4. Why did the Supreme Court reverse the Cantwells' convictions? Did it reject the state's interests?

5. The Court contrasted the unconstitutional Connecticut law with "general and non-discriminatory legislation." What did the Supreme Court have in mind? We will see this concept of "time, place, and manner restrictions" throughout the **Chapter**.

6. Note that the Supreme Court treated *Cantwell* as both a free speech and free exercise case. We will cover the Free Exercise Clause in **Chapter 2**, below.

7. Note as well that, by 1940, the Supreme Court confidently stated that "[t]he fundamental concept of liberty embodied in that Amendment embraces the liberties guaranteed by the First Amendment." This was only fifteen years after *Gitlow v. New York*, 268 U.S. 652 (1925), where the Court had incorporated the Free Speech Clause against the states.

3. "Expressive Conduct"

Unlike "pure speech," it may not be intuitive to you that expressive conduct is also protected by the First Amendment. From its earliest modern free speech cases, the Supreme Court has treated "expressive conduct," also known as "symbolic speech," as analogous to pure speech and accorded it similar protection. *Stromberg v. California*, 283 U.S. 359, 369–70 (1931); *see also West Va. State Bd. of Ed. v. Barnette*, 319 U.S. 624, 632 (1943) ("[T]he flag salute is a form of utterance."). The Supreme Court's inclusion of expressive conduct within the First Amendment's protection has been subject to strong criticism, *see, e.g., Street v. New York*, 394 U.S. 576, 610 (1969) (Black, J., dissenting), and support, *see, e.g.,* Eugene Volokh, *Symbolic Expression and the Original Meaning of the First Amendment*, 97 Geo. L.J. 1057 (2009) (arguing that the Free Speech Clause's original meaning included symbolic speech).

---

10. Compare *Schenck v. United States*, 249 U.S. 47, 52 [(1919)].

One of the primary reasons for this controversy is the concern that too-broad protection for expressive conduct will undermine government's ability to restrain unlawful activity. This tension—between, on the one hand, free speech, and, on the other hand, the Rule of Law—was displayed in the famous case of *United States v. O'Brien*, 391 U.S. 367 (1968), reprinted below:

United States v. O'Brien

391 U.S. 367 (1968)

Mr. Chief Justice Warren delivered the opinion of the Court.

On the morning of March 31, 1966, David Paul O'Brien and three companions burned their Selective Service registration certificates on the steps of the South Boston Courthouse. Immediately after the burning, members of the crowd began attacking O'Brien and his companions. An FBI agent ushered O'Brien to safety inside the courthouse. O'Brien stated to FBI agents that he had burned his registration certificate because of his beliefs, knowing that he was violating federal law....

For this act, O'Brien was indicted, tried, convicted, and sentenced in the United States District Court for the District of Massachusetts. He stated in argument to the jury that he burned the certificate publicly to influence others to adopt his antiwar beliefs....

Section 462(b)(3) ... was amended by Congress in 1965, so that at the time O'Brien burned his certificate an offense was committed by any person, "who forges, alters, knowingly destroys, knowingly mutilates, or in any manner changes any such certificate...." In the District Court, O'Brien argued that the 1965 Amendment prohibiting the knowing destruction or mutilation of certificates was unconstitutional because it was enacted to abridge free speech, and because it served no legitimate legislative purpose. The District Court rejected these arguments....

On appeal, the Court of Appeals for the First Circuit held the 1965 Amendment unconstitutional as a law abridging freedom of speech. [After reviewing the Amendment's legislative history, the court concluded that] the 1965 Amendment ran afoul of the First Amendment by singling out persons engaged in protests for special treatment....

... We hold that the 1965 Amendment is constitutional. We therefore vacate the judgment of the Court of Appeals....

I.

When a male reaches the age of 18, he is required by the Universal Military Training and Service Act to register with a local draft board. He is assigned a Selective Service number, and within five days he is issued a registration certificate. Subsequently, and based on a questionnaire completed by the registrant, he is assigned a classification denoting his eligibility for induction, and thereafter he is issued a Notice of Classification.

Both the registration and classification certificates are small white cards, approximately 2 by 3 inches. The registration certificate specifies the name of the registrant, the date of registration, and the number and address of the local board with which he is registered. Also inscribed upon it are the date and place of the registrant's birth, his residence at registration, his physical description, his signature, and his Selective Service number....

The classification certificate shows the registrant's name, Selective Service number, signature, and eligibility classification. It specifies whether he was so classified by his local board, an appeal board, or the President. It contains the address of his local board and the date the certificate was mailed.

Both the registration and classification certificates bear notices that the registrant must notify his local board in writing of every change in address, physical condition, and occupational, marital, family, dependency, and military status, and of any other fact which might change his classification. Both also contain a notice that the registrant's Selective Service number should appear on all communications to his local board.

Congress demonstrated its concern that certificates issued by the Selective Service System might be abused well before the 1965 Amendment here challenged. The 1948 Act itself prohibited many different abuses. In addition, regulations of the Selective Service System required registrants to keep both their registration and classification certificates in their personal possession at all times....

By the 1965 Amendment, Congress added to § 12(b)(3) ... the provision here at issue.... We note at the outset that the 1965 Amendment plainly does not abridge free speech on its face, and we do not understand O'Brien to argue otherwise. Amended § 12(b)(3) on its face ... deals with conduct having no connection with speech. It prohibits the knowing destruction of certificates issued by the Selective Service System, and there is nothing necessarily expressive about such conduct. The Amendment does not distinguish between public and private destruction, and it does not punish only destruction engaged in for the purpose of expressing views....

II.

O'Brien first argues that the 1965 Amendment is unconstitutional as applied to him because his act of burning his registration certificate was protected "symbolic speech" within the First Amendment. His argument is that the freedom of expression which the First Amendment guarantees includes all modes of "communication of ideas by conduct," and that his conduct is within this definition because he did it in "demonstration against the war and against the draft."

We cannot accept the view that an apparently limitless variety of conduct can be labeled "speech" whenever the person engaging in the conduct intends thereby to express an idea. However, even on the assumption that the alleged communicative element in O'Brien's conduct is sufficient to bring into play the First Amendment, it does not necessarily follow that the destruction of a registration certificate is constitutionally protected activity. This Court has held that when "speech" and "nonspeech" elements are combined in the same course of conduct, a sufficiently important governmental interest in regulating the nonspeech element can justify incidental limitations on First Amendment freedoms.... [W]e think it clear that a government regulation is sufficiently justified if it is within the constitutional power of the Government; if it furthers an important or substantial governmental interest; if the governmental interest is unrelated to the suppression of free expression; and if the incidental restriction on alleged First Amendment freedoms is no greater than is essential to the furtherance of that interest....

The constitutional power of Congress to raise and support armies and to make all laws necessary and proper to that end is broad and sweeping. The power of Congress to classify and conscript manpower for military service is "beyond question." Pursuant to this power, Congress may establish a system of registration for individuals liable for training and service. The issuance of certificates indicating the registration and eligibility classification of individuals is a legitimate and substantial administrative aid in the functioning of this system. And legislation to insure the continuing availability of issued certificates serves a legitimate and substantial purpose in the system's administration.

... Many of the [certificates'] purposes would be defeated by the certificates' destruction or mutilation. Among these are:

1. The registration certificate serves as proof that the individual described thereon has registered for the draft. The classification certificate shows the eligibility classification of a named but undescribed individual. Voluntarily displaying the two certificates is an easy and painless way for a young man to dispel a question as to whether he might be delinquent in his Selective Service obligations.... Additionally, in a time of national crisis, reasonable availability to each registrant of the two small cards assures a rapid and uncomplicated means for determining his fitness for immediate induction....

2. The information supplied on the certificates facilitates communication between registrants and local boards, simplifying the system and benefiting all concerned. To begin with, each certificate bears the address of the registrant's local board.... Further, each card bears the registrant's Selective Service number....

3. Both certificates carry continual reminders that the registrant must notify his local board of any change of address, and other specified changes in his status....

4. The regulatory scheme involving Selective Service certificates includes clearly valid prohibitions against the alteration, forgery, or similar deceptive misuse of certificates. The destruction or mutilation of certificates obviously increases the difficulty of detecting and tracing abuses such as these....

The many functions performed by Selective Service certificates establish beyond doubt that Congress has a legitimate and substantial interest in preventing their wanton and unrestrained destruction and assuring their continuing availability by punishing people who knowingly and wilfully destroy or mutilate them....

....

We think it apparent that the continuing availability to each registrant of his Selective Service certificates substantially furthers the smooth and proper functioning of the system that Congress has established to raise armies. We think it also apparent that the Nation has a vital interest in having a system for raising armies that functions with maximum efficiency and is capable of easily and quickly responding to continually changing circumstances. For these reasons, the Government has a substantial interest in assuring the continuing availability of issued Selective Service certificates.

It is equally clear that the 1965 Amendment specifically protects this substantial governmental interest. We perceive no alternative means that would more precisely and narrowly assure the continuing availability of issued Selective Service certificates than a law which prohibits their wilful mutilation or destruction. The 1965 Amendment prohibits such conduct and does nothing more. In other words, both the governmental interest and the operation of the 1965 Amendment are limited to the noncommunicative aspect of O'Brien's conduct. The governmental interest and the scope of the 1965 Amendment are limited to preventing harm to the smooth and efficient functioning of the Selective Service System. When O'Brien deliberately rendered unavailable his registration certificate, he wilfully frustrated this governmental interest. For this noncommunicative impact of his conduct, and for nothing else, he was convicted.

The case at bar is therefore unlike one where the alleged governmental interest in regulating conduct arises in some measure because the communication allegedly integral to the conduct is itself thought to be harmful. In *Stromberg v. People of State of California*, 283 U.S. 359 (1931), for example, this Court struck down a statutory phrase which punished people who expressed their "opposition to organized government" by displaying "any flag, badge, banner, or device." Since the statute there was aimed at suppressing communication it could not be sustained as a regulation of noncommunicative conduct.

In conclusion, we find that because of the Government's substantial interest in assuring the continuing availability of issued Selective Service certificates, because amended § 462(b) is an appropriately narrow means of protecting this interest and condemns only the independent noncommunicative impact of conduct within its reach, and because the noncommunicative impact of O'Brien's act of burning his registration certificate frustrated the Government's interest, a sufficient governmental interest has been shown to justify O'Brien's conviction.

III.

O'Brien finally argues that the 1965 Amendment is unconstitutional as enacted because what he calls the "purpose" of Congress was "to suppress freedom of speech." We reject this argument because under settled principles the purpose of Congress, as O'Brien uses that term, is not a basis for declaring this legislation unconstitutional.

It is a familiar principle of constitutional law that this Court will not strike down an otherwise constitutional statute on the basis of an alleged illicit legislative motive. As the Court long ago stated: "The decisions of this court from the beginning lend no support whatever to the assumption that the judiciary may restrain the exercise of lawful power on the assumption that a wrongful purpose or motive has caused the power to be exerted."

Inquiries into congressional motives or purposes are a hazardous matter. When the issue is simply the interpretation of legislation, the Court will look to statements by legislators for guidance as to the purpose of the legislature, because the benefit to sound decision-making in this circumstance is thought sufficient to risk the possibility of misreading Congress' purpose. It is entirely a different matter when we are asked to void a statute that is, under well-settled criteria, constitutional on its face, on the basis of what fewer than a handful of Congressmen said about it. What motivates one legislator to make a speech about a statute is not necessarily what motivates scores of others to enact it, and the stakes are sufficiently high for us to eschew guesswork. We decline to void essentially on the ground that it is unwise legislation which Congress had the undoubted power to enact and which could be reenacted in its exact form if the same or another legislator made a "wiser" speech about it.

… There was little floor debate on this legislation in either House. Only Senator Thurmond commented on its substantive features in the Senate. After his brief statement, and without any additional substantive comments, the bill passed the Senate. In the House debate only two Congressmen addressed themselves to the Amendment. The bill was passed after their statements without any further debate by a vote of 393 to 1. It is principally on the basis of the statements by these three Congressmen that O'Brien makes his congressional-"purpose" argument. We note that if we were to examine legislative purpose in the instant case, we would be obliged to consider not only these statements but also the more authoritative reports of the Senate and House Armed Services Committees. While both reports make clear a concern with the "defiant" destruction of so-called "draft cards" and with "open" encouragement to others to destroy their cards, both reports also indicate that this concern stemmed from an apprehension that unrestrained destruction of cards would disrupt the smooth functioning of the Selective Service System.

IV.

… Accordingly, we vacate the judgment of the Court of Appeals.

It is so ordered.

Mr. Justice Marshall took no part in the consideration or decision of these cases.

Mr. Justice Harlan, concurring. [Opinion omitted.]

Mr. Justice Douglas, dissenting. [Opinion omitted.]

Exercise 4:

1. In what way was O'Brien's freedom of speech limited by the federal government?

2. The Supreme Court assumed that "the alleged communicative element in O'Brien's conduct is sufficient to bring into play the First Amendment." Is that a reasonable assumption?

3. What test did the *O'Brien* Court articulate to evaluate restrictions on expressive conduct?

4. Was the challenged statute content neutral? In other words, did it regulate based on the speech's subject matter or viewpoint?

5. Was the challenged statute supported by an important governmental interest?

6. Articulate the chain of reasoning that tied the challenged statute to the federal power(s) and purpose(s) the regulation was said to advance. Is that chain too thin? Why or why not?

7. Chief Justice Warren claimed that the Court should refrain from inquiring into legislative purpose. What reasons did he provide for that position? Are those reasons persuasive?

8. Did the *O'Brien* Court's rejection of purpose inquiry fit with other areas of the law? If not, is there a way to justify the different treatment?

9. One practical effect of the *O'Brien* Test is that, so long as the government is regulating expressive conduct without reference to the content of the communicative component of the expressive conduct, the government has significant leeway. For example, a city could limit a pro-life rally in a city park to certain times, places, or manners, so long as it was doing so in a neutral way. Consequently, a city could prohibit the rally after 10 p.m., but it could not prohibit the rally because it was on the subject of abortion. These types of regulations—called time, place, and manner restrictions—are described in more detail, in Section I, below.

O'Brien pronounced the test to evaluate restrictions on expressive conduct, but the Court in *O'Brien* assumed that O'Brien's activity was, in fact, protected by the First Amendment. The *O'Brien* Court did not spell out criteria to determine what activity qualified for Free Speech Clause protection. *Spence v. Washington*, 418 U.S. 405 (1974), reprinted below, articulated the test the Supreme Court sketched to distinguished protected expressive conduct from unprotected conduct.

Spence v. Washington

418 U.S. 405 (1974)

PER CURIAM.

I

On May 10, 1970, appellant, a college student, hung his United States flag from the window of his apartment on private property in Seattle, Washington. The flag was upside down, and attached to the front and back was a peace symbol (i.e., a circle enclosing a trident) made of removable black tape. The window was above the ground floor. The flag measured approximately three by five feet and was plainly visible to passersby. The peace symbol occupied roughly half of the surface of the flag.

Three Seattle police officers observed the flag and entered the apartment house. They were met at the main door by appellant, who said: "I suppose you are here about the flag. I didn't know there was anything wrong with it. I will take it down." Appellant permitted the officers to enter his apartment, where they seized the flag and arrested him....

... [T]he State relied on the so-called "improper use" statute, Wash Rev. Code §9.86.020. This statute provides, in pertinent part:

"No person shall, in any manner, for exhibition or display:

"(1) Place or cause to be placed any word, figure, mark, picture, design, drawing or advertisement of any nature upon any flag, standard, color, ensign or shield of the United States or of this state ... or

"(2) Expose to public view any such flag, standard, color, ensign or shield upon which shall have been printed, painted or otherwise produced, or to which shall have been attached, appended, affixed or annexed any such word, figure, mark, picture, design, drawing or advertisement...."

Appellant took the stand in his own defense. He testified that he put a peace symbol on the flag and displayed it to public view as a protest against the invasion of Cambodia and the killings at Kent State University, events which occurred a few days prior to his arrest. He said that his purpose was to associate the American flag with peace instead of war and violence: "I felt there had been so much killing and that this was not what America stood for. I felt that the flag stood for America and I wanted people to know that I thought America stood for peace."

... The jury returned a verdict of guilty. The Washington Court of Appeals reversed the conviction. [T]he Washington Supreme Court reversed and reinstated the conviction.

II

... The undisputed facts are that appellant "wanted people to know that I thought America stood for peace." To be sure, appellant did not choose to articulate his views through printed or spoken words. It is therefore necessary to determine whether his activity was sufficiently imbued with elements of communication to fall within the scope of the First and Fourteenth Amendments, for as the Court noted in *United States v. O'Brien*, 391 U.S. 367, 376 (1968), "[w]e cannot accept the view that an apparently limitless variety of conduct can be labeled 'speech' whenever the person engaging in the conduct intends thereby to express an idea." But the nature of appellant's activity, combined with the factual context and environment in which it was undertaken, lead to the conclusion that he engaged in a form of protected expression.

The Court for decades has recognized the communicative connotations of the use of flags. In many of their uses flags are a form of symbolism comprising a "primitive but effective way of communicating ideas...," and "a short cut from mind to mind." *West Virginia State Board of Education v. Barnette*, 319 U.S. 624, 632 (1943). On this record there can be little doubt that appellant communicated through the use of symbols. The symbolism included not only the flag but also the superimposed peace symbol.

Moreover, the context in which a symbol is used for purposes of expression is important, for the context may give meaning to the symbol.... In this case, appellant's activity was roughly simultaneous with and concededly triggered by the Cambodian incursion and the Kent State tragedy, also issues of great public moment. A flag bearing a peace symbol and displayed upside down by a student today might be interpreted as nothing more than bizarre behavior, but it would have been difficult for the great majority of citizens to miss the drift of appellant's point at the time that he made it.

It may be noted, further, that this was not an act of mindless nihilism. Rather, it was a pointed expression of anguish by appellant about the then-current domestic and foreign affairs of his government. An intent to convey a particularized message was present, and in the surrounding circumstances the likelihood was great that the message would be understood by those who viewed it.

We are confronted then with a case of prosecution for the expression of an idea through activity. Accordingly, we must examine with particular care the interests advanced by appellee to support its prosecution. [The Supreme Court went on to hold that, as applied to Spence, the statute violated the Constitution.]

The judgment is reversed.

It is so ordered.

Judgment reversed.

Mr. Justice Blackmun concurs in the result.

Mr. Justice Douglas, concurring. [Opinion omitted.]

Mr. Chief Justice Burger, dissenting. [Opinion omitted.]

Mr. Justice Rehnquist, with whom The Chief Justice and Mr. Justice White join, dissenting. [Opinion omitted.]

Exercise 5:

1. What test did the Supreme Court articulate to differentiate protected expressive conduct from unprotected nonexpressive activity?

2. From where did the Court draw the test? Is the line drawn by the Supreme Court faithful to the Constitution's text? Its original meaning? Judicial precedent?

3. The *Spence* Test is meant to navigate a tension. On the one hand, expressive conduct has some of the same qualities as pure speech. It, for instance, communicates ideas and messages. On the other hand, conduct is different from speech in many ways, including its consequences. So, the Court did not wish to subject all criminal law to rigorous judicial scrutiny. Is the line drawn by the Supreme Court the appropriate line? Is there expressive activity that the *Spence* Test fails to protect that should be protected? Or, nonexpressive activity that is, but should not be protected?

4. The *Spence* Test is a relatively hard rule. Would it have been better for the Court to use a multifactor balancing test to ascertain whether particular activity is expressive or not?

Though *Spence's* underlying facts involved defacement of the United States Flag, the Supreme Court did not squarely face the constitutionality of bans on desecration of the American Flag until *Texas v. Johnson*, 491 U.S. 397 (1989), reprinted below. This was, and remains, one of the most controversial issues in constitutional law.

Texas v. Johnson
491 U.S. 397 (1989)

JUSTICE BRENNAN delivered the opinion of the Court.

I

While the Republican National Convention was taking place in Dallas in 1984, respondent Johnson participated in a political demonstration dubbed the "Republican War Chest Tour." As explained in literature distributed by the demonstrators and in speeches made by them, the purpose of this event was to protest the policies of the Reagan administration and of certain Dallas-based corporations. The demonstrators marched through the Dallas streets, chanting political slogans and stopping at several corporate locations to stage "die-ins" intended to dramatize the consequences of nuclear war. On several occasions they spray-painted the walls of buildings and overturned potted plants, but Johnson himself took no part in such activities. He did, however, accept an American flag handed to him by a fellow protestor who had taken it from a flagpole outside one of the targeted buildings.

The demonstration ended in front of Dallas City Hall, where Johnson unfurled the American flag, doused it with kerosene, and set it on fire. While the flag burned, the protestors chanted: "America, the red, white, and blue, we spit on you." After the demonstrators dispersed, a witness to the flag burning collected the flag's remains and buried them in his backyard. No one was physically injured or threatened with injury, though several witnesses testified that they had been seriously offended by the flag burning.

… Johnson alone was charged with a crime. The only criminal offense with which he was charged was the desecration of a venerated object in violation of Tex. Penal Code Ann. § 42.09(a)(3) (1989).[1] After a trial, he was convicted, sentenced to one year in prison, and fined $2,000. The Court of Appeals for the Fifth District of Texas at Dallas affirmed Johnson's conviction, but the Texas Court of Criminal Appeals reversed, holding that the State could not, consistent with the First Amendment, punish Johnson for burning the flag in these circumstances.

[We now affirm.]

II

Johnson was convicted of flag desecration for burning the flag rather than for uttering insulting words. This fact somewhat complicates our consideration of his conviction under the First Amendment. We must first determine whether Johnson's burning of the flag constituted expressive conduct, permitting him to invoke the First Amendment in challenging his conviction. See, *e.g., Spence v. Washington*, 418 U.S.

---

1. Texas Penal Code Ann. § 42.09 (1989) provides:

"§ 42.09. Desecration of Venerated Object

"(a) A person commits an offense if he intentionally or knowingly desecrates: …

"(3) a state or national flag."

405, 409–411 (1974). If his conduct was expressive, we next decide whether the State's regulation is related to the suppression of free expression. See, *e.g., United States v. O'Brien*, 391 U.S. 367, 377 (1968). If the State's regulation is not related to expression, then the less stringent standard we announced in *United States v. O'Brien* for regulations of noncommunicative conduct controls. If it is, then we are outside of *O'Brien*'s test, and we must ask whether this interest justifies Johnson's conviction under a more demanding standard.

The First Amendment literally forbids the abridgment only of "speech," but we have long recognized that its protection does not end at the spoken or written word.... [W]e have acknowledged that conduct may be "sufficiently imbued with elements of communication to fall within the scope of the First and Fourteenth Amendments," *Spence, supra*, at 409.

In deciding whether particular conduct possesses sufficient communicative elements to bring the First Amendment into play, we have asked whether "[a]n intent to convey a particularized message was present, and [whether] the likelihood was great that the message would be understood by those who viewed it." Especially pertinent to this case are our decisions recognizing the communicative nature of conduct relating to flags. Attaching a peace sign to the flag, *Spence, supra*, at 409–410; refusing to salute the flag, *West Va. St. Bd. of Educ. v. Barnette*, 319 U.S., [624,] 632 [(1943)]; and displaying a red flag, *Stromberg v. California*, 283 U.S. 359, 368–369 (1931), we have held, all may find shelter under the First Amendment. That we have had little difficulty identifying an expressive element in conduct relating to flags should not be surprising. The very purpose of a national flag is to serve as a symbol of our country.

We have not automatically concluded, however, that any action taken with respect to our flag is expressive. Instead, in characterizing such action for First Amendment purposes, we have considered the context in which it occurred.

The State of Texas conceded for purposes of its oral argument in this case that Johnson's conduct was expressive conduct. Johnson burned an American flag as part—indeed, as the culmination—of a political demonstration that coincided with the convening of the Republican Party and its renomination of Ronald Reagan for President. The expressive, overtly political nature of this conduct was both intentional and overwhelmingly apparent. At his trial, Johnson explained his reasons for burning the flag as follows: "The American Flag was burned as Ronald Reagan was being renominated as President. And a more powerful statement of symbolic speech, whether you agree with it or not, couldn't have been made at that time. It's quite a just position [juxtaposition]. We had new patriotism and no patriotism." In these circumstances, Johnson's burning of the flag was conduct "sufficiently imbued with elements of communication" to implicate the First Amendment.

III

The government generally has a freer hand in restricting expressive conduct than it has in restricting the written or spoken word. See *O'Brien*, 391 U.S. at 376–377.

Thus, although we have recognized that where "'speech' and 'nonspeech' elements are combined in the same course of conduct, a sufficiently important governmental interest in regulating the nonspeech element can justify incidental limitations on First Amendment freedoms," *O'Brien, supra,* at 376, we have limited the applicability of *O'Brien*'s relatively lenient standard to those cases in which "the governmental interest is unrelated to the suppression of free expression."

In order to decide whether *O'Brien*'s test applies here, therefore, we must decide whether Texas has asserted an interest in support of Johnson's conviction that is unrelated to the suppression of expression. The State offers two separate interests to justify this conviction: preventing breaches of the peace and preserving the flag as a symbol of nationhood and national unity. We hold that the first interest is not implicated on this record and that the second is related to the suppression of expression.

A

Texas claims that its interest in preventing breaches of the peace justifies Johnson's conviction for flag desecration. However, no disturbance of the peace actually occurred or threatened to occur because of Johnson's burning of the flag. The only evidence offered by the State at trial to show the reaction to Johnson's actions was the testimony of several persons who had been seriously offended by the flag burning.

The State's position, therefore, amounts to a claim that an audience that takes serious offense at particular expression is necessarily likely to disturb the peace and that the expression may be prohibited on this basis. Our precedents do not countenance such a presumption. On the contrary, they recognize that a principal "function of free speech under our system of government is to invite dispute. It may indeed best serve its high purpose when it induces a condition of unrest, creates dissatisfaction with conditions as they are, or even stirs people to anger." *Tinker v. Des Moines Independent Community School Dist.* 393 U.S. [503,] 508–509 [(1969)].

Thus, we have not permitted the government to assume that every expression of a provocative idea will incite a riot, but have instead required careful consideration of the actual circumstances surrounding such expression, asking whether the expression "is directed to inciting or producing imminent lawless action and is likely to incite or produce such action." *Brandenburg v. Ohio*, 395 U.S. 444, 447 (1969). To accept Texas' arguments that it need only demonstrate "the potential for a breach of the peace," and that every flag burning necessarily possesses that potential, would be to eviscerate our holding in *Brandenburg*. This we decline to do.

Nor does Johnson's expressive conduct fall within that small class of "fighting words" that are "likely to provoke the average person to retaliation, and thereby cause a breach of the peace." *Chaplinsky v. New Hampshire*, 315 U.S. 568, 574 (1942). No reasonable onlooker would have regarded Johnson's generalized expression of dissatisfaction with the policies of the Federal Government as a direct personal insult or an invitation to exchange fisticuffs.

We thus conclude that the State's interest in maintaining order is not implicated on these facts.

content-based

B

➤ The State also asserts an interest in preserving the flag as a symbol of nationhood and national unity. We are persuaded that this interest is related to expression in the case of Johnson's burning of the flag. The State, apparently, is concerned that such conduct will lead people to believe either that the flag does not stand for nationhood and national unity, but instead reflects other, less positive concepts, or that the concepts reflected in the flag do not in fact exist, that is, that we do not enjoy unity as a Nation. These concerns blossom only when a person's treatment of the flag communicates some message, and thus are related "to the suppression of free expression" within the meaning of *O'Brien*. We are thus outside of *O'Brien*'s test altogether.

IV

It remains to consider whether the State's interest in preserving the flag as a symbol of nationhood and national unity justifies Johnson's conviction.

Johnson was not, we add, prosecuted for the expression of just any idea; he was prosecuted for his expression of dissatisfaction with the policies of this country, expression situated at the core of our First Amendment values. Moreover, Johnson was prosecuted because he knew that his politically charged expression would cause "serious offense." If he had burned the flag as a means of disposing of it because it was dirty or torn, he would not have been convicted of flag desecration under this Texas law. The Texas law is thus not aimed at protecting the physical integrity of the flag in all circumstances, but is designed instead to protect it only against impairments that would cause serious offense to others.

Whether Johnson's treatment of the flag violated Texas law thus depended on the likely communicative impact of his expressive conduct. [T]his restriction on Johnson's expression is content based. Johnson's political expression was restricted because of the content of the message he conveyed. We must therefore subject the State's asserted interest in preserving the special symbolic character of the flag to "the most exacting scrutiny."

Texas argues that its interest in preserving the flag as a symbol of *nationhood* and *national unity* survives this close analysis. [T]he State's claim is that it has an interest in preserving the flag as a symbol of nationhood and national unity, a symbol with a determinate range of meanings. According to Texas, if one physically treats the flag in a way that would tend to cast doubt on either the idea that nationhood and national unity are the flag's referents or that national unity actually exists, the message conveyed thereby is a harmful one and therefore may be prohibited.[9]

---

9. Texas claims that "Texas is not endorsing, protecting, avowing or prohibiting any particular philosophy." If Texas means to suggest that its asserted interest does not prefer Democrats over Socialists, or Republicans over Democrats, for example, then it is beside the point, for Johnson does not rely on such an argument. He argues instead that the State's desire to maintain the flag as a symbol of nationhood and national unity assumes that there is only one proper view of the flag. Thus, if Texas means to argue that its interest does not prefer *any* viewpoint over another, it is mistaken; surely one's attitude toward the flag and its referents is a viewpoint.

If there is a bedrock principle underlying the First Amendment, it is that the government may not prohibit the expression of an idea simply because society finds the idea itself offensive or disagreeable. We have not recognized an exception to this principle even where our flag has been involved. Nor may the government, we have held, compel conduct that would evince respect for the flag. "To sustain the compulsory flag salute we are required to say that a Bill of Rights which guards the individual's right to speak his own mind, left it open to public authorities to compel him to utter what is not in his mind." *Barnette*, 319 U.S., at 6[24]. In *Spence*, we held that the same interest asserted by Texas here was insufficient to support a criminal conviction under a flag-misuse statute for the taping of a peace sign to an American flag. In short, nothing in our precedents suggests that a State may foster its own view of the flag by prohibiting expressive conduct relating to it.

Texas' focus on the precise nature of Johnson's expression, moreover, misses the point of our prior decisions: their enduring lesson, that the government may not prohibit expression simply because it disagrees with its message, is not dependent on the particular mode in which one chooses to express an idea. If we were to hold that a State may forbid flag burning wherever it is likely to endanger the flag's symbolic role, but allow it wherever burning a flag promotes that role[,] we would be saying that when it comes to impairing the flag's physical integrity, the flag itself may be used as a symbol ... only in one direction. We would be permitting a State to "prescribe what shall be orthodox" by saying that one may burn the flag to convey one's attitude toward it and its referents only if one does not endanger the flag's representation of nationhood and national unity.

To conclude that the government may permit designated symbols to be used to communicate only a limited set of messages would be to enter territory having no discernible or defensible boundaries. Could the government, on this theory, prohibit the burning of state flags? Of copies of the Presidential seal? Of the Constitution? In evaluating these choices under the First Amendment, how would we decide which symbols were sufficiently special to warrant this unique status? To do so, we would be forced to consult our own political preferences, and impose them on the citizenry, in the very way that the First Amendment forbids us to do.

It is not the State's ends, but its means, to which we object. It cannot be gainsaid that there is a special place reserved for the flag in this Nation, and thus we do not doubt that the government has a legitimate interest in making efforts to "preserv[e] the national flag as an unalloyed symbol of our country." Congress has, for example, enacted precatory regulations describing the proper treatment of the flag, and we cast no doubt on the legitimacy of its interest in making such recommendations. To say that the government has an interest in encouraging proper treatment of the flag, however, is not to say that it may criminally punish a person for burning a flag as a means of political protest.

We are fortified in today's conclusion by our conviction that forbidding criminal punishment for conduct such as Johnson's will not endanger the special role played by our flag or the feelings it inspires. Indeed, Texas' argument that the burning of an American flag " 'is an act having a high likelihood to cause a breach of the peace,' " and its statute's implicit assumption that physical mistreatment of the flag will lead to "serious offense," tend to confirm that the flag's special role is not in danger; if it were, no one would riot or take offense because a flag had been burned.

We are tempted to say, in fact, that the flag's deservedly cherished place in our community will be strengthened, not weakened, by our holding today. Our decision is a reaffirmation of the principles of freedom and inclusiveness that the flag best reflects, and of the conviction that our toleration of criticism such as Johnson's is a sign and source of our strength.... It is the Nation's resilience, not its rigidity, that Texas sees reflected in the flag — and it is that resilience that we reassert today.

The way to preserve the flag's special role is not to punish those who feel differently about these matters. It is to persuade them that they are wrong. And, precisely because it is our flag that is involved, one's response to the flag burner may exploit the uniquely persuasive power of the flag itself. We can imagine no more appropriate response to burning a flag than waving one's own, no better way to counter a flag burner's message than by saluting the flag that burns, no surer means of preserving the dignity even of the flag that burned than by — as one witness here did — according its remains a respectful burial. We do not consecrate the flag by punishing its desecration, for in doing so we dilute the freedom that this cherished emblem represents.

The judgment of the Texas Court of Criminal Appeals is therefore

Affirmed.

JUSTICE KENNEDY, concurring.

... I join [t]his opinion without reservation, but with a keen sense that this case, like others before us from time to time, exacts its personal toll.... The hard fact is that sometimes we must make decisions we do not like. We make them because they are right, right in the sense that the law and the Constitution, as we see them, compel the result. And so great is our commitment to the process that, except in the rare case, we do not pause to express distaste for the result, perhaps for fear of undermining a valued principle that dictates the decision. This is one of those rare cases.

CHIEF JUSTICE REHNQUIST, with whom JUSTICE WHITE and JUSTICE O'CONNOR join, dissenting.

For more than 200 years, the American flag has occupied a unique position as the symbol of our Nation, a uniqueness that justifies a governmental prohibition against flag burning in the way respondent Johnson did here.

At the time of the American Revolution, the flag served to unify the Thirteen Colonies at home, while obtaining recognition of national sovereignty abroad.... During the War of 1812, Francis Scott Key, a Washington lawyer, had been granted permission by the British to board one of their warships to negotiate the release of an American who had been taken prisoner. That night, waiting anxiously on the British ship, Key watched the British fleet firing on Fort McHenry. Finally, at daybreak, he saw the fort's American flag still flying; the British attack had failed. Intensely moved, he began to scribble on the back of an envelope the poem that became our national anthem....

The American flag played a central role in our Nation's most tragic conflict, when the North fought against the South. The lowering of the American flag at Fort Sumter was viewed as the start of the war.... In the First and Second World Wars, thousands of our countrymen died on foreign soil fighting for the American cause. At Iwo Jima in the Second World War, United States Marines fought hand to hand against thousands of Japanese[, and when they] reached the top of Mount Suribachi, they raised a piece of pipe upright and from one end fluttered a flag....

During the Korean war, the successful amphibious landing of American troops at Inchon was marked by the raising of an American flag within an hour of the event. Impetus for the enactment of the Federal Flag Desecration Statute in 1967 came from the impact of flag burnings in the United States on troop morale in Vietnam....

The flag symbolizes the Nation in peace as well as in war. It signifies our national presence on battleships, airplanes, military installations, and public buildings from the United States Capitol to the thousands of county courthouses and city halls throughout the country. Two flags are prominently placed in our courtroom. Countless flags are placed by the graves of loved ones each year on what was first called Decoration Day, and is now called Memorial Day. The flag is traditionally placed on the casket of deceased members of the Armed Forces, and it is later given to the deceased's family. Congress has provided that the flag be flown at half-staff upon the death of the President, Vice President, and other government officials "as a mark of respect to their memory." The flag identifies United States merchant ships, and "[t]he laws of the Union protect our commerce wherever the flag of the country may float."

No other American symbol has been as universally honored as the flag.... Both Congress and the States have enacted numerous laws regulating misuse of the American flag. With the exception of Alaska and Wyoming, all of the States now have statutes prohibiting the burning of the flag....

The American flag, then, ... has come to be the visible symbol embodying our Nation. It does not represent the views of any particular political party, and it does not represent any particular political philosophy. The flag is not simply another "idea" or "point of view" competing for recognition in the marketplace of ideas. Millions and millions of Americans regard it with an almost mystical reverence regardless of what sort of social, political, or philosophical beliefs they may have....

But the Court insists that the Texas statute prohibiting the public burning of the American flag infringes on respondent Johnson's freedom of expression. Such freedom, of course, is not absolute.... [As in *Chaplinsky v. New Hampshire*, 315, U.S. 568 (1942), h]ere it may equally well be said that the public burning of the American flag by Johnson was no essential part of any exposition of ideas, and at the same time it had a tendency to incite a breach of the peace. Johnson was free to make any verbal denunciation of the flag that he wished; indeed, he was free to burn the flag in private.

He could publicly burn other symbols of the Government or effigies of political leaders. He did lead a march through the streets of Dallas, and conducted a rally in front of the Dallas City Hall. He engaged in a "die-in" to protest nuclear weapons. He shouted out various slogans during the march. For none of these acts was he arrested or prosecuted; it was only when he proceeded to burn publicly an American flag stolen from its rightful owner that he violated the Texas statute....

Johnson's public burning of the flag in this case ... obviously did convey Johnson's bitter dislike of his country. But his act, like Chaplinsky's provocative words, conveyed nothing that could not have been conveyed and was not conveyed just as forcefully in a dozen different ways. As with "fighting words," so with flag burning, for purposes of the First Amendment: It is "no essential part of any exposition of ideas, and [is] of such slight social value as a step to truth that any benefit that may be derived from [it] is clearly outweighed" by the public interest in avoiding a probable breach of the peace....

The result of the Texas statute is obviously to deny one in Johnson's frame of mind one of many means of "symbolic speech." Far from being a case of "one picture being worth a thousand words," flag burning is the equivalent of an inarticulate grunt or roar that, it seems fair to say, is most likely to be indulged in not to express any particular idea, but to antagonize others.... The Texas statute deprived Johnson of only one rather inarticulate symbolic form of protest—a form of protest that was profoundly offensive to many—and left him with a full panoply of other symbols and every conceivable form of verbal expression to express his deep disapproval of national policy.... It was Johnson's use of this particular symbol, and not the idea that he sought to convey by it or by his many other expressions, for which he was punished....

The Court decides that the American flag is just another symbol, about which not only must opinions pro and con be tolerated, but for which the most minimal public respect may not be enjoined. The government may conscript men into the Armed Forces where they must fight and perhaps die for the flag, but the government may not prohibit the public burning of the banner under which they fight. I would uphold the Texas statute as applied in this case.

JUSTICE STEVENS, dissenting.

As the Court analyzes this case, it presents the question whether the State of Texas, or indeed the Federal Government, has the power to prohibit the public desecration of the American flag. The question is unique....

A country's flag is a symbol of more than "nationhood and national unity." It also signifies the ideas that characterize the society that has chosen that emblem as well as the special history that has animated the growth and power of those ideas.

So it is with the American flag. It is more than a proud symbol of the courage, the determination, and the gifts of nature that transformed 13 fledgling Colonies into a world power. It is a symbol of freedom, of equal opportunity, of religious tolerance, and of good will for other peoples who share our aspirations....

The value of the flag as a symbol cannot be measured. Even so, I have no doubt that the interest in preserving that value for the future is both significant and legitimate. [I]n my considered judgment, sanctioning the public desecration of the flag will tarnish its value—both for those who cherish the ideas for which it waves and for those who desire to don the robes of martyrdom by burning it. That tarnish is not justified by the trivial burden on free expression occasioned by requiring that an available, alternative mode of expression—including uttering words critical of the flag—be employed....

The ideas of liberty and equality have been an irresistible force in motivating leaders like Patrick Henry, Susan B. Anthony, and Abraham Lincoln, schoolteachers like Nathan Hale and Booker T. Washington, the Philippine Scouts who fought at Bataan, and the soldiers who scaled the bluff at Omaha Beach. If those ideas are worth fighting for—and our history demonstrates that they are—it cannot be true that the flag that uniquely symbolizes their power is not itself worthy of protection from unnecessary desecration.

Exercise 6:

1. Why did the majority classify flag burning by Johnson as protected expressive conduct? Was that conclusion right, or was Chief Justice Rehnquist's label—"inarticulate grunt"—a better application of the Spence Test? If Johnson's activity was expressive, what "particularized" message did he send? Was there a great likelihood that the intended audience would understand *that* message?

2. What reasons did the Court give for its ruling that Texas' ban on flag burning was content based? Did Chief Justice Rehnquist convince you otherwise?

3. Did Texas have a compelling state interest in protecting the American Flag? Was Chief Justice Rehnquist correct when he argued that the United States Flag was unique and that, therefore, Texas' flag protection law survived strict scrutiny?

4. The majority argued that the ban prohibited more speech than was necessary to preserve the American Flag's unique status: "We can imagine no more appropriate response to burning a flag than waving one's own, no better way to counter a flag burner's message than by saluting the flag that burns, no surer means of preserving the dignity even of the flag that burned than by ... according its remains a respectful burial." Is that true?

5. The *Johnson* Court contended that protecting the American Flag from destruction would open a Pandora's box: "To conclude that the government may permit designated symbols to be used to communicate only a limited set of messages would be to enter territory having no discernible or defensible boundaries. Could the government, on this theory, prohibit the burning of state flags? Of copies of the Presidential seal? Of the Constitution?" Is anyone proposing to prohibit burning—or is anyone burning, for that matter—presidential seals?

6. Relatedly, was the majority correct when it asserted that the Flag's "cherished place in our community will be strengthened" by its ruling? Does a community typically

"cherish[]" its valuable assets by permitting their destruction? Were Congress and forty-eight states mistaken about the best way to protect the Flag's status and role?

7. Which, if any, of the purposes of the First Amendment does protection of flag burning, assuming that it is expressive conduct, advance?

8. Justice Kennedy, in concurrence, expressed the tension he perceived between the Constitution's command, which he, as a judge, was required to follow, and his personal concern for the American Flag and that for which it stands. How should one resolve Justice Kennedy's tension? Did Justice Kennedy's opinion show that judges are not just "politicians in robes"? Does it show that the law constrains judges?

9. Similarly, note that Justice Scalia joined the majority, without comment. Indeed, Justice Scalia was the crucial fifth vote. Justice Scalia's personal policy preference was to ban flag burning. *See* Piers Morgan Tonight, *Interview with Antonin Scalia and Brian Garner*, July 18, 2012, *available at* http://transcripts.cnn.com/TRANSCRIPTS/1207/18/pmt.01.html ("[I]f I were king, I—I would not allow people to go about burning the American flag."). Does Justice Scalia's vote against his policy preference show that constitutional law, and the Supreme Court's articulation of it, is not "just politics," as critics often claim?

After *Texas v. Johnson* was decided, there was significant public debate on how, if at all, to respond. Two commonly-advanced courses of action were a constitutional amendment that would authorize Congress to proscribe destruction of the American Flag and a federal statute. Congress was never able to muster the requisite votes to send a proposed constitutional amendment to the states. However, it did pass the Flag Protection Act of 1989, 103 Stat. 777, 18 U.S.C. § 700. The Act stated: "Whoever knowingly mutilates, defaces, physically defiles, burns, maintains on the floor or ground, or tramples upon any flag of the United States shall be fined under this title or imprisoned for not more than one year, or both." *Id.* § 700(a)(1).

The Supreme Court struck down the Act in *United States v. Eichman*, 496 U.S. 310 (1990). The United States argued that the Act was content neutral, because the Act protected the Flag's physical integrity regardless of the content of expressive conduct. *Id.* at 315. The Court, following *Johnson's* construction of the Texas statute, ruled that the Act was content based and did not survive strict scrutiny. *Id.* at 315–18.

Another important area of the law, where the question of how to categorize activity for free speech purposes arose, is campaign finance regulation. The Supreme Court has addressed campaign finance regulation many times since Congress passed the Federal Elections Campaign Act of 1971, *codified at* 2 U.S.C. § 431 *et seq.* The Act, which was amended in 1974, was challenged by Senator Buckley in the case that bears his name, reprinted below. The Supreme Court answered two key questions: (1) are campaign contributions and expenditures "speech" protected by the Free Speech Clause?; and (2) to what extent, if any, and for what purposes, may the federal government limit campaign contributions or expenditures?

Buckley v. Valeo

424 U.S. 1 (1976)

PER CURIAM.

These appeals present constitutional challenges to the key provisions of the Federal Election Campaign Act of 1971 (Act), as amended in 1974.

... The statutes at issue summarized in broad terms, contain the following provisions: (8a) individual political contributions are limited to $1,000 to any single candidate per election, with an overall annual limitation of $25,000 by any contributor; independent expenditures by individuals and groups "relative to a clearly identified candidate" are limited to $1,000 a year; campaign spending by candidates for various federal offices and spending for national conventions by political parties are subject to prescribed limits; (b) contributions and expenditures above certain threshold levels must be reported and publicly disclosed; (c) a system for public funding of Presidential campaign activities is established; and (d) a Federal Election Commission is established to administer and enforce the legislation.

I. CONTRIBUTION AND EXPENDITURE LIMITATIONS

The intricate statutory scheme adopted by Congress to regulate federal election campaigns includes restrictions on political contributions and expenditures that apply broadly to all phases of and all participants in the election process. The major contribution and expenditure limitations in the Act prohibit individuals from contributing more than $25,000 in a single year or more than $1,000 to any single candidate for an election campaign and from spending more than $1,000 a year "relative to a clearly identified candidate." Other provisions restrict a candidate's use of personal and family resources in his campaign and limit the overall amount that can be spent by a candidate in campaigning for federal office.

... [T]he critical constitutional questions presented here go not to the basic power of Congress to legislate in this area, but to whether the specific legislation that Congress has enacted interferes with First Amendment freedoms....

A. General Principles

The Act's contribution and expenditure limitations operate in an area of the most fundamental First Amendment activities. Discussion of public issues and debate on the qualifications of candidates are integral to the operation of the system of government established by our Constitution. The First Amendment affords the broadest protection to such political expression in order "to assure [the] unfettered interchange of ideas for the bringing about of political and social changes desired by the people." *Roth v. United States*, 354 U.S. 476, 484 (1957). Although First Amendment protections are not confined to "the exposition of ideas," "there is practically universal agreement that a major purpose of that Amendment was to protect the free discussion of governmental affairs.... of course includ[ing] discussions of candidates...." This no more than reflects our "profound national commitment to the principle that debate on public issues should be uninhibited, robust, and wide-open," *New York Times Co. v.*

Sullivan, 376 U.S. 254, 270 (1964). In a republic where the people are sovereign, the ability of the citizenry to make informed choices among candidates for office is essential, for the identities of those who are elected will inevitably shape the course that we follow as a nation.

It is with these principles in mind that we consider the primary contentions of the parties.... Appellees contend that what the Act regulates is conduct, and that its effect on speech and association is incidental at most. Appellants respond that contributions and expenditures are at the very core of political speech, and that the Act's limitations thus constitute restraints on First Amendment liberty that are both gross and direct.

In upholding the constitutional validity of the Act's contribution and expenditure provisions on the ground that those provisions should be viewed as regulating conduct, not speech, the Court of Appeals relied upon *United States v. O'Brien*, 391 U.S. 367 (1968). We cannot share the view that the present Act's contribution and expenditure limitations are comparable to the restrictions on conduct upheld in *O'Brien*. The expenditure of money simply cannot be equated with such conduct as destruction of a draft card. Some forms of communication made possible by the giving and spending of money involve speech alone, some involve conduct primarily, and some involve a combination of the two. Yet this Court has never suggested that the dependence of a communication on the expenditure of money operates itself to introduce a non-speech element or to reduce the exacting scrutiny required by the First Amendment.... See *Bigelow v. Virginia*, 421 U.S. 809, 820 (1975); *New York Times Co. v. Sullivan*, *supra*, 376 U.S., at 266.

Even if the categorization of the expenditure of money as conduct were accepted, the limitations challenged here would not meet the *O'Brien* test because the governmental interests advanced in support of the Act involve "suppressing communication." The interests served by the Act include restricting the voices of people and interest groups who have money to spend and reducing the overall scope of federal election campaigns. Although the Act does not focus on the ideas expressed by persons or groups subject to its regulations, it is aimed in part at equalizing the relative ability of all voters to affect electoral outcomes by placing a ceiling on expenditures for political expression by citizens and groups. Unlike *O'Brien*, where the Selective Service System's administrative interest in the preservation of draft cards was wholly unrelated to their use as a means of communication, it is beyond dispute that the interest in regulating the alleged "conduct" of giving or spending money "arises in some measure because the communication allegedly integral to the conduct is itself thought to be harmful."

Nor can the Act's contribution and expenditure limitations be sustained, ... [as] reasonable time, place, and manner regulations, which do not discriminate among speakers or ideas, in order to further an important governmental interest unrelated to the restriction of communication.... The critical difference is that the present Act's contribution and expenditure limitations impose direct quantity restrictions on political communication and association by persons, groups, candidates, and political parties in addition to any reasonable time, place, and manner regulations otherwise imposed.[17]

A restriction on the amount of money a person or group can spend on political communication during a campaign necessarily reduces the quantity of expression by restricting the number of issues discussed, the depth of their exploration, and the size of the audience reached. This is because virtually every means of communicating ideas in today's mass society requires the expenditure of money. The distribution of the humblest handbill or leaflet entails printing, paper, and circulation costs. The electorate's increasing dependence on television, radio, and other mass media for news and information has made these expensive modes of communication indispensable instruments of effective political speech.

The expenditure limitations contained in the Act represent substantial rather than merely theoretical restraints on the quantity and diversity of political speech. The $1,000 ceiling on spending "relative to a clearly identified candidate," would appear to exclude all citizens and groups from any significant use of the most effective modes of communication.[20] ...

By contrast with a limitation upon expenditures for political expression, a limitation upon the amount that any one person or group may contribute to a candidate or political committee entails only a marginal restriction upon the contributor's ability to engage in free communication. A contribution serves as a general expression of support for the candidate and his views, but does not communicate the underlying basis for the support. The quantity of communication by the contributor does not increase perceptibly with the size of his contribution, since the expression rests solely on the undifferentiated, symbolic act of contributing. At most, the size of the contribution provides a very rough index of the intensity of the contributor's support for the candidate. A limitation on the amount of money a person may give to a candidate or campaign organization thus involves little direct restraint on his political communication, for it permits the symbolic expression of support evidenced by a contribution but does not in any way infringe the contributor's freedom to discuss candidates and issues. While contributions may result in political expression if spent by a candidate or an association to present views to the voters, the transformation of contributions into political debate involves speech by someone other than the contributor.

---

17. The nongovernmental appellees argue that just as the decibels emitted by a sound truck can be regulated consistently with the First Amendment, *Kovacs v. Cooper*, 336 U.S. 77 (1949), the Act may restrict the volume of dollars in political campaigns without impermissibly restricting freedom of speech. This comparison underscores a fundamental misconception. The decibel restriction upheld in *Kovacs* limited the manner of operating a soundtruck but not the extent of its proper use. By contrast, the Act's dollar ceilings restrict the extent of the reasonable use of virtually every means of communicating information.

20. The record indicates that one full-page advertisement in a daily edition of a certain metropolitan newspaper cost $6,971.04 almost seven times the annual limit on expenditures "relative to" a particular candidate imposed on the vast majority of individual citizens and associations.

Given the important role of contributions in financing political campaigns, contribution restrictions could have a severe impact on political dialogue if the limitations prevented candidates and political committees from amassing the resources necessary for effective advocacy. There is no indication, however, that the contribution limitations imposed by the Act would have any dramatic adverse effect on the funding of campaigns and political associations. The overall effect of the Act's contribution ceilings is merely to require candidates and political committees to raise funds from a greater number of persons and to compel people who would otherwise contribute amounts greater than the statutory limits to expend such funds on direct political expression, rather than to reduce the total amount of money potentially available to promote political expression.

In sum, although the Act's contribution and expenditure limitations both implicate fundamental First Amendment interests, its expenditure ceilings impose significantly more severe restrictions on protected freedoms of political expression and association than do its limitations on financial contributions.

B. Contribution Limitations

1. The $1,000 Limitation on Contributions by Individuals and Groups to Candidates and Authorized Campaign Committees

Section 608(b) provides that "no person shall make contributions to any candidate with respect to any election for Federal office which, in the aggregate, exceed $1,000." ... The restriction applies to aggregate amounts contributed to the candidate for each election with primaries, run-off elections, and general elections counted separately, and all Presidential primaries held in any calendar year treated together as a single election campaign.

(a)

[T]he primary First Amendment problem raised by the Act's contribution limitations is their restriction of one aspect of the contributor's freedom of political association. The Court's decisions involving associational freedoms establish that the right of association is a "basic constitutional freedom," that is "closely allied to freedom of speech and a right which, like free speech, lies at the foundation of a free society." See, e.g., *NAACP v. Alabama*, 357 U.S. [449,] 460–461 [(1958)].

... In view of the fundamental nature of the right to associate, governmental "action which may have the effect of curtailing the freedom to associate is subject to the closest scrutiny." Yet, it is clear that "[n]either the right to associate nor the right to participate in political activities is absolute." Even a "'significant interference' with protected rights of political association" may be sustained if the State demonstrates a sufficiently important interest and employs means closely drawn to avoid unnecessary abridgment of associational freedoms.

Appellees argue that the Act's restrictions on large campaign contributions are justified by three governmental interests. According to the parties and amici, the primary interest served by the limitations and, indeed, by the Act as a whole, is the prevention of corruption and the appearance of corruption spawned by the real or imagined coercive influence of large financial contributions on candidates' positions and on their actions if elected to office. Two "ancillary" interests underlying the Act are also allegedly furthered by the $1,000 limits on contributions. First, the limits serve to mute the voices of affluent persons and groups in the election process and thereby to equalize the relative ability of all citizens to affect the outcome of elections. Second, it is argued, the ceilings may to some extent act as a brake on the skyrocketing cost of political campaigns and thereby serve to open the political system more widely to candidates without access to sources of large amounts of money.

It is unnecessary to look beyond the Act's primary purpose to limit the actuality and appearance of corruption resulting from large individual financial contributions in order to find a constitutionally sufficient justification for the $1,000 contribution limitation. Under a system of private financing of elections, a candidate lacking immense personal or family wealth must depend on financial contributions from others to provide the resources necessary to conduct a successful campaign. The increasing importance of the communications media and sophisticated mass-mailing and polling operations to effective campaigning make the raising of large sums of money an ever more essential ingredient of an effective candidacy. To the extent that large contributions are given to secure a political quid pro quo from current and potential office holders, the integrity of our system of representative democracy is undermined. Although the scope of such pernicious practices can never be reliably ascertained, the deeply disturbing examples surfacing after the 1972 election demonstrate that the problem is not an illusory one.

Of almost equal concern as the danger of actual quid pro quo arrangements is the impact of the appearance of corruption stemming from public awareness of the opportunities for abuse inherent in a regime of large individual financial contributions. Here, Congress could legitimately conclude that the avoidance of the appearance of improper influence "is also critical ... if confidence in the system of representative Government is not to be eroded to a disastrous extent."

Appellants contend that the contribution limitations must be invalidated because bribery laws and narrowly drawn disclosure requirements constitute a less restrictive means of dealing with "proven and suspected quid pro quo arrangements." But laws making criminal the giving and taking of bribes deal with only the most blatant and specific attempts of those with money to influence governmental action. And while disclosure requirements serve many salutary purposes, Congress was surely entitled to conclude that disclosure was only a partial measure, and that contribution ceilings were a necessary legislative concomitant to deal with the reality or appearance of corruption inherent in a system permitting unlimited financial contributions, even when the identities of the contributors and the amounts of their contributions are fully disclosed.

The Act's $1,000 contribution limitation focuses precisely on the problem of large campaign contributions where the actuality and potential for corruption have been identified while leaving persons free to engage in independent political expression, to associate actively through volunteering their services, and to assist to a limited but nonetheless substantial extent in supporting candidates and committees with financial resources. Significantly, the Act's contribution limitations in themselves do not undermine to any material degree the potential for robust and effective discussion of candidates and campaign issues by individual citizens, associations, the institutional press, candidates, and political parties.

We find that, under the rigorous standard of review established by our prior decisions, the weighty interests served by restricting the size of financial contributions to political candidates are sufficient to justify the limited effect upon First Amendment freedoms caused by the $1,000 contribution ceiling.

. . . .

4. The $25,000 Limitation on Total Contributions During any Calendar Year

In addition to the $1,000 limitation on the nonexempt contributions that an individual may make to a particular candidate for any single election, the Act contains an overall $25,000 limitation on total contributions by an individual during any calendar year. §608(b)(3). The overall $25,000 ceiling does impose an ultimate restriction upon the number of candidates and committees with which an individual may associate himself by means of financial support. But this quite modest restraint upon protected political activity serves to prevent evasion of the $1,000 contribution limitation by a person who might otherwise contribute massive amounts of money to a particular candidate through the use of unearmarked contributions to political committees likely to contribute to that candidate, or huge contributions to the candidate's political party. The limited, additional restriction on associational freedom imposed by the overall ceiling is thus no more than a corollary of the basic individual contribution limitation that we have found to be constitutionally valid.

C. Expenditure Limitations

The Act's expenditure ceilings impose direct and substantial restraints on the quantity of political speech. The most drastic of the limitations restricts individuals and groups, including political parties that fail to place a candidate on the ballot, to an expenditure of $1,000 "relative to a clearly identified candidate during a calendar year." §608(e)(1). Other expenditure ceilings limit spending by candidates, §608(a), their campaigns, §608(c), and political parties in connection with election campaigns, §608(f). It is clear that a primary effect of these expenditure limitations is to restrict the quantity of campaign speech by individuals, groups, and candidates. The restrictions, while neutral as to the ideas expressed, limit political expression "at the core of our electoral process and of the First Amendment freedoms."

1. The $1,000 Limitation on Expenditures "Relative to a Clearly Identified Candidate"

… The plain effect of §608(e)(1) is to prohibit all individuals, who are neither candidates nor owners of institutional press facilities, and all groups, except political parties and campaign organizations, from voicing their views "relative to a clearly identified candidate" through means that entail aggregate expenditures of more than $1,000 during a calendar year. The provision, for example, would make it a federal criminal offense for a person or association to place a single one-quarter page advertisement "relative to a clearly identified candidate" in a major metropolitan newspaper.

. . . .

The discussion in Part I-A explains why the Act's expenditure limitations impose far greater restraints on the freedom of speech and association than do its contribution limitations....

We find that the governmental interest in preventing corruption and the appearance of corruption is inadequate to justify § 608(e)(1)'s ceiling on independent expenditures. First, assuming, arguendo, that large independent expenditures pose the same dangers of actual or apparent quid pro quo arrangements as do large contributions, § 608(e)(1) does not provide an answer that sufficiently relates to the elimination of those dangers. Unlike the contribution limitations' total ban on the giving of large amounts of money to candidates, § 608(e)(1) prevents only some large expenditures. So long as persons and groups eschew expenditures that in express terms advocate the election or defeat of a clearly identified candidate, they are free to spend as much as they want to promote the candidate and his views. It would naively underestimate the ingenuity and resourcefulness of persons and groups desiring to buy influence to believe that they would have much difficulty devising expenditures that skirted the restriction on express advocacy of election or defeat but nevertheless benefited the candidate's campaign. Yet no substantial societal interest would be served by a loophole-closing provision designed to check corruption that permitted unscrupulous persons and organizations to expend unlimited sums of money in order to obtain improper influence over candidates for elective office.

Second, the independent advocacy restricted by the provision does not presently appear to pose dangers of real or apparent corruption comparable to those identified with large campaign contributions. The parties defending § 608(e)(1) contend that it is necessary to prevent would-be contributors from avoiding the contribution limitations by the simple expedient of paying directly for media advertisements or for other portions of the candidate's campaign activities. Yet such controlled or coordinated expenditures are treated as contributions rather than expenditures under the Act. Section 608(b)'s contribution ceilings rather than § 608(e)(1)'s independent expenditure limitation prevent attempts to circumvent the Act through prearranged or coordinated expenditures amounting to disguised contributions. By contrast, § 608(e)(1) limits expenditures for express advocacy of candidates made totally independently of the candidate and his campaign. Unlike contributions, such independent expenditures may well provide little assistance to the candidate's campaign and indeed may prove counterproductive. The absence of prearrangement and coordination of an expenditure with the candidate or his agent not only undermines the value of the expenditure to the candidate, but also alleviates the danger that expenditures will be given as a quid pro quo for improper commitments from the candidate. Rather than preventing circumvention of the contribution limitations, § 608(e)(1) severely restricts all independent advocacy despite its substantially diminished potential for abuse.

While the independent expenditure ceiling thus fails to serve any substantial governmental interest in stemming the reality or appearance of corruption in the electoral process, it heavily burdens core First Amendment expression. Advocacy of the election or defeat of candidates for federal office is no less entitled to protection under the

First Amendment than the discussion of political policy generally or advocacy of the passage or defeat of legislation.

It is argued, however, that the ancillary governmental interest in equalizing the relative ability of individuals and groups to influence the outcome of elections serves to justify the limitation on express advocacy of the election or defeat of candidates imposed by § 608(e)(1)'s expenditure ceiling. But the concept that government may restrict the speech of some elements of our society in order to enhance the relative voice of others is wholly foreign to the First Amendment, which was designed "to secure the widest possible dissemination of information from diverse and antagonistic sources,'" and "'to assure unfettered interchange of ideas for the bringing about of political and social changes desired by the people.'" *New York Times Co. v. Sullivan*, *supra*, 376 U.S., at 266, 269. The First Amendment's protection against governmental abridgment of free expression cannot properly be made to depend on a person's financial ability to engage in public discussion.

For the reasons stated, we conclude that § 608(e)(1)'s independent expenditure limitation is unconstitutional under the First Amendment.

2. Limitation on Expenditures by Candidates from Personal or Family Resources

The Act also sets limits on expenditures by a candidate "from his personal funds, or the personal funds of his immediate family, in connection with his campaigns during any calendar year." § 608(a)(1). These ceilings vary from $50,000 for Presidential or Vice Presidential candidates to $35,000 for senatorial candidates, and $25,000 for most candidates for the House of Representatives.

The ceiling on personal expenditures by candidates on their own behalf imposes a substantial restraint on the ability of persons to engage in protected First Amendment expression. The candidate, no less than any other person, has a First Amendment right to engage in the discussion of public issues and vigorously and tirelessly to advocate his own election and the election of other candidates. Indeed, it is of particular importance that candidates have the unfettered opportunity to make their views known so that the electorate may intelligently evaluate the candidates' personal qualities and their positions on vital public issues before choosing among them on election day.... Section 608(a)'s ceiling on personal expenditures by a candidate in furtherance of his own candidacy thus clearly and directly interferes with constitutionally protected freedoms.

The primary governmental interest served by the Act the prevention of actual and apparent corruption of the political process does not support the limitation on the candidate's expenditure of his own personal funds. Indeed, the use of personal funds reduces the candidate's dependence on outside contributions and thereby counteracts the coercive pressures and attendant risks of abuse to which the Act's contribution limitations are directed.

The ancillary interest in equalizing the relative financial resources of candidates competing for elective office, therefore, provides the sole relevant rationale for § 608(a)'s expenditure ceiling. That interest is clearly not sufficient to justify the provision's infringement of fundamental First Amendment rights. First, the limitation may fail to promote financial equality among candidates. A candidate who spends less of his personal resources on his campaign may nonetheless outspend his rival as a result of more successful fundraising efforts.... Second, and more fundamentally, the First Amendment simply cannot tolerate § 608(a)'s restriction upon the freedom of a candidate to speak without legislative limit on behalf of his own candidacy. We therefore hold that § 608(a)'s restriction on a candidate's personal expenditures is unconstitutional.

3. Limitations on Campaign Expenditures

Section 608(c) places limitations on overall campaign expenditures by candidates seeking nomination for election and election to federal office....

No governmental interest that has been suggested is sufficient to justify the restriction on the quantity of political expression imposed by § 608(c)'s campaign expenditure limitations. The major evil associated with rapidly increasing campaign expenditures is the danger of candidate dependence on large contributions. The interest in alleviating the corrupting influence of large contributions is served by the Act's contribution limitations and disclosure provisions rather than by § 608(c)'s campaign expenditure ceilings.... There is no indication that the substantial criminal penalties for violating the contribution ceilings combined with the political repercussion of such violations will be insufficient to police the contribution provisions. Extensive reporting, auditing, and disclosure requirements applicable to both contributions and expenditures by political campaigns are designed to facilitate the detection of illegal contributions.

The interest in equalizing the financial resources of candidates competing for federal office is no more convincing a justification for restricting the scope of federal election campaigns. Given the limitation on the size of outside contributions, the financial resources available to a candidate's campaign, like the number of volunteers recruited, will normally vary with the size and intensity of the candidate's support. There is nothing invidious, improper, or unhealthy in permitting such funds to be spent to carry the candidate's message to the electorate. Moreover, the equalization of permissible campaign expenditures might serve not to equalize the opportunities of all candidates, but to handicap a candidate who lacked substantial name recognition or exposure of his views before the start of the campaign.

The campaign expenditure ceilings appear to be designed primarily to serve the governmental interests in reducing the allegedly skyrocketing costs of political campaigns. Appellees stressed statistics indicating that spending for federal election campaigns increased almost 300% between 1952 and 1972 in comparison with a 57.6% rise in the consumer price index during the same period. In any event, the mere growth in the cost of federal election campaigns in and of itself provides no basis for governmental restrictions on the quantity of campaign spending and the resulting limitation on the scope of federal campaigns. The First Amendment denies government the power to determine that spending to promote one's political views is wasteful, excessive, or unwise. In the free society ordained by our Constitution it is not the government, but the people individually as citizens and candidates and collectively as associations and political committees who must retain control over the quantity and range of debate on public issues in a political campaign.

For these reasons we hold that § 608(c) is constitutionally invalid.

In sum, the provisions of the Act that impose a $1,000 limitation on contributions to a single candidate, § 608(b)(1), a $5,000 limitation on contributions by a political committee to a single candidate, § 608(b)(2), and a $25,000 limitation on total contributions by an individual during any calendar year, § 608(b)(3), are constitutionally valid. These limitations, along with the disclosure provisions, constitute the Act's primary weapons against the reality or appearance of improper influence stemming from the dependence of candidates on large campaign contributions. The contribution ceilings thus serve the basic governmental interest in safeguarding the integrity of the electoral process without directly impinging upon the rights of individual citizens and candidates to engage in political debate and discussion. By contrast, the First Amendment requires the invalidation of the Act's independent expenditure ceiling, § 608(e)(1), its limitation on a candidate's expenditures from his own personal funds, § 608(a), and its ceilings on overall campaign expenditures, § 608(c). These provisions place substantial and direct restrictions on the ability of candidates, citizens, and associations to engage in protected political expression, restrictions that the First Amendment cannot tolerate.

II. REPORTING AND DISCLOSURE REQUIREMENTS

. . . .

In summary, we find no constitutional infirmities in the recordkeeping, reporting, and disclosure provisions of the Act.

III. PUBLIC FINANCING OF PRESIDENTIAL ELECTION CAMPAIGNS

. . . .

IV. THE FEDERAL ELECTION COMMISSION

[You reviewed this portion of the case in Volume 2.]

So ordered.

MR. JUSTICE STEVENS took no part in the consideration or decision of these cases.

MR. CHIEF JUSTICE BURGER, concurring in part and dissenting in part. [Opinion omitted.]

MR. JUSTICE WHITE, concurring in part and dissenting in part. [Opinion omitted.]

MR. JUSTICE MARSHALL, concurring in part and dissenting in part. [Opinion omitted.]

MR. JUSTICE BLACKMUN, concurring in part and dissenting in part. [Opinion omitted.]

MR. JUSTICE REHNQUIST, concurring in part and dissenting in part. [Opinion omitted.]

Exercise 7:

1. Describe the Act's campaign finance regulations. What are the different categories of restrictions and in what ways are those categories restricted?

2. For what reason(s) did Congress restrict these categories?

3. According to the Court, how did the Act infringe the right to free speech?

4. The Supreme Court ruled that monetary participation in political campaigns is protected speech, and not unprotected conduct. Why? How is giving money to a political candidate "speech"? Why is it not like burning a draft card, as in the *O'Brien* case?

5. The Federal Government argued that the Act's restrictions on money were content-neutral, time, place, and manner restrictions. The Government claimed that the Act's quantity limits did not restrict based on the speech's content; instead, the Act limited monetary participation regardless of the speaker's political perspective. How did the Court distinguish the Government's claims? How might you criticize the Court's argument?

6. What level of scrutiny did the Court apply to the restrictions? Why?

7. Was the Supreme Court correct to subject the Act's restrictions to heightened scrutiny? In what way was the Act content-based? Were its restrictions on the speech's subject matter or its viewpoint?

8. The Court distinguished between monetary contributions and monetary expenditures in its analysis. How did it justify that distinction? Was it proper to do so?

9. What governmental interests did the Federal Government proffer to support the Act's restrictions? Be specific when you describe the government's interests, because that will help us analyze whether the Supreme Court later narrowed the permissible governmental interests.

10. Which of the government's proffered interests did the Court determine were and were not sufficiently powerful? Did the Court adequately distinguish its treatment of the different interests?

11. Explain the Court's analysis for each interest and each category of restriction.

12. What role did the concept of "political speech" play in the Court's analysis?

13. According to the Court, which of the Free Speech Clause's purposes were implicated by the challenged Act's restrictions? In what way did these purposes impact the Court's analysis?

Buckley is the seminal case that set the baseline for future campaign finance cases. In particular, *Buckley*'s rulings on which governmental interests justified restrictions on political spending, and its different treatment of contribution and expenditure limitations, remains important today. Since *Buckley*, there has been significant activity on the Court. In *Austin v. Michigan Chamber of Commerce*, 494 U.S. 652 (1990), the Court concluded that the government may ban political speech based on a speaker's corporate identity. In that case, the Michigan Chamber of Commerce wanted to use its general treasury funds to run an ad supporting a specific candidate in a newspaper, but a Michigan law prohibited corporations from making independent expenditures that supported or opposed any candidate for state office. The Court upheld the law, finding that Michigan had a compelling interest in preventing "the corrosive and distorting effects of immense aggregations of wealth that are accumulated with the help of the corporate form and that have little or no correlation to the public's support for the corporation's political ideas." And in *McConnell v. Federal Election Comm'n*, 540 U.S. 93, 203–09 (2003), the Court directly relied on *Austin* in upholding limits on "electioneering communications" by corporations, *i.e.*, advertisements that are paid out of a corporation's general treasury fund and that expressly advocate for the election or defeat of candidates in federal elections.

Seven years later, in *Citizens United v. Federal Election Commission*, 558 U.S. 310 (2010), the Court reconsidered — and ultimately rejected — the reasoning underlying the holdings in *Austin* and *McConnell* regarding corporate speech. Specifically, the Court, in an opinion written by Justice Kennedy, struck down a federal law that "prohibit[ed] corporations and unions from using their general treasury funds to make independent expenditures for speech defined as an 'electioneering communication' or for speech expressly advocating the election or defeat of a candidate." *Id.* at 318–19. Citizens United, a nonprofit corporation, sought to release a 90-minute documentary called *Hillary: The Movie* about then-Senator Hillary Clinton, who was a candidate in the Democratic Party's 2008 presidential primary elections. Citizens United worried that the federal law precluded release of the film through video-on-demand within 30 days of the primary because of its ban on corporate-funded independent expenditures.

In concluding that the ban on independent expenditures by corporations violated the First Amendment, the Court emphasized that "[t]he First Amendment protects speech and speaker, and the ideas that flow from each" and that "political speech does not lose First Amendment protection 'simply because its source is a corporation.'" *Id.* at 341–42. Whereas *Austin* "sought to ... prevent corporations from obtaining 'an unfair advantage in the political marketplace,'" *Buckley* "rejected the premise that the Government has an interest 'in equalizing the relative ability of individuals and groups to influence the outcome of elections.'" *Id.* at 350. Moreover, the majority worried that *Austin* authorized broad restrictions on speakers and listeners, both of which contravened long-established First Amendment principles:

> *Austin* interferes with the "open marketplace" of ideas protected by the First Amendment. It permits the Government to ban the political speech of millions of associations of citizens. Most of these are small corporations without large amounts of wealth. This fact belies the Government's argument that the statute is justified on the ground that it prevents the "distorting effects of immense aggregations of wealth." It is not even aimed at amassed wealth....
> By suppressing the speech of manifold corporations, both for-profit and nonprofit, the Government prevents their voices and viewpoints from reach-

ing the public and advising voters on which persons or entities are hostile to their interests. Factions will necessarily form in our Republic, but the remedy of "destroying the liberty" of some factions is "worse than the disease." The Federalist No. 10 (J. Madison). Factions should be checked by permitting them all to speak, and by entrusting the people to judge what is true and what is false.

Id. at 354.

Not surprisingly given this view, the Court overturned *Austin*, concluding that "independent expenditures, including those made by corporations, do not give rise to corruption or the appearance of corruption ... [because b]y definition, an independent expenditure is political speech presented to the electorate that is not coordinated with a candidate. The fact that corporation, or any other speaker, is willing to spend money to try to persuade voters presupposes that the people have the ultimate influence over elected officials." *Id.* at 357, 360. Under *Citizens United*, however, the government still may "regulate corporate political speech through disclaimer and disclosure requirements." *Id.* at 319. Are such restrictions consistent with *Buckley* and *Citizens United*? After *Citizens United*, how may (and may not) the government regulate corporate and union monetary participation in elections?

Citizens United set off a firestorm of controversy, primarily focused on the status of corporate and union political contributions. Indeed, President Obama famously criticized *Citizens United* during his 2010 State of the Union Address. *See* Adam Liptak, *Supreme Court Gets a Rare Rebuke, in Front of Nation*, N.Y. TIMES, Jan. 29, 2010, at A12.

However, perhaps more importantly, from a long term legal perspective, *Citizens United* also suggested a narrower understanding of the key governmental interest in restricting campaign contributions: corruption. The *Citizens United* majority stated that "[w]hen *Buckley* identified ... corruption, that interest was limited to *quid pro quo* corruption." *Citizens United*, 558 U.S. at 359.

A plurality of the Court picked up this narrowed understanding in *McCutcheon v. Federal Election Comm'n*, 572 U.S. 185 (2014). Writing for the plurality, Justice Kennedy summarized the case law saying that: "We have said that government regulation may not target the general gratitude a candidate may feel toward those who support him or his allies, or the political access such support may afford. 'Ingratiation and access ... are not corruption.' They embody a central feature of democracy— that constituents support candidates who share their beliefs and interests, and candidates who are elected can be expected to be responsive to those concerns." *Id.* at 192. Justice Thomas concurred on the rationale that no anti-corruption interest justifies limiting campaign contributions or expenditures. *Id.* at 228–29.

4. Unprotected Activity

If regulated activity is not pure speech, and it is not expressive activity, then it is noncommunicative activity that is not protected by the Free Speech Clause.[97] For example, if a person is pulled over for driving over the speed limit while driving to work, and the driver did not intend his activity to communicate a message, and the "audience"—other drivers—would not understand a message, then the activity would not be protected by the Free Speech Clause.

Another example that has garnered a number of lower court decisions, but no Supreme Court case on point, is that nudity—by itself, and not as part of a larger work of art or coupled with some other expressive speech or activity—is noncommunicative and therefore unprotected activity. *See, e.g., South Fl. Beaches, Inc. v. Miami*, 734 F.2d 608, 610 (11th Cir. 1984). By contrast, the Supreme Court recently ruled that the act of signing a state referendum petition constituted protected speech because the act of signing "express[es] the view that the law subject to the petition should be overturned [or] ... the political view that the question should be considered 'by the whole electorate.'" *John Doe No. 1 v. Reed*, 561 U.S. 186, 195 (2010).

E. When Is the "Freedom of Speech" *Infringed*?

1. Introduction

In order for the government's[98] action to implicate the Free Speech Clause, it must "infringe" the freedom of speech. If the government's actions do not "infringe" free speech, then the government regulation is not subject to free speech scrutiny, and court review of the government's action will not require the government to justify its actions.[99]

In most cases, it is easy to discern whether the government has infringed free speech. For example, a flat government criminal prohibition on obscenity constitutes an infringement of speech. However, because of the pervasiveness of both speech and governmental regulation in American life, there are many situations where the government is regulating speech, though in a manner short of an absolute ban. For example, if the government increased the corporate tax, this tax would include publishers and newspapers, and would therefore limit their activities. Or, the government

---

97. Keep in mind that the activity may receive protection from other provisions of the Constitution—for instance, one of the Due Process Clauses.

98. Recall the State Action Doctrine, from Volume 5, which is that the Constitution limits only the government, and not private parties.

99. At least not under the Free Speech Clause. Of course, the government may still have to justify its actions under other constitutional provisions and doctrines.

would make speech slightly more expensive or slightly more inconvenient by requiring that all park users, including protestors, obtain a permit to utilize a public park.

The Supreme Court has stated that the government infringes the First Amendment when it "imposes a significant burden on expressive activity." *United States v. Nat'l Treasury Employees Union*, 513 U.S. 454, 469 (1995); *see also Lying v. UAW*, 485 U.S. 360, 365 (1988) ("directly and substantially interfere[]"). This test has both clear and less clear applications because what constitutes a "significant burden" is a judgment-laden concept that will vary depending on the circumstances.

One implication of this form of analysis is that there will be situations in which the government's infringement of free speech is constitutional. For example, as we saw in *Buckley*, the limit on campaign contributions, though an infringement, was constitutionally justified.

Below are some of the common categories of cases where the Supreme Court has ruled that government regulations infringe on speech.

2. Prior Restraints

The classic form of government infringement of the freedom of speech was the prior restraint. A prior restraint was a governmental order directing a person to not speak or publish. In the United Kingdom, prior restraints took the form of a licensing system under which the crown decided who could speak and what could be said. *See Thomas v. Chicago Park Dist.*, 534 U.S. 316, 320–21 (2002) (describing this). The Free Speech Clause's Framers and Ratifiers had this form of governmental regulation of speech in mind as the focal case of what they wished to prohibit.

Because of this history, prior restraints have been rare in the United States. One of the early Supreme Court free speech decisions, and the key prior restraint case, is *Near v. Minnesota*, 283 U.S. 697 (1931), reprinted below.

Near v. State of Minnesota ex rel. Olson
283 U.S. 697 (1931)

MR. CHIEF JUSTICE HUGHES delivered the opinion of the Court.

Chapter 285 of the Session Laws of Minnesota for the year 1925 provides for the abatement, as a public nuisance, of a "malicious, scandalous and defamatory newspaper, magazine or other periodical." Section 1 of the act is as follows:

> "Section 1. Any person who shall be engaged in the business of regularly or customarily producing, publishing or circulating, having in possession, selling or giving away[:] (a) an obscene, lewd and lascivious newspaper, magazine, or other periodical, or (b) a malicious, scandalous and defamatory newspaper, magazine or other periodical, is guilty of a nuisance, and all persons guilty of such nuisance may be enjoined, as hereinafter provided."

Section two provides that[,] whenever any such nuisance is committed or exists, the county attorney of any county where any such periodical is published or circulated may maintain an action in the district court of the county in the name of the state to enjoin perpetually the persons committing or maintaining any such nuisance from further committing or maintaining it. Upon such evidence as the court shall deem sufficient, a temporary injunction may be granted.... The court is empowered, as in other cases of contempt, to punish disobedience to a temporary or permanent injunction by fine or by imprisonment in the county jail for not more than twelve months.

Under this statute ([section 1,] clause (b)), the county attorney of Hennepin county brought this action to enjoin the publication of The Saturday Press, published by the defendants in the city of Minneapolis. The complaint alleged that the defendants published and circulated editions of that periodical which were "largely devoted to malicious, scandalous and defamatory articles" concerning Charles G. Davis, Frank W. Brunskill, the Minneapolis Tribune, the Minneapolis Journal, Melvin C. Passolt, George E. Leach, the Jewish Race, the members of the grand jury of Hennepin county impaneled in November, 1927, and then holding office, and other persons....

... [W]e deem it sufficient to say that the articles charged, in substance, that a Jewish gangster was in control of gambling, bootlegging, and racketeering in Minneapolis, and that law enforcing officers and agencies were not energetically performing their duties. Most of the charges were directed against the chief of police; he was charged with gross neglect of duty, illicit relations with gangsters, and with participation in graft. The county attorney was charged with knowing the existing conditions and with failure to take adequate measures to remedy them. The mayor was accused of inefficiency and dereliction. One member of the grand jury was stated to be in sympathy with the gangsters. A special grand jury and a special prosecutor were demanded to deal with the situation in general, and, in particular, to investigate an attempt to assassinate one Guilford, one of the original defendants, who, it appears from the articles, was shot by gangsters after the first issue of the periodical had been published. There is no question but that the articles made serious accusations against the public officers named and others in connection with the prevalence of crimes and the failure to expose and punish them.

[T]he defendant Near, the present appellant, answered the complaint. He expressly invoked the protection of the due process clause of the Fourteenth Amendment. The case then came on for trial. Judgment was thereupon entered adjudging that "the newspaper, magazine and periodical known as The Saturday Press," as a public nuisance, "be and is hereby abated." The judgment perpetually enjoined the defendants "from producing, editing, publishing, circulating, having in their possession, selling or giving away any publication whatsoever which is a malicious, scandalous or defamatory newspaper, as defined by law," and also "from further conducting said nuisance under the name and title of said The Saturday Press or any other name or title."

The defendant Near appealed from this judgment to the Supreme Court of the State, again asserting his right under the Federal Constitution, and the judgment was affirmed.... From the judgment as thus affirmed, the defendant Near appeals to this Court.

This statute, for the suppression as a public nuisance of a newspaper or periodical, is unusual, if not unique, and raises questions of grave importance transcending the local interests involved in the particular action. It is no longer open to doubt that the liberty of the press and of speech is within the liberty safeguarded by the due process clause of the Fourteenth Amendment from invasion by state action. *Gitlow v. New York*, 268 U.S. 652, 666 [(1925)]; *Stromberg v. California*, 283 U.S. 359, decided May 18, 1931. In maintaining this guaranty, the authority of the state to enact laws to promote the health, safety, morals, and general welfare of its people is necessarily admitted. The limits of this sovereign power must always be determined with appropriate regard to the particular subject of its exercise. Liberty of speech and of the press is not an absolute right, and the state may punish its abuse. Liberty, in each of its phases, has its history and connotation, and, in the present instance, the inquiry is as to the historic conception of the liberty of the press and whether the statute under review violates the essential attributes of that liberty.

The object of the statute is not punishment, in the ordinary sense, but suppression of the offending newspaper or periodical. The reason for the enactment, as the state court has said, is that prosecutions to enforce penal statutes for libel do not result in "efficient repression or suppression of the evils of scandal." It is the continued publication of scandalous and defamatory matter that constitutes the business and the declared nuisance. Under this statute, a publisher of a newspaper or periodical, undertaking to conduct a campaign to expose and to censure official derelictions, and devoting his publication principally to that purpose, must face not simply the possibility of a verdict against him in a suit or prosecution for libel, but a determination that his newspaper or periodical is a public nuisance to be abated, and that this abatement and suppression will follow unless he is prepared with legal evidence to prove the truth of the charges and also to satisfy the court that, in addition to being true, the matter was published with good motives and for justifiable ends. This suppression is accomplished by enjoining publication, and that restraint is the object and effect of the statute.

The statute not only operates to suppress the offending newspaper or periodical, but to put the publisher under an effective censorship. When a newspaper or periodical is found to be "malicious, scandalous and defamatory," and is suppressed as such, resumption of publication is punishable as a contempt of court by fine or imprisonment. Thus, where a newspaper or periodical has been suppressed because of the circulation of charges against public officers of official misconduct, it would seem to be clear that the renewal of the publication of such charges would constitute a contempt, and that the judgment would lay a permanent restraint upon the publisher, to escape which he must satisfy the court as to the character of a new publication. Whether he would be permitted again to publish matter deemed to be derogatory to the same or other public officers would depend upon the court's ruling. In the present instance the judgment restrained the defendants from "publishing, circulating, having in their possession, selling or giving away any publication whatsoever which is a malicious, scandalous or defamatory newspaper, as defined by law." The law gives no definition except that covered by the words "scandalous and defamatory," and publications charging official misconduct are of the class. While the court, answering the objection that the judgment was too broad, saw no reason for construing it as restraining the defendants "from operating a newspaper in harmony with the public welfare to which all must yield," and said that the defendants had not indicated "any desire to conduct their business in the usual and legitimate manner," the manifest inference is that, at least with respect to a new publication directed against official misconduct, the defendant would be held, under penalty of punishment for contempt as provided in the statute, to a manner of publication which the court considered to be "usual and legitimate" and consistent with the public welfare. This is of the essence of censorship.

The question is whether a statute authorizing such proceedings in restraint of publication is consistent with the conception of the liberty of the press as historically conceived and guaranteed. In determining the extent of the constitutional protection, it has been generally, if not universally, considered that it is the chief purpose of the guaranty to prevent previous restraints upon publication. The struggle in England, directed against the legislative power of the licenser, resulted in renunciation of the censorship of the press. The liberty deemed to be established was thus described by Blackstone: "The liberty of the press is indeed essential to the nature of a free state; but this consists in laying no previous restraints upon publications, and not in freedom from censure for criminal matter when published. Every freeman has an undoubted right to lay what sentiments he pleases before the public; to forbid this, is to destroy the freedom of the press; but if he publishes what is improper, mischievous or illegal, he must take the consequence of his own temerity." 4 Bl. Com. 151, 152. See Story on the Constitution, §§ 1884, 1889.

The criticism upon Blackstone's statement has not been because immunity from previous restraint upon publication has not been regarded as deserving of special emphasis, but chiefly because that immunity cannot be deemed to exhaust the conception of the liberty guaranteed by State and Federal Constitutions. The point of criticism has been "that the mere exemption from restraints cannot be all that is secured by the constitutional provisions," and that "the liberty of the press might be rendered a mockery and a delusion, and the phrase itself a by-word, if, while every man was at liberty to publish what he pleased, the public authorities might nevertheless punish him for harmless publications." 2 Cooley, Const. Lim. (8th Ed.) pp. 885. But it is recognized that punishment for the abuse of the liberty accorded to the press is essential to the protection of the public, and that the common-law rules that subject the libeler to responsibility for the public offense, as well as for the private injury, are not abolished by the protection extended in our Constitutions The law of criminal libel rests upon that secure foundation. There is also the conceded authority of courts to punish for contempt when publications directly tend to prevent the proper discharge of judicial functions. In the present case, we have no occasion to inquire as to the permissible scope of subsequent punishment. For whatever wrong the appellant has committed or may commit, by his publications, the state appropriately affords both public and private redress by its libel laws. As has been noted, the statute in question does not deal with punishments; it provides for no punishment, except in case of contempt for violation of the court's order, but for suppression and injunction [—] that is, for restraint upon publication.

The objection has also been made that the principle as to immunity from previous restraint is stated too broadly, if every such restraint is deemed to be prohibited. That is undoubtedly true; the protection even as to previous restraint is not absolutely unlimited. But the limitation has been recognized only in exceptional cases. "When a nation is at war many things that might be said in time of peace are such a hindrance to its effort that their utterance will not be endured so long as men fight and that no Court could regard them as protected by any constitutional right." *Schenck v. United States*, 249 U.S. 47, 52 [(1919)]. No one would question but that a government might prevent actual obstruction to its recruiting service or the publication of the sailing dates of transports or the number and location of troops. On similar grounds, the primary requirements of decency may be enforced against obscene publications. The security of the community life may be protected against incitements to acts of violence and the overthrow by force of orderly government.... These limitations are not applicable here....

The fact that for approximately one hundred and fifty years there has been almost an entire absence of attempts to impose previous restraints upon publications relating to the malfeasance of public officers is significant of the deep-seated conviction that such restraints would violate constitutional right. Public officers, whose character and conduct remain open to debate and free discussion in the press, find their remedies for false accusations in actions under libel laws providing for redress and punishment, and not in proceedings to restrain the publication of newspapers and periodicals. The general principle that the constitutional guaranty of the liberty of the press gives immunity from previous restraints has been approved in many decisions under the provisions of state constitutions.

The importance of this immunity has not lessened. While reckless assaults upon public men, and efforts to bring obloquy upon those who are endeavoring faithfully to discharge official duties, exert a baleful influence and deserve the severest condemnation in public opinion, it cannot be said that this abuse is greater, and it is believed to be less, than that which characterized the period in which our institutions took shape. Meanwhile, the administration of government has become more complex, the opportunities for malfeasance and corruption have multiplied, crime has grown to most serious proportions, and the danger of its protection by unfaithful officials and of the impairment of the fundamental security of life and property by criminal alliances and official neglect, emphasizes the primary need of a vigilant and courageous press, especially in great cities. The fact that the liberty of the press may be abused by miscreant purveyors of scandal does not make any the less necessary the immunity of the press from previous restraint in dealing with official misconduct. Subsequent punishment for such abuses as may exist is the appropriate remedy, consistent with constitutional privilege.

Equally unavailing is the insistence that the statute is designed to prevent the circulation of scandal which tends to disturb the public peace and to provoke assaults and the commission of crime. Charges of reprehensible conduct, and in particular of official malfeasance, unquestionably create a public scandal, but the theory of the constitutional guaranty is that even a more serious public evil would be caused by authority to prevent publication. There is nothing new in the fact that charges of reprehensible conduct may create resentment and the disposition to resort to violent means of redress, but this well-understood tendency did not alter the determination to protect the press against censorship and restrain upon publication.

For these reasons we hold the statute, so far as it authorized the proceedings in this action under clause (b) of section 1, to be an infringement of the liberty of the press guaranteed by the Fourteenth Amendment....

Judgment reversed.

Mr. Justice Butler (dissenting).

The decision of the Court in this case declares Minnesota and every other state powerless to restrain by injunction the business of publishing and circulating among the people malicious, scandalous, and defamatory periodicals that in due course of judicial procedure has been adjudged to be a public nuisance. It gives to freedom of the press a meaning and a scope not heretofore recognized, and construes "liberty" in the due process clause of the Fourteenth Amendment to put upon the states a federal restriction that is without precedent.

The Minnesota statute does not operate as a previous restraint on publication within the proper meaning of that phrase. It does not authorize administrative control in advance such as was formerly exercised by the licensers and censors, but prescribes a remedy to be enforced by a suit in equity. In this case there was previous publication made in the course of the business of regularly producing malicious, scandalous, and defamatory periodicals. The business and publications unquestionably constitute an abuse of the right of free press. The statute denounces the things done as a nuisance on the ground, as stated by the state Supreme Court, that they threaten morals, peace, and good order. There is no question of the power of the state to denounce such transgressions. The restraint authorized is only in respect of continuing to do what has been duly adjudged to constitute a nuisance. There is nothing in the statute purporting to prohibit publications that have not been adjudged to constitute a nuisance. It is fanciful to suggest similarity between the granting or enforcement of the decree authorized by this statute to prevent further publication of malicious, scandalous, and defamatory articles and the previous restraint upon the press by licensers as referred to by Blackstone and described in the history of the times to which he alludes.

The judgment should be affirmed.

Mr. Justice Van Devanter, Mr. Justice McReynolds, and Mr. Justice Sutherland concur in this opinion.

Exercise 8:

1. What about the challenged statute made it a prior restraint?

2. Why are prior restraints worse than other forms of speech restrictions?

3. The Supreme Court tied its ruling to the Free Speech Clause's original meaning. Did it describe that meaning correctly?

4. Keep in mind the Court's historical claim when we cover *New York Times v. Sullivan*, 376 U.S. 254 (1964), below in Section [H][4][d].

5. Why was the statute unconstitutional?

6. Who, the majority or dissent, better evaluated the costs and benefits of the Minnesota statute? Are Supreme Court justices the best officials to make such an evaluation? If you argue no, then who would be better?

7. Under what circumstances are prior restraints permissible, according to the Court?

8. Following the dissent's reasoning, what could a state *not* do? Is that an attractive interpretation of the Free Speech Clause?

Though judicial prior restraints, like the one at issue in *Near*, are rare today, they arise most frequently in the contexts of national security and publicity of trial proceedings, and the Supreme Court is very skeptical of them. *See, e.g., New York Times v. United States*, 403 U.S. 713 (1971) (refusing to grant an injunction to the United States to prevent publication of the *History of U.S. Decision-Making Process on Viet Nam Policy*, colloquially known as the Pentagon Papers); *Nebraska Press Ass'n v. Stuart*, 427 U.S. 539 (1976) (ruling that a criminal trial court order that restrained news media from publicizing the defendant's admissions to law enforcement violated the First Amendment).

Today, prior restraints most prominently come in the form of licensing systems for usage of public property. Cities, counties, states, and the federal government authorize usage of their public properties, and they commonly do so through permitting systems. The Supreme Court has a long line of case law evaluating the various licensing regimes. The Court, in *Thomas v. Chicago Park Dist.*, 534 U.S. 316 (2002), summarized this case law and utilized the test that governs these content-neutral permitting regimes. First, the licensing scheme must serve an important interest. For example, a licensing regime prevents double-booking of a park, and therefore avoids conflict among prospective speakers. Second, the scheme must contain clear licensing criteria that leave little discretion for the licensing authority. For instance, an ordinance may not permit denial of a permit for a nonspecific reason, such as "in the public interest," because that could hide an official's dislike of the petitioner's message. Third, the permitting scheme must contain adequate, expeditious, procedural protections, including prompt judicial review. *Id.* at 322–24.

The context of governmental licensing for public park usage is closely related to the broader context of content-neutral time, place, and manner restrictions in public fora, discussed below in Section [I][3].

3. Government Punishment Because of Speech

A common form of infringement of the Free Speech Clause is government punishment because of speech. The clearest example of such punishment is criminal prosecution premised on a defendant's speech.

For instance, during World War I, the federal government passed two statutes that targeted speech which undermined the war effort, the Espionage Act of June 15, 1917, and the Act of May 16, 1918. Among other things, the Acts punished "whoever, when the United States is at war, shall willfully cause or attempt mutiny, etc. to cause, or incite or attempt to incite, insubordination, disloyalty, mutiny, or refusal of duty, in the military or naval forces of the United States, or shall willfully obstruct or attempt to obstruct recruiting or enlistment service of the United States...." Act of May 16, 1918, 40 Stat. 553 (1918).

Famously, the United States prosecuted Eugene V. Debs for violation of the Acts. Debs was the major socialist party's candidate for president on five occasions, including against President Wilson. He was also a prominent and vocal opponent of American involvement in World War I, frequently publicly voicing his opposition. In *Debs v. United States*, 249 U.S. 211 (1919), the Supreme Court upheld Debs' conviction under the 1918 Act, which carried with it ten years' imprisonment (though President Harding later pardoned Debs).

4. Government Compels Speech

The Supreme Court has ruled that government compulsion to speak constitutes an infringement of the Free Speech Clause and generally has taken such compulsions to be unconstitutional. The reason for this is that the freedom of speech includes the freedom not to speak. Stated differently, the right to refrain from speaking is a complementary component of the broader concept of "individual freedom of mind." The problem is that government compulsion to speak comes in many forms. Standard issue license plates, such as Live Free or Die in New Hampshire, may require vehicle owners to carry a government-created and government-mandated message. *See Wooley v. Maynard*, 430 U.S. 705 (1977). Calls for fair or balanced news coverage, like a right-of-reply statute, may force newspapers or others to carry or promote a view or position that they do not support. *Miami Herald Pub. Co. v. Tornillo*, 418 U.S. 241 (1974). And even public accommodations laws, which are designed to protect certain individuals from discrimination, may oblige groups or individuals who are engaged in expressive activity to create or convey a particular government-approved message. *See Hurley v. Irish-American Gay, Lesbian, Bisexual Group of Boston*, 515 U.S. 557 (1995). The Court has struck down each of these speech compulsions.

As we saw above in the campaign finance context, though, not all speech compulsions are unconstitutional. Campaign finance laws require disclosure of campaign monies and survive strict scrutiny. With respect to the forced contribution of money to an organization or group, the Court previously recognized three exceptions to the general rule that such compulsions are unconstitutional: compelled contributions to public sector unions, *Abood v. Detroit Bd. of Educ.*, 431 U.S. 209 (1977); required fees that lawyers must pay to state bars (for things like attorney discipline or developing ethical codes), *Keller v. State Bar*, 496 U.S. 1 (1990); and mandatory student fees to public universities, *Board of Regents of Univ. of Wisc. Sys. v. Southworth*, 529 U.S. 217 (2000). As discussed in the second case in this section, the viability of these exceptions is in flux in the wake of *Janus v. American Fed. of State, Cty., and Municipal Employees, Coucil 31*, 138 S. Ct. 2448 (2018), which expressly overturned *Abood*.

This line of compelled speech cases stretches back to the New Deal period. The Supreme Court initially ruled, in *Minersville Sch. Dist. v. Gobitis*, 310 U.S. 586 (1940), that a public school district could constitutionally require student participation in a flag salute and Pledge of Allegiance ceremony. A brief three years later, however, the Supreme Court reversed course in a classic case, reprinted below.

West Virginia State Board of Education v. Barnette
319 U.S. 624 (1943)

MR. JUSTICE JACKSON delivered the opinion of the Court.

Following the decision by this Court on June 3, 1940, in *Minersville School District v. Gobitis*, 310 U.S. 586 [(1940)], the West Virginia legislature amended its statutes to require all schools therein to conduct courses of instruction in history, civics, and in the Constitutions of the United States and of the State "for the purpose of teaching, fostering and perpetuating the ideals, principles and spirit of Americanism, and increasing the knowledge of the organization and machinery of the government." ...

The Board of Education on January 9, 1942, adopted a resolution containing recitals taken largely from the Court's *Gobitis* opinion and ordering that the salute to the flag become "a regular part of the program of activities in the public schools," that all teachers and pupils "shall be required to participate in the salute honoring the Nation represented by the Flag; provided, however, that refusal to salute the Flag be regarded as an Act of insubordination, and shall be dealt with accordingly." ... What is now required is the "stiff-arm" salute while the following is repeated: "I pledge allegiance to the Flag of the United States of America and to the Republic for which it stands; one Nation, indivisible, with liberty and justice for all."

Failure to conform is "insubordination" dealt with by expulsion. Readmission is denied by statute until compliance. Meanwhile the expelled child is "unlawfully absent" and may be proceeded against as a delinquent. His parents or guardians are liable to prosecution, and if convicted are subject to fine not exceeding $50 and jail term not exceeding thirty days.

Appellees ... brought suit in the United States District Court for themselves and others similarly situated asking its injunction to restrain enforcement of these laws and regulations against Jehovah's Witnesses. The Witnesses are an unincorporated body teaching that the obligation imposed by law of God is superior to that of laws enacted by temporal government. Their religious beliefs include a literal version of

Exodus, Chapter 20, verses 4 and 5, which says: "Thou shalt not make unto thee any graven image, or any likeness of anything that is in heaven above, or that is in the earth beneath, or that is in the water under the earth; thou shalt not bow down thyself to them nor serve them." They consider that the flag is an "image" within this command. For this reason they refuse to salute it.

Children of this faith have been expelled from school. Officials threaten to send them to reformatories maintained for criminally inclined juveniles. Parents of such children have been prosecuted and are threatened with prosecutions for causing delinquency.

The Board of Education moved to dismiss the complaint. The cause was submitted on the pleadings to a District Court of three judges. It restrained enforcement as to the plaintiffs and those of that class. The Board of Education brought the case here by direct appeal.

This case calls upon us to reconsider a precedent decision. Before turning to the *Gobitis* case, however, it is desirable to notice certain characteristics by which this controversy is distinguished.

As the present CHIEF JUSTICE said in dissent in the *Gobitis* case, the State may "require teaching by instruction and study of all in our history and in the structure and organization of our government, including the guaranties of civil liberty which tend to inspire patriotism and love of country." Here, however, we are dealing with a compulsion of students to declare a belief. They are not merely made acquainted with the flag salute so that they may be informed as to what it is or even what it means. The issue here is whether this slow and easily neglected route to aroused loyalties constitutionally may be short-cut by substituting a compulsory salute and slogan....

There is no doubt that, in connection with the pledges, the flag salute is a form of utterance. Symbolism is a primitive but effective way of communicating ideas. The use of an emblem or flag to symbolize some system, idea, institution, or personality, is a short cut from mind to mind. Causes and nations, political parties, lodges and ecclesiastical groups seek to knit the loyalty of their followings to a flag or banner, a color or design. The State announces rank, function, and authority through crowns and maces, uniforms and black robes; the church speaks through the Cross, the Crucifix, the altar and shrine, and clerical raiment. Symbols of State often convey political ideas just as religious symbols come to convey theological ones. Associated with many of these symbols are appropriate gestures of acceptance or respect: a salute, a bowed or bared head, a bended knee. A person gets from a symbol the meaning he puts into it, and what is one man's comfort and inspiration is another's jest and scorn.

Over a decade ago Chief Justice Hughes led this Court in holding that the display of a red flag as a symbol of opposition by peaceful and legal means to organized government was protected by the free speech guaranties of the Constitution. *Stromberg v. California*, 283 U.S. 359 [(1931)]. Here it is the State that employs a flag as a symbol of adherence to government as presently organized. It requires the individual to communicate by word and sign his acceptance of the political ideas it thus bespeaks. Objection to this form of communication when coerced is an old one, well known to the framers of the Bill of Rights.

It is also to be noted that the compulsory flag salute and pledge requires affirmation of a belief and an attitude of mind. It is now a commonplace that censorship or suppression of expression of opinion is tolerated by our Constitution only when the expression presents a clear and present danger. [H]ere the power of compulsion is invoked without any allegation that remaining passive during a flag salute ritual creates a clear and present danger that would justify an effort even to muffle expression....

Whether the First Amendment to the Constitution will permit officials to order observance of ritual of this nature does not depend upon whether as a voluntary exercise we would think it to be good, bad or merely innocuous. Any credo of nationalism is likely to include what some disapprove or to omit what others think essential, and to give off different overtones as it takes on different accents or interpretations. If official power exists to coerce acceptance of any patriotic creed, what it shall contain cannot be decided by courts, but must be largely discretionary with the ordaining authority, whose power to prescribe would no doubt include power to amend....

The question which underlies the flag salute controversy is whether such a ceremony so touching matters of opinion and political attitude may be imposed upon the individual by official authority under powers committed to any political organization under our Constitution. We examine rather than assume existence of this power and, against this broader definition of issues in this case, re-examine specific grounds assigned for the *Gobitis* decision.

1. It was said that the flag-salute controversy confronted the Court with "the problem which Lincoln cast in memorable dilemma: 'Must a government of necessity be too strong for the liberties of its people, or too weak to maintain its own existence?" and that the answer must be in favor of strength.

It may be doubted whether Mr. Lincoln would have thought that the strength of government to maintain itself would be impressively vindicated by our confirming power of the state to expel a handful of children from school. Such oversimplification, so handy in political debate, often lacks the precision necessary to postulates of judicial reasoning. If validly applied to this problem, the utterance cited would resolve every issue of power in favor of those in authority and would require us to override every liberty thought to weaken or delay execution of their policies.

Government of limited power need not be anemic government. Assurance that rights are secure tends to diminish fear and jealousy of strong government, and by making us feel safe to live under it makes for its better support. Without promise of a limiting Bill of Rights it is doubtful if our Constitution could have mustered enough strength to enable its ratification. To enforce those rights today is not to choose weak government over strong government. It is only to adhere as a means of strength to individual freedom of mind in preference to officially disciplined uniformity for which history indicates a disappointing and disastrous end.

The subject now before us exemplifies this principle. Free public education, if faithful to the ideal of secular instruction and political neutrality, will not be partisan or enemy of any class, creed, party, or faction. If it is to impose any ideological discipline, however, each party or denomination must seek to control, or failing that, to weaken the influence of the educational system....

2. It was also considered in the *Gobitis* case that functions of educational officers in states, counties and school districts were such that to interfere with their authority "would in effect make us the school board for the country."

The Fourteenth Amendment, as now applied to the States, protects the citizen against the State itself and all of its creatures — Boards of Education not excepted. These have, of course, important, delicate, and highly discretionary functions, but none that they may not perform within the limits of the Bill of Rights. That they are educating the young for citizenship is reason for scrupulous protection of Constitutional freedoms of the individual, if we are not to strangle the free mind at its source and teach youth to discount important principles of our government as mere platitudes.

Such Boards are numerous and their territorial jurisdiction often small. But small and local authority may feel less sense of responsibility to the Constitution, and agencies of publicity may be less vigilant in calling it to account. There are village tyrants as well as village Hampdens, but none who acts under color of law is beyond reach of the Constitution.

3. The *Gobitis* opinion reasoned that this is a field "where courts possess no marked and certainly no controlling competence," that it is committed to the legislatures as well as the courts to guard cherished liberties and that it is constitutionally appropriate to "fight out the wise use of legislative authority in the forum of public opinion and before legislative assemblies rather than to transfer such a contest to the judicial arena," since all the "effective means of inducing political changes are left free."

The very purpose of a Bill of Rights was to withdraw certain subjects from the vicissitudes of political controversy, to place them beyond the reach of majorities and officials and to establish them as legal principles to be applied by the courts. One's right to life, liberty, and property, to free speech, a free press, freedom of worship and assembly, and other fundamental rights may not be submitted to vote; they depend on the outcome of no elections.

... The test of legislation which collides with the Fourteenth Amendment, because it also collides with the principles of the First, is much more definite than the test when only the Fourteenth is involved. Much of the vagueness of the due process clause disappears when the specific prohibitions of the First become its standard. [F]reedoms of speech and of press, of assembly, and of worship ... are susceptible of restriction only to prevent grave and immediate danger to interests which the state may lawfully protect....

Nor does our duty to apply the Bill of Rights to assertions of official authority depend upon our possession of marked competence in the field where the invasion of rights occurs. True, the task of translating the majestic generalities of the Bill of

Rights, conceived as part of the pattern of liberal government in the eighteenth century, into concrete restraints on officials dealing with the problems of the twentieth century, is one to disturb self-confidence. These principles grew in soil which also produced a philosophy that the individual was the center of society, that his liberty was attainable through mere absence of governmental restraints, and that government should be entrusted with few controls and only the mildest supervision over men's affairs. We must transplant these rights to a soil in which the laissez-faire concept or principle of non-interference has withered at least as to economic affairs, and social advancements are increasingly sought through closer integration of society and through expanded and strengthened governmental controls. These changed conditions often deprive precedents of reliability and cast us more than we would choose upon our own judgment. But we act in these matters not by authority of our competence but by force of our commissions. We cannot, because of modest estimates of our competence in such specialties as public education, withhold the judgment that history authenticates as the function of this Court when liberty is infringed.

4. Lastly, and this is the very heart of the *Gobitis* opinion, it reasons that "National unity is the basis of national security," that the authorities have "the right to select appropriate means for its attainment," and hence reaches the conclusion that such compulsory measures toward "national unity" are constitutional....

National unity as an end which officials may foster by persuasion and example is not in question. The problem is whether under our Constitution compulsion as here employed is a permissible means for its achievement.

Struggles to coerce uniformity of sentiment in support of some end thought essential to their time and country have been waged by many good as well as by evil men. Nationalism is a relatively recent phenomenon but at other times and places the ends have been racial or territorial security, support of a dynasty or regime, and particular plans for saving souls. As first and moderate methods to attain unity have failed, those bent on its accomplishment must resort to an ever-increasing severity. As governmental pressure toward unity becomes greater, so strife becomes more bitter as to whose unity it shall be. Probably no deeper division of our people could proceed from any provocation than from finding it necessary to choose what doctrine and whose program public educational officials shall compel youth to unite in embracing. Ultimate futility of such attempts to compel coherence is the lesson of every such effort from the Roman drive to stamp out Christianity as a disturber of its pagan unity, the Inquisition, as a means to religious and dynastic unity, the Siberian exiles as a means to Russian unity, down to the fast failing efforts of our present totalitarian enemies. Those who begin coercive elimination of dissent soon find themselves exterminating dissenters. Compulsory unification of opinion achieves only the unanimity of the graveyard.

It seems trite but necessary to say that the First Amendment to our Constitution was designed to avoid these ends by avoiding these beginnings. There is no mysticism in the American concept of the State or of the nature or origin of its authority. We set up government by consent of the governed, and the Bill of Rights denies those in power any legal opportunity to coerce that consent. Authority here is to be controlled by public opinion, not public opinion by authority.

The case is made difficult not because the principles of its decision are obscure but because the flag involved is our own. Nevertheless, we apply the limitations of the Constitution with no fear that freedom to be intellectually and spiritually diverse or even contrary will disintegrate the social organization. To believe that patriotism will not flourish if patriotic ceremonies are voluntary and spontaneous instead of a compulsory routine is to make an unflattering estimate of the appeal of our institutions to free minds. We can have intellectual individualism and the rich cultural diversities that we owe to exceptional minds only at the price of occasional eccentricity and abnormal attitudes. When they are so harmless to others or to the State as those we deal with here, the price is not too great. But freedom to differ is not limited to things that do not matter much. That would be a mere shadow of freedom. The test of its substance is the right to differ as to things that touch the heart of the existing order.

If there is any fixed star in our constitutional constellation, it is that no official, high or petty, can prescribe what shall be orthodox in politics, nationalism, religion, or other matters of opinion or force citizens to confess by word or act their faith therein. If there are any circumstances which permit an exception, they do not now occur to us.

We think the action of the local authorities in compelling the flag salute and pledge transcends constitutional limitations on their power and invades the sphere of intellect and spirit which it is the purpose of the First Amendment to our Constitution to reserve from all official control.

The decision of this Court in *Minersville School District v. Gobitis* [is] overruled, and the judgment enjoining enforcement of the West Virginia Regulation is

Affirmed.

Mr. Justice Roberts and Mr. Justice Reed [dissenting. Opinion omitted.]

Mr. Justice Black and Mr. Justice Douglas, concurring. [Opinion omitted.]

Mr. Justice Murphy, concurring. [Opinion omitted.]

Mr. Justice Frankfurter, dissenting.

One who belongs to the most vilified and persecuted minority in history is not likely to be insensible to the freedoms guaranteed by our Constitution. Were my purely personal attitude relevant I should whole-heartedly associate myself with the general libertarian views in the Court's opinion, representing as they do the thought and action of a lifetime. But as judges we are neither Jew nor Gentile, neither Catholic nor agnostic. We owe equal attachment to the Constitution and are equally bound by our judicial obligations whether we derive our citizenship from the earliest or the latest immigrants to these shores. As a member of this Court I am not justified in writing my private notions of policy into the Constitution, no matter how deeply I may cherish them or how mischievous I may deem their disregard. The duty of a judge who must decide which of two claims before the Court shall prevail, that of a

State to enact and enforce laws within its general competence or that of an individual to refuse obedience because of the demands of his conscience, is not that of the ordinary person. It can never be emphasized too much that one's own opinion about the wisdom or evil of a law should be excluded altogether when one is doing one's duty on the bench. The only opinion of our own even looking in that direction that is material is our opinion whether legislators could in reason have enacted such a law. In the light of all the circumstances, including the history of this question in this Court, it would require more daring than I possess to deny that reasonable legislators could have taken the action which is before us for review. Most unwillingly, therefore, I must differ from my brethren with regard to legislation like this. I cannot bring my mind to believe that the "liberty" secured by the Due Process Clause gives this Court authority to deny to the State of West Virginia the attainment of that which we all recognize as a legitimate legislative end, namely, the promotion of good citizenship, by employment of the means here chosen.

One's conception of the Constitution cannot be severed from one's conception of a judge's function in applying it. The Court has no reason for existence if it merely reflects the pressures of the day. Our system is built on the faith that men set apart for this special function, freed from the influences of immediacy and from the deflections of worldly ambition, will become able to take a view of longer range than the period of responsibility entrusted to Congress and legislatures. We are dealing with matters as to which legislators and voters have conflicting views. Are we as judges to impose our strong convictions on where wisdom lies? That which three years ago had seemed to five successive Courts to lie within permissible areas of legislation is now outlawed by the deciding shift of opinion of two Justices. What reason is there to believe that they or their successors may not have another view a few years hence? Is that which was deemed to be of so fundamental a nature as to be written into the Constitution to endure for all times to be the sport of shifting winds of doctrine? ...

In the past this Court has from time to time set its views of policy against that embodied in legislation by finding laws in conflict with what was called the "spirit of the Constitution". Such undefined destructive power was not conferred on this Court by the Constitution. Before a duly enacted law can be judicially nullified, it must be forbidden by some explicit restriction upon political authority in the Constitution. Equally inadmissible is the claim to strike down legislation because to us as individuals it seems opposed to the "plan and purpose" of the Constitution. That is too tempting a basis for finding in one's personal views the purposes of the Founders.

The uncontrollable power wielded by this Court brings it very close to the most sensitive areas of public affairs. As appeal from legislation to adjudication becomes more frequent, and its consequences more far-reaching, judicial self-restraint becomes more and not less important, lest we unwarrantably enter social and political domains wholly outside our concern. I think I appreciate fully the objections to the law before us. But to deny that it presents a question upon which men might reasonably differ appears to me to be intolerance. And since men may so reasonably differ, I deem it beyond my constitutional power to assert my view of the wisdom of this law against the view of the State of West Virginia.

Of course patriotism cannot be enforced by the flag salute. But neither can the liberal spirit be enforced by judicial invalidation of illiberal legislation. Our constant preoccupation with the constitutionality of legislation rather than with its wisdom tends to preoccupation of the American mind with a false value. The tendency of focusing attention on constitutionality is to make constitutionality synonymous with wisdom, to regard a law as all right if it is constitutional. Such an attitude is a great enemy of liberalism. Particularly in legislation affecting freedom of thought and freedom of speech much which should offend a free-spirited society is constitutional. Reliance for the most precious interests of civilization, therefore, must be found outside of their vindication in courts of law. Only a persistent positive translation of the faith of a free society into the convictions and habits and actions of a community is the ultimate reliance against unabated temptations to fetter the human spirit.

Exercise 9:

1. What specifically, in the Supreme Court's view, were the coercive aspects of the School Board's flag salute and pledge exercise?

2. Why did the Free Speech Clause protect *not* speaking?

3. Why did the Free Speech Clause protect the Barnetts' refusal, according to the Court?

4. Applying the *Spence* Test, is the Barnetts' activity of the flag salute constitutionally protected expressive conduct?

5. What levels of scrutiny did the majority and Justice Frankfurter apply? Which is appropriate?

6. The majority claimed that legally mandated exercises, like the flag salute and Pledge of Allegiance, in fact *undermine* loyalty to the government. Is that true? How did the justices know? Were the Justices better able to know than, for example, the West Virginia legislature or the School Board?

7. Is the *Barnette* Court's holding consistent with the purposes of the Free Speech Clause?

8. The majority pointed to the legal sanctions that backed the School Board's salute and pledge orders. What if the School Board had instead issued this rule: "To foster the ideals, principles and spirit of Americanism, and increasing the knowledge of the organization and machinery of the government, classes shall begin every day with a strictly voluntary salute and pledge of allegiance. Any student not wishing to participate may sit or stand in respectful silence during this exercise." Would this exercise violate the Free Speech Clause?

9. Did the *Barnette* Court improperly inject the Supreme Court into local educational policy that is better left to the states and local school boards?

10. Relatedly, to justify his decision to exercise judicial review in this case, Justice Jackson stated that "small and local authority may feel less sense of responsibility to

the Constitution." Is that true? Less responsibility than what other governmental institutions? How did Justice Jackson know?

11. Justice Jackson famously stated in *Barnette* that: "The very purpose of a Bill of Rights was to withdraw certain subjects from the vicissitudes of political controversy, to place them beyond the reach of majorities and officials and to establish them as legal principles to be applied by the courts. One's right to life, liberty, and property, to free speech, a free press, freedom of worship and assembly, and other fundamental rights may not be submitted to vote; they depend on the outcome of no elections." Under Justice Jackson's view, what is the scope of constitutional judicial review? What role, in Justice Jackson's view, do legislatures and executives have in implementing the Bill of Rights? Are his conclusions correct, or are Justice Frankfurter's contrary views, in dissent?

12. What is the limit to the Supreme Court's reasoning? The Court stated that "the State may 'require teaching by instruction and study of all in our history and in the structure and organization of our government, including the guaranties of civil liberty which tend to inspire patriotism and love of country.'" Is that qualification consistent with the Court's analysis? Why or why not?

13. Justice Frankfurter was an immigrant from Austria who taught at Harvard Law School for a quarter century before President Roosevelt appointed him to the Supreme Court. As Justice Frankfurter acknowledged, "I ... whole-heartedly associate myself with the general libertarian views in the Court's opinion," but he chided the Court for "writing [its] private notions of policy into the Constitution." Was Justice Frankfurter's accusation correct? How do you know? If he was correct, did the Court act improperly?

14. Suppose a state enforces its public accommodations law against a baker, who designs and creates custom wedding cakes, in a way that would require the baker to make a custom-designed wedding cake for a same-sex marriage. The baker objects, contending that when applied against him, the public accommodations law compels him to create expression and, therefore, convey a message with which he disagrees (based on his sincerely held religious beliefs). Setting aside any First Amendment religion claims, does the state's public accommodations law violate the baker's First Amendment speech rights? *See Craig v. Masterpiece Cakeshop, Inc.*, 370 P.3d 272 (Colo. Ct. App. 2015) (overturned on non-speech grounds). What if the state law was applied against a stationer, who created custom-made wedding invitations and declined to make such invitations for a same-sex couple? *See Brush & Nib Studio, LC v. City of Phoenix*, 247 Ariz. 269 (2019). A florist? *See State of Washington v. Arlene's Flowers, Inc.*, 441 P.3d 1203 (Wash. 2019).

In addition to the factual scenario in cases like *Barnette*—where individuals are forced to speak—the Supreme Court has extended its holding to the related context of the right to associate. This occurs in two main ways. First, the Supreme Court has ruled that the government may not force an expressive association to accept members that will alter the association's message. For instance, the Court ruled that New Jersey could not force the Boy Scouts to accept openly-gay scoutmasters because doing so would alter the Boy Scouts' message of morality. *Boy Scouts of America v. Dale*, 530 U.S. 640 (2000).

Second, the Supreme Court has ruled that the right to association limits the government's ability to force an association to identify its members. In the seminal case of *NAACP v. Alabama ex rel. Patterson*, 357 U.S. 449 (1958), the Court ruled that Alabama could not force the state NAACP to provide its membership list because the disclosure would chill membership.

More recently, the Court has demonstrated a willingness to reconsider whether forced contributions to certain groups (such as unions, state bars, or student governments), which then may use the money to engage in speech with which a public employee, attorney, or student disagrees, are constitutional. In *Janus*, which is excerpted below, the Court overturned a 40 year old precedent and held that requiring public employees to pay "agency fees" to unions is unconstitutional even if those fees are used only for speech that is "germane" to the organization's activities (such as collective bargaining). As you read *Janus*, consider whether such mandatory contributions burden First Amendment speech rights and whether the government has an adequate justification for requiring such mandatory contributions in the union or any other context.

Janus v. American Federation of State, County and Municipal Employees, Council 31

138 S. Ct. 2448 (2018)

Justice Alito delivered the opinion of the Court.

Under Illinois law, public employees are forced to subsidize a union, even if they choose not to join and strongly object to the positions the union takes in collective bargaining and related activities. We conclude that this arrangement violates the free speech rights of nonmembers by compelling them to subsidize private speech on matters of substantial public concern.

We upheld a similar law in *Abood v. Detroit Bd. of Ed.*, 431 U.S. 209 (1977), and we recognize the importance of following precedent unless there are strong reasons for not doing so. But there are very strong reasons in this case.... *Abood* is therefore overruled.

I

A

Under the Illinois Public Labor Relations Act (IPLRA), employees of the State and its political subdivisions are permitted to unionize. If a majority of the employees in a bargaining unit vote to be represented by a union, that union is designated as the exclusive representative of all the employees. Employees in the unit are not obligated to join the union selected by their co-workers, but whether they join or not, that union is deemed to be their sole permitted representative.

Employees who decline to join the union are not assessed full union dues but must instead pay what is generally called an "agency fee," which amounts to a percentage of the union dues. Under *Abood,* nonmembers may be charged for the portion of union dues attributable to activities that are "germane to [the union's] duties as collective-bargaining representative," but nonmembers may not be required to fund the union's political and ideological projects. 431 U.S., at 235. In labor-law parlance, the outlays in the first category are known as "chargeable" expenditures, while those in the latter are labeled "nonchargeable."

As illustrated by the record in this case, unions charge nonmembers, not just for the cost of collective bargaining *per se,* but also for many other supposedly connected activities. Here, the nonmembers were told that they had to pay for "[l]obbying," "[s]ocial and recreational activities," "advertising," "[m]embership meetings and conventions," and "litigation," as well as other unspecified "[s]ervices" that "may ultimately inure to the benefit of the members of the local bargaining unit." The total chargeable amount for nonmembers was 78.06% of full union dues.

B

Petitioner Mark Janus is employed by the Illinois Department of Healthcare and Family Services as a child support specialist. The employees in his unit are among the 35,000 public employees in Illinois who are represented by respondent American Federation of State, County, and Municipal Employees, Council 31 (Union). Janus refused to join the Union because he opposes "many of the public policy positions that [it] advocates," including the positions it takes in collective bargaining. Janus believes that the Union's "behavior in bargaining does not appreciate the current fiscal crises in Illinois and does not reflect his best interests or the interests of Illinois citizens." Therefore, if he had the choice, he "would not pay any fees or otherwise subsidize [the Union]." Under his unit's collective-bargaining agreement, however, he was required to pay an agency fee of $44.58 per month—which would amount to about $535 per year.

The amended complaint claims that all "nonmember fee deductions are coerced political speech" and that "the First Amendment forbids coercing any money from the nonmembers." Respondents moved to dismiss the amended complaint, correctly recognizing that the claim it asserted was foreclosed by *Abood.* The District Court granted the motion, and the Court of Appeals for the Seventh Circuit affirmed.

Janus then sought review in this Court, asking us to overrule *Abood* and hold that public-sector agency-fee arrangements are unconstitutional. We granted certiorari to consider this important question.

III

A

The First Amendment, made applicable to the States by the Fourteenth Amendment, forbids abridgment of the freedom of speech. We have held time and again that freedom of speech "includes both the right to speak freely and the right to refrain from speaking at all." *Wooley v. Maynard,* 430 U.S. 705, 714 (1977). The right to eschew association for expressive purposes is likewise protected. *Roberts v. United States Jaycees*, 468 U.S. 609, 623 (1984) ("Freedom of association ... plainly presupposes a freedom not to associate"). As Justice Jackson memorably put it [in *West Va. Bd. of Educ. v. Barnette*]: "If there is any fixed star in our constitutional constellation, it is that no official, high or petty, can prescribe what shall be orthodox in politics, nationalism, religion, or other matters of opinion or *force citizens to confess by word or act their faith therein.*" (emphasis added).

Free speech serves many ends. It is essential to our democratic form of government, see, *e.g., Garrison v. Louisiana*, 379 U.S. 64, 74–75 (1964), and it furthers the search for truth, see, *e.g., Thornhill v. Alabama*, 310 U.S. 88, 95 (1940). Whenever the Federal Government or a State prevents individuals from saying what they think on important matters or compels them to voice ideas with which they disagree, it undermines these ends.

When speech is compelled, however, additional damage is done. In that situation, individuals are coerced into betraying their convictions. Forcing free and independent individuals to endorse ideas they find objectionable is always demeaning, and for this reason, one of our landmark free speech cases said that a law commanding "involuntary affirmation" of objected-to beliefs would require "even more immediate and urgent grounds" than a law demanding silence.

Compelling a person to *subsidize* the speech of other private speakers raises similar First Amendment concerns. As Jefferson famously put it, "to compel a man to furnish contributions of money for the propagation of opinions which he disbelieves and abhor[s] is sinful and tyrannical." A Bill for Establishing Religious Freedom, in 2 Papers of Thomas Jefferson 545 (J. Boyd ed. 1950) (emphasis deleted and footnote omitted). We have therefore recognized that a "significant impingement on First Amendment rights" occurs when public employees are required to provide financial support for a union that "takes many positions during collective bargaining that have powerful political and civic consequences."

Because the compelled subsidization of private speech seriously impinges on First Amendment rights, it cannot be casually allowed. Our free speech cases have identified "levels of scrutiny" to be applied in different contexts. [In the context of compulsory subsidized commercial speech,] prior precedent applied what we characterized as "exacting" scrutiny, a less demanding test than the "strict" scrutiny that might be thought to apply outside the commercial sphere. Under "exacting" scrutiny, we noted, a compelled subsidy must "serve a compelling state interest that cannot be achieved through means significantly less restrictive of associational freedoms."

[In this case,] we again find it unnecessary to decide the issue of strict scrutiny because the Illinois scheme cannot survive under even the more permissive [exacting scrutiny] standard applied in [our prior cases].

B

In *Abood*, the main defense of the agency-fee arrangement was that it served the State's interest in "labor peace." By "labor peace," the *Abood* Court meant avoidance of the conflict and disruption that it envisioned would occur if the employees in a unit were represented by more than one union. In such a situation, the Court predicted, "inter-union rivalries" would foster "dissension within the work force," and the employer could face "conflicting demands from different unions." Confusion would ensue if the employer entered into and attempted to "enforce two or more agreements specifying different terms and conditions of employment." And a settlement with one union would be "subject to attack from [a] rival labor organizatio[n]."

We assume that "labor peace," in this sense of the term, is a compelling state interest, but *Abood* cited no evidence that the pandemonium it imagined would result if agency fees were not allowed, and it is now clear that *Abood*'s fears were unfounded. The *Abood* Court assumed that designation of a union as the exclusive representative of all the employees in a unit and the exaction of agency fees are inextricably linked, but that is simply not true.

The federal employment experience is illustrative. Under federal law, a union chosen by majority vote is designated as the exclusive representative of all the employees, but federal law does not permit agency fees. See 5 U.S.C. §§ 7102, 7111(a), 7114(a). Nevertheless, nearly a million federal employees — about 27% of the federal work force — are union members. The situation in the Postal Service is similar. Although permitted to choose an exclusive representative, Postal Service employees are not required to pay an agency fee and about 400,000 are union members. Likewise, millions of public employees in the 28 States that have laws generally prohibiting agency fees are represented by unions that serve as the exclusive representatives of all the employees. Whatever may have been the case 41 years ago when *Abood* was handed down, it is now undeniable that "labor peace" can readily be achieved "through means significantly less restrictive of associational freedoms" than the assessment of agency fees.

C

In addition to the promotion of "labor peace," *Abood* cited "the risk of 'free riders'" as justification for agency fees. Respondents and some of their *amici* endorse this reasoning, contending that agency fees are needed to prevent nonmembers from enjoying the benefits of union representation without shouldering the costs.

Petitioner strenuously objects to this free-rider label. He argues that he is not a free rider on a bus headed for a destination that he wishes to reach but is more like a person shanghaied for an unwanted voyage.

Whichever description fits the majority of public employees who would not subsidize a union if given the option, avoiding free riders is not a compelling interest. As we have noted, "free-rider arguments ... are generally insufficient to overcome First Amendment objections." To hold otherwise across the board would have startling consequences. Many private groups speak out with the objective of obtaining government action that will have the effect of benefiting nonmembers. May all those who are thought to benefit from such efforts be compelled to subsidize this speech?

Suppose that a particular group lobbies or speaks out on behalf of what it thinks are the needs of senior citizens or veterans or physicians, to take just a few examples. Could the government require that all seniors, veterans, or doctors pay for that service even if they object? It has never been thought that this is permissible. "[P]rivate speech often furthers the interests of nonspeakers," but "that does not alone empower the state to compel the speech to be paid for." *Lehnert v. Ferris Faculty Assn.,* 500 U.S. 507, 556 (1991) (Scalia, J., concurring in judgment in part and dissenting in part). In simple terms, the First Amendment does not permit the government to compel a person to pay for another party's speech just because the government thinks that the speech furthers the interests of the person who does not want to pay.

Those supporting agency fees contend that the situation here is different because unions are statutorily required to "represen[t] the interests of all public employees in the unit," whether or not they are union members. Why might this matter?

We can think of two possible arguments. It might be argued that a State has a compelling interest in requiring the payment of agency fees because (1) unions would otherwise be unwilling to represent nonmembers or (2) it would be fundamentally unfair to require unions to provide fair representation for nonmembers if nonmembers were not required to pay. Neither of these arguments is sound.

First, it is simply not true that unions will refuse to serve as the exclusive representative of all employees in the unit if they are not given agency fees. As noted, unions represent millions of public employees in jurisdictions that do not permit agency fees. No union is ever compelled to seek that designation. On the contrary, designation as exclusive representative is avidly sought. Why is this so?

Even without agency fees, designation as the exclusive representative confers many benefits. As noted, that status gives the union a privileged place in negotiations over wages, benefits, and working conditions. Not only is the union given the exclusive right to speak for all the employees in collective bargaining, but the employer is required by state law to listen to and to bargain in good faith with only that union. Designation as exclusive representative thus "results in a tremendous increase in the power" of the union. In addition, a union designated as exclusive representative is often granted special privileges, such as obtaining information about employees and having dues and fees deducted directly from employee wages. The collective-bargaining agreement in this case guarantees a long list of additional privileges.

These benefits greatly outweigh any extra burden imposed by the duty of providing fair representation for nonmembers. What this duty entails, in simple terms, is an obligation not to "act solely in the interests of [the union's] own members." ... What does this mean when it comes to the negotiation of a contract? The union may not negotiate a collective-bargaining agreement that discriminates against nonmembers, but the union's bargaining latitude would be little different if state law simply prohibited public employers from entering into agreements that discriminate in that way.

What about the representation of nonmembers in grievance proceedings? Representation of nonmembers furthers the union's interest in keeping control of the ad-

ministration of the collective-bargaining agreement, since the resolution of one employee's grievance can affect others. And when a union controls the grievance process,
it may, as a practical matter, effectively subordinate "the interests of [an] individual
employee ... to the collective interests of all employees in the bargaining unit."

In any event, whatever unwanted burden is imposed by the representation of nonmembers in disciplinary matters can be eliminated "through means significantly less
restrictive of associational freedoms" than the imposition of agency fees. Individual
nonmembers could be required to pay for that service or could be denied union representation altogether.[6] Thus, agency fees cannot be sustained on the ground that
unions would otherwise be unwilling to represent nonmembers.

Nor can such fees be justified on the ground that it would otherwise be unfair to
require a union to bear the duty of fair representation. That duty is a necessary concomitant of the authority that a union seeks when it chooses to serve as the exclusive
representative of all the employees in a unit. As explained, designating a union as
the exclusive representative of nonmembers substantially restricts the nonmembers'
rights. Protection of their interests is placed in the hands of the union, and if the
union were free to disregard or even work against those interests, these employees
would be wholly unprotected.

In sum, we do not see any reason to treat the free-rider interest any differently in
the agency-fee context than in any other First Amendment context. We therefore
hold that agency fees cannot be upheld on free-rider grounds.

IV

A

[Implicitly acknowledging the weakness of *Abood*'s own reasoning,] the Union respondent [proffers an] originalist defense of *Abood*. According to this argument,
Abood was correctly decided because the First Amendment was not originally understood to provide *any* protection for the free speech rights of public employees.

As an initial matter, we doubt that the Union — or its members — actually want
us to hold that public employees have "*no* [free speech] rights." Nor, in any event,
does the First Amendment's original meaning support the Union's claim. The Union
offers no persuasive founding-era evidence that public employees were understood
to lack free speech protections. The only early *speech* restrictions the Union identifies
are an 1806 statute prohibiting military personnel from using "'contemptuous or
disrespectful words against the President'" and other officials, and an 1801 directive
limiting electioneering by top government employees. But those examples at most
show that the government was understood to have power to limit employee speech

---

6. There is precedent for such arrangements. Some States have laws providing that, if an employee
with a religious objection to paying an agency fee "requests the [union] to use the grievance procedure
or arbitration procedure on the employee's behalf, the [union] is authorized to charge the employee
for the reasonable cost of using such procedure." *E.g.*, Cal. Govt.Code Ann. §3546.3. This more
tailored alternative, if applied to other objectors, would prevent free ridership while imposing a lesser
burden on First Amendment rights.

that threatened important governmental interests (such as maintaining military discipline and preventing corruption)—not that public employees' speech was entirely unprotected.

Ultimately, the Union relies, not on founding-era evidence, but on dictum from a 1983 opinion of this Court stating that, "[f]or most of th[e 20th] century, the unchallenged dogma was that a public employee had no right to object to conditions placed upon the terms of employment—including those which restricted the exercise of constitutional rights." *Connick v. Myers*, 461 U.S. 138, 143 [(1983)]. Even on its own terms, this dictum about 20th-century views does not purport to describe how the First Amendment was understood in 1791. And a careful examination of the decisions by this Court that *Connick* cited to support its dictum reveals that none of them rested on the facile premise that public employees are unprotected by the First Amendment. Instead, they considered (much as we do today) whether particular speech restrictions were "necessary to protect" fundamental government interests.

The Union has also failed to show that, even if public employees enjoyed free speech rights, the First Amendment was nonetheless originally understood to allow forced subsidies like those at issue here. We can safely say that, at the time of the adoption of the First Amendment, no one gave any thought to whether public-sector unions could charge nonmembers agency fees. Entities resembling labor unions did not exist at the founding, and public-sector unions did not emerge until the mid-20th century. The idea of public-sector unionization and agency fees would astound those who framed and ratified the Bill of Rights. Thus, the Union cannot point to any accepted founding-era practice that even remotely resembles the compulsory assessment of agency fees from public-sector employees.

In short, the Union has offered no basis for concluding that *Abood* is supported by the original understanding of the First Amendment.

VI

[The majority's lengthy discussion of stare decisis is omitted.]

VII

For these reasons, States and public-sector unions may no longer extract agency fees from nonconsenting employees.[28] ... This procedure violates the First Amendment and cannot continue. Neither an agency fee nor any other payment to the union may

---

28. [Footnote moved—ed.] Unfortunately, the dissent sees the need to resort to accusations that we are acting like "black-robed rulers" who have shut down an "energetic policy debate." We certainly agree that judges should not "overrid[e] citizens' choices" or "pick the winning side"—unless the Constitution commands that they do so. But when a federal or state law violates the Constitution, the American doctrine of judicial review requires us to enforce the Constitution. Here, States with agency-fee laws have abridged fundamental free speech rights. In holding that these laws violate the Constitution, we are simply enforcing the First Amendment as properly understood, "[t]he very purpose of [which] was to withdraw certain subjects from the vicissitudes of political controversy, to place them beyond the reach of majorities and officials and to establish them as legal principles to be applied by the courts." *Barnette*, 319 U.S. at 638.

be deducted from a nonmember's wages, nor may any other attempt be made to collect such a payment, unless the employee affirmatively consents to pay. By agreeing to pay, nonmembers are waiving their First Amendment rights, and such a waiver cannot be presumed. Rather, to be effective, the waiver must be freely given and shown by "clear and compelling" evidence. Unless employees clearly and affirmatively consent before any money is taken from them, this standard cannot be met.

Abood was wrongly decided and is now overruled. The judgment of the United States Court of Appeals for the Seventh Circuit is reversed, and the case is remanded for further proceedings consistent with this opinion.

It is so ordered.

JUSTICE SOTOMAYOR, dissenting. [opinion omitted]

JUSTICE KAGAN, with whom JUSTICE GINSBURG, JUSTICE BREYER, and JUSTICE SOTOMAYOR join, dissenting.

For over 40 years, *Abood* struck a stable balance between public employees' First Amendment rights and government entities' interests in running their workforces as they thought proper. Under that decision, a government entity could require public employees to pay a fair share of the cost that a union incurs when negotiating on their behalf over terms of employment. But no part of that fair-share payment could go to any of the union's political or ideological activities.

That holding fit comfortably with this Court's general framework for evaluating claims that a condition of public employment violates the First Amendment. The Court's decisions have long made plain that government entities have substantial latitude to regulate their employees' speech—especially about terms of employment—in the interest of operating their workplaces effectively. *Abood* allowed governments to do just that. While protecting public employees' expression about non-workplace matters, the decision enabled a government to advance important managerial interests—by ensuring the presence of an exclusive employee representative to bargain with. Far from an "anomaly," the *Abood* regime was a paradigmatic example of how the government can regulate speech in its capacity as an employer.

Not any longer. Today, the Court succeeds in its 6-year campaign to reverse *Abood*. Its decision will have large-scale consequences. Public employee unions will lose a secure source of financial support. State and local governments that thought fair-share provisions furthered their interests will need to find new ways of managing their workforces. Across the country, the relationships of public employees and employers will alter in both predictable and wholly unexpected ways.

II

Unlike the majority, I see nothing "questionable" about *Abood*'s analysis. The decision's account of why some government entities have a strong interest in agency fees (now often called fair-share fees) is fundamentally sound. And the balance *Abood* struck between public employers' interests and public employees' expression is right at home in First Amendment doctrine.

A

Abood's reasoning about governmental interests has three connected parts. First, exclusive representation arrangements benefit some government entities because they can facilitate stable labor relations. In particular, such arrangements eliminate the potential for inter-union conflict and streamline the process of negotiating terms of employment. Second, the government may be unable to avail itself of those benefits unless the single union has a secure source of funding. The various tasks involved in representing employees cost money; if the union doesn't have enough, it can't be an effective employee representative and bargaining partner. And third, agency fees are often needed to ensure such stable funding. That is because without those fees, employees have every incentive to free ride on the union dues paid by others.

Because of that legal duty, the union cannot give special advantages to its own members. And that in turn creates a collective action problem of nightmarish proportions. Everyone—not just those who oppose the union, but also those who back it—has an economic incentive to withhold dues; only altruism or loyalty—as *against* financial self-interest—can explain why an employee would pay the union for its services. And so emerged *Abood*'s rule allowing fair-share agreements: That rule ensured that a union would receive sufficient funds, despite its legally imposed disability, to effectively carry out its duties as exclusive representative of the government's employees.

The majority's initial response to this reasoning is simply to dismiss it. "[F]ree rider arguments," the majority pronounces, "are generally insufficient to overcome First Amendment objections." "To hold otherwise," it continues, "would have startling consequences" because "[m]any private groups speak out" in ways that will "benefit[] nonmembers." But that disregards the defining characteristic of *this* free-rider argument—that unions, unlike those many other private groups, must serve members and non-members alike. Groups advocating for "senior citizens or veterans" (to use the majority's examples) have no legal duty to provide benefits to all those individuals: They can spur people to pay dues by conferring all kinds of special advantages on their dues-paying members. Unions are—by law—in a different position, as this Court has long recognized.... That special feature was what justified *Abood*: "Where the state imposes upon the union a duty to deliver services, it may permit the union to demand reimbursement for them."

The majority's fallback argument purports to respond to the distinctive position of unions, but still misses *Abood*'s economic insight. The gist of the account is that "designation as the exclusive representative confers many benefits," which outweigh the costs of providing services to non-members. But that response avoids the key question, which is whether unions without agency fees will be *able to* (not whether they will *want to*) carry on as an effective exclusive representative. And as to that question, the majority again fails to reckon with how economically rational actors behave—in public as well as private workplaces. Without a fair-share agreement, the class of union non-members spirals upward. Employees (including those who love the union) realize that they can get the same benefits even if they let their memberships expire. And as more and more stop paying dues, those left must take up the financial slack (and anyway, begin to feel like suckers)—so they too quit the union. And when the vicious cycle finally ends, chances are that the union will lack the resources to effectively perform the responsibilities of an exclusive representative—or, in the worst case, to perform them at all. The result is to frustrate the interests of every government entity that thinks a strong exclusive-representation scheme will promote stable labor relations.

IV

There is no sugarcoating today's opinion. The majority overthrows a decision entrenched in this Nation's law—and in its economic life—for over 40 years. As a result, it prevents the American people, acting through their state and local officials, from making important choices about workplace governance. And it does so by weaponizing the First Amendment, in a way that unleashes judges, now and in the future, to intervene in economic and regulatory policy.

The majority has overruled *Abood* because it wanted to pick the winning side in what should be—and until now, has been—an energetic policy debate. Some state and local governments (and the constituents they serve) think that stable unions promote healthy labor relations and thereby improve the provision of services to the public. Other state and local governments (and their constituents) think, to the contrary, that strong unions impose excessive costs and impair those services. Americans have debated the pros and cons for many decades—in large part, by deciding whether to use fair-share arrangements. Yesterday, 22 States were on one side, 28 on the other (ignoring a couple of in-betweeners). Today, that healthy—that democratic—debate ends.

And maybe most alarming, the majority has chosen the winners by turning the First Amendment into a sword, and using it against workaday economic and regulatory policy. Today is not the first time the Court has wielded the First Amendment in such an aggressive way. See, *e.g., National Institute of Family and Life Advocates v. Becerra,* 138 S. Ct. 2361 (2018) (invalidating a law requiring medical and counseling facilities to provide relevant information to users). And it threatens not to be the last. Speech is everywhere—a part of every human activity (employment, health care, securities trading, you name it). For that reason, almost all economic and regulatory policy affects or touches speech. So the majority's road runs long. And at every stop are black-robed rulers overriding citizens' choices. The First Amendment was meant for better things. It was meant not to undermine but to protect democratic governance—including over the role of public-sector unions.

Exercise 10:

1. Is the majority correct that compelled speech is worse (*i.e.,* imposes "additional damage") than speech restrictions? Is that true always? Sometimes? How should the dissent respond?

2. Does compelling an individual to subsidize the speech of private speakers raise the same concerns? Does the dissent agree with the majority on this point? For the

dissent, does it depend on the type of speech for which the money will be used? If so, why does that matter? Which types of speech can compelled contributions be used for under the dissent's analysis?

3. If the majority and dissent disagree that the agency fee requirement infringes on First Amendment rights, then they must either apply different standards of review or apply the same standard differently. Which is it? Articulate the test or tests that the majority and dissent use in *Janus*.

4. For the majority, does the compelled contribution requirement fall because the government lacks a sufficiently important purpose? Because the requirement is not properly tailored to the government's alleged interest? Both?

5. Does it matter that public employers are imposing the agency fees? Stated differently, should the compelled speech analysis be different when the government is acting as employer?

6. In *Keller v. State Bar*, 496 U.S. 1 (1990), the Court followed *Abood* and held that attorney bar dues are constitutional if such compelled contributions are used for purposes that are "germane" to the state bar's regulating the legal profession or improving the quality of legal services. Such mandatory contributions cannot constitutionally be used to fund the bar's political or ideological speech. Suppose that, after graduating law school and passing the bar, you start your legal practice, receive a notice from your state bar stating that you owe a certain amount in bar fees, and decide to challenge the assessment, citing *Janus*. In the wake of *Janus*, is *Keller* still good law? How will you argue that *Janus* is controlling such that the bar fee is unconstitutional? How might the state bar (perhaps invoking the dissent's position in *Janus*) distinguish the mandatory bar fees from union dues?

7. Suppose that a university charges each student an "activity fee," which is distributed to student organizations across campus in a viewpoint-neutral way. Even though the activity fees are not used to support the student government's political speech or other ideological activities, a second-year student objects to the mandatory charge and properly files an action challenging the activity fee. In the university context, will the student win? Does such an assessment infringe the student's First Amendment rights (given that some moneys go to groups with which she disagrees)? Should the majority's analysis in *Janus* control? Or does the dissent's position have even greater force in the context of post-secondary education? *See Bd. of Regents v. Southworth*, 529 U.S. 217 (2000).

Assume for the sake of this exercise that the Supreme Court strikes down student activity fees based on the majority's reasoning in *Janus*. Assume further that a public university then does away with its $200 student activity fee and instead increases its tuition by $200. The university then takes the additional tuition revenue and gives that money to the student government to carry out its various activities on campus. Would this cure any potential First Amendment problem under *Janus*? Should it? Does such an arrangement serve as a lesser restrictive means or simply show that the dissent's position is stronger than the majority suggests?

8. What if the government imposes a tax on certain individuals and then uses that revenue to fund its own speech activity? Should the Court view that as a form of compelled speech that the First Amendment forbids? *See Johanns v. Livestock Marketing Ass'n*, 544 U.S. 550 (2005) (analyzing the USDA's "Beef, It's What's for Dinner" advertising campaign).

5. Government Makes Speaking (More) Costly

The government may also infringe the freedom of speech when it increases the cost of speaking. This occurs in two main ways. First, the government may remove the monetary benefits one would otherwise receive from speech. Second, the government may impose monetary liability for one's speech.

The Supreme Court has repeatedly ruled that denial of compensation for speech infringes the freedom of speech, such as in the case reprinted below.

Simon & Schuster, Inc. v. Members of the New York State Crime Victims Board
502 U.S. 105 (1991)

JUSTICE O'CONNOR delivered the opinion of the Court.

New York's "Son of Sam" law requires that an accused or convicted criminal's income from works describing his crime be deposited in an escrow account. These funds are then made available to the victims of the crime and the criminal's other creditors. We consider whether this statute is consistent with the First Amendment.

I

This case began in 1986, when the Board first became aware of the contract between petitioner Simon & Schuster and admitted organized crime figure Henry Hill.... Hill was arrested in 1980. In exchange for immunity from prosecution, he testified against many of his former colleagues. Since his arrest, he has lived under an assumed name in an unknown part of the country.

In August 1981, Hill entered into a contract with author Nicholas Pileggi for the production of a book about Hill's life. The following month, Hill and Pileggi signed a publishing agreement with Simon & Schuster, Inc. Under the agreement, Simon & Schuster agreed to make payments to both Hill and Pileggi....

Wiseguy was published in January 1986. The book depicts, in colorful detail, the day-to-day existence of organized crime, primarily in Hill's first-person narrative. *Wiseguy* was a commercial success: Within 19 months of its publication, more than a million copies were in print. A few years later, the book was converted into a film called Goodfellas, which won a host of awards.

From Henry Hill's perspective, however, the publicity generated by the book's success proved less desirable. The Crime Victims Board learned of *Wiseguy* in January 1986, soon after it was published.

C

On January 31, the Board ordered Simon & Schuster ... to furnish copies of any contracts it had entered into with Hill, to provide the dollar amounts and dates of all payments it had made to Hill, and to suspend all payments to Hill in the future. Simon & Schuster complied with this order. By that time, Simon & Schuster had paid Hill's literary agent $96,250 in advances and royalties on Hill's behalf, and was holding $27,958 for eventual payment to Hill.

The Board reviewed the book and the contract, and determined that Simon & Schuster had violated the law. The Board ordered Hill to turn over the payments he had already received, and ordered Simon & Schuster to turn over all money payable to Hill at the time or in the future.

Simon & Schuster brought suit in August 1987, seeking a declaration that the Son of Sam law violates the First Amendment and an injunction barring the statute's enforcement....

II

A statute is presumptively inconsistent with the First Amendment if it imposes a financial burden on speakers because of the content of their speech. As we emphasized in invalidating a content-based magazine tax: "[O]fficial scrutiny of the content of publications as the basis for imposing a tax is entirely incompatible with the First Amendment's guarantee of freedom of the press."

... It is but one manifestation of a far broader principle: "Regulations which permit the Government to discriminate on the basis of the content of the message cannot be tolerated under the First Amendment." *Police Dept. of Chicago v. Mosley*, 408 U.S. 92, 95 (1972). In the context of financial regulation, it bears repeating, that the government's ability to impose content-based burdens on speech raises the specter that the government may effectively drive certain ideas or viewpoints from the marketplace. The First Amendment presumptively places this sort of discrimination beyond the power of the government....

The Son of Sam law is such a content-based statute. It singles out income derived from expressive activity for a burden the State places on no other income, and it is directed only at works with a specified content. Whether the First Amendment "speaker" is considered to be Henry Hill, whose income the statute places in escrow because of the story he has told, or Simon & Schuster, which can publish books about crime with the assistance of only those criminals willing to forgo remuneration for at least five years, the statute plainly imposes a financial disincentive only on speech of a particular content.

The Son of Sam law establishes a financial disincentive to create or publish works with a particular content. In order to justify such differential treatment, "the State must show that its regulation is necessary to serve a compelling state interest and is narrowly drawn to achieve that end."

....

The judgment of the Court of Appeals is accordingly

Reversed.

Justice Thomas took no part in the consideration or decision of this case.

Justice Blackmun, concurring in the judgment. [Opinion omitted.]

Justice Kennedy, concurring in the judgment. [Opinion omitted.]

Exercise 11:

1. What was the financial cost imposed by New York state?

2. On a scale of 1 to 10, with 10 being the most onerous, how weighty was that cost? Is that enough of a cost to "infringe" freedom of speech?

3. Why, according to the Supreme Court, should it treat governmental cost-imposing measures, as infringing the freedom of speech?

———————

The Supreme Court has also ruled that government imposition of civil liability for speech infringes the freedom of speech. *New York Times v. Sullivan*, 376 U.S. 254, 283 (1964). This occurs most frequently in the context of tort liability premised on speech, such as libel, invasion of privacy, and intentional infliction of emotional distress, which we will cover below, in Section [H][4][d].

6. Other Forms of Government Pressure to Speak or Not to Speak

Criminal prosecution and civil fines are relatively direct and substantial burdens on speech. However, there are a wide variety of other forms that government pressure to speak, or not speak, can take. The case law in this area is mixed. On the one hand, the Supreme Court ruled that requiring movies to carry the label "propaganda" did not infringe the Free Speech Clause. *Meese v. Keene*, 481 U.S. 465 (1987). On the other hand, the Court ruled that a state commission sending a letter to a bookseller asking the bookseller to cease selling an "objectionable" book, and stating that it had a duty to recommend obscenity prosecutions to the attorney general, infringed the freedom of speech. *Bantam Books, Inc. v. Sullivan*, 372 U.S. 58 (1963).

7. Government Conditions Discretionary Benefits on Speech

The pervasiveness of government, coupled with governments' desire to reach preferred policy goals, frequently results in government conditioning benefits in exchange for the recipients doing or not doing something. For instance, the federal government conditioned money to states for highway building and maintenance on the states adopting a drinking age of twenty-one. *See, e.g., South Dakota v. Dole*, 483 U.S. 203 (1987) (upholding this condition).

For a long time, the Supreme Court did not police such conditions. During this period, the Court relied on a distinction between privileges and rights: the government could condition benefits on the relinquishment of a privilege, but it could not condition a benefit on the relinquishment of a right. A major practical consequence of this approach was that the government could condition the grant of discretionary benefits for almost any reason. For instance, since employment with the government was a privilege, governmental employment could be conditioned on a number of bases. Justice Holmes famously ruled, in *McAuliffe v. City of New Bedford*, 29 N.E. 517 (Mass. 1892), that a city could fire a police officer because the police officer violated a prohibition on political participation. "The petitioner may have a constitutional right to talk politics, but he has no constitutional right to be a policeman." *Id.* at 517. Gradually, the Supreme Court rejected the rights-privileges distinction.

In its place, the Supreme Court adopted the unconstitutional conditions doctrine.[100] The unconstitutional conditions doctrine states that the government may not condition the grant of a discretionary benefit on the relinquishment of a constitutional right. *Regan v. Taxation with Representation of Wash.*, 461 U.S. 540, 545 (1983); *Perry v. Sindermann*, 408 U.S. 593, 597 (1972). Though easy to state, this doctrine is notoriously challenging because the Supreme Court *has* permitted conditioned grants, and it is difficult to synthesize the Court's case law in this area.[101]

The major reason why the doctrine is knotty is that the Court is attempting to navigate two — to its mind — unpalatable extremes. On the one hand, the Court is reluctant to permit any and all conditions because, given governments' massive resources, they could undermine constitutional rights through pervasive conditioning of grants. On the other hand, the Court is also reluctant to forbid all conditions because they are effective tools of public policy. The unconstitutional conditions doctrine is the Supreme Court's attempted resolution of the tension.

For our purposes, the key point is that, at some point, a condition becomes so coercive that it constitutes an "infringement." This occurs when the condition is a "penalty," and not a "subsidy." Stated differently, the government can condition subsidies, but not impose a penalty on speech. This line, at best, is opaque, and the Supreme Court has struggled to apply it in a principled manner.

The seminal case in the free speech context, *Speiser v. Randall*, 357 U.S. 513 (1958), is reprinted below. Afterward is *Rust v. Sullivan*, 500 U.S. 173 (1991), which reaches a different result.

---

100. Two important articles on the doctrine are Richard A. Epstein, *Unconstitutional Conditions, State Power, and the Limits of Consent*, 102 HARV. L. REV. 4 (1988); Kathleen M. Sullivan, *Unconstitutional Conditions*, 102 HARV. L. REV. 1413 (1989).

101. It is likely that you have, or will encounter the unconstitutional conditions doctrine in many of your other classes as well. For example, in administrative law, you may come across it in the procedural due process context. *E.g.*, *Bailey v. Richardson*, 182 F.2d 46 (D.C. Cir. 1950) (ruling that government employment was not property protected by the Fifth Amendment Due Process Clause).

Speiser v. Randall

357 U.S. 513 (1958)

MR. JUSTICE BRENNAN delivered the opinion of the Court.

The appellants are honorably discharged veterans of World War II who claimed the veterans' property-tax exemption provided by Art. XIII, § 1 1/4, of the California Constitution. Under California law applicants for such exemption must annually complete a standard form of application and file it with the local assessor. The form was revised in 1954 to add an oath by the applicant: "I do not advocate the overthrow of the Government of the United States or of the State of California by force or violence or other unlawful means, nor advocate the support of a foreign Government against the United States in event of hostilities." Each refused to subscribe the oath and struck it from the form which he executed and filed for the tax year 1954–1955. Each contended that the exaction of the oath as a condition of obtaining a tax exemption was forbidden by the Federal Constitution. The respective assessors denied the exemption solely for the refusal to execute the oath. The Supreme Court of California sustained the assessors' actions against the appellants' claims of constitutional invalidity....

It cannot be gainsaid that a discriminatory denial of a tax exemption for engaging in speech is a limitation on free speech. It is settled that speech can be effectively limited by the exercise of the taxing power. To deny an exemption to claimants who engage in certain forms of speech is in effect to penalize them for such speech. Its deterrent effect is the same as if the State were to fine them for this speech. The appellees are plainly mistaken in their argument that, because a tax exemption is a "privilege" or "bounty," its denial may not infringe speech. This contention did not prevail before the California courts, which recognized that conditions imposed upon the granting of privileges or gratuities must be "reasonable." It has been said that Congress may not by withdrawal of mailing privileges place limitations upon the freedom of speech which if directly attempted would be unconstitutional. This Court has similarly rejected the contention that speech was not abridged when the sole restraint on its exercise was withdrawal of the opportunity to invoke the facilities of the National Labor Relations Board, or the opportunity for public employment So here, the denial of a tax exemption for engaging in certain speech necessarily will have the effect of coercing the claimants to refrain from the proscribed speech. The denial is "frankly aimed at the suppression of dangerous ideas."

Reversed and remanded.

MR. JUSTICE BURTON concurs in the result.

THE CHIEF JUSTICE took no part in the consideration or decision of this case.

MR. JUSTICE DOUGLAS, with whom MR. JUSTICE BLACK agrees, concurring. [Opinion omitted.]

MR. JUSTICE CLARK, dissenting. [Opinion omitted.]

Exercise 12:

1. What was the condition imposed by California, and in exchange for what?

2. On a scale of 1 to 10, with 10 being the most onerous, how costly was the condition? Is that enough of a cost to infringe freedom of speech?

3. In your view, was the condition so costly that it precluded veterans from the benefit?

4. Why was the condition a "penalty" and not a subsidy, according to the Court?

Rust v. Sullivan

500 U.S. 173 (1991)

CHIEF JUSTICE REHNQUIST delivered the opinion of the Court.

These cases concern a facial challenge to Department of Health and Human Services (HHS) regulations which limit the ability of Title X fund recipients to engage in abortion-related activities....

IA

In 1970, Congress enacted Title X of the Public Health Service Act (Act), which provides federal funding for family-planning services. The Act authorizes the Secretary to "make grants to and enter into contracts with public or nonprofit private entities to assist in the establishment and operation of voluntary family planning projects which shall offer a broad range of acceptable and effective family planning methods and services." Section 1008 of the Act provides that "[n]one of the funds appropriated under this subchapter shall be used in programs where abortion is a method of family planning." That restriction was intended to ensure that Title X funds would "be used only to support preventive family planning services, population research, infertility services, and other related medical, informational, and educational activities." H.R. Conf. Rep. No. 91-1667, p. 8 (1970).

In 1988, the Secretary promulgated new regulations. The regulations clarify, through the definition of the term "family planning," that Congress intended Title X funds "to be used only to support *preventive* family planning services." The regulations attach three principal conditions on the grant of federal funds for Title X projects. First, the regulations specify that a "Title X project may not provide counseling concerning the use of abortion as a method of family planning or provide referral for abortion as a method of family planning." Title X projects must refer every pregnant client "for appropriate prenatal and/or social services by furnishing a list of available providers that promote the welfare of mother and unborn child." ... Second, the regulations broadly prohibit a Title X project from engaging in activities that "encourage, promote or advocate abortion as a method of family planning." Third, the regulations require that Title X projects be organized so that they are "physically and financially separate" from prohibited abortion activities.

B

Petitioners are Title X grantees and doctors who supervise Title X funds suing on behalf of themselves and their patients. Petitioners challenged the regulations on the grounds that they violate the First Amendment rights of Title X clients and of Title X health providers.... [T]he District Court rejected petitioners' constitutional challenges to the regulations and granted summary judgment in favor of the Secretary. A panel of the Court of Appeals for the Second Circuit affirmed.

III

Petitioners contend that the regulations violate the First Amendment by impermissibly discriminating based on viewpoint because they prohibit "all discussion about abortion as a lawful option — while compelling the clinic or counselor to provide information that promotes continuing a pregnancy to term." They assert that the regulations violate free speech rights by impermissibly imposing "viewpoint-discriminatory conditions on government subsidies" and thus "penalize speech funded with non-Title X monies." Because "Title X continues to fund speech ancillary to pregnancy testing in a manner that is not evenhanded with respect to views and information about abortion, it invidiously discriminates on the basis of viewpoint." ...

There is no question but that the statutory prohibition contained in § 1008 is constitutional. Here the Government is exercising the authority it possesses to subsidize family planning services which will lead to conception and childbirth, and declining to "promote or encourage abortion." The Government can, without violating the Constitution, selectively fund a program to encourage certain activities it believes to be in the public interest, without at the same time funding an alternative program which seeks to deal with the problem in another way. In so doing, the Government has not discriminated on the basis of viewpoint; it has merely chosen to fund one activity to the exclusion of the other. "[A] legislature's decision not to subsidize the exercise of a fundamental right does not infringe the right." *Regan* [*v. Taxation with Representation of Wash.*], 461 U.S. [540], 549 [(1983)]. "A refusal to fund protected activity, without more, cannot be equated with the imposition of a 'penalty' on that activity."

The challenged regulations are designed to ensure that the limits of the federal program are observed. The Title X program is designed not for prenatal care, but to encourage family planning. A doctor who wished to offer prenatal care to a project patient who became pregnant could properly be prohibited from doing so because such service is outside the scope of the federally funded program. The regulations prohibiting abortion counseling and referral are of the same ilk; a doctor employed by the project may be prohibited in the course of his project duties from counseling abortion or referring for abortion. This is not a case of the Government "suppressing a dangerous idea," but of a prohibition on a project grantee or its employees from engaging in activities outside of the project's scope.

To hold that the Government unconstitutionally discriminates on the basis of viewpoint when it chooses to fund a program dedicated to advance certain permissible goals, because the program in advancing those goals necessarily discourages alternative goals, would render numerous Government programs constitutionally suspect. When Congress established a National Endowment for Democracy to encourage other countries to adopt democratic principles, it was not constitutionally required to fund a program to encourage competing lines of political philosophy such as communism and fascism. Petitioners' assertions ultimately boil down to the position that if the government chooses to subsidize one protected right, it must subsidize analogous counterpart rights. But the Court has soundly rejected that proposition. *Regan v. Taxation with Representation of Wash.* Within far broader limits than petitioners are willing to concede, when the Government appropriates public funds to establish a program it is entitled to define the limits of that program.

Petitioners also contend that the restrictions on the subsidization of abortion-related speech contained in the regulations are impermissible because they condition the receipt of a benefit, in these cases Title X funding, on the relinquishment of a constitutional right, the right to engage in abortion advocacy and counseling....

Rationale

Petitioners' [argument] is unavailing, however, because the Government is not denying a benefit to anyone, but is instead simply insisting that public funds be spent for the purposes for which they were authorized. The Secretary's regulations do not force the Title X grantee to give up abortion-related speech; they merely require that the grantee keep such activities separate and distinct from Title X activities. Title X expressly distinguishes between a Title X *grantee* and a Title X *project*. The grantee, which normally is a health-care organization, may receive funds from a variety of sources for a variety of purposes. The grantee receives Title X funds, however, for the specific and limited purpose of establishing and operating a Title X project. The regulations govern the scope of the Title X *project's* activities, and leave the grantee unfettered in its other activities. The Title X *grantee* can continue to perform abortions, provide abortion-related services, and engage in abortion advocacy; it simply is required to conduct those activities through programs that are separate and independent from the project that receives Title X funds.

In contrast, our "unconstitutional conditions" cases involve situations in which the Government has placed a condition on the *recipient* of the subsidy rather than on a particular program or service, thus effectively prohibiting the recipient from engaging in the protected conduct outside the scope of the federally funded program. Similarly, in *Regan* we held that Congress could, in the exercise of its spending power, reasonably refuse to subsidize the lobbying activities of tax-exempt charitable organizations by prohibiting such organizations from using tax-deductible contributions to support their lobbying efforts. In so holding, we explained that such organizations remained free "to receive deductible contributions to support ... nonlobbying activit[ies]." ... Given that alternative, the Court concluded that "Congress has not infringed any First Amendment rights or regulated any First Amendment activity[; it] has simply chosen not to pay for [appellee's] lobbying." The condition that federal funds will be used only to further the purposes of a grant does not violate constitutional rights....

Holding

This is not to suggest that funding by the Government, even when coupled with the freedom of the fund recipients to speak outside the scope of the Government-funded project, is invariably sufficient to justify Government control over the content of expression.

Justice Blackmun, with whom Justice Marshall joins, with whom Justice Stevens joins as to Parts II and III, and with whom Justice O'Connor joins as to Part I, dissenting.

Until today, the Court never has upheld viewpoint-based suppression of speech simply because that suppression was a condition upon the acceptance of public funds. Whatever may be the Government's power to condition the receipt of its largess upon the relinquishment of constitutional rights, it surely does not extend to a condition that suppresses the recipient's cherished freedom of speech based solely upon the content or viewpoint of that speech. *Speiser v. Randall*, 357 U.S. 513, 518–519 (1958) ("To deny an exemption to claimants who engage in certain forms of speech is in effect to penalize them for such speech.... The denial is 'frankly aimed at the suppression of dangerous ideas.'")...."Above all else, the First Amendment means that government has no power to restrict expression because of its message, its ideas, its subject matter, or its content."

It cannot seriously be disputed that the counseling and referral provisions at issue in the present cases constitute content-based regulation of speech. Title X grantees may provide counseling and referral regarding any of a wide range of family planning and other topics, save abortion.

The regulations are also clearly viewpoint based. While suppressing speech favorable to abortion with one hand, the Secretary compels antiabortion speech with the other. For example, the Department of Health and Human Services' own description of the regulations makes plain that "Title X projects are *required* to facilitate access to prenatal care and social services, including adoption services, [...] while making it abundantly clear that the project is not permitted to promote abortion by facilitating access to abortion through the referral process." 53 Fed. Reg. 2927 (1988). Moreover, the regulations command that a project refer for prenatal care each woman diagnosed as pregnant, irrespective of the woman's expressed desire to continue or terminate her pregnancy. If a client asks directly about abortion, a Title X physician or counselor is required to say, in essence, that the project does not consider abortion to be an appropriate method of family planning. Both requirements are antithetical to the First Amendment.

Remarkably, the majority concludes that "the Government has not discriminated on the basis of viewpoint; it has merely chosen to fund one activity to the exclusion of the other." ... By refusing to fund those family-planning projects that advocate abortion *because* they advocate abortion, the Government plainly has targeted a particular viewpoint. The majority's reliance on the fact that the regulations pertain solely to funding decisions simply begs the question. Clearly, there are some bases upon which government may not rest its decision to fund or not to fund. For example, the Members of the majority surely would agree that government may not base its decision to support an activity upon considerations of race. As demonstrated above, our cases make clear that ideological viewpoint is a similarly repugnant ground upon which to base funding decisions.

JUSTICE STEVENS, dissenting. [Opinion omitted.]

JUSTICE O'CONNOR, dissenting. [Opinion omitted.]

Exercise 13:

1. What was the condition imposed by the federal government, and in exchange for what?

2. On a scale of 1 to 10, with 10 being the most onerous, how costly was the condition? Is that enough of a cost to infringe freedom of speech?

3. In your view, was the condition so costly that it precluded Title X program participants from the benefit?

4. Is the condition at issue in *Rust* a penalty or subsidy, according to the Court? Why?

5. Is *Rust* consistent with *Speiser*?

6. Which perspective on governmental conditions is closer to and better advances the First Amendment: *Speiser*'s or *Rust*'s, and why?

7. Assuming, for purposes of this question, that you believe that there should be an unconstitutional conditions doctrine (at least in the free speech context), where would you draw the line? At the same place the Supreme Court has drawn it? Or, somewhere else? Defend your line, and explain how your line avoids the slippery slope identified by the majority.

8. We will see below, in Section [G][5], that later cases have interpreted *Rust* as part of what is called the government speech doctrine. As described below, government speech is when the government expresses its views, and the Free Speech Clause does not limit government speech.

In 2001, the Supreme Court decided *Legal Services Corp. v. Velazquez*, 531 U.S. 533 (2001). There, the federal government provided money to the Legal Services Corporation which, in turn, provided grants to local organizations to provide legal services to indigent clients. Congress imposed the condition that the federal monies to the Corporation would not be used to challenge welfare laws. The Court distinguished *Rust* on multiple axes, and ruled that the condition violated the Free Speech Clause. Citing *Speiser*, the Court summarized its reasoning:

> Congress was not required to fund an LSC attorney to represent indigent clients; and when it did so, it was not required to fund the whole range of legal representations or relationships. The LSC and the United States, however, in effect ask us to permit Congress to define the scope of the litigation it funds to exclude certain vital theories and ideas. The attempted restriction is designed to insulate the Government's interpretation of the Constitution from judicial

challenge. The Constitution does not permit the Government to confine litigants and their attorneys in this manner. We must be vigilant when Congress imposes rules and conditions which in effect insulate its own laws from legitimate judicial challenge. Where private speech is involved, even Congress' antecedent funding decision cannot be aimed at the suppression of ideas thought inimical to the Government's own interest.

Id. at 548–49. Are *Speiser*, *Rust*, and *Velazquez* consistent?

F. Vagueness and Overbreadth

1. Introduction

Vagueness and overbreadth are related doctrines that one may use to challenge infringements of the freedom of speech. They are relatively unattached to other free speech doctrines, so they receive their own treatment here.

A law is vague if a reasonable person would not know what speech a law permits or forbids. A law is overbroad if it regulates substantially more protected speech than is necessary to effectively regulate the unprotected speech. Laws may be both vague and overbroad. Can you think of such a law?

2. Vagueness

Vagueness is the legal doctrine that requires reasonable clarity of free speech restrictions. The doctrine states that, "a statute which either forbids or requires the doing of an act in terms so vague that men of common intelligence must necessarily guess at its meaning and differ as to its application," is impermissibly vague. *Connally v. General Constr. Co.*, 269 U.S. 385, 391 (1926); *see also Grayned v. City of Rockford*, 408 U.S. 104, 108 (1972) (stating that "we insist that laws give the person of ordinary intelligence a reasonable opportunity to know what is prohibited, so that he may act accordingly"). This doctrine ensures that free speech restrictions are sufficiently clear so that the speaker can know, with confidence, what is legal, and therefore speak robustly. Stated differently, the clarity required by vagueness doctrine avoids "chilling" speech. Also, the doctrine also prevents arbitrary governmental limits on speech, by narrowing official discretion, and, relatedly, providing for robust judicial review.

For example, a City of Cincinnati ordinance stated: "It shall be unlawful for three or more persons to assemble … on any of the sidewalks, street corners, vacant lots, or mouths of alleys, and there conduct themselves in a manner annoying to persons passing by…." The Supreme Court ruled that this ordinance was unconstitutionally vague in *Cincinnati v. Coates*, 402 U.S. 611 (1971). "In our opinion this ordinance is unconstitutionally vague because it subjects the exercise of the right of assembly to an unascertainable standard…. Conduct that annoys some people does not annoy others. Thus, the ordinance is vague, not in the sense that it requires a person to conform his conduct to an imprecise but comprehensible normative standard, but rather in the sense that no standard of conduct is specified at all. As a result, 'men of common intelligence must necessarily guess at its meaning.'" *Id.* at 614.

3. Overbreadth

The overbreadth doctrine states that a speech regulation may not regulate substantially more protected speech than necessary to effectively regulate unprotected speech. "The overbreadth doctrine prohibits the Government from banning unprotected speech if a substantial amount of protected speech is prohibited or chilled in the process." *Ashcroft v. Free Speech Coalition*, 535 U.S. 234, 255 (2002). As described by the Court in the important case of *Broadrick v. Oklahoma*, 413 U.S. 601, 615 (1973), "the overbreadth of a statute must not only be real, but substantial as well, judged in relation to the statute's plainly legitimate sweep."

A key facet of the overbreadth doctrine is that it permits one whose own speech is *not* limited by a purportedly unconstitutional speech restriction, to challenge the speech restriction. Because of this, overbreadth is an exception to the usual standing rules you learned in Volume 1, which prohibit third-party standing. *United States v. Raines*, 362 U.S. 17, 21 (1960).

A good example of overbreadth occurred in *Gooding v. Wilson*, 405 U.S. 518 (1972). There, the Supreme Court ruled that the challenged statute, which stated, "[a]ny person who shall, without provocation, use to or of another, and in his presence ... opprobrious words or abusive language, tending to cause a breach of the peace ... shall be guilty of a misdemeanor," was unconstitutionally overbroad because it prohibited more speech than constitutionally proscribable "fighting words." (You will cover Fighting Words in Part [H][3][b], below.) The Court focused on the breadth of the words "opprobrious" and "abusive."

G. Content-Based and Content-Neutral Regulations

1. Introduction

Thus far, you have learned that the Constitution's protection for free speech is triggered when the government regulates communicative activity—either pure speech or expressive conduct—in such a way that it has "infringed" the speaker's speech.

Once you have reached this point, you must next apply *the* key doctrine in modern free speech law: the distinction between content-based and content-neutral regulations of speech. Though this distinction plays a crucial role in the Supreme Court's case law, it is of relatively recent origin. The seminal case is reprinted below:

Police Department of the City of Chicago v. Mosley

408 U.S. 92 (1972)

MR. JUSTICE MARSHALL delivered the opinion of the Court.

At issue in this case is the constitutionality of the following Chicago ordinance:

"A person commits disorderly conduct when he knowingly:

"(i) Pickets or demonstrates on a public way within 150 feet of any primary or secondary school building while the school is in session..., provided, that this subsection does not prohibit the peaceful picketing of any school involved in a labor dispute...." Municipal Code, c. 193-1(i).

The suit was brought by Earl Mosley, a federal postal employee, who for seven months prior to the enactment of the ordinance had frequently picketed Jones Commercial High School in Chicago. During school hours and usually by himself, Mosley would walk the public sidewalk adjoining the school, carrying a sign that read: "Jones High School practices black discrimination. Jones High School has a black quota." His lonely crusade was always peaceful, orderly, and quiet, and was conceded to be so by the city of Chicago.

On March 26, 1968, Chapter 193-1(i) was passed, to become effective on April 5. On April 4, the day before the ordinance became effective, Mosley ended his picketing next to the school. Thereafter, he brought this action in the United States District Court for the Northern District of Illinois. He alleged a violation of constitutional rights in that (1) the statute punished activity protected by the First Amendment; and (2) by exempting only peaceful labor picketing from its general prohibition against picketing, the statute denied him "equal protection of the law in violation of the First and Fourteenth Amendments...."

After a hearing, the District Court granted a directed verdict dismissing the complaint. The Seventh Circuit reversed.... We hold that the ordinance is unconstitutional because it makes an impermissible distinction between labor picketing and other peaceful picketing.

I

The city of Chicago exempts peaceful labor picketing from its general prohibition on picketing next to a school. The question we consider here is whether this selective exclusion from a public place is permitted. Our answer is "No."

Because Chicago treats some picketing differently from others, we analyze this ordinance in terms of the Equal Protection Clause of the Fourteenth Amendment. Of course, the equal protection claim in this case is closely intertwined with First Amendment interests; the Chicago ordinance affects picketing, which is expressive conduct; moreover, it does so by classifications formulated in terms of the subject of the picketing.... [T]he crucial question is whether there is an appropriate governmental interest suitably furthered by the differential treatment.

The central problem with Chicago's ordinance is that it describes permissible picketing in terms of its subject matter. Peaceful picketing on the subject of a school's labor-management dispute is permitted, but all other peaceful picketing is prohibited. The operative distinction is the message on a picket sign. But, above all else, the First Amendment means that government has no power to restrict expression because of its message, its ideas, its subject matter, or its content. *Cohen v. California*, 403 U.S. 15, 24 (1971); *New York Times Co. v. Sullivan*, 376 U.S. 254, 269–270 (1964); *NAACP v. Button*, 371 U.S. 415, 445 (1963). To permit the continued building of our politics and culture, and to assure self-fulfillment for each individual, our people are guaranteed the right to express any thought, free from government censorship. The essence of this forbidden censorship is content control. Any restriction on expressive activity because of its content would completely undercut the "profound national commitment to the principle that debate on public issues should be uninhibited, robust, and wide-open."

Necessarily, then, under the Equal Protection Clause, not to mention the First Amendment itself, government may not grant the use of a forum to people whose views it finds acceptable, but deny use to those wishing to express less favored or more controversial views. And it may not select which issues are worth discussing or debating in public facilities. There is an "equality of status in the field of ideas," and government must afford all points of view an equal opportunity to be heard. Once a forum is opened up to assembly or speaking by some groups, government may not prohibit others from assembling or speaking on the basis of what they intend to say. Selective exclusions from a public forum may not be based on content alone, and may not be justified by reference to content alone.

II

This is not to say that all picketing must always be allowed. We have continually recognized that reasonable "time, place and manner" regulations of picketing may be necessary to further significant governmental interests. [T]here may be sufficient regulatory interests justifying selective exclusions or distinctions among pickets. Conflicting demands on the same place may compel the State to make choices among potential users and uses. And the State may have a legitimate interest in prohibiting some picketing to protect public order. But these justifications for selective exclusions from a public forum must be carefully scrutinized. Because picketing plainly involves expressive conduct within the protection of the First Amendment, discriminations among pickets must be tailored to serve a substantial governmental interest.

III

In this case, the ordinance itself describes impermissible picketing not in terms of time, place, and manner, but in terms of subject matter. The regulation "thus slip[s] from the neutrality of time, place, and circumstance into a concern about content." This is never permitted. In spite of this, Chicago urges that the ordinance is not improper content censorship, but rather a device for preventing disruption of the school....

Although preventing school disruption is a city's legitimate concern, Chicago itself has determined that peaceful labor picketing during school hours is not an undue interference with school. Therefore, under the Equal Protection Clause, Chicago may not maintain that other picketing disrupts the school unless that picketing is clearly more disruptive than the picketing Chicago already permits. Cf. *Tinker v. Des Moines Independent Community School District*, 393 U.S. 503, 511 (1969). If peaceful labor picketing is permitted, there is no justification for prohibiting all nonlabor picketing, both peaceful and nonpeaceful. "Peaceful" nonlabor picketing, however the term "peaceful" is defined, is obviously no more disruptive than "peaceful" labor picketing. But Chicago's ordinance permits the latter and prohibits the former. Such unequal treatment is exactly what [i]s condemned.

Similarly, we reject the city's argument that, although it permits peaceful labor picketing, it may prohibit all nonlabor picketing because, as a class, nonlabor picketing is more prone to produce violence than labor picketing. Predictions about imminent disruption from picketing involve judgments appropriately made on an individualized basis, not by means of broad classifications, especially those based on subject matter. Freedom of expression, and its intersection with the guarantee of equal protection, would rest on a soft foundation indeed if government could distinguish among picketers on such a wholesale and categorical basis. Some labor picketing is peaceful, some disorderly; the same is true of picketing on other themes. No labor picketing could be more peaceful or less prone to violence than Mosley's solitary vigil....

The Equal Protection Clause requires that statutes affecting First Amendment interests be narrowly tailored to their legitimate objectives. Chicago may not vindicate its interest in preventing disruption by the wholesale exclusion of picketing on all but one preferred subject. Given what Chicago tolerates from labor picketing, the excesses of some nonlabor picketing may not be controlled by a broad ordinance prohibiting both peaceful and violent picketing. Such excesses "can be controlled by narrowly drawn statutes," focusing on the abuses and dealing evenhandedly with picketing regardless of subject matter. Chicago's ordinance imposes a selective restriction on expressive conduct far "greater than is essential to the furtherance of [a substantial governmental] interest." *United States v. O'Brien*, 391 U.S. 367, 377 (1968). Far from being tailored to a substantial governmental interest, the discrimination among pickets is based on the content of their expression. Therefore, under the Equal Protection Clause, it may not stand.

The judgment is affirmed.

MR. JUSTICE BLACKMUN and MR. JUSTICE REHNQUIST concur in the result.

MR. CHIEF JUSTICE BURGER, concurring.

I join the Court's opinion but with the reservation that some of the language used in the discussion of the First Amendment could, if read out of context, be misleading. Numerous holdings of this Court attest to the fact that the First Amendment does not literally mean that we "are guaranteed the right to express any thought, free from government censorship." This statement is subject to some qualifications, as for example those of *Roth v. United States*, 354 U.S. 476 (1957); *Chaplinsky v. New Hampshire*, 315 U.S. 568 (1942).

Exercise 14:

1. *Mosley* is a seminal case because the Supreme Court's language expressly and strongly identified the distinction between content-based and content-neutral speech regulations as the "essence" of free speech. From where did the Court draw that distinction?

2. If you were going to argue for a narrow application of the content-based, content-neutral distinction, how would you do so?

3. What purposes does protection of free speech advance, according to Justice Marshall?

4. The content-based, content-neutral distinction dominates free speech case law. Does it fit with the Free Speech Clause's original meaning? The Clause's purposes?

5. Is the distinction a good idea?

6. Though the *Mosley* Court used labels like "content" and "subject matter" to distinguish a category of speech regulations from another category of "neutral" regulations, it did not define those terms. What counts as a "content" regulation or restriction based on "subject matter"?

Though, at first blush, the content-based, content-neutral distinction articulated in *Mosley* may appear to be a relatively easy-to-apply rule, it often has proved to be difficult. In many cases, the Supreme Court has fractured when applying the distinction. Consider, for instance, the law at issue in *Hill v. Colorado*, 530 U.S. 703 (2000), which made it unlawful for any person within 100 feet of any health care facility "to 'knowingly approach' within eight feet of another person, without that person's consent, 'for the purpose of passing a leaflet or handbill to, displaying a sign to, or engaging in oral protest, education, or counseling with such other person.'" Petitioners, who sought to engage in sidewalk counseling within 100 feet of the entrance to abortion facilities and places that referred women to such facilities, claimed that the statute was (1) content-based because "[t]he content of the speech must be examined to determine whether it 'constitutes oral protest, counseling and education'" and (2) viewpoint-based "because the statute 'makes it likely that prosecution will occur based on displeasure with the position taken by the speaker.'"

Drawing on *Ward v. Rock Against Racism*, 491 U.S. 781, 791 (1989), the *Hill* majority stated that "'the principle inquiry in determining content neutrality ... is whether the government has adopted a regulation of speech because of disagreement with the message it conveys.'" The Court concluded that the statute was constitutional because it (1) was "a regulation of the places where some speech may occur," not of speech; (2) "appl[ied] equally to all demonstrators, regardless of viewpoint, and the statutory language makes no reference to the content of the speech;" and (3) furthered "the State's interests in protecting access and privacy, and providing the police with clear guidelines, [which] are unrelated to the content of the demonstrators' speech." In response to the Petitioners' argument that the statute was nevertheless content-based because government officials would have to evaluate the content of the communication to determine whether it was part of an oral protest, education, or counseling, the Court held that the statute "simply establishes a minor place restriction on an extremely broad category of communications with unwilling listeners. Instead of drawing distinctions based on the subject that the approaching speaker may wish to address, the statute applies equally to used car salesmen, animal rights activists, fundraisers, environmentalists, and missionaries. Each can attempt to educate unwilling listeners on any subject, but without consent may not approach within eight feet to do so."

In his dissent, Justice Scalia argued that the statute was "obviously and undeniably" content-based: "A speaker wishing to approach another for the purpose of communicating *any* message except one of protest, education, or counseling may do so without first securing the other's consent. Whether a speaker must obtain permission before approaching within eight feet—and whether he will be sent to prison for failing to do so—depends entirely on *what he intends to say* when he gets there." Given that the purpose of the statute was "to protect '[t]he unwilling listener's interest in avoiding unwanted communication,'" it precluded speech based on its communicative impact—the effect of certain speech on its hearer—which for Scalia is a content-based distinction: "This singling out of presumptively 'unwelcome' communications fits precisely the description of prohibited regulation [because it] 'targets the *direct impact* of a particular category of speech, not a secondary feature that happens to be associated with that type of speech.'"

As you read the following case, consider whether and how the majority's analysis differs from the Court's reasoning in *Hill*.

McCullen v. Coakley

573 U.S. 464 (2014)

CHIEF JUSTICE ROBERTS delivered the opinion of the Court.

[The Massachusetts Reproductive Health Care Facilities Act (the "Act")] makes it a crime to knowingly stand on a "public way or sidewalk" within 35 feet of an entrance or driveway to any place, other than a hospital, where abortions are performed. Petitioners are individuals who approach and talk to women outside such facilities, attempting to dissuade them from having abortions. The statute prevents petitioners from doing so near the facilities' entrances. The Act exempts (1) "persons entering or leaving such facility"; (2) "employees or agents of such facility acting within the scope of their employment"; (3) "law enforcement, ambulance, firefighting, ... and other municipal agents acting within the scope of their employment"; and (4) "persons using the public sidewalk or street right-of-way adjacent to such facility solely for the purpose of reaching a destination other than such facility."

I

B

Some of the individuals who stand outside Massachusetts abortion clinics are fairly described as protestors, who express their moral or religious opposition to abortion through signs and chants or, in some cases, more aggressive methods such as face-to-face confrontation. Petitioners take a different tack. They attempt to engage women approaching the clinics in what they call "sidewalk counseling," which involves offering information about alternatives to abortion and help pursuing those options. Petitioner Eleanor McCullen, for instance, will typically initiate a conversation this way: "Good morning, may I give you my literature? Is there anything I can do for you? I'm available if you have any questions." If the woman seems receptive, McCullen will provide additional information. McCullen and the other petitioners consider it essential to maintain a caring demeanor, a calm tone of voice, and direct eye contact during these exchanges. Such interactions, petitioners believe, are a much more effective means of dissuading women from having abortions than confrontational methods such as shouting or brandishing signs, which in petitioners' view tend only to antagonize their intended audience. In unrefuted testimony, petitioners say they have collectively persuaded hundreds of women to forgo abortions.

The buffer zones have displaced petitioners from their previous positions outside the clinics. Before the Act was amended to create the buffer zones, petitioners stood near the entryway to the foyer. Now a buffer zone—marked by a painted arc and a sign—surrounds the entrance. This zone extends 23 feet down the sidewalk in one direction, 26 feet in the other, and outward just one foot short of the curb. The upshot is that petitioners are effectively excluded from a 56-foot-wide expanse of the public sidewalk in front of the clinic.

Petitioners at all three clinics claim that the buffer zones have considerably hampered their counseling efforts. Although they have managed to conduct some counseling and to distribute some literature outside the buffer zones—particularly at the Boston clinic—they say they have had many fewer conversations and distributed many fewer leaflets since the zones went into effect.

The second statutory exemption allows clinic employees and agents acting within the scope of their employment to enter the buffer zones. Relying on this exemption, the Boston clinic uses "escorts" to greet women as they approach the clinic, accompanying them through the zones to the clinic entrance. Petitioners claim that the escorts sometimes thwart petitioners' attempts to communicate with patients by blocking petitioners from handing literature to patients, telling patients not to "pay any attention" or "listen to" petitioners, and disparaging petitioners as "crazy."

II

By its very terms, the Massachusetts Act regulates access to "public way[s]" and "sidewalk[s]." These places—which we have labeled "traditional public fora"—"'have immemorially been held in trust for the use of the public and, time out of mind, have been used for purposes of assembly, communicating thoughts between citizens, and discussing public questions.'"

It is no accident that public streets and sidewalks have developed as venues for the exchange of ideas. Even today, they remain one of the few places where a speaker can be confident that he is not simply preaching to the choir. With respect to other means of communication, an individual confronted with an uncomfortable message can always turn the page, change the channel, or leave the Web site. Not so on public streets and sidewalks. There, a listener often encounters speech he might otherwise tune out. In light of the First Amendment's purpose "to preserve an uninhibited marketplace of ideas in which truth will ultimately prevail," this aspect of traditional public fora is a virtue, not a vice.

Thus, even though the Act says nothing about speech on its face, there is no doubt—and respondents do not dispute—that it restricts access to traditional public fora and is therefore subject to First Amendment scrutiny. In particular, the guiding First Amendment principle that the "government has no power to restrict expression because of its message, its ideas, its subject matter, or its content" applies with full force in a traditional public forum. As a general rule, in such a forum the government may not "selectively ... shield the public from some kinds of speech on the ground that they are more offensive than others."

We have, however, afforded the government somewhat wider leeway to regulate features of speech unrelated to its content. "[E]ven in a public forum the government may impose reasonable restrictions on the time, place, or manner of protected speech, provided the restrictions 'are justified without reference to the content of the regulated speech, that they are narrowly tailored to serve a significant governmental interest, and that they leave open ample alternative channels for communication of the information.'"

III

Petitioners contend that the Act is not content neutral for two independent reasons: First, they argue that it discriminates against abortion-related speech because it establishes buffer zones only at clinics that perform abortions. Second, petitioners contend that the Act, by exempting clinic employees and agents, favors one viewpoint about abortion over the other. If either of these arguments is correct, then the Act must satisfy strict scrutiny—that is, it must be the least restrictive means of achieving a compelling state interest.

A

The Act applies only at a "reproductive health care facility," defined as "a place, other than within or upon the grounds of a hospital, where abortions are offered or performed." Given this definition, petitioners argue, "virtually all speech affected by the Act is speech concerning abortion," thus rendering the Act content based.

We disagree. To begin, the Act does not draw content-based distinctions on its face. The Act would be content based if it required "enforcement authorities" to "examine the content of the message that is conveyed to determine whether" a violation has occurred. But it does not. Whether petitioners violate the Act "depends" not "on what they say," but simply on where they say it. Indeed, petitioners can violate the Act merely by standing in a buffer zone, without displaying a sign or uttering a word.

It is true, of course, that by limiting the buffer zones to abortion clinics, the Act has the "inevitable effect" of restricting abortion-related speech more than speech on other subjects. But a facially neutral law does not become content based simply because it may disproportionately affect speech on certain topics. On the contrary, "[a] regulation that serves purposes unrelated to the content of expression is deemed neutral, even if it has an incidental effect on some speakers or messages but not others." The question in such a case is whether the law is "'justified without reference to the content of the regulated speech.'"

The Massachusetts Act is. Its stated purpose is to "increase forthwith public safety at reproductive health care facilities." Respondents have articulated similar purposes before this Court—namely, "public safety, patient access to healthcare, and the unobstructed use of public sidewalks and roadways." It is not the case that "[e]very objective indication shows that the provision's primary purpose is to restrict speech that opposes abortion."

We have previously deemed the foregoing concerns to be content neutral. Obstructed access and congested sidewalks are problems no matter what caused them. A group of individuals can obstruct clinic access and clog sidewalks just as much when they loiter as when they protest abortion or counsel patients.

To be clear, the Act would not be content neutral if it were concerned with undesirable effects that arise from "the direct impact of speech on its audience" or "[l]isteners' reactions to speech." If, for example, the speech outside Massachusetts abortion clinics caused offense or made listeners uncomfortable, such offense or discomfort would not give the Commonwealth a content-neutral justification to restrict the speech. All of the problems identified by the Commonwealth here, however, arise irrespective of any listener's reactions. Whether or not a single person reacts to abortion protestors' chants or petitioners' counseling, large crowds outside abortion clinics can still compromise public safety, impede access, and obstruct sidewalks.

Petitioners do not really dispute that the Commonwealth's interests in ensuring safety and preventing obstruction are, as a general matter, content neutral. But petitioners note that these interests "apply outside every building in the State that hosts any activity that might occasion protest or comment," not just abortion clinics. By choosing to pursue these interests only at abortion clinics, petitioners argue, the Massachusetts Legislature evinced a purpose to "single[] out for regulation speech about one particular topic: abortion."

We cannot infer such a purpose from the Act's limited scope. The Massachusetts Legislature amended the Act in 2007 in response to a problem that was, in its experience, limited to abortion clinics. There was a record of crowding, obstruction, and even violence outside such clinics. There were apparently no similar recurring problems associated with other kinds of healthcare facilities, let alone with "every building in the State that hosts any activity that might occasion protest or comment." In light of the limited nature of the problem, it was reasonable for the Massachusetts Legislature to enact a limited solution. When selecting among various options for combating a particular problem, legislatures should be encouraged to choose the one that restricts less speech, not more.

Justice Scalia objects that the statute does restrict more speech than necessary, because "only one [Massachusetts abortion clinic] is known to have been beset by the problems that the statute supposedly addresses." But there are no grounds for inferring content-based discrimination here simply because the legislature acted with respect to abortion facilities generally rather than proceeding on a facility-by-facility basis. On these facts, the poor fit noted by Justice Scalia goes to the question of narrow tailoring, which we consider below.

B

Petitioners also argue that the Act is content based because it exempts four classes of individuals, one of which comprises "employees or agents of [a reproductive healthcare] facility acting within the scope of their employment." This exemption, petitioners say, favors one side in the abortion debate and thus constitutes viewpoint discrimination—an "egregious form of content discrimination."

There is nothing inherently suspect about providing some kind of exemption to allow individuals who work at the clinics to enter or remain within the buffer zones. In particular, the exemption cannot be regarded as simply a carve-out for the clinic escorts; it also covers employees such as the maintenance worker shoveling a snowy sidewalk or the security guard patrolling a clinic entrance.

Given the need for an exemption for clinic employees, the "scope of their employment" qualification simply ensures that the exemption is limited to its purpose of allowing the employees to do their jobs. It performs the same function as the identical "scope of their employment" restriction on the exemption for "law enforcement, ambulance, fire-fighting, construction, utilities, public works and other municipal agents." The limitation instead makes clear—with respect to both clinic employees and municipal agents—that exempted individuals are allowed inside the zones only to perform those acts authorized by their employers. There is no suggestion in the record that any of the clinics authorize their employees to speak about abortion in the buffer zones.

It would be a very different question if it turned out that a clinic authorized escorts to speak about abortion inside the buffer zones. In that case, the escorts would not seem to be violating the Act because the speech would be within the scope of their employment. The Act's exemption for clinic employees would then facilitate speech on only one side of the abortion debate—a clear form of viewpoint discrimination that would support an as-applied challenge to the buffer zone at that clinic.

We thus conclude that the Act is neither content nor viewpoint based and therefore need not be analyzed under strict scrutiny.

IV

Even though the Act is content neutral, it still must be "narrowly tailored to serve a significant governmental interest." [B]y demanding a close fit between ends and means, the tailoring requirement prevents the government from too readily "sacrific[ing] speech for efficiency."

For a content-neutral time, place, or manner regulation to be narrowly tailored, it must not "burden substantially more speech than is necessary to further the government's legitimate interests." Such a regulation, unlike a content-based restriction of speech, "need not be the least restrictive or least intrusive means of" serving the government's interests. But the government still "may not regulate expression in such a manner that a substantial portion of the burden on speech does not serve to advance its goals."

A

We have previously recognized the legitimacy of the government's interests in "ensuring public safety and order, promoting the free flow of traffic on streets and sidewalks, protecting property rights, and protecting a woman's freedom to seek pregnancy-related services." The buffer zones clearly serve these interests.

At the same time, the buffer zones impose serious burdens on petitioners' speech. At each of the clinics where petitioners attempt to counsel patients, the zones carve out a significant portion of the adjacent public sidewalks, pushing petitioners well back from the clinics' entrances and driveways. The zones thereby compromise petitioners' ability to initiate the close, personal conversations that they view as essential to "sidewalk counseling."

For example, in uncontradicted testimony, McCullen explained that she often cannot distinguish patients from passersby outside the Boston clinic in time to initiate a conversation before they enter the buffer zone. And even when she does manage to begin a discussion outside the zone, she must stop abruptly at its painted border, which she believes causes her to appear "untrustworthy" or "suspicious." Given these limitations, McCullen is often reduced to raising her voice at patients from outside the zone—a mode of communication sharply at odds with the compassionate message she wishes to convey.

Although McCullen claims that she has persuaded about 80 women not to terminate their pregnancies since the 2007 amendment, she also says that she reaches "far fewer people" than she did before the amendment. The buffer zones have also made it substantially more difficult for petitioners to distribute literature to arriving patients. As explained, because petitioners in Boston cannot readily identify patients before they enter the zone, they often cannot approach them in time to place literature near their hands—the most effective means of getting the patients to accept it. In short, the Act operates to deprive petitioners of their two primary methods of communicating with patients....

[W]hile the First Amendment does not guarantee a speaker the right to any particular form of expression, some forms—such as normal conversation and leafletting on a public sidewalk—have historically been more closely associated with the transmission of ideas than others. When the government makes it more difficult to engage in these modes of communication, it imposes an especially significant First Amendment burden.

It is thus no answer to say that petitioners can still be "seen and heard" by women within the buffer zones. If all that the women can see and hear are vociferous opponents of abortion, then the buffer zones have effectively stifled petitioners' message.

B

1

The buffer zones burden substantially more speech than necessary to achieve the Commonwealth's asserted interests. [T]he Act is truly exceptional: Respondents and their *amici* identify no other State with a law that creates fixed buffer zones around abortion clinics. That of course does not mean that the law is invalid. It does, however, raise concern that the Commonwealth has too readily forgone options that could serve its interests just as well, without substantially burdening the kind of speech in which petitioners wish to engage.

That is the case here. The Commonwealth's interests include ensuring public safety outside abortion clinics, preventing harassment and intimidation of patients and clinic staff, and combating deliberate obstruction of clinic entrances. The Act itself contains a separate provision that prohibits much of this conduct. If Massachusetts determines that broader prohibitions along the same lines are necessary, it could enact legislation similar to the federal Freedom of Access to Clinic Entrances Act of 1994, which subjects to both criminal and civil penalties anyone who "by force or threat of force or by physical obstruction, intentionally injures, intimidates or interferes with ... any person ... in order to intimidate such person ... from, obtaining or providing reproductive health services." These measures are, of course, in addition to available generic criminal statutes forbidding assault, breach of the peace, trespass, vandalism, and the like.

We have previously noted the First Amendment virtues of targeted injunctions as alternatives to broad, prophylactic measures. Such an injunction "regulates the activities, and perhaps the speech, of a group," but only "because of the group's past *actions* in the context of a specific dispute between real parties." Moreover, given the equitable nature of injunctive relief, courts can tailor a remedy to ensure that it restricts no more speech than necessary focus[ing] on the precise individuals and the precise conduct causing a particular problem. The Act, by contrast, categorically excludes non-exempt individuals from the buffer zones, unnecessarily sweeping in innocent individuals and their speech.

According to respondents, even when individuals do not deliberately obstruct access to clinics, they can inadvertently do so simply by gathering in large numbers. But the Commonwealth could address that [congestion] problem through more targeted means. Some localities, for example, have ordinances that require crowds blocking a clinic entrance to disperse when ordered to do so by the police, and that forbid the individuals to reassemble within a certain distance of the clinic for a certain period.

[Furthermore, t]he portions of the record that respondents cite to support the anticongestion interest pertain mainly to one place at one time: the Boston Planned Parenthood clinic on Saturday mornings. Respondents point us to no evidence that individuals regularly gather at other clinics, or at other times in Boston, in sufficiently large groups to obstruct access. For a problem shown to arise only once a week in one city at one clinic, creating 35-foot buffer zones at every clinic across the Commonwealth is hardly a narrowly tailored solution.

2

Respondents have but one reply: "We have tried other approaches, but they do not work." Respondents emphasize the history in Massachusetts of obstruction at abortion clinics, and the Commonwealth's allegedly failed attempts to combat such obstruction with injunctions and individual prosecutions.

We cannot accept that contention. Although respondents claim that Massachusetts "tried other laws already on the books," they identify not a single prosecution brought under those laws within at least the last 17 years. And while they also claim that the Commonwealth "tried injunctions," the last injunctions they cite date to the 1990s. In short, the Commonwealth has not shown that it seriously undertook to address the problem with less intrusive tools readily available to it. Nor has it shown that it considered different methods that other jurisdictions have found effective.

Respondents contend that given the "widespread" nature of the problem, it is simply not "practicable" to rely on individual prosecutions and injunctions. But far from being "widespread," the problem appears from the record to be limited principally to the Boston clinic on Saturday mornings. Moreover, by their own account, the police appear perfectly capable of singling out lawbreakers. The legislative testimony preceding the 2007 Act revealed substantial police and video monitoring at the clinics, especially when large gatherings were anticipated.... Attorney General Coakley relied on video surveillance to show legislators conduct she thought was "clearly against the law." If Commonwealth officials can compile an extensive record of obstruction and harassment to support their preferred legislation, we do not see why they cannot do the same to support injunctions and prosecutions against those who might deliberately flout the law.

[Respondents also argue that some of] the alternatives we have identified ... require a showing of intentional or deliberate obstruction, intimidation, or harassment, which is often difficult to prove. As Captain Evans predicted in his legislative testimony, fixed buffer zones would "make our job so much easier."

Of course they would. But that is not enough to satisfy the First Amendment. To meet the requirement of narrow tailoring, the government must demonstrate that alternative measures that burden substantially less speech would fail to achieve the government's interests, not simply that the chosen route is easier. A painted line on the sidewalk is easy to enforce, but the prime objective of the First Amendment is not efficiency. In any case, we do not think that showing intentional obstruction is nearly so difficult in this context as respondents suggest. To determine whether a protestor intends to block access to a clinic, a police officer need only order him to move. If he refuses, then there is no question that his continued conduct is knowing or intentional.

For similar reasons, respondents' reliance on our decision in *Burson v. Freeman*[, 504 U.S. 191 (1992),] is misplaced. There, we upheld a state statute that established 100-foot buffer zones outside polling places on election day within which no one could display or distribute campaign materials or solicit votes. We approved the buffer zones as a valid prophylactic measure, noting that existing "[i]ntimidation and interference laws fall short of serving a State's compelling interests because they 'deal with only the most blatant and specific attempts' to impede elections." Such laws were insufficient because "[v]oter intimidation and election fraud are ... difficult to detect." Obstruction of abortion clinics and harassment of patients, by contrast, are anything but subtle.

We also noted in *Burson* that under state law, "law enforcement officers generally are barred from the vicinity of the polls to avoid any appearance of coercion in the electoral process," with the result that "many acts of interference would go undetected." Not so here. Again, the police maintain a significant presence outside Massachusetts abortion clinics. The buffer zones in *Burson* were justified because less restrictive measures were inadequate. Respondents have not shown that to be the case here.

Justice Scalia, with whom Justice Kennedy and Justice Thomas join, concurring in the judgment.

[Justice Scalia argued that the Court's discussion of content-neutrality was unnecessary before explaining his reasons for taking the Act to be content-based.]

II. The Statue is Content Based and Fails Strict Scrutiny

A. Application to Abortion Clinics Only

"[T]he public spaces outside of [abortion-providing] facilities ha[ve] become, by necessity and by virtue of this Court's decisions, a forum of last resort for those who oppose abortion." It blinks reality to say, as the majority does, that a blanket prohibition on the use of streets and sidewalks where speech on only one politically controversial topic is likely to occur—and where that speech can most effectively be communicated—is not content based. Would the Court exempt from strict scrutiny a law banning access to the streets and sidewalks surrounding the site of the Republican National Convention? Or those used annually to commemorate the 1965 Selma-to-Montgomery civil rights marches? Or those outside the Internal Revenue Service? Surely not.

The majority says, correctly enough, that a facially neutral speech restriction escapes strict scrutiny, even when it "may disproportionately affect speech on certain topics," so long as it is "justified without reference to the content of the regulated speech." ...

The majority points only to the statute's stated purpose of increasing "'public safety'" at abortion clinics and to the additional aims articulated by respondents before this Court—namely, protecting "'patient access to healthcare ... and the unobstructed use of public sidewalks and roadways.'" Really? Does a statute become "justified without reference to the content of the regulated speech" simply because the statute itself and those defending it in court *say* that it is? Every objective indication shows that the provision's primary purpose is to restrict speech that opposes abortion.

[T]he majority [might have] defend[ed] the statute's peculiar targeting by arguing that those locations regularly face the safety and access problems that it says the Act was designed to solve. But the majority does not make that argument because it would be untrue. [A]lthough the statute applies to all abortion clinics in Massachusetts, only one is known to have been beset by the problems that the statute supposedly addresses.

Whether the statute "restrict[s] more speech than necessary" in light of the problems that it allegedly addresses, it is also relevant—powerfully relevant—to whether the law is really directed to safety and access concerns or rather to the suppression of a particular type of speech. Showing that a law that suppresses speech on a specific subject is so far-reaching that it applies even when the asserted non-speech-related problems are not present is persuasive evidence that the law is content based.

The structure of the Act also indicates that it rests on content-based concerns. The goals of "public safety, patient access to healthcare, and the unobstructed use of public sidewalks and roadways," are already achieved by an earlier-enacted subsection of the statute, which provides criminal penalties for "[a]ny person who knowingly obstructs, detains, hinders, impedes or blocks another person's entry to or exit from a repro-ductive health care facility." As the majority recognizes, that provision is easy to enforce. Thus, the speech-free zones carved out by subsection (b) add nothing to safety and access; what they achieve, and what they were obviously designed to achieve, is the suppression of speech opposing abortion.

Further contradicting the Court's fanciful defense of the Act is the fact that sub-section (b) was enacted as a more easily enforceable substitute for a prior provision. As the majority acknowledges, that [prior] provision was "modeled on a ... Colorado law that this Court had upheld in *Hill*." And in that case, the Court recognized that the statute in question was directed at the suppression of unwelcome speech, vindi-cating what *Hill* called "[t]he unwilling listener's interest in avoiding unwanted com-munication." The Court held that interest to be content neutral.

The provision at issue here was indisputably meant to serve the same interest in protecting citizens' supposed right to avoid speech that they would rather not hear. In concluding that the statute is content based and therefore subject to strict scrutiny, I necessarily conclude that *Hill* should be overruled. *Hill* stands in contradiction to our First Amendment jurisprudence. Protecting People from speech they do not want to hear is not a function that the First Amendment allows the government to undertake in the public streets and sidewalks.

One final thought regarding *Hill* : It can be argued, and it should be argued in the next case, that by stating that "the Act would not be content neutral if it were concerned with undesirable effects that arise from '[l]isteners' reactions to speech'" and then holding the Act unconstitutional for being insufficiently tailored to safety and access concerns, the Court itself has *sub silentio* (and perhaps inadvertently) overruled *Hill*. The unavoidable implication of that holding is that protection against unwelcome speech cannot justify restrictions on the use of public streets and sidewalks.

B. Exemption for Abortion-Clinic Employees or Agents

[T]he Act exempts "employees or agents" of an abortion clinic "acting within the scope of their employment."

It goes without saying that "[g]ranting waivers to favored speakers (or denying them to disfavored speakers) would of course be unconstitutional." Is there any serious doubt that *abortion-clinic employees or agents* "acting within the scope of their employment" near clinic entrances may—indeed, often will—speak in favor of abortion ("You are doing the right thing")? Or speak in opposition to the message of abortion opponents—saying, for example, that "this is a safe facility" to rebut the statement that it is not? The Court's contrary assumption is simply incredible. And the majority makes no attempt to establish the further necessary proposition that abortion-clinic employees and agents do not engage in nonspeech activities directed to the suppression of antiabortion speech by hampering the efforts of counselors to speak to prospective clients. Are we to believe that a clinic employee sent out to "escort" prospective clients into the building would not seek to prevent a counselor like Eleanor McCullen from communicating with them? He could pull a woman away from an approaching counselor, cover her ears, or make loud noises to drown out the counselor's pleas.

The Court takes the peculiar view that, so long as the clinics have not specifically authorized their employees to speak in favor of abortion (or, presumably, to impede antiabortion speech), there is no viewpoint discrimination. But it is axiomatic that "where words are employed in a statute which had at the time a well-known meaning at common law or in the law of this country[,] they are presumed to have been used in that sense unless the context compels to the contrary." The phrase "scope of employment" is a well-known common-law concept that includes "[t]he range of reasonable and foreseeable activities that an employee engages in while carrying out the employer's business." The employer need not specifically direct or sanction each aspect of an employee's conduct for it to qualify. [I]t is implausible that clinics would bar escorts from engaging in the sort of activity mentioned above. Moreover, a statute that forbids one side but not the other to convey its message does not become viewpoint neutral simply because the favored side chooses voluntarily to abstain from activity that the statute permits.

There is not a shadow of a doubt that the assigned or foreseeable conduct of a clinic employee or agent can include both speaking in favor of abortion rights and countering the speech of people like petitioners. Indeed, as the majority acknowledges, the trial record includes testimony that escorts at the Boston clinic "expressed views about abortion to the women they were accompanying, thwarted petitioners' attempts to speak and hand literature to the women, and disparaged petitioners in various ways," including by calling them "'crazy.'" … The dangers that the Web site [for the Planned Parenthood League of Massachusetts (which operates the three abortion facilities where petitioners attempt to counsel women)] attributes to "protestors" are related entirely to speech, not to safety or access. "Protestors," it reports, "hold signs, try to speak to patients entering the building, and distribute literature that can be misleading." The "safe space" provided by escorts is protection from that speech.

JUSTICE ALITO, concurring in the judgment.

A clinic may direct or authorize an employee or agent, while within the zone, to express favorable views about abortion or the clinic, and if the employee exercises that authority, the employee's conduct is perfectly lawful. In short, petitioners and other critics of a clinic are silenced, while the clinic may authorize its employees to express speech in support of the clinic and its work.

Consider this entirely realistic situation. A woman enters a buffer zone and heads haltingly toward the entrance. A sidewalk counselor, such as petitioners, enters the buffer zone, approaches the woman and says, "If you have doubts about an abortion, let me try to answer any questions you may have. The clinic will not give you good information." At the same time, a clinic employee, as instructed by the management, approaches the same woman and says, "Come inside and we will give you honest answers to all your questions." The sidewalk counselor and the clinic employee expressed opposing viewpoints, but only the first violated the statute.

Or suppose that the issue is not abortion but the safety of a particular facility. Suppose that there was a recent report of a botched abortion at the clinic. A non-employee may not enter the buffer zone to warn about the clinic's health record, but an employee may enter and tell prospective clients that the clinic is safe.

It is clear on the face of the Massachusetts law that it discriminates based on viewpoint. Speech in favor of the clinic and its work by employees and agents is permitted; speech criticizing the clinic and its work is a crime. This is blatant viewpoint discrimination.

Exercise 15:

1. Why does the Court conclude that the statute in *McCullen* is content neutral? Is the *McCullen* majority adopting the same analysis as the majority in *Hill* with respect to content-neutrality? Are both statutes subject-matter and viewpoint neutral? On their face, are the statutes content neutral? Were they adopted for a content-neutral purpose?

2. Would the statute in *Hill* survive the scrutiny analysis that the *McCullen* majority applied to Massachusetts's content-neutral statute? Stated differently, is the Colorado statute in *Hill* "narrowly tailored to serve a significant governmental interest" under *McCullen*?

3. Does *McCullen* override *Hill sub silencio*? Are the two opinions consistent?

4. If a statute is content-based or neutral on its face, and it has the opposite purpose — e.g., facially content neutral but with a content-based purpose — how should the Court treat that statute? Was that the situation in *McCullen*? In *Hill*? Is this what makes one or both cases difficult?

5. Why does Justice Scalia believe that *Hill* is inconsistent with the Court's First Amendment speech jurisprudence? Is he correct?

6. Justice Scalia's dissent in *Hill* colorfully charged the majority with utilizing the "'ad hoc nullification machine' that the Court has set in motion to push aside whatever doctrines of constitutional law stand in the way of th[e] highly favored practice [of abortion]." In *McCullen*, he made a similar charge: "Today's opinion carries forward this Court's practice of giving abortion-rights advocates a pass when it comes to suppressing the free-speech rights of their opponents. There is an entirely separate,

abridged edition of the First Amendment applicable to speech against abortion." Is Justice Scalia correct? What evidence can you muster to support and/or to contradict Justice Scalia's claim?

7. Could you draft a statute that is clearly content-neutral, and which would acheive Colorado's and Massachusetts' ostensible goals of safe access to medical facilities? If so, does that suggest that Colorado and Massachusetts really wished to suppress pro-life speech?

2. The Distinction Further Explained: Subject Matter and Viewpoint Discrimination

The distinction between content-based regulations of speech, and those that are content neutral, has one further wrinkle: a regulation is content based if it is *either*: (1) subject-matter based, or (2) viewpoint based. A speech regulation is subject-matter based if it restricts subjects of speech. Similarly, a regulation is viewpoint based if it restricts speech because of the speaker's viewpoint.[102]

These two types of content-based speech regulation are related in a way best exemplified by a hypothetical licensing system for public use of a public park for expressive purposes. If the licensing system authorized public rally permits for all subjects—for example, the war on terror, global warming, the size of government—except for abortion, then the licensing system would be content based because it proscribed the subject of abortion. If, however, the licensing system issued permits for all subjects including, now, abortion, but denied permits for pro-life protestors, then the licensing system would be a viewpoint-based regulation of speech. It permitted the pro-choice viewpoint on the subject of abortion, but proscribed the pro-life viewpoint.

As with the distinction between content-based and content-neutral restrictions, the Supreme Court sometimes struggles to apply the distinction between subject matter and viewpoint. For instance, in *Boos v. Barry*, 485 U.S. 312 (1988), the Court ruled that a statute, which prohibited "the display of any sign within 500 feet of a foreign embassy if that sign tends to bring that foreign government into 'public odium' or 'public disrepute,'" was subject-matter based. While, in *Rosenberger v. Rector and Visitors of the University of Virginia*, 515 U.S. 819 (1995), the Court found that a school funding prohibition for student groups that "'primarily promote[] or manifest[] a particular belie[f] in or about a deity or an ultimate reality,'" was viewpoint based.

In run-of-the-mill cases, the distinction between subject matter and viewpoint is not determinative, because the existence of either one will make a regulation content based. However, the distinction does play a crucial role in the government subsidy context. There, the Supreme Court has developed the rule that the government may make subject-matter distinctions between what it will and will not fund, but it may

---

102. There are also some cases, including *Citizens United*, covered above, in which the Supreme Court has stated that speaker identity is also a basis upon which to conclude a regulation is content based.

not make viewpoint distinctions. For example, in *National Endowment for the Arts v. Finley*, 524 U.S. 569 (1998), the Court upheld a funding requirement—"taking into consideration general standards of decency and respect for the diverse beliefs and values of the American public"—because it was not viewpoint based. The Court summarized its conclusion:

> [T]he "decency and respect" criteria do not silence speakers by expressly "threaten[ing] censorship of ideas." Thus, we do not perceive a realistic danger that § 954(d)(1) will compromise First Amendment values. As respondents' own arguments demonstrate, the considerations that the provision introduces, by their nature, do not engender the kind of directed viewpoint discrimination that would prompt this Court to invalidate a statute on its face. Respondents assert, for example, that "[o]ne would be hard-pressed to find two people in the United States who could agree on what the 'diverse beliefs and values of the American public' are, much less on whether a particular work of art 'respects' them"; and they claim that "'[d]ecency' is likely to mean something very different to a septegenarian in Tuscaloosa and a teenager in Las Vegas." The NEA likewise views the considerations enumerated in § 954(d)(1) as susceptible to multiple interpretations.... Accordingly, the provision does not introduce considerations that, in practice, would effectively preclude or punish the expression of particular views. Indeed, one could hardly anticipate how "decency" or "respect" would bear on grant applications in categories such as funding for symphony orchestras.

Id. at 583.

3. How to Determine If a Regulation Is Content Based or Content Neutral

a. Facially Content Based and Facially Content Neutral

If a government regulation of speech is facially content based, it is generally treated as content based. A regulation is facially content based if its terms identify speech for positive or negative treatment based on the speech's content. For example, a city ordinance that states, "No war-related protests are permitted in Central Park," is facially content based, because a subject of speech—"war-related"—is proscribed. Likewise, a regulation is facially content based if its terms identify speech based on the speech's viewpoint.

If a government regulation is facially content neutral, it will typically be treated as content neutral, although as the case below indicates there are two possible exceptions to this general rule. A regulation is facially content neutral when the regulation's terms do not identify regulated speech based on the speech's content. For instance, a city ordinance that states, "No protests, rallies, or demonstrations, between the hours of 10 p.m. and 8 a.m. in Central Park," is facially content neutral, because all speech, regardless of subject matter or viewpoint, is regulated; no matter what your view of gun rights—pro-gun control or pro-gun freedom—you cannot hold a protest at 11 p.m. But what about a sign ordinance that distinguishes between and among various types of signs (ideological, political, and temporary directional signs that indicate the way to particular types of events)? Is such an ordinance content-neutral or content-based? The Court addressed this specific issue in the following case.

Reed v. Town of Gilbert
576 U.S. 155 (2015)

Justice Thomas delivered the opinion of the Court.

The [Gilbert, Arizona] Sign Code identifies various categories of signs based on the type of information they convey, then subjects each category to different restrictions. One of the categories is "Temporary Directional Signs Relating to a Qualifying Event," loosely defined as signs directing the public to a meeting of a nonprofit group. The Code imposes more stringent restrictions on these signs than it does on signs conveying other messages. We hold that these provisions are content-based regulations of speech that cannot survive strict scrutiny.

I

A

The Sign Code prohibits the display of outdoor signs anywhere within the Town without a permit, but it then exempts 23 categories of signs from that requirement. Three categories of exempt signs are particularly relevant here.

The first is "Ideological Sign[s]." This category includes any "sign communicating a message or ideas for noncommercial purposes that is not a Construction Sign, Directional Sign, Temporary Directional Sign Relating to a Qualifying Event, Political Sign, Garage Sale Sign, or a sign owned or required by a governmental agency." Of the three categories discussed here, the Code treats ideological signs most favorably, allowing them to be up to 20 square feet in area and to be placed in all "zoning districts" without time limits.

The second category is "Political Sign[s]." This includes any "temporary sign designed to influence the outcome of an election called by a public body." The Code allows the placement of political signs up to 16 square feet on residential property and up to 32 square feet on nonresidential property, undeveloped municipal property, and "rights-of-way." These signs may be displayed up to 60 days before a primary election and up to 15 days following a general election.

The third category is "Temporary Directional Signs Relating to a Qualifying Event." This includes any "Temporary Sign intended to direct pedestrians, motorists, and other passersby to a 'qualifying event.'" A "qualifying event" is defined as any "assembly, gathering, activity, or meeting sponsored, arranged, or promoted by a religious, charitable, community service, educational, or other similar non-profit organization." Temporary directional signs may be no larger than six square feet.

They may be placed on private property or on a public right-of-way, but no more than four signs may be placed on a single property at any time. And, they may be displayed no more than 12 hours before the "qualifying event" and no more than 1 hour afterward.

B

Petitioners Good News Community Church (Church) and its pastor, Clyde Reed, wish to advertise the time and location of their Sunday church services. The Church is a small, cash-strapped entity that owns no building, so it holds its services at elementary schools or other locations in or near the Town. In order to inform the public about its services, which are held in a variety of different locations, the Church began placing 15 to 20 temporary signs around the Town, frequently in the public right-of-way abutting the street. The signs typically displayed the Church's name, along with the time and location of the upcoming service. Church members would post the signs early in the day on Saturday and then remove them around midday on Sunday. The display of these signs has proved to be an economical and effective way for the Church to let the community know where its services are being held each week.

This practice caught the attention of the Town's Sign Code compliance manager, who twice cited the Church for violating the Code [provisions dealing with] the time limits for displaying its temporary directional signs [and] the Church's failure to include the date of the event on the signs.

II

A

Under th[e First Amendment], a government "has no power to restrict expression because of its message, its ideas, its subject matter, or its content." Content-based laws—those that target speech based on its communicative content—are presumptively unconstitutional and may be justified only if the government proves that they are narrowly tailored to serve compelling state interests.

Government regulation of speech is content based if a law applies to particular speech because of the topic discussed or the idea or message expressed. This commonsense meaning of the phrase "content based" requires a court to consider whether a regulation of speech "on its face" draws distinctions based on the message a speaker conveys. Some facial distinctions based on a message are obvious, defining regulated speech by particular subject matter, and others are more subtle, defining regulated speech by its function or purpose. Both are distinctions drawn based on the message a speaker conveys, and, therefore, are subject to strict scrutiny.

Our precedents have also recognized a separate and additional category of laws that, though facially content neutral, will be considered content-based regulations of speech: laws that cannot be "'justified without reference to the content of the regulated speech,'" or that were adopted by the government "because of disagreement with the message [the speech] conveys." Those laws, like those that are content based on their face, must also satisfy strict scrutiny.

B

The Town's Sign Code is content based on its face. It defines "Temporary Directional Signs" on the basis of whether a sign conveys the message of directing the public to church or some other "qualifying event." It defines "Political Signs" on the basis of whether a sign's message is "designed to influence the outcome of an election." And it defines "Ideological Signs" on the basis of whether a sign "communicat[es] a message or ideas" that do not fit within the Code's other categories. It then subjects each of these categories to different restrictions.

The restrictions in the Sign Code that apply to any given sign thus depend entirely on the communicative content of the sign. If a sign informs its reader of the time and place a book club will discuss John Locke's Two Treatises of Government, that sign will be treated differently from a sign expressing the view that one should vote for one of Locke's followers in an upcoming election, and both signs will be treated differently from a sign expressing an ideological view rooted in Locke's theory of government. More to the point, the Church's signs inviting people to attend its worship services are treated differently from signs conveying other types of ideas. On its face, the Sign Code is a content-based regulation of speech.

C

A law that is content based on its face is subject to strict scrutiny regardless of the government's benign motive, content-neutral justification, or lack of "animus toward the ideas contained" in the regulated speech. We have thus made clear that "'[i]llicit legislative intent is not the *sine qua non* of a violation of the First Amendment,'" and a party opposing the government "need adduce 'no evidence of an improper censorial motive.'" In other words, an innocuous justification cannot transform a facially content-based law into one that is content neutral.

That is why we have repeatedly considered whether a law is content neutral on its face *before* turning to the law's justification or purpose. Because strict scrutiny applies either when a law is content based on its face or when the purpose and justification for the law are content based, a court must evaluate each question before it concludes that the law is content neutral and thus subject to a lower level of scrutiny.

The First Amendment requires no less. Innocent motives do not eliminate the danger of censorship presented by a facially content-based statute, as future government officials may one day wield such statutes to suppress disfavored speech. That is why the First Amendment expressly targets the operation of the laws — i.e., the "abridg[ement] of speech" — rather than merely the motives of those who enacted them. "'The vice of content-based legislation … is not that it is always used for invidious, thought-control purposes, but that it lends itself to use for those purposes.'"

In the Town's view, a sign regulation that "does not censor or favor particular viewpoints or ideas" cannot be content based. Government discrimination among viewpoints — or the regulation of speech based on "the specific motivating ideology or the opinion or perspective of the speaker" — is a "more blatant" and "egregious form of content discrimination." But it is well established that "[t]he First Amendment's hostility to content-based regulation extends not only to restrictions on particular viewpoints, but also to prohibition of public discussion of an entire topic."

Thus, a speech regulation targeted at specific subject matter is content based even if it does not discriminate among viewpoints within that subject matter. The Town's Sign Code ... singles out specific subject matter for differential treatment, even if it does not target viewpoints within that subject matter. Ideological messages are given more favorable treatment than messages concerning a political candidate, which are themselves given more favorable treatment than messages announcing an assembly of like-minded individuals. That is a paradigmatic example of content-based discrimination.

Here, the Code singles out signs bearing a particular message: the time and location of a specific event. This type of ordinance may seem like a perfectly rational way to regulate signs, but a clear and firm rule governing content neutrality is an essential means of protecting the freedom of speech, even if laws that might seem "entirely reasonable" will sometimes be "struck down because of their content-based nature."

III

Because the Town's Sign Code imposes content-based restrictions on speech, those provisions can stand only if they survive strict scrutiny, "'which requires the Government to prove that the restriction furthers a compelling interest and is narrowly tailored to achieve that interest.'" [The majority concluded that the sign ordinance failed strict scrutiny—eds.]

IV

Our decision today will not prevent governments from enacting effective sign laws. Not "all distinctions" are subject to strict scrutiny, only *content-based* ones are. Laws that are *content neutral* are instead subject to lesser scrutiny.

The Town has ample content-neutral options available to resolve problems with safety and aesthetics. For example, its current Code regulates many aspects of signs that have nothing to do with a sign's message: size, building materials, lighting, moving parts, and portability. [Furthermore], the presence of certain signs may be essential, both for vehicles and pedestrians, to guide traffic or to identify hazards and ensure safety. A sign ordinance narrowly tailored to the challenges of protecting the safety of pedestrians, drivers, and passengers—such as warning signs marking hazards on private property, signs directing traffic, or street numbers associated with private houses—well might survive strict scrutiny. The signs at issue in this case, including political and ideological signs and signs for events, are far removed from those purposes. As discussed above, they are facially content based and are neither justified by traditional safety concerns nor narrowly tailored.

JUSTICE ALITO, with whom JUSTICE KENNEDY and JUSTICE SOTOMAYOR join, concurring.

I join the opinion of the Court but add a few words of further explanation. Content-based laws merit [strict scrutiny] because they present, albeit sometimes in a subtler form, the same dangers as laws that regulate speech based on viewpoint. Limiting speech based on its "topic" or "subject" favors those who do not want to disturb the status quo. Such regulations may interfere with democratic self-government and the search for truth.

This does not mean, however, that municipalities are powerless to enact and enforce reasonable sign regulations.

In addition to regulating signs put up by private actors, government entities may ... put up all manner of signs to promote safety, as well as directional signs and signs pointing out historic sites and scenic spots. Properly understood, today's decision will not prevent cities from regulating signs in a way that fully protects public safety and serves legitimate esthetic objectives.

Justice Breyer, concurring in the judgment.

In my view, the category "content discrimination" is better considered in many contexts, including here, as a rule of thumb, rather than as an automatic "strict scrutiny" trigger, leading to almost certain legal condemnation.

To use content discrimination to trigger strict scrutiny sometimes makes perfect sense. There are cases in which the Court has found content discrimination an unconstitutional method for suppressing a viewpoint. And there are cases where the Court has found content discrimination to reveal that rules governing a traditional public forum are, in fact, not a neutral way of fairly managing the forum in the interest of all speakers. In these types of cases, strict scrutiny is often appropriate, and content discrimination has thus served a useful purpose.

But content discrimination, while helping courts to identify unconstitutional suppression of expression, cannot and should not *always* trigger strict scrutiny. I readily concede, for example, that content discrimination, as a conceptual tool, can sometimes reveal weaknesses in the government's rationale for a rule that limits speech. If, for example, a city looks to litter prevention as the rationale for a prohibition against placing newsracks dispensing free advertisements on public property, why does it exempt other newsracks causing similar litter? I also concede that, whenever government disfavors one kind of speech, it places that speech at a disadvantage, potentially interfering with the free marketplace of ideas and with an individual's ability to express thoughts and ideas that can help that individual determine the kind of society in which he wishes to live, help shape that society, and help define his place within it.

Nonetheless, in these latter instances to use the presence of content discrimination automatically to trigger strict scrutiny and thereby call into play a strong presumption against constitutionality goes too far. That is because virtually all government activities involve speech, many of which involve the regulation of speech. Regulatory programs almost always require content discrimination. And to hold that such content discrimination triggers strict scrutiny is to write a recipe for judicial management of ordinary government regulatory activity.

Consider a few examples of speech regulated by government that inevitably involve content discrimination, but where a strong presumption against constitutionality has no place. Consider governmental regulation of securities, *e.g.,* 15 U.S.C. §78*l* (requirements for content that must be included in a registration statement); of energy conservation labeling-practices, *e.g.,* 42 U.S.C. §6294 (requirements for content that must be included on labels of certain consumer electronics); of prescription drugs, *e.g.,* 21 U.S.C. §353(b)(4)(A) (requiring a prescription drug label to bear the symbol "Rx only"); … of signs at petting zoos, *e.g.,* N.Y. Gen. Bus. Law Ann. §399-ff(3) (West Cum. Supp. 2015) (requiring petting zoos to post a sign at every exit "'strongly recommend[ing] that persons wash their hands upon exiting the petting zoo area'"); and so on.

Nor can the majority avoid the application of strict scrutiny to all sorts of justifiable governmental regulations by relying on this Court's many subcategories and exceptions to the rule. The Court has said, for example, that we should apply less strict standards to "commercial speech." But I have great concern that many justifiable instances of "content-based" regulation are noncommercial. The Court has also said that "government speech" escapes First Amendment strictures. But regulated speech is typically private speech, not government speech.

I recognize that the Court could escape the problem by watering down the force of the presumption against constitutionality that "strict scrutiny" normally carries with it. But, in my view, doing so will weaken the First Amendment's protection in instances where "strict scrutiny" should apply in full force.

The better approach is to generally treat content discrimination as a strong reason weighing against the constitutionality of a rule where a traditional public forum, or where viewpoint discrimination, is threatened, but elsewhere treat it as a rule of thumb, finding it a helpful, but not determinative legal tool, in an appropriate case, to determine the strength of a justification. I would use content discrimination as a supplement to a more basic analysis, which, tracking most of our First Amendment cases, asks whether the regulation at issue works harm to First Amendment interests that is disproportionate in light of the relevant regulatory objectives. Answering this question requires examining the seriousness of the harm to speech, the importance of the countervailing objectives, the extent to which the law will achieve those objectives, and whether there are other, less restrictive ways of doing so. Admittedly, this approach does not have the simplicity of a mechanical use of categories. But it does permit the government to regulate speech in numerous instances where the voters have authorized the government to regulate and where courts should hesitate to substitute judicial judgment for that of administrators.

Here, regulation of signage along the roadside, for purposes of safety and beautification is at issue. There is no traditional public forum nor do I find any general effort to censor a particular viewpoint. Consequently, the specific regulation at issue does not warrant "strict scrutiny."

JUSTICE KAGAN, with whom JUSTICE GINSBURG and JUSTICE BREYER join, concurring in the judgment.

Countless cities and towns across America have adopted ordinances regulating the posting of signs, while exempting certain categories of signs based on their subject matter. Given the Court's analysis, many sign ordinances of that kind are now in jeopardy. [A]lthough the majority holds out hope that some sign laws with subject-matter exemptions "might survive" that stringent review, the likelihood is that most will be struck down. After all, it is the "rare case[] in which a speech restriction withstands strict scrutiny." The consequence — unless courts water down strict scrutiny to something unrecognizable — is that our communities will find themselves in an unenviable bind: They will have to either repeal the exemptions that allow for helpful signs on streets and sidewalks, or else lift their sign restrictions altogether and resign themselves to the resulting clutter.

This Court's decisions articulate two important and related reasons for subjecting content-based speech regulations to the most exacting standard of review. The first is "to preserve an uninhibited marketplace of ideas in which truth will ultimately prevail." The second is to ensure that the government has not regulated speech "based on hostility — or favoritism — towards the underlying message expressed." Yet the subject-matter exemptions included in many sign ordinances do not implicate those concerns. Allowing residents, say, to install a light bulb over "name and address" signs but no others does not distort the marketplace of ideas. Nor does that different treatment give rise to an inference of impermissible government motive.

We apply strict scrutiny to facially content-based regulations of speech, in keeping with the rationales just described, when there is any "realistic possibility that official suppression of ideas is afoot." That is always the case when the regulation facially differentiates on the basis of viewpoint. It is also the case (except in non-public or limited public forums) when a law restricts "discussion of an entire topic" in public debate. And we have recognized that such subject-matter restrictions, even though viewpoint-neutral on their face, may "suggest[] an attempt to give one side of a debatable public question an advantage in expressing its views to the people." ... When that is realistically possible — when the restriction "raises the specter that the Government may effectively drive certain ideas or viewpoints from the marketplace" — we insist that the law pass the most demanding constitutional test.

But when that is not realistically possible, we may do well to relax our guard so that "entirely reasonable" laws imperiled by strict scrutiny can survive. To do its intended work, of course, the category of content-based regulation triggering strict scrutiny must sweep more broadly than the actual harm; that category exists to create a buffer zone guaranteeing that the government cannot favor or disfavor certain viewpoints. But that buffer zone need not extend forever. We can administer our content-regulation doctrine with a dose of common sense, so as to leave standing laws that in no way implicate its intended function.

The Town of Gilbert's defense of its sign ordinance — most notably, the law's distinctions between directional signs and others — does not pass strict scrutiny, or intermediate scrutiny, or even the laugh test. The Town, for example, provides no reason at all for prohibiting more than four directional signs on a property while placing no limits on the number of other types of signs. Similarly, the Town offers no coherent justification for restricting the size of directional signs to 6 square feet while allowing other signs to reach 20 square feet. The absence of any sensible basis for these and other distinctions dooms the Town's ordinance under even the intermediate scrutiny that the Court typically applies to "time, place, or manner" speech regulations. Accordingly, there is no need to decide in this case whether strict scrutiny applies to every sign ordinance in every town across this country containing a subject-matter exemption.

As the years go by, courts will discover that thousands of towns have such ordinances, many of them "entirely reasonable." And as the challenges to them mount, courts will have to invalidate one after the other. And courts will strike down those democratically enacted local laws even though no one—certainly not the majority—has ever explained why the vindication of First Amendment values requires that result.

Exercise 16:

1. The majority identifies two ways in which a speech regulation can be content-based on its face. What are they? The majority also highlights two ways in which an ostensibly content-neutral regulation can be content-based. Identify both ways. Was the Town of Gilbert's ordinance facially content neutral or facially content based?

2. How might an ordinance define speech based on its function or purpose? Can you provide an example of such an ordinance? Can you give an example of an ordinance that is both facially content neutral and that can be justified without reference to the content of the regulated speech? Suppose a town generally restricts signs but provides an exception for "signs advertising a one-time event" such as a fall festival or a school fundraiser. Would such a law be subject to strict scrutiny? Could it survive such heightened review?

3. Looking through the lens of *Reed*, was the Colorado statute in *Hill* content neutral or content based? In *Reed*, the majority did not cite the majority opinion in *Hill*; instead, the *Reed* majority cited the dissenting opinions in *Hill* that Justices Kennedy and Scalia authored. What, if anything, might that tell us about the status of *Hill*? Are *Reed* and *Hill* consistent? Interestingly, the *Reed* majority also did not invoke *City of Renton v. Playtime Theatres, Inc.*, which is excerpted below. When you read *Playtime Theatres*, consider whether the *Reed* majority should have discussed *Playtime Theatres*, which the *Reed* dissent invoked to support its claim that a lower level of scrutiny should apply to certain facially content-based ordinances that reveal "not even a hint of bias or censorship."

4. Under the majority's view, is an ordinance content-based if it treats "all messages announcing an assembly of like-minded individuals" on signs the same? In the wake of *Reed*, must the government treat all ideological signs, signs of political candidates, and signs announcing assemblies in the same fashion? If the government attempts to impose different requirements for different types of signs, can it ever survive strict scrutiny? Who has the better argument on this point, Justice Alito or Justice Kagan? Which types of distinctions between and among signs might survive?

5. The Town of Gilbert articulated two interests to justify its sign ordinance—aesthetic appeal and traffic safety. Assume for the sake of argument that both of these interests are compelling. Are the ordinances narrowly tailored? If you represented the Town of Gilbert, how would you argue that the ordinances are narrowly tailored? What is (are) the strongest argument(s) that the ordinances fails strict scrutiny?

6. The *Reed* majority explains that "a law that is content based on its face is subject to strict scrutiny regardless of the government's benign motive, content-neutral justification, or lack of animus toward the ideas contained in the regulated speech." If the government acts with a benign or good motive, why should the Court not apply a lower level of review? What level of scrutiny would Justice Kagan apply to such laws? With whom do you agree?

7. What is the standard that Justice Breyer articulates in his concurrence? How does it differ from the position that Justice Kagan articulates in her concurrence (and which Justice Breyer joined)? Might they lead to different results in particular cases? Which position provides a more manageable standard for courts? Is one or both better or worse than the rule that the majority adopts?

8. Restrictions on symbolic expression are treated like content-based laws if the limitations are predicated on the communicative impact of that symbolic expression. Flag burning in *Texas v. Johnson*, 491 U.S. 397 (1989), and the wearing of black armbands in *Tinker v. Des Moines Indep. Comm. Sch. Dist.*, 393 U.S. 503 (1969), are prime examples of restrictions based on the message that the symbolic expression communicates. *See, e.g., Johnson*, 491 U.S. at 411 ("The Texas law ... is designed to protect [the flag] only against impairments that would cause serious offense to others ... [and] thus depend[s] on the likely communicative impact of his expressive conduct."). Such restrictions, therefore, are subject to strict scrutiny.

9. Suppose a federal statute makes it a crime to "knowingly provid[e] material support or resources to a foreign organization," which support and resources are defined to include "instruction or teaching designed to impart a specific skill, as opposed to general knowledge." *See* 18 U.S.C. §2339B. Does this statute regulate conduct such that the lower standard from *United States v. O'Brien* should apply, or does it impose a content-based regulation of speech? Provide an argument for each position, and explain which side has the stronger position post-*Reed*. *See Holder v. Humanitarian Law Project*, 561 U.S. 1 (2010).

b. The Role of Purpose

The Supreme Court's cases on what role, if any, purpose plays in its determination of content neutrality, are difficult to synthesize. In some cases, the Court stated, purpose is irrelevant to the inquiry. "It is a familiar principle of constitutional law that this Court will not strike down an otherwise constitutional statute on the basis of an alleged illicit legislative motive." *United States v. O'Brien*, 391 U.S. 367, 383 (1968). In others, however, the Court relied on purpose to determine whether a regulation was content based. *See, e.g., Texas v. Johnson*, 491 U.S. 397, 406–07, 410 (1989) (concluding that Texas' "interest in preserving the flag as a symbol of nationhood and national unity" is content based).

The Supreme Court has varied its treatment of a speech regulation because of legislative purpose. For instance, as discussed below in *City of Renton v. Playtime Theatres, Inc.*, 475 U.S. 41 (1986), the "secondary effects" doctrine permits the Court to label a facially content-based regulation, content neutral. Similarly, a content-based purpose has caused the Supreme Court to treat a facially content-neutral regulation as content based. Following the earlier example of a content-neutral park regulation, assume that the city council passed the ordinance because it had learned that an anti-poverty "sleep-in" was going to take place in the hypothetical Central Park, and wished to prevent it. The city's purpose is content based because it issued the regulation to suppress one subject of speech.

In *Turner Broadcasting Sys. v. FCC*, 512 U.S. 622 (1994), below, the Supreme Court engaged in an extended discussion of the relationship between a regulation's text and its purpose.

Turner Broadcasting System, Inc. v. Federal Communications Commission

512 U.S. 622 (1994)

Justice Kennedy announced the judgment of the Court and delivered the opinion of the Court, except as to Part III-B.

Sections 4 and 5 of the Cable Television Consumer Protection and Competition Act of 1992 require cable television systems to devote a portion of their channels to the transmission of local broadcast television stations. This case presents the question whether these provisions abridge the freedom of speech or of the press, in violation of the First Amendment.

I

. . . .

B

On October 5, 1992, Congress overrode a Presidential veto to enact the Cable Television Consumer Protection and Competition Act of 1992.... At issue in this case is the constitutionality of the so-called must-carry provisions, contained in §§ 4 and 5 of the Act.... Section 4 requires carriage of "local commercial television stations," defined to include all full power television broadcasters, other than those qualifying as "noncommercial educational" stations under § 5, that operate within the same television market as the cable system. Section 5 of the Act imposes similar requirements regarding the carriage of local public broadcast television stations, referred to in the Act as local "noncommercial educational television stations."

Taken together, therefore, §§ 4 and 5 subject all but the smallest cable systems nationwide to must-carry obligations, and confer must-carry privileges on all full power broadcasters operating within the same television market as a qualified cable system.

C

Congress enacted the 1992 Cable Act after conducting three years of hearings on the structure and operation of the cable television industry. In brief, Congress found that the physical characteristics of cable transmission, compounded by the increasing concentration of economic power in the cable industry, are endangering the ability of over-the-air broadcast television stations to compete for a viewing audience and thus for necessary operating revenues. Congress determined that regulation of the market for video programming was necessary to correct this competitive imbalance.

Congress concluded that unless cable operators are required to carry local broadcast stations, "[t]here is a substantial likelihood that ... additional local broadcast signals will be deleted, repositioned, or not carried"; the "marked shift in market share" from broadcast to cable will continue to erode the advertising revenue base which sustains free local broadcast television; and that, as a consequence, "the economic viability of free local broadcast television and its ability to originate quality local programming will be seriously jeopardized."

D

Soon after the Act became law, appellants filed these five consolidated actions in the United States District Court for the District of Columbia against the United States and the Federal Communications Commission (hereinafter referred to collectively as the Government), challenging the constitutionality of the must-carry provisions. Appellants are numerous cable programmers and cable operators. [A] three-judge District Court convened to hear the actions.... [T]he District Court, in a divided opinion, granted summary judgment in favor of the Government, ruling that the must-carry provisions are consistent with the First Amendment.

This direct appeal followed.

II

There can be no disagreement on an initial premise: Cable programmers and cable operators engage in and transmit speech, and they are entitled to the protection of the speech and press provisions of the First Amendment. Through "original programming or by exercising editorial discretion over which stations or programs to include in its repertoire," cable programmers and operators "see[k] to communicate messages on a wide variety of topics and in a wide variety of formats." By requiring cable systems to set aside a portion of their channels for local broadcasters, the must-carry rules regulate cable speech in two respects: The rules reduce the number of channels over which cable operators exercise unfettered control, and they render it more difficult for cable programmers to compete for carriage on the limited channels remaining. Nevertheless, because not every interference with speech triggers the same degree of scrutiny under the First Amendment, we must decide at the outset the level of scrutiny applicable to the must-carry provisions.

B

At the heart of the First Amendment lies the principle that each person should decide for himself or herself the ideas and beliefs deserving of expression, consideration, and adherence. Our political system and cultural life rest upon this ideal. See *Cohen v. California*, 403 U.S. 15, 24 (1971); *West Virginia Bd. of Ed. v. Barnette*, 319 U.S. 624, 638, 640–642 (1943). Government action that stifles speech on account of its message, or that requires the utterance of a particular message favored by the Government, contravenes this essential right. Laws of this sort pose the inherent risk that the Government seeks not to advance a legitimate regulatory goal, but to suppress unpopular ideas or information or manipulate the public debate through coercion rather than persuasion. These restrictions "rais[e] the specter that the Government may effectively drive certain ideas or viewpoints from the marketplace."

For these reasons, the First Amendment, subject only to narrow and well-understood exceptions, does not countenance governmental control over the content of messages expressed by private individuals. *R.A.V. v. St. Paul*, 505 U.S. 377, 382–383 (1992); *Texas v. Johnson*, 491 U.S. 397, 414 (1989). Our precedents thus apply the most exacting scrutiny to regulations that suppress, disadvantage, or impose differential burdens upon speech because of its content. In contrast, regulations that are unrelated to the content of speech are subject to an intermediate level of scrutiny, because in most cases they pose a less substantial risk of excising certain ideas or viewpoints from the public dialogue.

Deciding whether a particular regulation is content based or content neutral is not always a simple task. We have said that the "principal inquiry in determining content neutrality ... is whether the government has adopted a regulation of speech because of [agreement or] disagreement with the message it conveys." *Ward v. Rock Against Racism*, 491 U.S. 781, 791 (1989). The purpose, or justification, of a regulation will often be evident on its face. But while a content-based purpose may be sufficient in certain circumstances to show that a regulation is content based, it is not necessary to such a showing in all cases. Nor will the mere assertion of a content-neutral purpose be enough to save a law which, on its face, discriminates based on content.

As a general rule, laws that by their terms distinguish favored speech from disfavored speech on the basis of the ideas or views expressed are content based. See, *e.g., Boos v. Barry*, 485 U.S. 312, 318–319 (1988). By contrast, laws that confer benefits or impose burdens on speech without reference to the ideas or views expressed are in most instances content neutral.

C

Insofar as they pertain to the carriage of full-power broadcasters, the must-carry rules, on their face, impose burdens and confer benefits without reference to the content of speech. Although the provisions interfere with cable operators' editorial discretion by compelling them to offer carriage to a certain minimum number of broadcast stations, the extent of the interference does not depend upon the content of the cable operators' programming. The rules impose obligations upon all operators regardless of the programs or stations they now offer or have offered in the past. Nothing in the Act imposes a restriction, penalty, or burden by reason of the views, programs, or stations the cable operator has selected or will select. The number of channels a cable operator must set aside depends only on the operator's channel capacity; hence, an operator cannot avoid or mitigate its obligations under the Act by altering the programming it offers to subscribers.

The must-carry provisions also burden cable programmers by reducing the number of channels for which they can compete. But, again, this burden is unrelated to content, for it extends to all cable programmers irrespective of the programming they choose to offer viewers. And finally, the privileges conferred by the must-carry provisions are also unrelated to content. The rules benefit all full power broadcasters who request carriage-be they commercial or noncommercial, independent or network affiliated, English or Spanish language, religious or secular. The aggregate effect of the rules is thus to make every full power commercial and noncommercial broadcaster eligible for must-carry, provided only that the broadcaster operates within the same television market as a cable system.

It is true that the must-carry provisions distinguish between speakers in the television programming market. But they do so based only upon the manner in which speakers transmit their messages to viewers, and not upon the messages they carry: Broadcasters, which transmit over the airwaves, are favored, while cable programmers, which do not, are disfavored. Cable operators, too, are burdened by the carriage obligations, but only because they control access to the cable conduit. So long as they are not a subtle means of exercising a content preference, speaker distinctions of this nature are not presumed invalid under the First Amendment.

That the must-carry provisions, on their face, do not burden or benefit speech of a particular content does not end the inquiry. Our cases have recognized that even a regulation neutral on its face may be content based if its manifest purpose is to regulate speech because of the message it conveys. *Ward*, 491 U.S., at 791–792; cf. *Church of Lukumi Babalu Aye, Inc. v. Hialeah*, 508 U.S. 520, 534–535 (1993).

Appellants contend, in this regard, that the must-carry regulations are content-based because Congress' purpose in enacting them was to promote speech of a favored content. We do not agree. Our review of the Act and its various findings persuades us that Congress' overriding objective in enacting must-carry was not to favor programming of a particular subject matter, viewpoint, or format, but rather to preserve access to free television programming for the 40 percent of Americans without cable.

[T]he must-carry provisions are not designed to favor or disadvantage speech of any particular content. Rather, they are meant to protect broadcast television from what Congress determined to be unfair competition by cable systems. In enacting the provisions, Congress sought to preserve the existing structure of the Nation's broadcast television medium while permitting the concomitant expansion and development of cable television, and, in particular, to ensure that broadcast television remains available as a source of video programming for those without cable.

III

A

We agree with the District Court that the appropriate standard by which to evaluate the constitutionality of must-carry is the intermediate level of scrutiny applicable to content-neutral restrictions that impose an incidental burden on speech. See *Ward v. Rock Against Racism*, 491 U.S. 781 (1989); *United States v. O'Brien*, 391 U.S. 367 (1968).

Under *O'Brien*, a content-neutral regulation will be sustained if "it furthers an important or substantial governmental interest; if the governmental interest is unrelated to the suppression of free expression; and if the incidental restriction on alleged First Amendment freedoms is no greater than is essential to the furtherance of that interest." To satisfy this standard, a regulation need not be the least speech-restrictive means of advancing the Government's interests. "Rather, the requirement of narrow tailoring is satisfied 'so long as the … regulation promotes a substantial government interest that would be achieved less effectively absent the regulation.'" *Ward, supra*, 491 U.S., at 799.

Congress declared that the must-carry provisions serve three interrelated interests: (1) preserving the benefits of free, over-the-air local broadcast television, (2) promoting the widespread dissemination of information from a multiplicity of sources, and (3) promoting fair competition in the market for television programming.… [W]e have no difficulty concluding that each of them is an important governmental interest.

[T]he importance of local broadcasting outlets "can scarcely be exaggerated, for broadcasting is demonstrably a principal source of information and entertainment for a great part of the Nation's population." Although cable and other technologies have ushered in alternatives to broadcast television, nearly 40 percent of American households still rely on broadcast stations as their exclusive source of television programming. Likewise, assuring that the public has access to a multiplicity of information sources is a governmental purpose of the highest order, for it promotes values central to the First Amendment.…

Finally, the Government's interest in eliminating restraints on fair competition is always substantial, even when the individuals or entities subject to particular regulations are engaged in expressive activity protected by the First Amendment.

B

That the Government's asserted interests are important in the abstract does not mean, however, that the must-carry rules will in fact advance those interests.

Thus, in applying *O'Brien* scrutiny we must ask first whether the Government has adequately shown that the economic health of local broadcasting is in genuine jeopardy and in need of the protections afforded by must-carry. Assuming an affirmative answer to the foregoing question, the Government still bears the burden of showing that the remedy it has adopted does not "burden substantially more speech than is necessary to further the government's legitimate interests." *Ward*, 491 U.S., at 799. On the state of the record developed thus far, and in the absence of findings of fact from the District Court, we are unable to conclude that the Government has satisfied either inquiry.

Without a more substantial elaboration in the District Court of the predictive or historical evidence upon which Congress relied, or the introduction of some additional evidence to establish that the dropped or repositioned broadcasters would be at serious risk of financial difficulty, we cannot determine whether the threat to broadcast television is real enough to overcome the challenge to the provisions made by these appellants....

Finally, the record fails to provide any judicial findings concerning the availability and efficacy of "constitutionally acceptable less restrictive means" of achieving the Government's asserted interests.

In sum, because there are genuine issues of material fact still to be resolved on this record, we hold that the District Court erred in granting summary judgment in favor of the Government. [W]e think it necessary to permit the parties to develop a more thorough factual record, and to allow the District Court to resolve any factual disputes remaining, before passing upon the constitutional validity of the challenged provisions.

The judgment below is vacated, and the case is remanded for further proceedings consistent with this opinion.

It is so ordered.

JUSTICE BLACKMUN, concurring. [Opinion omitted.]

JUSTICE STEVENS, concurring in part and concurring in the judgment. [Opinion omitted.]

JUSTICE O'CONNOR, with whom JUSTICE SCALIA and JUSTICE GINSBURG join, and with whom JUSTICE THOMAS joins as to Parts I and III, concurring in part and dissenting in part.

Under the First Amendment, it is normally not within the government's power to decide who may speak and who may not. The government does have the power to impose content-neutral time, place, and manner restrictions, but this is in large part precisely because such restrictions apply to all speakers. Laws that treat all speakers equally are relatively poor tools for controlling public debate, and their very generality creates a substantial political check that prevents them from being unduly burdensome. Laws that single out particular speakers are substantially more dangerous, even when they do not draw explicit content distinctions.

But looking at the statute at issue, I cannot avoid the conclusion that its preference for broadcasters over cable programmers is justified with reference to content. The findings, enacted by Congress as § 2 of the Act make this clear. "There is a substantial governmental and First Amendment interest in promoting a diversity of views provided through multiple technology media." "[P]ublic television provides educational and informational programming to the Nation's citizens, thereby advancing the Government's compelling interest in educating its citizens." "A primary objective and benefit of our Nation's system of regulation of television broadcasting is the local origination of programming. There is a substantial governmental interest in ensuring its continuation."...

In determining whether a broadcast station should be eligible for must-carry in a particular market, the Federal Communications Commission (FCC) must "afford

particular attention to the value of localism by taking into account such factors as . . .
whether any other [eligible station] provides news coverage of issues of concern to
such community or provides carriage or coverage of sporting and other events of interest to the community." . . . Moreover, the Act distinguishes between commercial
television stations and noncommercial educational television stations, giving special
benefits to the latter.

Preferences for diversity of viewpoints, for localism, for educational programming,
and for news and public affairs all make reference to content. They may not reflect
hostility to particular points of view, or a desire to suppress certain subjects because
they are controversial or offensive. They may be quite benignly motivated. But benign
motivation, we have consistently held, is not enough to avoid the need for strict
scrutiny of content-based justifications. The First Amendment does more than just
bar government from intentionally suppressing speech of which it disapproves. It
also generally prohibits the government from excepting certain kinds of speech from
regulation because it thinks the speech is especially valuable. See, *e.g., Police Dept. of
Chicago v. Mosley*, 408 U.S. 92, 96 (1972).

This is why the Court is mistaken in concluding that the interest in diversity is
content neutral. Indeed, the interest is not "related to the *suppression* of free expression," but that is not enough for content neutrality. The interest in giving labor picketers an exemption from a general picketing ban, see *Mosley, supra*, is not related to
the suppression of speech. But [it is] related to the *content* of speech — to its communicative impact. The interest in ensuring access to a multiplicity of diverse and
antagonistic sources of information, no matter how praiseworthy, is directly tied to
the content of what the speakers will likely say.

Justice Ginsburg, concurring in part and dissenting in part. [Opinion omitted.]

Exercise 17:

1. In what ways, or how, is the regulated cable operators' cable services "speech"?

2. How did the Act "infringe" the cable operators' "freedom of speech"?

3. What analysis did the Supreme Court articulate to evaluate whether the Act was
content based or neutral?

4. What role did purpose inquiry play in the Court's prescribed analysis?

5. According to the Court, were the Act's restrictions on cable operators content
based or neutral? Why?

6. To what level of scrutiny did the Court subject the Act?

7. Explain the Court's application of that level of scrutiny.

8. From the dissenters' perspective, in what way was the Act's must-carry requirement content based? Was it subject matter, viewpoint, or both?

Though the Supreme Court in *Turner Broadcasting* admonished that, "[n]or will . . .
a content-neutral purpose be enough to save a law which, on its face, discriminates

based on content," there is a well-established doctrine in which that occurs. The Supreme Court's most prominent use of purpose resulted in what has become known as the "secondary effects" doctrine. The doctrine found its most prominent statement in *City of Renton v. Playtime Theatres, Inc.*, 475 U.S. 41 (1986), reprinted below.

City of Renton v. Playtime Theatres, Inc.
475 U.S. 41 (1986)

JUSTICE REHNQUIST delivered the opinion of the Court.

In May 1980, the Mayor of Renton, a city of approximately 32,000 people located just south of Seattle, suggested to the Renton City Council that it consider the advisability of enacting zoning legislation dealing with adult entertainment uses. No such uses existed in the city at that time. Upon the Mayor's suggestion, the City Council referred the matter to the city's Planning and Development Committee. The Committee held public hearings, reviewed the experiences of Seattle and other cities, and received a report from the City Attorney's Office advising as to developments in other cities.

In April 1981, acting on the basis of the Planning and Development Committee's recommendation, the City Council enacted Ordinance No. 3526. The ordinance prohibited any "adult motion picture theater" from locating within 1,000 feet of any residential zone, single- or multiple-family dwelling, church, or park, and within one mile of any school. The term "adult motion picture theater" was defined as "[a]n enclosed building used for presenting motion picture films, video cassettes, cable television, or any other such visual media, distinguished or characteri[zed] by an emphasis on matter depicting, describing or relating to 'specified sexual activities' or 'specified anatomical areas'... for observation by patrons therein."

In early 1982, respondents acquired two existing theaters in downtown Renton, with the intention of using them to exhibit feature-length adult films. The theaters were located within the area proscribed by Ordinance No. 3526. At about the same time, respondents filed [a] lawsuit challenging the ordinance on First and Fourteenth Amendment grounds, and seeking declaratory and injunctive relief....

[The District Court entered summary judgment in favor of Renton.] ... Relying on *Young v. American Mini Theatres, Inc.*, 427 U.S. 50 (1976), and *United States v. O'Brien*, 391 U.S. 367 (1968), the court held that the Renton ordinance did not violate the First Amendment. The Court of Appeals for the Ninth Circuit reversed.

This Court has long held that regulations enacted for the purpose of restraining speech on the basis of its content presumptively violate the First Amendment. See *Police Dept. of Chicago v. Mosley*, 408 U.S. 92, 95, 98–99 (1972). On the other hand, so-called "content-neutral" time, place, and manner regulations are acceptable so long as they are designed to serve a substantial governmental interest and do not unreasonably limit alternative avenues of communication.

At first glance, the Renton ordinance, like the ordinance in *American Mini Theatres*, does not appear to fit neatly into either the "content-based" or the "content-neutral" category. To be sure, the ordinance treats theaters that specialize in adult films differently from other kinds of theaters. Nevertheless, as the District Court concluded, the Renton ordinance is aimed not at the *content* of the films shown at "adult motion picture theatres," but rather at the *secondary effects* of such theaters on the surrounding community. The District Court found that the City Council's "*predominate* concerns" were with the secondary effects of adult theaters, and not with the content of adult films themselves. The District Court's finding as to "predominate" intent, left undisturbed by the Court of Appeals, is more than adequate to establish that the city's pursuit of its zoning interests here was unrelated to the suppression of free expression.

The ordinance by its terms is designed to prevent crime, protect the city's retail trade, maintain property values, and generally "[protect] and [preserve] the quality of [the city's] neighborhoods, commercial districts, and the quality of urban life," not to suppress the expression of unpopular views....

In short, the Renton ordinance is completely consistent with our definition of "content-neutral" speech regulations as those that "are *justified* without reference to the content of the regulated speech." The ordinance does not contravene the fundamental principle that underlies our concern about "content-based" speech regulations: that "government may not grant the use of a forum to people whose views it finds acceptable, but deny use to those wishing to express less favored or more controversial views." *Mosley, supra,* 408 U.S., at 95–96.

The appropriate inquiry in this case, then, is whether the Renton ordinance is designed to serve a substantial governmental interest and allows for reasonable alternative avenues of communication. It is clear that the ordinance meets such a standard. As a majority of this Court recognized in *American Mini Theatres,* a city's "interest in attempting to preserve the quality of urban life is one that must be accorded high respect." Exactly the same vital governmental interests are at stake here.

The Court of Appeals ruled, however, that because the Renton ordinance was enacted without the benefit of studies specifically relating to "the particular problems or needs of Renton," the city's justifications for the ordinance were "conclusory and speculative." We think the Court of Appeals imposed on the city an unnecessarily rigid burden of proof. The record in this case reveals that Renton relied heavily on the experience of, and studies produced by, the city of Seattle.

We hold that Renton was entitled to rely on the experiences of Seattle and other cities. The First Amendment does not require a city, before enacting such an ordinance, to conduct new studies or produce evidence independent of that already generated by other cities, so long as whatever evidence the city relies upon is reasonably believed to be relevant to the problem that the city addresses. That was the case here.

We also find no constitutional defect in the method chosen by Renton to further its substantial interests. Cities may regulate adult theaters by dispersing them, as in Detroit, or by effectively concentrating them, as in Renton. "It is not our function to appraise the wisdom of [the city's] decision to require adult theaters to be separated rather than concentrated in the same areas.... [T]he city must be allowed a reasonable opportunity to experiment with solutions to admittedly serious problems." Moreover, the Renton ordinance is "narrowly tailored" to affect only that category of theaters shown to produce the unwanted secondary effects.

Respondents contend that the Renton ordinance is "under-inclusive," in that it fails to regulate other kinds of adult businesses that are likely to produce secondary effects similar to those produced by adult theaters. That Renton chose first to address the potential problems created by one particular kind of adult business in no way suggests that the city has "singled out" adult theaters for discriminatory treatment. We simply have no basis on this record for assuming that Renton will not, in the future, amend its ordinance to include other kinds of adult businesses that have been shown to produce the same kinds of secondary effects as adult theaters. See *Williamson v. Lee Optical Inc.*, 348 U.S. 483, 488–489 (1955).

Finally, turning to the question whether the Renton ordinance allows for reasonable alternative avenues of communication, we note that the ordinance leaves some 520 acres, or more than five percent of the entire land area of Renton, open to use as adult theater sites. The District Court found that the 520 acres of land consists of "[a]mple, accessible real estate[.]" In our view, the First Amendment requires only that Renton refrain from effectively denying respondents a reasonable opportunity to open and operate an adult theater within the city, and the ordinance before us easily meets this requirement.

JUSTICE BLACKMUN concurs in the result.

JUSTICE BRENNAN, with whom JUSTICE MARSHALL joins, dissenting.

I

The fact that adult movie theaters may cause harmful "secondary" land-use effects may arguably give Renton a compelling reason to regulate such establishments; it does not mean, however, that such regulations are content neutral.... In this case, both the language of the ordinance and its dubious legislative history belie the Court's conclusion that "the city's pursuit of its zoning interests here was unrelated to the suppression of free expression."

A

The ordinance discriminates on its face against certain forms of speech based on content. Movie theaters specializing in "adult motion pictures" may not be located within 1,000 feet of any residential zone, single- or multiple-family dwelling, church, park, or school. Other motion picture theaters, and other forms of "adult entertainment," such as bars, massage parlors, and adult bookstores, are not subject to the same restrictions. This selective treatment strongly suggests that Renton was interested not in controlling the "secondary effects" associated with adult businesses, but in discriminating against adult theaters based on the content of the films they exhibit.

B

Shortly *after* this lawsuit commenced, the Renton City Council amended the ordinance, adding a provision explaining that its intention in adopting the ordinance had been "to promote the City of Renton's great interest in protecting and preserving the quality of its neighborhoods, commercial districts, and the quality of urban life through effective land use planning."

Prior to the amendment, there was no indication that the ordinance was designed to address any "secondary effects" a single adult theater might create. In addition to the suspiciously coincidental timing of the amendment, many of the City Council's "findings" do not relate to legitimate land-use concerns. As the Court of Appeals observed, "many of the stated reasons for the ordinance were no more than expressions of dislike for the subject matter." That some residents may be offended by the *content* of the films shown at adult movie theaters cannot form the basis for state regulation of speech.

The City Council conducted no studies, and heard no expert testimony, on how the protected uses [such as schools, churches, parks, or residences] would be affected by the presence of an adult movie theater, and never considered whether residents' concerns could be met by "restrictions that are less intrusive on protected forms of expression."

The Court holds that Renton was entitled to rely on the experiences of cities like Detroit and Seattle, which had enacted special zoning regulations for adult entertainment businesses after studying the adverse effects caused by such establishments. However, it never actually reviewed any of the studies conducted by those cities. Renton had no basis for determining if any of the "findings" made by these cities were relevant to *Renton's* problems or needs. Moreover, since Renton ultimately adopted zoning regulations different from either Detroit or Seattle, these "studies" provide no basis for assessing the effectiveness of the particular restrictions adopted under the ordinance.

Exercise 18:

1. What is Playtime's speech? Did the ordinance infringe on Playtime's freedom of speech?

2. Why did the Supreme Court find that Renton's zoning ordinance was content neutral?

3. Is it true that "adult entertainment" causes harmful "secondary effects"? How did Renton know? How did the Court know? Is that an adequate basis for the Court's conclusion?

4. Is the Secondary Effects Doctrine consistent with the broader body of free speech doctrine and its purpose(s)?

5. What standard of review did the *Renton* Court use to evaluate Renton's ordinance? Was that the proper level of scrutiny?

6. What governmental interests supported Renton's ordinance? Is that a weighty enough interest?

7. How directly did Renton's ordinance advance its interests?

8. What channels remained open for the regulated speech?

One of the major criticisms of the Secondary Effects Doctrine is that it is difficult to cabin its scope in a principled manner. A critic could argue that the government can nearly always proffer a purpose that is content neutral, as the *Renton* Court defined the term. For example, Texas could have argued that it prohibited flag desecration, not because it disagreed with the content of the message sent by flag burners, but because of the likely secondary harm that would result from the desecration of the flag and that, therefore, its ban was content neutral. The federal government proffered this line of argument in *Boos v. Barry*, 485 U.S. 312 (1988), to support a provision of the District of Columbia Code that precluded "the display of any sign within 500 feet of a foreign embassy if that sign tends to bring that foreign government into 'public odium' or 'public disrepute.'" *Id.* at 315. Three individuals sought to carry signs criticizing the governments of the Soviet Union and Nicaragua on public sidewalks within 500 feet of the embassies of those governments

Following *Renton*, the government argued, *inter alia*, that its real concern was with preventing the secondary effects of such speech activity, "namely, our international law obligation to shield diplomats from speech that offends their dignity." *Id.* at 320. The Court distinguished the two cases, limiting *Renton* to situations where "the justifications for regulation have nothing to do with content, *i.e.*, the desire to suppress crime has nothing to do with the actual films being shown inside adult movie theaters." *Id.* According to *Boos*, *Renton* did not apply to "[r]egulations that focus on the direct impact of speech on its audience" because such regulations were not content neutral. *Id.* at 321. The Court concluded that the sign restriction in *Boos* was content based because it restricted speech due to its communicative impact on listeners, not the secondary effects of picket signs within 500 feet of embassies: "[The Respondents] do not point to congestion, to interference with ingress or egress, to visual clutter, or to the need to protect the security of embassies. Rather, they rely on the need to protect the dignity of foreign diplomatic personnel by shielding them from speech that is critical of their governments. This justification focuses *only* on the content of the speech and the direct impact that speech has on its listeners." *Id.*

Given that the ordinance imposed a content-based restriction on political speech in a public forum, the Court applied strict scrutiny. Even assuming that the government's interest in protecting the dignity of foreign diplomatic personnel was compelling, the Court concluded that the law was not narrowly tailored to serve that interest. Consistent with another federal law implementing the Vienna Convention, Congress could have prohibited only "willful acts or attempts to 'intimidate, coerce, threaten, or harass a foreign official.'" *Id.* at 324. Thus, the law was not the least restrictive way to advance the government's alleged interest. Did the *Boos* Court adequately distinguish *Renton*? Did it successfully cabin the reach of the Secondary Effects Doctrine? Should the doctrine be limited in this way? Why or why not?

Up to this point, you have learned that the key doctrine in the Supreme Court's free speech cases is the distinction between content-neutral and content-based regulations of speech. You have also seen some examples of the Court's struggles applying the distinction in a principled manner. Given these challenges, should the Supreme Court continue to utilize the distinction? If not, how should the Court implement the Free Speech Clause's protections?

4. Key Effect of the Distinction between Content-Based and Content-Neutral Regulations: Strict Scrutiny and Intermediate Scrutiny

a. Introduction

The determination that a government regulation of speech is content based or content neutral carries major implications. The most important is that content-based restrictions on speech generally receive "strict scrutiny" review, while content-neutral restrictions receive "intermediate scrutiny" review. Whether the challenged governmental action regulates pure speech or expressive conduct, the result is similar. *See, e.g., Clark v. Community for Creative Non-Violence*, 468 U.S. 288, 298 (1984) (noting that the *O'Brien* test is analogous to intermediate scrutiny).

b. Strict Scrutiny

You have seen the standard of review labeled strict scrutiny in many other contexts including, most prominently, substantive due process and equal protection. Strict scrutiny in the context of free speech law usually results in a holding that the challenged government regulation of speech is unconstitutional. According to the Supreme Court, when a government regulation infringes on speech based on the speech's content, the government must show that the speech restriction is supported by a compelling state interest and that the restriction is narrowly tailored to achieve that interest. *Turner Broad. Sys., Inc., v. FCC*, 512 U.S. 622, 642 (1994). We have already reviewed a number of cases where the Supreme Court utilized this analysis, including *Texas v. Johnson, Citizens United v. FEC, Simon & Schuster, Inc. v. Members of the New York State Crime Victims Board*, and *Boos v. Barry*. Below is one of the Court's most recent applications of strict scrutiny, which involves a state restriction on the sale of violent video games. As you read this case, consider whether the majority or the dissent has the better view of strict scrutiny.

Brown v. Entertainment Merchants Association

564 U.S. 786 (2011)

Justice Scalia delivered the opinion of the Court.

I

Cal. Civ. Code Ann. §§ 1746–1746.5 [the "Act"] prohibits the sale or rental of "violent video games" to minors, and requires their packaging to be labeled "18." The Act covers games "in which the range of options available to a player includes killing, maiming, dismembering, or sexually assaulting an image of a human being, if those acts are depicted" in a manner that "[a] reasonable person, considering the game as a whole, would find appeals to a deviant or morbid interest of minors," that is "patently offensive to prevailing standards in the community as to what is suitable for minors," and that "causes the game, as a whole, to lack serious literary, artistic, political, or scientific value for minors." Violation of the Act is punishable by a civil fine of up to $1,000.

II

California correctly acknowledges that video games qualify for First Amendment protection. The Free Speech Clause exists principally to protect discourse on public matters, but we have long recognized that it is difficult to distinguish politics from entertainment, and dangerous to try. "Everyone is familiar with instances of propaganda through fiction. What is one man's amusement, teaches another's doctrine." Like the protected books, plays, and movies that preceded them, video games communicate ideas — and even social messages — through many familiar literary devices (such as characters, dialogue, plot, and music) and through features distinctive to the medium (such as the player's interaction with the virtual world). That suffices to confer First Amendment protection.[4] Under our Constitution, "esthetic and moral judgments about art and literature ... are for the individual to make, not for the Government to decree, even with the mandate or approval of a majority." And whatever the challenges of applying the Constitution to ever-advancing technology, "the basic principles of freedom of speech and the press, like the First Amendment's command, do not vary" when a new and different medium for communication appears.

The most basic of those principles is this: "[A]s a general matter, ... government has no power to restrict expression because of its message, its ideas, its subject matter, or its content." There are of course exceptions. " 'From 1791 to the present,'... the First Amendment has 'permitted restrictions upon the content of speech in a few limited areas,' and has never 'include[d] a freedom to disregard these traditional limitations.' " These limited areas — such as obscenity, *Roth v. United States*, 354 U.S. 476, 483 (1957), incitement, *Brandenburg v. Ohio*, 395 U.S. 444, 447–49 (1969) (*per curiam*), and fighting words, *Chaplinsky v. New Hampshire*, 315 U.S. 568, 572 (1942) — represent "well-defined and narrowly limited classes of speech, the prevention and punishment of which have never been thought to raise any Constitutional problem."

Last Term, in *Stevens*, we held that new categories of unprotected speech may not be added to the list by a legislature that concludes certain speech is too harmful to be tolerated. [*United States v. Stevens*, 559 U.S. 460 (2010).] *Stevens* concerned a federal statute purporting to criminalize the creation, sale, or possession of certain depictions of animal cruelty. We held that statute to be an impermissible content-based restriction on speech. There was no American tradition of forbidding the *depiction of* animal cruelty — though States have long had laws against *committing* it.

---

4. [Footnote moved — ed.] Crudely violent video games, tawdry TV shows, and cheap novels and magazines are no less forms of speech than The Divine Comedy, and restrictions upon them must survive strict scrutiny. Even if we can see in them "nothing of any possible value to society..., they are as much entitled to the protection of free speech as the best of literature."

"Maybe there are some categories of speech that have been historically unprotected, but have not yet been specifically identified or discussed as such in our case law." But without persuasive evidence that a novel restriction on content is part of a long (if heretofore unrecognized) tradition of proscription, a legislature may not revise the "judgment [of] the American people," embodied in the First Amendment, "that the benefits of its restrictions on the Government outweigh the costs."

[The majority then considered — and rejected — California's argument that strict scrutiny should not apply because the State's restriction on violent video games should be viewed as an extension of the obscenity exception.]

III

Because the Act imposes a restriction on the content of protected speech, it is invalid unless California can demonstrate that it passes strict scrutiny — that is, unless it is justified by a compelling government interest and is narrowly drawn to serve that interest. The State must specifically identify an "actual problem" in need of solving, and the curtailment of free speech must be actually necessary to the solution. That is a demanding standard. "It is rare that a regulation restricting speech because of its content will ever be permissible."

California cannot meet that standard. California relies primarily on the research of Dr. Craig Anderson and a few other research psychologists whose studies purport to show a connection between exposure to violent video games and harmful effects on children. These studies have been rejected by every court to consider them, and with good reason: They do not prove that violent video games *cause* minors to *act* aggressively (which would at least be a beginning). Instead, "[n]early all of the research is based on correlation, not evidence of causation, and most of the studies suffer from significant, admitted flaws in methodology." They show at best some correlation between exposure to violent entertainment and minuscule real-world effects, such as children's feeling more aggressive or making louder noises in the few minutes after playing a violent game than after playing a nonviolent game.

Even taking for granted Dr. Anderson's conclusions that violent video games produce some effect on children's feelings of aggression, those effects are both small and indistinguishable from effects produced by other media. In his testimony in a similar lawsuit, Dr. Anderson admitted that the "effect sizes" of children's exposure to violent video games are "about the same" as that produced by their exposure to violence on television. And he admits that the *same* effects have been found when children watch cartoons starring Bugs Bunny or the Road Runner, or when they play video games like Sonic the Hedgehog that are rated "E" (appropriate for all ages), or even when they "vie[w] a picture of a gun."[8]

---

8. Nor is JUSTICE ALITO correct in attributing to us the view that "violent video games really present no serious problem." Perhaps they do present a problem, and perhaps none of us would allow our own children to play them. But there are all sorts of "problems" — some of them surely more serious than this one — that cannot be addressed by governmental restriction of free expression: for example, the problem of encouraging anti-Semitism (*National Socialist Party of America v. Skokie,*

Of course, California has (wisely) declined to restrict Saturday morning cartoons, the sale of games rated for young children, or the distribution of pictures of guns. The consequence is that its regulation is wildly underinclusive when judged against its asserted justification, which in our view is alone enough to defeat it. Underinclusiveness raises serious doubts about whether the government is in fact pursuing the interest it invokes, rather than disfavoring a particular speaker or viewpoint. Here, California has singled out the purveyors of video games for disfavored treatment—at least when compared to booksellers, cartoonists, and movie producers—and has given no persuasive reason why.

The Act is also seriously underinclusive in another respect—and a respect that renders irrelevant the contentions of the concurrence and the dissents that video games are qualitatively different from other portrayals of violence. The California Legislature is perfectly willing to leave this dangerous, mind-altering material in the hands of children so long as one parent (or even an aunt or uncle) says it's OK. And there are not even any requirements as to how this parental or avuncular relationship is to be verified; apparently the child's or putative parent's, aunt's, or uncle's say-so suffices. That is not how one addresses a serious social problem.

California claims that the Act is justified in aid of parental authority: By requiring that the purchase of violent video games can be made only by adults, the Act ensures that parents can decide what games are appropriate. At the outset, we note our doubts that punishing third parties for conveying protected speech to children *just in case* their parents disapprove of that speech is a proper governmental means of aiding parental authority. Accepting that position would largely vitiate the rule that "only in relatively narrow and well-defined circumstances may government bar public dissemination of protected materials to [minors]."

But leaving that aside, California cannot show that the Act's restrictions meet a substantial need of parents who wish to restrict their children's access to violent video games but cannot do so. The video-game industry has in place a voluntary rating system designed to inform consumers about the content of games. This system does much to ensure that minors cannot purchase seriously violent games on their own, and that parents who care about the matter can readily evaluate the games their children bring home. Filling the remaining modest gap in concerned-parents' control can hardly be a compelling state interest.

And finally, the Act's purported aid to parental authority is vastly overinclusive. Not all of the children who are forbidden to purchase violent video games on their own have parents who *care* whether they purchase violent video games. While some of the legislation's effect may indeed be in support of what some parents of the restricted children actually want, its entire effect is only in support of what the State

---

432 U.S. 43 (1977)), the problem of spreading a political philosophy hostile to the Constitution (*Noto v. United States,* 367 U.S. 290 (1961)), or the problem of encouraging disrespect for the Nation's flag (*Texas v. Johnson,* 491 U.S. 397 (1989)).

thinks parents *ought* to want. This is not the narrow tailoring to "assisting parents" that restriction of First Amendment rights requires.

* * *

California's effort to regulate violent video games is the latest episode in a long series of failed attempts to censor violent entertainment for minors. Our task is only to say whether or not such works constitute a "well-defined and narrowly limited clas[s] of speech, the prevention and punishment of which have never been thought to raise any Constitutional problem" (the answer plainly is no); and if not, whether the regulation of such works is justified by that high degree of necessity we have described as a compelling state interest (it is not). Even where the protection of children is the object, the constitutional limits on governmental action apply.

Justice Alito, with whom The Chief Justice joins, concurring in the judgment.

The California statute that is before us in this case represents a pioneering effort to address what the state legislature and others regard as a potentially serious social problem: the effect of exceptionally violent video games on impressionable minors, who often spend countless hours immersed in the alternative worlds that these games create. [Justice Alito concluded that the Act was unconstitutionally vague and then contended that a more narrowly drawn statute might be constitutional.]

II

B

Citing the video-game industry's voluntary rating system, the Court argues that the California law does not "meet a substantial need of parents who wish to restrict their children's access to violent video games but cannot do so." The Court does not mention the fact that the industry adopted this system in response to the threat of federal regulation, a threat that the Court's opinion may now be seen as largely eliminating. Nor does the Court acknowledge that compliance with this system at the time of the enactment of the California law left much to be desired—or that future enforcement may decline if the video-game industry perceives that any threat of government regulation has vanished. Nor does the Court note, as Justice Breyer points out, that many parents today are simply not able to monitor their children's use of computers and gaming devices.

C

[T]he Court is far too quick to dismiss the possibility that the experience of playing video games (and the effects on minors of playing violent video games) may be very different from anything that we have seen before.

Today's most advanced video games create realistic alternative worlds in which millions of players immerse themselves for hours on end. These games feature visual imagery and sounds that are strikingly realistic, and in the near future video-game graphics may be virtually indistinguishable from actual video footage. It is also forecast that video games will soon provide sensory feedback. By wearing a special vest or other device, a player will be able to experience physical sensations supposedly felt by a character on the screen. Some *amici* who support respondents foresee the day when " 'virtual-reality shoot-'em-ups' " will allow children to " 'actually feel the splatting blood from the blown-off head' " of a victim.

Persons who play video games also have an unprecedented ability to participate in the events that take place in the virtual worlds that these games create. Players can create their own video-game characters and can use photos to produce characters that closely resemble actual people. A person playing a sophisticated game can make a multitude of choices and can thereby alter the course of the action in the game. While the action in older games was often directed with buttons or a joystick, players dictate the action in newer games by engaging in the same motions that they desire a character in the game to perform. For example, a player who wants a video-game character to swing a baseball bat—either to hit a ball or smash a skull—could bring that about by simulating the motion of actually swinging a bat.

In some of these games, the violence is astounding. Victims by the dozens are killed with every imaginable implement, including machine guns, shotguns, clubs, hammers, axes, swords, and chainsaws. Victims are dismembered, decapitated, disemboweled, set on fire, and chopped into little pieces. They cry out in agony and beg for mercy. Blood gushes, splatters, and pools. Severed body parts and gobs of human remains are graphically shown. In some games, points are awarded based, not only on the number of victims killed, but on the killing technique employed.

It also appears that there is no antisocial theme too base for some in the video-game industry to exploit. There are games in which a player can take on the identity and reenact the killings carried out by the perpetrators of the murders at Columbine High School and Virginia Tech. The objective of one game is to rape a mother and her daughters; in another, the goal is to rape Native American women. There is a game in which players engage in "ethnic cleansing" and can choose to gun down African-Americans, Latinos, or Jews. In still another game, players attempt to fire a rifle shot into the head of President Kennedy as his motorcade passes by the Texas School Book Depository.

If the technological characteristics of the sophisticated games that are likely to be available in the near future are combined with the characteristics of the most violent games already marketed, the result will be games that allow troubled teens to experience in an extraordinarily personal and vivid way what it would be like to carry out unspeakable acts of violence.

The Court is untroubled by this possibility. According to the Court, the "interactive" nature of video games is "nothing new" because "all literature is interactive." [But] video games are "far more concretely interactive." [O]nly an extraordinarily imaginative reader who reads a description of a killing in a literary work will experience that event as vividly as he might if he played the role of the killer in a video game. To take an example, think of a person who reads the passage in Crime and Punishment in which Raskolnikov kills the old pawn broker with an axe. Compare that reader with a video-game player who creates an avatar that bears his own image; who sees a realistic image of the victim and the scene of the killing in high definition and in three dimensions;

who is forced to decide whether or not to kill the victim and decides to do so; who then pretends to grasp an axe, to raise it above the head of the victim, and then to bring it down; who hears the thud of the axe hitting her head and her cry of pain; who sees her split skull and feels the sensation of blood on his face and hands. For most people, the two experiences will not be the same.

When all of the characteristics of video games are taken into account, there is certainly a reasonable basis for thinking that the experience of playing a video game may be quite different from the experience of reading a book, listening to a radio broadcast, or viewing a movie. And if this is so, then for at least some minors, the effects of playing violent video games may also be quite different. The Court acts prematurely in dismissing this possibility out of hand. If differently framed statutes are enacted by the States or by the Federal Government, we can consider the constitutionality of those laws when cases challenging them are presented to us.

JUSTICE THOMAS, dissenting.

The Court's decision today does not comport with the original public understanding of the First Amendment. The majority strikes down, as facially unconstitutional, a state law that prohibits the direct sale or rental of certain video games to minors because the law "abridg[es] the freedom of speech." But I do not think the First Amendment stretches that far. The practices and beliefs of the founding generation establish that "the freedom of speech," as originally understood, does not include a right to speak to minors (or a right of minors to access speech) without going through the minors' parents or guardians.

I

When interpreting a constitutional provision, "the goal is to discern the most likely public understanding of [that] provision at the time it was adopted." Because the Constitution is a written instrument, "its meaning does not alter." "That which it meant when adopted, it means now."

In my view, the "practices and beliefs held by the Founders" reveal another category of excluded speech: speech to minor children bypassing their parents. The historical evidence shows that the founding generation believed parents had absolute authority over their minor children and expected parents to use that authority to direct the proper development of their children. It would be absurd to suggest that such a society understood "the freedom of speech" to include a right to speak to minors (or a corresponding right of minors to access speech) without going through the minors' parents. [Justice Thomas' detailed discussion of the historical evidence relating to parental authority to raise and educate their children is omitted.]

II

A

In light of this history, the Framers could not possibly have understood "the freedom of speech" to include an unqualified right to speak to minors. As a consequence, I do not believe that laws limiting such speech—for example, by requiring parental consent to speak to a minor—"abridg[e] the freedom of speech" within the original meaning of the First Amendment.

B

Although much has changed in this country since the Revolution, the notion that parents have authority over their children and that the law can support that authority persists today. For example, at least some States make it a crime to lure or entice a minor away from the minor's parent. Every State in the Union still establishes a minimum age for marriage without parental or judicial consent. And minors remain subject to curfew laws across the country and cannot unilaterally consent to most medical procedures.

The Court's constitutional jurisprudence "historically has reflected Western civilization concepts of the family as a unit with broad parental authority over minor children." Under that case law, "legislature[s] [can] properly conclude that parents and others, teachers for example, who have ... primary responsibility for children's well-being are entitled to the support of laws designed to aid discharge of that responsibility."

III

Under any of this Court's standards for a facial First Amendment challenge, this one must fail. Even assuming that video games are speech, in most applications the California law does not implicate the First Amendment. All that the law does is prohibit the direct sale or rental of a violent video game to a minor by someone other than the minor's parent, grandparent, aunt, uncle, or legal guardian. Where a minor has a parent or guardian, as is usually true, the law does not prevent that minor from obtaining a violent video game with his parent's or guardian's help. In the typical case, the only speech affected is speech that bypasses a minor's parent or guardian. Because such speech does not fall within "the freedom of speech" as originally understood, California's law does not ordinarily implicate the First Amendment and is not facially unconstitutional.

JUSTICE BREYER, dissenting.

Applying traditional First Amendment analysis, I would uphold the statute as constitutional on its face and would consequently reject the industries' facial challenge.

I

B

In determining whether the statute is unconstitutional, the special First Amendment category I find relevant is the category of "protection of children." This Court has held that the "power of the state to control the conduct of children reaches beyond the scope of its authority over adults." And the "'regulatio[n] of communication addressed to [children] need not conform to the requirements of the [F]irst [A]mendment in the same way as those applicable to adults.'"

III

Like the majority, I believe that the California law must be "narrowly tailored" to further a "compelling interest," without there being a "less restrictive" alternative that would be "at least as effective." I would not apply this strict standard "mechanically." Rather, in applying it, I would evaluate the degree to which the statute injures speech-related interests, the nature of the potentially-justifying "compelling interests," the degree to which the statute furthers that interest, the nature and effectiveness of possible alternatives, and, in light of this evaluation, whether, overall, "the statute works speech-related harm out of proportion to the benefits that the statute seeks to provide."

A

California's law imposes no more than a modest restriction on expression. The statute prevents no one from playing a video game, it prevents no adult from buying a video game, and it prevents no child or adolescent from obtaining a game provided a parent is willing to help. All it prevents is a child or adolescent from buying, without a parent's assistance, a gruesomely violent video game of a kind that the industry *itself* tells us it wants to keep out of the hands of those under the age of 17.

Nor is the statute, if upheld, likely to create a precedent that would adversely affect other media, say films, or videos, or books. A typical video game involves a significant amount of physical activity. And pushing buttons that achieve an interactive, virtual form of target practice (using images of human beings as targets), while containing an expressive component, is not just like watching a typical movie.

B

The interest that California advances in support of the statute is compelling. As this Court has previously described that interest, it consists of both (1) the "basic" parental claim "to authority in their own household to direct the rearing of their children," which makes it proper to enact "laws designed to aid discharge of [parental] responsibility," and (2) the State's "independent interest in the well-being of its youth." And where these interests work in tandem, it is not fatally "underinclusive" for a State to advance its interests in protecting children against the special harms present in an interactive video game medium through a default rule that still allows parents to provide their children with what their parents wish.

At the same time, there is considerable evidence that California's statute significantly furthers this compelling interest ["in protecting the physical and psychological well-being of minors"]. Video games can help develop habits, accustom the player to performance of the task, and reward the player for performing that task well. Why else would the Armed Forces incorporate video games into its training?

There are many scientific studies that support California's views. Social scientists, for example, have found *causal* evidence that playing these games results in harm. Longitudinal studies, which measure changes over time, have found that increased exposure to violent video games causes an increase in aggression over the same period. Experimental studies in laboratories have found that subjects randomly assigned to play a violent video game subsequently displayed more characteristics of aggression than those who played nonviolent games.

Surveys of 8th and 9th grade students have found a correlation between playing violent video games and aggression. Cutting-edge neuroscience has shown that "virtual violence in video game playing results in those neural patterns that are considered characteristic for aggressive cognition and behavior." And "meta-analyses," *i.e.,* studies of all the studies, have concluded that exposure to violent video games "was positively associated with aggressive behavior, aggressive cognition, and aggressive affect," and that "playing violent video games is a *causal* risk factor for long-term harmful outcomes."

Some of these studies take care to explain in a commonsense way why video games are potentially more harmful than, say, films or books or television. In essence, they say that the closer a child's behavior comes, not to watching, but to *acting* out horrific violence, the greater the potential psychological harm.

Experts debate the conclusions of all these studies. Like many, perhaps most, studies of human behavior, each study has its critics, and some of those critics have produced studies of their own in which they reach different conclusions. I, like most judges, lack the social science expertise to say definitively who is right. But associations of public health professionals who do possess that expertise have reviewed many of these studies and found a significant risk that violent video games, when compared with more passive media, are particularly likely to cause children harm ... : "Studies of these rapidly growing and ever-more-sophisticated types of media have indicated that the effects of child-initiated virtual violence may be *even more profound than those of passive media* such as television. In many games the child or teenager is 'embedded' in the game and uses a 'joystick' (handheld controller) that enhances both the experience and the aggressive feelings."

Unlike the majority, I would find sufficient grounds in these studies and expert opinions for this Court to defer to an elected legislature's conclusion that the video games in question are particularly likely to harm children. The majority, in reaching its own, opposite conclusion about the validity of the relevant studies, grants the legislature no deference at all.

C

I can find no "less restrictive" alternative to California's law that would be "at least as effective." The majority points to a voluntary alternative: The industry tries to prevent those under 17 from buying extremely violent games by labeling those games with an "M" (Mature) and encouraging retailers to restrict their sales to those 17 and older. But this voluntary system has serious enforcement gaps. [A]s of the FTC's most recent update to Congress, 20% of those under 17 are still able to buy M-rated video games, and, breaking down sales by store, one finds that this number rises to nearly 50% in the case of one large national chain. And the industry could easily revert back to the substantial noncompliance that existed in 2004, particularly after today's broad ruling reduces the industry's incentive to police itself.

The industry also argues for an alternative technological solution, namely "filtering at the console level." Brief for Respondents 53. But it takes only a quick search of the Internet to find guides explaining how to circumvent any such technological controls. YouTube viewers, for example, have watched one of those guides (called "How to bypass parental controls on the Xbox 360") more than 47,000 times.

IV

This case is ultimately less about censorship than it is about education. Our Constitution cannot succeed in securing the liberties it seeks to protect unless we can raise future generations committed cooperatively to making our system of government work. Education, however, is about choices. Sometimes, children need to learn by making choices for themselves. Other times, choices are made for children—by their parents, by their teachers, and by the people acting democratically through their governments. In my view, the First Amendment does not disable government from helping parents make such a choice here—a choice not to have their children buy extremely violent, interactive video games, which they more than reasonably fear pose only the risk of harm to those children.

Exercise 19:

1. How does the majority determine whether a category of speech should fall outside the protection of the First Amendment? Are history and tradition a proper way to make this determination? Is this historical approach the only way? How do Justice Thomas and Justice Breyer argue for excepting violent video games from the generally broad protection afforded speech under the First Amendment?

2. If speech directed at minors involving sex can be prohibited, *see Ginsberg v. New York*, 390 U.S. 629 (1968), why cannot a state also limit speech to minors that takes the form of (extremely) violent video games?

3. The majority and Justice Breyer both claim to be applying strict scrutiny. Do they actually use the same test? If so, why do they reach opposite conclusions? If not, what are the relevant differences between the strict scrutiny standard that the majority employs and the one Justice Breyer uses?

4. The majority contends that the California law is underinclusive in at least two ways. What are those ways? How does Justice Breyer respond to such arguments? Which side has the better position on underinclusiveness and why?

5. The Entertainment Software Rating Board (the "ESRB") has established a voluntary rating system that assigns age-specific ratings to each video game—*e.g.*, EC (Early Childhood); E (Everyone); E10+ (Everyone 10 and older); T (Teens); M (17 and older); and AO (Adults Only—18 and older). In light of this rating system, does the California law substantially advance the state's interest in helping parents control which video games their children purchase or use? Why does Justice Breyer take the remaining gap in concerned-parents' control over the materials their children access to be compelling?

6. The City of Jacksonville enacts an ordinance that prohibits drive-in movie theaters from showing films containing nudity if the drive-in theater's screen is visible from a public street or place. What level of scrutiny should apply? Does the ordinance survive that level of scrutiny? *See Erznoznik v. City of Jacksonville*, 422 U.S. 205 (1977).

7. An Illinois statute generally prohibits the picketing of residences but exempts "the peaceful picketing of a place of employment involved in a labor dispute." Several

individuals are convicted under the statute for participating in a peaceful demonstration on the public sidewalk in front of the home of the Mayor of Chicago, protesting the Mayor's alleged failure to support the busing of schoolchildren to achieve racial integration. The state asserts its interest in protecting residential privacy. Is the Illinois statute constitutional? *See Carey v. Brown*, 447 U.S. 455 (1980).

8. Canon 7C(1) of the Florida Code of Judicial Conduct imposes limits on fundraising in judicial elections. Specifically, Canon 7C(1) states that a candidate for judicial office "shall not personally solicit campaign funds, or solicit attorneys for publicly stated support, but may establish committees ... [that solicit and spend] funds for the candidate's campaign and [that] obtain public statements of support." A judicial candidate drafts, signs, and distributes a letter to local voters announcing her candidacy, which states: "An early contribution of $25, $50, $100, $250, or $500 made payable to my campaign will help raise the funds needed to launch the campaign and get our message out to the public. I thank you in advance for your support in meeting the primary election fundraising goals." The Florida Bar files a complaint against her, and the candidate is publicly reprimanded and assessed the costs of the proceeding. On appeal, should the Court find the Canon constitutional? *See Williams-Yulee v. Florida Bar*, 575 U.S. 433 (2015).

c. Intermediate Scrutiny

Though you have also encountered the standard of review labeled intermediate scrutiny in other contexts, its use in free speech law is similar, though slightly different. In free speech law, the government bears the burden of showing that the challenged content-neutral regulation: (1) serves a significant or important governmental interest; (2) utilizes means that are "narrowly tailored"; and (3) leaves open ample alternative channels for communication. *Ward v. Rock Against Racism*, 491 U.S. 781 (1989), below, clarified this test.

Ward v. Rock Against Racism
491 U.S. 781 (1989)

JUSTICE KENNEDY delivered the opinion of the Court.

In the southeast portion of New York City's Central Park, about 10 blocks upward from the park's beginning point at 59th Street, there is an amphitheater and stage structure known as the Naumberg Acoustic Bandshell. The bandshell faces west across the remaining width of the park. In close proximity to the bandshell, and lying within the directional path of its sound, is a grassy open area called the Sheep Meadow. The city has designated the Sheep Meadow as a quiet area for passive recreations like reclining, walking, and reading. Just beyond the park, and also within the potential sound range of the bandshell, are the apartments and residences of Central Park West.

This case arises from the city's attempt to regulate the volume of amplified music at the bandshell so the performances are satisfactory to the audience without intruding upon those who use the Sheep Meadow or live on Central Park West....

The city's regulation requires bandshell performers to use sound-amplification equipment and a sound technician provided by the city. The challenge to this volume control technique comes from the sponsor of a rock concert. The trial court sustained the noise control measures, but the Court of Appeals for the Second Circuit reversed. We granted certiorari to resolve the important First Amendment issues presented by the case.

I

Rock Against Racism, respondent in this case, is an unincorporated association which, in its own words, is "dedicated to the espousal and promotion of antiracist views." Each year from 1979 through 1986, RAR has sponsored a program of speeches and rock music at the bandshell. RAR has furnished the sound equipment and sound technician used by the various performing groups at these annual events.

Over the years, the city received numerous complaints about excessive sound amplification at respondent's concerts from park users and residents of areas adjacent to the park. On some occasions RAR was less than cooperative when city officials asked that the volume be reduced....

The city then undertook to develop comprehensive New York City Parks Department Use Guidelines for the Naumberg Bandshell. A principal problem to be addressed by the guidelines was controlling the volume of amplified sound at bandshell events. A major concern was that at some bandshell performances the event sponsors had been unable to "provide the amplification levels required and 'crowds unhappy with the sound became disappointed or unruly.'" The city found that this problem had several causes, including inadequate sound equipment, sound technicians who were either unskilled at mixing sound outdoors or unfamiliar with the acoustics of the bandshell and its surroundings, and the like. Because some performers compensated for poor sound mix by raising volume, these factors tended to exacerbate the problem of excess noise.

The city considered various solutions to the sound-amplification problem. The idea of a fixed decibel limit for all performers using the bandshell was rejected because the impact on listeners of a single decibel level is not constant, but varies in response to changes in air temperature, foliage, audience size, and like factors. The city also rejected the possibility of employing a sound technician to operate the equipment provided by the various sponsors of bandshell events, because the city's technician might have had difficulty satisfying the needs of sponsors while operating unfamiliar, and perhaps inadequate, sound equipment. Instead, the city concluded that the most effective way to achieve adequate but not excessive sound amplification would be for the city to furnish high quality sound equipment and retain an independent, experienced sound technician for all performances at the bandshell. After an extensive search the city hired a private sound company capable of meeting the needs of all the varied users of the bandshell.

The Use Guidelines were promulgated on March 21, 1986. After learning that it would be expected to comply with the guidelines at its upcoming annual concert in May 1986, respondent [went] to the District Court and filed a motion for an injunction against the enforcement of certain aspects of the guidelines. The District Court preliminarily enjoined enforcement of the sound-amplification rule on May 1, 1986.

Under the protection of the injunction, and alone among users of the bandshell in the 1986 season, RAR was permitted to use its own sound equipment and technician, just as it had done in prior years. RAR's 1986 concert again generated complaints about excessive noise from park users and nearby residents.

After the concert, respondent amended its complaint to seek damages and a declaratory judgment striking down the guidelines as facially invalid. After hearing five days of testimony about various aspects of the guidelines, the District Court issued its decision upholding the sound-amplification guideline.

The Court of Appeals reversed.... We granted certiorari to clarify the legal standard applicable to governmental regulation of the time, place, or manner of protected speech. Because the Court of Appeals erred in requiring the city to prove that its regulation was the least intrusive means of furthering its legitimate governmental interests, and because the ordinance is valid on its face, we now reverse.

II

Music is one of the oldest forms of human expression. From Plato's discourse in the Republic to the totalitarian state in our own times, rulers have known its capacity to appeal to the intellect and to the emotions, and have censored musical compositions to serve the needs of the state. The Constitution prohibits any like attempts in our own legal order. Music, as a form of expression and communication, is protected under the First Amendment. In the case before us the performances apparently consisted of remarks by speakers, as well as rock music, but the case has been presented as one in which the constitutional challenge is to the city's regulation of the musical aspects of the concert; and, based on the principle we have stated, the city's guideline must meet the demands of the First Amendment. The parties do not appear to dispute that proposition.

... [T]he city justifies its guideline as a regulatory measure to limit and control noise. Here the bandshell was open, apparently, to all performers; and we decide the case as one in which the bandshell is a public forum for performances in which the government's right to regulate expression is subject to the protections of the First Amendment. *Perry Education Assn. v. Perry Local Educators' Assn.*, 460 U.S. 37, 45 (1983). Our cases make clear, however, that even in a public forum the government may impose reasonable restrictions on the time, place, or manner of protected speech, provided the restrictions "are justified without reference to the content of the regulated speech, that they are narrowly tailored to serve a significant governmental interest, and that they leave open ample alternative channels for communication of the information." We consider these requirements in turn.

A

The principal inquiry in determining content neutrality, in speech cases generally and in time, place, or manner cases in particular, is whether the government has adopted a regulation of speech because of disagreement with the message it conveys. The government's purpose is the controlling consideration. A regulation that serves purposes unrelated to the content of expression is deemed neutral, even if it has an incidental effect on some speakers or messages but not others. See *Renton v. Playtime Theatres, Inc.*, 475 U.S. 41 (1986). Government regulation of expressive activity is content neutral so long as it is "*justified* without reference to the content of the regulated speech."

The principal justification for the sound-amplification guideline is the city's desire to control noise levels at bandshell events, in order to retain the character of the Sheep Meadow and its more sedate activities, and to avoid undue intrusion into residential areas and other areas of the park. This justification for the guideline "ha[s] nothing to do with content," and it satisfies the requirement that time, place, or manner regulations be content neutral.

B

The city's regulation is also "narrowly tailored to serve a significant governmental interest." Despite respondent's protestations to the contrary, it can no longer be doubted that government "ha[s] a substantial interest in protecting its citizens from unwelcome noise." This interest is perhaps at its greatest when government seeks to protect " 'the well-being, tranquility, and privacy of the home,' " but it is by no means limited to that context, for the government may act to protect even such traditional public forums as city streets and parks from excessive noise.

We think it also apparent that the city's interest in ensuring the sufficiency of sound amplification at bandshell events is a substantial one. The record indicates that inadequate sound amplification has had an adverse affect on the ability of some audiences to hear and enjoy performances at the bandshell.

The Court of Appeals erred in sifting through all the available or imagined alternative means of regulating sound volume in order to determine whether the city's solution was "the least intrusive means." This "less-restrictive-alternative analysis … has never been a part of the inquiry into the validity of a time, place, and manner regulation." Instead, our cases quite clearly hold that restrictions on the time, place, or manner of protected speech are not invalid "simply because there is some imaginable alternative that might be less burdensome on speech."

The Court of Appeals apparently drew its least-intrusive-means requirement from *United States v. O'Brien*, 391 U.S., at 377, the case in which we established the standard for judging the validity of restrictions on expressive conduct. The court's reliance was misplaced, however, for we have held that the *O'Brien* test "in the last analysis is little, if any, different from the standard applied to time, place, or manner restrictions." …

Lest any confusion on the point remain, we reaffirm today that a regulation of the time, place, or manner of protected speech must be narrowly tailored to serve the government's legitimate, content-neutral interests but that it need not be the least restrictive or least intrusive means of doing so.[6] Rather, the requirement of narrow

---

6. Respondent contends that our decision last Term in *Boos v. Barry*, 485 U.S. 312 (1988), supports the conclusion that "a regulation is neither precisely drawn nor 'narrowly tailored' if less intrusive means than those employed are available." In *Boos* we concluded that the government regulation at issue was "not narrowly tailored; a less restrictive alternative is readily available." In placing reliance

tailoring is satisfied "so long as the ... regulation promotes a substantial government interest that would be achieved less effectively absent the regulation." To be sure, this standard does not mean that a time, place, or manner regulation may burden substantially more speech than is necessary to further the government's legitimate interests.... So long as the means chosen are not substantially broader than necessary to achieve the government's interest, however, the regulation will not be invalid simply because a court concludes that the government's interest could be adequately served by some less-speech-restrictive alternative.

It is undeniable that the city's substantial interest in limiting sound volume is served in a direct and effective way by the requirement that the city's sound technician control the mixing board during performances. Absent this requirement, the city's interest would have been served less well, as is evidenced by the complaints about excessive volume generated by respondent's past concerts. The Court of Appeals erred in failing to defer to the city's reasonable determination that its interest in controlling volume would be best served by requiring bandshell performers to utilize the city's sound technician.

The city's second content-neutral justification for the guideline, that of ensuring "that the sound amplification [is] sufficient to reach all listeners within the defined concert ground," also supports the city's choice of regulatory methods. By providing competent sound technicians and adequate amplification equipment, the city eliminated the problems of inexperienced technicians and insufficient sound volume that had plagued some bandshell performers in the past. Considering these proffered justifications together, therefore, it is apparent that the guideline directly furthers the city's legitimate governmental interests and that those interests would have been less well served in the absence of the sound-amplification guideline.

C

The final requirement, that the guideline leave open ample alternative channels of communication, is easily met. Indeed, in this respect the guideline is far less restrictive than regulations we have upheld in other cases, for it does not attempt to ban any particular manner or type of expression at a given place or time. Cf. *Renton v. Playtime Theatres, Inc.*, 475 U.S., at 53–54. Rather, the guideline continues to permit expressive activity in the bandshell, and has no effect on the quantity or content of that expression beyond regulating the extent of amplification. That the city's limitations on volume may reduce to some degree the potential audience for respondent's speech is of no consequence, for there has been no showing that the remaining avenues of communication are inadequate.

---

on *Boos*, however, respondent ignores a crucial difference between that case and this. The regulation we invalidated in *Boos* was a content-based ban on displaying signs critical of foreign governments; such content-based restrictions on political speech "must be subjected to the most exacting scrutiny." While time, place, or manner regulations must also be "narrowly tailored" in order to survive First Amendment challenge, we have never applied strict scrutiny in this context. As a result, the same degree of tailoring is not required of these regulations, and least-restrictive-alternative analysis is wholly out of place.

III

The city's sound-amplification guideline is narrowly tailored to serve the substantial and content-neutral governmental interests of avoiding excessive sound volume and providing sufficient amplification within the bandshell concert ground, and the guideline leaves open ample channels of communication. Accordingly, it is valid under the First Amendment as a reasonable regulation of the place and manner of expression. The judgment of the Court of Appeals is

Reversed.

Justice Blackmun concurs in the result.

Justice Marshall, with whom Justice Brennan and Justice Stevens join, dissenting.

No one can doubt that government has a substantial interest in regulating the barrage of excessive sound that can plague urban life. Unfortunately, the majority plays to our shared impatience with loud noise to obscure the damage that it does to our First Amendment rights. Until today, a key safeguard of free speech has been government's obligation to adopt the least intrusive restriction necessary to achieve its goals. By abandoning the requirement that time, place, and manner regulations must be narrowly tailored, the majority replaces constitutional scrutiny with mandatory deference. The majority's willingness to give government officials a free hand in achieving their policy ends extends so far as to permit, in this case, government control of speech in advance of its dissemination. Because New York City's Use Guidelines (Guidelines) are not narrowly tailored to serve its interest in regulating loud noise, and because they constitute an impermissible prior restraint, I dissent.

Exercise 20:

1. What was RAR's protected "speech"? Why was RAR's "speech" protected by the freedom of speech?

2. How did the challenged regulations "infringe" RAR's protected speech?

3. Describe the analysis utilized by Justice Kennedy to evaluate the challenged regulation. Pay particular attention to the narrow tailoring analysis.

4. What part of the majority's analysis did the dissent challenge? Why? Whose position is more faithful to the Free Speech Clause's history and purposes?

5. Relatedly, should free speech doctrine defer to governmental judgments about narrow tailoring of their speech restrictions to their government goals?

6. What was New York's substantial governmental interest?

7. Why was New York's sound amplification regulation "narrowly tailored"?

8. What alternative channels of communication did RAR have?

9. Make an argument that New York's Guidelines constituted an unconstitutional prior restraint.

Intermediate scrutiny of content-neutral regulations of speech can occur in many contexts. For example, *O'Brien* involved a content-neutral prohibition on draft card destruction.

The context in which it is frequently applied is time, place, and manner restrictions in a public forum. A time, place, and manner restriction, as its label indicates, is content neutral, and focuses not on the speech's subject matter or viewpoint, but on when, where, and how the speech occurs. A classic example is a prohibition on "sound trucks," where a loudspeaker is placed on a vehicle to advertise goods or political candidates. Such a regulation limits the manner by which speech is conveyed; it limits its loudness. *See Kovacs v. Cooper*, 336 U.S. 77 (1949) (upholding a conviction under a municipal ordinance banning sound trucks). We will review public forum doctrine, and time, place, and manner restrictions, in more detail, below, in Part [I][3].

5. Government Speech

In the early-1990s, the Supreme Court began—inchoately at first—articulating what has become known as the government speech doctrine. This Doctrine states that the Free Speech Clause does not apply to the government's own speech. This means that, when the government is speaking, the doctrines you learned earlier— such as the rule that content-based regulations generally receive strict scrutiny—do not apply.

One of the difficulties with the doctrine is identifying when the government is actually speaking. This difficulty is especially acute when the government claims as its own the speech of nongovernmental actors. For example, in *Rust v. Sullivan*, 500 U.S. 173 (1991), reviewed above in Part [E][7], the Supreme Court faced a challenge to federal funding limitations that prohibited recipients of Title X family planning funds from advocating abortion as a method of family planning. The Court ruled that such restrictions did not violate the Free Speech Clause, though one of the questions was whether the speech in question was that of the federal government or of the funding recipients.

A recent explanation and application of the doctrine is reprinted below.

Pleasant Grove City, Utah v. Summum

555 U.S. 460 (2009)

Justice Alito delivered the opinion of the Court.

This case presents the question whether the Free Speech Clause of the First Amendment entitles a private group to insist that a municipality permit it to place a permanent monument in a city park in which other donated monuments were previously erected. The Court of Appeals held that the municipality was required to accept the monument because a public park is a traditional public forum. We conclude, however, that although a park is a traditional public forum for speeches and other transitory expressive acts, the display of a permanent monument in a public park is not a form of expression to which forum analysis applies. Instead, the placement of a permanent monument in a public park is best viewed as a form of government speech and is therefore not subject to scrutiny under the Free Speech Clause.

I

A

Pioneer Park (or Park) is a 2.5-acre public park located in the Historic District of Pleasant Grove City (or City) in Utah. The Park currently contains 15 permanent displays, at least 11 of which were donated by private groups or individuals. These include an historic granary, a wishing well, the City's first fire station, a September 11 monument, and a Ten Commandments monument donated by the Fraternal Order of Eagles in 1971.

Respondent Summum is a religious organization founded in 1975 and headquartered in Salt Lake City, Utah. On two separate occasions in 2003, Summum's president wrote a letter to the City's mayor requesting permission to erect a "stone monument," which would contain "the Seven Aphorisms of SUMMUM" and be similar in size and nature to the Ten Commandments monument. The City denied the requests and explained that its practice was to limit monuments in the Park to those that "either (1) directly relate to the history of Pleasant Grove, or (2) were donated by groups with longstanding ties to the Pleasant Grove community." The following year, the City passed a resolution putting this policy into writing.

In May 2005, respondent's president again wrote to the mayor asking to erect a monument, but the letter did not describe the monument, its historical significance, or Summum's connection to the community. The city council rejected this request.

B

In 2005, respondent filed this action against the City asserting, among other claims, that petitioners had violated the Free Speech Clause of the First Amendment by accepting the Ten Commandments monument but rejecting the proposed Seven Aphorisms monument. After the District Court denied Summum's preliminary injunction request, respondent appealed, pressing solely its free speech claim. A panel of the Tenth Circuit reversed.

We granted certiorari, and now reverse.

II

No prior decision of this Court has addressed the application of the Free Speech Clause to a government entity's acceptance of privately donated, permanent monuments for installation in a public park, and the parties disagree sharply about the line of precedents that governs this situation. Petitioners contend that the pertinent cases are those concerning government speech. Respondent, on the other hand, agrees with the Court of Appeals panel that the applicable cases are those that analyze private speech in a public forum. The parties' fundamental disagreement thus centers on the nature of petitioners' conduct when they permitted privately donated monuments to be erected in Pioneer Park. Were petitioners engaging in their own expressive conduct? Or were they providing a forum for private speech?

A

If petitioners were engaging in their own expressive conduct, then the Free Speech Clause has no application. The Free Speech Clause restricts government regulation of private speech; it does not regulate government speech. A government entity has the right to "speak for itself." "[I]t is entitled to say what it wishes," *Rosenberger v. Rector and Visitors of Univ. of Va.*, 515 U.S. 819, 833 (1995), and to select the views that it wants to express. See *Rust v. Sullivan*, 500 U.S. 173, 194 (1991); *National Endowment for Arts v. Finley*, 524 U.S. 569, 598 (1998) (Scalia, J., concurring in judgment) ("It is the very business of government to favor and disfavor points of view"). Indeed, it is not easy to imagine how government could function if it lacked this freedom. "If every citizen were to have a right to insist that no one paid by public funds express a view with which he disagreed, debate over issues of great concern to the public would be limited to those in the private sector, and the process of government as we know it radically transformed."

A government entity may exercise this same freedom to express its views when it receives assistance from private sources for the purpose of delivering a government-controlled message. See *Rosenberger, supra*, at 833 (a government entity may "regulate the content of what is or is not expressed ... when it enlists private entities to convey its own message").

This does not mean that there are no restraints on government speech. For example, government speech must comport with the Establishment Clause. The involvement of public officials in advocacy may be limited by law, regulation, or practice. And of course, a government entity is ultimately "accountable to the electorate and the political process for its advocacy."

B

[Justice Alito summarized public forum doctrine.]

III

There may be situations in which it is difficult to tell whether a government entity is speaking on its own behalf or is providing a forum for private speech, but this case does not present such a situation. Permanent monuments displayed on public property typically represent government speech.

Governments have long used monuments to speak to the public. Since ancient times, kings, emperors, and other rulers have erected statues of themselves to remind their subjects of their authority and power. Triumphal arches, columns, and other monuments have been built to commemorate military victories and sacrifices and other events of civic importance. A monument, by definition, is a structure that is designed as a means of expression. When a government entity arranges for the construction of a monument, it does so because it wishes to convey some thought or instill some feeling in those who see the structure. Neither the Court of Appeals nor respondent disputes the obvious proposition that a monument that is commissioned and financed by a government body for placement on public land constitutes government speech.

Just as government-commissioned and government-financed monuments speak for the government, so do privately financed and donated monuments that the government accepts and displays to the public on government land. It certainly is not common for property owners to open up their property for the installation of permanent monuments that convey a message with which they do not wish to be associated. And because property owners typically do not permit the construction of such monuments on their land, persons who observe donated monuments routinely—and reasonably—interpret them as conveying some message on the property owner's behalf. In this context, there is little chance that observers will fail to appreciate the identity of the speaker. This is true whether the monument is located on private property or on public property.

We think it is fair to say that throughout our Nation's history, the general government practice with respect to donated monuments has been one of selective receptivity. A great many of the monuments that adorn the Nation's public parks were financed with private funds or donated by private parties. Sites managed by the National Park Service contain thousands of privately designed or funded commemorative objects, including the Statue of Liberty, the Marine Corps War Memorial (the Iwo Jima monument), and the Vietnam Veterans Memorial. States and cities likewise have received thousands of donated monuments.

But while government entities regularly accept privately funded or donated monuments, they have exercised selectivity…. Across the country, "municipalities generally exercise editorial control over donated monuments through prior submission requirements, design input, requested modifications, written criteria, and legislative approvals of specific content proposals."

Public parks are often closely identified in the public mind with the government unit that owns the land. City parks—ranging from those in small towns, like Pioneer Park in Pleasant Grove City, to those in major metropolises, like Central Park in New York City—commonly play an important role in defining the identity that a city projects to its own residents and to the outside world. Accordingly, cities and other jurisdictions take some care in accepting donated monuments…. The monuments that are accepted, therefore, are meant to convey and have the effect of conveying a government message, and they thus constitute government speech.

IV

A

In this case, it is clear that the monuments in Pleasant Grove's Pioneer Park represent government speech. Although many of the monuments were not designed or built by the City and were donated in completed form by private entities, the City decided to accept those donations and to display them in the Park. Respondent does not claim that the City ever opened up the Park for the placement of whatever permanent monuments might be offered by private donors. Rather, the City has "effectively controlled" the messages sent by the monuments in the Park by exercising "final approval authority" over their selection. The City has selected those monuments that it wants to display for the purpose of presenting the image of the City that it wishes to project to all who frequent the Park; it has taken ownership of most of the monuments in the Park, including the Ten Commandments monument that is the focus of respondent's concern; and the City has now expressly set forth the criteria it will use in making future selections.

B

Respondent voices the legitimate concern that the government speech doctrine not be used as a subterfuge for favoring certain private speakers over others based on viewpoint. Respondent's suggested solution is to require a government entity accepting a privately donated monument to go through a formal process of adopting a resolution publicly embracing "the message" that the monument conveys.

We see no reason for imposing a requirement of this sort.

V

In sum, we hold that the City's decision to accept certain privately donated monuments while rejecting respondent's is best viewed as a form of government speech. As a result, the City's decision is not subject to the Free Speech Clause, and the Court of Appeals erred in holding otherwise. We therefore reverse.

It is so ordered.

JUSTICE STEVENS, with whom JUSTICE GINSBURG joins, concurring. [Opinion omitted.]

JUSTICE SCALIA, with whom JUSTICE THOMAS joins, concurring. [Opinion omitted.]

JUSTICE BREYER, concurring. [Opinion omitted.]

JUSTICE SOUTER, concurring in the judgment. [Opinion omitted.]

Exercise 21:

1. According to Justice Alito's opinion for the Court, how does one distinguish government speech from private speech?

2. What legal and policy reasons did the Court provide to support its conclusion that government speech is not restricted by the Free Speech Clause? Is either set of reasons persuasive to you? For instance, does the Court's precedent support a government speech doctrine? Or, do the Free Speech Clause's purposes support the doctrine? What are some potential negative consequences of the doctrine?

3. In *Summum*, what was the speech in question—government or private speech—and why? In particular, how did the Court account for the fact that the Ten Commandments monument was donated to the City by a private party?

4. Why could the Court not regulate governmental monuments through the doctrine of content-neutral, time, place, and manner restrictions, which would require application of intermediate scrutiny?

5. A closely-related issue in the lower courts, and in the Supreme Court Justices' minds (in parts of the case not reproduced here), was whether the City's inclusion of a Ten Commandments monument in its park violated the Establishment Clause. Though the City of Pleasant Grove "won" this case, how does its victory here set it up for an Establishment Clause challenge? (You will be able to better answer this question once you have covered **Chapter 3**.)

Matal v. Tam
137 S. Ct. 1744 (2017)

JUSTICE ALITO announced the judgment of the Court and delivered the opinion of the Court with respect to Parts I, II, and III-A, and an opinion with respect to Parts III-B, III-C, and IV, in which THE CHIEF JUSTICE, JUSTICE THOMAS, and JUSTICE BREYER join.

This case concerns a dance-rock band's application for federal trademark registration of the band's name, "The Slants." "Slants" is a derogatory term for persons of Asian descent, and members of the band are Asian-Americans. But the band members believe that by taking that slur as the name of their group, they will help to "reclaim" the term and drain its denigrating force.

The Patent and Trademark Office (PTO) denied the application based on a provision of federal law prohibiting the registration of trademarks that may "disparage ... or bring ... into contemp[t] or disrepute" any "persons, living or dead." 15 U.S.C. § 1052(a) [the "disparagement clause"]. We now hold that this provision violates the Free Speech Clause of the First Amendment. It offends a bedrock First Amendment principle: Speech may not be banned on the ground that it expresses ideas that offend.

I

A

"The principle underlying trademark protection is that distinctive marks—words, names, symbols, and the like—can help distinguish a particular artisan's goods from those of others." A trademark "designate [s] the goods as the product of a particular trader" and "protect[s] his good will against the sale of another's product as his." It helps consumers identify goods and services that they wish to purchase, as well as those they want to avoid.

"[F]ederal law does not create trademarks." Trademarks and their precursors have ancient origins, and trademarks were protected at common law and in equity at the time of the founding of our country. There are now more than two million marks that have active federal certificates of registration. This system of federal registration helps to ensure that trademarks are fully protected and supports the free flow of commerce. "[N]ational protection of trademarks is desirable," we have explained, "because trademarks foster competition and the maintenance of quality by securing to the producer the benefits of good reputation."

B

Federal registration, however, "confers important legal rights and benefits on trademark owners who register their marks." Registration on the principal register (1) "serves as 'constructive notice of the registrant's claim of ownership' of the mark," (2) "is 'prima facie evidence of the validity of the registered mark and of the registration of the mark, of the owner's ownership of the mark, and of the owner's exclusive right to use the registered mark in commerce on or in connection with the goods or services specified in the certificate,' " and (3) can make a mark " 'incontestable' once a mark has been registered for five years." Registration also enables the trademark holder "to stop the importation into the United States of articles bearing an infringing mark."

D

Simon Tam is the lead singer of "The Slants." He chose this moniker in order to "reclaim" and "take ownership" of stereotypes about people of Asian ethnicity. The group "draws inspiration for its lyrics from childhood slurs and mocking nursery rhymes" and has given its albums names such as "The Yellow Album" and "Slanted Eyes, Slanted Hearts."

Tam sought federal registration of "THE SLANTS," on the principal register, but an examining attorney at the PTO rejected the request, applying the PTO's two-part framework and finding that "there is ... a substantial composite of persons who find the term in the applied-for mark offensive." The examining attorney relied in part on the fact that "numerous dictionaries define 'slants' or 'slant-eyes' as a derogatory or offensive term." The examining attorney also relied on a finding that "the band's name has been found offensive numerous times"—citing a performance that was canceled because of the band's moniker and the fact that "several bloggers and commenters to articles on the band have indicated that they find the term and the applied-for mark offensive."

III

A

[T]he First Amendment does not say that Congress and other government entities must abridge their own ability to speak freely. And our cases recognize that "[t]he Free Speech Clause ... does not regulate government speech." " '[T]he First Amendment forbids the government to regulate speech in ways that favor some viewpoints or ideas at the expense of others,' " but imposing a requirement of viewpoint-neutrality on government speech would be paralyzing. When a government entity embarks on a course of action, it necessarily takes a particular viewpoint and rejects others. The Free Speech Clause does not require government to maintain viewpoint neutrality when its officers and employees speak about that venture. [For example,] the First Amendment did not demand that the Government balance the message of [World War II posters urging enlistment, the purchase of war bonds, and the conservation of scarce resources] by producing and distributing posters encouraging Americans to refrain from engaging in these activities.

But [i]f private speech could be passed off as government speech by simply affixing a government seal of approval, government could silence or muffle the expression of disfavored viewpoints. For this reason, we must exercise great caution before extending our government-speech precedents.

The Federal Government does not dream up these [trade]marks, and it does not edit marks submitted for registration. Except as required by the statute involved here, an examiner may not reject a mark based on the viewpoint that it appears to express. Thus, unless that section is thought to apply, an examiner does not inquire whether any viewpoint conveyed by a mark is consistent with Government policy or whether any such viewpoint is consistent with that expressed by other marks already on the principal register. Instead, if the mark meets the Lanham Act's viewpoint-neutral requirements, registration is mandatory.

In light of all this, it is far-fetched to suggest that the content of a registered mark is government speech. If the federal registration of a trademark makes the mark government speech, the Federal Government is babbling prodigiously and incoherently. It is saying many unseemly things. It is expressing contradictory views. [The Court compared the registered marks "Abolish Abortion" with "I stand with Planned Parenthood" and "Capitalism Is Not Moral, Not Fair, and Not Freedom" with "Capitalism Ensuring Innovation."] It is unashamedly endorsing a vast array of commercial products and services. And it is providing Delphic advice to the consuming public. For example, if trademarks represent government speech, what does the Government have in mind when it advises Americans to "make.believe" (Sony), "Think different" (Apple), "Just do it" (Nike), or "Have it your way" (Burger King)? Was the Government warning about a coming disaster when it registered the mark "EndTime Ministries"?

The PTO has made it clear that registration does not constitute approval of a mark. And it is unlikely that more than a tiny fraction of the public has any idea what federal registration of a trademark means.

None of our government speech cases even remotely supports the idea that registered trademarks are government speech. Holding that the monuments in the park represented government speech [in *Pleasant Grove City, Utah v. Summum*, 555 U.S. 460 (2009)], we cited many factors. Governments have used monuments to speak to the public since ancient times; parks have traditionally been selective in accepting and displaying donated monuments; parks would be overrun if they were obligated to accept all monuments offered by private groups; "[p]ublic parks are often closely identified in the public mind with the government unit that owns the land"; and "[t]he monuments that are accepted ... are meant to convey and have the effect of conveying a government message."

Trademarks share none of these characteristics. Trademarks have not traditionally been used to convey a Government message. With the exception of the enforcement of [the disparagement clause], the viewpoint expressed by a mark has not played a role in the decision whether to place it on the principal register. And there is no evidence that the public associates the contents of trademarks with the Federal Government.

This brings us to the case on which the Government relies most heavily, *Walker* [*v. Texas Div., Sons of Confederate Veterans, Inc.*, 576 U.S. 200 (2015)], which likely marks the outer bounds of the government-speech doctrine. Holding that the messages on Texas specialty license plates are government speech, the *Walker* Court cited three factors distilled from *Summum*. First, license plates have long been used by the States to convey state messages. Second, license plates "are often closely identified in the public mind" with the State, since they are manufactured and owned by the State, generally designed by the State, and serve as a form of "government ID." Third, Texas "maintain[ed] direct control over the messages conveyed on its specialty plates." As explained above, none of these factors are present in this case.

Holding that the registration of a trademark converts the mark into government speech would constitute a huge and dangerous extension of the government-speech doctrine. For if the registration of trademarks constituted government speech, other systems of government registration could easily be characterized in the same way.

Perhaps the most worrisome implication of the Government's argument concerns the system of copyright registration. If federal registration makes a trademark government speech and thus eliminates all First Amendment protection, would the registration of the copyright for a book produce a similar transformation?

The Government attempts to distinguish copyright on the ground that it is " 'the engine of free expression,' " but as this case illustrates, trademarks often have an expressive content. Companies spend huge amounts to create and publicize trademarks that convey a message. It is true that the necessary brevity of trademarks limits what they can say. But powerful messages can sometimes be conveyed in just a few words.

Trademarks are private, not government, speech.

B

We next address the Government's argument that this case is governed by cases in which this Court has upheld the constitutionality of government programs that subsidized speech expressing a particular viewpoint. [G]overnment is not required to subsidize activities that it does not wish to promote.

[T]he decisions on which the Government relies [*Rust v. Sullivan* and *National Endowment for Arts v. Finley*] all involved cash subsidies or their equivalent for family planning services[,] cash grants to artists[, or] tax benefits [as in *Regan v. Taxation with Representation of Washington*].

The federal registration of a trademark is nothing like the programs at issue in these cases. The PTO does not pay money to parties seeking registration of a mark. Quite the contrary is true: An applicant for registration must pay the PTO a filing fee of $225–$600. And to maintain federal registration, the holder of a mark must pay a fee of $300–$500 every 10 years. The Federal Circuit concluded that these fees have fully supported the registration system for the past 27 years.

The Government responds that registration provides valuable non-monetary benefits that "are directly traceable to the resources devoted by the federal government to examining, publishing, and issuing certificates of registration for those marks." But just about every government service requires the expenditure of government funds. This is true of services that benefit everyone, like police and fire protection, as well as services that are utilized by only some, *e.g.*, the adjudication of private lawsuits and the use of public parks and highways.

Trademark registration is not the only government registration scheme. For example, the Federal Government registers copyrights and patents. State governments and their subdivisions register the title to real property and security interests; they issue driver's licenses, motor vehicle registrations, and hunting, fishing, and boating licenses or permits.

Cases like *Rust* and *Finley* are not instructive in analyzing the constitutionality of restrictions on speech imposed in connection with such services.

C

Potentially more analogous [to the present case] are cases in which a unit of government creates a limited public forum for private speech. When government creates such a forum, in either a literal or "metaphysical" sense, some content- and speaker-based restrictions may be allowed. However, even in such cases, what we have termed "viewpoint discrimination" is forbidden.

Our cases use the term "viewpoint" discrimination in a broad sense, and in that sense, the disparagement clause discriminates on the bases of "viewpoint." To be sure, the clause evenhandedly prohibits disparagement of all groups. It applies equally to marks that damn Democrats and Republicans, capitalists and socialists, and those arrayed on both sides of every possible issue. It denies registration to any mark that is offensive to a substantial percentage of the members of any group. But in the sense relevant here, that is viewpoint discrimination: Giving offense is a viewpoint.

We have said time and again that "the public expression of ideas may not be prohibited merely because the ideas are themselves offensive to some of their hearers." *Street v. New York,* 394 U.S. 576, 592 (1969). *See also Texas v. Johnson,* 491 U.S. 397, 414 (1989) ("If there is a bedrock principle underlying the First Amendment, it is that the government may not prohibit the expression of an idea simply because society finds the idea itself offensive or disagreeable").

For this reason, the disparagement clause cannot be saved by analyzing it as a type of government program in which some content- and speaker-based restrictions are permitted.

IV

[W]e [also] must confront a dispute between the parties on the question whether trademarks are commercial speech and are thus subject to the relaxed scrutiny outlined in *Central Hudson Gas & Elec. Corp. v. Public Serv. Comm'n of N.Y.,* 447 U.S. 557 (1980). We need not resolve this debate between the parties because the disparagement clause cannot withstand even *Central Hudson* review. Under *Central Hudson,* a restriction of speech must serve "a substantial interest," and it must be "narrowly drawn." This means, among other things, that "[t]he regulatory technique may extend only as far as the interest it serves." The disparagement clause fails this requirement.

[T]he Government asserts an interest in preventing "'underrepresented groups'" from being "'bombarded with demeaning messages in commercial advertising.'" [The] unmistakable thrust [of the government's position] is this: The Government has an interest in preventing speech expressing ideas that offend. And, as we have explained, that idea strikes at the heart of the First Amendment. Speech that demeans on the basis of race, ethnicity, gender, religion, age, disability, or any other similar ground is hateful; but the proudest boast of our free speech jurisprudence is that we protect the freedom to express "the thought that we hate."

The second interest asserted is protecting the orderly flow of commerce. Commerce, we are told, is disrupted by trademarks that "involv[e] disparagement of race, gender, ethnicity, national origin, religion, sexual orientation, and similar demographic classification." Such trademarks are analogized to discriminatory conduct, which has been recognized to have an adverse effect on commerce.

A simple answer to this argument is that the disparagement clause is not "narrowly drawn" to drive out trademarks that support invidious discrimination. The clause reaches any trademark that disparages *any person, group, or institution.* It applies to trademarks like the following: "Down with racists," "Down with sexists," "Down with homophobes." It is not an anti-discrimination clause; it is a happy-talk clause. In this way, it goes much further than is necessary to serve the interest asserted.

There is also a deeper problem with the argument that commercial speech may be cleansed of any expression likely to cause offense. The commercial market is well stocked with merchandise that disparages prominent figures and groups, and the line between commercial and non-commercial speech is not always clear, as this case illustrates. If affixing the commercial label permits the suppression of any speech that may lead to political or social "volatility," free speech would be endangered.

JUSTICE GORSUCH took no part in the consideration or decision of this case.

JUSTICE KENNEDY, with whom JUSTICE GINSBURG, JUSTICE SOTOMAYOR, and JUSTICE KAGAN join, concurring in part and concurring in the judgment. [Opinion omitted.]

JUSTICE THOMAS, concurring in part and concurring in the judgment [omitted].

Exercise 22:

1. According to Justice Alito's opinion, how does one distinguish government speech from private speech? Are the tests for government speech articulated in *Summum* and *Walker* the same? How do they differ? Why are trademarks not government speech?

2. Why does the majority believe it "must exercise great caution before extending our government speech precedents"? If the First Amendment Speech Clause does not apply to government speech, what provides a check on such government expression? Why is this check not sufficient to check abuses of government speech?

3. Under the Court's precedents, including *Matal v. Tam*, can the government ever prohibit speech that offends a listener or viewer? Should the government be able to ban such speech under certain circumstances? Can you provide some examples of

such speech? Would such a restriction constitute an impermissible viewpoint-based restriction under *Matal*?

4. Why does Justice Alito contend that trademarks should not be viewed the same as government programs that subsidize speech expressing a particular viewpoint? Is his argument convincing? If trademarks confer the benefits that the Court identifies in its opinion, why are not these non-monetary benefits a type of government subsidy?

5. Should trademarks be viewed as a form of commercial speech? What are the government's interest in regulating such speech even if it is commercial? Why does each justification fail even the "relaxed scrutiny" set out in *Central Hudson*?

6. A federal statute created a program of paid advertising "to advance the image and desirability of beef and beef products." Many of the ads included the trademarked slogan, "Beef, It's What's for Dinner." Under the program, Congress and the Secretary of Agriculture provided guidelines for the ads, Department of Agriculture officials attended the meetings at which the content of specific ads was discussed, and the Secretary could edit or reject any proposed ad. The program was paid for by a $1 per-head assessment (or "checkoff") on all sales or importation of cattle and a comparable assessment on imported beef products. Does the program constitute government speech or the speech of the cattle producers who sell the beef? Does it matter if most people had no idea that the government helped to create and controlled the content of the ad campaign? *See Johanns v. Livestock Marketing Assoc.*, 544 U.S. 550, 561 (2005).

7. In *Rust v. Sullivan*, covred previously, the Court considered the constitutionality of Title X of the Public Health Service Act (the "Act") under which the federal government issued grants to non-profit health-care organizations "to assist in the establishment and operation of voluntary family planning projects [to] offer a broad range of acceptable and effective family planning methods and services." The governing regulations of the Act prohibited Title X projects from advocating abortion as a method of family planning and required grantees to ensure that their Title X projects were "physically and financially separate" from their other projects that engaged in the prohibited activities. Were Title X's voluntary family planning projects government speech under *Summum* and *Matal*? Did Title X discriminate based on viewpoint?

H. Categories of Protected, Unprotected, and Less-Protected Speech

1. Introduction

Thus far, you have learned that a lot hinges on whether a speech regulation is characterized as content based or content neutral. This Section introduces you to the second major component of free speech doctrine: the Supreme Court's categorical approach to speech.

Throughout the twentieth century, the Supreme Court identified categories of speech — particular subject matters — that it held where *un*protected by the Free

Speech Clause, or *less* protected by the Clause. For example, in a series of cases stretching back to at least 1915, *Fox v. Washington*, 236 U.S. 273 (1915), the Supreme Court held that incitement of others to engage in illegal activity is not protected speech. *See Schenck v. United States*, 249 U.S. 47 (1919) (ruling that speech constituted a "clear and present danger" of illegal obstruction of the draft and therefore was not protected by the First Amendment); *Frohwerk v. United States*, 249 U.S. 204 (1919) (same); *Debs v. United States*, 249 U.S. 211 (1919) (same); *Abrams v. United States*, 250 U.S. 616 (1919) (same).

The Court's categorical approach to speech protection is very important to your analysis. Assume that a person is engaged in pure speech. Assume further that the government has prohibited this speech because of its content, and has therefore infringed the freedom of speech. At this point, you would normally evaluate the speech restriction under strict scrutiny. However, now assume that the speech in question was unprotected—for instance, it was incitement to illegal activity. Instead of applying strict scrutiny, you would conclude that the government's regulation was constitutional, because the Free Speech Clause provided no protection to that speech.[103]

There are a number of ways to justify the categorical approach. One could argue that, for each category of speech—as a category, and not for individual instances of such speech—the harm caused by the speech outweighs the value it brings. Another, related approach, is to find that the category of speech does not advance the Free Speech Clause's purposes. One could also conclude that the Free Speech Clause does not protect a category of speech because it was never protected in the history and tradition of the Clause.

The Supreme Court's categorical approach to speech has been and remains subject to significant criticism. Given the Court's repeated and recent affirmation of its categorical approach to unprotected speech, it is unlikely that the Court will abandon it any time soon. *See, e.g., Brown v. Entm't Merchs. Ass'n*, 131 S. Ct. 2729, 2733 (2011) ("From 1791 to the present, the First Amendment has permitted restrictions upon the content of speech in a few limited areas, and has never include[d] a freedom to disregard these traditional limitations.") (quotations omitted). At the same time, the Supreme Court has been steadfast in recent years, refusing every invitation to create new categories of unprotected speech, or expanding existing categories. Indeed, the little movement there has been in the Court's doctrine, is toward narrowing the existing categories. *E.g., R.A.V. v. St. Paul*, 505 U.S. 377 (1992).

The Supreme Court has identified five main categories of unprotected speech, and four primary categories of less-protected speech.[104] We will review each category below, after looking at protected speech.

---

103. With the caveat that the regulation would have to comply with the requirement articulated in *R.A.V. v. St. Paul*, 505 U.S. 377 (1992), that the regulation is not content based *within* the category of otherwise-unprotected speech. This caveat is discuss below, in Part [H][6].

104. Be aware that there are other reasonable ways to organize these categories of speech. For instance, one could separate out one of the categories identified here into two separate categories, or one could combine two of these categories as part of one broader category.

Before proceeding, it is worth thinking about whether the Court's categorical approach is the best way to implement the Free Speech Clause. There are two basic possible approaches that commentators have offered: the absolutist approach, and the balancing approach. The absolutist approach would require protecting all speech. The balancing approach would, by contrast, look at each instance of speech regulation (or classes of similar speech regulations) and determine whether the costs of the speech outweigh its benefits. Which approach — an absolutist, or a balancing approach — is best for free speech law? Why? Which approach is closest to the Court's categorical approach?

2. Protected Speech

The strong norm in free speech law is that speech is protected by the Free Speech Clause. One particularly strong manifestation of this protection is in the context of "political" speech. Political speech is speech regarding candidates, elections, and political issues. Though the subject matter of political speech does not have its own, discrete, doctrinal role to play in the Supreme Court's analysis — it does not make a separate appearance in any of the doctrines you will learn in this **Chapter** — its existence in a case is noted by the Court and influences the Court's analysis.

For example, in *Republican Party of Minn. v. White*, 536 U.S. 765 (2002), the Supreme Court faced a challenge by a candidate for the Minnesota Supreme Court to Minnesota's "announce clause": a " 'candidate for a judicial office, including an incumbent judge,' shall not 'announce his or her views on disputed legal or political issues.' " *Id.* at 768. The Court ruled that the announce clause violated freedom of speech and stated, at the beginning of its analysis, that: "As the Court of Appeals recognized, the announce clause both prohibits speech on the basis of its content and burdens a category of speech that is 'at the core of our First Amendment freedoms' — speech about the qualifications of candidates for public office." *Id.* at 774. Though the fact that the regulated speech was political did not change the mode of analysis — strict scrutiny — it seemed to influence the Court's application of strict scrutiny through especially rigorous scrutiny. You have seen a similar influence in earlier cases, such as *Citizens United v. FEC*.

3. Unprotected Speech

a. Incitement to Illegal Activity

Incitement to illegal activity occurs when one incites others to engage in illegal activity. For example, after the rise of international communism, many of these cases involved members of communist organizations that advocated the overthrow of the United States government and elimination of private property through violent means.

The first major Supreme Court cases to state and utilize this exception to free speech protection occurred during World War I. Congress passed the 1917 and 1918 Espionage Acts to protect the war effort, and the defendants in a series of cases were prosecuted for violating those Acts. *Schenck v. United States*, 249 U.S. 47 (1919); *Fro-*

hwerk v. United States, 249 U.S. 204 (1919); *Debs v. United States*, 249 U.S. 211 (1919); *Abrams v. United States*, 250 U.S. 616 (1919).

In this line of cases, the Supreme Court articulated the Clear and Present Danger Test. The Test stated that, speech was not protected—it constituted incitement of illegal activity—if: (1) there was a high likelihood; (2) of imminent; and (3) substantial, harm. The Clear and Present Danger Test was relatively unprotective of speech. Can you see why?

Later, beginning in the 1920s, states passed so-called syndicalism statutes that outlawed advocacy of the violent overthrow of the government and private property. During this time period, the Supreme Court broadened the category of unprotected incitement of illegal activity by articulating the Reasonableness Test. Under the Reasonableness Test, government could punish speech that incited unlawful activity so long as the speech prohibition was rationally related to a legitimate state interest. This Test incorporated great deference to government judgments and was analogous to the due process rational basis test. Using this Test, the Supreme Court generally upheld prosecutions. *See, e.g.*, *Gitlow v. New York*, 268 U.S. 652 (1925) (upholding the conviction in a case where the "Left Wing Section of the Socialist Party" advocated violent and unlawful overthrow of the government).

Then, as the Cold War hardened in the late-1940s, the Supreme Court adopted another version of the Clear and Present Danger Test. This Test looked at two factors: the likelihood of harm and the severity of harm caused by the prohibited speech. Under this Test, if the severity of potential harm was great, then the government could proscribe the speech even if the likelihood of the harm coming to pass was low. This made the Test less protective of speech advocating the violent overthrow of government because the potential harm was so severe. The unprotectiveness of this version of the Clear and Present Danger Test was compounded because, unlike the Test's initial formulation, immediacy was not a factor. *See Dennis v. United States*, 341 U.S. 494 (1951) (upholding conviction under the Smith Act, 18 U.S.C. § 2385, for conspiring to organize the Communist Party of the United States to advocate the violent overthrow of the United States government).

After a period of uncertainty, *see, e.g.*, *Yates v. United States*, 354 U.S. 298 (1957) (overturning a conviction under the Smith Act for incitement of violent overthrow of the government); *Noto v. United States*, 367 U.S. 290 (1961) (same), in 1969, the Supreme Court decided the famous case of *Brandenburg v. Ohio*, 395 U.S. 444 (1969), and articulated the current test for the incitement to illegal activity exception.

Brandenburg v. Ohio

395 U.S. 444 (1969)

PER CURIAM.

The appellant, a leader of a Ku Klux Klan group, was convicted under the Ohio Criminal Syndicalism statute.... Ohio Rev. Code Ann. § 2923.13. He was fined $1,000 and sentenced to one to 10 years' imprisonment. The appellant challenged the constitutionality of the criminal syndicalism statute under the First and Fourteenth Amendments to the United States Constitution, but the intermediate appellate court of Ohio affirmed his conviction without opinion. The Supreme Court of Ohio dismissed his appeal, sua sponte, "for the reason that no substantial constitutional question exists herein." Appeal was taken to this Court. We reverse.

The record shows that a man, identified at trial as the appellant, telephoned an announcer-reporter on the staff of a Cincinnati television station and invited him to come to a Ku Klux Klan "rally" to be held at a farm in Hamilton County. With the cooperation of the organizers, the reporter and a cameraman attended the meeting and filmed the events.…

The prosecution's case rested on the films and on testimony identifying the appellant as the person who communicated with the reporter and who spoke at the rally. The State also introduced into evidence several articles appearing in the film, including a pistol, a rifle, a shotgun, ammunition, a Bible, and a red hood worn by the speaker in the films.

One film showed 12 hooded figures, some of whom carried firearms. They were gathered around a large wooden cross, which they burned. No one was present other than the participants and the newsmen who made the film. Most of the words uttered during the scene were incomprehensible when the film was projected, but scattered phrases could be understood that were derogatory of Negroes and, in one instance, of Jews. Another scene on the same film showed the appellant, in Klan regalia, making a speech. The speech, in full, was as follows:

> "This is an organizers' meeting. We have had quite a few members here today which are — we have hundreds, hundreds of members throughout the State of Ohio. The Klan has more members in the State of Ohio than does any other organization. We're not a revengent organization, but if our President, our Congress, our Supreme Court, continues to suppress the white, Caucasian race, it's possible that there might have to be some revengeance taken.

> "We are marching on Congress July the Fourth, four hundred thousand strong. From there we are dividing into two groups, one group to march on St. Augustine, Florida, the other group to march into Mississippi. Thank you."

The second film showed six hooded figures one of whom, later identified as the appellant, repeated a speech very similar to that recorded on the first film. [O]ne sentence was added: "Personally, I believe the nigger should be returned to Africa, the Jew returned to Israel." Though some of the figures in the films carried weapons, the speaker did not.

The Ohio Criminal Syndicalism Statute was enacted in 1919. From 1917 to 1920, identical or quite similar laws were adopted by 20 States and two territories. In 1927, this Court sustained the constitutionality of California's Criminal Syndicalism Act, the text of which is quite similar to that of the laws of Ohio. *Whitney v. California*, 274 U.S. 357 (1927). The Court upheld the statute on the ground that, without more, "advocating" violent means to effect political and economic change involves such danger to the security of the State that the State may outlaw it. But *Whitney* has been thoroughly discredited by later decisions. See *Dennis v. United States*, 341 U.S. 494, at 507 (1951). These later decisions have fashioned the principle that the constitutional guarantees of free speech and free press do not permit a State to forbid or proscribe advocacy of the use of force or of law violation except where such advocacy is directed to inciting or producing imminent lawless action and is likely to incite or produce such action. "[T]he mere abstract teaching * * * of the moral propriety or even moral necessity for a resort to force and violence, is not the same as preparing a group for violent action and steeling it to such action." A statute which fails to draw this distinction impermissibly intrudes upon the freedoms guaranteed by the First and Fourteenth Amendments.

Measured by this test, Ohio's Criminal Syndicalism Act cannot be sustained. The Act punishes persons who "advocate or teach the duty, necessity, or propriety" of violence "as a means of accomplishing industrial or political reform"; or who publish or circulate or display any book or paper containing such advocacy; or who "justify" the commission of violent acts "with intent to exemplify, spread or advocate the propriety of the doctrines of criminal syndicalism"; or who "voluntarily assemble" with a group formed "to teach or advocate the doctrines of criminal syndicalism." Neither the indictment nor the trial judge's instructions to the jury in any way refined the statute's bald definition of the crime in terms of mere advocacy not distinguished from incitement to imminent lawless action.

Accordingly, we are here confronted with a statute which, by its own words and as applied, purports to punish mere advocacy and to forbid, on pain of criminal punishment, assembly with others merely to advocate the described type of action. Such a statute falls within the condemnation of the First and Fourteenth Amendments. The contrary teaching of *Whitney v. California*, cannot be supported, and that decision is therefore overruled.

MR. JUSTICE BLACK, concurring. [Opinion omitted.]

MR. JUSTICE DOUGLAS, concurring. [Opinion omitted.]

Exercise 23:

1. What test did the Supreme Court adopt to distinguish between constitutionally protected "advocacy" and constitutionally proscribable incitement?

2. How is this test different from, and similar to, earlier tests, described above? Relatedly, what speech might this test protect, that earlier tests did not?

3. What are the relative costs and benefits of the *Brandenburg* Test compared to the earlier tests?

4. What speech does this Test *not* protect? For example, what if one person proposes to another person to engage in a bank robbery that evening? Or, what if a speaker publicly advocates a group of people to immediately take control of a nearby police station?

b. Fighting Words

Fighting words is a category of words "which by their very utterance inflict injury or tend to incite an immediate breach of the peace." *Chaplinsky v. New Hampshire*, 315 U.S. 568 (1942). The category of fighting words is subject to significant uncertainty, both regarding whether it remains a category of unprotected speech and, if it does, what the scope of the exception is.

Chaplinsky, the seminal case discussing fighting words, is reprinted below. Later cases, which have unsettled this area of the law, are discussed after *Chaplinsky*. The later case law pushes the fighting words category in multiple conflicting directions. First, the case law requires that punishable fighting words must be directed at a particular person or persons. Second, proscriptions on fighting words cannot be vague. Third, fighting words proscriptions cannot make content-based judgments among fighting words. Despite this uncertainty, the Supreme Court continues to cite approvingly to the category generally and *Chaplinsky* in particular. *E.g.*, *Brown v. Entm't Merchs. Ass'n*, 564 U.S. 786, 791 (2011); *Virginia v. Black*, 538 U.S. 343, 358 (2003).

Chaplinsky v. New Hampshire

315 U.S. 568 (1942)

Mr. Justice Murphy delivered the opinion of the Court.

Appellant, a member of the sect known as Jehovah's Witnesses, was convicted in the municipal court of Rochester, New Hampshire, for violation of Chapter 378, § 2, of the Public Laws of New Hampshire: "No person shall address any offensive, derisive or annoying word to any other person who is lawfully in any street or other public place, nor call him by any offensive or derisive name, nor make any noise or exclamation in his presence and hearing with intent to deride, offend or annoy him, or to prevent him from pursuing his lawful business or occupation."

The complaint charged that appellant "with force and arms, in a certain public place in said city of Rochester, to wit, on the public sidewalk on the easterly side of Wakefield Street, near unto the entrance of the City Hall, did unlawfully repeat, the words following, addressed to the complainant, that is to say, 'You are a God damned racketeer' and 'a damned Fascist and the whole government of Rochester are Fascists or agents of Fascists' the same being offensive, derisive and annoying words and names".

He was found guilty and the judgment of conviction was affirmed by the Supreme Court of the State. By motions and exceptions, appellant raised the questions that the statute was invalid under the Fourteenth Amendment of the Constitution of the United States in that it placed an unreasonable restraint on freedom of speech, freedom of the press, and freedom of worship, and because it was vague and indefinite. These contentions were overruled and the case comes here on appeal.

There is no substantial dispute over the facts. Chaplinsky was distributing the literature of his sect on the streets of Rochester on a busy Saturday afternoon. Members of the local citizenry complained to the City Marshal, Bowering, that Chaplinsky was denouncing all religion as a "racket". Bowering told them that Chaplinsky was lawfully engaged, and then warned Chaplinsky that the crowd was getting restless. Some time later a disturbance occurred and the traffic officer on duty at the busy intersection started with Chaplinsky for the police station, but did not inform him that he was under arrest or that he was going to be arrested. On the way they encountered Marshal Bowering who had been advised that a riot was under way and was therefore hurrying to the scene. Bowering repeated his earlier warning to Chaplinsky who then addressed to Bowering the words set forth in the complaint.

Chaplinsky's version of the affair was slightly different. He testified that when he met Bowering, he asked him to arrest the ones responsible for the disturbance. In reply Bowering cursed him and told him to come along. Appellant admitted that he said the words charged in the complaint with the exception of the name of the Deity.

Allowing the broadest scope to the language and purpose of the Fourteenth Amendment, it is well understood that the right of free speech is not absolute at all times and under all circumstances.[2] There are certain well-defined and narrowly limited classes of speech, the prevention and punishment of which have never been thought to raise any Constitutional problem. These include the lewd and obscene, the profane, the libelous, and the insulting or "fighting" words—those which by their very utterance inflict injury or tend to incite an immediate breach of the peace.[4] It has been well observed that such utterances are no essential part of any exposition of ideas, and are of such slight social value as a step to truth that any benefit that may be derived from them is clearly outweighed by the social interest in order and morality. "Resort to epithets or personal abuse is not in any proper sense communication of information or opinion safeguarded by the Constitution, and its punishment as a criminal act would raise no question under that instrument."

The state statute here challenged comes to us authoritatively construed by the highest court of New Hampshire.... [T]he state court declared that the statute's purpose was to preserve the public peace, no words being "forbidden except such as have a direct tendency to cause acts of violence by the person to whom, individually, the remark is addressed". It was further said: "The word 'offensive' is not to be defined in terms of what a particular addressee thinks. * * * The test is what men of common intelligence would understand would be words likely to cause an average addressee to fight. * * * The English language has a number of words and expressions which by general consent are 'fighting words' when said without a disarming smile. * * * Such words, as ordinary men know, are likely to cause a fight. So are threatening, profane or obscene revilings. Derisive and annoying words can be taken as coming within the purview of the statute as heretofore interpreted only

---

2. *Schenck v. United States*, 249 U.S. 47 [(1919)]; *Whitney v. California*, 274 U.S. 357, 373 [(1927)] (Brandeis, J., concurring).

4. [Zachariah] Chafee, *Free Speech in the United States* (1941), 149.

when they have this characteristic of plainly tending to excite the addressee to a breach of the peace. * * * The statute, as construed, does no more than prohibit the face-to-face words plainly likely to cause a breach of the peace by the addressee, words whose speaking constitute a breach of the peace by the speaker — including 'classical fighting words', words in current use less 'classical' but equally likely to cause violence, and other disorderly words, including profanity, obscenity and threats."

We are unable to say that the limited scope of the statute as thus construed contravenes the constitutional right of free expression. It is a statute narrowly drawn and limited to define and punish specific conduct lying within the domain of state power, the use in a public place of words likely to cause a breach of the peace. This conclusion necessarily disposes of appellant's contention that the statute is so vague and indefinite as to render a conviction thereunder a violation of due process. A statute punishing verbal acts, carefully drawn so as not unduly to impair liberty of expression, is not too vague for a criminal law.

Nor can we say that the application of the statute to the facts disclosed by the record substantially or unreasonably impinges upon the privilege of free speech. Argument is unnecessary to demonstrate that the appellations "damn racketeer" and "damn Fascist" are epithets likely to provoke the average person to retaliation, and thereby cause a breach of the peace.

Exercise 24:

1. What is the scope of the fighting words exception? Is there a list of "fighting words"? Are fighting words judged by the particular target of fighting words or by an objective standard? Do fighting words even exist today? Should they?

2. What is the source of the fighting words exception?

3. The Supreme Court identified *two* types of fighting words that are not protected by the Constitution; what are those types? Should both categories be unprotected?

4. Suppose that a speaker is giving a talk on a controversial topic in a busy public area and that a crowd begins to gather. Some members of the crowd become agitated, yelling and shouting at the speaker and those in the crowd that support her. Should the police be allowed to stop the speaker (whose words might seem to be leading to a ruckus) or should they stop the upset listeners from disrupting the speaker, or both?

Some might contend that the facts of this case show that the speaker's words "tend to incite an immediate breach of the peace" because a disturbance is starting to break out. And if the speaker's words actually constitute fighting words under *Chaplinsky*, then the police can stop her speech. But notice also that if *Chaplinsky* is interpreted broadly, there is the threat of what has become known as a "heckler's veto." If an audience's reaction is sufficient to permit government officials to stifle the speech of a speaker, then those who disagree with the speaker may be incentivized to cause trouble or to react violently so as to show that the speaker's words tended to (and actually did) cause a breach of the peace—hence, creating a "veto" power on the speaker's expression.

Outside the context of fighting words, though, the Court has been wary to permit the government to restrain speakers based on the actual or anticipated reaction of listeners, generally requiring the government to control the crowd and its response rather than silencing the speaker. For example, in *Terminiello v. City of Chicago*, 337 U.S. 1 (1949), the Court overturned the conviction of a speaker who had made inflammatory comments to listeners inside an auditorium and to others outside the venue, which led to a riot. The Court explained that one of the functions of the First Amendment "is to invite dispute" and that free speech "may indeed best serve its high purpose when it induces a condition of unrest, creates dissatisfaction with conditions as they are, or even stirs people to anger." *Id.* at 4. Thus, there is an important (even if unclear) line between fighting words, which are not protected, and other forms of speech that offends others, which generally are protected.

———

Though no Supreme Court case has repudiated the fighting words exception, and the Court continues to reference fighting words as a category of unprotected speech, three developments in the case law have significantly narrowed the category's scope, and perhaps have fatally undermined the category. First, the Supreme Court ruled in *Cohen v. California*, 403 U.S. 15, 20 (1971), that fighting words must be "directed to the person of the hearer."[10] Cohen's actions—walking through a courthouse with a four-letter word on his jacket protesting the Vietnam war draft—was not directed at any particular person, and therefore was not unprotected speech. This significantly narrowed the universe of speech which was subject to the fighting words exception.

Second, the Supreme Court held that fighting words prohibitions may not be constitutionally vague. For instance, in *Gooding v. Wilson*, 405 U.S. 518 (1972), the Supreme Court ruled that Georgia's fighting words statute was unconstitutionally vague. "[T]he statute must be carefully drawn or be authoritatively construed to punish only unprotected speech and not be susceptible of application to protected expression." *Id.* at 522. The challenge posed by this ruling is that it is difficult for governments to state, with sufficient specificity, what words qualify as fighting words. This can be seen from the Supreme Court's own abstract description of fighting words in *Chaplinsky*.

The challenge posed by vagueness limits is compounded by the third development in the important case of *R.A.V. v. St. Paul*, 505 U.S. 377 (1992). We will review *R.A.V.* in more detail below, in Section [H][6]. Here, however, it is sufficient to note that the Court in *R.A.V.* prohibited content-based distinctions *within* the category of otherwise-unprotected fighting words. The challenged city ordinance banned fighting words that caused harm "on the basis of race, color, creed, religion or gender." The Supreme Court ruled that this selective banning of fighting words

———

10. *Cohen* is discussed more fully below, in Section [H][4][c].

was content based without sufficient justification. Today, to ban fighting words, the government must achieve sufficient specificity to avoid unconstitutional vagueness, while, at the same time, avoiding such specificity that the government runs afoul of *R.A.V.*

c. True Threats

True threats is a category related to incitement and fighting words. As you will see in the case that follows, the Supreme Court has described true threats as "statements where the speaker means to communicate a serious expression of an intent to commit an act of unlawful violence to a particular individual or group of individuals." *Virginia v. Black*, 538 U.S. 343, 359 (2003). The Supreme Court has stated that the exception for true threats "protect[s] individuals from the fear of violence" and "from the disruption that fear engenders," in addition to protecting people "from the possibility that the threatened violence will occur." *R.A.V. v. St. Paul*, 505 U.S. 377, 388 (1992). As you read the case below, consider (1) how the true threats category differs from incitement and fighting words and (2) what is the minimum *mens rea* required for a threat conviction under the First Amendment.

Virginia v. Black
538 U.S. 343 (2003)

JUSTICE O'CONNOR delivered the opinion of the Court with respect to Parts I, II, and III, and an opinion with respect to Parts IV and V, in which THE CHIEF JUSTICE, JUSTICE STEVENS, and JUSTICE BREYER join.

In this case we consider whether the Commonwealth of Virginia's statute banning cross burning with "an intent to intimidate a person or group of persons" violates the First Amendment. We conclude that while a State, consistent with the First Amendment, may ban cross burning carried out with the intent to intimidate, the provision in the Virginia statute treating any cross burning as prima facie evidence of intent to intimidate renders the statute unconstitutional in its current form.

I

Respondents Barry Black, Richard Elliott, and Jonathan O'Mara were convicted separately of violating Virginia's cross-burning statute, § 18.2-423. That statute provides:

> It shall be unlawful for any person or persons, with the intent of intimidating any person or group of persons, to burn, or cause to be burned, a cross on the property of another, a highway or other public place. Any such burning of a cross shall be prima facie evidence of an intent to intimidate a person or group of persons.

On August 22, 1998, Barry Black led a Ku Klux Klan rally in Carroll County, Virginia. Twenty-five to thirty people attended this gathering, which occurred on private property with the permission of the owner, who was in attendance.

At the conclusion of the rally, the crowd circled around a 25- to 30-foot cross. The cross was [in an open field] between 300 and 350 yards away from the road. According to the sheriff, the cross "then all of a sudden … went up in a flame." As the cross burned, the Klan played Amazing Grace over the loudspeakers. [Rebecca] Sechrist [who was related to the owner of the property where the rally took place and who watched the rally from a nearby lawn] stated that the cross burning made her feel "awful" and "terrible."

When the sheriff observed the cross burning, he informed his deputy that they needed to "find out who's responsible and explain to them that they cannot do this in the State of Virginia." The sheriff then went down the driveway, entered the rally, and asked "who was responsible for burning the cross." Black responded, "I guess I am because I'm the head of the rally." The sheriff then told Black, "[T]here's a law in the State of Virginia that you cannot burn a cross and I'll have to place you under arrest for this."

Black was charged with burning a cross with the intent of intimidating a person or group of persons, in violation of § 18.2-423. At his trial, the jury was instructed that "intent to intimidate means the motivation to intentionally put a person or a group of persons in fear of bodily harm. Such fear must arise from the willful conduct of the accused rather than from some mere temperamental timidity of the victim." The trial court also instructed the jury that "the burning of a cross by itself is sufficient evidence from which you may infer the required intent." The jury found Black guilty.

II

From the [early 1900s], cross burnings have been used to communicate both threats of violence and messages of shared ideology. Often, the [Ku Klux] Klan used cross burnings as a tool of intimidation and a threat of impending violence. [The Court provided examples of the Klan's burning crosses to target mostly blacks but also Jews and union members.] These cross burnings embodied threats to people whom the Klan deemed antithetical to its goals. And these threats had special force given the long history of Klan violence.

Throughout the history of the Klan, cross burnings have also remained potent symbols of shared group identity and ideology. The burning cross became a symbol of the Klan itself and a central feature of Klan gatherings [at which] cross burning became the climax of the rally or the initiation. Posters advertising an upcoming Klan rally often featured a Klan member holding a cross. Typically, a cross burning would start with a prayer followed by the singing of Onward Christian Soldiers. The Klan would then light the cross on fire, as the members raised their left arm toward the burning cross and sang The Old Rugged Cross. Throughout the Klan's history, the Klan continued to use the burning cross in their ritual ceremonies.

To this day, regardless of whether the message is a political one or whether the message is also meant to intimidate, the burning of a cross is a "symbol of hate." And while cross burning sometimes carries no intimidating message, at other times the intimidating message is the *only* message conveyed. For example, when a cross burning is directed at a particular person not affiliated with the Klan, the burning cross often serves as a message of intimidation, designed to inspire in the victim a fear of bodily harm. Moreover, the history of violence associated with the Klan shows that the possibility of injury or death is not just hypothetical. The person who burns a cross directed at a particular person often is making a serious threat, meant to coerce the victim to comply with the Klan's wishes unless the victim is willing to risk the wrath of the Klan. Indeed, as the case of respondent Elliott indicate[s], individuals without Klan affiliation who wish to threaten or menace another person sometimes use cross burning because of this association between a burning cross and violence.

In sum, while a burning cross does not inevitably convey a message of intimidation, often the cross burner intends that the recipients of the message fear for their lives. And when a cross burning is used to intimidate, few if any messages are more powerful.

III

A

The hallmark of the protection of free speech is to allow "free trade in ideas" — even ideas that the overwhelming majority of people might find distasteful or discomforting. Thus, the First Amendment "ordinarily" denies a State "the power to prohibit dissemination of social, economic and political doctrine which a vast majority of its citizens believes to be false and fraught with evil consequence." The First Amendment affords protection to symbolic or expressive conduct as well as to actual speech.

The protections afforded by the First Amendment, however, are not absolute, and we have long recognized that the government may regulate certain categories of expression consistent with the Constitution. The First Amendment permits "restrictions upon the content of speech in a few limited areas, which are 'of such slight social value as a step to truth that any benefit that may be derived from them is clearly outweighed by the social interest in order and morality.'"

Thus, for example, a State may punish those words "which by their very utterance inflict injury or tend to incite an immediate breach of the peace." We have consequently held that fighting words — "those personally abusive epithets which, when addressed to the ordinary citizen, are, as a matter of common knowledge, inherently likely to provoke violent reaction" — are generally proscribable under the First Amendment. Furthermore, "the constitutional guarantees of free speech and free press do not permit a State to forbid or proscribe advocacy of the use of force or of law violation except where such advocacy is directed to inciting or producing imminent lawless action and is likely to incite or produce such action." And the First Amendment also permits a State to ban a "true threat." *Watts v. United States,* 394 U.S. 705, 708 (1969); *R.A.V. v. City of St. Paul,* [505 U.S. 377], 388 [(1992)] ("[T]hreats of violence are outside the First Amendment").

"True threats" encompass those statements where the speaker means to communicate a serious expression of an intent to commit an act of unlawful violence to a particular individual or group of individuals. See *Watts,* [394 U.S.] at 708 ("political hyberbole" is not a true threat). The speaker need not actually intend to carry out the threat. Rather, a prohibition on true threats "protect[s] individuals from the fear of violence" and "from the disruption that fear engenders," in addition to protecting people "from the possibility that the threatened violence will occur." Intimidation in the constitutionally proscribable sense of the word is a type of true threat, where a speaker directs a threat to a person or group of persons with the intent of placing the victim in fear of bodily harm or death. Respondents do not contest that some cross burnings fit within this meaning of intimidating speech, and rightly so. [T]he history of cross burning in this country shows that cross burning is often intimidating, intended to create a pervasive fear in victims that they are a target of violence.

B

[T]he burning of a cross is symbolic expression. The reason why the Klan burns a cross at its rallies, or individuals place a burning cross on someone else's lawn, is that the burning cross represents the message that the speaker wishes to communicate. Individuals burn crosses as opposed to other means of communication because cross burning carries a message in an effective and dramatic manner.

The First Amendment permits Virginia to outlaw cross burnings done with the intent to intimidate because burning a cross is a particularly virulent form of intimidation. Instead of prohibiting all intimidating messages, Virginia may choose to regulate this subset of intimidating messages in light of cross burning's long and pernicious history as a signal of impending violence. Thus, just as a State may regulate only that obscenity which is the most obscene due to its prurient content, so too may a State choose to prohibit only those forms of intimidation that are most likely to inspire fear of bodily harm. A ban on cross burning carried out with the intent to intimidate and is proscribable under the First Amendment.

IV

The prima facie evidence provision, as interpreted by the jury instruction [in Barry Black's case], renders the statute unconstitutional. As construed by the jury instruction, the prima facie provision strips away the very reason why a State may ban cross burning with the intent to intimidate. The prima facie evidence provision permits a jury to convict in every cross-burning case in which defendants exercise their constitutional right not to put on a defense. And even where a defendant like Black presents a defense, the prima facie evidence provision makes it more likely that the jury will find an intent to intimidate regardless of the particular facts of the case. The provision permits the Commonwealth to arrest, prosecute, and convict a person based solely on the fact of cross burning itself.

It is apparent that the provision as so interpreted "'would create an unacceptable risk of the suppression of ideas.'" The act of burning a cross may mean that a person is engaging in constitutionally proscribable intimidation. But that same act may mean only that the person is engaged in core political speech. The prima facie evidence provision in this statute blurs the line between these two meanings of a burning cross. As interpreted by the jury instruction, the provision chills constitutionally protected political speech because of the possibility that the Commonwealth will prosecute— and potentially convict—somebody engaging only in lawful political speech at the core of what the First Amendment is designed to protect.

As the history of cross burning indicates, a burning cross is not always intended to intimidate. Rather, sometimes the cross burning is a statement of ideology, a symbol of group solidarity. It is a ritual used at Klan gatherings, and it is used to represent the Klan itself. Thus, "[b]urning a cross at a political rally would almost certainly be protected expression." Indeed, occasionally a person who burns a cross does not intend to express either a statement of ideology or intimidation. Cross burnings have appeared in movies such as Mississippi Burning, and in plays such as the stage adaptation of Sir Walter Scott's The Lady of the Lake.

The prima facie provision makes no effort to distinguish among these different types of cross burnings. It does not distinguish between a cross burning at a public rally or a cross burning on a neighbor's lawn. It does not treat the cross burning directed at an individual differently from the cross burning directed at a group of like-minded believers. It allows a jury to treat a cross burning on the property of another with the owner's acquiescence in the same manner as a cross burning on the property of another without the owner's permission.

It may be true that a cross burning, even at a political rally, arouses a sense of anger or hatred among the vast majority of citizens who see a burning cross. But this sense of anger or hatred is not sufficient to ban all cross burnings. The prima facie evidence provision in this case ignores all of the contextual factors that are necessary to decide whether a particular cross burning is intended to intimidate. The First Amendment does not permit such a shortcut....

JUSTICE STEVENS, concurring. [Opinion omitted.]

JUSTICE SCALIA, with whom JUSTICE THOMAS joins as to Parts I and II, concurring in part, concurring in the judgment in part, and dissenting in part. [Opinion omitted.]

JUSTICE SOUTER, with whom JUSTICE KENNEDY and JUSTICE GINSBURG join, concurring in the judgment in part and dissenting in part. [Opinion omitted.]

JUSTICE THOMAS, dissenting.

I

Although I agree with the majority's conclusion that it is constitutionally permissible to "ban ... cross burning carried out with the intent to intimidate," I believe that the majority errs in imputing an expressive component to the activity in question. In my view, whatever expressive value cross burning has, the legislature simply wrote it out by banning only intimidating conduct undertaken by a particular means. A conclusion that the statute prohibiting cross burning with intent to intimidate sweeps beyond a prohibition on certain conduct into the zone of expression overlooks not only the words of the statute but also reality.

B

In our culture, cross burning has almost invariably meant lawlessness and understandably instills in its victims well-grounded fear of physical violence.* Although the

---

* [Text moved from section I.A.—ed.]

Klan was disbanded at the national level in 1944, a series of cross burnings in Virginia took place between 1949 and 1952. Most of the crosses were burned on the lawns of black families, who either were business owners or lived in predominantly white neighborhoods. At least one of the cross burnings was accompanied by a shooting. These incidents were, in the words of the time, "*terroristic [sic]*" and "un-American act[s], designed to *intimidate* Negroes from seeking their rights as citizens."

In February 1952, in light of this series of cross burnings and attendant reports that the Klan, "long considered dead in Virginia, is being revitalized in Richmond," Governor Battle announced that "Virginia 'might well consider passing legislation' to restrict the activities of the Ku Klux Klan." As newspapers reported at the time, the bill was "to ban the burning of crosses and other similar evidences of *terrorism.*" The bill was presented to the House of Delegates by a former FBI agent and future two-term Governor, Delegate Mills E. Godwin, Jr. "Godwin said law and order in the State were impossible if organized groups could *create fear by intimidation.*"

It strains credulity to suggest that a state legislature that adopted a litany of segregationist laws self-contradictorily intended to squelch the segregationist message. Even for segregationists, violent and terroristic conduct, the Siamese twin of cross burning, was intolerable. The ban on cross burning with intent to intimidate demonstrates that even segregationists understood the difference between intimidating and terroristic conduct and racist expression. It is simply beyond belief that, in passing the statute now under review, the Virginia Legislature was concerned with anything but penalizing conduct it must have viewed as particularly vicious.

Accordingly, this statute prohibits only conduct, not expression. And, just as one cannot burn down someone's house to make a political point and then seek refuge in the First Amendment, those who hate cannot terrorize and intimidate to make their point. In light of my conclusion that the statute here addresses only conduct, there is no need to analyze it under any of our First Amendment tests.

Exercise 25:

1. As the Supreme Court makes clear, true threats fall outside the protection of the First Amendment, but what types of expression constitute "true" threats?

2. The majority in *Black* states that intimidation can be a true threat "where a speaker directs a threat to a person or group of persons with the intent of placing the victim in fear of bodily harm or death." Must a speaker have the intent—the purpose—of putting others in fear? Or should the *mens rea* requirement be recklessness? Negligence? While *Black* suggests that purpose is required, several lower courts have adopted negligence as the standard. And while the Supreme Court concluded that negligence was not sufficient under the federal threats statute, it did not resolve the constitutional *mens rea* standard for true threats. *See Elonis v. United States*, 135 S. Ct. 2001 (2015).

3. Recently, some governments have attempted to utilize the true threats category (along with fighting words) to limit what it called hate speech. The Supreme Court has not yet recognized a hate speech exception to the First Amendment. Should it? What would that argument look like? How might *Black* support or hinder such an argument?

4. In *Watts v. United States*, 394 U.S. 705 (1969), which is cited in *Black*, the Court explained that threats are protected if a reasonable person would understand them to be hyperbole. In *Watts*, the petitioner, an 18-year-old who had received his draft classification as 1-A, had said at a public rally that "[i]f they ever make me carry a rifle the first man I want to get in my sights is L.B.J." *Id.* at 706. He was charged under a federal statute that prohibited "knowingly and willfully ... [making] any threat to take the life of or to inflict bodily harm upon the President." *Id.* at 705. The Court concluded that these statements did not constitute a true threat: "We do not believe that the kind of political hyperbole indulged in by petitioner fits within that statutory term [of true threat]. For we must interpret the language Congress chose 'against the background of a profound national commitment to the principle that debate on public issues should be uninhibited, robust, and wide-open, and that it may well include vehement, caustic, and sometimes unpleasantly sharp attacks on government and public officials.' The language of the political arena, like the language used in labor disputes is often vituperative, abusive, and inexact. We agree with petitioner that his only offense here was 'a kind of very crude offensive method of stating a political opposition to the President.' Taken in context, and regarding the expressly conditional nature of the statement and the reaction of the listeners, we do not see how it could be interpreted otherwise." *Id.* at 708.

5. The Supreme Court also has held that the First Amendment protects threats of a lawful boycott or of possible social ostracism: "It is not disputed that a major purpose of the boycott in this case was to influence governmental action.... [T]he petitioners certainly foresaw—and directly intended—that the merchants would sustain economic injury as a result of their campaign.... The right of the States to regulate economic activity could not justify a complete prohibition against a nonviolent, politically motivated boycott designed to force governmental and economic change and to effectuate rights guaranteed by the Constitution itself." *NAACP v. Claiborne Hardware Co.*, 458 U.S. 886, 914 (1982). While lawful boycotts are protected, violent ones are not: "The First Amendment does not protect violence.... No federal rule of law restricts a State from imposing tort liability for business losses that are caused by violence and by threats of violence. When such conduct occurs in the context of constitutionally protected activity, however, 'precision of regulation' is demanded." *Id.* at 916.

6. Suppose a pro-life organization protests abortion providers by publicly disclosing their names and addresses on posters and on its web site. One such poster, known as the Deadly Dozen poster, is captioned "GUILTY" at the top, beneath which in slightly smaller print the poster indicates "OF CRIMES AGAINST HUMANITY." Under the heading "THE DEADLY DOZEN," the poster identifies thirteen abortion providers, three of whom file suit under the Freedom of Access to Clinics Entrances Act (FACE), which gives aggrieved persons a right of action against whoever by "threat of force ... intentionally ... intimidates ... any person because that person is or has been ... providing reproductive health services." The poster lists the names and home addresses of the doctors and offers a "$5,000 REWARD" "for information leading to arrest, conviction, and revocation of license to practice medicine." At the bottom, the poster bears the legend "ABORTIONIST" in large, bold typeface. Suppose also

that the "GUILTY" posters are circulated roughly three months after another group in another State had posted a series of "WANTED" and "unWANTED" posters that had identified other doctors who performed abortions and who were subsequently murdered by violent third parties who were not associated with the other group or the defendant organization in this case. As a result of these past acts of violence, the FBI offers protection to the doctors identified on the Deadly Dozen poster the day after it is released and advises them to wear bulletproof vests and take other security precautions. Do the posters constitute true threats on their face? In the context of the prior posters in other states and the murder of other doctors? *See Planned Parenthood of the Columbia/Willamette, Inc. v. American Coalition of Life Advocates*, 290 F.3d 1058 (9th Cir. 2002) (holding in a 6–5 *en banc* decision that the poster constituted a true threat).

d. Obscenity

Though the Supreme Court long stated that obscene material was not protected by the Free Speech Clause, *e.g.*, *Chaplinsky v. New Hampshire*, 315 U.S. 568 (1942), it was not until *Roth v. United States*, 354 U.S. 476, 485 (1957), that the Supreme Court directly held that obscenity was unprotected. The Court reasoned that the Free Speech Clause's history and original meaning did not protect obscenity, *id.* at 483, and that obscene materials are "utterly without redeeming social importance." *Id.* at 484.

The *Roth* Court's holding was clear—obscene materials do not merit First Amendment protection—however, the Court's definition of obscenity was itself unclear. The Court defined obscenity as "material which deals with sex in a manner appealing to prurient interest." *Id.* at 487. Prurient interest, in turn, was defined as "material having a tendency to excite lustful thoughts." *Id.* at 487 n.20.

Following *Roth*, the Supreme Court was inundated with challenges to convictions under state and federal obscenity laws. The Court badly fractured both on what standard to apply and whether the particular subject matter in each case constituted obscenity. *E.g.*, *Jacobellis v. Ohio*, 378 U.S. 184, 197 (1964); *Memoirs v. Massachusetts*, 383 U.S. 413 (1966). The Supreme Court even resorted to the unusual policy of summarily reversing obscenity convictions when a cobbled-together majority of the Court agreed on application of their various standards. *E.g.*, *Redrup v. New York*, 386 U.S. 767 (1967) (per curium); *see also Miller v. California*, 413 U.S. 15, 22 n.3 (1973) (noting that this summary reversal procedure was utilized in thirty-one cases). It was in this trying context that an exasperated Justice Stewart famously stated: "It is possible to read the Court's opinion in *Roth v. United States*…, 354 U.S. 476, in a variety of ways. In saying this, I imply no criticism of the Court, which … was faced with the task of trying to define what may be indefinable. I have reached the conclusion … that under the First and Fourteenth Amendments criminal laws in this area are constitutionally limited to hard-core pornography. I shall not today attempt further to define the kinds of material I understand to be embraced within that shorthand description; and perhaps I could never succeed in intelligibly doing so. But I know it when I see it, and the motion picture involved in this case is not that." *Jacobellis v. Ohio*, 378 U.S. 184, 197 (1964) (Stewart, J., concurring) (internal citations omitted).

Many commentators expected the Supreme Court to abandon *Roth* and rule that obscenity was protected. However, in *Miller v. California*, 413 U.S. 15 (1973), the Supreme Court adopted the test that still governs today.

Miller v. California
413 U.S. 15 (1973)

MR. CHIEF JUSTICE BURGER delivered the opinion of the Court.

This is one of a group of "obscenity-pornography" cases being reviewed by the Court in a re-examination of standards enunciated in earlier cases involving what Mr. Justice Harlan called "the intractable obscenity problem."

Appellant conducted a mass mailing campaign to advertise the sale of illustrated books, euphemistically called "adult" material. After a jury trial, he was convicted of violating California Penal Code § 311.2(a), a misdemeanor, by knowingly distributing obscene matter, and the Appellate Department, Superior Court of California, County of Orange, summarily affirmed the judgment without opinion. Appellant's conviction was specifically based on his conduct in causing five unsolicited advertising brochures to be sent through the mail in an envelope addressed to a restaurant in Newport Beach, California. The envelope was opened by the manager of the restaurant and his mother. They had not requested the brochures; they complained to the police.

The brochures advertise four books entitled "Intercourse," "Man-Woman," "Sex Orgies Illustrated," and "An Illustrated History of Pornography," and a film entitled "Marital Intercourse." While the brochures contain some descriptive printed material, primarily they consist of pictures and drawings very explicitly depicting men and women in groups of two or more engaging in a variety of sexual activities, with genitals often prominently displayed.

I

... [S]ince the Court now undertakes to formulate standards more concrete than those in the past, it is useful for us to focus on two of the landmark cases in the somewhat tortured history of the Court's obscenity decisions. In *Roth v. United States*, 354 U.S. 476 (1957), the Court sustained a conviction under a federal statute punishing the mailing of "obscene, lewd, lascivious or filthy ..." materials. The key to that holding was the Court's rejection of the claim that obscene materials were protected by the First Amendment.

Apart from the initial formulation in the *Roth* case, no majority of the Court has at any given time been able to agree on a standard to determine what constitutes obscene, pornographic material subject to regulation under the States' police power.

II

This much has been categorically settled by the Court, that obscene material is unprotected by the First Amendment. *Roth v. United States*, 354 U.S., at 485. We acknowledge, however, the inherent dangers of undertaking to regulate any form of expression. State statutes designed to regulate obscene materials must be carefully limited. As a result, we now confine the permissible scope of such regulation to works which depict or describe sexual conduct. That conduct must be specifically defined by the applicable state law, as written or authoritatively construed.

The basic guidelines for the trier of fact must be: (a) whether "the average person, applying contemporary community standards" would find that the work, taken as a whole, appeals to the prurient interest, (b) whether the work depicts or describes, in a patently offensive way, sexual conduct specifically defined by the applicable state law; and (c) whether the work, taken as a whole, lacks serious literary, artistic, political, or scientific value. If a state law that regulates obscene material is thus limited, as written or construed, the First Amendment values applicable to the States through the Fourteenth Amendment are adequately protected by the ultimate power of appellate courts to conduct an independent review of constitutional claims when necessary.

We emphasize that it is not our function to propose regulatory schemes for the States. That must await their concrete legislative efforts. It is possible, however, to give a few plain examples of what a state statute could define for regulation under part (b) of the standard announced in this opinion, *supra*:

(a) Patently offensive representations or descriptions of ultimate sexual acts, normal or perverted, actual or simulated.

(b) Patently offensive representation or descriptions of masturbation, excretory functions, and lewd exhibition of the genitals.

Sex and nudity may not be exploited without limit by films or pictures exhibited or sold in places of public accommodation any more than live sex and nudity can be exhibited or sold without limit in such public places.[8] At a minimum, prurient, patently offensive depiction or description of sexual conduct must have serious literary, artistic, political, or scientific value to merit First Amendment protection. For example, medical books for the education of physicians and related personnel necessarily use graphic illustrations and descriptions of human anatomy. In resolving the inevitably sensitive questions of fact and law, we must continue to rely on the jury system, accompanied by the safeguards that judges, rules of evidence, presumption of innocence, and other protective features provide.

It is certainly true that the absence, since *Roth*, of a single majority view of this Court as to proper standards for testing obscenity has placed a strain on both state and federal courts. But today, for the first time since *Roth* was decided in 1957, a majority of this Court has agreed on concrete guidelines to isolate "hard core" pornography from expression protected by the First Amendment.

---

8. Although we are not presented here with the problem of regulating lewd public conduct itself, the States have greater power to regulate nonverbal, physical conduct than to suppress depictions or descriptions of the same behavior. *United States v. O'Brien*, 391 U.S. 367 (1968).

III

Under a National Constitution, fundamental First Amendment limitations on the powers of the States do not vary from community to community, but this does not mean that there are, or should or can be, fixed, uniform national standards of precisely what appeals to the "prurient interest" or is "patently offensive." These are essentially questions of fact, and our Nation is simply too big and too diverse for this Court to reasonably expect that such standards could be articulated for all 50 States in a single formulation, even assuming the prerequisite consensus exists. When triers of fact are asked to decide whether "the average person, applying contemporary community standards" would consider certain materials "prurient," it would be unrealistic to require that the answer be based on some abstract formulation. The adversary system, with lay jurors as the usual ultimate fact finders in criminal prosecutions, has historically permitted triers of fact to draw on the standards of their community, guided always by limiting instructions on the law. To require a State to structure obscenity proceedings around evidence of a national "community standard" would be an exercise in futility.... We hold that the requirement that the jury evaluate the materials with reference to "contemporary standards of the State of California" serves this protective purpose and is constitutionally adequate.

IV

The dissenting Justices sound the alarm of repression. But, in our view, to equate the free and robust exchange of ideas and political debate with commercial exploitation of obscene material demeans the grand conception of the First Amendment and its high purposes in the historic struggle for freedom. The First Amendment protects works which, taken as a whole, have serious literary, artistic, political, or scientific value, regardless of whether the government or a majority of the people approve of the ideas these works represent. But the public portrayal of hard-core sexual conduct for its own sake, and for the ensuing commercial gain, is a different matter.

There is no evidence, empirical or historical, that the stern 19th century American censorship of public distribution and display of material relating to sex in any way limited or affected expression of serious literary, artistic, political, or scientific ideas. On the contrary, it is beyond any question that the era following Thomas Jefferson to Theodore Roosevelt was an "extraordinarily vigorous period," not just in economics and politics, but in belles lettres and in "the outlying fields of social and political philosophies."

The judgment of the Appellate Department of the Superior Court, Orange County, California, is vacated and the case remanded to that court for further proceedings not inconsistent with the First Amendment standards established by this opinion.

Vacated and remanded.

Mr. Justice Douglas, dissenting.

I

Today we leave open the way for California to send a man to prison for distributing brochures that advertise books and a movie under freshly written standards defining obscenity which until today's decision were never the part of any law. [T]he Court retreats from the earlier formulations of the constitutional test and undertakes to make new definitions. The difficulty is that we do not deal with constitutional terms, since "obscenity" is not mentioned in the Constitution or Bill of Rights. And the First Amendment makes no such exception from "the press" which it undertakes to protect nor, as I have said on other occasions, is an exception necessarily implied, for there was no recognized exception to the free press at the time the Bill of Rights was adopted which treated "obscene" publications differently from other types of papers, magazines, and books. So there are no constitutional guidelines for deciding what is and what is not "obscene." The Court is at large because we deal with tastes and standards of literature. What shocks me may be sustenance for my neighbor. What causes one person to boil up in rage over one pamphlet or movie may reflect only his neurosis, not shared by others. We deal here with a regime of censorship which, if adopted, should be done by constitutional amendment after full debate by the people.

III

The idea that the First Amendment permits government to ban publications that are "offensive" to some people puts an ominous gloss on freedom of the press. That test would make it possible to ban any paper or any journal or magazine in some benighted place. The First Amendment was designed "to invite dispute," to induce "a condition of unrest," to "create dissatisfaction with conditions as they are," and even to stir "people' to anger." The idea that the First Amendment permits punishment for ideas that are "offensive" to the particular judge or jury sitting in judgment is astounding.... The tendency throughout history has been to subdue the individual and to exalt the power of government. The use of the standard "offensive" gives authority to government that cuts the very vitals out of the First Amendment.

Mr. Justice Brennan, with whom Mr. Justice Stewart and Mr. Justice Marshall join, dissenting. [Opinion omitted.]

Exercise 26:

1. What is the test articulated by the *Miller* Court to identify unprotected obscene speech?

2. Does the *Miller* test provide the clarity lacking under *Roth*? Or, is it so vague that it too will provide a vehicle for speech suppression?

3. Does the *Miller* test draw the line between protected and unprotected speech in the correct place? If not, where should the line be?

4. Does the use of local community standards to determine whether the work "appeals to the prurient interest" undermine the First Amendment?

5. What does "taken as a whole" mean? Is it an entire exhibit, or one painting in an exhibit? Is it one scene from a movie, or the entire movie?

6. Was it appropriate for the Supreme Court to create such as detailed "test"? Was the Court inappropriately acting like a legislature?

7. Why did the Supreme Court struggle with the definition of obscenity for almost twenty years?

8. Does the logic of Justice Douglas' dissent lead to no limits on obscene materials? If so, is that result consistent with the Clause's original meaning, purposes, and the Court's precedent?

The Supreme Court's fullest justification for not protecting obscene speech is found in a case decided the same day as *Miller*:

Paris Adult Theatre I v. Slaton
413 U.S. 49 (1973)

MR. CHIEF JUSTICE BURGER delivered the opinion of the Court.

Petitioners are two Atlanta, Georgia, movie theaters and their owners and managers, operating in the style of "adult" theaters. On December 28, 1970, respondents, the local state district attorney and the solicitor for the local state trial court, filed civil complaints in that court alleging that petitioners were exhibiting to the public for paid admission two allegedly obscene films, contrary to Georgia Code Ann. §26-2101.[1] The two films in question, "Magic Mirror" and "It All Comes Out in the End," depict sexual conduct characterized by the Georgia Supreme Court as "hard core pornography" leaving "little to the imagination."

On January 13, 1971, 15 days after the proceedings began, the films were produced by petitioners at a jury-waived trial. Certain photographs, also produced at trial, were stipulated to portray the single entrance to both Paris Adult Theatre I and Paris Adult Theatre II as it appeared at the time of the complaints. These photographs show a conventional, inoffensive theater entrance, without any pictures, but with signs indicating that the theaters exhibit "Atlanta's Finest Mature Feature Films." On the door itself is a sign saying: "Adult Theatre—You must be 21 and able to prove it. If viewing the nude body offends you, Please Do Not Enter." On April 12, 1971, the trial judge dismissed respondents' complaints.

On appeal, the Georgia Supreme Court unanimously reversed. It held that the films were without protection under the First Amendment.

I

It should be clear from the outset that we do not undertake to tell the States what they must do, but rather to define the area in which they may chart their own course

----

1. Georgia Code Ann. §26-2101 reads in relevant part:
   "Distributing obscene materials.
   "(b) Material is obscene if considered as a whole, applying community standards, its pre-dominant appeal is to prurient interest, that is, a shameful or morbid interest in nudity, sex or excretion, and utterly without redeeming social value and if, in addition, it goes sub-stantially beyond customary limits of candor in describing or representing such matters...."

in dealing with obscene material. This Court has consistently held that obscene material is not protected by the First Amendment as a limitation on the state police power by virtue of the Fourteenth Amendment. *Miller v. California*, 413 U.S. 15, 23–25 [(1973)]; *Roth v. United States*, 354 U.S. 476, 485 (1957).

Today, in *Miller v. California, supra*, we have sought to clarify the constitutional definition of obscene material subject to regulation by the States, and we vacate and remand this case for reconsideration in light of Miller.

II

We categorically disapprove the theory, apparently adopted by the trial judge, that obscene, pornographic films acquire constitutional immunity from state regulation simply because they are exhibited for consenting adults only. Although we have often pointedly recognized the high importance of the state interest in regulating the exposure of obscene materials to juveniles and unconsenting adults, see *Miller v. California, supra*, 413 U.S., at 18–20; *Stanley v. Georgia*, 394 U.S. [557], 567 [(1969)], this Court has never declared these to be the only legitimate state interests permitting regulation of obscene material. The States have a long-recognized legitimate interest in regulating the use of obscene material in local commerce and in all places of public accommodation. "In an unbroken series of cases extending over a long stretch of this Court's history it has been accepted as a postulate that 'the primary requirements of decency may be enforced against obscene publications.' *Near v. Minnesota ex rel. Olson*, 283 U.S. 697, 716 (1931)."

In particular, we hold that there are legitimate state interests at stake in stemming the tide of commercialized obscenity, even assuming it is feasible to enforce effective safeguards against exposure to juveniles and to passersby.[7] Rights and interests "other than those of the advocates are involved." These include the interest of the public in the quality of life and the total community environment, the tone of commerce in the great city centers, and, possibly, the public safety itself. The Hill-Link Minority Report of the Commission on Obscenity and Pornography indicates that there is at least an arguable correlation between obscene material and crime.[8]

But, it is argued, there are no scientific data which conclusively demonstrate that exposure to obscene material adversely affects men and women or their society.

---

7. An "adult" bookstore, dealing in obscene books, magazines, and pictures, cannot realistically make this claim. The Hill-Link Minority Report of the Commission on Obscenity and Pornography emphasizes evidence that, although most pornography may be bought by elders, "the heavy users and most highly exposed people to pornography are adolescent females (among women) and adolescent and young adult males (among men)." The Report of the Commission on Obscenity and Pornography 401 (1970). The legitimate interest in preventing exposure of juveniles to obscene materials cannot be fully served by simply barring juveniles from the immediate physical premises of "adult" book stores, when there is a flourishing "outside business" in these materials.

8. The Report of the Commission on Obscenity and Pornography 390–412 (1970). Congress and the legislatures of every State have enacted measures to restrict the distribution of erotic and pornographic material, [and] justify these controls by reference to evidence that antisocial behavior may result in part from reading obscenity.

It is urged on behalf of the petitioners that, absent such a demonstration, [this] kind of state regulation is "impermissible." We reject this argument. It is not for us to resolve empirical uncertainties underlying state legislation, save in the exceptional case where that legislation plainly impinges upon rights protected by the Constitution itself. Although there is no conclusive proof of a connection between antisocial behavior and obscene material, the legislature of Georgia could quite reasonably determine that such a connection does or might exist. In deciding Roth, this Court implicitly accepted that a legislature could legitimately act on such a conclusion to protect "the social interest in order and morality." *Roth v. United States*, 354 U.S., at 485, quoting *Chaplinsky v. New Hampshire*, 315 U.S. 568, 572 (1942).

From the beginning of civilized societies, legislators and judges have acted on various unprovable assumptions. Such assumptions underlie much lawful state regulation of commercial and business affairs. The same is true of the federal securities and antitrust laws and a host of federal regulations. Understandably those who entertain an absolutist view of the First Amendment find it uncomfortable to explain why rights of association, speech, and press should be severely restrained in the marketplace of goods and money, but not in the marketplace of pornography.

If we accept the unprovable assumption that a complete education requires the reading of certain books, and the well nigh universal belief that good books, plays, and art lift the spirit, improve the mind, enrich the human personality, and develop character, can we then say that a state legislature may not act on the corollary assumption that commerce in obscene books, or public exhibitions focused on obscene conduct, have a tendency to exert a corrupting and debasing impact leading to antisocial behavior? The sum of experience, including that of the past two decades, affords an ample basis for legislatures to conclude that a sensitive, key relationship of human existence, central to family life, community welfare, and the development of human personality, can be debased and distorted by crass commercial exploitation of sex. Nothing in the Constitution prohibits a State from reaching such a conclusion and acting on it legislatively simply because there is no conclusive evidence or empirical data.

It is argued that individual 'free will' must govern, even in activities beyond the protection of the First Amendment and other constitutional guarantees of privacy, and that government cannot legitimately impede an individual's desire to see or acquire obscene plays, movies, and books. We do indeed base our society on certain assumptions that people have the capacity for free choice. Most exercises of individual free choice—those in politics, religion, and expression of ideas—are explicitly protected by the Constitution. Totally unlimited play for free will, however, is not allowed in our or any other society. We have just noted, for example, that neither the First Amendment nor "free will" precludes States from having "blue sky" laws to regulate what sellers of securities may write or publish about their wares. Such laws are to protect the weak, the uninformed, the unsuspecting, and the gullible from the exercise of their own volition. Nor do modern societies leave disposal of garbage and sewage up to the individual "free will," but impose regulation to protect both public health and the appearance of public places.

The States, of course, may follow a "laissez-faire" policy and drop all controls on commercialized obscenity, if that is what they prefer, just as they can ignore consumer protection in the marketplace, but nothing in the Constitution compels the States to do so with regard to matters falling within state jurisdiction. "We do not sit as a super-legislature to determine the wisdom, need, and propriety of laws that touch economic problems, business affairs, or social conditions." *Griswold v. Connecticut*, 381 U.S. 479, 482 (1965).

It is asserted, however, that standards for evaluating state commercial regulations are inapposite in the present context, as state regulation of access by consenting adults to obscene material violates the constitutionally protected right to privacy enjoyed by petitioners' customers. [I]t is unavailing to compare a theater, open to the public for a fee, with the private home of Stanley v. Georgia, 394 U.S., at 568, and the marital bedroom of *Griswold v. Connecticut, supra*, 381 U.S., at 485–486. This Court, has, on numerous occasions, refused to hold that commercial ventures such as a motion-picture house are "private" for the purpose of civil rights litigation and civil rights statutes. See *Heart of Atlanta Motel, Inc. v. United States*, 379 U.S. 241, 247, 260–261 (1964).

To summarize, we have today reaffirmed the basic holding of *Roth v. United States, supra*, that obscene material has no protection under the First Amendment. See *Miller v. California*. We have directed our holdings, not at thoughts or speech, but at depiction and description of specifically defined sexual conduct that States may regulate within limits designed to prevent infringement of First Amendment rights. We have also reaffirmed that commerce in obscene material is unprotected by any constitutional doctrine of privacy. In this case we hold that the States have a legitimate interest in regulating commerce in obscene material and in regulating exhibition of obscene material in places of public accommodation, including so-called "adult" theaters from which minors are excluded. In light of these holdings, nothing precludes the State of Georgia from the regulation of the allegedly obscene material exhibited in Paris Adult Theatre I or II, provided that the applicable Georgia law, as written or authoritatively interpreted by the Georgia courts, meets the First Amendment standards set forth in *Miller v. California, supra*, 413 U.S., at 23–25.

Vacated and remanded.

Mr. Justice Douglas, dissenting. [Opinion omitted.]

Mr. Justice Brennan, with whom Mr. Justice Stewart and Mr. Justice Marshall join, dissenting.

This case requires the Court to confront once again the vexing problem of reconciling state efforts to suppress sexually oriented expression with the protections of the First Amendment, as applied to the States through the Fourteenth Amendment. No other aspect of the First Amendment has, in recent years, demanded so substantial a commitment of our time, generated such disharmony of views, and remained so resistant to the formulation of stable and manageable standards. I am convinced that the approach initiated 16 years ago in *Roth v. United States*, 354 U.S. 476 (1957), and culminating in the Court's decision today, cannot bring stability to this area of the law without jeopardizing fundamental First Amendment values, and I have concluded that the time has come to make a significant departure from that approach.

Exercise 27:

1. What is the Supreme Court's justification for ruling that obscenity is not protected by the Free Speech Clause? Evaluate the Supreme Court's argument.

2. The Supreme Court also suggested that exposure to obscene material may cause other social problems, such as crime. This claim was, and remains, controversial. What evidence would be sufficient to support that link? Assume that there is no conclusive evidence on a causal connection, though there is some evidence that could plausibly support the connection. How should the Court treat legislative judgment in that scenario?

3. Relatedly, the Supreme Court argued that this was an area of constitutional law where the states retained freedom to regulate or not regulate as they saw fit. Why, according to the Court? What are the merits and demerits to this position?

4. Is the Supreme Court's explanation for why government may prohibit obscenity consistent with other areas of constitutional law? For example, is the Supreme Court's claim in *Paris Adult Theatre* that "complete education requires the reading of certain books, and the well nigh universal belief that good books, plays, and art lift the spirit, improve the mind, enrich the human personality, and develop character" consistent with the *Casey* Court's statement that "[a]t the heart of liberty is the right to define one's own concept of existence, of meaning, of the universe, and of the mystery of human life. Beliefs about these matters could not define the attributes of personhood were they formed under compulsion of the State"? *Planned Parenthood v. Casey*, 505 U.S. 833, 851 (1992). If they are inconsistent, which is the more attractive view?

5. Is the Supreme Court's claim that "complete education requires the reading of certain books, and the well nigh universal belief that good books, plays, and art lift the spirit, improve the mind, enrich the human personality, and develop character" true? How would one support or disprove that claim?

6. The majority claimed that the Court's substantive due process precedent did not entail a right to obscenity, though its argument was thin. How would you make that argument? Is it persuasive?

––––––––––

The Supreme Court has ruled that the government cannot prohibit possession of obscene materials, at least in the context of one's home. In *Stanley v. Georgia*, 394 U.S. 557, 572 (1969), the Court held that the First Amendment right to receive information, coupled with "the right to be let alone," required protection for possession of obscene material. *Id.* at 564. *Stanley* is in tension with other cases, though it has not been overruled.

First, *Stanley* does not fit well with *Paris Adult Theatre*'s rationale for not protecting obscenity. If, as *Paris Adult Theatre* argued, obscenity is without value and harms its "consumers" and the broader culture, then viewing obscenity in one's house falls within that rationale. Second, later cases have limited *Stanley*. *See, e.g., United States v. Reidel*, 402 U.S. 351 (1971) (holding that the First Amendment did not protect distribution of obscene material, distinguishing *Stanley*). Third, as you will see below, *Stanley* is in tension with the Supreme Court's ruling that the government may criminalize possession of child pornography.

e. Child Pornography

A category of speech distinct from obscenity, which also falls outside the protection of the Free Speech Clause, is child pornography. The Supreme Court defined this category in the 1982 case that follows:

New York v. Ferber

458 U.S. 747 (1982)

JUSTICE WHITE delivered the opinion of the Court.

At issue in this case is the constitutionality of a New York criminal statute which prohibits persons from knowingly promoting sexual performances by children under the age of 16 by distributing material which depicts such performances.

I

In recent years, the exploitive use of children in the production of pornography has become a serious national problem. The Federal Government and 47 States have sought to combat the problem with statutes specifically directed at the production of child pornography. Thirty-five States and the United States Congress have also passed legislation prohibiting the distribution of such materials.... At issue in this case is § 263.15, defining a class D felony: "A person is guilty of promoting a sexual performance by a child when, knowing the character and content thereof, he produces, directs or promotes any performance which includes sexual conduct by a child less than sixteen years of age."

This case arose when Paul Ferber, the proprietor of a Manhattan bookstore specializing in sexually oriented products, sold two films to an undercover police officer. The films are devoted almost exclusively to depicting young boys masturbating. Ferber was indicted on two counts of violating § 263.15. After a jury trial, Ferber was found guilty of the two counts under § 263.15, which did not require proof that the films were obscene. Ferber's convictions were affirmed without opinion by the Appellate Division of the New York.

The New York Court of Appeals reversed, holding that § 263.15 violated the First Amendment. We granted the State's petition for certiorari.

II

The Court of Appeals proceeded on the assumption that the standard of obscenity, which follows the guidelines enunciated in *Miller v. California*, 413 U.S. 15 (1973), constitutes the appropriate line dividing protected from unprotected expression by which to measure a regulation directed at child pornography.

The Court of Appeals' assumption was not unreasonable in light of our decisions. This case, however, constitutes our first examination of a statute directed at and limited to depictions of sexual activity involving children. We believe our inquiry should begin with the question of whether a State has somewhat more freedom in proscribing works which portray sexual acts or lewd exhibitions of genitalia by children.

A

In *Chaplinsky v. New Hampshire*, 315 U.S. 568 (1942), the Court laid the foundation for the excision of obscenity from the realm of constitutionally protected expression:

> "There are certain well-defined and narrowly limited classes of speech, the prevention and punishment of which have never been thought to raise any Constitutional problem. These include the lewd and obscene.... It has been well observed that such utterances are no essential part of any exposition of ideas, and are of such slight social value as a step to truth that any benefit that may be derived from them is clearly outweighed by the social interest in order and morality."

B

The *Miller* standard, like its predecessors, was an accommodation between the State's interests in protecting the "sensibilities of unwilling recipients" from exposure to pornographic material and the dangers of censorship inherent in unabashedly content-based laws.... For the following reasons, we are persuaded that the States are entitled to greater leeway in the regulation of pornographic depictions of children.

First. It is evident beyond the need for elaboration that a State's interest in "safeguarding the physical and psychological well-being of a minor" is "compelling." "A democratic society rests, for its continuance, upon the healthy, well-rounded growth of young people into full maturity as citizens." *Prince v. Massachusetts*, 321 U.S. 158 (1944). Accordingly, we have sustained legislation aimed at protecting the physical and emotional well-being of youth even when the laws have operated in the sensitive area of constitutionally protected rights. In *Prince v. Massachusetts*, the Court held that a statute prohibiting use of a child to distribute literature on the street was valid notwithstanding the statute's effect on a First Amendment activity. Most recently, we held that the Government's interest in the "well-being of its youth" justified special treatment of indecent broadcasting received by adults as well as children. *FCC v. Pacifica Foundation*, 438 U.S. 726 (1978).

The prevention of sexual exploitation and abuse of children constitutes a government objective of surpassing importance. The legislative findings accompanying passage of the New York laws reflect this concern:

"[There] has been a proliferation of exploitation of children as subjects in sexual performances. The care of children is a sacred trust and should not be abused by those who seek to profit through a commercial network based upon the exploitation of children." 1977 N.Y. Laws, ch. 910, § 1.

We shall not second-guess this legislative judgment. Respondent has not intimated that we do so. Suffice it to say that virtually all of the States and the United States have passed legislation proscribing the production of or otherwise combating "child pornography." The legislative judgment, as well as the judgment found in the relevant literature, is that the use of children as subjects of pornographic materials is harmful to the physiological, emotional, and mental health of the child.[9] That judgment, we think, easily passes muster under the First Amendment....

Second. The distribution of photographs and films depicting sexual activity by juveniles is intrinsically related to the sexual abuse of children in at least two ways. First, the materials produced are a permanent record of the children's participation and the harm to the child is exacerbated by their circulation. Second, the distribution network for child pornography must be closed if the production of material which requires the sexual exploitation of children is to be effectively controlled. Indeed, there is no serious contention that the legislature was unjustified in believing that it is difficult, if not impossible, to halt the exploitation of children by pursuing only those who produce the photographs and movies. While the production of pornographic materials is a low-profile, clandestine industry, the need to market the resulting products requires a visible apparatus of distribution. The most expeditious if not the only practical method of law enforcement may be to dry up the market for this material by imposing severe criminal penalties on persons selling, advertising, or otherwise promoting the product. Thirty-five States and Congress have concluded that restraints on the distribution of pornographic materials are required in order to effectively combat the problem, and there is a body of literature and testimony to support these legislative conclusions.

Respondent argues that it is enough for the State to prohibit the distribution of materials that are legally obscene under the *Miller* test. The *Miller* standard, like all general definitions of what may be banned as obscene, does not reflect the State's particular and more compelling interest in prosecuting those who promote the sexual exploitation of children. Thus, the question under the *Miller* test bears no connection to the issue of whether a child has been physically or psychologically harmed in the production of the work. Similarly, a sexually explicit depiction need not be "patently offensive" in order to have required the sexual exploitation of a child for its production. In addition, a work which, taken on the whole, contains serious literary, artistic, po-

---

9. "[T]he use of children as ... subjects of pornographic materials is very harmful to both the children and the society as a whole." S. Rep. No. 95-438, p. 5 (1977), U.S. Code Cong. & Admin. News 1978, p. 42. It has been found that sexually exploited children are unable to develop healthy affectionate relationships in later life, have sexual dysfunctions, and have a tendency to become sexual abusers as adults. Sexual molestation by adults is often involved in the production of child sexual performances.

litical, or scientific value may nevertheless embody the hardest core of child pornography. We therefore cannot conclude that the *Miller* standard is a satisfactory solution to the child pornography problem.

Third. The advertising and selling of child pornography provide an economic motive for and are thus an integral part of the production of such materials, an activity illegal throughout the Nation. "It rarely has been suggested that the constitutional freedom for speech and press extends its immunity to speech or writing used as an integral part of conduct in violation of a valid criminal statute." We note that were the statutes outlawing the employment of children in these films and photographs fully effective, and the constitutionality of these laws has not been questioned, the First Amendment implications would be no greater than that presented by laws against distribution: enforceable production laws would leave no child pornography to be marketed.

Fourth. The value of permitting live performances and photographic reproductions of children engaged in lewd sexual conduct is exceedingly modest, if not *de minimis.* We consider it unlikely that visual depictions of children performing sexual acts or lewdly exhibiting their genitals would often constitute an important and necessary part of a literary performance or scientific or educational work. As a state judge in this case observed, if it were necessary for literary or artistic value, a person over the statutory age who perhaps looked younger could be utilized. Simulation outside of the prohibition of the statute could provide another alternative. Nor is there any question here of censoring a particular literary theme or portrayal of sexual activity. The First Amendment interest is limited to that of rendering the portrayal somewhat more "realistic" by utilizing or photographing children.

Fifth. Recognizing and classifying child pornography as a category of material outside the protection of the First Amendment is not incompatible with our earlier decisions. [I]t is not rare that a content-based classification of speech has been accepted because it may be appropriately generalized that within the confines of the given classification, the evil to be restricted so overwhelmingly outweighs the expressive interests, if any, at stake, that no process of case-by-case adjudication is required. When a definable class of material, such as that covered by § 263.15, bears so heavily and pervasively on the welfare of children engaged in its production, we think the balance of competing interests is clearly struck and that it is permissible to consider these materials as without the protection of the First Amendment.

C

There are, of course, limits on the category of child pornography which is unprotected by the First Amendment. As with all legislation in this sensitive area, the conduct to be prohibited must be adequately defined by the applicable state law, as written or authoritatively construed. Here the nature of the harm to be combated requires that the state offense be limited to works that *visually* depict sexual conduct by children below a specified age.

We note that the distribution of descriptions or other depictions of sexual conduct, not otherwise obscene, which do not involve live performance or photographic or other visual reproduction of live performances, retains First Amendment protection. As with obscenity laws, criminal responsibility may not be imposed without some element of scienter on the part of the defendant.

D

We hold that § 263.15 sufficiently describes a category of material the production and distribution of which is not entitled to First Amendment protection. It also follows that the State is not barred by the First Amendment from prohibiting the distribution of unprotected materials produced outside the State.

IV

The judgment of the New York Court of Appeals is reversed, and the case is remanded to that court for further proceedings not inconsistent with this opinion.

[I]n my view application of § 263.15 or any similar statute to depictions of children that in themselves do have serious literary, artistic, scientific, or medical value, would violate the First Amendment. As the Court recognizes, the limited classes of speech, the suppression of which does not raise serious First Amendment concerns, have two attributes. They are of exceedingly "slight social value," and the State has a compelling interest in their regulation. The First Amendment value of depictions of children that are in themselves serious contributions to art, literature, or science, is, by definition, simply not "*de minimis*." At the same time, the State's interest in suppression of such materials is likely to be far less compelling. For the Court's assumption of harm to the child resulting from the "permanent record" and "circulation" of the child's "participation," lacks much of its force where the depiction is a serious contribution to art or science. The production of materials of serious value is not the "low-profile, clandestine industry" that according to the Court produces purely pornographic materials.

With this understanding, I concur in the Court's judgment in this case.

JUSTICE STEVENS, concurring in the judgment. [Opinion omitted.]

Exercise 28:

1. Why did the Supreme Court hold that child pornography was unprotected by the Free Speech Clause?

2. Justice White argued that a category of speech, child pornography, was unprotected by the Free Speech Clause because, as a category, the value of such speech was outweighed by the speech's cost. Is that judgment accurate? What evidence persuaded the Justices? Are the justices the best officials to make that judgment?

3. Why did the Court note the actions of the federal and state governments limiting child pornography?

4. Thinking back to the purported purposes of free speech, which of those purposes support and which are in tension with the Supreme Court's ruling?

5. Why did the cases governing obscenity, such as *Miller v. California*, 413 U.S. 15 (1973), not decide this case?

6. Why did it take until 1982 for the Supreme Court to face the question whether child pornography was protected under the Free Speech Clause?

7. Under the Court's ruling, what may the government prohibit? Production of child pornography? Its distribution?

8. What is Justice Brennan's position on protection for child pornography? Is he suggesting that such protection should depend on case-by-case analysis in each case, or is he proposing that the category of unprotected child pornography is narrower than that identified by the majority?

Later, in *Osborne v. Ohio*, 495 U.S. 103 (1990), the Supreme Court ruled that Ohio's ban on the possession of child pornography was constitutional. The Court found that "[i]t is ... surely reasonable for the State to conclude that it will decrease the production of child pornography if it penalizes those who possess and view the product, thereby decreasing demand." *Id.* at 109–110. As in *Ferber*, therefore, reducing possession of child pornography would reduce its production and attendant harms. In reaching this conclusion, the Court distinguished *Stanley v. Georgia*, discussed above, characterizing *Stanley* as a "narrow holding." *Id.* at 108.

The category of child pornography is firmly entrenched as unprotected by the Constitution. However, its scope remains uncertain. In particular, and in response to the proliferation of child pornography on the internet, the federal government passed the Child Pornography Prevention Act of 1996, 18 U.S.C. § 2251 *et seq.*, that proscribed images that appeared to depict child pornography, but which were made without children, for instance, with computer-generated images of children. The Supreme Court, in a fractured opinion, struck down the Act because the speech prohibited by the act was not the result of or would not result in harm to children, and therefore the Act was overbroad. *Ashcroft v. Free Speech Coalition*, 535 U.S. 234, 250 (2002).

Congress thereafter drafted the Prosecutorial Remedies and Other Tools to End the Exploitation of Children Today (PROTECT) Act of 2003, 18 U.S.C. § 2252A. This Act prohibits the knowing pandering and solicitation of material that "reflects the belief, or that is intended to cause another to believe" the material is child pornography. *Id.* § 2252A(a)(3)(B). In other words, the Act did not require that the pandered or solicited material be produced with children. The Supreme Court concluded that "offers to provide or requests to obtain child pornography are categorically excluded from the First Amendment." *United States v. Williams*, 553 U.S. 285, 299 (2008).

f. Speech Integral to Criminal Conduct

The Supreme Court also has held that the First Amendment does not protect speech integral to criminal (or unlawful) conduct, although the scope of this exception from protection remains somewhat unclear. The exception traces its modern roots back to at least *Giboney v. Empire Storage & Ice Co.*, 336 U.S. 490 (1949). In *Giboney*, a local union attempted to get all nonunion retail ice peddlers to join the union. As part of its plan, the union sought agreements from all wholesale ice distributors that they would not sell to nonunion ice peddlers. Empire Storage & Ice refused, and the union began picketing Empire with "the sole immediate object ... to compel Empire to agree to stop selling ice to nonunion peddlers." *Id.* at 492. Empire secured an injunction against the union under a Missouri law that criminalized "any ... combination ... or understanding ... in restraint of trade or competition in the ... transportation, manufacture, purchase or sale of any product or commodity." *Id.* at 491 n.1. The Supreme Court upheld the Missouri law, rejecting the union's claim "that the constitutional freedom for speech and press extends its immunity to speech or writing used as an integral part of conduct in violation of a valid criminal statute.... [C]onduct otherwise unlawful is [not] always immune from state regulation because an integral part of that conduct is carried on by display of placards by peaceful picketers." *Id.* at 498. According to the Court, "it has never been deemed an abridgement of freedom of speech ... to make a course of conduct illegal merely because the conduct was in part initiated, evidenced, or carried out by means of language, either spoken, written, or printed." *Id.* at 502.

More recently, the Court has invoked *Giboney* and the speech integral to criminal conduct exception in *Rumsfeld v. FAIR*, 547 U.S. 47, 62 (2006), and *United States v. Williams*, 553 U.S. 285, 297 (2008) (citing *Giboney* for the proposition that "[o]ffers to engage in illegal transactions are categorically excluded from First Amendment protection"). Yet *Williams* also confirmed the "important distinction between a proposal to engage in illegal activity and the abstract advocacy of illegality"—while the former is not protected, the latter is. *Id.* at 298–99. Thus, as *Williams* expressly notes, a child pornography statute may be constitutional if it "does not prohibit advocacy of child pornography, but only offers to provide or requests to obtain it." *Id.* at 299.

In the case that follows, the majority suggests that the child pornography exception, while a separate and distinct category of unprotected speech, is a particular (and perhaps unique) instance of the speech integral to criminal/unlawful conduct exception. Under this exception, then, the government may be able to restrict speech that seeks to cause or perhaps tends to cause certain unlawful conduct (other than the restricted speech itself) such as the restraint of trade in *Giboney* or the sexual abuse of children in *Ferber*.

At the same time, though, the majority indicates a reluctance to expand the categories of unprotected speech beyond the "historic and traditional categories long familiar to the bar" (*i.e.*, the types of exceptions discussed in this section), suggesting that any speech restrictions must be narrowly defined so as not to preclude speech that might inform or persuade individuals who will not engage in unlawful conduct. Thus, while the Court recently has reinvigorated the speech integral to unlawful conduct exception, the justices have not interpreted it broadly to encompass wide swaths of speech. Consequently, if a case involves restrictions on speech that falls outside the established categories of unprotected speech, the government might advance at least two related arguments: that a certain type of speech is integral to unlawful conduct (and, therefore, falls within that historic and traditional category), on that the specific prohibited speech is just like one of the long-recognized categories and, accordingly, should be treated the same way. As you read the following case, consider which argument(s) the government makes to support the federal ban on crush videos and how the majority and dissent evaluate the government's argument(s).

United States v. Stevens

559 U.S. 460 (2010)

CHIEF JUSTICE ROBERTS delivered the opinion of the Court.

Congress enacted 18 U.S.C. §48 to criminalize the commercial creation, sale, or possession of certain depictions of animal cruelty. The statute does not address underlying acts harmful to animals, but only portrayals of such conduct. The question presented is whether the prohibition in the statute is consistent with the freedom of speech guaranteed by the First Amendment. *Issue*

I

Section 48 establishes a criminal penalty of up to five years in prison for anyone who knowingly "creates, sells, or possesses a depiction of animal cruelty," if done "for commercial gain" in interstate or foreign commerce. A depiction of "animal cruelty" is defined as one "in which a living animal is intentionally maimed, mutilated, tortured, wounded, or killed," if that conduct violates federal or state law where "the creation, sale, or possession takes place." In what is referred to as the "exceptions clause," the law exempts from prohibition any depiction "that has serious religious, political, scientific, educational, journalistic, historical, or artistic value."

The legislative background of §48 focused primarily on the interstate market for "crush videos." According to the House Committee Report on the bill, such videos feature the intentional torture and killing of helpless animals, including cats, dogs, monkeys, mice, and hamsters. Crush videos often depict women slowly crushing animals to death "with their bare feet or while wearing high heeled shoes," sometimes while "talking to the animals in a kind of dominatrix patter" over "[t]he cries and squeals of the animals, obviously in great pain." Apparently these depictions "appeal to persons with a very specific sexual fetish who find them sexually arousing or otherwise exciting." The acts depicted in crush videos are typically prohibited by the animal cruelty laws enacted by all 50 States and the District of Columbia. But crush videos rarely disclose the participants' identities, inhibiting prosecution of the underlying conduct.

This case, however, involves an application of §48 to depictions of animal fighting. Dogfighting, for example, is unlawful in all 50 States and the District of Columbia and has been restricted by federal law since 1976. Robert J. Stevens ran a business, "Dogs of Velvet and Steel," and an associated Web site, through which he sold videos of pit bulls engaging in dogfights and attacking other animals. Among these videos were Japan Pit Fights and Pick-A-Winna: A Pit Bull Documentary, which include contemporary footage of dogfights in Japan (where such conduct is allegedly legal) as well as footage of American dogfights from the 1960's and 1970's. A third video,

Catch Dogs and Country Living, depicts the use of pit bulls to hunt wild boar, as well as a "gruesome" scene of a pit bull attacking a domestic farm pig. On the basis of these videos, Stevens was indicted on three counts of violating §48.

II

The Government's primary submission is that §48 necessarily complies with the Constitution because the banned depictions of animal cruelty, as a class, are categorically unprotected by the First Amendment. We disagree.

"[A]s a general matter, the First Amendment means that government has no power to restrict expression because of its message, its ideas, its subject matter, or its content." Section 48 explicitly regulates expression based on content: The statute restricts "visual [and] auditory depiction[s]," such as photographs, videos, or sound recordings, depending on whether they depict conduct in which a living animal is intentionally harmed. As such, §48 is "'presumptively invalid,' and the Government bears the burden to rebut that presumption."

"From 1791 to the present," however, the First Amendment has "permitted restrictions upon the content of speech in a few limited areas," and has never "include[d] a freedom to disregard these traditional limitations." These "historic and traditional categories long familiar to the bar"—including obscenity, defamation, fraud, incitement, and speech integral to criminal conduct, *Giboney v. Empire Storage & Ice Co.,* 336 U.S. 490, 498 (1949)—are "well-defined and narrowly limited classes of speech, the prevention and punishment of which have never been thought to raise any Constitutional problem."

The Government argues that "depictions of animal cruelty" should be added to the list. It contends that depictions of "illegal acts of animal cruelty" that are "made, sold, or possessed for commercial gain" necessarily "lack expressive value," and may accordingly "be regulated as *unprotected* speech." The claim is not just that Congress may regulate depictions of animal cruelty subject to the First Amendment, but that these depictions are outside the reach of that Amendment altogether.

As the Government notes, the prohibition of animal cruelty itself has a long history in American law, starting with the early settlement of the Colonies. But we are unaware of any similar tradition excluding *depictions* of animal cruelty from "the freedom of speech" codified in the First Amendment, and the Government points us to none.

The Government contends that categories of speech may be exempted from the First Amendment's protection without any long-settled tradition of subjecting that speech to regulation. Instead, the Government points to Congress's "'legislative judgment that ... depictions of animals being intentionally tortured and killed [are] of such minimal redeeming value as to render [them] unworthy of First Amendment protection'" and asks the Court to uphold the ban on the same basis. The Government thus proposes that a claim of categorical exclusion should be considered under a simple balancing test: "Whether a given category of speech enjoys First Amendment protection depends upon a categorical balancing of the value of the speech against its societal costs."

As a free-floating test for First Amendment coverage, that sentence is startling and dangerous. The First Amendment's guarantee of free speech does not extend only to categories of speech that survive an ad hoc balancing of relative social costs and benefits. The First Amendment itself reflects a judgment by the American people that the benefits of its restrictions on the Government outweigh the costs. Our Constitution forecloses any attempt to revise that judgment simply on the basis that some speech is not worth it. The Constitution is not a document "prescribing limits, and declaring that those limits may be passed at pleasure."

When we have identified categories of speech as fully outside the protection of the First Amendment, it has not been on the basis of a simple cost-benefit analysis. In *Ferber,* for example, we classified child pornography as such a category. We noted that the State of New York had a compelling interest in protecting children from abuse, and that the value of using children in these works (as opposed to simulated conduct or adult actors) was *de minimis.* But our decision did not rest on this "balance of competing interests" alone. We made clear that *Ferber* presented a special case: The market for child pornography was "intrinsically related" to the underlying abuse, and was therefore "an integral part of the production of such materials, an activity illegal throughout the Nation." As we noted, " '[i]t rarely has been suggested that the constitutional freedom for speech and press extends its immunity to speech or writing used as an integral part of conduct in violation of a valid criminal statute.' " *Ferber* thus grounded its analysis in a previously recognized, long-established category of unprotected speech, and our subsequent decisions have shared this understanding. See *Osborne v. Ohio,* 495 U.S. 103, 110 (1990); *Ashcroft v. Free Speech Coalition,* 535 U.S. 234, 249–250 (2002).

Our decisions in *Ferber* and other cases cannot be taken as establishing a freewheeling authority to declare new categories of speech outside the scope of the First Amendment. Maybe there are some categories of speech that have been historically unprotected, but have not yet been specifically identified or discussed as such in our case law. But if so, there is no evidence that "depictions of animal cruelty" is among them. We need not foreclose the future recognition of such additional categories to reject the Government's highly manipulable balancing test as a means of identifying them.

III

[The court ruled that §48 was unconstitutionally overbroad.]

Justice Alito, dissenting.

IV

A

1

It is undisputed that the *conduct* depicted in crush videos may constitutionally be prohibited. All 50 States and the District of Columbia have enacted statutes prohibiting animal cruelty. But before the enactment of §48, the underlying conduct depicted in crush videos was nearly impossible to prosecute. These videos, which "often appeal to persons with a very specific sexual fetish" were made in secret, generally without a live audience, and "the faces of the women inflicting the torture in the material often were not shown, nor could the location of the place where the cruelty was being inflicted or the date of the activity be ascertained from the depiction." Thus, law enforcement authorities often were not able to identify the parties responsible for the torture. In the rare instances in which it was possible to identify and find the perpetrators, they "often were able to successfully assert as a defense that the State could not prove its jurisdiction over the place where the act occurred or that the actions depicted took place within the time specified in the State statute of limitations."

In light of the practical problems thwarting the prosecution of the creators of crush videos under state animal cruelty laws, Congress concluded that the only effective way of stopping the underlying criminal conduct was to prohibit the commercial exploitation of the videos of that conduct.

2

The First Amendment protects freedom of speech, but it most certainly does not protect violent criminal conduct, even if engaged in for expressive purposes. Crush videos present a highly unusual free speech issue because they are so closely linked with violent criminal conduct. The videos record the commission of violent criminal acts, and it appears that these crimes are committed for the sole purpose of creating the videos.

The most relevant of our prior decisions is *Ferber*, which concerned child pornography. The Court there held that child pornography is not protected speech, and I believe that *Ferber*'s reasoning dictates a similar conclusion here.

In *Ferber,* an important factor—I would say the most important factor—was that child pornography involves the commission of a crime that inflicts severe personal injury to the "children who are made to engage in sexual conduct for commercial purposes.'" The *Ferber* Court repeatedly described the production of child pornography as child "abuse," "molestation," or "exploitation." ... [I]n *Ferber* "[t]he production of the work, not its content, was the target of the statute."

Second, *Ferber* emphasized the fact that these underlying crimes could not be effectively combated without targeting the distribution of child pornography. As the Court put it, "the distribution network for child pornography must be closed if the production of material which requires the sexual exploitation of children is to be effectively controlled." The Court added:

> "[T]here is no serious contention that the legislature was unjustified in believing that it is difficult, if not impossible, to halt the exploitation of children by pursuing only those who produce the photographs and movies.... The most expeditious if not the only practical method of law enforcement may be to dry up the market for this material by imposing severe criminal penalties on persons selling, advertising, or otherwise promoting the product."

Third, the *Ferber* Court noted that the value of child pornography "is exceedingly modest, if not *de minimis*," and that any such value was "overwhelmingly outweigh[ed]" by "the evil to be restricted."

All three of these characteristics are shared by § 48, as applied to crush videos. First, the conduct depicted in crush videos is criminal in every State and the District of Columbia. Thus, any crush video made in this country records the actual commission of a criminal act that inflicts severe physical injury and excruciating pain and ultimately results in death.

Second, the criminal acts shown in crush videos cannot be prevented without targeting the conduct prohibited by § 48 — the creation, sale, and possession for sale of depictions of animal torture with the intention of realizing a commercial profit.

Finally, the harm caused by the underlying crimes vastly outweighs any minimal value that the depictions might conceivably be thought to possess. Section 48 reaches only the actual recording of acts of animal torture; the statute does not apply to verbal descriptions or to simulations. And, unlike the child pornography statute in *Ferber*, § 48(b) provides an exception for depictions having any "serious religious, political, scientific, educational, journalistic, historical, or artistic value."

It must be acknowledged that § 48 differs from a child pornography law in an important respect: preventing the abuse of children is certainly much more important than preventing the torture of the animals used in crush videos. But while protecting children is unquestionably *more* important than protecting animals, the Government also has a compelling interest in preventing the torture depicted in crush videos.

Section 48's ban on trafficking in crush videos also helps to enforce the criminal laws and to ensure that criminals do not profit from their crimes. We have already judged that taking the profit out of crime is a compelling interest. See *Simon & Schuster, Inc. v. Members of N.Y. State Crime Victims Bd.*, 502 U.S. 105, 119 (1991).

In short, *Ferber* is the case that sheds the most light on the constitutionality of Congress' effort to halt the production of crush videos. Applying the principles set forth in *Ferber*, I would hold that crush videos are not protected by the First Amendment. [Justice Alito applied the same *Ferber* framework to depictions of brutal animal fights — ed.]

Exercise 29:

1. In *Chaplinsky v. New Hampshire*, 315 U.S. 568, 572 (1942), the Court indicated that low-value speech, such as fighting words, is "no essential part of any exposition of ideas, and [is] of such slight social value as a step to truth that any benefit that may be derived from [it] is clearly outweighed by the social interest in order and morality." Are crush videos an "essential part of any exposition of ideas"? If not, why is the majority so reluctant to hold that such videos are low-value speech and, therefore, unprotected?

2. Given that the Court uses balancing tests in other areas of constitutional law, why is the majority worried about adopting a balancing test in the free speech context? Are the majority's concerns justified?

3. Is the sale, distribution, or possession of crush videos "speech that is integral to criminal conduct"? Are crush videos similar enough to child pornography that regulations on the former should be treated the same as regulations on the latter?

How does Justice Alito answer these questions? How does the majority respond? Who has the better argument on this point and why?

4. How would Justice Alito argue that § 48 is constitutional as applied to depictions of dogfights (or other brutal animal fights)? Should *Ferber* govern the constitutional analysis of the federal ban on dogfights? On crush videos? The majority leaves open the possibility a more narrowly drawn statute — one "limited to crush videos or other depictions of extreme animal cruelty" — might be constitutional. How would you draft such a statute?

4. Less-Protected Speech

a. Introduction

Unlike the categories of speech covered above in Section 3, the categories of speech we are going to cover in Section 4 are protected speech. For each category discussed below, the Supreme Court has created a category-specific approach to the speech. You need to learn the analysis proper to each category.

b. Commercial Speech

For most of American history, commercial speech was heavily regulated and did not receive First Amendment protection. *Valentine v. Chrestensen*, 316 U.S. 52 (1942). Then, in 1975, the Supreme Court reversed course and ruled that commercial speech did receive free speech protection. *Bigelow v. Virginia*, 421 U.S. 809, 818 (1975), though some doubt remained regarding the holding because of language in the opinion. *Id.* at 822–25. The following year, however, the Supreme Court definitively ruled that commercial speech was protected by the Free Speech Clause.

Virginia State Board of Pharmacy v. Virginia Citizens Consumer Council Inc.
425 U.S. 748 (1976)

MR. JUSTICE BLACKMUN delivered the opinion of the Court.

The plaintiff-appellees in this case attack, as violative of the First and Fourteenth Amendments, that portion of § 54-524.35 of Va. Code Ann. (1974), which provides that a pharmacist licensed in Virginia is guilty of unprofessional conduct if he "(3) publishes, advertises or promotes, directly or indirectly, in any manner whatsoever, any amount, price, fee, premium, discount, rebate or credit terms ... for any drugs which may be dispensed only by prescription." The three-judge District Court declared the quoted portion of the statute "void and of no effect," and enjoined the defendant-appellants, the Virginia State Board of Pharmacy and the individual members of that Board, from enforcing it.

I

The "practice of pharmacy" is statutorily declared to be "a professional practice affecting the public health, safety and welfare," and to be "subject to regulation and control in the public interest." Va. Code Ann. §54-524.2(a) (1974). Indeed, the practice is subject to extensive regulation aimed at preserving high professional standards. The regulatory body is the appellant Virginia State Board of Pharmacy. The Board is also the licensing authority.

Inasmuch as only a licensed pharmacist may dispense prescription drugs in Virginia, advertising or other affirmative dissemination of prescription drug price information is effectively forbidden in the State.

Certainly that information may be of value. Drug prices in Virginia, for both prescription and nonprescription items, strikingly vary from outlet to outlet even within the same locality. It is stipulated, for example, that in Richmond "the cost of 40 Achromycin tablets ranges from $2.59 to $6.00, a difference of 140% [Sic]," and that in the Newport News-Hampton area the cost of tetracycline ranges from $1.20 to $9.00, a difference of 650%.

IV

The appellants contend that the advertisement of prescription drug prices is outside the protection of the First Amendment because it is "commercial speech." There can be no question that in past decisions the Court has given some indication that commercial speech is unprotected. Last Term, in *Bigelow v. Virginia*, 421 U.S. 809 (1975), the notion of unprotected "commercial speech" all but passed from the scene. Here, the question whether there is a First Amendment exception for "commercial speech" is squarely before us. Our pharmacist does not wish to editorialize on any subject, cultural, philosophical, or political.... The "idea" he wishes to communicate is simply this: "I will sell you the X prescription drug at the Y price." Our question, then, is whether this communication is wholly outside the protection of the First Amendment.   *Issue*

V

We begin with several propositions that already are settled or beyond serious dispute. It is clear, for example, that speech does not lose its First Amendment protection because money is spent to project it, as in a paid advertisement of one form or another. *Buckley v. Valeo*, 424 U.S. 1, 35–59 (1976); *New York Times Co. v. Sullivan*, 376 U.S., [254,] 266 [(1964)]. Speech likewise is protected even though it is carried in a form that is "sold" for profit, and even though it may involve a solicitation to purchase or otherwise pay or contribute money. *New York Times Co. v. Sullivan, supra; NAACP v. Button*, 371 U.S. 415, 429 (1963); *Cantwell v. Connecticut*, 310 U.S. 296, 306–307 (1940).

If there is a kind of commercial speech that lacks all First Amendment protection, therefore, it must be distinguished by its content. Yet the speech whose content deprives it of protection cannot simply be speech on a commercial subject. No one would contend that our pharmacist may be prevented from being heard on the subject of whether, in general, pharmaceutical prices should be regulated, or their advertisement forbidden. Nor can it be dispositive that a commercial advertisement is noneditorial, and merely reports a fact. Purely factual matter of public interest may claim protection.

Our question is whether speech which does "no more than propose a commercial transaction," is so removed from any "exposition of ideas," *Chaplinsky v. New Hampshire*, 315 U.S. 568, 572 (1942), and from "'truth, science, morality, and arts in general, in its diffusion of liberal sentiments on the administration of Government,'" *Roth v. United States*, 354 U.S. 476, 484 (1957), that it lacks all protection. Our answer is that it is not.

ISSUE 2

Focusing first on the individual parties to the transaction that is proposed in the commercial advertisement, we may assume that the advertiser's interest is a purely economic one. That hardly disqualifies him from protection under the First Amendment. The interests of the contestants in a labor dispute are primarily economic, but it has long been settled that both the employee and the employer are protected by the First Amendment when they express themselves on the merits of the dispute in order to influence its outcome.

As to the particular consumer's interest in the free flow of commercial information, that interest may be as keen, if not keener by far, than his interest in the day's most urgent political debate. Appellees' case in this respect is a convincing one. Those whom the suppression of prescription drug price information hits the hardest are the poor, the sick, and particularly the aged. A disproportionate amount of their income tends to be spent on prescription drugs; yet they are the least able to learn, by shopping from pharmacist to pharmacist, where their scarce dollars are best spent. When drug prices vary as strikingly as they do, information as to who is charging what becomes more than a convenience. It could mean the alleviation of physical pain or the enjoyment of basic necessities.

Generalizing, society also may have a strong interest in the free flow of commercial information. Even an individual advertisement, though entirely "commercial," may be of general public interest. Obviously, not all commercial messages contain the same or even a very great public interest element. There are few to which such an element, however, could not be added. Our pharmacist, for example, could cast himself as a commentator on store-to-store disparities in drug prices, giving his own and those of a competitor as proof. We see little point in requiring him to do so, and little difference if he does not.

Moreover, there is another consideration that suggests that no line between publicly "interesting" or "important" commercial advertising and the opposite kind could ever be drawn. Advertising, however tasteless and excessive it sometimes may seem, is nonetheless dissemination of information as to who is producing and selling what product, for what reason, and at what price. So long as we preserve a predominantly free enterprise economy, the allocation of our resources in large measure will be made through numerous private economic decisions. It is a matter of public interest that those decisions, in the aggregate, be intelligent and well informed. To this end, the free flow of commercial information is indispensable. And if it is indispensable to the proper allocation of resources in a free enterprise system, it is also indispensable to the formation of intelligent opinions as to how that system ought to be regulated or altered. Therefore, even if the First Amendment were thought to be primarily an instrument to enlighten public decisionmaking in a democracy, we could not say that the free flow of information does not serve that goal.

Arrayed against these substantial individual and societal interests are a number of justifications for the advertising ban. These have to do principally with maintaining a high degree of professionalism on the part of licensed pharmacists.[21] Indisputably, the State has a strong interest in maintaining that professionalism. It is exercised in a number of ways for the consumer's benefit.

Price advertising, it is argued, will place in jeopardy the pharmacist's expertise and, with it, the customer's health. It is claimed that the aggressive price competition that will result from unlimited advertising will make it impossible for the pharmacist to supply professional services in the compounding, handling, and dispensing of prescription drugs. It is also claimed that prices might not necessarily fall as a result of advertising. If one pharmacist advertises, others must, and the resulting expense will inflate the cost of drugs. It is further claimed that advertising will lead people to shop for their prescription drugs among the various pharmacists who offer the lowest prices, and the loss of stable pharmacist-customer relationships will make individual attention and certainly the practice of monitoring impossible. Finally, it is argued that damage will be done to the professional image of the pharmacist.

The strength of these proffered justifications is greatly undermined by the fact that high professional standards, to a substantial extent, are guaranteed by the close regulation to which pharmacists in Virginia are subject. And this case concerns the retail sale by the pharmacist more than it does his professional standards. Surely, any pharmacist guilty of professional dereliction that actually endangers his customer will promptly lose his license.

[I]t is seen that the State's protectiveness of its citizens rests in large measure on the advantages of their being kept in ignorance. The advertising ban does not directly affect professional standards one way or the other. It affects them only through the reactions it is assumed people will have to the free flow of drug price information. There is no claim that the advertising ban in any way prevents the cutting of corners by the pharmacist who is so inclined. That pharmacist is likely to cut corners in any event. The only effect the advertising ban has on him is to insulate him from price competition and to open the way for him to make a substantial, and perhaps even excessive, profit in addition to providing an inferior service. The more painstaking pharmacist is also protected but, again, it is a protection based in large part on public ignorance.

It appears to be feared that if the pharmacist who wishes to provide low cost, and assertedly low quality, services is permitted to advertise, he will be taken up on his

---

21. An argument not advanced by the Board, either in its brief or in the testimony proffered prior to summary judgment, but which on occasion has been made to other courts, is that the advertisement of low drug prices will result in overconsumption and in abuse of the advertised drugs. The argument prudently has been omitted. By definition, the drugs at issue here may be sold only on a physician's prescription. We do not assume, as apparently the dissent does, that simply because low prices will be freely advertised, physicians will overprescribe, or that pharmacists will ignore the prescription requirement.

offer by too many unwitting customers. They will choose the low-cost, low-quality service and drive the "professional" pharmacist out of business. They will respond only to costly and excessive advertising, and end up paying the price. They will go from one pharmacist to another, following the discount, and destroy the pharmacist-customer relationship. They will lose respect for the profession because it advertises. All this is not in their best interests, and all this can be avoided if they are not permitted to know who is charging what.

There is, of course, an alternative to this highly paternalistic approach. That alternative is to assume that this information is not in itself harmful, that people will perceive their own best interests if only they are well enough informed, and that the best means to that end is to open the channels of communication rather than to close them. If they are truly open, nothing prevents the "professional" pharmacist from marketing his own assertedly superior product, and contrasting it with that of the low-cost, high-volume prescription drug retailer. But the choice among these alternative approaches is not ours to make or the Virginia General Assembly's. It is precisely this kind of choice, between the dangers of suppressing information, and the dangers of its misuse if it is freely available, that the First Amendment makes for us. Virginia is free to require whatever professional standards it wishes of its pharmacists; it may subsidize them or protect them from competition in other ways. But it may not do so by keeping the public in ignorance of the entirely lawful terms that competing pharmacists are offering. In this sense, the justifications Virginia has offered for suppressing the flow of prescription drug price information, far from persuading us that the flow is not protected by the First Amendment, have reinforced our view that it is. We so hold.

VI

In concluding that commercial speech, like other varieties, is protected, we of course do not hold that it can never be regulated in any way. Some forms of commercial speech regulation are surely permissible. We mention a few only to make clear that they are not before us and therefore are not foreclosed by this case.

There is no claim that prescription drug price advertisements are forbidden because they are false or misleading in any way. Untruthful speech, commercial or otherwise, has never been protected for its own sake. Obviously, much commercial speech is not provably false, or even wholly false, but only deceptive or misleading. We foresee no obstacle to a State's dealing effectively with this problem.[24] The First Amendment,

---

24. In concluding that commercial speech enjoys First Amendment protection, we have not held that it is wholly undifferentiable from other forms. There are commonsense differences between speech that does "no more than propose a commercial transaction," and other varieties. Even if the differences do not justify the conclusion that commercial speech is valueless, and thus subject to complete suppression by the State, they nonetheless suggest that a different degree of protection is necessary to insure that the flow of truthful and legitimate commercial information is unimpaired. The truth of commercial speech, for example, may be more easily verifiable by its disseminator than, let us say, news reporting or political commentary, in that ordinarily the advertiser seeks to disseminate information about a specific product or service that he himself provides and presumably knows more about than anyone else. Also, commercial speech may be more durable than other kinds. Since advertising is the sine qua non of commercial profits, there is little likelihood of its being chilled by

as we construe it today does not prohibit the State from insuring that the stream of commercial information flow[s] cleanly as well as freely.

Also, there is no claim that the transactions proposed in the forbidden advertisements are themselves illegal in any way.

What is at issue is whether a State may completely suppress the dissemination of concededly truthful information about entirely lawful activity, fearful of that information's effect upon its disseminators and its recipients. Reserving other questions, we conclude that the answer to this one is in the negative.

The judgment of the District Court is affirmed.

[Affirmed.]

Mr. Justice Stevens took no part in the consideration or decision of this case.

Mr. Chief Justice Burger, concurring. [Opinion omitted.]

Mr. Justice Stewart, concurring. [Opinion omitted.]

Mr. Justice Rehnquist, dissenting.

The logical consequences of the Court's decision in this case, a decision which elevates commercial intercourse between a seller hawking his wares and a buyer seeking to strike a bargain to the same plane as has been previously reserved for the free marketplace of ideas, are far reaching indeed. Under the Court's opinion the way will be open not only for dissemination of price information but for active promotion of prescription drugs, liquor, cigarettes, and other products the use of which it has previously been thought desirable to discourage. Now, however, such promotion is protected by the First Amendment so long as it is not misleading or does not promote an illegal product or enterprise. In coming to this conclusion, the Court has overruled a legislative determination that such advertising should not be allowed and has done so on behalf of a consumer group which is not directly disadvantaged by the statute in question.

II

The Court speaks of the consumer's interest in the free flow of commercial information, particularly in the case of the poor, the sick, and the aged. It goes on to observe that "society also may have a strong interest in the free flow of commercial information." One need not disagree with either of these statements in order to feel that they should presumptively be the concern of the Virginia Legislature, which sits to balance these and other claims in the process of making laws such as the one here under attack. The Court speaks of the importance in a "predominantly free enterprise economy" of intelligent and well-informed decisions as to allocation of resources.

---

proper regulation and forgone entirely. Attributes such as these, the greater objectivity and hardiness of commercial speech, may make it less necessary to tolerate inaccurate statements for fear of silencing the speaker. They may also make it appropriate to require that a commercial message appear in such a form, or include such additional information, warnings, and disclaimers, as are necessary to prevent its being deceptive.

While there is again much to be said for the Court's observation as a matter of desirable public policy, there is certainly nothing in the United States Constitution which requires the Virginia Legislature to hew to the teachings of Adam Smith in its legislative decisions regulating the pharmacy profession.

The Court insists that the rule it lays down is consistent even with the view that the First Amendment is "primarily an instrument to enlighten public decisionmaking in a democracy." I had understood this view to relate to public decisionmaking as to political, social, and other public issues, rather than the decision of a particular individual as to whether to purchase one or another kind of shampoo. It is undoubtedly arguable that many people in the country regard the choice of shampoo as just as important as who may be elected to local, state, or national political office, but that does not automatically bring information about competing shampoos within the protection of the First Amendment. It is one thing to say that the line between strictly ideological and political commentaries and other kinds of commentary is difficult to draw, and that the mere fact that the former may have in it an element of commercialism does not strip it of First Amendment protection. See *New York Times Co. v. Sullivan*, 376 U.S. 254 (1964). But it is another thing to say that because that line is difficult to draw, we will stand at the other end of the spectrum and reject out of hand the observation of so dedicated a champion of the First Amendment as Mr. Justice Black that the protections of that Amendment do not apply to a "'merchant' who goes from door to door 'selling pots.'"

[The Majority's] line simply makes no allowance whatever for what appears to have been a considered legislative judgment in most States that while prescription drugs are a necessary and vital part of medical care and treatment, there are sufficient dangers attending their widespread use that they simply may not be promoted in the same manner as hair creams, deodorants, and toothpaste. The very real dangers that general advertising for such drugs might create in terms of encouraging, even though not sanctioning, illicit use of them by individuals for whom they have not been prescribed, or by generating patient pressure upon physicians to prescribe them, are simply not dealt with in the Court's opinion. If prescription drugs may be advertised, they may be advertised on television during family viewing time. Nothing we know about the acquisitive instincts of those who inhabit every business and profession to a greater or lesser extent gives any reason to think that such persons will not do everything they can to generate demand for these products in much the same manner and to much the same degree as demand for other commodities has been generated.

Both Congress and state legislatures have by law sharply limited the permissible dissemination of information about some commodities because of the potential harm resulting from those commodities, even though they were not thought to be sufficiently demonstrably harmful to warrant outright prohibition of their sale. Current prohibitions on television advertising of liquor and cigarettes are prominent in this category, but apparently under the Court's holding so long as the advertisements are not deceptive they may no longer be prohibited.

Exercise 30:

1. What is the Court's (implicit) test for differentiating between commercial and noncommercial speech?

2. What reasons did the Supreme Court provide for its conclusion that the Free Speech Clause protected commercial speech? What reasons did Justice Rehnquist offer to conclude that commercial speech should be unprotected?

3. What reasons did the Court provide to support its conclusion that some commercial speech is subject to no protection?

4. Are the majority's statements that false or misleading commercial speech may be prohibited consistent with its reasons for protecting commercial speech in the first instance?

5. What less restrictive means did the Court identify that Virginia may utilize to reach its stated goals? Were these actually adequate to meet Virginia's goals?

6. Justice Rehnquist, in dissent, argued that the Virginia legislature is best suited to evaluate the costs and benefits of commercial pharmaceutical advertising; is he or the majority correct? Whose position is more consistent with the New Deal and, particularly, *Carolene Products* Footnote 4 (which you may have covered in Chapter 3 of Volume 5)? *See United States v. Carolene Products Co.*, 304 U.S. 144, 153 n.4 (1938).

7. Justice Rehnquist identified a parade of horrors that, he predicted, would result from the Court's extending free speech protection to commercial speech. Have his predictions come true?

After *Virginia State Board of Pharmacy*, it was clear that commercial speech received protection — albeit something less than full free speech protection — though it was not yet clear what standard distinguished commercial from noncommerical speech. The prohibited speech in *Virginia State Board of Pharmacy* involved what one might call the core of commercial speech: the pharmacists proposed to consumers to sell a product at a particular price. What about speech, however, that mixes this type of core commercial speech with noncommerical aspects? The Supreme Court provided the test to adjudicate these situations in the case reprinted below.

Bolger v. Youngs Drug Products Corp.

463 U.S. 60 (1983)

Justice Marshall delivered the opinion of the Court.

Title 39 U.S.C. § 3001(e)(2) prohibits the mailing of unsolicited advertisements for contraceptives. The District Court held that, as applied to appellee's mailings, the statute violates the First Amendment. We affirm.

I

Appellee Youngs Drug Products Corporation (Youngs) is engaged in the manufacture, sale and distribution of contraceptives. This litigation resulted from Youngs' decision to undertake a campaign of unsolicited mass mailings to members of the public. In conjunction with its wholesalers and retailers, Youngs seeks to mail to the public on an unsolicited basis three types of materials:

- multi-page, multi-item flyers promoting a large variety of products available at a drug store, including prophylactics;

- flyers exclusively or substantially devoted to promoting prophylactics;

- informational pamphlets discussing the desirability and availability of prophylactics in general or Youngs' products in particular.[4]

[The Government brought this direct appeal.]

II

Beginning with *Bigelow v. Virginia*, 421 U.S. 809 (1975), this Court extended the protection of the First Amendment to commercial speech. Nonetheless, our decisions have recognized "the 'commonsense' distinction between speech proposing a commercial transaction, which occurs in an area traditionally subject to government regulation, and other varieties of speech." Thus, we have held that the Constitution accords less protection to commercial speech than to other constitutionally safeguarded forms of expression. *Central Hudson Gas & Electric Corp. v. Public Service Comm'n of New York*, 447 U.S. 557, 562–563 (1980); *Virginia State Board of Pharmacy v. Virginia Citizens Consumer Council, Inc.*, 425 U.S. 748, 771–772, n. 24 (1976).

Most of appellee's mailings fall within the core notion of commercial speech — "speech which does 'no more than propose a commercial transaction.'" *Virginia State Board of Pharmacy v. Virginia Citizens Consumer Council, Inc.*, 425 U.S., at 762. Youngs' informational pamphlets, however, cannot be characterized merely as proposals to engage in commercial transactions. Their proper classification as commercial or non-commercial speech thus presents a closer question. The mere fact that these pamphlets are conceded to be advertisements clearly does not compel the conclusion that they are commercial speech. See *New York Times v. Sullivan*, 376 U.S. 254, 265–266 (1964). Similarly, the reference to a specific product does not by itself render the pamphlets commercial speech. Finally, the fact that Youngs has an economic motivation for mailing the pamphlets would clearly be insufficient by itself to turn the materials into commercial speech. See *Bigelow v. Virginia*, 421 U.S. 809, 818 (1975).

The combination of *all* these characteristics, however, provides strong support for the District Court's conclusion that the informational pamphlets are properly characterized as commercial speech. The mailings constitute commercial speech notwith-

---

4. In the District Court, Youngs offered two examples of informational pamphlets. The first, entitled "Condoms and Human Sexuality," is a 12-page pamphlet describing the use, manufacture, desirability, and availability of condoms, and providing detailed descriptions of various Trojan-brand condoms manufactured by Youngs. The second, entitled "Plain Talk about Venereal Disease," is an eight-page pamphlet discussing at length the problem of venereal disease and the use and advantages of condoms in aiding the prevention of venereal disease. The only identification of Youngs or its products is at the bottom of the last page of the pamphlet, which states that the pamphlet has been contributed as a public service by Youngs, the distributor of Trojan-brand prophylactics.

standing the fact that they contain discussions of important public issues such as venereal disease and family planning. A company has the full panoply of protections available to its direct comments on public issues, so there is no reason for providing similar constitutional protection when such statements are made in the context of commercial transactions. Advertisers should not be permitted to immunize false or misleading product information from government regulation simply by including references to public issues.

We conclude, therefore, that all of the mailings in this case are entitled to the qualified but nonetheless substantial protection accorded to commercial speech.

JUSTICE BRENNAN took no part in the decision of this case.

JUSTICE REHNQUIST, with whom JUSTICE O'CONNOR joins, concurring in the judgment. [Opinion omitted.]

JUSTICE STEVENS, concurring in the judgment. [Opinion omitted.]

Exercise 31:

1. What test did the *Bolger* Court articulate to distinguish commercial from non-commerical speech?

2. Apply that test to each of Youngs' three types of materials.

Thus far, you have learned that commercial speech is protected free speech, and you have learned how to distinguish between commercial and other speech. Below, in *Central Hudson*, you will learn the test articulated by the Supreme Court to evaluate restrictions on commercial speech.

Central Hudson Gas & Electrical Corporation v. Public Service Commission of New York

447 U.S. 557 (1980)

MR. JUSTICE POWELL delivered the opinion of the Court.

Issue This case presents the question whether a regulation of the Public Service Commission of the State of New York violates the First and Fourteenth Amendments because it completely bans promotional advertising by an electrical utility.

I

In December 1973, the Commission, appellee here, ordered electric utilities in New York State to cease all advertising that "promot[es] the use of electricity." The order was based on the Commission's finding that "the interconnected utility system in New York State does not have sufficient fuel stocks or sources of supply to continue furnishing all customer demands for the 1973–1974 winter."

Three years later, when the fuel shortage had eased, the Commission requested comments from the public on its proposal to continue the ban on promotional advertising. After reviewing the public comments, the Commission extended the prohibition in a Policy Statement issued on February 25, 1977.

The Policy Statement divided advertising expenses "into two broad categories: promotional—advertising intended to stimulate the purchase of utility services—and institutional and informational, a broad category inclusive of all advertising not clearly intended to promote sales." The Commission declared all promotional advertising contrary to the national policy of conserving energy. It acknowledged that the ban is not a perfect vehicle for conserving energy. For example, the Commission's order prohibits promotional advertising to develop consumption during periods when demand for electricity is low. By limiting growth in "off-peak" consumption, the ban limits the "beneficial side effects" of such growth in terms of more efficient use of existing powerplants.

The Commission's order explicitly permitted "informational" advertising designed to encourage "*shifts* of consumption" from peak demand times to periods of low electricity demand. Informational advertising would not seek to increase aggregate consumption, but would invite a leveling of demand throughout any given 24-hour period.

Appellant challenged the order in state court, arguing that the Commission had restrained commercial speech in violation of the First and Fourteenth Amendments. The Commission's order was upheld by the trial court and at the intermediate appellate level. The New York Court of Appeals affirmed. [We now reverse.]

II

The Commission's order restricts only commercial speech, that is, expression related solely to the economic interests of the speaker and its audience. *Virginia Pharmacy Board v. Virginia Citizens Consumer Council*, 425 U.S. 748, 762 (1976). The First Amendment, as applied to the States through the Fourteenth Amendment, protects commercial speech from unwarranted governmental regulation. *Virginia Pharmacy Board*, 425 U.S., at 761–762.

Nevertheless, our decisions have recognized "the 'commonsense' distinction between speech proposing a commercial transaction, which occurs in an area traditionally subject to government regulation, and other varieties of speech." The Constitution therefore accords a lesser protection to commercial speech than to other constitutionally guaranteed expression. The protection available for particular commercial expression turns on the nature both of the expression and of the governmental interests served by its regulation.

In commercial speech cases, a four-part analysis has developed. At the outset, we must determine whether the expression is protected by the First Amendment. For commercial speech to come within that provision, it at least must concern lawful activity and not be misleading. Next, we ask whether the asserted governmental interest is substantial. If both inquiries yield positive answers, we must determine whether the regulation directly advances the governmental interest asserted, and whether it is not more extensive than is necessary to serve that interest.

III

We now apply this four-step analysis for commercial speech to the Commission's arguments in support of its ban on promotional advertising.

A

The Commission does not claim that the expression at issue either is inaccurate or relates to unlawful activity.

B

The Commission offers two state interests as justifications for the ban on promotional advertising. The first concerns energy conservation. Any increase in demand for electricity—during peak or off-peak periods—means greater consumption of energy. In view of our country's dependence on energy resources beyond our control, no one can doubt the importance of energy conservation. Plainly, therefore, the state interest asserted is substantial.

The Commission also argues that promotional advertising will aggravate inequities caused by the failure to base the utilities' rates on marginal cost. The utilities argued to the Commission that if they could promote the use of electricity in periods of low demand, they would improve their utilization of generating capacity. The Commission responded that promotion of off-peak consumption also would increase consumption during peak periods. If peak demand were to rise, the absence of marginal cost rates would mean that the rates charged for the additional power would not reflect the true costs of expanding production. Instead, the extra costs would be borne by all consumers through higher overall rates. Without promotional advertising, the Commission stated, this inequitable turn of events would be less likely to occur. The choice among rate structures involves difficult and important questions of economic supply and distributional fairness. The State's concern that rates be fair and efficient represents a clear and substantial governmental interest.

C

Next, we focus on the relationship between the State's interests and the advertising ban. Under this criterion, the Commission's laudable concern over the equity and efficiency of appellant's rates does not provide a constitutionally adequate reason for restricting protected speech. The link between the advertising prohibition and appellant's rate structure is, at most, tenuous. The impact of promotional advertising on the equity of appellant's rates is highly speculative. Advertising to increase off-peak usage would have to increase peak usage, while other factors that directly affect the fairness and efficiency of appellant's rates remained constant. Such conditional and remote eventualities simply cannot justify silencing appellant's promotional advertising.

In contrast, the State's interest in energy conservation is directly advanced by the Commission order at issue here. There is an immediate connection between advertising and demand for electricity. Central Hudson would not contest the advertising ban unless it believed that promotion would increase its sales. Thus, we find a direct link between the state interest in conservation and the Commission's order.

D

We come finally to the critical inquiry in this case: whether the Commission's complete suppression of speech ordinarily protected by the First Amendment is no more extensive than necessary to further the State's interest in energy conservation. The Commission's order reaches all promotional advertising, regardless of the impact of the touted service on overall energy use. But the energy conservation rationale, as important as it is, cannot justify suppressing information about electric devices or services that would cause no net increase in total energy use. In addition, no showing has been made that a more limited restriction on the content of promotional advertising would not serve adequately the State's interests.

The Commission's order prevents appellant from promoting electric services that would reduce energy use by diverting demand from less efficient sources, or that would consume roughly the same amount of energy as do alternative sources. In neither situation would the utility's advertising endanger conservation or mislead the public. To the extent that the Commission's order suppresses speech that in no way impairs the State's interest in energy conservation, the Commission's order violates the First and Fourteenth Amendments and must be invalidated.

The Commission also has not demonstrated that its interest in conservation cannot be protected adequately by more limited regulation of appellant's commercial expression. To further its policy of conservation, the Commission could attempt to restrict the format and content of Central Hudson's advertising. It might, for example, require that the advertisements include information about the relative efficiency and expense of the offered service, both under current conditions and for the foreseeable future. In the absence of a showing that more limited speech regulation would be ineffective, we cannot approve the complete suppression of Central Hudson's advertising.

IV

Accordingly, the judgment of the New York Court of Appeals is

Reversed.

MR. JUSTICE BRENNAN, concurring in the judgment. [Opinion omitted.]

MR. JUSTICE BLACKMUN, with whom MR. JUSTICE BRENNAN joins, concurring in the judgment. [Opinion omitted.]

MR. JUSTICE STEVENS, with whom MR. JUSTICE BRENNAN joins, concurring in the judgment. [Opinion omitted.]

MR. JUSTICE REHNQUIST, dissenting. [Opinion omitted.]

Exercise 32:

1. What test did the *Central Hudson* Court articulate to evaluate regulations of commercial speech?

2. The Supreme Court quickly agreed with New York that its two asserted state interests were substantial. What process of analysis led the Court to this conclusion? Do you agree with the Court's conclusion?

3. The Court concluded that the speech regulation was unconstitutional. Did the Court find that the regulation was over- and/or under-inclusive? Explain.

4. Use the *Central Hudson* Test to evaluate hypothetical television advertising bans on legal, though (potentially) harmful substances and activities such as cigarettes, alcohol, and gambling.

———————

There is an ongoing debate, on and off the Supreme Court, over the status of commercial speech. A number of justices and commentators have argued that commercial speech should receive the same protection as other speech categories. They claim that the less-preferred position of commercial speech is a relic of the New Deal's distaste for economic activities. Thus far, there has not been sufficient weight behind this view to alter commercial speech's status.

c. Profanity/Indecent Speech

Profanity and indecent speech are forms of offensive speech that include swear words and sexually explicit words. For many years, profanity and indecent speech were legally regulated and punished. The Supreme Court, in *Chaplinsky v. New Hampshire*, 315 U.S. 568, 571 (1942), included profanity within its influential listing of categories of unprotected speech. The Supreme Court switched course most famously in the case of *Cohen v. California*, 403 U.S. 15 (1971), reprinted below, and ruled that profane and indecent speech are protected by the First Amendment, though not in all contexts, as the notes afterward will describe.

Cohen v. California
403 U.S. 15 (1971)

MR. JUSTICE HARLAN delivered the opinion of the Court.

This case may seem at first blush too inconsequential to find its way into our books, but the issue it presents is of no small constitutional significance.

Appellant Paul Robert Cohen was convicted in the Los Angeles Municipal Court of violating that part of California Penal Code § 415 which prohibits "maliciously and willfully disturb[ing] the peace or quiet of any neighborhood or person * * * by * * * offensive conduct * * *." He was given 30 days' imprisonment. The facts upon which his conviction rests are detailed in the opinion of the Court of Appeal of California as follows:

> "On April 26, 1968, the defendant was observed in the Los Angeles County Courthouse in the corridor outside of division 20 of the municipal court wearing a jacket bearing the words 'Fuck the Draft' which were plainly visible. There were women and children present in the corridor. The defendant was arrested. The defendant testified that he wore the jacket knowing that the words were on the jacket as a means of informing the public of the depth of his feelings against the Vietnam War and the draft."

> "The defendant did not engage in, nor threaten to engage in, nor did anyone as the result of his conduct in fact commit or threaten to commit any

act of violence. The defendant did not make any loud or unusual noise, nor was there any evidence that he uttered any sound prior to his arrest."

In affirming the conviction the Court of Appeal held that "offensive conduct" means "behavior which has a tendency to provoke others to acts of violence or to in turn disturb the peace," and that the State had proved this element because, on the facts of this case, "[i]t was certainly reasonably foreseeable that such conduct might cause others to rise up to commit a violent act against the person of the defendant or attempt to forceably remove his jacket." The California Supreme Court declined review by a divided vote. We now reverse.

I

In order to lay hands on the precise issue which this case involves, it is useful first to canvass various matters which this record does not present.

The conviction quite clearly rests upon the asserted offensiveness of the words Cohen used to convey his message to the public. The only "conduct" which the State sought to punish is the fact of communication. Thus, we deal here with a conviction resting solely upon "speech," not upon any separately identifiable conduct which allegedly was intended by Cohen to be perceived by others as expressive of particular views but which, on its face, does not necessarily convey any message and hence arguably could be regulated without effectively repressing Cohen's ability to express himself. Cf. *United States v. O'Brien*, 391 U.S. 367 (1968). Further, the State certainly lacks power to punish Cohen for the underlying content of the message the inscription conveyed. Cohen could not, consistently with the First and Fourteenth Amendments, be punished for asserting the evident position on the inutility or immorality of the draft his jacket reflected.

Appellant's conviction, then, rests squarely upon his exercise of the "freedom of speech" protected from arbitrary governmental interference by the Constitution and can be justified, if at all, only as a valid regulation of the manner in which he exercised that freedom, not as a permissible prohibition on the substantive message it conveys. This does not end the inquiry, of course, for the First and Fourteenth Amendments have never been thought to give absolute protection to every individual to speak whenever or wherever he pleases or to use any form of address in any circumstances that he chooses. In this vein, too, however, we think it important to note that several issues typically associated with such problems are not presented here.

[T]his case cannot be said to fall within those relatively few categories of instances where prior decisions have established the power of government to deal more comprehensively with certain forms of individual expression simply upon a showing that such a form was employed. This is not, for example, an obscenity case. *Roth v. United States*, 354 U.S. 476 (1957). It cannot plausibly be maintained that this vulgar allusion to the Selective Service System would conjure up such psychic stimulation in anyone likely to be confronted with Cohen's crudely defaced jacket.

This Court has also held that the States are free to ban the simple use, without a demonstration of additional justifying circumstances, of so-called "fighting words," those personally abusive epithets which, when addressed to the ordinary citizen, are, as a matter of common knowledge, inherently likely to provoke violent reaction. *Chaplinsky v. New Hampshire*, 315 U.S. 568 (1942). While the four-letter word displayed by Cohen in relation to the draft is not uncommonly employed in a personally provocative fashion, in this instance it was clearly not "directed to the person of the hearer." *Cantwell v. Connecticut*, 310 U.S. 296, 309 (1940). No individual actually or likely to be present could reasonably have regarded the words on appellant's jacket as a direct personal insult. Nor do we have here an instance of the exercise of the State's police power to prevent a speaker from intentionally provoking a given group to hostile reaction. Cf. *Feiner v. New York*, 340 U.S. 315 (1951). There is, as noted above, no showing that anyone who saw Cohen was in fact violently aroused or that appellant intended such a result.

Finally, in arguments before this Court much has been made of the claim that Cohen's distasteful mode of expression was thrust upon unwilling or unsuspecting viewers, and that the State might therefore legitimately act as it did in order to protect the sensitive from otherwise unavoidable exposure to appellant's crude form of protest. Of course, the mere presumed presence of unwitting listeners or viewers does not serve automatically to justify curtailing all speech capable of giving offense. While this Court has recognized that government may properly act in many situations to prohibit intrusion into the privacy of the home of unwelcome views and ideas which cannot be totally banned from the public dialogue, we have at the same time consistently stressed that "we are often 'captives' outside the sanctuary of the home and subject to objectionable speech." The ability of government, consonant with the Constitution, to shut off discourse solely to protect others from hearing it is, in other words, dependent upon a showing that substantial privacy interests are being invaded in an essentially intolerable manner. Any broader view of this authority would effectively empower a majority to silence dissidents simply as a matter of personal predilections.

In this regard, persons confronted with Cohen's jacket were in a quite different posture than, say, those subjected to the raucous emissions of sound trucks blaring outside their residences. Those in the Los Angeles courthouse could effectively avoid further bombardment of their sensibilities simply by averting their eyes. And, while it may be that one has a more substantial claim to a recognizable privacy interest when walking through a courthouse corridor than, for example, strolling through Central Park, surely it is nothing like the interest in being free from unwanted expression in the confines of one's own home. Given the subtlety and complexity of the factors involved, if Cohen's "speech" was otherwise entitled to constitutional protection, we do not think the fact that some unwilling "listeners" in a public building may have been briefly exposed to it can serve to justify this breach of the peace conviction where, as here, there was no evidence that persons powerless to avoid appellant's conduct did in fact object to it, and where that portion of the statute upon which Cohen's conviction rests evinces no concern, either on its face or as construed by the California courts, with the special plight of the captive auditor, but, instead, indiscriminately sweeps within its prohibitions all "offensive conduct" that disturbs "any neighborhood or person."

II

Against this background, the issue flushed by this case stands out in bold relief. It is whether California can excise, as "offensive conduct," one particular scurrilous epithet from the public discourse, either upon the theory of the court below that its use is inherently likely to cause violent reaction or upon a more general assertion that the States, acting as guardians of public morality, may properly remove this offensive word from the public vocabulary.

The rationale of the California court is plainly untenable. At most it reflects an "undifferentiated fear or apprehension of disturbance [which] is not enough to overcome the right to freedom of expression." *Tinker v. Des Moines Indep. Community School Dist.*, 393 U.S. 503, 508 (1969). We have been shown no evidence that substantial numbers of citizens are standing ready to strike out physically at whoever may assault their sensibilities with execrations like that uttered by Cohen. There may be some persons about with such lawless and violent proclivities, but that is an insufficient base upon which to erect, consistently with constitutional values, a governmental power to force persons who wish to ventilate their dissident views into avoiding particular forms of expression.

Admittedly, it is not so obvious that the First and Fourteenth Amendments must be taken to disable the States from punishing public utterance of this unseemly expletive in order to maintain what they regard as a suitable level of discourse within the body politic. We think, however, that examination and reflection will reveal the shortcomings of a contrary viewpoint.

At the outset, we cannot overemphasize that, in our judgment, most situations where the State has a justifiable interest in regulating speech will fall within one or more of the various established exceptions, discussed above but not applicable here, to the usual rule that governmental bodies may not prescribe the form or content of individual expression. Equally important to our conclusion is the constitutional backdrop against which our decision must be made. The constitutional right of free expression is powerful medicine in a society as diverse and populous as ours. It is designed and intended to remove governmental restraints from the arena of public discussion, putting the decision as to what views shall be voiced largely into the hands of each of us, in the hope that use of such freedom will ultimately produce a more capable citizenry and more perfect polity and in the belief that no other approach would comport with the premise of individual dignity and choice upon which our political system rests. See *Whitney v. California*, 274 U.S. 357, 375–377 (1927) (Brandeis, J., concurring).

To many, the immediate consequence of this freedom may often appear to be only verbal tumult, discord, and even offensive utterance. These are, however, within established limits, in truth necessary side effects of the broader enduring values which the process of open debate permits us to achieve. That the air may at times seem filled with verbal cacophony is, in this sense not a sign of weakness but of strength. We cannot lose sight of the fact that, in what otherwise might seem a trifling and annoying instance of individual distasteful abuse of a privilege, these fundamental societal values are truly implicated.

Against this perception of the constitutional policies involved, we discern certain more particularized considerations that peculiarly call for reversal of this conviction. First, the principle contended for by the State seems inherently boundless. How is one to distinguish this from any other offensive word? Surely the State has no right to cleanse public debate to the point where it is grammatically palatable to the most squeamish among us. Yet no readily ascertainable general principle exists for stopping short of that result were we to affirm the judgment below. For, while the particular four-letter word being litigated here is perhaps more distasteful than most others of its genre, it is nevertheless often true that one man's vulgarity is another's lyric. Indeed, we think it is largely because governmental officials cannot make principled distinctions in this area that the Constitution leaves matters of taste and style so largely to the individual.

Additionally, we cannot overlook the fact, because it is well illustrated by the episode involved here, that much linguistic expression serves a dual communicative function: it conveys not only ideas capable of relatively precise, detached explication, but otherwise inexpressible emotions as well. In fact, words are often chosen as much for their emotive as their cognitive force. We cannot sanction the view that the Constitution, while solicitous of the cognitive content of individual speech has little or no regard for that emotive function which practically speaking, may often be the more important element of the overall message sought to be communicated.

Finally, and in the same vein, we cannot indulge the facile assumption that one can forbid particular words without also running a substantial risk of suppressing ideas in the process. Indeed, governments might soon seize upon the censorship of particular words as a convenient guise for banning the expression of unpopular views. We have been able, as noted above, to discern little social benefit that might result from running the risk of opening the door to such grave results.

It is, in sum, our judgment that, absent a more particularized and compelling reason for its actions, the State may not, consistently with the First and Fourteenth Amendments, make the simple public display here involved of this single four-letter expletive a criminal offense. Because that is the only arguably sustainable rationale for the conviction here at issue, the judgment below must be reversed.

Conclusion

Reversed.

Mr. Justice Blackmun, with whom The Chief Justice and Mr. Justice Black join.

Cohen's absurd and immature antic, in my view, was mainly conduct and little speech. The California Court of Appeal appears so to have described it, and I cannot characterize it otherwise. Further, the case appears to me to be well within the sphere of *Chaplinsky v. New Hampshire*, 315 U.S. 568 (1942), where Mr. Justice Murphy, a known champion of First Amendment freedoms, wrote for a unanimous bench. As a consequence, this Court's agonizing over First Amendment values seem misplaced and unnecessary.

Mr. Justice White concurs in [omitted] Paragraph 2 of Mr. Justice Blackmun's dissenting opinion.

Exercise 33:

1. Did *Cohen* engage in pure speech or expressive conduct?

2. How did California "infringe" Cohen's freedom of speech?

3. Why is profane and indecent speech protected, according to Justice Harlan? Is protecting profane speech consistent with the Free Speech Clause's original meaning and purposes?

4. Was Cohen's profane and indecent speech valuable, as the Court concluded? Or, was it, as Justice Rehnquist argued in *Texas v. Johnson*, 491 U.S. 397, 432 (1989), "an inarticulate grunt or roar"?

5. In what contexts or under what conditions may the government limit or prohibit profane and indecent speech, after *Cohen*?

6. Argue that California should have been able to punish Cohen for his speech, because of the context in which the challenged speech occurred.

7. What if a city wished to ban racial epithets? Would it be constitutional under *Cohen*? How could you construct such a ban to make it consonant with *Cohen*?

Following *Cohen*, the Supreme Court has carved out situations where the government can regulate profane and indecent speech. There are three general situations when the government may regulate such speech: (1) to protect captive audiences, especially in the home; (2) to protect minors, especially (though not only) in the school context; and (3) on some forms of media.

As Justice Harlan noted, "government may properly act in many situations to prohibit intrusion into the privacy of the home of unwelcome views and ideas which cannot be totally banned from the public dialogue.... The ability of government, consonant with the Constitution, to shut off discourse solely to protect others from hearing it is, in other words, dependent upon a showing that substantial privacy interests are being invaded in an essentially intolerable manner." It remains unclear how broadly this exception extends beyond the home. *See, e.g., Erznoznik v. City of Jacksonville*, 422 U.S. 205 (1975) (ruling that a prohibition of nude movies at drive-in theatres could not be justified based on protecting captive audiences because an offended passer-by could "avert his eyes").

The Supreme Court has frequently ruled that protecting minors justifies restricting profane and indecent speech. In *Morse v. Frederick*, 551 U.S. 393 (2007), the Supreme Court ruled that a school could expel students who displayed a large banner that bore the words "BONG HiTS 4 JESUS." The Court ruled that the suspended students' "First

Amendment rights were circumscribed 'in light of the special characteristics of the school environment.'" *Id.* at 405. Therefore, the school's suspension was constitutional.

Third, the Supreme Court created a media-by-media approach to profane and indecent speech. The Court has held that the government may restrict such speech over broadcast media, such as broadcast television and radio. *FCC v. Pacifica Foundation*, 438 U.S. 726 (1978). The Supreme Court explained that the broadcast media entered into private spaces, such as homes, and that it reached unwilling listeners, including children. *Id.* at 748–49. However, the Supreme Court has also distinguished other media—telephones, cable television, and the internet—and ruled that the government does not possess the same power to regulate indecent and profane speech over them, at least without a compelling interest. *See Sable Commc'ns v. FCC*, 492 U.S. 115 (1989) (telephone); *Denver Area Educ. Telecomms. Consortium, Inc v. FCC*, 518 U.S. 727 (1996) (cable); *Reno v. American Civil Liberties Union*, 521 U.S. 844 (1997) (internet). The Court, in these cases, generally argued that these media did not present the same problems with captive audiences and children.

d. Tortious Speech

Speech may harm a person's reputation. For this reason, American tort law has compensated and punished based on such speech. Like profanity and indecent speech, for most of American history, tortious speech was unprotected by the freedom of speech. Then, in 1964, the Court issued *New York Times v. Sullivan*, 376 U.S. 254 (1964), which held that the First Amendment limited tort liability based on speech. However, unlike profanity and indecent speech, since then, the Supreme Court has articulated a complex body of doctrine to determine when and under what circumstances tort liability may be premised on speech. Therefore, tortious speech is protected, but there is not one test or standard to ascertain that protection. Here, because of the complexity of this area of law, you are introduced to it; for full coverage of this area of the law, you should take an advanced class dedicated to the First Amendment.

New York Times Company v. Sullivan
376 U.S. 254 (1964)

MR. JUSTICE BRENNAN delivered the opinion of the Court.

We are required in this case to determine for the first time the extent to which the constitutional protections for speech and press limit a State's power to award damages in a libel action brought by a public official against critics of his official conduct.

Respondent L.B. Sullivan is one of the three elected Commissioners of the City of Montgomery, Alabama. He brought this civil libel action against the four individual petitioners, who are Negroes and Alabama clergymen, and against petitioner the New York Times Company. A jury in the Circuit Court of Montgomery County awarded him damages of $500,000, the full amount claimed, against all the petitioners, and the Supreme Court of Alabama affirmed.

Respondent's complaint alleged that he had been libeled by statements in a full-page advertisement that was carried in the New York Times on March 29, 1960. Entitled "Heed Their Rising Voices," the advertisement began by stating that "As the whole world knows by now, thousands of Southern Negro students are engaged in widespread non-violent demonstrations in positive affirmation of the right to live in human dignity as guaranteed by the U.S. Constitution and the Bill of Rights." It went on to charge that "in their efforts to uphold these guarantees, they are being met by an unprecedented wave of terror by those who would deny and negate that document which the whole world looks upon as setting the pattern for modern freedom. * * *" Succeeding paragraphs purported to illustrate the "wave of terror" by describing certain alleged events.

Of the 10 paragraphs of text in the advertisement, the third and a portion of the sixth were the basis of respondent's claim of libel. Third paragraph: "In Montgomery, Alabama, after students sang 'My Country, 'Tis of Thee' on the State Capitol steps, their leaders were expelled from school, and truckloads of police armed with shotguns and tear-gas ringed the Alabama State College Campus. When the entire student body protested to state authorities by refusing to re-register, their dining hall was padlocked in an attempt to starve them into submission."

Sixth paragraph: "Again and again the Southern violators have answered Dr. King's peaceful protests with intimidation and violence. They have bombed his home almost killing his wife and child. They have assaulted his person. They have arrested him seven times-for 'speeding,' 'loitering' and similar 'offenses.' And now they have charged him with 'perjury'—a felony under which they could imprison him for ten years. * * *"

Although neither off these statements mentions respondent by name, he contended that the word "police" in the third paragraph referred to him as the Montgomery Commissioner who supervised the Police Department. As to the sixth paragraph, he contended that since arrests are ordinarily made by the police, the paragraph would be read as accusing the Montgomery police, and hence him, of answering Dr. King's protests with "intimidation and violence," bombing his home, assaulting his person, and charging him with perjury.

It is uncontroverted that some of the statements contained in the two paragraphs were not accurate descriptions of events which occurred in Montgomery. Respondent was allowed to prove that he had not participated in the events described.

Respondent made no effort to prove that he suffered actual pecuniary loss as a result of the alleged libel. The trial judge submitted the case to the jury under instructions that the statements in the advertisement were "libelous per se," so that petitioners might be held liable if the jury found that they had published the advertisement and that the statements were made "of and concerning" respondent.

The jury was instructed that, because the statements were libelous per se, "the law * * * implies legal injury from the bare fact of publication itself," "falsity and malice are presumed," "general damages need not be alleged or proved but are presumed," and "punitive damages may be awarded by the jury even though the amount of actual damages is neither found nor shown." An award of punitive damages—as distinguished from "general" damages, which are compensatory in nature—apparently requires proof of actual malice under Alabama law. The judge rejected petitioners' contention that his rulings abridged the freedoms of speech and of the press that are guaranteed by the First and Fourteenth Amendments.

[T]he Supreme Court of Alabama sustained the trial judge's rulings and instructions in all respects. We reverse the judgment. We hold that the rule of law applied by the Alabama courts is constitutionally deficient for failure to provide the safeguards for freedom of speech and of the press that are required by the First and Fourteenth Amendments in a libel action brought by a public official against critics of his official conduct.

II.

Respondent relies heavily, as did the Alabama courts, on statements of this Court to the effect that the Constitution does not protect libelous publications.[6] Those statements do not foreclose our inquiry here. None of the cases sustained the use of libel laws to impose sanctions upon expression critical of the official conduct of public officials. In deciding the question now, we are compelled by neither precedent nor policy.

The general proposition that freedom of expression upon public questions is secured by the First Amendment has long been settled by our decisions. The constitutional safeguard, we have said, "was fashioned to assure unfettered interchange of ideas for the bringing about of political and social changes desired by the people." The First Amendment, said Judge Learned Hand, "presupposes that right conclusions are more likely to be gathered out of a multitude of tongues, than through any kind of authoritative selection. To many this is, and always will be, folly; but we have staked upon it our all." *United States v. Associated Press*, 52 F. Supp. 362, 372 (D.N.Y.1943).

Thus we consider this case against the background of a profound national commitment to the principle that debate on public issues should be uninhibited, robust, and wide-open, and that it may well include vehement, caustic, and sometimes unpleasantly sharp attacks on government and public officials. The present advertisement, as an expression of grievance and protest on one of the major public issues of our time, would seem clearly to qualify for the constitutional protection. The question is whether it forfeits that protection by the falsity of some of its factual statements and by its alleged defamation of respondent.

Authoritative interpretations of the First Amendment guarantees have consistently refused to recognize an exception for any test of truth—and especially one that puts the burden of proving truth on the speaker. The constitutional protection does not turn upon "the truth, popularity, or social utility of the ideas and beliefs which are offered." As Madison said, "Some degree of abuse is inseparable from the proper use

---

6. *Roth v. United States*, 354 U.S. 476, 486–487 [(1957)]; *Chaplinsky v. New Hampshire*, 315 U.S. 568, 572 [(1942)]; *Near v. Minnesota*, 283 U.S. 697 [(1931)].

of every thing; and in no instance is this more true than in that of the press." 4 Elliot's Debates on the Federal Constitution (1876), p. 571.[13]

Injury to official reputation error affords no more warrant for repressing speech that would otherwise be free than does factual error. Criticism of their official conduct does not lose its constitutional protection merely because it is effective criticism and hence diminishes their official reputations.

If neither factual error nor defamatory content suffices to remove the constitutional shield from criticism of official conduct, the combination of the two elements is no less inadequate. This is the lesson to be drawn from the great controversy over the Sedition Act of 1798, 1 Stat. 596, which first crystallized a national awareness of the central meaning of the First Amendment. See Levy, Legacy of Suppression (1960), at 258 et seq. The Act allowed the defendant the defense of truth, and provided that the jury were to be judges both of the law and the facts. Despite these qualifications, the Act was vigorously condemned as unconstitutional in an attack joined in by Jefferson and Madison [i]n the famous Virginia Resolutions of 1798.

Madison prepared the Report in support of the protest. His premise was that the Constitution created a form of government under which "The people, not the government, possess the absolute sovereignty." The structure of the government dispersed power in reflection of the people's distrust of concentrated power, and of power itself at all levels. This form of government was "altogether different" from the British form, under which the Crown was sovereign and the people were subjects. "Is it not natural and necessary, under such different circumstances," he asked, "that a different degree of freedom in the use of the press should be contemplated?" The right of free public discussion of the stewardship of public officials was thus, in Madison's view, a fundamental principle of the American form of government.

Although the Sedition Act was never tested in this Court, the attack upon its validity has carried the day in the court of history. Fines levied in its prosecution were repaid by Act of Congress on the ground that it was unconstitutional. Jefferson, as President, pardoned those who had been convicted and sentenced under the Act and remitted their fines. The invalidity of the Act has also been assumed by Justices of this Court. See Holmes, J., dissenting and joined by Brandeis, J., in *Abrams v. United States*, 250 U.S. 616, 630 [(1919)]. See also Cooley, Constitutional Limitations (8th ed., Carrington, 1927), pp. 899–900; Chafee, Free Speech in the United States (1942), pp. 27–28. These views reflect a broad consensus that the Act, because of the

---

13. See also Mill, On Liberty (Oxford: Blackwell, 1947), at 47:

"* * * [T]o argue sophistically, to suppress facts or arguments, to misstate the elements of the case, or misrepresent the opposite opinion * * * all this, even to the most aggravated degree, is so continually done in perfect good faith, by persons who are not considered, and in many other respects may not deserve to be considered, ignorant or incompetent, that it is rarely possible, on adequate grounds, conscientiously to stamp the misrepresentation as morally culpable; and still less could law presume to interfere with this kind of controversial misconduct."

restraint it imposed upon criticism of government and public officials, was inconsistent with the First Amendment.

What a State may not constitutionally bring about by means of a criminal statute is likewise beyond the reach of its civil law of libel. The fear of damage awards under a rule such as that invoked by the Alabama courts here may be markedly more inhibiting than the fear of prosecution under a criminal statute. [Due process] safeguards are not available to the defendant in a civil action. The judgment awarded in this case—without the need for any proof of actual pecuniary loss—was one thousand times greater than the maximum fine provided by the Alabama criminal statute. And since there is no double-jeopardy limitation applicable to civil lawsuits, this is not the only judgment that may be awarded against petitioners for the same publication. Whether or not a newspaper can survive a succession of such judgments, the pall of fear and timidity imposed upon those who would give voice to public criticism is an atmosphere in which the First Amendment freedoms cannot survive.

The state rule of law is not saved by its allowance of the defense of truth. A rule compelling the critic of official conduct to guarantee the truth of all his factual assertions—and to do so on pain of libel judgments virtually unlimited in amount—leads to a comparable "self-censorship." Allowance of the defense of truth, with the burden of proving it on the defendant, does not mean that only false speech will be deterred.[19] Under such a rule, would-be critics of official conduct may be deterred from voicing their criticism, even though it is believed to be true and even though it is in fact true, because of doubt whether it can be proved in court or fear of the expense of having to do so. They tend to make only statements which "steer far wider of the unlawful zone." The rule thus dampens the vigor and limits the variety of public debate. It is inconsistent with the First and Fourteenth Amendments.

The constitutional guarantees require, we think, a federal rule that prohibits a public official from recovering damages for a defamatory falsehood relating to his official conduct unless he proves that the statement was made with "actual malice"—that is, with knowledge that it was false or with reckless disregard of whether it was false or not.

III.

We hold today that the Constitution delimits a State's power to award damages for libel in actions brought by public officials against critics of their official conduct. Since this is such an action, the rule requiring proof of actual malice is applicable. While Alabama law apparently requires proof of actual malice for an award of punitive damages, where general damages are concerned malice is "presumed." Such a presumption is inconsistent with the federal rule. Since the trial judge did not instruct the jury to differentiate between general and punitive damages, it may be that the

---

19. Even a false statement may be deemed to make a valuable contribution to public debate, since it brings about "the clearer perception and livelier impression of truth, produced by its collision with error." Mill, On Liberty (Oxford: Blackwell, 1947), at 15; see also Milton, *Areopagitica*, in Prose Works (Yale, 1959), Vol. II, at 561.

verdict was wholly an award of one or the other. But it is impossible to know, in view of the general verdict returned. Because of this uncertainty, the judgment must be reversed and the case remanded.

Since respondent may seek a new trial, we deem that considerations of effective judicial administration require us to review the evidence in the present record to determine whether it could constitutionally support a judgment for respondent. This Court's duty is not limited to the elaboration of constitutional principles; we must also in proper cases review the evidence to make certain that those principles have been constitutionally applied. This is such a case.

We think the evidence against the Times supports at most a finding of negligence in failing to discover the misstatements, and is constitutionally insufficient to show the recklessness that is required for a finding of actual malice.

The judgment of the Supreme Court of Alabama is reversed and the case is remanded to that court for further proceedings not inconsistent with this opinion.

Reversed and remanded.

MR. JUSTICE BLACK, with whom MR. JUSTICE DOUGLAS joins (concurring).

I agree with the Court that the Fourteenth Amendment made the First applicable to the States. This means to me that since the adoption of the Fourteenth Amendment a State has no more power than the Federal Government to use a civil libel law or any other law to impose damages for merely discussing public affairs and criticizing public officials. The power of the United States to do that is, in my judgment, precisely nil. Such was the general view held when the First Amendment was adopted and ever since. Congress never has sought to challenge this viewpoint by passing any civil libel law.

MR. JUSTICE GOLDBERG, with whom MR. JUSTICE DOUGLAS joins (concurring in the result).

. . . .

For these reasons, I strongly believe that the Constitution accords citizens and press an unconditional freedom to criticize official conduct. It necessarily follows that in a case such as this, where all agree that the allegedly defamatory statements related to official conduct, the judgments for libel cannot constitutionally be sustained.

Exercise 34:

1. What was the state action in this case that was subject to the Fourteenth Amendment?

2. How was the *New York Times*'s freedom of speech infringed?

3. What test did the Supreme Court articulate to evaluate defamation claims premised on harmful speech?

4. Apply each element of the test to the facts of this case.

5. The test laid out by the Court is robustly speech protective. Did it strike the right balance between the harms caused by defamation and the benefits of freedom

of speech? What evidence can you point to that supports your conclusion? What, if anything, does the fact that other countries strike the balance differently—more protective of reputational interests—suggest?

6. The concurring justices advocated for an absolute bar to all defamation actions against public officials premised on speech. Should the majority have adopted this standard instead?

7. Upon what tools of interpretation did the Supreme Court rely to conclude that the freedom of speech limited defamation actions?

8. The Court repeatedly quoted John Stuart Mill's famous book, *On Liberty*. To what end? One could easily find a similarly famous book and author with a different perspective, so how much weight, if any, should one assign to such an "authority"?

———————

In the years following *New York Times v. Sullivan*, the Supreme Court created nuanced rules on when the *New York Times* test applied, depending on variables such as whether the plaintiff is a public official or private party, whether the speech is a matter of public concern, and with different state of mind requirements. It has also limited a variety of tort actions, including intentional infliction of emotional distress, false light, invasion of privacy, and the right of publicity. In doing so, the Court has created a complex set of related analyses that you would cover in an advanced First Amendment course.

e. Sexually-Explicit Speech

Sexually explicit speech is sexual expression that does not constitute obscenity or child pornography. Generally, the Supreme Court has held that sexually explicit speech is constitutionally protected, but it is less protected. An important case in this line is *Young v. American Mini Theatres*, 427 U.S. 50 (1976). Like *Renton v. Playtime Threatres, Inc.*, 475 U.S. 41 (1986), discussed earlier, *Young* involved restrictive zoning of "adult" entertainment. Justice Stevens, writing for the Court, expressly stated that sexually explicit speech is less valuable, and therefore deserving of less protection. "[F]ew of us would march our sons and daughters off to war to preserve the citizen's right to see 'Specified Sexual Activities' exhibited in the theaters of our choice. Even though the First Amendment protects communication in this area from total suppression, we hold that the State may legitimately use the content of these materials as the basis for placing them in a different classification from other motion pictures." *Id.* at 70.

Earlier, we saw that the Supreme Court created the Secondary Effects Doctrine for the zoning of adult entertainment businesses. *Renton v. Playtime Threatres, Inc.*, 475 U.S. 41 (1986). This allowed relatively vigorous regulation—though not prohibition—of sexually explicit speech. We saw this as well in the context of indecent speech, where the Court, though generally protecting indecent speech, carved out situations where the government could regulate and prohibit indecent speech, such as in schools. The Supreme Court's less favorable treatment of sexually explicit speech in these contexts is of-a-piece with the Court's generally less favorable treatment of sexually explicit speech. *See also City of Erie v. Pap's A.M.*, 529 U.S. 277 (2000) (upholding a ban on nude dancing, though without a majority rationale).

Though the Court has expressly and implicitly provided less protection to sexually explicit speech, there is not one rule or test applicable to all contexts. Instead, you should know that the Court's approach to the regulation of sexually explicit speech is context specific. For instance, in the zoning context, you should apply the Secondary Effects Doctrine.

5. New Categories of Unprotected and Lesser-Protected Speech?

The Supreme Court's categorical approach to speech protection has, as one of its results, the continuing possibility that the Court may announce additional categories of unprotected or less-protected speech. In recent years, such claims have reached the Court in a number of cases. Uniformly, however, the Supreme Court has refused to create new, or expand, categorical exceptions to the freedom of speech. *See Brown v. Entertainment Merchs. Ass'n*, 131 S. Ct. 2729 (2011) (declining to create a new category of unprotected violent speech aimed at children when addressing California's regulation of violent video games); *Snyder v. Phelps*, 131 S. Ct. 1207 (2011) (ruling that the First Amendment prevented the father of a deceased soldier from recovering for intentional infliction of emotional distress from virulent funeral protestors); *United States v. Stevens*, 559 U.S. 460 (2010) (declining to create a new category of unprotected depiction of animal cruelty). Indeed, Justice Scalia, writing for the Court in *Stevens*, bluntly stated: "Our decisions ... cannot be taken as establishing a freewheeling authority to declare new categories of speech outside the scope of the First Amendment. Maybe there are some categories of speech that have been historically unprotected, but have not yet been specifically identified or discussed as such in our case law.... We need not foreclose the future recognition of such additional categories to reject the Government's highly manipulable balancing test as a means of identifying them." *Stevens*, 559 U.S. at 472.

The Court's reasoning focused on both the value of freedom of speech and the historically defined contours of categories of unprotected speech. Therefore, it is unlikely the Supreme Court will identify new or expand existing categories of unprotected or less-protected speech. This is especially the case given the acknowledged low value of the speech at issue in the three recent cases.

6. *R.A.V. v. St. Paul*, and Content-Based Restrictions *within* Categories of Unprotected and Less-Protected Speech

Up to this point in our review of the Supreme Court's categorical approach to speech protection, we have operated on the assumption that unprotected speech was completely free from protection by the Free Speech Clause. However, the Supreme Court, in *R.A.V. v. St. Paul*, 505 U.S. 377 (1992), introduced a significant qualification on that operative assumption. As you will see in the complicated opinion below, the Supreme Court ruled that the Free Speech Clause also prohibited content-based distinctions *within* the categories of unprotected speech themselves.

R.A.V. v. City of St. Paul, Minnesota
505 U.S. 377 (1992)

JUSTICE SCALIA delivered the opinion of the Court.

In the predawn hours of June 21, 1990, petitioner and several other teenagers allegedly assembled a crudely made cross by taping together broken chair legs. They then allegedly burned the cross inside the fenced yard of a black family that lived across the street from the house where petitioner was staying. [O]ne of the two provisions under which respondent city of St. Paul chose to charge petitioner (then a juvenile) was the St. Paul Bias-Motivated Crime Ordinance, St. Paul, Minn., Legis. Code § 292.02 (1990), which provides:

> "Whoever places on public or private property a symbol, object, appellation, characterization or graffiti, including, but not limited to, a burning cross or Nazi swastika, which one knows or has reasonable grounds to know arouses anger, alarm, or resentment in others on the basis of race, color, creed, religion or gender commits disorderly conduct and shall be guilty of a misdemeanor."

Petitioner moved to dismiss this count on the ground that the St. Paul ordinance was substantially overbroad and impermissibly content based and therefore facially invalid under the First Amendment. The trial court granted this motion, but the Minnesota Supreme Court reversed. That court rejected petitioner's overbreadth claim because the modifying phrase "arouses anger, alarm, or resentment in others" limited the reach of the ordinance to conduct that amounts to "fighting words," *i.e.*, "conduct that itself inflicts injury or tends to incite immediate violence...," *In re Welfare of R.A.V.*, 464 N.W.2d 507, 510 (Minn.1991) (citing *Chaplinsky v. New Hampshire*, 315 U.S. 568, 572 (1942)), and therefore the ordinance reached only expression "that the first amendment does not protect[.]" The court also concluded that the ordinance was not impermissibly content based. We granted certiorari.

I

In construing the St. Paul ordinance, we accept the Minnesota Supreme Court's authoritative statement that the ordinance reaches only those expressions that constitute "fighting words" within the meaning of *Chaplinsky*. We conclude that the ordinance is facially unconstitutional in that it prohibits otherwise permitted speech solely on the basis of the subjects the speech addresses.

The First Amendment generally prevents government from proscribing speech, see, *e.g.*, *Cantwell v. Connecticut*, 310 U.S. 296, 309–311 (1940), or even expressive conduct, see, *e.g.*, *Texas v. Johnson*, 491 U.S. 397, 406 (1989), because of disapproval of the ideas expressed. Content-based regulations are presumptively invalid. *Consolidated Edison Co. of N.Y. v. Public Serv. Comm'n of N.Y.*, 447 U.S. 530, 536 (1980); *Police Dept. of Chicago v. Mosley*, 408 U.S. 92, 95 (1972). From 1791 to the present, however, our society, like other free but civilized societies, has permitted restrictions upon the content of speech in a few limited areas, which are "of such slight social value as a step to truth that any benefit that may be derived from them is clearly outweighed by the social interest in order and morality." *Chaplinsky, supra*, 315 U.S., at 572. See, *e.g., Roth v. United States*, 354 U.S. 476 (1957) (obscenity); *Beauharnais v. Illinois*, 343 U.S. 250 (1952) (defamation); *Chaplinsky v. New Hampshire, supra* (" 'fighting' words"). Our decisions since the 1960's have narrowed the scope of the traditional categorical exceptions for defamation, see *New York Times Co. v. Sullivan*, 376 U.S. 254 (1964), and for obscenity, see *Miller v. California*, 413 U.S. 15 (1973), but a limited categorical approach has remained an important part of our First Amendment jurisprudence.

We have sometimes said that these categories of expression are "not within the area of constitutionally protected speech," *Roth, supra*, 354 U.S., at 483; *Beauharnais, supra*, 343 U.S., at 266; *Chaplinsky, supra*, 315 U.S., at 571–572; or that the "protection of the First Amendment does not extend" to them. Such statements must be taken in context, however, and are no more literally true than is the occasionally repeated shorthand characterizing obscenity "as not being speech at all[.]" What they mean is that these areas of speech can, consistently with the First Amendment, be regulated *because of their constitutionally proscribable content* (obscenity, defamation, etc.)—not that they are categories of speech entirely invisible to the Constitution, so that they may be made the vehicles for content discrimination unrelated to their distinctively proscribable content. Thus, the government may proscribe libel; but it may not make the further content discrimination of proscribing *only* libel critical of the government.... Our cases surely do not establish the proposition that the First Amendment imposes no obstacle whatsoever to regulation of particular instances of such proscribable expression, so that the government "may regulate [them] freely[.]" That would mean that a city council could enact an ordinance prohibiting only those legally obscene works that contain criticism of the city government or, indeed, that do not include endorsement of the city government. Such a simplistic, all-or-nothing-at-all approach to First Amendment protection is at odds with common sense and with our jurisprudence as well. It is not true that "fighting words" have at most a "*de minimis*" expressive content, or that their content is *in all respects* "worthless and undeserving of constitutional protection"; sometimes they are quite expressive indeed. We have not said that they constitute "*no* part of the expression of ideas," but only that they constitute "no *essential* part of any exposition of ideas." *Chaplinsky, supra*, 315 U.S., at 572 (emphasis added).

The proposition that a particular instance of speech can be proscribable on the basis of one feature (*e.g.*, obscenity) but not on the basis of another (*e.g.*, opposition to the city government) is commonplace and has found application in many contexts. We have long held, for example, that nonverbal expressive activity can be banned because of the action it entails, but not because of the ideas it expresses—so that burning a flag in violation of an ordinance against outdoor fires could be punishable, whereas burning a flag in violation of an ordinance against dishonoring the flag is not. See *Johnson*, 491 U.S., at 406–407. Similarly, we have upheld reasonable "time, place, or manner" restrictions, but only if they are "justified without reference to the content of the regulated speech." And just as the power to proscribe particular speech on the basis of a noncontent element (*e.g.*, noise) does not entail the power to proscribe the same speech on the basis of a content element; so also, the power to proscribe it on the basis of *one* content element (*e.g.*, obscenity) does not entail the power to proscribe it on the basis of *other* content elements.

In other words, the exclusion of "fighting words" from the scope of the First Amendment simply means that, for purposes of that Amendment, the unprotected features of the words are, despite their verbal character, essentially a "nonspeech" element of communication. Fighting words are thus analogous to a noisy sound truck: Each is a "mode of speech"; both can be used to convey an idea; but neither has, in and of itself, a claim upon the First Amendment. As with the sound truck, however, so also with fighting words: The government may not regulate use based on hostility — or favoritism — towards the underlying message expressed.

In our view, the First Amendment imposes a "content discrimination" limitation upon a State's prohibition of proscribable speech. There is no problem whatever, for example, with a State's prohibiting obscenity (and other forms of proscribable expression) only in certain media or markets, for although that prohibition would be "underinclusive," it would not discriminate on the basis of content. See, *e.g.*, *Sable Communications*, 492 U.S. [115,] 124–126 [(1989)] (upholding 47 U.S.C. §223(b)(1), which prohibits obscene *telephone* communications).

Even the prohibition against content discrimination that we assert the First Amendment requires is not absolute. It applies differently in the context of proscribable speech than in the area of fully protected speech. The rationale of the general prohibition, after all, is that content discrimination "raises the specter that the Government may effectively drive certain ideas or viewpoints from the marketplace[.]" But content discrimination among various instances of a class of proscribable speech often does not pose this threat.

When the basis for the content discrimination consists entirely of the very reason the entire class of speech at issue is proscribable, no significant danger of idea or viewpoint discrimination exists. Such a reason, having been adjudged neutral enough to support exclusion of the entire class of speech from First Amendment protection, is also neutral enough to form the basis of distinction within the class. To illustrate: A State might choose to prohibit only that obscenity which is the most patently offensive *in its prurience* — *i.e.*, that which involves the most lascivious displays of sexual activity. But it may not prohibit, for example, only that obscenity which includes offensive *political* messages. And the Federal Government can criminalize only those threats of violence that are directed against the President, see 18 U.S.C. §871 — since the reasons why threats of violence are outside the First Amendment (protecting individuals from the fear of violence, from the disruption that fear engenders, and from the possibility that the threatened violence will occur) have special force when applied to the person of the President. But the Federal Government may not criminalize only those threats against the President that mention his policy on aid to inner cities....

Another valid basis for according differential treatment to even a content-defined subclass of proscribable speech is that the subclass happens to be associated with particular "secondary effects" of the speech, so that the regulation is "*justified* without reference to the content of the ... speech," *Renton v. Playtime Theatres, Inc.*, 475 U.S. 41, 48 (1986). A State could, for example, permit all obscene live performances except those involving minors. Moreover, since words can in some circumstances violate laws directed not against speech but against conduct (a law against treason, for example, is violated by telling the enemy the Nation's defense secrets), a particular content-based subcategory of a proscribable class of speech can be swept up incidentally within the reach of a statute directed at conduct rather than speech. See *O'Brien*, 391 U.S., at 376–377. Thus, for example, sexually derogatory "fighting words," among other words, may produce a violation of Title VII's general prohibition against sexual discrimination in employment practices, 42 U.S.C. § 2000e-2. Where the government does not target conduct on the basis of its expressive content, acts are not shielded from regulation merely because they express a discriminatory idea or philosophy.

These bases for distinction refute the proposition that the selectivity of the restriction is "even arguably 'conditioned upon the sovereign's agreement with what a speaker may intend to say.'" There may be other such bases as well. Indeed, to validate such selectivity (where totally proscribable speech is at issue) it may not even be necessary to identify any particular "neutral" basis, so long as the nature of the content discrimination is such that there is no realistic possibility that official suppression of ideas is afoot. (We cannot think of any First Amendment interest that would stand in the way of a State's prohibiting only those obscene motion pictures with blue-eyed actresses.) Save for that limitation, the regulation of "fighting words," like the regulation of noisy speech, may address some offensive instances and leave other, equally offensive, instances alone.

II

Applying these principles to the St. Paul ordinance, we conclude that, even as narrowly construed by the Minnesota Supreme Court, the ordinance is facially unconstitutional. Although the phrase in the ordinance, "arouses anger, alarm, or resentment in others," has been limited by the Minnesota Supreme Court's construction to reach only those symbols or displays that amount to "fighting words," the remaining, unmodified terms make clear that the ordinance applies only to "fighting words" that insult, or provoke violence, "on the basis of race, color, creed, religion or gender." Displays containing abusive invective, no matter how vicious or severe, are permissible unless they are addressed to one of the specified disfavored topics. Those who wish to use "fighting words" in connection with other ideas — to express hostility, for example, on the basis of political affiliation, union membership, or homosexuality — are not covered. The First Amendment does not permit St. Paul to impose special prohibitions on those speakers who express views on disfavored subjects.

In its practical operation, moreover, the ordinance goes even beyond mere content discrimination, to actual viewpoint discrimination. Displays containing some words — odious racial epithets, for example — would be prohibited to proponents of all views.

But "fighting words" that do not themselves invoke race, color, creed, religion, or gender-aspersions upon a person's mother, for example—would seemingly be usable *ad libitum* in the placards of those arguing *in favor* of racial, color, etc., tolerance and equality, but could not be used by those speakers' opponents. One could hold up a sign saying, for example, that all "anti-Catholic bigots" are misbegotten; but not that all "papists" are, for that would insult and provoke violence "on the basis of religion." St. Paul has no such authority to license one side of a debate to fight freestyle, while requiring the other to follow Marquis of Queensberry rules.

What we have here, it must be emphasized, is not a prohibition of fighting words that are directed at certain persons or groups (which would be *facially* valid if it met the requirements of the Equal Protection Clause); but rather, a prohibition of fighting words that contain (as the Minnesota Supreme Court repeatedly emphasized) messages of "bias-motivated" hatred and in particular, as applied to this case, messages "based on virulent notions of racial supremacy." One must wholeheartedly agree with the Minnesota Supreme Court that "[i]t is the responsibility, even the obligation, of diverse communities to confront such notions in whatever form they appear," but the manner of that confrontation cannot consist of selective limitations upon speech. St. Paul's brief asserts that a general "fighting words" law would not meet the city's needs because only a content-specific measure can communicate to minority groups that the "group hatred" aspect of such speech "is not condoned by the majority." Brief for Respondent 25. The point of the First Amendment is that majority preferences must be expressed in some fashion other than silencing speech on the basis of its content.

The content-based discrimination reflected in the St. Paul ordinance comes within neither any of the specific exceptions to the First Amendment prohibition we discussed earlier nor a more general exception for content discrimination that does not threaten censorship of ideas. It assuredly does not fall within the exception for content discrimination based on the very reasons why the particular class of speech at issue (here, fighting words) is proscribable. As explained earlier, the reason why fighting words are categorically excluded from the protection of the First Amendment is not that their content communicates any particular idea, but that their content embodies a particularly intolerable (and socially unnecessary) *mode* of expressing *whatever* idea the speaker wishes to convey. St. Paul has not singled out an especially offensive mode of expression—it has not, for example, selected for prohibition only those fighting words that communicate ideas in a threatening (as opposed to a merely obnoxious) manner. Rather, it has proscribed fighting words of whatever manner that communicate messages of racial, gender, or religious intolerance. Selectivity of this sort creates the possibility that the city is seeking to handicap the expression of particular ideas. That possibility would alone be enough to render the ordinance presumptively invalid, but St. Paul's comments and concessions in this case elevate the possibility to a certainty.

St. Paul argues that the ordinance comes within another of the specific exceptions we mentioned, the one that allows content discrimination aimed only at the "secondary effects" of the speech, see *Renton v. Playtime Theatres, Inc.*, 475 U.S. 41 (1986).

According to St. Paul, the ordinance is intended to "protect against the victimization of a person or persons who are particularly vulnerable because of their membership in a group that historically has been discriminated against." [I]t is clear that the St. Paul ordinance is not directed to secondary effects within the meaning of *Renton*. As we said in *Boos v. Barry*, 485 U.S. 312 (1988), "Listeners' reactions to speech are not the type of 'secondary effects' we referred to in *Renton*." "The emotive impact of speech on its audience is not a 'secondary effect.' "[7]

Finally, St. Paul and its *amici* defend the conclusion of the Minnesota Supreme Court that, even if the ordinance regulates expression based on hostility towards its protected ideological content, this discrimination is nonetheless justified because it is narrowly tailored to serve compelling state interests. Specifically, they assert that the ordinance helps to ensure the basic human rights of members of groups that have historically been subjected to discrimination, including the right of such group members to live in peace where they wish. We do not doubt that these interests are compelling, and that the ordinance can be said to promote them. But the "danger of censorship" presented by a facially content-based statute requires that that weapon be employed only where it is "*necessary* to serve the asserted [compelling] interest[.]" The existence of adequate content-neutral alternatives thus "undercut[s] significantly" any defense of such a statute, casting considerable doubt on the government's protestations that "the asserted justification is in fact an accurate description of the purpose and effect of the law[.]" The dispositive question in this case, therefore, is whether content discrimination is reasonably necessary to achieve St. Paul's compelling interests; it plainly is not. An ordinance not limited to the favored topics, for example, would have precisely the same beneficial effect. In fact the only interest distinctively served by the content limitation is that of displaying the city council's special hostility towards the particular biases thus singled out. That is precisely what the First Amendment forbids. The politicians of St. Paul are entitled to express that hostility—but not through the means of imposing unique limitations upon speakers who (however benightedly) disagree.

Let there be no mistake about our belief that burning a cross in someone's front yard is reprehensible. But St. Paul has sufficient means at its disposal to prevent such behavior without adding the First Amendment to the fire.

JUSTICE WHITE, with whom JUSTICE BLACKMUN and JUSTICE O'CONNOR join, and with whom JUSTICE STEVENS joins except as to Part I-A, concurring in the judgment.

I agree with the majority that the judgment of the Minnesota Supreme Court should be reversed. However, our agreement ends there.

---

7. St. Paul has not argued in this case that the ordinance merely regulates that subclass of fighting words which is most likely to provoke a violent response. But even if one assumes (as appears unlikely) that the categories selected may be so described, that would not justify selective regulation under a "secondary effects" theory. The only reason why such expressive conduct would be especially correlated with violence is that it conveys a particularly odious message; because the "chain of causation" thus *necessarily* "run[s] through the persuasive effect of the expressive component" of the conduct, it is clear that the St. Paul ordinance regulates on the basis of the "primary" effect of the speech—*i.e.*, its persuasive (or repellant) force.

I

A

This Court's decisions have plainly stated that expression falling within certain limited categories so lacks the values the First Amendment was designed to protect that the Constitution affords no protection to that expression. *Chaplinsky v. New Hampshire*, 315 U.S. 568 (1942), made the point in the clearest possible terms. Thus, as the majority concedes, this Court has long held certain discrete categories of expression to be proscribable on the basis of their content. For instance, the Court has held that the individual who falsely shouts "fire" in a crowded theater may not claim the protection of the First Amendment. The Court has concluded that neither child pornography nor obscenity is protected by the First Amendment. And the Court has observed that, "[l]eaving aside the special considerations when public officials [and public figures] are the target, a libelous publication is not protected by the Constitution."

All of these categories are content based. But the Court has held that the First Amendment does not apply to them because their expressive content is worthless or of *de minimis* value to society. This categorical approach has provided a principled and narrowly focused means for distinguishing between expression that the government may regulate freely and that which it may regulate on the basis of content only upon a showing of compelling need.

It is inconsistent to hold [as the majority does] that the government may proscribe an entire category of speech because the content of that speech is evil, but that the government may not treat a subset of that category differently without violating the First Amendment; the content of the subset is by definition worthless and undeserving of constitutional protection.

The majority's observation that fighting words are "quite expressive indeed," is no answer. Fighting words are not a means of exchanging views, rallying supporters, or registering a protest; they are directed against individuals to provoke violence or to inflict injury. Therefore, a ban on all fighting words or on a subset of the fighting words category would restrict only the social evil of hate speech, without creating the danger of driving viewpoints from the marketplace.

Therefore, the Court's insistence on inventing its brand of First Amendment under inclusiveness puzzles me. [T]he Court's new "underbreadth" creation serves no desirable function. Instead, it permits, indeed invites, the continuation of expressive conduct that in this case is evil and worthless in First Amendment terms, until the city of St. Paul cures the underbreadth by adding to its ordinance a catchall phrase such as "and all other fighting words that may constitutionally be subject to this ordinance."

Any contribution of this holding to First Amendment jurisprudence is surely a negative one, since it necessarily signals that expressions of violence, such as the message of intimidation and racial hatred conveyed by burning a cross on someone's lawn, are of sufficient value to outweigh the social interest in order and morality that has traditionally placed such fighting words outside the First Amendment....

B

In a second break with precedent, the Court refuses to sustain the ordinance even though it would survive under the strict scrutiny applicable to other protected expression. Under the majority's view, a narrowly drawn, content-based ordinance could never pass constitutional muster if the object of that legislation could be accomplished by banning a wider category of speech. This appears to be a general renunciation of strict scrutiny review, a fundamental tool of First Amendment analysis.

Although the First Amendment does not apply to categories of unprotected speech, such as fighting words, the Equal Protection Clause requires that the regulation of unprotected speech be rationally related to a legitimate government interest. Turning to the St. Paul ordinance and assuming, *arguendo*, as the majority does, that the ordinance is not constitutionally overbroad, there is no question that it would pass equal protection review. The ordinance proscribes a subset of "fighting words," those that injure "on the basis of race, color, creed, religion or gender." This selective regulation reflects the city's judgment that harms based on race, color, creed, religion, or gender are more pressing public concerns than the harms caused by other fighting words. In light of our Nation's long and painful experience with discrimination, this determination is plainly reasonable. Indeed, as the majority concedes, the interest is compelling.

JUSTICE BLACKMUN, concurring in the judgment. [Opinion omitted.]

JUSTICE STEVENS, with whom JUSTICE WHITE and JUSTICE BLACKMUN join as to Part I, concurring in the judgment. [Opinion omitted.]

Exercise 35:

1. What is the rule you take from *R.A.V.*? Are there any exceptions to it?

2. From what bases did the Court draw that rule?

3. Justice Scalia's conclusion that the Free Speech Clause protects speech within the categories of *un*protected speech from content-based discrimination is elegantly argued. Describe the doctrinal obstacles Justice Scalia had to overcome to reach this conclusion. For example, what cases stood in his way? And, what doctrines were in tension with his conclusion?

4. Next, describe the different strands of argument that Justice Scalia synthesized to overcome those obstacles and justify his conclusion.

5. We will see, in **Chapter 3**, Justice Scalia authored a structurally similar opinion, *Employment Division v. Smith*, 494 U.S. 872 (1990), where he reworked the Court's free exercise case law in a similar—and similarly controversial—manner.

6. Is there a slippery-slope problem with *R.A.V.*'s holding? For instance, will it undermine the categories of unprotected speech? Justice Scalia's opinion evidences this concern. How does he respond?

7. Is the Court's holding in *R.A.V.* consistent with First Amendment purposes?

8. Explain the majority's application of strict scrutiny to St. Paul's ordinance.

9. What arguments did Justice White make against the majority's rule? Evaluate who had the better of the arguments.

10. Draft a fighting words prohibition that is constitutional after *R.A.V.*

11. Does *R.A.V.* prohibit hate speech restrictions?

I. Public Forum Doctrine

1. Introduction

Public forum doctrine is the analysis the Supreme Court utilizes when evaluating speech on government-owned property. Public forum doctrine is the Court's mechanism to navigate the tension between two competing goals. First, the government (typically) utilizes its property for a public purpose, so the Court wishes to preserve the government's ability to do so. Second, free speech needs space—both physical, like parks, and nonphysical, such as student activity funds—so the Court wishes to ensure adequate room for speech. Public forum doctrine attempts to accommodate both of these goals.

Public forum doctrine originated in the 1930s, when the Supreme Court began applying the First Amendment to the states via incorporation. At its inception, public forum doctrine was relatively speech protective compared both to the prior law governing speech on government-owned property and compared to other facets of free speech law.

The Supreme Court had decided *Davis v. Massachusetts*, 167 U.S. 43 (1897), in 1897. Massachusetts prosecuted Davis for a public address he delivered on the Boston Common without the legally required permit from the city's mayor. The Supreme Court ruled that the government's ownership of the public park entitled Massachusetts to determine on what conditions, if any, speech could occur: "The right to absolutely exclude all right to use necessarily includes the authority to determine under what circumstances such use may be availed of, as the greater power contains the lesser." *Id.* at 48. The Court followed the holding and reasoning of the Massachusetts Supreme Judicial Court in an opinion authored by Justice Holmes. Justice Holmes famously wrote: "For the legislature absolutely or conditionally to forbid public speaking in a highway or public park is no more an infringement of the rights of a member of the public than for the owner of a private house to forbid it in his house." *Commonwealth v. Davis*, 39 N.E. 113, 113 (Mass. 1895).

At the same time, the Court's early free speech cases governing incitement to illegal activity, which you covered in Section [H][3][a], provided modest protection to free speech. In *Gitlow v. New York*, 268 U.S. 652 (1925), for instance, the Supreme Court upheld Gitlow's conviction for publishing *The Left Wing Manifesto* and *The Revolutionary Age*, where Gitlow advocated the illegal overthrow of the government. *Id.* at 654–56. The Court held that Gitlow's conviction was a reasonable exercise of New York's police powers. *Id.* at 669–70. "[W]hen the legislative body has determined generally, in the constitutional exercise of its discretion, that utterances of a certain kind involve such danger of substantive evil that they may be punished, the question whether any specific utterance coming within the prohibited class is likely, in and of itself, to bring about the substantive evil, is not open to consideration." *Id.* at 670.

Against this background, it is not surprising that the Supreme Court provides robust protection for speech in traditional public fora in the seminal case that follows.

Hague v. Committee for Industrial Organization
307 U.S. 496 (1939)

Mr. Justice Butler:

The judgment of the court in this case is that the decree is modified and as modified affirmed. Mr. Justice Frankfurter and Mr. Justice Douglas took no part in the consideration or decision of the case. Mr. Justice Roberts has an opinion in which Mr. Justice Black concurs, and Mr. Justice Stone an opinion in which Mr. Justice Reed concurs. The Chief Justice concurs in an opinion. Mr. Justice McReynolds and Mr. Justice Butler dissent for reasons stated in opinions by them respectively.

Mr. Justice Roberts delivered an opinion in which Mr. Justice Black concurred.

The respondents, individual citizens, unincorporated labor organizations composed of such citizens and a membership corporation, brought suit in the United States District Court against the petitioners, the Mayor, the Director of Public Safety, and the Chief of Police of Jersey City, New Jersey, and the Board of Commissioners, the governing body of the city.

The bill alleges that the petitioners have denied respondents the right to hold lawful meetings in Jersey City. It further alleges that the petitioners have discriminated against the respondents by prohibiting and interfering with distribution of leaflets and pamphlets by the respondents while permitting others to distribute similar printed matter; that the petitioners have caused respondents to be arrested for distributing printed matter in the streets, and have caused them, and their associates, to be carried beyond the limits of the city or to remote places therein, and have compelled them to board ferry boats destined for New York; have arrested and prosecuted respondents for attempting to distribute such printed matter; and have threatened that if respondents attempt to hold public meetings in the city to discuss rights afforded by the National Labor Relations Act, they would be arrested. The bill further alleges that petitioners have consistently refused to issue any permits for meetings to be held by, or sponsored by, respondents, and have thus prevented the holding of such meetings ...; that the respondents' sole purpose is to explain to workingmen the purposes of the National Labor Relations act, the benefits to be derived from it, and the aid which the Committee for Industrial Organization would furnish workingmen to that end; and all the activities in which they seek to engage in Jersey City were, and are, to be performed peacefully, without intimidation, fraud, violence, or other unlawful methods.

The bill charges that the petitioners have deprived respondents of the privileges of free speech and peaceable assembly secured to them, as citizens of the United

States, by the Fourteenth Amendment. It prays an injunction against continuance of petitioners' conduct.

After trial upon the merits the District Court entered a decree in favor of respondents. The findings are that the petitioners, as officials, have adopted and enforced a deliberate policy of forbidding the respondents and their associates from communicating their views respecting the National Labor Relations Act to the citizens of Jersey City by holding meetings or assemblies in the open air and at public places; that there is no competent proof that the proposed speakers have ever spoken at an assembly where a breach of the peace occurred or at which any utterances were made which violated the canons of proper discussion or gave occasion for disorder consequent upon what was said; that there is no competent proof that the parks of Jersey City are dedicated to any general purpose other than the recreation of the public and that there is competent proof that the municipal authorities have granted permits to various persons other than the respondents to speak at meetings in the streets of the city.

The court concluded that the petitioners' official policy and acts were in violation of the Fourteenth Amendment. The Circuit Court of Appeals affirmed.

[I]t is clear that the right peaceably to assemble and to discuss these topics, and to communicate respecting them, whether orally or in writing, is a privilege inherent in citizenship of the United States which the Amendment protects. In the *Slaughter-House Cases* it was said, [83 U.S. (]16 Wall.[) 36,] 79 [(1872)]: "The right to peaceably assemble and petition for redress of grievances, the privilege of the writ of habeas corpus, are rights of the citizen guaranteed by the Federal Constitution." … Citizenship of the United States would be little better than a name if it did not carry with it the right to discuss national legislation and the benefits, advantages, and opportunities to accrue to citizens therefrom. All of the respondents' proscribed activities had this single end and aim.

What has been said demonstrates that, in the light of the facts found, privileges and immunities of the individual respondents as citizens of the United States, were infringed by the petitioners, by virtue of their official positions, under color of ordinances of Jersey City, unless, as petitioners contend, the city's ownership of streets and parks is as absolute as one's ownership of his home, with consequent power altogether to exclude citizens from the use thereof, or unless, though the city holds the streets in trust for public use, the absolute denial of their use to the respondents is a valid exercise of the police power.

The findings of fact negative the latter assumption. In support of the former the petitioners rely upon *Davis v. Massachusetts*, 167 U.S. 43 [(1897)]. The ordinance there in question apparently had a different purpose from that of the one here challenged, for it was not directed solely at the exercise of the right of speech and assembly, but was addressed as well to other activities, not in the nature of civil rights, which doubtless might be regulated or prohibited as respects their enjoyment in parks. In the instant case the ordinance deals only with the exercise of the right of assembly for the purpose of communicating views entertained by speakers, and is not a general measure to promote the public convenience in the use of the streets or parks.

We have no occasion to determine whether, on the facts disclosed, the *Davis* Case was rightly decided, but we cannot agree that it rules the instant case. Wherever the title of streets and parks may rest, they have immemorially been held in trust for the use of the public and, time out of mind, have been used for purposes of assembly, communicating thoughts between citizens, and discussing public questions. Such use of the streets and public places has, from ancient times, been a part of the privileges, immunities, rights, and liberties of citizens. The privilege of a citizen of the United States to use the streets and parks for communication of views on national questions may be regulated in the interest of all; it is not absolute, but relative, and must be exercised in subordination to the general comfort and convenience, and in consonance with peace and good order; but it must not, in the guise of regulation, be abridged or denied.

We think the court below was right in holding the ordinance void upon its face. It does not make comfort or convenience in the use of streets or parks the standard of official action. It enables the Director of Safety to refuse a permit on his mere opinion that such refusal will prevent "riots, disturbances or disorderly assemblage." It can thus, as the record discloses, be made the instrument of arbitrary suppression of free expression of views on national affairs for the prohibition of all speaking will undoubtedly "prevent" such eventualities. But uncontrolled official suppression of the privilege cannot be made a substitute for the duty to maintain order in connection with the exercise of the right.

MR. JUSTICE STONE. [Opinion omitted.]

MR. CHIEF JUSTICE HUGHES, concurring. [Opinion omitted.]

MR. JUSTICE McREYNOLDS. [Opinion omitted.]

MR. JUSTICE BUTLER.

I am of opinion that the challenged ordinance is not void on its face; that in principle it does not differ from the Boston ordinance, as applied and upheld by this Court, speaking through Mr. Justice White, in *Davis v. Massachusetts*, 167 U.S. 43 [(1897)], affirming the Supreme Judicial Court of Massachusetts, speaking through Mr. Justice Holmes, in *Commonwealth v. Davis*, 39 N.E. 113 [(Mass. 1895)], and that the decree of the Circuit Court of Appeals should be reversed.

Exercise 36:

1. What was it about the location at which the CIO wished to speak and distribute printed literature that prompted the Supreme Court to conclude that CIO's activities were protected?

2. How broad was the Supreme Court's holding in *Hague*? For instance, to what property did it apply? Also, what limits, if any, may the government impose on speaking in public parks?

3. Did the Supreme Court overrule *Davis v. Massachusetts*?

4. Assuming that *Hague* is inconsistent with *Davis*, which of the two respective approaches is better?

2. Types of Public Fora

The major modern case where the Supreme Court described the contours of public forum analysis is *Perry v. Perry*, 460 U.S. 37 (1983), reprinted below.

Perry Education Association v.
Perry Local Educators' Association
460 U.S. 37 (1983)

Justice White delivered the opinion of the Court.

Perry Education Association is the duly elected exclusive bargaining representative for the teachers of the Metropolitan School District of Perry Township, Ind. A collective-bargaining agreement with the Board of Education provided that Perry Education Association, but no other union, would have access to the interschool mail system and teacher mailboxes in the Perry Township schools. The issue in this case is whether the denial of similar access to the Perry Local Educators' Association, a rival teacher group, violates the First and Fourteenth Amendments.

I

The Metropolitan School District of Perry Township, Ind., operates a public school system of 13 separate schools. Each school building contains a set of mailboxes for the teachers. Interschool delivery by school employees permits messages to be delivered rapidly to teachers in the district. The primary function of this internal mail system is to transmit official messages among the teachers and between the teachers and the school administration. In addition, teachers use the system to send personal messages and individual school building principals have allowed delivery of messages from various private organizations.[2]

Prior to 1977, both the Perry Education Association (PEA) and the Perry Local Educators' Association (PLEA) represented teachers in the school district and apparently had equal access to the interschool mail system. In 1977, PLEA challenged PEA's status as *de facto* bargaining representative for the Perry Township teachers by filing an election petition with the Indiana Education Employment Relations Board (Board). PEA won the election and was certified as the exclusive representative, as provided by Indiana law.

The Board permits a school district to provide access to communication facilities to the union selected for the discharge of the exclusive representative duties of representing the bargaining unit and its individual members without having to provide equal access to rival unions. Following the election, PEA and the school district negotiated a labor contract in which the school board gave PEA "access to teachers' mailboxes in which to insert material" and the right to use the interschool mail delivery system to the extent that the school district incurred no extra expense by such use.

---

2. Local parochial schools, church groups, YMCAs, and Cub Scout units have used the system. The record does not indicate whether any requests for use have been denied, nor does it reveal whether permission must separately be sought for every message that a group wishes delivered to the teachers.

The labor agreement noted that these access rights were being accorded to PEA "acting as the representative of the teachers" and went on to stipulate that these access rights shall not be granted to any other "school employee organization" — a term of art defined by Indiana law to mean "any organization which has school employees as members and one of whose primary purposes is representing school employees in dealing with their employer."

The exclusive-access policy applies only to use of the mailboxes and school mail system. PLEA is not prevented from using other school facilities to communicate with teachers. PLEA may post notices on school bulletin boards; may hold meetings on school property after school hours; and may, with approval of the building principals, make announcements on the public address system. Of course, PLEA also may communicate with teachers by word of mouth, telephone, or the United States mail. Moreover, under Indiana law, the preferential access of the bargaining agent may continue only while its status as exclusive representative is insulated from challenge. While a representation contest is in progress, unions must be afforded equal access to such communication facilities.

PLEA and two of its members filed this action against PEA and individual members of the Perry Township School Board. Plaintiffs contended that PEA's preferential access to the internal mail system violates the First Amendment and the Equal Protection Clause of the Fourteenth Amendment. Upon cross-motions for summary judgment, the district court entered judgment for the defendants. The Court of Appeals for the Seventh Circuit reversed.

The PEA now seeks review of this judgment by way of appeal.

III

The primary question presented is whether the First Amendment, applicable to the states by virtue of the Fourteenth Amendment, is violated when a union that has been elected by public school teachers as their exclusive bargaining representative is granted access to certain means of communication, while such access is denied to a rival union. There is no question that constitutional interests are implicated by denying PLEA use of the interschool mail system. "It can hardly be argued that either students or teachers shed their constitutional rights to freedom of speech or expression at the schoolhouse gate." *Tinker v. Des Moines School District*, 393 U.S. 503, 506 (1969). The First Amendment's guarantee of free speech applies to teacher's mailboxes as surely as it does elsewhere within the school, *Tinker v. Des Moines School District*, and on sidewalks outside, *Police Department of Chicago v. Mosely*, 408 U.S. 92 (1972). But this is not to say that the First Amendment requires equivalent access to all parts of a school building in which some form of communicative activity occurs. The existence of a right of access to public property and the standard by which limitations upon such a right must be evaluated differ depending on the character of the property at issue.

A

In places which by long tradition or by government fiat have been devoted to assembly and debate, the rights of the state to limit expressive activity are sharply circumscribed. At one end of the spectrum are streets and parks which "have immemorially been held in trust for the use of the public, and, time out of mind, have been used for purposes of assembly, communicating thoughts between citizens, and discussing public questions." *Hague v. CIO*, 307 U.S. 496, 515 (1939). In these quintessential public forums, the government may not prohibit all communicative activity. For the state to enforce a content-based exclusion it must show that its regulation is necessary to serve a compelling state interest and that it is narrowly drawn to achieve that end. The state may also enforce regulations of the time, place, and manner of expression which are content-neutral, are narrowly tailored to serve a significant government interest, and leave open ample alternative channels of communication. *Cantwell v. Connecticut*, 310 U.S. 296 (1940); *Schneider v. State of New Jersey*, 308 U.S. 147 (1939).

A second category consists of public property which the state has opened for use by the public as a place for expressive activity. The Constitution forbids a state to enforce certain exclusions from a forum generally open to the public even if it was not required to create the forum in the first place. *Widmar v. Vincent*, 454 U.S. 263 (1981) (university meeting facilities).[7] Although a state is not required to indefinitely retain the open character of the facility, as long as it does so it is bound by the same standards as apply in a traditional public forum. Reasonable time, place and manner regulations are permissible, and a content-based prohibition must be narrowly drawn to effectuate a compelling state interest.

Public property which is not by tradition or designation a forum for public communication is governed by different standards. We have recognized that the "First Amendment does not guarantee access to property simply because it is owned or controlled by the government." In addition to time, place, and manner regulations, the state may reserve the forum for its intended purposes, communicative or otherwise, as long as the regulation on speech is reasonable and not an effort to suppress expression merely because public officials oppose the speaker's view. As we have stated on several occasions, "[the] State, no less than a private owner of property, has power to preserve the property under its control for the use to which it is lawfully dedicated."

The school mail facilities at issue here fall within this third category. The Court of Appeals recognized that Perry School District's interschool mail system is not a traditional public forum: "We do not hold that a school's internal mail system is a public forum in the sense that a school board may not close it to all but official business if it chooses." Nor do the parties dispute that, as the District Court observed, the "normal and intended function [of the school mail facilities] is to facilitate internal communication of school related matters to teachers." The internal mail system, at least by policy, is not held open to the general public. It is instead PLEA's position that the school mail facilities have become a "limited public forum" from which it

---

7. A public forum may be created for a limited purpose such as use by certain groups, *e.g.*, *Widmar v. Vincent*, 454 U.S. 263 (1981) (student groups), or for the discussion of certain subjects.

may not be excluded because of the periodic use of the system by private non-school connected groups, and PLEA's own unrestricted access to the system prior to PEA's certification as exclusive representative.

Neither of these arguments is persuasive. The use of the internal school mail by groups not affiliated with the schools is no doubt a relevant consideration. If by policy or by practice the Perry School District has opened its mail system for indiscriminate use by the general public, then PLEA could justifiably argue a public forum has been created. This, however, is not the case. As the case comes before us, there is no indication in the record that the school mailboxes and interschool delivery system are open for use by the general public. Permission to use the system to communicate with teachers must be secured from the individual building principal. There is no court finding or evidence in the record which demonstrates that this permission has been granted as a matter of course to all who seek to distribute material. We can only conclude that the schools do allow some outside organizations such as the YMCA, Cub Scouts, and other civic and church organizations to use the facilities. This type of selective access does not transform government property into a public forum.

Moreover, even if we assume that by granting access to the Cub Scouts, YMCAs, and parochial schools, the school district has created a "limited" public forum, the constitutional right of access would in any event extend only to other entities of similar character. While the school mail facilities thus might be a forum generally open for use by the Girl Scouts, the local boys' club and other organizations that engage in activities of interest and educational relevance to students, they would not as a consequence be open to an organization such as PLEA, which is concerned with the terms and conditions of teacher employment.

Because the school mail system is not a public forum, the School District had no "constitutional obligation per se to let any organization use the school mail boxes." In the Court of Appeals' view, however, the access policy adopted by the Perry schools favors a particular viewpoint, that of the PEA, on labor relations, and consequently must be strictly scrutinized regardless of whether a public forum is involved. There is, however, no indication that the school board intended to discourage one viewpoint and advance another. We believe it is more accurate to characterize the access policy as based on the *status* of the respective unions rather than their views. Implicit in the concept of the nonpublic forum is the right to make distinctions in access on the basis of subject matter and speaker identity. These distinctions may be impermissible in a public forum but are inherent and inescapable in the process of limiting a nonpublic forum to activities compatible with the intended purpose of the property. The touchstone for evaluating these distinctions is whether they are reasonable in light of the purpose which the forum at issue serves.

B

The differential access provided PEA and PLEA is reasonable because it is wholly consistent with the district's legitimate interest in "preserv[ing] the property ... for the use to which it is lawfully dedicated." Use of school mail facilities enables PEA to perform effectively its obligations as exclusive representative of *all* Perry Township teachers. Conversely, PLEA does not have any official responsibility in connection with the school district and need not be entitled to the same rights of access to school mailboxes. We observe that providing exclusive access to recognized bargaining representatives is a permissible labor practice in the public sector. We have previously noted that the "designation of a union as exclusive representative carries with it great responsibilities. Moreover, exclusion of the rival union may reasonably be considered a means of insuring labor-peace within the schools.

The Court of Appeals accorded little or no weight to PEA's special responsibilities. In its view these responsibilities, while justifying PEA's access, did not justify denying equal access to PLEA. The Court of Appeals would have been correct if a public forum were involved here. But the internal mail system is not a public forum. As we have already stressed, when government property is not dedicated to open communication the government may — without further justification — restrict use to those who participate in the forum's official business.

Finally, the reasonableness of the limitations on PLEA's access to the school mail system is also supported by the substantial alternative channels that remain open for union-teacher communication to take place. These means range from bulletin boards to meeting facilities to the United States mail. During election periods, PLEA is assured of equal access to all modes of communication. There is no showing here that PLEA's ability to communicate with teachers is seriously impinged by the restricted access to the internal mail system....

The judgment of the Court of Appeals is

Reversed.

JUSTICE BRENNAN, with whom JUSTICE MARSHALL, JUSTICE POWELL, and JUSTICE STEVENS join, dissenting.

In this case, the intent to discriminate can be inferred from the effect of the policy, which is to deny an effective channel of communication to the respondents, and from other facts in the case. In addition, the petitioner's status has nothing to do with whether viewpoint discrimination in fact has occurred. If anything, the petitioner's status is relevant to the question of whether the exclusive access policy can be justified, not to whether the board has discriminated among viewpoints.

Addressing the question of viewpoint discrimination directly it is clear that the exclusive access policy discriminates on the basis of viewpoint. The Court of Appeals found that "the access policy adopted by the Perry schools, in form a speaker restriction, favors a particular viewpoint on labor relations in the Perry schools : the teachers inevitably will receive from [the petitioner] self-laudatory descriptions of its activities on their behalf and will be denied the critical perspective offered by [the respondents]." This assessment of the effect of the policy is eminently reasonable.

On a practical level, the only reason for the petitioner to seek an exclusive access policy is to deny its rivals access to an effective channel of communication. No other group is explicitly denied access to the mail system. In fact, as the Court points out, many other groups have been granted access to the system. Apparently, access is denied to the respondents because of the likelihood of their expressing points of view different from the petitioner's on a range of subjects. The very argument the petitioner advances in support of the policy, the need to preserve labor peace, also indicates that the access policy is not viewpoint-neutral.

In short, the exclusive access policy discriminates against the respondents based on their viewpoint. This sort of discrimination amounts to censorship and infringes the First Amendment rights of the respondents.

Exercise 37:

1. How did the school district's policy "infringe" on PLEA's freedom of speech?

2. What are the three types of fora described by the Supreme Court in *Perry*?

3. How does one distinguish into which forum a particular piece of government property falls? What rule or factors did the Court provide?

4. What legal rules govern each type of forum?

5. Here, in *Perry*, the school district permitted a number of groups to utilize the mail system. Why did the Court determine that this was a nonpublic forum, instead of a limited public forum?

6. Upon what basis did the Court hold that the school district's exclusion of PLEA was not viewpoint based?

7. Thinking back to the purposes of free speech protection, is *Perry* consonant with those purposes? Is *Perry* a reasonable accommodation to the practical reality of government needing to function?

––––––––––

Though *Perry* remains explication of the types of fora, the Court recently introduced some changes (and uncertainty) in *Christian Legal Society v. Martinez*, 561 U.S. 661 (2010). There, the Hastings College of Law instituted an antidiscrimination policy for its student groups called an "all-comers" policy. This policy required all student groups to accept any students as members and leaders. The Christian Legal Society, which required its group leaders to agree to a statement of faith, sued Hastings for violation of its freedom of speech.

The Supreme Court restated its public forum doctrine in the course of deciding CLS's claim. The Court stated that there were three types of fora: "traditional public forums"; "designated public forums"; and "limited public forums." *Id.* at 2984 n.11. *See also Pleasant Grove City v. Summum*, 555 U.S. 460, 469–70 (2009) (providing a similar listing). This listing is slightly different from *Perry*'s in two main ways: first, in *Perry*, the limited public forum was considered a subtype of designated public forum, while in *CLS* it is an entirely separate forum; and, second, in *Perry*, the third type of forum was a nonpublic forum, while in CLS it is the limited public forum. *See also* Lyrissa Lidsky, *Public Forum 2.0*, 91 B.U. L. Rev. 1975, 1976–93 (2011) (describing the changes in the doctrine). These changes were recently confirmed by the

Court in *Walker v. Texas Div., Sons of Confederate Veterans, Inc.*, 576 U.S. 200 (2015), reprinted after the following notes.

Below, we will discuss in more detail the rules governing each type of forum.

3. Traditional Public Forum

The Supreme Court famously stated that a traditional public forum is government property that has "immemorially been held in trust for the use of the public and, time out of mind, have been used for purposes of assembly, communicating thoughts between citizens, and discussing public questions." *Hague v. Committee for Indus. Org.*, 307 U.S. 496, 515 (1939). The paradigm examples of traditional public fora are streets, sidewalks, and parks. "[W]e have repeatedly referred to public streets as the archetype of a traditional public forum," noting that "'[t]ime out of mind' public streets and sidewalks have been used for public assembly and debate." *Frisby v. Schultz*, 487 U.S. 474, 480 (1988). The scope of this type of forum is not likely to expand beyond these traditional locations. *International Soc'y for Krishna Consciousness, Inc. v. Lee*, 505 U.S. 672, 680–81 (1992).

Government regulation of speech in a traditional public forum is subject to the same rules you learned earlier. Content-based regulations are subject to strict scrutiny, and content-neutral regulations are subject to intermediate scrutiny. Content-neutral regulations also are known, in public forum doctrine, as time, place, and manner restrictions. Such regulations do not target a speaker's subject matter or viewpoint; instead, time, place, and manner regulations focus on the nonspeech characteristics of speech such as: What time did it occur?; Where did it occur?; and How loud was the speech?

4. Designated Public Forum

The government may also create—designate—a public forum out of its property that was not otherwise open to speech. "[A] public forum may be created by government designation of a place or channel of communication for use by the public at large for assembly and speech, for use by certain speakers, or for the discussion of certain subjects." *Cornelius v. N.A.A.C.P. Legal Defense and Educ. Fund, Inc.*, 473 U.S. 788, 802 (1985). The Free Speech Clause does not require the government to designate public fora, and the government may close designated public fora. *Id.* However, when there is a designated public forum, the same rules that apply to traditional public fora apply here as well. Thus, the key difference between a traditional and a designated public forum is that the government need not open, or continue, a designated public forum.

5. Limited Forum

The limited public forum, like the designated public forum, is created by the government. However, unlike the designated public forum, a limited public forum is "limited to use by certain groups or dedicated solely to the discussion of certain sub-jects." *Pleasant Grove City*, 555 U.S. at 470. Unlike the two prior fora, the government is entitled to restrict speech within the limited public forum to maintain the forum's purpose, so long as the restrictions are reasonable in light of the forum and viewpoint neutral. *Rosenberger v. Rector & Visitors of Univ. of Va.*, 515 U.S. 819, 829 (1995). This means that the government can exclude subjects of speech and categories of speakers (again, subject to the requirements of reasonableness and viewpoint neu-trality) from the forum.

There are two distinct facets to limited public forum doctrine: (1) the *scope* of the forum, and (2) restrictions *internal* to the forum. *See, e.g., American Civil Liberties Union v. Mote*, 423 F.3d 438, 444 (4th Cir. 2005) (explaining this distinction). You should treat this as a two-step analysis. First, you should determine whether the limited public forum's scope is reasonable and viewpoint neutral. Second, if a speaker falls *within* a limited public forum's scope, then you should evaluate the speaker's exclusion using strict scrutiny.

The first facet looks at the *scope* of a limited public forum, or *externally*. This facet evaluates whether the scope of the forum is reasonable and viewpoint neutral. For example, the local public school could decide to open its classrooms, after school hours, to school-related activities (a subject of speech). This limited public forum is limited in time (after hours), location (classrooms), and subject matter (school-related activities). For instance, students could hold their school chess club in a room. But the school could exclude a local political party from holding its meeting in a room. Or, a local public school could decide to open its classrooms, after school hours, to members of the local community (a category of speakers). This would permit local political parties to hold meetings in the rooms. But the school could ex-clude someone from outside the community.

However, our hypothetical school cannot exclude speech on the basis of viewpoint. For example, if the school opened its classrooms, after school hours, to school-related activities, and excluded a student Bible club from the forum, then that viewpoint-based exclusion would violate the freedom of speech. *See Good News Club v. Milford Central Sch. Dist.*, 533 U.S. 98 (2001) (presenting this situation). Also, our hypothetical school cannot unreasonably exclude speech. For instance, a school's exclusion of the subject of math would be unreasonable in light of the forum's purpose (even though this exclusion was not viewpoint based).

The second facet of limited public forum doctrine looks at regulations *internally*, from the perspective of the forum's scope. This facet evaluates exclusion of a speaker who is within an otherwise included category of speech or speakers. This type of ex-clusion is subject to strict scrutiny. Stated differently, within the bounds of the limited forum created by the government, speech restrictions are subject to strict scrutiny. For example, assume our hypothetical school opened its classrooms, after school hours, to school children. Assume also that the school refused to allow the student fencing club to meet because fencing encouraged violence. This exclusion would be subject to strict scrutiny because the students were within the parameters of the school's limited public forum. The school would have to argue that its exclusion was narrowly tailored to serve a compelling state interest.

6. Nonpublic Forum

The nonpublic forum is most other government property; it is the default category for government property. *Compare* Aaron H. Caplan, *Invasion of the Public Forum Doctrine*, 46 WILLAMETTE L. REV. 647, 655–66 (2010) (criticizing this claim, though acknowledging that it is widely shared by courts and scholars). Government speech restrictions for nonpublic fora must be reasonable in light of a forum's purpose and be viewpoint neutral. For the vast array of the government's use of its own property, this is the applicable rule. For instance, the government could prohibit picketing in a post office lobby because that restriction would be reasonable — it would preserve the Post Office's use of the lobby for patrons — and viewpoint neutral — picketing on any subject or from any viewpoint is prohibited. *See also United States v. Kokinda*, 497 U.S. 720 (1990) (ruling that a Post Office prohibition on solicitation on its premises was a constitutional regulation of a nonpublic forum); *Brown v. Glines*, 444 U.S. 348 (1980) (upholding the constitutionality of Air Force regulations that required base commander approval prior to circulating petitions on base).

7. Government Property That Is Not a Forum

The government's property is not a forum of any type when the government uses that property to communicate its own message. For these uses of government property, the Free Speech Clause simply does not apply, so even the minimal limits we saw in the nonpublic forum context (reasonable and viewpoint neutral) have no application. This is a manifestation of the Government Speech Doctrine, which you saw in Part [G][5], above, and is best exemplified by *Pleasant Grove City, Utah v. Summum*, 555 U.S. 460 (2009), and the case that follows, *Walker v. Tex. Div., Sons of Confederate Veterans, Inc. See also Arkansas Educ. Television Comm'n v. Forbes*, 523 U.S. 666 (1998) (suggesting that a public television station's broadcast day is not a forum of any type). In these cases, the government did not create a forum for private speech; instead, it used its property for its own speech. *See, e.g., Santa Fe Indep. Sch. Dist. v. Doe*, 530 U.S. 290 (2000) (concluding that the challenged school prayer was the school district's speech, not that of students).

A recent case to address public forum doctrine is reprinted below.

Walker v. Texas Division, Sons of Confederate Veterans, Inc.
576 U.S. 200 (2015)

JUSTICE BREYER delivered the opinion of the Court.

Texas offers automobile owners a choice between ordinary and specialty license plates. Those who want the State to issue a particular specialty plate may propose a plate design, comprising a slogan, a graphic, or (most commonly) both. If the Texas Department of Motor Vehicles Board approves the design, the State will make it available for display on vehicles registered in Texas [generally for an annual fee].

In this case, the Texas Division of the Sons of Confederate Veterans proposed a specialty license plate design featuring a Confederate battle flag. [The relevant statute says that the Board "may refuse to create a new specialty license plate" for a number of reasons, for example "if the design might be offensive to any member of the public ... or for any other reason established by rule."] The Board rejected the proposal [explaining that it had found "it necessary to deny th[e] plate design application, specifically the confederate flag portion of the design, because public comments ha[d] shown that many members of the general public find the design offensive, and because such comments are reasonable."] We must decide whether that rejection violated the Constitution's free speech guarantees. We conclude that it did not.

II

When government speaks, it is not barred by the Free Speech Clause from determining the content of what it says. That freedom in part reflects the fact that it is the democratic electoral process that first and foremost provides a check on government speech. Thus, government statements (and government actions and programs that take the form of speech) do not normally trigger the First Amendment rules designed to protect the marketplace of ideas. Instead, the Free Speech Clause helps produce informed opinions among members of the public, who are then able to influence the choices of a government that, through words and deeds, will reflect its electoral mandate.

Were the Free Speech Clause interpreted otherwise, government would not work. How could a state government effectively develop programs designed to encourage and provide vaccinations, if officials also had to voice the perspective of those who oppose this type of immunization? "[I]t is not easy to imagine how government could function if it lacked th[e] freedom" to select the messages it wishes to convey.

That is not to say that a government's ability to express itself is without restriction. Constitutional and statutory provisions outside of the Free Speech Clause may limit government speech. And the Free Speech Clause itself may constrain the government's speech if, for example, the government seeks to compel private persons to convey the government's speech. But, as a general matter, when the government speaks it is entitled to promote a program, to espouse a policy, or to take a position. In doing so, it represents its citizens and it carries out its duties on their behalf.

III

In our view, specialty license plates issued pursuant to Texas's statutory scheme convey government speech. We conclude here, as we did [in *Summum*], that our precedents regarding government speech (and not our precedents regarding forums for private speech) provide the appropriate framework through which to approach the case. [The majority then recounted the facts and government speech analysis from *Summum*, which is excerpted on Section [G][5], *supra*.]

B

Our analysis in *Summum* leads us to the conclusion that here, too, government speech is at issue. First, the history of license plates shows that, insofar as license plates have conveyed more than state names and vehicle identification numbers, they long have communicated messages from the States. Over the years, state plates have included the phrases "North to the Future" (Alaska), "Keep Florida Green" (Florida), "Hoosier Hospitality" (Indiana), "The Iodine Products State" (South Carolina), "Green Mountains" (Vermont), and "America's Dairyland" (Wisconsin). States have used license plate slogans to urge action, to promote tourism, and to tout local industries.

Second, Texas license plate designs "are often closely identified in the public mind with the [State]." Each Texas license plate is a government article serving the governmental purposes of vehicle registration and identification. The governmental nature of the plates is clear from their faces: The State places the name "TEXAS" in large letters at the top of every plate. Moreover, the State requires Texas vehicle owners to display license plates, and every Texas license plate is issued by the State.

Texas license plates are, essentially, government IDs. And issuers of ID "typically do not permit" the placement on their IDs of "message[s] with which they do not wish to be associated." Consequently, "persons who observe" designs on IDs "routinely — and reasonably — interpret them as conveying some message on the [issuer's] behalf."

Third, Texas maintains direct control over the messages conveyed on its specialty plates. Texas law provides that the State "has sole control over the design, typeface, color, and alphanumeric pattern for all license plates." § 504.005. The Board must approve every specialty plate design proposal before the design can appear on a Texas plate. Accordingly, like the city government in *Summum*, Texas "has 'effectively controlled' the messages [conveyed] by exercising 'final approval authority' over their selection."

This final approval authority allows Texas to choose how to present itself and its constituency. Thus, Texas offers plates celebrating the many educational institutions attended by its citizens. But it need not issue plates deriding schooling. Texas offers plates that pay tribute to the Texas citrus industry. But it need not issue plates praising Florida's oranges as far better. And Texas offers plates that say "Fight Terrorism." But it need not issue plates promoting al Qaeda.

C

According to SCV, the State does not engage in expressive activity [at least with respect to the designs (comprising slogans and graphics) that were initially proposed by private parties], but rather provides a forum for private speech by making license plates available to display the private parties' designs. We cannot agree.

We have previously used what we have called "forum analysis" to evaluate government restrictions on purely private speech that occurs on government property. But forum analysis is misplaced here. Because the State is speaking on its own behalf, the First Amendment strictures that attend the various types of government-established forums do not apply.

The parties agree that Texas's specialty license plates are not a "traditional public forum," such as a street or a park, "which ha[s] immemorially been held in trust for the use of the public and, time out of mind, ha[s] been used for purposes of assembly, communicating thoughts between citizens, and discussing public questions." "The Court has rejected the view that traditional public forum status extends beyond its historic confines." And state-issued specialty license plates lie far beyond those confines.

It is equally clear that Texas's specialty plates are neither a "'designated public forum,'" which exists where "government property that has not traditionally been regarded as a public forum is intentionally opened up for that purpose," nor a "limited public forum," which exists where a government has "reserv[ed a forum] for certain groups or for the discussion of certain topics." A government "does not create a public forum by inaction or by permitting limited discourse, but only by intentionally opening a nontraditional forum for public discourse." And in order "to ascertain whether [a government] intended to designate a place not traditionally open to assembly and debate as a public forum," this Court "has looked to the policy and practice of the government" and to "the nature of the property and its compatibility with expressive activity."

Texas's policies and the nature of its license plates indicate that the State did not intend its specialty license plates to serve as either a designated public forum or a limited public forum. First, the State exercises final authority over each specialty license plate design. This authority militates against a determination that Texas has created a public forum. Second, Texas takes ownership of each specialty plate design, making it particularly untenable that the State intended specialty plates to serve as a forum for public discourse. Finally, Texas license plates have traditionally been used for government speech, are primarily used as a form of government ID, and bear the State's name. These features of Texas license plates indicate that Texas explicitly associates itself with the speech on its plates.

For similar reasons, we conclude that Texas's specialty license plates are not a "nonpublic for[um]," which exists "[w]here the government is acting as a proprietor, managing its internal operations." With respect to specialty license plate designs, Texas is not simply managing government property, but instead is engaging in expressive conduct. As we have described, we reach this conclusion based on the historical context, observers' reasonable interpretation of the messages conveyed by Texas specialty plates, and the effective control that the State exerts over the design selection process. Texas's specialty license plate designs "are meant to convey and have the effect of conveying a government message." They "constitute government speech."

The fact that private parties take part in the design and propagation of a message does not extinguish the governmental nature of the message or transform the government's role into that of a mere forum-provider. In *Summum*, private entities "financed and donated monuments that the government accept[ed] and display[ed] to the public." Here, similarly, private parties propose designs that Texas may accept and display on its license plates. In this case, as in *Summum*, the "government entity may exercise [its] freedom to express its views" even "when it receives assistance from private sources for the purpose of delivering a government-controlled message."

Of course, Texas allows many more license plate designs than the city in *Summum* allowed monuments. Texas's desire to communicate numerous messages does not mean that the messages conveyed are not Texas's own.

Additionally, the fact that Texas vehicle owners pay annual fees in order to display specialty license plates does not imply that the plate designs are merely a forum for private speech. While some nonpublic forums provide governments the opportunity to profit from speech, the existence of government profit alone is insufficient to trigger forum analysis. Thus, if the city in *Summum* had established a rule that organizations wishing to donate monuments must also pay fees to assist in park maintenance, we do not believe that the result in that case would have been any different.

Finally, we note that this case does not resemble other cases in which we have identified a nonpublic forum. This case is not like *Perry Ed. Assn.,* where we found a school district's internal mail system to be a nonpublic forum for private speech. There, it was undisputed that a number of private organizations, including a teachers' union, had access to the mail system. It was therefore clear that private parties, and not only the government, used the system to communicate. Here, by contrast, each specialty license plate design is formally approved by and stamped with the imprimatur of Texas. Nor is this case like *Lehman*]v. *Shaker Heights*, 418 U.S. 298 (1974)], where we found the advertising space on city buses to be a nonpublic forum. There, the messages were located in a context (advertising space) that is traditionally available for private speech. And the advertising space, in contrast to license plates, bore no indicia that the speech was owned or conveyed by the government.

IV

Our determination that Texas's specialty license plate designs are government speech does not mean that the designs do not also implicate the free speech rights of private persons. But here, compelled private speech is not at issue. And just as Texas cannot require SCV to convey "the State's ideological message," SCV cannot force Texas to include a Confederate battle flag on its specialty license plates.

Justice Alito, with whom The Chief Justice, Justice Scalia, and Justice Kennedy join, dissenting.

Unfortunately, the Court's decision categorizes private speech as government speech and thus strips it of all First Amendment protection. The Court holds that all the privately created messages on the many specialty plates issued by the State of Texas convey a government message rather than the message of the motorist displaying the plate.

This capacious understanding of government speech takes a large and painful bite out of the First Amendment. Specialty plates may seem innocuous. They make motorists happy, and they put money in a State's coffers. But the precedent this case sets is dangerous. While all license plates unquestionably contain *some* government speech (*e.g.,* the name of the State and the numbers and/or letters identifying the vehicle), the State of Texas has converted the remaining space on its specialty plates into little mobile billboards on which motorists can display their own messages. And what Texas did here was to reject one of the messages that members of a private group wanted to post on some of these little billboards because the State thought that many of its citizens would find the message offensive. That is blatant viewpoint discrimination. [Justice Alito explained why specialty license plates are not government speech under *Summum*.]

III

What Texas has done by selling space on its license plates is to create what we have called a limited public forum. It has allowed state property (*i.e.,* motor vehicle license plates) to be used by private speakers according to rules that the State prescribes. Under the First Amendment, however, those rules cannot discriminate on the basis of viewpoint. But that is exactly what Texas did here. The Board rejected Texas SCV's design, "specifically the confederate flag portion of the design, because public comments have shown that many members of the general public find the design offensive, and because such comments are reasonable." These statements indisputably demonstrate that the Board denied Texas SCV's design because of its viewpoint.

The Confederate battle flag is a controversial symbol. To the Texas Sons of Confederate Veterans, it is said to evoke the memory of their ancestors and other soldiers who fought for the South in the Civil War. To others, it symbolizes slavery, segregation, and hatred. Whatever it means to motorists who display that symbol and to those who see it, the flag expresses a viewpoint. The Board rejected the plate design because it concluded that many Texans would find the flag symbol offensive. That was pure viewpoint discrimination.

If the Board's candid explanation of its reason for rejecting the SCV plate were not alone sufficient to establish this point, the Board's approval of the Buffalo Soldiers plate at the same meeting dispels any doubt. The proponents of both the SCV and Buffalo Soldiers plates saw them as honoring soldiers who served with bravery and honor in the past. To the opponents of both plates, the images on the plates evoked painful memories. The Board rejected one plate and approved the other.

The Board's decision cannot be saved by its suggestion that the plate, if allowed, "could distract or disturb some drivers to the point of being unreasonably dangerous." This rationale cannot withstand strict scrutiny. Other States allow specialty plates with the Confederate Battle Flag, and Texas has not pointed to evidence that these plates have led to incidents of road rage or accidents. Texas does not ban bumper stickers bearing the image of the Confederate battle flag. Nor does it ban any of the many other bumper stickers that convey political messages and other messages that are capable of exciting the ire of those who loathe the ideas they express.

Messages that are proposed by private parties and placed on Texas specialty plates are private speech, not government speech. Texas cannot forbid private speech based on its viewpoint. That is what it did here. Because the Court approves this violation of the First Amendment, I respectfully dissent.

Exercise 38:

1. Does the majority in *Walker* provide an exhaustive or non-exhaustive list of factors for determining whether speech is that of the government? What other factors might be relevant?

2. In Texas, vehicle owners can choose from more than 350 different specialty plates. If you sat by the side of a Texas highway and focused on the license plates of the vehicles that passed by, you would see a wide range of specialty plates. Would you attribute the messages on the specialty license plates to Texas (which authorized the plates), the owner of the vehicle (who selected the plate), or both? What is the majority's response? Do you agree with the majority? Should the way in which third parties interpret the speech affect the Court's government speech analysis?

3. Are monuments in public parks the same as specialty license plates? In what ways do they differ? Should these differences make a constitutional difference? Why or why not?

4. Are specialty license plates better viewed as government speech (as the majority contends) or as private speech in a limited public forum (as the dissent claims)?

5. Suppose the State of North Carolina erects electronic billboards along its highways and begins to post government messages on the billboards (*e.g.*, amber alert information or public safety messages like "Life goes by fast enough — there is no need to speed"). Over time, North Carolina decides that it could generate much needed revenue by allowing private entities and individuals to purchase the right to post their own messages on these billboards — provided that the state liked the proposed messages and did not find them too controversial. Would such a program be constitutional under *Walker*? Is it just like Texas's specialty license plate program, which might be viewed as authorizing miniature (and mobile) billboards?

6. Many states allow personalized plates, which frequently are called vanity plates. Under these personalization programs, a vehicle owner may request a particular alphanumeric pattern for use as a plate number (*e.g.*, "L8 AGN" or "BU2FUL"). The state frequently retains the power to deny the request. Suppose Michigan law prohibits any letter-number combination that carries a "connotation offensive to good taste and decency," including expressions of hate for political parties and most other things. James Davis, a graduate of the University of Michigan, requests a "H8 OHIO ST" vanity plate, which the state subsequently rejects. Mr. Davis sues, claiming that the denial of his requested vanity plate violates the First Amendment. In light of *Walker*, is he correct? What type of forum is at issue when dealing with vanity plates as opposed to specialty plates? What standard should the court apply to Michigan's regulation of vanity plates?

7. For the dissent, Texas engaged in viewpoint discrimination by rejecting the Sons of Confederate Veterans' proposed specialty plate. Why did Texas's action fail strict scrutiny?

8. Erosion of Distinctiveness of Public Forum Doctrine

Since the 1970s, public forum doctrine has lost much of its distinctiveness because the architectonic distinction between content-based and content-neutral regulations has colonized many aspects of free speech law. Whereas in 1939, when *Hague* was decided, the Supreme Court's ruling was relatively speech protective, today, the Court's general free speech doctrine is relatively speech protective.

As a result, public forum doctrine generally makes a difference in analysis and outcome in two situations. First, public forum doctrine may make a difference to analysis in the context of a challenge to the *scope* of the limited public forum. Normally, the government may not utilize content-based speech regulations, including both subject-matter and viewpoint regulations. However, when constructing the scope of a limited public forum, the government may make subject-matter distinctions. What this means pragmatically is that, if the government would otherwise lose a case because its speech regulation was content based and therefore subject to strict scrutiny, because the government's subject-matter discrimination occurred regarding the scope of a limited public forum, it would win the case (assuming that the scope was also viewpoint neutral and reasonable).

Second, public forum doctrine may change the result in the context of a nonpublic forum. There, the government can make otherwise-prohibited subject-matter based distinctions excluding speech from the forum. What this means pragmatically, is that, if the government would otherwise lose a case because its speech regulation was content based and therefore subject to strict scrutiny, since the government's subject-matter discrimination occurred within a nonpublic forum, it would win the case (assuming that the regulation was also viewpoint neutral and reasonable).

Outside of these situations, public forum doctrine will generally not change your analysis of a free speech issue.

9. The Relationship Between Public Forum Doctrine and Religious Speech

One of the continuing flash-points in the Supreme Court's public forum doctrine has been the place of religious speech in public fora. There are two key issues in this context: first, to what extent must the government treat religious speech the same as nonreligious speech in a public forum; and second, to what extent does the Establishment Clause require the government to exclude religious speech from a public forum? This subsection addresses the first issue, while **Chapter 3** considers the second issue.

In a series of cases, stretching back to the 1970s, *Healy v. James*, 408 U.S. 169 (1972) (ruling that a university could not exclude a student group, Students for Democratic Action, because of the group's viewpoint), and gaining steam in the 1980s, *Widmar v. Vincent*, 454 U.S. 263 (1981) (ruling that a university could not exclude a religious student group), the Supreme Court has ruled that the government must treat religious speech identically to nonreligious speech and that limitations on religious speech may violate the Free Speech Clause. This line of cases culminated in the following case:

Rosenberger v.
Rector and Visitors of the University of Virginia
515 U.S. 819 (1995)

JUSTICE KENNEDY delivered the opinion of the Court.

The University of Virginia, an instrumentality of the Commonwealth for which it is named and thus bound by the First and Fourteenth Amendments, authorizes the payment of outside contractors for the printing costs of a variety of student publications. It withheld any authorization for payments on behalf of petitioners for the sole reason that their student paper "primarily promotes or manifests a particular belie[f] in or about a deity or an ultimate reality." That the paper did promote or manifest views within the defined exclusion seems plain enough. The challenge is to the University's regulation and its denial of authorization, the case raising issues under the Speech and Establishment Clauses of the First Amendment.

I

Before a student group is eligible to submit bills from its outside contractors for payment by the fund described below, it must become a "Contracted Independent Organization" (CIO). CIO status is available to any group the majority of whose members are students, whose managing officers are fulltime students, and that complies with certain procedural requirements. A CIO must file its constitution with the University; must pledge not to discriminate in its membership; and must include in dealings with third parties and in all written materials a disclaimer, stating that the CIO is independent of the University and that the University is not responsible for the CIO.

All CIO's may exist and operate at the University, but some are also entitled to apply for funds from the Student Activities Fund (SAF). Established and governed by University Guidelines, the purpose of the SAF is to support a broad range of extracurricular student activities that "are related to the educational purpose of the University." The SAF receives its money from a mandatory fee of $14 per semester assessed to each full-time student.

The Guidelines recognize 11 categories of student groups that may seek payment to third-party contractors because they "are related to the educational purpose of the University of Virginia." One of these is "student news, information, opinion, entertainment, or academic communications media groups." The Guidelines also specify, however, that the costs of certain activities of CIO's that are otherwise eligible for funding will not be reimbursed by the SAF. The student activities that are excluded from SAF support [include] religious activities, [which are] ... defined as any activity that "primarily promotes or manifests a particular belie[f] in or about a deity or an ultimate reality."

If an organization seeks SAF support, it must submit its bills to the Student Council, which pays the organization's creditors upon determining that the expenses are appropriate. No direct payments are made to the student groups.

Petitioners' organization, Wide Awake Productions (WAP), qualified as a CIO. Formed by petitioner Ronald Rosenberger and other undergraduates in 1990, WAP was established "[t]o publish a magazine of philosophical and religious expression," "[t]o facilitate discussion which fosters an atmosphere of sensitivity to and tolerance of Christian viewpoints," and "[t]o provide a unifying focus for Christians of multicultural backgrounds." WAP publishes Wide Awake: A Christian Perspective at the University of Virginia. The paper's Christian viewpoint was evident from the first issue, in which its editors wrote that the journal "offers a Christian perspective on both personal and community issues, especially those relevant to college students at the University of Virginia." The editors committed the paper to a two-fold mission: "to challenge Christians to live, in word and deed, according to the faith they proclaim and to encourage students to consider what a personal relationship with Jesus Christ means."

WAP had acquired CIO status soon after it was organized. This is an important consideration in this case, for had it been a "religious organization," WAP would not have been accorded CIO status. As defined by the Guidelines, a "[r]eligious [o]rganization" is "an organization whose purpose is to practice a devotion to an acknowledged ultimate reality or deity."

A few months after being given CIO status, WAP requested the SAF to pay its printer $5,862 for the costs of printing its newspaper. The Appropriations Committee of the Student Council denied WAP's request on the ground that Wide Awake was a "religious activity" within the meaning of the Guidelines.... WAP appealed the denial to the full Student Council, contending that WAP met all the applicable Guidelines and that denial of SAF support on the basis of the magazine's religious perspective violated the Constitution. The appeal was denied without further comment, and WAP appealed to the next level, the Student Activities Committee. In a letter signed by the Dean of Students, the committee sustained the denial of funding. [WAP subsequently filed an action in the United States District Court for the Western District of Virginia, and the Fourth Circuit ultimately concluded that, although content-based, the University's discrimination "was justified by the 'compelling interest in maintaining strict separation of church and state.'"]

II

It is axiomatic that the government may not regulate speech based on its substantive content or the message it conveys. Other principles follow from this precept. In the realm of private speech or expression, government regulation may not favor one speaker over another. Discrimination against speech because of its message is presumed to be unconstitutional. When the government targets not subject matter, but particular views taken by speakers on a subject, the violation of the First Amendment is all the more blatant. Viewpoint discrimination is thus an egregious form of content discrimination. The government must abstain from regulating speech when the specific motivating ideology or the opinion or perspective of the speaker is the rationale for the restriction.

These principles provide the framework forbidding the State to exercise viewpoint discrimination, even when the limited public forum is one of its own creation.... The necessities of confining a forum to the limited and legitimate purposes for which it was created may justify the State in reserving it for certain groups or for the discussion of certain topics. Once it has opened a limited forum, however, the State must respect the lawful boundaries it has itself set. The State may not exclude speech where its distinction is not "reasonable in light of the purpose [served by the forum]," nor may it discriminate against speech on the basis of its viewpoint. Thus, in determining whether the State is acting to preserve the limits of the forum it has created so that the exclusion of a class of speech is legitimate, we have observed a distinction between, on the one hand, content discrimination, which may be permissible if it preserves the purposes of that limited forum, and, on the other hand, viewpoint discrimination, which is presumed impermissible when directed against speech otherwise within the forum's limitations.

The SAF is a forum more in a metaphysical than in a spatial or geographic sense, but the same principles are applicable. The most recent and most apposite case is our decision in *Lamb's Chapel* [*v. Center Moriches Union Free School Dist.*, 508 U.S. 384 (1993)]. There, a school district had opened school facilities for use after school hours by community groups for a wide variety of social, civic, and recreational purposes. The district, however, had enacted a formal policy against opening facilities to groups for religious purposes. Invoking its policy, the district rejected a request from a group desiring to show a film series addressing various child-rearing questions from a "Christian perspective." Our conclusion was unanimous: "[I]t discriminates on the basis of viewpoint to permit school property to be used for the presentation of all views about family issues and childrearing except those dealing with the subject matter from a religious standpoint."

The University insists that the Guidelines draw lines based on content, not viewpoint. As we have noted, discrimination against one set of views or ideas is but a subset or particular instance of the more general phenomenon of content discrimination. And, it must be acknowledged, the distinction is not a precise one. It is, in a sense, something of an understatement to speak of religious thought and discussion as just a viewpoint, as distinct from a comprehensive body of thought. The nature of our origins and destiny and their dependence upon the existence of a divine being have been subjects of philosophic inquiry throughout human history. We conclude, nonetheless, that here, as in *Lamb's Chapel*, viewpoint discrimination is the proper way to interpret the University's objections to Wide Awake. By the very terms of the SAF prohibition, the University does not exclude religion as a subject matter but selects for disfavored treatment those student journalistic efforts with religious editorial viewpoints. Religion may be a vast area of inquiry, but it also provides, as it did here, a specific premise, a perspective, a standpoint from which a variety of subjects may be discussed and considered. The prohibited perspective, not the general subject matter, resulted in the refusal to make third-party payments, for the subjects discussed were otherwise within the approved category of publications.

If the topic of debate is, for example, racism, then exclusion of several views on that problem is just as offensive to the First Amendment as exclusion of only one. It is as objectionable to exclude both a theistic and an atheistic perspective on the debate as it is to exclude one, the other, or yet another political, economic, or social viewpoint. The dissent's declaration that debate is not skewed so long as multiple voices are silenced is simply wrong; the debate is skewed in multiple ways.

[I]n *Rust v. Sullivan, supra,* we upheld the government's prohibition on abortion-related advice applicable to recipients of federal funds for family planning counseling. There, the government did not create a program to encourage private speech but instead used private speakers to transmit specific information pertaining to its own program. We recognized that when the government appropriates public funds to promote a particular policy of its own it is entitled to say what it wishes.

It does not follow, however, that viewpoint-based restrictions are proper when the University does not itself speak or subsidize transmittal of a message it favors but instead expends funds to encourage a diversity of views from private speakers. A holding that the University may not discriminate based on the viewpoint of private persons whose speech it facilitates does not restrict the University's own speech, which is controlled by different principles.

The distinction between the University's own favored message and the private speech of students is evident in the case before us. The University itself has taken steps to ensure the distinction in the agreement each CIO must sign. The University declares that the student groups eligible for SAF support are not the University's agents, are not subject to its control, and are not its responsibility. Having offered to pay the third-party contractors on behalf of private speakers who convey their own messages, the University may not silence the expression of selected viewpoints.

Vital First Amendment speech principles are at stake here. The first danger to liberty lies in granting the State the power to examine publications to determine whether or not they are based on some ultimate idea and, if so, for the State to classify them. The second, and corollary, danger is to speech from the chilling of individual thought and expression.... For the University, by regulation, to cast disapproval on particular viewpoints of its students risks the suppression of free speech and creative inquiry in one of the vital centers for the Nation's intellectual life, its college and university campuses.

The prohibition on funding on behalf of publications that "primarily promot[e] or manifes[t] a particular belie[f] in or about a deity or an ultimate reality," in its ordinary and commonsense meaning, has a vast potential reach. The term "promotes" as used here would comprehend any writing advocating a philosophic position that rests upon a belief in a deity or ultimate reality. And the term "manifests" would bring within the scope of the prohibition any writing that is explicable as resting upon a premise that presupposes the existence of a deity or ultimate reality. Were the prohibition applied with much vigor at all, it would bar funding of essays by hypothetical student contributors named Plato, Spinoza, and Descartes. And if the regulation covers, as the University says it does those student journalistic efforts that primarily manifest or promote a belief that there is no deity and no ultimate reality, then under-graduates named Karl Marx, Bertrand Russell, and Jean-Paul Sartre would likewise have some of their major essays excluded from student publications. If any manifestation of beliefs in first principles disqualifies the writing, as seems to be the case, it is indeed difficult to name renowned thinkers whose writings would be accepted, save perhaps for articles disclaiming all connection to their ultimate philosophy. Plato could contrive perhaps to submit an acceptable essay on making pasta or peanut butter cookies, provided he did not point out their (necessary) imperfections.

[After reviewing the University's claim that the Establishment Clause required the University to exclude WAP, the Supreme Court concluded that "[t]o obey the Establishment Clause, it was not necessary for the University to deny eligibility to student publications because of their viewpoint."]

JUSTICE O'CONNOR, concurring. [Opinion omitted.]

JUSTICE THOMAS, concurring. [Opinion omitted.]

JUSTICE SOUTER, with whom JUSTICE STEVENS, JUSTICE GINSBURG, and JUSTICE BREYER join, dissenting. [Opinion omitted.]

Exercise 39:

1. What is the forum identified by the Supreme Court that the University created? What are its contours? Who and what is included, and excluded, from it?

2. What *type* of forum did the University create? What facts suggested to the Court that it was this type of forum and not another?

3. Does public forum analysis make sense applied to the nonphysical "forum" created by the University?

4. Did this case concern speech within the scope of the University's forum, or was this a question about the forum's scope itself?

5. According to the Court, did this case concern subject-matter or viewpoint discrimination? What was Justice Kennedy's argument supporting his conclusion? Are you persuaded?

6. How would you distinguish this case from other cases where the Supreme Court has permitted the government to make content-based distinctions, such as *Rust v. Sullivan* and *NEA v. Finley*?

Chapter 2

The Free Exercise Clause

A. Introduction

Unlike the Supreme Court's complex free speech doctrine, its Free Exercise Clause case law has a relatively simple trajectory: (1) beginning in the 1940s, the Supreme Court moved toward significant protection for free exercise claims up through the early-1970s; and (2) the Supreme Court moved toward and ultimately adopted the relatively unprotective *Smith* Rule in *Employment Division v. Smith*, 494 U.S. 872 (1990). Since *Smith*, there has been significant federal and state *legislative* activity that more robustly protects religious liberty. There has been, however, little movement on the Supreme Court to limit *Smith* until recently. In 2019, four Justices (Justices Thomas, Alito, Gorsuch, and Kavanaugh) indicated a willingness to revisit *Smith*. *See Kennedy v. Bremerton School District*, 139 S. Ct. 634 (2019) (Alito, J., concurring in denial of certiorari). Accordingly, the Court already has begun receiving more and more petitions for certiorari asking the Court to reconsider *Smith*, and it may just be a matter of time before these justices find (what they take to be) an appropriate challenge to *Smith* and grant certiorari.

Exercise 1:

Apply the first four forms of argument to the Free Exercise Clause.

1. Looking at the Constitution's text, what information do you gather regarding "free exercise"? What is protected? From what is free exercise protected? How extensively is free exercise protected?

2. Looking at the Constitution's structure, what do you learn about "free exercise"? Do structural principles broaden or narrow the Constitution's protection for free exercise? In what way? How much?

3. Reviewing evidence of the Constitution's original meaning, what does it tell you about "free exercise"? What did you learn beyond the Clause's text and structure?

4. Do the materials following adoption of the Constitution offer any insight into free exercise?

In the Supreme Court's modern case law, the key case is *Smith*. There, the Supreme Court articulated the (in)famous *Smith* Rule: neutral, generally applicable laws, that incidentally burden religious exercise, are subject to rational basis review under the Free Exercise Clause.

As you read the materials below, some of the issues to consider include:

What is the Supreme Court's current definition of "religion"?

Is this definition of "religion" based on the original meaning, tradition, and/or precedent?

Should nontheistic belief systems receive the same free exercise protection as theistic religious belief systems?

What does "free exercise" include? Religious beliefs only? Religiously-motived actions too? If so, all, or just some religiously-motivated actions?

What does it mean for the government to "prohibit[ ]" religious exercise? Is a complete ban on a religious practice necessary, or will something less suffice?

Must a law that restricts or bans a religious practice do so *because* it is a religious practice to count as "prohibiting," or is the government's purpose irrelevant?

What is the distinction between religious beliefs and religiously-motivated action?

What role does this distinction play in current doctrine?

What is the origin for this distinction?

What purpose(s) does the distinction serve?

What is the *Smith* Rule?

Is the *Smith* Rule faithful to the Free Exercise Clause's original meaning? Tradition? The Supreme Court's pre-*Smith* precedent?

What purpos(es) does the *Smith* Rule serve?

What exceptions are there to the *Smith* Rule?

What further exception(s) to the *Smith* Rule should the Court articulate?

B. Original Meaning of the Free Exercise Clause

The United States has always been a relatively religious nation, and the Constitution reflects that fact in a number of ways including via its protection for the "free exercise" of "religion."[1] The Free Exercise Clause also reflects the initial, and subsequently expanding, religious diversity of the American people.

The major axis of contention regarding the original meaning of the Free Exercise Clause has been whether and, if so, under what conditions, does the Clause entitle one to an exemption from a law that burdens one's religious exercise?[2] This Part

---

1. U.S. CONST., amend. I.

2. A separate, though related, question is whether the Free Exercise Clause authorizes *judicially-crafted* religious exemptions from neutral laws. Scholars have debated this separate question as well, but it is beyond the scope of this brief Introduction, which is focused on the Clause's original meaning and not its institutional implementation.

focuses on the historical evidence that bears on that question.[3] The historical evidence and scholarly commentary on the Clause's original meaning is voluminous;[4] this Section is a brief introduction to the main evidence and arguments.

The United States was the inheritor of many different perspectives on religious liberty, and many of the colonies and, later, states, approached religious liberty differently.[5] With time, religious pluralism developed more readily in some colonies and states than others, so that, by the time of the Revolution, state approaches to religious exercise ranged on a spectrum.[6]

Prior to 1791, nearly all of the states in the United States constitutionally protected religious exercise, usually through their newly-adopted Constitutions.[7] New York's 1777 Constitution had a typical religious exercise clause: "... the free exercise and enjoyment of religious profession and worship, without discrimination or preference, shall forever hereafter be allowed, within this State, to all mankind: *Provided*, That the liberty of conscience, hereby granted, shall not be so construed as to excuse acts of licentiousness, or justify practices inconsistent with the peace or safety of this State."[8]

---

3. The two best pieces of historical scholarship on this issue, from the two respective major positions, are Michael W. McConnell, *The Origins and Historical Understanding of Free Exercise of Religion*, 103 Harv. L. Rev. 1409 (1990) (arguing for religious exemptions); *see also* Michael W. McConnell, *Free Exercise Revisionism and the* Smith *Decision*, 57 U. Chi. L. Rev. 1109 (1990) (making a briefer argument against *Smith*), and Gerard V. Bradley, *Beguiled: Free Exercise Exemptions and the Siren Song of Liberalism*, 20 Hofstra L. Rev. 245 (1991) (arguing against religious exemptions).

A shorter, but influential piece is Philip A. Hamburger, *A Constitutional Right of Religious Exemptions: An Historical Perspective*, 60 Geo. Wash. L. Rev. 915 (1992) (arguing against religious exemptions); *see also* William P. Marshall, *The Case Against the Constitutionally Compelled Free Exercise Exemption*, 40 Case W. Res. L. Rev. 357 (1990) (making a host of arguments against religious exemptions). For an earlier piece by a respected scholar, see Philip B. Kurland, *The Origins of the Religion Clauses of the Constitution*, 27 Wm. & Mary L. Rev. 839 (1986). The scholarly consensus, though not without a significant minority view, is that the exemption conception of the Free Exercise Clause is correct, though many of the scholars who hold this conception do so for reasons other than the Clause's original meaning. *See* Steven H. Aden & Lee J. Strang, *When a "Rule" Doesn't Rule: The Failure of the* Oregon Employment Division v. Smith *"Hybrid-Rights Exemption"*, 108 Penn. St. L. Rev. 573, 574–76, 581–87 (2003) (summarizing the post-*Smith* scholarship). This Introduction to the Clause's original meaning does not cover the changes to the meaning of "free exercise" and "establishment" that occurred up to the time of the ratification of the Fourteenth Amendment. For excellent accounts of this history, see Kurt T. Lash, *The Second Adoption of the Free Exercise Clause: Religious Exemptions Under the Fourteenth Amendment*, 88 Nw. U.L. Rev. 1106 (1994); Kurt T. Lash, *The Second Adoption of the Establishment Clause: The Rise of the Nonestablishment Principle*, 27 Ariz. St. L.J. 1085 (1995).

4. *Compare* Jeffrey Shulman, Essay, *The Siren Song of History: Originalism and the Religion Clauses*, 27 J.L. & Rel. 163 (2012) (concluding that originalism cannot deliver on its promise to provide historical determinacy on the original meaning of the Religion Clauses).

5. *See* McConnell, *supra* note 3, at 1421–30 (describing various approaches to religious liberty in the United States).

6. *Id.*

7. *Id.* at 1456.

8. N.Y. Const. of 1777, art. XXXVIII, *reprinted in* 7 Sources and Documents of United States Constitutions 178 (William F. Swindler ed., 1978).

Two key facets of New York's religious liberty protection are: (1) its specification and limitation of what is protected—only "religious profession and worship"—and; (2) its proviso. Most of the state law protections for religious liberty, like New York's, contained clauses that limited their scope by conditioning protection of religious beliefs and exercise "provided he doth not disturb the public peace," in the words of New Hampshire's 1784 Constitution.[9] The Northwest Ordinance, adopted in 1787, took a similar approach: "[n]o person demeaning himself in a peaceable and orderly manner shall ever be molested on account of his mode of worship or religious sentiments in the said territory."[10]

Professor Philip Hamburger has argued that these provisos "included more than just nonpeaceful behavior.... According to long tradition ... the phrase 'contra pacem' became associated with the notion of violation of the law."[11] Indeed, many of the state constitutional protections contained provisos that were very broad.[12] Maryland's, for instance, exempted from protection those who "shall infringe the laws of morality, or injure others in their natural, civil or religious rights."[13] This conditioning of religious liberty was also exemplified by contemporary statements by the Framers and Ratifiers.[14] This approach to religious liberty, which conditioned it, was challenged in some states, such as Virginia, and by some prominent Americans, such as Thomas Jefferson.[15]

Virginia engaged in a detailed and influential debate over religious exercise at the onset of the Revolution. During the debates over Virginia's 1776 Declaration of Rights, George Mason's initial draft of the religious liberty provision stated: "all men should enjoy the fullest toleration in the exercise of religion ... unless, under colour of religion, any man disturb the peace, the happiness, or safety of society."[16] This formulation fit many of the state provisions we discussed above, because it had a relatively broad condition on free exercise: "disturb the peace, happiness, or safety of society."

---

9. N.H. Const. of 1784, pt. I, art. V. The earliest protections for religious exercise contained similar provisos. For instance, the 1641 Rhode Island legislature limited religious liberty in this manner: "provided that it not be directly repugnant to the government or laws established." McConnell, *supra* note 3, at 1426.

10. Northwest Ordinance, art. I (1787).

11. Hamburger, *supra* note 3, at 918–19; *but see* McConnell, *supra* note 3, at 1447–48 (arguing that the provisos showed that government could withhold religious exemptions only in narrow circumstances).

12. *See* Hamburger, *supra* note 3, at 918–26 (arguing that the caveats in state religious liberty clauses were broadly understood to *not* protect illegal actions).

13. Md. Decl. of Rights of 1776, art. 33; *see also* S.C. Const. of 1790, art. VIII, §1 (excluding "licentiousness").

14. *See* Oliver Ellsworth, *A Landholder*, Con. Courant, Dec. 17, 1787, *in* 14 Documentary History of the Ratification of the Constitution 449 (John P. Kaminski & Gaspare J. Saladino eds., 1983) ("If he be a good and peaceable citizen, he is liable to no penalties or incapacities on account of his religious sentiments.").

15. *See* Hamburger, *supra* note 3, at 923–24 (describing Georgia, Kentucky, Pennsylvania, and Virginia, as holding this view).

16. George Mason, *Committee Draft of the Virginia Declaration of Rights, reprinted in* 1 Papers of George Mason 1725–1792, at 284–85 (Robert A. Rutland ed., 1970).

It also fit John Locke's conception of religious exercise, discussed below, as a form of toleration of religious activity by the civil authorities. James Madison then introduced an amended version of Virginia's religious liberty provision: "all men are equally entitled to the full and free exercise of [religion] ... unless under color of religion the preservation of equal liberty, and the existence of the State be manifestly endangered."[17] Madison's proposal expanded religious liberty in two ways: (1) it moved away from "toleration" of religion; and (2) it narrowed the conditions placed on religious exercise. Ultimately, the Virginia legislature adopted the following provision for religious exercise: "all men are equally entitled to the free exercise of religion, according to the dictates of conscience."[18] Notably, this final version did not condition religious exercise.

Religious dissenters of the time, anxious to rebut any claims or perceptions that their religious doctrines courted anarchy, often argued *against* religious exemptions.[19] For instance, Baptist leader John Leland stated that "[t]o indulge [Baptist ministers] with an exemption from taxes and bearing arms is a tempting emolument. The law should be silent about them; protect them as citizens, not as sacred officers, for the civil law knows no sacred religious officers."[20] Likewise, the Presbyterian Synod of New York and Philadelphia adopted the following resolution, in 1788: "Infidelity or difference in religion, doth not make void the magistrate's just and legal authority, nor free people from their due obedience to him."[21]

State law protections for (a subset of) religiously-motivated actions and for religious beliefs fit the thought of the influential English political theorist, John Locke.[22] Locke's core claim, in his *A Letter Concerning Toleration*, was that religious authorities governed the truth about "the world to come," while civil authorities were "confined to the care of the things of this world."[23] Locke distinguished between civil laws that proscribed actions *because of* the actions' religious motivations, and civil laws that proscribed actions for non-religious reasons.[24] He argued that the state did not possess the power to enact the first class of laws, though it did have the authority to enact the latter category because "the law is not made about a religion, but a political matter."[25] Therefore, the government could legislate for the public good of the community, even if such

---

17. 1 THE PAPERS OF JAMES MADISON 174–75 (William T. Hutchinson & William M. E. Rachal, eds., Chicago: University of Chicago Press, 1962).

18. THE VIRGINIA DECLARATION OF RIGHTS § 16 (1776).

19. *See* Hamburger, *supra* note 3, at 942 (making this argument).

20. John Leland, *The Rights of Conscience Inalienable, and Therefore, Religious Opinions Not Cognizable by Law* (1791), *in* THE WRITINGS OF THE LATE ELDER JOHN LELAND 188 (N.Y. 1845).

21. THE CONSTITUTION OF THE PRESBYTERIAN CHURCH IN THE UNITED STATES OF AMERICA 26 (1792).

22. Both Professors McConnell and Bradley make use of Locke's claims to support their respective positions.

23. John Locke, *A Letter Concerning Toleration, in* 6 THE WORKS OF JOHN LOCKE 12–13, 19 (London 1823, reprint ed., 1963).

24. John Locke, *A Letter Concerning Toleration, in* JOHN LOCKE: THE SECOND TREATISE OF GOVERNMENT AND A LETTER CONCERNING TOLERATION 147–48 (J.W. Gough ed., 1976).

25. *Id.*

laws had the incidental effect of limiting religiously-motivated action.[26] Importantly, according to Locke, when religious and civil authority came into conflict, "[t]he private judgment of any person concerning a law enacted in political matters, for the public good, does not take away the obligation of the law, nor deserve a dispensation."[27]

James Madison was influential, not only in the Framing and Ratification of the Constitution, but was also a major contributor to Americans' evolving thought on religious liberty, particularly through his participation in Virginia's debates on religion, discussed above. Madison's most famous contribution was his 1785 *Memorial and Remonstrance Against Religious Assessments,*[28] which went beyond Locke's theoretical place for religion. There, Madison argued that individuals were entitled to religious exercise, as a matter of right, not toleration, because religion is one's "duty towards the Creator," which is "precedent both in order of time and degree of obligation, to the claims of Civil Society."[29] There is some possible support for this more capacious understanding of religious liberty among a few other influential Americans at the time.[30]

Five states that ratified the Constitution proposed amendments that protected religious exercise. Typical among them was Virginia's: "all men have an equal, natural, and unalienable right to the free exercise of religion, according to the dictates of conscience...."[31] Other states proposed related language.[32]

James Madison, following his promise made during the ratification debates to the Anti-Federalists[33] to provide a bill of rights, introduced the initial draft of what became the Free Exercise Clause in the first session of the First Congress, on June 8, 1789. Madison's initial language stated: "The civil rights of none shall be abridged on account of religious belief or worship, nor shall any national religion be established, nor shall the full and equal rights of conscience be in any manner, or on any pretext, infringed."[34] Madison's proposal was sent to a select committee, on which he sat, that returned the following text to the House: "The civil rights of none shall be abridged on account of religious belief or worship, no religion shall be established by law, nor

---

26. Hamburger, *supra* note 3, at 922, 938.

27. John Locke, *A Letter Concerning Toleration, in* 6 THE WORKS OF JOHN LOCKE 43 (London 1823, reprint ed. 1963).

28. James Madison, *Memorial and Remonstrance Against Religious Assessments, reprinted in* 2 THE WRITINGS OF JAMES MADISON 1783–1787, at 184–85 (Gaillard Hunt ed., 1901).

29. *Id.*

30. *See* Vincent Phillip Munoz, *The Original Meaning of the Free Exercise Clause: The Evidence from the First Congress,* 31 HARV. J.L. & PUB. POL'Y 1083, 1094 (2008) (discussing, though not adopting, the claim that Thomas Jefferson and George Washington followed this view).

31. 3 THE DEBATES IN THE SEVERAL STATE CONVENTIONS ON THE ADOPTION OF THE FEDERAL CONSTITUTION AS RECOMMENDED BY THE GENERAL CONVENTION AT PHILADELPHIA IN 1787, at 657–61 (Jonathan Elliot ed., 2d ed. 1888).

32. *See* Munoz, *supra* note 30, at 1101–02 (describing the texts).

33. *See, e.g., Letters from The Federal Farmer No. 4,* POUGHKEEPSIE COUNTRY J., Oct. 12, 1787, *reprinted in* 2 THE COMPLETE ANTI-FEDERALIST 245, 250 (Herbert J. Storing ed., 1981) (articulating the Anti-Federalist concern for religious liberty).

34. 1 ANNALS OF CONG. 451 (Joseph Gales ed., 1834).

shall the equal rights of conscience be infringed."[35] Ultimately, after multiple revisions in both the House and the Senate, typically with little comment and primarily regarding the language governing establishments, Congress settled on the current text.[36] Similarly, there was little recorded debate in the state ratification conventions on the Free Exercise Clause.[37]

The text ultimately adopted—"Congress shall make no law"—itself suggested no entitlement to exemptions from generally applicable laws. The Clause's bar was a class prohibition. It *pro*scribed Congress from doing a class of acts: prohibiting religious exercise. It did not *pre*scribe a different phenomenon—making exemptions from general laws.[38]

The First Congress also debated whether to adopt a constitutional amendment to provide an exemption from militia service for members of religious sects that objected to military service.[39] This followed on the heels of proposals by three states for such an amendment.[40] James Madison introduced the following proposed amendment: "… but no person religiously scrupulous shall be compelled to bear arms."[41] Two facets of this complex debate are pertinent to our purposes: first, both houses of Congress rejected a constitutional religious exemption from the duty to bear arms; and, second, proponents of the constitutional exemption did not reference or appeal to the earlier and contemporaneous debate on the Free Exercise Clause's text. This suggests that members of Congress did not believe that free exercise entitled one to exemption from general laws.[42]

The Quakers, more formally known as the Religious Society of Friends, played a prominent role in the early discussions of the Free Exercise Clause and state law analogues, particularly in Pennsylvania.[43] The Quakers' religious beliefs prohibited them

---

35. *Id.* at 757.

36. *See* Munoz, *supra* note 30, at 1105–09 (describing the text's evolution); McConnell, *supra* note 3, at 1480–85 (same).

37. *See* Munoz, *supra* note 30, at 1085 (finding that "the drafting of the Free Exercise Clause sheds almost no light on the text's original meaning").

38. *Compare* Allan Ides, *The Test of the Free Exercise Clause as a Measure of* Employment Division v. Smith and *the Religious Freedom Restoration Act*, 51 Wash. & Lee L. Rev. 135 (1994) (arguing that the Clause's text contained two key ambiguities).

39. *See* Munoz, *supra* note 30, at 1109–19 (reviewing this historical episode and concluding that Congress' rejection of an exemption "provide[s] strong evidence against the exemption interpretation of the Free Exercise Clause").

40. *Id.* at 1111.

41. 1 Annals of Cong. 451 (Joseph Gales ed., 1834). For a survey of the congressional debate on this proposed amendment see Munoz, *supra* note 30, at 1110–19.

42. Munoz, *supra* note 30, at 1117–18; *but see* McConnell, *supra* note 3, at 1501 (arguing that this debate did not show that the Free Exercise Clause did not require religious exemptions).

43. For an overview of the legal dispute between Pennsylvania Quakers and Pennsylvania revolutionaries over whether Quakers could be compelled to serve in the revolutionary army, or procure a substitute, or were legally privileged from any such service because of their religious scruples against armed conflict, see Philip Hamburger, *Religious Freedom in Philadelphia*, 54 Emory L.J. 1603 (205); *see also* Bradley, *supra* note 3, at 302–04 (discussing the Pennsylvania experience).

from participating in armed conflict. This caused the Quakers to seek religious exemptions from military duty requirements. They enjoyed widespread success, as many colonies, and later states, exempted religious groups, such as the Quakers, from military service.[44] For example, the Continental Congress passed the following resolution in 1775: "As there are some people, who, from religious principles, cannot bear arms in any case, this Congress intend no violence to their consciences, but earnestly recommend it to them, to contribute liberally in this time of universal calamity ... which they can consistently with their religious principles."[45]

In Pennsylvania, where the Quakers had a long and prominent history stretching back to William Penn, the founder of Pennsylvania and a Quaker himself, the Quakers sought exemption from newly-independent Pennsylvania's military service requirement during the Revolution.[46] The Quakers' conception of religious liberty was that religious beliefs exempted believers from contrary civil laws, including military service and even the requirement to purchase a substitute for military service.[47] The Pennsylvania Assembly's (and the Pennsylvania state constitution's drafters') conception of religious liberty, however, was one of equal treatment of religion under the law.[48] Therefore, the Assembly and state constitution required conscientious objectors to military service to pay an equivalent.[49] Article VIII of the Pennsylvania Declaration of Rights stated: "Nor can any man who is conscientiously scrupulous of bearing arms, be justly compelled thereto, if he will pay such equivalent."[50] This suggested that the concept of free exercise did not require exemptions from general laws.

The early case law applying state law analogues to the Free Exercise Clause strongly intimated that the Clause did not require exemptions.[51] The Pennsylvania Supreme Court summarized the legal doctrine governing religious exemptions in 1848: "[T]he right of conscience ... 'is simply a right to worship ...; to adopt any creed or hold any opinion whatever, or to support any religion; and to do or forbear to do any act for conscience' sake, the doing or forbearing of which is not prejudicial to the public weal."[52]

There were few cases that addressed free exercise exemption claims, and those that did, rejected such claims. Three of the relatively more common types of cases to address religious exemption claims involved witness competency, blasphemy, and Sab-

---

44. McConnell, *supra* note 3, at 1468.

45. Resolution of July 18, 1775, *reprinted in* 2 JOURNALS OF THE CONTINENTAL CONGRESS, 1774–1789, at 187, 189 (Worthington C. Ford ed., 1905).

46. Hamburger, *supra* note 3, at 1608–28.

47. *Id.* at 1612–14.

48. *Id.* at 1621–26.

49. *Id.*

50. PA. CONST. OF 1776, Declaration of Rights, art. VIII.

51. *See* Munoz, *supra* note 30, at 1099 ("[N]o antebellum state court interpreted constitutional protections of religious free exercise to grant exemptions."); *see also* McConnell, *supra* note 3, at 1503–11 (reviewing the cases and acknowledging that they "point against exemptions").

52. Specht v. Commonwealth, 8 Pa. 312, 322 (1848).

batarians.[53] In each class of cases, courts typically ruled that religious exercise claims did not exempt religious believers from generally applicable laws.[54]

The witness competency cases implicated free exercise because some religious sects refused to swear oaths utilized by courts to ensure truthful testimony. Courts rejected such claims because, "in the development of facts, and the ascertainment of truth, human tribunals have a right to interfere [with religion]."[55] Blasphemy cases implicated free exercise because the defendants in these cases argued that they were being punished for their expression of their religious beliefs. Courts rejected these claims as well because "an offense which outrages the feelings of the community so far as to endanger the public peace, may be prohibited by the legislature."[56] Sabbatarians invoked free exercise to justify their wish to engage in gainful activity on Sunday or not engage in such activity on Saturday. Courts rejected Sabbatarian exemption requests:

> The constitution of this state secures freedom of conscience and equality of religious right. No man, living under the protection of our institutions, can be coerced to profess any form of religious belief, or to practise any peculiar mode of worship, in preference to another. In this respect, the Christian, the Jew, the Mohammedan, and the Pagan, are alike entitled to protection. Nay, the Infidel, who madly rejects all belief in a Divine Essence, may safely do so, in reference to civil punishment, so long as he refrains from the wanton and malicious proclamation of his opinions with intent to outrage the moral and religious convictions of a community, the vast majority of whom are Christians. But beyond this, conscientious doctrines and practices can claim no immunity from the operation of general laws made for the government and to promote the welfare of the whole people.[57]

Indeed, the Supreme Court did not directly face a claimed religious exercise exemption for nearly a century, until 1878 in *Reynolds v. United States*.[58] And, as you will see below, it there rejected the claim. Not until 1963 did the Court accept such a claim.[59]

Much of the evidence utilized by scholars to support a pro-exemption interpretation of the Free Exercise Clause is the relatively widespread practice of non-judicial exemptions for religious believers.[60] For instance, the original Constitution contained the Religious Tests Clause, which exempted office-holders from the generally applicable

---

53. *See* Bradley, *supra* note 3, at 273–85 (discussing these cases).

54. *But see* People v. Phillips, N.Y. Ct. Gen. Sess. 1813, *reprinted in Privileged Communications to Clergyman*, 1 Cath. Law. 199–209 (1955).

55. Jackson v. Gridley, 18 Johns. 98, 106 (N.Y. Sup. Ct. 1820).

56. State v. Chandler, 2 Del. (2 Harr.) 553 (1837).

57. Specht v. Commonwealth, 8 Pa. 312, 322 (1848); *see also* City Council v. Benjamin, 32 S.C.L. (2 Strob) 508 (1846) (rejecting a Sabbatarian's religious exemption claim).

58. Reynolds v. United States, 98 U.S. 145 (1879).

59. *See* Bradley, *supra* note 3, at 272 (making the claim in this paragraph).

60. McConnell, *supra* note 3, at 1466.

Article VI oath requirement.[61] Similarly, the North Carolina ratification convention proposed an amendment that would exempt religious believers from military service: "That any person religiously scrupulous of bearing arms ought to be exempted, upon payment of an equivalent."[62] However, legislatively-granted exemptions may also have been motivated by nonconstitutional motives, such as respect for others' religious beliefs.[63] Furthermore, the existence of free exercise clauses and conscientious objector exemptions in the same state constitutions showed that Americans at the time did not believe that free exercise entitled religious pacifists to exemptions from neutral conscription laws.[64]

On balance, the historical evidence shows that the Free Exercise Clause's original meaning did not exempt religiously-motivated activity from general laws — laws that did not target activity because of its religious motivation — that incidentally burdened religiously-motived conduct.[65]

A last, further piece of evidence in support of this conclusion is that the Supreme Court's first major free exercise case, in 1878, *Reynolds v. United States*, adopted this interpretation of the Clause.[66] Only after the New Deal, and at the height of the Warren Court, did the Supreme Court, in *Sherbert v. Verner*,[67] shift to the pro-exemption interpretation of the Clause. It did so, without examining the Clause's history or original meaning.[68] Instead, the *Sherbert* Court's analysis was of-a-piece with contemporaneous Warren Court fundamental right analysis.

Exercise 2:

1. What is the original meaning of the Free Exercise Clause? What evidence supports your conclusion? What evidence points against your conclusion? Are you confident about your judgment?

2. Is the evidence regarding the Clause's original meaning determinate enough for judges today to rely on it?

3. One of the key disputes between proponents of the pro-exemption interpretation of the Free Exercise Clause and the opponents of religious exemptions from general laws, is whether contemporaneous legislative exemptions, both federal and state, are

---

61. U.S. Const., art. VI.

62. N.C. Proposal for a Declaration of Rights, § 19, *in* 4 Jonathan Elliot, The Debates in the Several State Conventions on the Adoption of the Federal Constitution 244 (1941).

63. *See* Hamburger, *supra* note 3, at 929 (making this argument).

64. *See* Ellis M. West, *The Right to Religion-Based Exemptions in Early America: The Case of Rel. Conscientious Objectors to Conscription*, 10 J.L. & Rel. 367 (1994) (making this argument).

65. Professor McConnell's scholarship makes the strongest case for the pro-exemption view. Professor McConnell, however, acknowledged that, even in his view, the evidence supporting his position is thin: "Without overstating the force of the evidence, however, it is possible to say that the modern doctrine of free exercise exemptions is more consistent with the original understanding than is a position that leads only to the facial neutrality of legislation." McConnell, *supra* note 3, at 1512; *see also id.* at 1513 (describing the post-1791 case law as "tend[ing] to point against exemptions").

66. Reynolds v. United States, 98 U.S. 145 (1879).

67. Sherbert v. Verner, 374 U.S. 398 (1963).

68. McConnell, *supra* note 3, at 1413; Munoz, *supra* note 30, at 1087.

evidence that federal judges have the authority to craft religious exemptions. Explain arguments on both sides, using text, structure, history, and precedent.

4. Does the protection afforded religious exercise by the Free Exercise Clause make sense today, in a society with greater religious pluralism, including a significant minority of nonbelievers?

5. Relatedly, assuming that you wished to defend some category of religious exemptions, what policy arguments would you make to support your position? To what extent, if any, could the Clause's framers and ratifiers accept your policy arguments?

C. What Counts as a "Religion"?

Though this is likely to come as a surprise, there is no generally-agreed upon definition of "religion," for First Amendment purposes.[69] For most of American history, the definition of religion utilized by the Supreme Court and federal courts was unselfconsciously theistic. *Davis v. Beason*, 133 U.S. 333, 342 (1890). Then, in two cases in 1965 and 1970, the Supreme Court suggested that a theistic definition of religion would itself violate the Establishment Clause, so the Court then utilized a nontheistic definition of religion in the context of statutory interpretation. *See Welsh v. United States*, 398 U.S. 333 (1970) (ruling that a conscientious objector's nontheistic beliefs constituted a religion for purposes of the selective service act); *United States v. Seeger*, 380 U.S. 163 (1965) (same).

Though *Welsh* and *Seeger* involved statutory definitions of religion, and not the meaning of "religion" in the First Amendment, many later courts and commentators have read the cases' reasoning relatively broadly to apply to the First Amendment. However, since then, the Supreme Court has not definitively weighed in on the constitutional definition of "religion" and, as we will see in **Chapter 3**, the Establishment Clause reasoning utilized in *Welsh* and *Seeger* has been undermined in the years since 1970 by contrary trends in the case law. At this point, therefore, there is no definition of "religion" clearly established in the Supreme Court's case law. For a review of the history of the Supreme Court's definition of religion, and a description of "religion['s]" original meaning, see Lee J. Strang, *The Meaning of "Religion" in the First Amendment*, 40 Duquesne L. Rev. 181 (2002) (arguing that the original meaning of "religion" is: belief in a deity, with duties in this life, and a future state of rewards and punishments);

---

69. If you studied the Incorporation Doctrine, covered in Volume 5, you will recall that the Supreme Court ruled that the Fourteenth Amendment's Due Process Clause "incorporated" most of the Bill of Rights. *See, e.g.*, Gitlow v. New York, 268 U.S. 652, 666 (1925) ("For present purposes we may and do assume that freedom of speech and of the press—which are protected by the First Amendment from abridgment by Congress—are among the fundamental personal rights and 'liberties' protected by the due process clause of the Fourteenth Amendment from impairment by the States."). The Supreme Court accomplished incorporation of the Free Exercise Clause via *Cantwell v. Connecticut*, 310 U.S. 296, 303 (1940) ("The First Amendment declares that Congress shall make no law respecting an establishment of religion or prohibiting the free exercise thereof. The Fourteenth Amendment has rendered the legislatures of the states as incompetent as Congress to enact such laws.").

Lee J. Strang, *The Original Meaning of "religion" in the First Amendment: A Test Case for Originalism's Utilization of Corpus Linguistics*, 2017 BYU L. Rev. 1683 (updating the analysis).

A key strategy employed by the Supreme Court to avoid having to definitively rule on the contours of the meaning of "religion" is avoidance. The Supreme Court has instructed that federal courts must refrain from inquiring into the reasonableness of religious belief systems. This pronouncement occurred most prominently in *United States v. Ballard*, 322 U.S. 78 (1944), reprinted below.

United States v. Ballard

322 U.S. 78 (1944)

Mr. Justice Douglas delivered the opinion of the Court.

Respondents were indicted and convicted for using, and conspiring to use, the mails to defraud. The indictment charged a scheme to defraud by organizing and promoting the I Am movement through the use of the mails. The charge was that certain designated corporations were formed, literature distributed and sold, funds solicited, and memberships in the I Am movement sought 'by means of false and fraudulent representations, pretenses and promises'. The false representations charged were eighteen in number. It is sufficient at this point to say that they covered respondents' alleged religious doctrines or beliefs. The following are representative:

> "that Guy W. Ballard, now deceased, alias Saint Germain, Jesus, George Washington, and Godfre Ray King, had been selected and thereby designated by the alleged 'ascertained masters,' Saint Germain, as a divine messenger; and that the words of 'ascended masters' and the words of the alleged divine entity, Saint Germain, would be transmitted to mankind through the medium of the said Guy W. Ballard;

> "that Guy W. Ballard, during his lifetime, and Edna W. Ballard, and Donald Ballard, by reason of their alleged high spiritual attainments and righteous conduct, had been selected as divine messengers through which the words of the alleged 'ascended masters,' including the alleged Saint Germain, would be communicated to mankind under the teachings commonly known as the 'I Am' movement;

> "that Guy W. Ballard, during his lifetime, and Edna W. Ballard and Donald Ballard had, by reason of supernatural attainments, the power to heal persons of ailments and diseases and to make well persons afflicted with any diseases, injuries, or ailments, and did falsely represent to persons intended to be defrauded that the three designated persons had the ability and power to cure persons of those diseases normally classified as curable and also of diseases which are ordinarily classified by the medical profession as being incurable diseases; and did further represent that the three designated persons had in fact cured either by the activity of one, either, or all of said persons, hundreds of persons afflicted with diseases and ailments."

After enumerating the eighteen misrepresentations the indictment also alleged: "At the time of making all of the afore-alleged representations by the defendants, and each of them, the defendants, and each of them, well knew that all of said aforementioned representations were false and untrue and were made with the intention on the part of the defendants, and each of them, to cheat, wrong, and defraud persons intended to be defrauded, and to obtain from persons intended to be defrauded by the defendants, money, property, and other things of value and to convert the same to the use and the benefit of the defendants, and each of them[.]" ...

There was a demurrer and a motion to quash each of which asserted that the indictment attacked the religious beliefs of respondents and sought to restrict the free exercise of their religion in violation of the Constitution of the United States. These motions were denied by the District Court. Early in the trial, however, objections were raised to the admission of certain evidence concerning respondents' religious beliefs. The court conferred with counsel in absence of the jury and with the acquiescence of counsel for the United States and for respondents confined the issues on this phase of the case to the question of the good faith of respondents. At the request of counsel for both sides the court advised the jury of that action in the following language:

"Now, gentlemen, here is the issue in this case: First, the defendants in this case made certain representations of belief in a divinity and in a supernatural power. Some of the teachings of the defendants, representations, might seem extremely improbable to a great many people.... Whether that is true or not is not the concern of this Court and is not the concern of the jury—and they are going to be told so in their instructions. As far as this Court sees the issue, it is immaterial what these defendants preached or wrote or taught in their classes. They are not going to be permitted to speculate on the actuality of the happening of those incidents. Now, I think I have made that as clear as I can. Therefore, the religious beliefs of these defendants cannot be an issue in this court.

"The issue is: Did these defendants honestly and in good faith believe those things? If they did, they should be acquitted. I cannot make it any clearer than that. If these defendants did not believe those things, did not believe the things that they wrote, the things that they preached, but used the mail for the purpose of getting money, the jury should find them guilty. Therefore, gentlemen, religion cannot come into this case."

The Circuit Court of Appeals reversed the judgment of conviction and granted a new trial. In its view the restriction of the issue in question to that of good faith was error. Its reason was that the scheme to defraud alleged in the indictment was that respondents made the eighteen alleged false representations; and that to prove that defendants devised the scheme described in the indictment "it was necessary to prove that they schemed to make some, at least, of the [eighteen] representations * * * and that some, at least, of the representations which they schemed to make were false."

The case is here on a petition for a writ of certiorari which we granted because of the importance of the question presented.

As we have noted, the Circuit Court of Appeals held that the question of the truth of the representations concerning respondent's religious doctrines or beliefs should have been submitted to the jury. But on whichever basis that court rested its action, we do not agree that the truth or verity of respondents' religious doctrines or beliefs should have been submitted to the jury. Whatever this particular indictment might require, the First Amendment precludes such a course, as the United States seems to concede. "The law knows no heresy, and is committed to the support of no dogma, the establishment of no sect." The First Amendment has a dual aspect. It not only "forestalls compulsion by law of the acceptance of any creed or the practice of any form of worship" but also "safeguards the free exercise of the chosen form of religion." "Thus the Amendment embraces two concepts,—freedom to believe and freedom to act. The first is absolute but, in the nature of things, the second cannot be." Freedom of thought, which includes freedom of religious belief, is basic in a society of free men. It embraces the right to maintain theories of life and of death and of the hereafter which are rank heresy to followers of the orthodox faiths. Heresy trials are foreign to our Constitution. Men may believe what they cannot prove. They may not be put to the proof of their religious doctrines or beliefs. Religious experiences which are as real as life to some may be incomprehensible to others. Yet the fact that they may be beyond the ken of mortals does not mean that they can be made suspect before the law. Many take their gospel from the New Testament. But it would hardly be supposed that they could be tried before a jury charged with the duty of determining whether those teachings contained false representations. The miracles of the New Testament, the Divinity of Christ, life after death, the power of prayer are deep in the religious convictions of many. If one could be sent to jail because a jury in a hostile environment found those teachings false, little indeed would be left of religious freedom. The Fathers of the Constitution were not unaware of the varied and extreme views of religious sects, of the violence of disagreement among them, and of the lack of any one religious creed on which all men would agree. They fashioned a charter of government which envisaged the widest possible toleration of conflicting views. Man's relation to his God was made no concern of the state. He was granted the right to worship as he pleased and to answer to no man for the verity of his religious views. The religious views espoused by respondents might seem incredible, if not preposterous, to most people. But if those doctrines are subject to trial before a jury charged with finding their truth or falsity, then the same can be done with the religious beliefs of any sect. When the triers of fact undertake that task, they enter a forbidden domain. The First Amendment does not select any one group or any one type of religion for preferred treatment. It puts them all in that position. So we conclude that the District Court ruled properly when it withheld from the jury all questions concerning the truth or falsity of the religious beliefs or doctrines of respondents.

Mr. Chief Justice Stone, dissenting.

I am not prepared to say that the constitutional guaranty of freedom of religion affords immunity from criminal prosecution for the fraudulent procurement of money by false statements as to one's religious experiences, more than it renders polygamy or libel immune from criminal prosecution. I cannot say that freedom of thought and worship includes freedom to procure money by making knowingly false statements about one's religious experiences. To go no further, if it were shown that a defendant in this case had asserted as a part of the alleged fraudulent scheme, that he had physically shaken hands with St. Germain in San Francisco on a day named, or that, as the indictment here alleges, by the exertion of his spiritual power he "had in fact cured * * * hundreds of persons afflicted with diseases and ailments", I should not doubt that it would be open to the Government to submit to the jury proof that he had never been in San Francisco and that no such cures had ever been effected.

Mr. Justice Roberts and Mr. Justice Frankfurter join in this opinion.

Mr. Justice Jackson, dissenting. [Opinion omitted.]

Exercise 3:

1. Which of the defendants' religious beliefs, if any, do you find "improbable"; why?

2. If you find some of the defendants' religious beliefs improbable, does that fact make it difficult for you to evaluate whether the defendants articulated those beliefs fraudulently? Would it be difficult for a jury to do so?

3. Why did the Supreme Court instruct the federal courts to refrain from inquiring into the veracity of a party's religious beliefs? Are those reasons persuasive?

4. Is Chief Justice Stone wrong, in dissent, when he argued that a civil court could entertain evidence that a purported event—e.g., the decedent had shaken hands with St. Germain at a particular place and time—did or did not occur?

5. Construct a slippery-slope argument that supports the majority's ruling. What bad consequences are likely to follow, if federal courts inquire into the veracity of religious believers' beliefs?

6. On the other hand, what bad consequences are likely to follow from the *Ballard* Court's approach?

7. What is the source of the Court's injunction against inquiring into the veracity of religious beliefs? The Free Exercise Clause? The Establishment Clause? Something else?

D. When Is the "Free Exercise" of "Religion" *Infringed*?

As in the free speech context, covered in **Chapter 1**, a preliminary question faced in free exercise cases is whether the government—federal, state, or local—has "infringed" on a private party's free exercise right. This infringement requirement derives from the text of the Free Exercise Clause, which proscribes "prohibit[ions]" on free exercise. If the government's actions do not "infringe" free exercise, then the government regulation is not subject to free exercise scrutiny, and the government need not justify its actions.

In many situations, it is easy to discern whether the government has infringed free exercise. For example, a flat government prohibition on religious worship infringes on religious exercise. However, given that both religious exercise and governmental regulation are pervasive in American life, there are many situations where the government acts in a way that limits religious exercise, though in a manner that does not result in an absolute ban.

The Supreme Court has stated that the government infringes the First Amendment when it "imposes a significant burden" on First Amendment activity. *United States v. Nat'l Treasury Employees Union*, 513 U.S. 454, 469 (1995). This test has both clear and less clear applications, because what constitutes a "significant burden" is a judgment-laden concept that may vary depending on the circumstances.

Prior to *Smith*, this preliminary infringement analysis was particularly important because, if a challenged governmental action infringed on religious exercise, it was subject to strict scrutiny. Post-*Smith*, governmental infringement of religious exercise is typically subject to rational basis review. For this reason, many critics of the Supreme Court's pre-*Smith* approach argued that, prior to *Smith*, the Supreme Court was reluctant to find that a challenged action infringed religious exercise. A case such critics frequently pointed to is reprinted below.

Lyng v. Northwest Indian Cemetery Protective Association
485 U.S. 439 (1988)

Justice O'Connor delivered the opinion of the Court.

This case requires us to consider whether the First Amendment's Free Exercise Clause prohibits the Government from permitting timber harvesting in, or constructing a road through, a portion of a National Forest that has traditionally been used for religious purposes by members of three American Indian tribes in northwestern California. We conclude that it does not.

I

As part of a project to create a paved 75-mile road linking two California towns, Gasquet and Orleans, the United States Forest Service has upgraded 49 miles of previously unpaved roads on federal land. In order to complete this project (the G-O road), the Forest Service must build a 6-mile paved segment through the Chimney Rock section of the Six Rivers National Forest. That section of the forest is situated between two other portions of the road that are already complete.

In 1977, the Forest Service issued a draft environmental impact statement that discussed proposals for upgrading an existing unpaved road that runs through the

Chimney Rock area. In response to comments on the draft statement, the Forest Service commissioned a study of American Indian cultural and religious sites in the area. The Chimney Rock area has historically been used for religious purposes by Yurok, Karok, and Tolowa Indians. The commissioned study, which was completed in 1979, found that the entire area "is significant as an integral and indispensible part of Indian religious conceptualization and practice." ... The study concluded that constructing a road along any of the available routes "would cause serious and irreparable damage to the sacred areas which are an integral and necessary part of the belief systems and lifeway of Northwest California Indian peoples."

In 1982, the Forest Service decided not to adopt this recommendation. The Regional Forester selected a route that avoided archeological sites and was removed as far as possible from the sites used by contemporary Indians for specific spiritual activities. Alternative routes that would have avoided the Chimney Rock area altogether were rejected because they would have required the acquisition of private land, had serious soil stability problems, and would in any event have traversed areas having ritualistic value to American Indians.

A panel of the Ninth Circuit affirmed in part [the District Court's permanent injunction prohibiting the Government from constructing the Chimney Rock section of the G-O road]. Relying primarily on the Forest Service's own commissioned study, the majority found that construction of the Chimney Rock section of the G-O road would have significant, though largely indirect, adverse effects on Indian religious practices. The majority concluded that the Government had failed to demonstrate a compelling interest in the completion of the road, and that it could have abandoned the road without thereby creating "a religious preserve for a single group in violation of the establishment clause."

III

A

It is undisputed that the Indian respondents' beliefs are sincere and that the Government's proposed actions will have severe adverse effects on the practice of their religion. Those respondents contend that the burden on their religious practices is heavy enough to violate the Free Exercise Clause unless the Government can demonstrate a compelling need to complete the G-O road or to engage in timber harvesting in the Chimney Rock area. We disagree.

In *Bowen v. Roy*, 476 U.S. 693 (1986), we considered a challenge to a federal statute that required the States to use Social Security numbers in administering certain welfare programs. Two applicants for benefits under these programs contended that their religious beliefs prevented them from acceding to the use of a Social Security number for their 2-year-old daughter because the use of a numerical identifier would "'rob the spirit' of [their] daughter and prevent her from attaining greater spiritual power." Similarly, in this case, it is said that disruption of the natural environment caused by the G-O road will diminish the sacredness of the area in question and create distractions that will interfere with "training and ongoing religious experience of individuals using [sites within] the area for personal medicine and growth … and as integrated parts of a system of religious belief and practice which correlates ascending degrees of personal power with a geographic hierarchy of power." The Court rejected this kind of challenge in *Roy*:

> "The Free Exercise Clause simply cannot be understood to require the Government to conduct its own internal affairs in ways that comport with the religious beliefs of particular citizens. Just as the Government may not insist that [the Roys] engage in any set form of religious observance, so [they] may not demand that the Government join in their chosen religious practices by refraining from using a number to identify their daughter.
>
> "The Free Exercise Clause affords an individual protection from certain forms of governmental compulsion; it does not afford an individual a right to dictate the conduct of the Government's internal procedures."

The building of a road on publicly owned land cannot meaningfully be distinguished from the use of a Social Security number in *Roy*. In both cases, the challenged Government action would interfere significantly with private persons' ability to pursue spiritual fulfillment according to their own religious beliefs. In neither case, however, would the affected individuals be coerced by the Government's action into violating their religious beliefs; nor would either governmental action penalize religious activity by denying any person an equal share of the rights, benefits, and privileges enjoyed by other citizens.

It is true that this Court has repeatedly held that indirect coercion or penalties on the free exercise of religion, not just outright prohibitions, are subject to scrutiny under the First Amendment. Thus, for example, [in *Sherbert*] ineligibility for unemployment benefits, based solely on a refusal to violate the Sabbath, has been analogized to a fine imposed on Sabbath worship. This does not and cannot imply that incidental effects of government programs, which may make it more difficult to practice certain religions but which have no tendency to coerce individuals into acting contrary to their religious beliefs, require government to bring forward a compelling justification for its otherwise lawful actions. The crucial word in the constitutional text is "prohibit."

Whatever may be the exact line between unconstitutional prohibitions on the free exercise of religion and the legitimate conduct by government of its own affairs, the location of the line cannot depend on measuring the effects of a governmental action on a religious objector's spiritual development. The Government does not dispute, and we have no reason to doubt, that the logging and road-building projects at issue in this case could have devastating effects on traditional Indian religious practices. The Indians use this area, as they have used it for a very long time, to conduct a wide variety of specific rituals that aim to accomplish their religious goals. According to their beliefs, the rituals would not be efficacious if conducted at other sites than the ones traditionally used.

However much we might wish that it were otherwise, government simply could not operate if it were required to satisfy every citizen's religious needs and desires. A broad range of government activities—from social welfare programs to foreign aid to conservation projects—will always be considered essential to the spiritual well-being of some citizens, often on the basis of sincerely held religious beliefs. Others will find the very same activities deeply offensive, and perhaps incompatible with their own search for spiritual fulfillment and with the tenets of their religion. The First Amendment must apply to all citizens alike, and it can give to none of them a veto over public programs that do not prohibit the free exercise of religion. The Constitution does not, and courts cannot, offer to reconcile the various competing demands on government, many of them rooted in sincere religious belief, that inevitably arise in so diverse a society as ours. That task, to the extent that it is feasible, is for the legislatures and other institutions. Cf. The Federalist No. 10 (suggesting that the effects of religious factionalism are best restrained through competition among a multiplicity of religious sects).

The Constitution does not permit government to discriminate against religions that treat particular physical sites as sacred, and a law prohibiting the Indian respondents from visiting the Chimney Rock area would raise a different set of constitutional questions. Whatever rights the Indians may have to the use of the area, however, those rights do not divest the Government of its right to use what is, after all, *its* land.

JUSTICE KENNEDY took no part in the consideration or decision of this case.

JUSTICE BRENNAN, with whom JUSTICE MARSHALL and JUSTICE BLACKMUN join, dissenting.

II

[T]he Court argues that the First Amendment bars only outright prohibitions, indirect coercion, and penalties on the free exercise of religion. All other "incidental effects of government programs," it concludes, simply do not give rise to constitutional concerns. Since our recognition nearly half a century ago that restraints on religious conduct implicate the concerns of the Free Exercise Clause, we have never suggested that the protections of the guarantee are limited to so narrow a range of governmental burdens. The land-use decision challenged here will restrain respondents from practicing their religion as surely and as completely as any of the governmental actions we have struck down in the past, and the Court's efforts simply to define away respondents' injury as nonconstitutional are both unjustified and ultimately unpersuasive.

A

[I]n *Wisconsin v. Yoder*, 406 U.S. 205 (1972), we struck down a state compulsory school attendance law on free exercise grounds ... because of "the *impact* that compulsory high school attendance could have on the continued survival of Amish communities." Detailed as their religious rules are, however, the parents in *Yoder* did not argue that their religion expressly proscribed public education beyond the eighth grade. By exposing Amish children "to a 'worldly' influence in conflict with their beliefs," and by removing those children "from their community, physically and emotionally, during the crucial and formative adolescent period of life" when Amish beliefs are inculcated, the compulsory school law posed "a very real threat of undermining the Amish community and religious practice."

I thus cannot accept the Court's premise that the form of the government's restraint on religious practice, rather than its effect, controls our constitutional analysis. Respondents here have demonstrated that construction of the G-O road will completely frustrate the practice of their religion, for as the lower courts found, the proposed construction activities will virtually destroy respondents' religion, and will therefore necessarily force them into abandoning those practices altogether. Indeed, the Government's proposed activities will restrain religious practice to a far greater degree here than in any of the cases cited by the Court today. None of the religious adherents in *Hobbie* [*v. Unemployment Appeals Commission of Florida*, 480 U.S. 136 (1987)], *Thomas* [*v. Review Board, Indiana Employment Security Div.*, 450 U.S. 707 (1981)], and *Sherbert*, for example, claimed or could have claimed that the denial of unemployment benefits rendered the practice of their religions impossible; at most, the challenged laws made those practices more expensive. Here, in stark contrast, respondents have claimed—and proved—that the desecration of the high country will prevent religious leaders from attaining the religious power or medicine indispensable to the success of virtually all their rituals and ceremonies. Here the threat posed by the desecration of sacred lands that are indisputably essential to respondents' religious practices is both more direct and more substantial than that raised by a compulsory school law that simply exposed Amish children to an alien value system.

Ultimately, the Court's coercion test turns on a distinction between governmental actions that compel affirmative conduct inconsistent with religious belief, and those governmental actions that prevent conduct consistent with religious belief. In my view, such a distinction is without constitutional significance. The crucial word in the constitutional text, as the Court itself acknowledges, is "prohibit," a comprehensive term that in no way suggests that the intended protection is aimed only at governmental actions that coerce affirmative conduct. Nor does the Court's distinction comport with the principles animating the constitutional guarantee: religious freedom is threatened no less by governmental action that makes the practice of one's chosen faith impossible than by governmental programs that pressure one to engage in conduct inconsistent with religious beliefs. The Court attempts to explain the line it draws by arguing that the protections of the Free Exercise Clause "cannot depend on measuring the effects of a governmental action on a religious objector's spiritual development," for in a society as diverse as ours, the Government cannot help but offend the "religious needs and desires" of some citizens. While I agree that governmental action that simply offends religious sensibilities may not be challenged under the Clause, we have recognized that laws that frustrate or inhibit religious *practice*— trigger the protections of the constitutional guarantee. The harm to the practitioners is the same regardless of the manner in which the government restrains their religious expression, and the Court's fear that an "effects" test will permit religious adherents to challenge governmental actions they merely find "offensive" in no way justifies its refusal to recognize the constitutional injury citizens suffer when governmental action not only offends but actually restrains their religious practices.

Exercise 4:

1. Identify the harm caused to the Indian tribes' religious exercise. On a scale of one to ten, with ten being the most harmful, how harmful was the challenged governmental action? Is that sufficient to constitute infringement?

2. What test did the Court utilize to determine that the plaintiffs' religious practices were not "infringed"?

3. Did the United States government's actions "significant[ly] burden" the tribes' religious exercise? If you answered no, then what other or additional restrictions would be more burdensome to the tribes' religious exercise than the destruction caused by the road? If you answered yes, then why did the Supreme Court rule as it did?

4. Was the *Lyng* Court really evaluating the merits of the tribes' religious liberty claims under the guise of determining whether the tribes' religious exercise was infringed? If you believe so, what evidence supports that conclusion?

5. Did the Court adequately distinguish the tribes' claim from those presented by the Amish in *Yoder*, or by the Seventh Day Adventist in *Sherbert*?

6. How does or should the dissent respond to the majority's slippery slope argument that accepting the tribes' claim would entail accepting a wide variety and large number of future claims against government programs that conflict with the claimants' religious beliefs?

E. When Is the "Free Exercise" of "Religion" *Violated*?

1. Introduction

Throughout the history of the Supreme Court's interpretation of the Free Exercise Clause, the Court has rigorously protected religious *belief*. The Court protects religious beliefs from both governmental actions that directly target religious beliefs and those that indirectly affect religious beliefs.

The Court's case law is not consistent, however, on the extent to which the Free Exercise Clause protects religiously-motivated *action*. At different times, the Supreme Court has afforded religiously-motivated actions more or less protection, and the Court has utilized different analyses to evaluate governmental limits on religious action.

The cases below highlight three different approaches that the Court has taken regarding religiously-motivated action. First, the Court provided relatively little protection. Second, it adopted the strict scrutiny analysis you learned in Volume 5 to provide relatively robust protection for religiously-motivated activity. Third, and most recently, the Court reverted back to its original position: relatively little protection for religiously-motivated activity.

The first major Supreme Court case to apply the Free Exercise Clause is reprinted below.

Reynolds v. United States

98 U.S. (8 Otto) 145 (1878)

Mr. Chief Justice Waite delivered the opinion of the court.

The assignments of error, when grouped, present the following questions:—

5. Should the accused have been acquitted if he married the second time, because he believed it to be his religious duty?

On the trial, the plaintiff in error, the accused, proved that at the time of his alleged second marriage he was, and for many years before had been, a member of the Church of Jesus Christ of Latter-Day Saints, commonly called the Mormon Church, and a believer in its doctrines; that it was an accepted doctrine of that church "that it was the duty of male members of said church, circumstances permitting, to practise polygamy; and also that the members of the church believed that the practice of polygamy was directly enjoined upon the male members thereof by the Almighty God; that the failing or refusing to practise polygamy by such male members of said church, when circumstances would admit, would be punished, and that the penalty for such failure and refusal would be damnation in the life to come." He also proved "that he had received permission from the recognized authorities in said church to enter into polygamous marriage; that Daniel H. Wells, one having authority in said church to perform the marriage ceremony, married the said defendant, to some woman by the name of Schofield."

Upon this proof he asked the court to instruct the jury that if they found from the evidence that he "was married as charged—if he was married—in pursuance of and in conformity with what he believed at the time to be a religious duty, that the verdict must be 'not guilty.'" This request was refused.

Upon this charge and refusal to charge the question is raised, whether religious belief can be accepted as a justification of an overt act made criminal by the law of the land. The inquiry is not as to the power of Congress to prescribe criminal laws for the Territories, but as to the guilt of one who knowingly violates a law which has been properly enacted, if he entertains a religious belief that the law is wrong.

Congress cannot pass a law for the government of the Territories which shall prohibit the free exercise of religion. The first amendment to the Constitution expressly forbids such legislation. The question to be determined is, whether the law now under consideration comes within this prohibition.

The word "religion" is not defined in the Constitution. We must go elsewhere, therefore, to ascertain its meaning, and nowhere more appropriately, we think, than to the history of the times in the midst of which the provision was adopted. The precise point of the inquiry is, what is the religious freedom which has been guaranteed.

Before the adoption of the Constitution, attempts were made in some of the colonies and States to legislate not only in respect to the establishment of religion, but in respect to its doctrines and precepts as well. The people were taxed, against their will, for the support of religion, and sometimes for the support of particular sects to whose tenets they could not and did not subscribe. Punishments were prescribed for a failure to attend upon public worship, and sometimes for entertaining heretical opinions. The controversy upon this general subject was animated in many of the States, but seemed at last to culminate in Virginia. In 1784, the House of Delegates of that State having under consideration "a bill establishing provision for teachers of the Christian religion," postponed it until the next session, and directed that the bill should be published and distributed, and that the people be requested "to signify their opinion respecting the adoption of such a bill at the next session of assembly."

This brought out a determined opposition. Amongst others, Mr. Madison prepared a "Memorial and Remonstrance," in which he demonstrated "that religion, or the duty we owe the Creator," was not within the cognizance of civil government. At the next session the proposed bill was not only defeated, but another, "for establishing religious freedom," drafted by Mr. Jefferson, was passed. In the preamble of this act religious freedom is defined; and after a recital "that to suffer the civil magistrate to intrude his powers into the field of opinion, and to restrain the profession or propagation of principles on supposition of their ill tendency, is a dangerous fallacy which at once destroys all religious liberty," it is declared "that it is time enough for the rightful purposes of civil government for its officers to interfere when principles break out into overt acts against peace and good order." In these two sentences is found the true distinction between what properly belongs to the church and what to the State.

In a little more than a year after the passage of this statute the convention met which prepared the Constitution of the United States. Of this convention Mr. Jefferson was not a member, he being then absent as minister to France. Five of the States, while adopting the Constitution, proposed amendments. Three—New Hampshire, New York, and Virginia—included in one form or another a declaration of religious freedom in the changes they desired to have made, as did also North Carolina, where the convention at first declined to ratify the Constitution until the proposed amendments were acted upon. Accordingly, at the first session of the first Congress the amendment now under consideration was proposed with others by Mr. Madison. It met the views of the advocates of religious freedom, and was adopted. Mr. Jefferson afterwards, in reply to an address to him by a committee of the Danbury Baptist Association, took occasion to say: "Believing with you that religion is a matter which lies solely between man and his God; that he owes account to none other for his faith or his worship; that the legislative powers of the government reach actions only, and not opinions,—I contemplate with sovereign reverence that act of the whole American people which declared that their legislature should 'make no law respecting an establishment of religion or prohibiting the free exercise thereof,' thus building a wall of separation between church and State. Coming as this does from an acknowledged leader of the advocates of the measure, it may be accepted almost as an authoritative declaration of the scope and effect of the amendment thus secured. Congress was deprived of all legislative power over mere opinion, but was left free to reach actions which were in violation of social duties or subversive of good order.

Polygamy has always been odious among the northern and western nations of Europe, and, until the establishment of the Mormon Church, was almost exclusively a feature of the life of Asiatic and of African people. At common law, the second marriage was always void, and from the earliest history of England polygamy has been treated as an offence against society.

By the statute of James I, the offence, if committed in England or Wales, was made punishable in the civil courts, and the penalty was death. As this statute was limited in its operation to England and Wales, it was at a very early period re-enacted, generally with some modifications, in all the colonies. In connection with the case we are now considering, it is a significant fact that on the 8th of December, 1788, after the passage of the act establishing religious freedom, and after the convention of Virginia had recommended as an amendment to the Constitution of the United States the declaration in a bill of rights that "all men have an equal, natural, and unalienable right to the free exercise of religion, according to the dictates of conscience," the legislature of that State substantially enacted the statute of James I, death penalty included. From that day to this we think it may safely be said there never has been a time in any State of the Union when polygamy has not been an offence against society, cognizable by the civil courts and punishable with more or less severity. In the face of all this evidence, it is impossible to believe that the constitutional guaranty of religious freedom was intended to prohibit legislation in respect to this most important feature of social life. Marriage, while from its very nature a sacred obligation, is nevertheless, in most civilized nations, a civil contract, and usually regulated by law. Upon it society may be said to be built, and out of its fruits spring social relations and social obligations and duties, with which government is necessarily required to deal. In fact, according as monogamous or polygamous marriages are allowed, do we find the principles on which the government of the people, to a greater or less extent, rests. Professor [Francis] Lieber says, polygamy leads to the patriarchal principle, and which, when applied to large communities, fetters the people in stationary despotism, while that principle cannot long exist in connection with monogamy. Chancellor Kent observes that this remark is equally striking and profound. 2 [JAMES] KENT, COM[MENTARIES ON AMERICAN LAW] 81, note (*e*). [T]here cannot be a doubt that, unless restricted by some form of constitution, it is within the legitimate scope of the power of every civil government to determine whether polygamy or monogamy shall be the law of social life under its dominion.

In our opinion, the statute immediately under consideration is within the legislative power of Congress. It is constitutional and valid as prescribing a rule of action for all those residing in the Territories, and in places over which the United States have exclusive control. This being so, the only question which remains is, whether those who make polygamy a part of their religion are excepted from the operation of the statute. Laws are made for the government of actions, and while they cannot interfere with mere religious belief and opinions, they may with practices. Suppose one believed that human sacrifices were a necessary part of religious worship, would it be seriously contended that the civil government under which he lived could not interfere to prevent a sacrifice? Or if a wife religiously believed it was her duty to burn herself upon the funeral pile of her dead husband, would it be beyond the power of the civil government to prevent her carrying her belief into practice?

So here, as a law of the organization of society under the exclusive dominion of the United States, it is provided that plural marriages shall not be allowed. Can a man excuse his practices to the contrary because of his religious belief? To permit this would be to make the professed doctrines of religious belief superior to the law of the land, and in effect to permit every citizen to become a law unto himself. Government could exist only in name under such circumstances.

Here the accused knew he had been once married, and that his first wife was living. He also knew that his second marriage was forbidden by law. When, therefore, he married the second time, he is presumed to have intended to break the law. And the breaking of the law is the crime. The only defence of the accused in this case is his belief that the law ought not to have been enacted. It matters not that his belief was a part of his professed religion: it was still belief, and belief only.

Upon a careful consideration of the whole case, we are satisfied that no error was committed by the court below.

Judgment affirmed.

MR. JUSTICE FIELD. [Opinion omitted.]

Exercise 5:

1. What definition of "religion" did the Supreme Court (implicitly) utilize?

2. What did the Free Exercise Clause protect: religious belief and/or religiously-motivated actions?

3. What justifications did the Supreme Court provide for its interpretation of the Clause's scope, in particular, for not extending the Clause's protection to religiously-motivated action in conflict with a general criminal prohibition?

4. Was the law under which Reynolds was prosecuted neutral? In other words, did it prohibit conduct without regard for religion, or did it target religiously-motivated activity?

5. *Should* the fact that a person's actions are sincerely religiously motivated excuse that person from compliance with neutral laws? Some subset of those laws? For example, many religious groups believe in faith healing. If members of such a group attempted to faith-heal their child, who subsequently died, should the Free Exercise Clause exempt them from prosecution for their child's death?

6. If you studied Congress' enumerated powers in Volume 3, under what power did Congress pass the act that forbade polygamy under which Reynolds was prosecuted?

7. Note that *Reynolds* is one of those cases where the First Amendment itself, and not via incorporation through the Fourteenth Amendment, is working.

2. Rise of Strict Scrutiny for Infringement of Free Exercise

The story of the Supreme Court's treatment of free exercise in the twentieth century is the rise and decline of strict scrutiny of religious freedom claims. If you covered Volume 5, you saw that, during the so-called Lochner Era, the Supreme Court decided two cases that, collectively, protected religious liberty under the doctrine of Substantive Due Process. The first, *Meyer v. Nebraska*, 262 U.S. 390 (1923), involved a state prosecution of a parochial school teacher who taught German to students in violation of a state statute. The Court struck down this statute. Two years later, the Supreme Court decided a similar case, *Pierce v. Society of Sisters*, 268 U.S. 510 (1925), where the Court struck down an Oregon statute that effectively outlawed nonpublic primary education. Though the Court's analysis in these cases was substantive due process, later cases relied on them to articulate heightened scrutiny of restrictions on religious liberty. *See, e.g., Wisconsin v. Yoder*, 406 U.S. 205, 222, 232 (1972) (citing *Meyer* and *Pierce*).

The New Deal Court, now relying explicitly on the First Amendment and the Free Exercise Clause, also decided cases that the Court later built on to establish strict scrutiny. *Cantwell v. Connecticut*, 310 U.S. 296, 303–04 (1940), covered in **Chapter 1**, struck down, on religious liberty grounds, the prosecution of Jehovah's Witnesses for public proselytization. Similarly, in *West Va. St. Bd. of Educ. v. Barnette*, 319 U.S. 624, 634–35, 642 (1943), also covered in **Chapter 1**, the Court reversed the prosecution of Jehovah's Witnesses for refusal to salute the American Flag in school. Both cases today are seen primarily in free speech terms, though the facts, rhetoric, and reasoning of the opinions also contained prominent religious exercise facets.

Building on those Lochner Era and New Deal cases, the Supreme Court's protection for religious exercise reached its high point in the 1960s through early-1970s. During this period, the Court ruled that, like other individual rights—such as free speech and the right to vote—it would subject restrictions on religious exercise to strict scrutiny. Below is the case that definitively stated that ruling, followed by one of the Court's most famous free exercise cases.

Sherbert v. Verner

374 U.S. 398 (1963)

MR. JUSTICE BRENNAN delivered the opinion of the Court.

Appellant, a member of the Seventh-day Adventist Church was discharged by her South Carolina employer because she would not work on Saturday, the Sabbath Day of her faith.[1] When she was unable to obtain other employment because she would not take Saturday work, she filed a claim for unemployment compensation benefits under the South Carolina Unemployment Compensation Act. That law provides that, to be eligible for benefits, a claimant must be "able to work and * * * is available for work"; and, further, that a claimant is ineligible for benefits "[i]f * * * he has failed,

---

1. No question has been raised in this case concerning the sincerity of appellant's religious beliefs.

without good cause * * * to accept available suitable work when offered him by the employment office or the employer * * *." The appellee Employment Security Commission, in administrative proceedings under the statute, found that appellant's restriction upon her availability for Saturday work brought her within the provision disqualifying for benefits insured workers who fail, without good cause, to accept "suitable work when offered * * *." The Commission's finding was sustained by the Court of Common Pleas for Spartanburg County. That court's judgment was in turn affirmed by the South Carolina Supreme Court, which rejected appellant's contention that, as applied to her, the disqualifying provisions of the South Carolina statute abridged her right to the free exercise of her religion secured under the Free Exercise Clause of the First Amendment through the Fourteenth Amendment. We reverse the judgment of the South Carolina Supreme Court.

I.

The door of the Free Exercise Clause stands tightly closed against any governmental regulation of religious beliefs as such, *Cantwell v. Connecticut*, 310 U.S. 296 [(1940)]. Government may neither compel affirmation of a repugnant belief, nor penalize or discriminate against individuals or groups because they hold religious views abhorrent to the authorities, nor employ the taxing power to inhibit the dissemination of particular religious views. On the other hand, the Court has rejected challenges under the Free Exercise Clause to governmental regulation of certain overt acts prompted by religious beliefs or principles, for "even when the action is in accord with one's religious convictions, [it] is not totally free from legislative restrictions." The conduct or actions so regulated have invariably posed some substantial threat to public safety, peace or order. See, e.g., *Reynolds v. United States*, 98 U.S. 145 [(1879)]; *Jacobson v. Massachusetts*, 197 U.S. 11 [(1905)]; *Prince v. Massachusetts*, 321 U.S. 158 [(1944)].

Plainly enough, appellant's conscientious objection to Saturday work constitutes no conduct prompted by religious principles of a kind within the reach of state legislation. If, therefore. the decision of the South Carolina Supreme Court is to withstand appellant's constitutional challenge, it must be either because her disqualification as a beneficiary represents no infringement by the State of her constitutional rights of free exercise, or because any incidental burden on the free exercise of appellant's religion may be justified by a "compelling state interest in the regulation of a subject within the State's constitutional power to regulate * * *." *NAACP v. Button*, 371 U.S. 415, 438 [(1963)].

II.

We turn first to the question whether the disqualification for benefits imposes any burden on the free exercise of appellant's religion. We think it is clear that it does. In a sense the consequences of such a disqualification to religious principles and practices may be only an indirect result of welfare legislation within the State's general competence to enact; it is true that no criminal sanctions directly compel appellant to work a six-day week. But this is only the beginning, not the end, of our inquiry. For "[i]f the purpose or effect of a law is to impede the observance of one or all religions or is to discriminate invidiously between religions, that law is constitutionally invalid even though the burden may be characterized as being only indirect." Here not only is it apparent that appellant's declared ineligibility for benefits derives solely from the practice of her religion, but the pressure upon her to forego that practice is unmistakable. The ruling forces her to choose between following the precepts of her religion and forfeiting benefits, on the one hand, and abandoning one of the precepts of her religion in order to accept work, on the other hand. Governmental imposition of such a choice puts the same kind of burden upon the free exercise of religion as would a fine imposed against appellant for her Saturday worship.

Nor may the South Carolina court's construction of the statute be saved from constitutional infirmity on the ground that unemployment compensation benefits are not appellant's "right" but merely a "privilege." It is too late in the day to doubt that the liberties of religion and expression may be infringed by the denial of or placing of conditions upon a benefit or privilege. [T]o condition the availability of benefits upon this appellant's willingness to violate a cardinal principle of her religious faith effectively penalizes the free exercise of her constitutional liberties.

III.

We must next consider whether some compelling state interest enforced in the eligibility provisions of the South Carolina statute justifies the substantial infringement of appellant's First Amendment right. It is basic that no showing merely of a rational relationship to some colorable state interest would suffice; in this highly sensitive constitutional area, "[o]nly the gravest abuses, endangering paramount interest, give occasion for permissible limitation[.]" No such abuse or danger has been advanced in the present case. The appellees suggest no more than a possibility that the filing of fraudulent claims by unscrupulous claimants feigning religious objections to Saturday work might not only dilute the unemployment compensation fund but also hinder the scheduling by employers of necessary Saturday work. But that possibility is not apposite here because no such objection appears to have been made before the South Carolina Supreme Court, and we are unwilling to assess the importance of an asserted state interest without the views of the state court. Nor, if the contention had been made below, would the record appear to sustain it; there is no proof whatever to warrant such fears of malingering or deceit. Even if consideration of such evidence is not foreclosed by the prohibition against judicial inquiry into the truth or falsity of religious beliefs, *United States v. Ballard*, 322 U.S. 78 [(1944)] — it is highly doubtful whether such evidence would be sufficient to warrant a substantial infringement of religious liberties. For even if the possibility of spurious claims did threaten to dilute the fund and disrupt the scheduling of work, it would plainly be incumbent upon the appellees to demonstrate that no alternative forms of regulation would combat such abuses without infringing First Amendment rights.[7]

---

7. We note that before the instant decision, state supreme courts had, without exception, granted benefits to persons who were physically available for work but unable to find suitable employment

In these respects, then, the state interest asserted in the present case is wholly dissimilar to the interests which were found to justify the less direct burden upon religious practices in *Braunfeld v. Brown*, [366 U.S. 599 (1961)]. The Court recognized that the Sunday closing law which that decision sustained undoubtedly served "to make the practice of [the Orthodox Jewish merchants'] religious beliefs more expensive[.]" But the statute was nevertheless saved by a countervailing factor which finds no equivalent in the instant case—a strong state interest in providing one uniform day of rest for all workers. That secular objective could be achieved, the Court found, only by declaring Sunday to be that day of rest. Requiring exemptions for Sabbatarians, while theoretically possible, appeared to present an administrative problem of such magnitude, or to afford the exempted class so great a competitive advantage, that such a requirement would have rendered the entire statutory scheme unworkable. In the present case no such justifications underlie the determination of the state court that appellant's religion makes her ineligible to receive benefits.

Reversed and remanded.

MR. JUSTICE DOUGLAS, concurring. [Opinion omitted.]

MR. JUSTICE STEWART, concurring in the result. [Opinion omitted.]

MR. JUSTICE HARLAN, whom MR. JUSTICE WHITE joins, dissenting.

In the present case all that the state court has done is to apply accepted principles. Since virtually all of the mills in the Spartanburg area were operating on a six-day week, the appellant was "unavailable for work," and thus ineligible for benefits, when personal considerations prevented her from accepting employment on a full-time basis in the industry and locality in which she had worked. The fact that these personal considerations sprang from her religious convictions was wholly without relevance to the state court's application of the law. Thus in no proper sense can it be said that the State discriminated against the appellant on the basis of her religious beliefs or that she was denied benefits because she was a Seventh-day Adventist. She was denied benefits just as any other claimant would be denied benefits who was not "available for work" for personal reasons.

Exercise 6:

1. The majority and dissenting justices disagreed about whether Sherbert's free exercise right was substantially infringed by South Carolina's refusal to provide unemployment benefits to her. Explain the respective positions of the majority and dissent, and argue which one is the better position.

2. Was the Court's conclusion that Sherbert's free exercise right was infringed, consistent with the *Lying* Court's different conclusion regarding the tribes' religious practices?

---

solely because of a religious prohibition against Saturday work. Of the 47 States which have eligibility provisions similar to those of the South Carolina statute, only 28 appear to have given administrative rulings concerning the eligibility of persons whose religious convictions prevented them from accepting available work. Twenty-two of those States have held such persons entitled to benefits.

3. Using the criteria the Supreme Court has articulated to determine whether strict scrutiny was appropriate in other contexts—such as a history of discrimination, the adequacy of political process, or the importance of a right—should the Court have ruled that restrictions on free exercise receive strict scrutiny?

4. The majority ruled that South Carolina did not meet strict scrutiny. Explain the Court's reasoning.

5. The *Sherbert* Court looked to the rulings and practices of the states to help it evaluate South Carolina's claim that it had to deny Sherbert's request for unemployment compensation to prevent fraudulent claims. How does the Court's reference to state practices support the Court's judgment on whether South Carolina's denial is "narrowly tailored"? Is it appropriate for the United States Supreme Court to rely on state court decisions when interpreting the U.S. Constitution?

6. The *Sherbert* Court distinguished *Braunfeld v. Brown*, 366 U.S. 599 (1961), where the Court had previously upheld Sunday closing laws. Upon what basis did the Court do so? Are you persuaded?

7. Should we be concerned that the majority's application of strict scrutiny to Sherbert's Free Exercise Clause claim could lead to plaintiffs from other faiths challenging other laws? The United States has many people with many different religious commitments, some of which are in conflict with common and/or important laws: everything from the relatively innocuous to the relatively important. Does *Sherbert's* use of strict scrutiny threaten the Rule of Law by opening the door to successful claims for religious exemptions from common laws?

Following *Sherbert*, the conventional wisdom was that the right to free exercise of religion was treated identically to other fundamental rights that received strict scrutiny review by the Supreme Court. However, the major case during this period, though notable for its interesting facts, was opaque in its reasoning. In particular, it was not clear whether the Court employed *Sherbert's* strict scrutiny analysis. That case is reprinted below.

Wisconsin v. Yoder

406 U.S. 205 (1972)

MR. CHIEF JUSTICE BURGER delivered the opinion of the Court.

Respondents Jonas Yoder and Wallace Miller are members of the Old Order Amish religion. They and their families are residents of Green County, Wisconsin. Wisconsin's compulsory school-attendance law required them to cause their children to attend public or private school until reaching age 16 but the respondents declined to send their children, ages 14 and 15, to school after they complete[d] the eighth grade.

On complaint of the school district administrator for the public schools, respondents were charged, tried, and convicted of violating the compulsory-attendance law in Green County Court and were fined the sum of $5 each. Respondents defended on the ground that the application of the compulsory-attendance law violated their rights under the First and Fourteenth Amendments. The trial testimony showed that respondents believed, in accordance with the tenets of Old Order Amish communities generally, that their children's attendance at high school, public or private, was contrary to the Amish religion and way of life. They believed that by sending their children to high school, they would not only expose themselves to the danger of the censure of the church community, but, as found by the county court, also endanger their own salvation and that of their children. The State stipulated that respondents' religious beliefs were sincere.

A feature of Old Order Amish communities is their devotion to a life in harmony with nature and the soil, as exemplified by the simple life of the early Christian era that continued in America during much of our early national life. Amish beliefs require members of the community to make their living by farming or closely related activities. Broadly speaking, the Old Order Amish religion pervades and determines the entire mode of life of its adherents. Their conduct is regulated in great detail by the Ordnung, or rules, of the church community.

Amish objection to formal education beyond the eighth grade is firmly grounded in these central religious concepts. They object to the high school, and higher education generally, because the values they teach are in marked variance with Amish values and the Amish way of life; they view secondary school education as an impermissible exposure of their children to a "wordly" influence in conflict with their beliefs. The high school tends to emphasize intellectual and scientific accomplishments, self-distinction, competitiveness, worldly success, and social life with other students. Amish society emphasizes informal learning-through-doing; a life of "goodness," rather than a life of intellect; wisdom, rather than technical knowledge; community welfare, rather than competition; and separation from, rather than integration with, contemporary worldly society.

Formal high school education beyond the eighth grade is contrary to Amish beliefs also because it takes them away from their community, physically and emotionally, during the crucial and formative adolescent period of life. During this period, the children must acquire Amish attitudes favoring manual work and self-reliance and the specific skills needed to perform the adult role of an Amish farmer or housewife. They must learn to enjoy physical labor.

On the basis of such considerations, Dr. Hostetler[, an expert,] testified that compulsory high school attendance could not only result in great psychological harm to Amish children, because of the conflicts it would produce, but would also, in his opinion, ultimately result in the destruction of the Old Order Amish church community as it exists in the United States today. The testimony of Dr. Donald A. Erickson, an expert witness on education, also showed that the Amish succeed in preparing their high school age children to be productive members of the Amish community. The evidence also showed that the Amish have an excellent record as law-abiding and generally self-sufficient members of society.

I

There is no doubt as to the power of a State, having a high responsibility for education of its citizens, to impose reasonable regulations for the control and duration of basic education. See, e.g., *Pierce v. Society of Sisters*, 268 U.S. 510, 534 (1925). Providing public schools ranks at the very apex of the function of a State. Yet even this paramount responsibility was, in *Pierce*, made to yield to the right of parents to provide an equivalent education in a privately operated system. As that case suggests, the values of parental direction of the religious upbringing and education of their children in their early and formative years have a high place in our society. See also *Meyer v. Nebraska*, 262 U.S. 390 (1923). Thus, a State's interest in universal education, however highly we rank it, is not totally free from a balancing process when it impinges on fundamental rights and interests, such as those specifically protected by the Free Exercise Clause of the First Amendment, and the traditional interest of parents with respect to the religious upbringing of their children so long as they, in the words of *Pierce*, "prepare [them] for additional obligations."

It follows that in order for Wisconsin to compel school attendance beyond the eighth grade against a claim that such attendance interferes with the practice of a legitimate religious belief, it must appear either that the State does not deny the free exercise of religious belief by its requirement, or that there is a state interest of sufficient magnitude to override the interest claiming protection under the Free Exercise Clause.

The essence of all that has been said and written on the subject is that only those interests of the highest order and those not otherwise served can overbalance legitimate claims to the free exercise of religion.

II

We come then to the quality of the claims of the respondents. In evaluating those claims we must be careful to determine whether the Amish religious faith and their mode of life are, as they claim, inseparable and interdependent. A way of life, however virtuous and admirable, may not be interposed as a barrier to reasonable state regulation of education if it is based on purely secular considerations; to have the protection of the Religion Clauses, the claims must be rooted in religious belief. Although a determination of what is a "religious" belief or practice entitled to constitutional protection may present a most delicate question [as in *United States v. Ballard*, 322 U.S. 78 (1944)], the very concept of ordered liberty precludes allowing every person to make his own standards on matters of conduct in which society as a whole has important interests. Thus, if the Amish asserted their claims because of their subjective evaluation and rejection of the contemporary secular values accepted by the majority, their claims would not rest on a religious basis.

Giving no weight to such secular considerations, however, we see that the record in this case abundantly supports the claim that the traditional way of life of the Amish is not merely a matter of personal preference, but one of deep religious conviction, shared by an organized group, and intimately related to daily living. That the Old Order Amish daily life and religious practice stem from their faith is shown by the fact that it is in response to their literal interpretation of the Biblical injunction from the Epistle of Paul to the Romans, "be not conformed to this world...." This command is fundamental to the Amish faith. Moreover, for the Old Order Amish, religion is not simply a matter of theocratic belief. As the expert witnesses explained, the Old Order Amish religion pervades and determines virtually their entire way of life, regulating it with the detail of the Talmudic diet through the strictly enforced rules of the church community....

As the record so strongly shows, the values and programs of the modern secondary school are in sharp conflict with the fundamental mode of life mandated by the Amish religion. The conclusion is inescapable that secondary schooling, by exposing Amish children to worldly influences in terms of attitudes, goals, and values contrary to beliefs, and by substantially interfering with the religious development of the Amish child and his integration into the way of life of the Amish faith community at the crucial adolescent stage of development, contravenes the basic religious tenets and practice of the Amish faith, both as to the parent and the child.

The impact of the compulsory-attendance law on respondents' practice of the Amish religion is not only severe, but inescapable, for the Wisconsin law affirmatively compels them, under threat of criminal sanction, to perform acts undeniably at odds with fundamental tenets of their religious beliefs. It carries with it precisely the kind of objective danger to the free exercise of religion that the First Amendment was designed to prevent. As the record shows, compulsory school attendance to age 16 for Amish children carries with it a very real threat of undermining the Amish community and religious practice as they exist today; they must either abandon belief and be assimilated into society at large, or be forced to migrate to some other and more tolerant region.

III

[The State's] position is that the State's interest in universal compulsory formal secondary education to age 16 is so great that it is paramount to the undisputed claims of respondents that their mode of preparing their youth for Amish life is an essential part of their religious belief and practice.

Wisconsin concedes that under the Religion Clauses religious beliefs are absolutely free from the State's control, but it argues that "actions," even though religiously grounded, are outside the protection of the First Amendment. But our decisions have rejected the idea that religiously grounded conduct is always outside the protection of the Free Exercise Clause. It is true that activities of individuals, even when religiously based, are often subject to regulation by the States in the exercise of their undoubted power to promote the health, safety, and general welfare, or the Federal Government in the exercise of its delegated powers. See, e.g., *Prince v. Massachusetts*, 321 U.S. 158 (1944); *Reynolds v. United States*, 98 U.S. 145 (1879). But to agree that religiously grounded conduct must often be subject to the broad police power of the State is not to deny that there are areas of conduct protected by the Free Exercise Clause of the First Amendment and thus beyond the power of the State to control, even under regulations of general applicability. E.g., *Sherbert v. Verner*, 374 U.S. 398 (1963); *Cantwell v. Connecticut*, 310 U.S. 296, 303–304 (1940). This case, therefore, does not become easier because respondents were convicted for their "actions" in refusing to send their children to the public high school; in this context belief and action cannot be neatly confined in logic-tight compartments.

Nor can this case be disposed of on the grounds that Wisconsin's requirement for school attendance to age 16 applies uniformly to all citizens of the State and does not, on its face, discriminate against religions or a particular religion, or that it is motivated by legitimate secular concerns. A regulation neutral on its face may, in its application, nonetheless offend the constitutional requirement for governmental neutrality if it unduly burdens the free exercise of religion. *Sherbert v. Verner.*

We turn, then, to the State's broader contention that its interest in its system of compulsory education is so compelling that even the established religious practices of the Amish must give way. Where fundamental claims of religious freedom are at stake, we must searchingly examine the interests that the State seeks to promote by its requirement for compulsory education to age 16, and the impediment to those objectives that would flow from recognizing the claimed Amish exemption.

The State advances two primary arguments in support of its system of compulsory education. It notes that some degree of education is necessary to prepare citizens to participate effectively and intelligently in our open political system if we are to preserve freedom and independence. Further, education prepares individuals to be self-reliant and self-sufficient participants in society. We accept these propositions.

However, the evidence adduced by the Amish in this case is persuasively to the effect that an additional one or two years of formal high school for Amish children in place of their long-established program of informal vocational education would do little to serve those interests. It is one thing to say that compulsory education for a year or two beyond the eighth grade may be necessary when its goal is the preparation of the child for life in modern society as the majority live, but it is quite another if the goal of education be viewed as the preparation of the child for life in the separated agrarian community that is the keystone of the Amish faith.

The State attacks respondents' position as one fostering "ignorance" from which the child must be protected by the State. No one can question the State's duty to protect children from ignorance but this argument does not square with the facts disclosed in the record. [T]his record strongly shows that the Amish community has been a highly successful social unit within our society[.] Its members are productive and very law-abiding members of society; they reject public welfare in any of its usual modern forms. The Congress itself recognized their self-sufficiency by authorizing exemption of such groups as the Amish from the obligation to pay social security taxes.[11]

It is neither fair nor correct to suggest that the Amish are opposed to education beyond the eighth grade level. What this record shows is that they are opposed to

---

11. The record in this case establishes without contradiction that the Green County Amish had never been known to commit crimes, that none had been known to receive public assistance, and that none were unemployed.

conventional formal education of the type provided by a certified high school because it comes at the child's crucial adolescent period of religious development.

The State, however, supports its interest in providing an additional one or two years of compulsory high school education to Amish children because of the possibility that some such children will choose to leave the Amish community, and that if this occurs they will be ill-equipped for life. The State argues that if Amish children leave their church they should not be in the position of making their way in the world without the education available in the one or two additional years the State requires. However, on this record, that argument is highly speculative. There is no specific evidence of the loss of Amish adherents by attrition, nor is there any showing that upon leaving the Amish community Amish children, with their practical agricultural training and habits of industry and self-reliance, would become burdens on society because of educational shortcomings. To the contrary, not only do the Amish accept the necessity for formal schooling through the eighth grade level, but continue to provide what has been characterized by the undisputed testimony of expert educators as an "ideal" vocational education for their children in the adolescent years.

Insofar as the State's claim rests on the view that a brief additional period of formal education is imperative to enable the Amish to participate effectively and intelligently in our democratic process, it must fall. The Amish alternative to formal secondary school education has enabled them to function effectively in their day-to-day life under self-imposed limitations on relations with the world, and to survive and prosper in contemporary society as a separate, sharply identifiable and highly self-sufficient community for more than 200 years in this country. In itself this is strong evidence that they are capable of fulfilling the social and political responsibilities of citizenship without compelled attendance beyond the eighth grade at the price of jeopardizing their free exercise of religious belief.

The independence and successful social functioning of the Amish community for a period approaching almost three centuries and more than 200 years in this country are strong evidence that there is at best a speculative gain, in terms of meeting the duties of citizenship, from an additional one or two years of compulsory formal education. Against this background it would require a more particularized showing from the State on this point to justify the severe interference with religious freedom such additional compulsory attendance would entail.

IV

This case, of course, is not one in which any harm to the physical or mental health of the child or to the public safety, peace, order, or welfare has been demonstrated or may be properly inferred. The record is to the contrary.

Contrary to the suggestion of the dissenting opinion of MR. JUSTICE DOUGLAS, our holding today in no degree depends on the assertion of the religious interest of the child as contrasted with that of the parents. It is the parents who are subject to prosecution here for failing to cause their children to attend school, and it is their right of free exercise, not that of their children, that must determine Wisconsin's power to impose criminal penalties on the parent. The dissent argues that a child who expresses a desire to attend public high school in conflict with the wishes of his parents should not be prevented from doing so. There is no reason for the Court to consider that point since it is not an issue in the case. The children are not parties to this litigation. The State has at no point tried this case on the theory that respondents were preventing their children from attending school against their expressed desires, and indeed the record is to the contrary. The State's position from the outset has been that it is empowered to apply its compulsory-attendance law to Amish parents in the same manner as to other parents — that is, without regard to the wishes of the child. That is the claim we reject today.

Our holding in no way determines the proper resolution of possible competing interests of parents, children, and the State in an appropriate state court proceeding in which the power of the State is asserted on the theory that Amish parents are preventing their minor children from attending high school despite their expressed desires to the contrary. Recognition of the claim of the State in such a proceeding would, of course, call into question traditional concepts of parental control over the religious upbringing and education of their minor children recognized in this Court's past decisions. It is clear that such an intrusion by a State into family decisions in the area of religious training would give rise to grave questions of religious freedom comparable to those raised here and those presented in *Pierce v. Society of Sisters*, 268 U.S. 510 (1925). On this record we neither reach nor decide those issues.

Indeed it seems clear that if the State is empowered, as parens patriae, to "save" a child from himself or his Amish parents by requiring an additional two years of compulsory formal high school education, the State will in large measure influence, if not determine, the religious future of the child. Even more markedly than in *Prince*, therefore, this case involves the fundamental interest of parents, as contrasted with that of the State, to guide the religious future and education of their children. The history and culture of Western civilization reflect a strong tradition of parental concern for the nurture and upbringing of their children. This primary role of the parents in the upbringing of their children is now established beyond debate as an enduring American tradition.

However read, the Court's holding in *Pierce* stands as a charter of the rights of parents to direct the religious upbringing of their children. And, when the interests of parenthood are combined with a free exercise claim of the nature revealed by this record, more than merely a "reasonable relation to some purpose within the competency of the State" is required to sustain the validity of the State's requirement under the First Amendment. To be sure, the power of the parent, even when linked to a free exercise claim, may be subject to limitation under *Prince* if it appears that parental decisions will jeopardize the health or safety of the child, or have a potential for significant social burdens. But in this case, the record strongly indicates that accommodating the religious objections of the Amish by forgoing one, or at most two, additional years of compulsory education will not impair the physical or mental health of the child, or result in an inability to be self-supporting or to discharge the duties and responsibilities of citizenship, or in any other way materially detract from the welfare of society.

Mr. Justice Powell and Mr. Justice Rehnquist took no part in the consideration or decision of this case.

Mr. Justice Stewart, with whom Mr. Justice Brennan joins, concurring. [Opinion omitted.]

Mr. Justice White, with whom Mr. Justice Brennan and Mr. Justice Stewart join, concurring. [Opinion omitted.]

Mr. Justice Douglas, dissenting in part.

I

I agree with the Court that the religious scruples of the Amish are opposed to the education of their children beyond the grade schools, yet I disagree with the Court's conclusion that the matter is within the dispensation of parents alone. The Court's analysis assumes that the only interests at stake in the case are those of the Amish parents on the one hand, and those of the State on the other. The difficulty with this approach is that, despite the Court's claim, the parents are seeking to vindicate not only their own free exercise claims, but also those of their high-school-age children.

[I]t is essential to reach the question to decide the case because no analysis of religious-liberty claims can take place in a vacuum. If the parents in this case are allowed a religious exemption, the inevitable effect is to impose the parents' notions of religious duty upon their children. Where the child is mature enough to express potentially conflicting desires, it would be an invasion of the child's rights to permit such an imposition without canvassing his views. As the child has no other effective forum, it is in this litigation that his rights should be considered. And, if an Amish child desires to attend high school, and is mature enough to have that desire respected, the State may well be able to override the parents' religiously motivated objections.

Religion is an individual experience. It is not necessary, nor even appropriate, for every Amish child to express his views on the subject in a prosecution of a single adult. Crucial, however, are the views of the child whose parent is the subject of the suit. Frieda Yoder has in fact testified that her own religious views are opposed to high-school education. But Frieda Yoder's views may not be those of Vernon Yutzy or Barbara Miller. I must dissent, therefore, as to respondents Adin Yutzy and Wallace Miller as their motion to dismiss also raised the question of their children's religious liberty.

II

This issue has never been squarely presented before today. Our opinions are full of talk about the power of the parents over the child's education. Recent cases, however, have clearly held that the children themselves have constitutionally protectible interests. These children are "persons" within the meaning of the Bill of Rights. We have so held over and over again. In *Tinker v. Des Moines Independent Community School District*, 393 U.S. 503 [(1969)], we dealt with 13-year-old, 15-year-old, and 16-year-old students who wore armbands to public schools and were disciplined for doing so.

On this important and vital matter of education, I think the children should be entitled to be heard. While the parents, absent dissent, normally speak for the entire family, the education of the child is a matter on which the child will often have decided views. He may want to be a pianist or an astronaut or an oceanographer. To do so he will have to break from the Amish tradition.[2]

It is the future of the student, not the future of the parents, that is imperiled by today's decision. If a parent keeps his child out of school beyond the grade school, then the child will be forever barred from entry into the new and amazing world of diversity that we have today. The child may decide that that is the preferred course, or he may rebel. It is the student's judgment, not his parents', that is essential if we are to give full meaning to what we have said about the Bill of Rights and of the right of students to be masters of their own destiny. If he is harnessed to the Amish way of life by those in authority over him and if his education is truncated, his entire life may be stunted and deformed. The child, therefore, should be given an opportunity to be heard before the State gives the exemption which we honor today.

Exercise 7:

1. Why did Chief Justice Burger spend so much time detailing the Amish's history, practices, and beliefs?

2. What other religious belief systems, if any, could receive the same protection as the Amish for their religiously-motivated way of life? Or are the Amish unique?

3. How, according to the Supreme Court, did Wisconsin's compulsory education law infringe on Yoder's free exercise of religion?

4. Wisconsin argued that the Free Exercise Clause did not protect Yoder's religiously-motivated *activity* (as opposed to *belief*, which the Clause did protect). Articulate Wisconsin's argument and its supporting bases. How did the Supreme Court respond?

5. What analysis did the *Yoder* Court employ to evaluate Yoder's Free Exercise Clause claim? What is the source of that analysis? Is that the appropriate analysis?

6. What was Wisconsin's compelling state interest it argued was advanced by its compulsory education law? Did the Court agree?

7. Was Wisconsin's compulsory education law sufficiently tailored to achieve Wisconsin's state interest? Why or why not?

8. You can get a feel for the burden on the state in contexts of strict scrutiny from the Court's rejection of Wisconsin's claim that it must provide more-than-eighth grade education because some Amish children leave the community and would be without the education necessary to thrive outside of the Amish community. The majority's response was that the state had failed to provide sufficient empirical evidence of its point. The Court did not deny that members of the Amish community leave

---

2. A significant number of Amish children do leave the Old Order. Professor Hostetler notes that [i]n one Pennsylvania church, he observed a defection rate of 30%. Rates up to 50% have been reported by others.

the community; how could it? Instead, the Court concluded that the state's failure to provide evidence of such departures and the quantity of such departures fatally undermined the state's argument.

9. What are the limits to the Court's reasoning? In particular, under what circumstances may a state limit parental control over children?

10. Does the majority's citation to and reliance on Lochner Era cases, such as *Pierce* and *Meyer* make *Yoder* an illegitimate decision? If not, do you believe that *Lochner* was legitimate?

11. The majority and Justice Douglas, in dissent, engaged in a now-famous debate over the constitutional relationship between the Amish parents and their children. Explain each side's position in this debate. Whose position is correct?

12. Assume that you agreed with Justice Douglas' position. How, in practice, would a state adjudicate whether a particular child should be able to attend high school, contrary to that child's parents' wishes? Would the child bring a lawsuit? What standard would a court employ to decide the child's claim? Who would bear the burden? Do these questions undercut Justice Douglas' position?

13. Is there a way to cabin the scope of Justice Douglas' position so that it does not undermine the right of parents to rear their children, as articulated in *Pierce* and *Meyer*?

14. Justice Douglas stated that "[r]eligion is an individual experience." Is that true? Justice Douglas did not cite a source for this claim; what source would one cite to support this claim? Or is the claim so obvious that judges may take judicial notice of it?

15. Keep Justice Douglas' characterization of religion in mind next chapter, when we review the Establishment Clause. Does at least some of the disagreement in that area of law stem from different conceptions of the nature of religion as an individual or communal experience?

16. The Supreme Court rejected Wisconsin's argument that the Free Exercise Clause did not protect the Yoder because the state's compulsory school attendance law applied to all Wisconsin children: "A regulation neutral on its face may, in its application, nonetheless offend the constitutional requirement for governmental neutrality if it unduly burdens the free exercise of religion." Keep this response in mind as we read the next case.

———————

Following *Yoder*, the Supreme Court continued to face free exercise challenges to federal and state laws. Some of these the Court accepted, and others it rejected, though the Court appeared to hew very closely to *Sherbert* by approving only those claims in the unemployment compensation context, *Thomas v. Review Board of the Indiana Employment Security Division*, 450 U.S. 707 (1981); *Hobbie v. Unemployment Appeals Commission of Florida*, 480 U.S. 136 (1987), and rejecting claims outside that context, *United States v. Lee*, 455 U.S. 252 (1982); *Bowen v. Roy*, 476 U.S. 693 (1986); *Goldman v. Weinberger*, 475 U.S. 503 (1986); *Lyng v. Northwest Indian Cemetery Pro-*

tective Ass'n, 485 U.S. 439 (1988). Throughout this period, the Court continued to utilize the analysis set out in *Sherbert*.

F. The *Smith* Rule

1. *Employment Division v. Smith*

Then came an unexpected bombshell in 1990, *Employment Division v. Smith*, 494 U.S. 872 (1990). No one anticipated *Smith* to transform free exercise law. It appeared to be a run-of-the-mill claim for a free exercise exemption from state law that infringed on religious exercise. The parties in their briefs and during oral argument employed the standard *Sherbert* analysis. Therefore, the Supreme Court's articulation of the *Smith* Rule stunned everyone.

Employment Division, Department of Human Resources of Oregon v. Smith

494 U.S. 872 (1990)

JUSTICE SCALIA delivered the opinion of the Court.

This case requires us to decide whether the Free Exercise Clause of the First Amendment permits the State of Oregon to include religiously inspired peyote use within the reach of its general criminal prohibition on use of that drug, and thus permits the State to deny unemployment benefits to persons dismissed from their jobs because of such religiously inspired use.

I

Oregon law prohibits the knowing or intentional possession of a "controlled substance" unless the substance has been prescribed by a medical practitioner. Ore. Rev. Stat. §475.992(4) (1987). The law defines "controlled substance" as a drug classified in the Federal Controlled Substances Act, as modified by the State Board of Pharmacy. Persons who violate this provision by possessing a controlled substance listed on Schedule I are "guilty of a Class B felony." As compiled by the State Board of Pharmacy, Schedule I contains the drug peyote, a hallucinogen.

Respondents Alfred Smith and Galen Black (hereinafter respondents) were fired from their jobs with a private drug rehabilitation organization because they ingested peyote for sacramental purposes at a ceremony of the Native American Church, of which both are members. When respondents applied to petitioner Employment Division (hereinafter petitioner) for unemployment compensation, they were determined to be ineligible for benefits because they had been discharged for work-related "misconduct." The Oregon Court of Appeals reversed that determination, holding that the denial of benefits violated respondents' free exercise rights under the First Amendment.

[T]he Oregon Supreme Court held that respondents' religiously inspired use of peyote fell within the prohibition of the Oregon statute. It then considered whether that prohibition was valid under the Free Exercise Clause, and concluded that it was not. The court [held] that the State could not deny unemployment benefits to respondents for having engaged in that practice.

II

Respondents' claim for relief rests on our decisions in *Sherbert v. Verner*, in which we held that a State could not condition the availability of unemployment insurance on an individual's willingness to forgo conduct required by his religion. Now that the Oregon Supreme Court has confirmed that Oregon does prohibit the religious use of peyote, we proceed to consider whether that prohibition is permissible under the Free Exercise Clause.

A

The Free Exercise Clause of the First Amendment provides that "Congress shall make no law respecting an establishment of religion, or *prohibiting the free exercise thereof....*" U.S. Const., Amdt. 1 (emphasis added.) The free exercise of religion means, first and foremost, the right to believe and profess whatever religious doctrine one desires. Thus, the First Amendment obviously excludes all "governmental regulation of religious *beliefs* as such." The government may not compel affirmation of religious belief, punish the expression of religious doctrines it believes to be false, impose special disabilities on the basis of religious views or religious status, or lend its power to one or the other side in controversies over religious authority or dogma.

But the "exercise of religion" often involves not only belief and profession but the performance of (or abstention from) physical acts: assembling with others for a worship service, participating in sacramental use of bread and wine, proselytizing, abstaining from certain foods or certain modes of transportation. It would be true, we think (though no case of ours has involved the point), that a State would be "prohibiting the free exercise [of religion]" if it sought to ban such acts or abstentions only when they are engaged in for religious reasons, or only because of the religious belief that they display. It would doubtless be unconstitutional, for example, to ban the casting of "statues that are to be used for worship purposes," or to prohibit bowing down before a golden calf.

Respondents in the present case, however, seek to carry the meaning of "prohibiting the free exercise [of religion]" one large step further. They contend that their religious motivation for using peyote places them beyond the reach of a criminal law that is not specifically directed at their religious practice, and that is concededly constitutional as applied to those who use the drug for other reasons. They assert, in other words, that "prohibiting the free exercise [of religion]" includes requiring any individual to observe a generally applicable law that requires (or forbids) the performance of an act that his religious belief forbids (or requires). As a textual matter, we do not think the words must be given that meaning. It is no more necessary to regard the collection of a general tax, for example, as "prohibiting the free exercise [of religion]" by those citizens who believe support of organized government to be sinful, than it is to regard the same tax as "abridging the freedom ... of the press" of those publishing companies that must pay the tax as a condition of staying in business. It is a permissible reading of the text, in the one case as in the other, to say that if prohibiting the exercise of religion (or burdening the activity of printing) is not the object of the tax but merely the incidental effect of a generally applicable and otherwise valid provision, the First Amendment has not been offended. *Citizen Publishing Co. v. United States*, 394 U.S. 131, 139 (1969) (upholding application of antitrust laws to press).

We have never held that an individual's religious beliefs excuse him from compliance with an otherwise valid law prohibiting conduct that the State is free to regulate. On the contrary, the record of more than a century of our free exercise jurisprudence contradicts that proposition. We first had occasion to assert that principle in *Reynolds v. United States*, 98 U.S. 145 (1879), where we rejected the claim that criminal laws against polygamy could not be constitutionally applied to those whose religion commanded the practice. "Laws," we said, "are made for the government of actions, and while they cannot interfere with mere religious belief and opinions, they may with practices. Can a man excuse his practices to the contrary because of his religious belief? To permit this would be to make the professed doctrines of religious belief superior to the law of the land, and in effect to permit every citizen to become a law unto himself."

Subsequent decisions have consistently held that the right of free exercise does not relieve an individual of the obligation to comply with a "valid and neutral law of general applicability on the ground that the law proscribes (or prescribes) conduct that his religion prescribes (or proscribes)." In *Prince v. Massachusetts*, 321 U.S. 158 (1944), we held that a mother could be prosecuted under the child labor laws for using her children to dispense literature in the streets, her religious motivation notwithstanding. *Braunfeld v. Brown*, 366 U.S. 599 (1961), upheld Sunday-closing laws against the claim that they burdened the religious practices of persons whose religions compelled them to refrain from work on other days.

Our most recent decision involving a neutral, generally applicable regulatory law that compelled activity forbidden by an individual's religion was *United States v. Lee*, 455 U.S. [252,] 258–261 [(1982)]. There, an Amish employer, on behalf of himself and his employees, sought exemption from collection and payment of Social Security taxes on the ground that the Amish faith prohibited participation in governmental support programs. We rejected the claim that an exemption was constitutionally required. There would be no way, we observed, to distinguish the Amish believer's objection to Social Security taxes from the religious objections that others might have to the collection or use of other taxes.

The only decisions in which we have held that the First Amendment bars application of a neutral, generally applicable law to religiously motivated action have involved not the Free Exercise Clause alone, but the Free Exercise Clause in conjunction with other constitutional protections, such as freedom of speech and of the press, see *Cantwell v. Connecticut*, or the right of parents, acknowledged in *Pierce v. Society of Sisters* to direct the education of their children, see *Wisconsin v. Yoder*. And it is easy to envision a case in which a challenge on freedom of association grounds would likewise be reinforced by Free Exercise Clause concerns.

The present case does not present such a hybrid situation, but a free exercise claim unconnected with any communicative activity or parental right. Respondents urge us to hold, quite simply, that when otherwise prohibitable conduct is accompanied by religious convictions, not only the convictions but the conduct itself must be free from governmental regulation. We have never held that, and decline to do so now. There being no contention that Oregon's drug law represents an attempt to regulate religious beliefs, the communication of religious beliefs, or the raising of one's children in those beliefs, the rule to which we have adhered ever since *Reynolds* plainly controls.

B

Respondents argue that even though exemption from generally applicable criminal laws need not automatically be extended to religiously motivated actors, at least the claim for a religious exemption must be evaluated under the balancing test set forth in *Sherbert v. Verner*. Applying that test we have, on three occasions, invalidated state unemployment compensation rules that conditioned the availability of benefits upon an applicant's willingness to work under conditions forbidden by his religion. See *Sherbert v. Verner; Thomas v. Review Bd. of Indiana Employment Security Div.*, 450 U.S. 707 (1981); *Hobbie v. Unemployment Appeals Comm'n of Florida*, 480 U.S. 136 (1987). We have never invalidated any governmental action on the basis of the *Sherbert* test except the denial of unemployment compensation. Although we have sometimes purported to apply the *Sherbert* test in contexts other than that, we have always found the test satisfied, see *United States v. Lee*, 455 U.S. 252 (1982); *Gillette v. United States*, 401 U.S. 437 (1971). In recent years we have abstained from applying the *Sherbert* test (outside the unemployment compensation field) at all. In *Bowen v. Roy*, 476 U.S. 693 (1986), we declined to apply *Sherbert* analysis to a federal statutory scheme that required benefit applicants and recipients to provide their Social Security numbers. In *Lyng v. Northwest Indian Cemetery Protective Assn.*, 485 U.S. 439 (1988), we declined to apply *Sherbert* analysis to the Government's logging and road construction activities on lands used for religious purposes by several Native American Tribes, even though it was undisputed that the activities "could have devastating effects on traditional Indian religious practices[.]" In *Goldman v. Weinberger*, 475 U.S. 503 (1986), we rejected application of the *Sherbert* test to military dress regulations that forbade the wearing of yarmulkes.

Even if we were inclined to breathe into *Sherbert* some life beyond the unemployment compensation field, we would not apply it to require exemptions from a generally applicable criminal law. The *Sherbert* test, it must be recalled, was developed in a context that lent itself to individualized governmental assessment of the reasons for the relevant conduct. As the plurality pointed out in *Roy*, our decisions in the unemployment cases stand for the proposition that where the State has in place a system of individual exemptions, it may not refuse to extend that system to cases of "religious hardship" without compelling reason.

Whether or not the decisions are that limited, they at least have nothing to do with an across-the-board criminal prohibition on a particular form of conduct. Although, as noted earlier, we have sometimes used the *Sherbert* test to analyze free exercise challenges to such laws, we have never applied the test to invalidate one. We conclude today that the sounder approach, and the approach in accord with the vast majority of our precedents, is to hold the test inapplicable to such challenges. The government's ability to enforce generally applicable prohibitions of socially harmful conduct, like its ability to carry out other aspects of public policy, "cannot depend on measuring the effects of a governmental action on a re-ligious objector's spiritual development." To make an individual's obligation to obey such a law contingent upon the law's coincidence with his religious beliefs, except where the State's interest is "compelling"—permitting him, by virtue of his beliefs, "to become a law unto himself"—contradicts both constitutional tradition and common sense.

The "compelling government interest" requirement seems benign, because it is fa-miliar from other fields. But using it as the standard that must be met before the government may accord different treatment on the basis of race, or before the gov-ernment may regulate the content of speech, is not remotely comparable to using it for the purpose asserted here. What it produces in those other fields—equality of treatment and an unrestricted flow of contending speech—are constitutional norms; what it would produce here—a private right to ignore generally applicable laws— is a constitutional anomaly.[3]

Nor is it possible to limit the impact of respondents' proposal by requiring a "com-pelling state interest" only when the conduct prohibited is "central" to the individual's religion. It is no more appropriate for judges to determine the "centrality" of religious beliefs before applying a "compelling interest" test in the free exercise field, than it would be for them to determine the "importance" of ideas before applying the "com-pelling interest" test in the free speech field. What principle of law or logic can be brought to bear to contradict a believer's assertion that a particular act is "central" to his personal faith? Repeatedly and in many different contexts, we have warned that

---

3. JUSTICE O'CONNOR suggests that "[t]here is nothing talismanic about neutral laws of general applicability," and that all laws burdening religious practices should be subject to compelling-interest scrutiny because "the First Amendment unequivocally makes freedom of religion, like freedom from race discrimination and freedom of speech, a 'constitutional nor[m],' not an 'anomaly.'" But this com-parison with other fields supports, rather than undermines, the conclusion we draw today. Just as we subject to the most exacting scrutiny laws that make classifications based on race, or on the content of speech, so too we strictly scrutinize governmental classifications based on religion. But we have held that race-neutral laws that have the *effect* of disproportionately disadvantaging a particular racial group do not thereby become subject to compelling-interest analysis under the Equal Protection Clause, see *Washington v. Davis*, 426 U.S. 229 (1976); and we have held that generally applicable laws unconcerned with regulating speech that have the *effect* of interfering with speech do not thereby be-come subject to compelling-interest analysis under the First Amendment. Our conclusion that generally applicable, religion-neutral laws that have the effect of burdening a particular religious practice need not be justified by a compelling governmental interest is the only approach compatible with these precedents.

courts must not presume to determine the place of a particular belief in a religion or the plausibility of a religious claim.

If the "compelling interest" test is to be applied at all, then, it must be applied across the board, to all actions thought to be religiously commanded. Moreover, if "compelling interest" really means what it says (and watering it down here would subvert its rigor in the other fields where it is applied), many laws will not meet the test. Any society adopting such a system would be courting anarchy, but that danger increases in direct proportion to the society's diversity of religious beliefs, and its determination to coerce or suppress none of them. Precisely because "we are a cosmopolitan nation made up of people of almost every conceivable religious preference," and precisely because we value and protect that religious divergence, we cannot afford the luxury of deeming *presumptively invalid*, as applied to the religious objector, every regulation of conduct that does not protect an interest of the highest order. The rule respondents favor would open the prospect of constitutionally required religious exemptions from civic obligations of almost every conceivable kind—ranging from compulsory military service, to the payment of taxes, to health and safety regulation such as manslaughter and child neglect laws, compulsory vaccination laws, drug laws, and traffic laws, to social welfare legislation such as minimum wage laws, child labor laws, animal cruelty laws, environmental protection laws, and laws providing for equality of opportunity for the races. The First Amendment's protection of religious liberty does not require this.

Values that are protected against government interference through enshrinement in the Bill of Rights are not thereby banished from the political process. Just as a society that believes in the negative protection accorded to the press by the First Amendment is likely to enact laws that affirmatively foster the dissemination of the printed word, so also a society that believes in the negative protection accorded to religious belief can be expected to be solicitous of that value in its legislation as well. It is therefore not surprising that a number of States [including Arizona, Colorado, and New Mexico] have made an exception to their drug laws for sacramental peyote use. But to say that a nondiscriminatory religious-practice exemption is permitted, or even that it is desirable, is not to say that it is constitutionally required, and that the appropriate occasions for its creation can be discerned by the courts. It may fairly be said that leaving accommodation to the political process will place at a relative disadvantage those religious practices that are not widely engaged in; but that unavoidable consequence of democratic government must be preferred to a system in which each conscience is a law unto itself or in which judges weigh the social importance of all laws against the centrality of all religious beliefs.

Because respondents' ingestion of peyote was prohibited under Oregon law, and because that prohibition is constitutional, Oregon may, consistent with the Free Exercise Clause, deny respondents unemployment compensation when their dismissal results from use of the drug.

JUSTICE O'CONNOR, with whom JUSTICE BRENNAN, JUSTICE MARSHALL, and JUSTICE BLACKMUN join as to Parts I and II, concurring in the judgment.

II

A

As the Court recognizes, the "free *exercise*" of religion often, if not invariably, re-quires the performance of (or abstention from) certain acts. "[B]elief and action can-not be neatly confined in logic-tight compartments." Because the First Amendment does not distinguish between religious belief and religious conduct, conduct motivated by sincere religious belief, like the belief itself, must be at least presumptively protected by the Free Exercise Clause.

The Court today, however, interprets the Clause to permit the government to prohibit, without justification, conduct mandated by an individual's religious beliefs, so long as that prohibition is generally applicable. But a law that prohibits certain conduct—conduct that happens to be an act of worship for someone—manifestly does prohibit that person's free exercise of his religion. A person who is barred from engaging in religiously motivated conduct is barred from freely exercising his religion.

The Court responds that generally applicable laws are "one large step" removed from laws aimed at specific religious practices. The First Amendment, however, does not distinguish between laws that are generally applicable and laws that target par-ticular religious practices. Indeed, few States would be so naive as to enact a law directly prohibiting or burdening a religious practice as such. Our free exercise cases have all concerned generally applicable laws that had the effect of significantly bur-dening a religious practice.

To say that a person's right to free exercise has been burdened, of course, does not mean that he has an absolute right to engage in the conduct. Under our established First Amendment jurisprudence, we have recognized that the freedom to act, unlike the freedom to believe, cannot be absolute. Instead, we have respected both the First Amendment's express textual mandate and the governmental interest in regulation of conduct by requiring the government to justify any substantial burden on religiously motivated conduct by a compelling state interest and by means narrowly tailored to achieve that interest. [JUSTICE O'CONNOR cited ten cases, including *Sherbert* and *Yoder*.] The compelling interest test effectuates the First Amendment's command that religious liberty is an independent liberty, that it occupies a preferred position, and that the Court will not permit encroachments upon this liberty, whether direct or indirect, unless required by clear and compelling governmental interests "of the highest order[.]"

The Court attempts to support its narrow reading of the Clause by claiming that "[w]e have never held that an individual's religious beliefs excuse him from compliance with an otherwise valid law prohibiting conduct that the State is free to regulate." But as the Court later notes, as it must, in cases such as *Cantwell* and *Yoder* we have in fact interpreted the Free Exercise Clause to forbid application of a generally applicable prohibition to religiously motivated conduct. Indeed, in *Yoder* we expressly rejected the interpretation the Court now adopts:

"But to agree that religiously grounded conduct must often be subject to the broad police power of the State is not to deny that there are areas of conduct protected by the Free Exercise Clause of the First Amendment and thus beyond the power of the State to control, *even under regulations of general applicability.* . . .

"A regulation neutral on its face may, in its application, nonetheless offend the constitutional requirement for government neutrality if it unduly burdens the free exercise of religion."

The Court endeavors to escape from our decisions in *Cantwell* and *Yoder* by labeling them "hybrid" decisions, but there is no denying that both cases expressly relied on the Free Exercise Clause, and that we have consistently regarded those cases as part of the mainstream of our free exercise jurisprudence. Moreover, in each of the other cases cited by the Court to support its categorical rule, we rejected the particular constitutional claims before us only after carefully weighing the competing interests. See *Prince v. Massachusetts*, 321 U.S. 158, 168–170 (1944) (state interest in regulating children's activities justifies denial of religious exemption from child labor laws); *Braunfeld v. Brown*, 366 U.S. 599, 608–609 (1961) (state interest in uniform day of rest justifies denial of religious exemption from Sunday closing law); *Lee*, 455 U.S., at 258–259 (state interest in comprehensive Social Security system justifies denial of religious exemption from mandatory participation requirement). That we rejected the free exercise claims in those cases hardly calls into question the applicability of First Amendment doctrine in the first place. Indeed, it is surely unusual to judge the vitality of a constitutional doctrine by looking to the win-loss record of the plaintiffs who happen to come before us.

B

Legislatures, of course, have always been "left free to reach actions which were in violation of social duties or subversive of good order." Yet because of the close relationship between conduct and religious belief, "[i]n every case the power to regulate must be so exercised as not, in attaining a permissible end, unduly to infringe the protected freedom." Once it has been shown that a government regulation or criminal prohibition burdens the free exercise of religion, we have consistently asked the government to demonstrate that unbending application of its regulation to the religious objector "is essential to accomplish an overriding governmental interest," or represents "the least restrictive means of achieving some compelling state interest[.]" To me, the sounder approach—the approach more consistent with our role as judges to decide each case on its individual merits—is to apply this test in each case to determine whether the burden on the specific plaintiffs before us is constitutionally significant and whether the particular criminal interest asserted by the State before us is compelling. Even if, as an empirical matter, a government's criminal laws might usually serve a compelling interest in health, safety, or public order, the First Amendment at least requires a case-by-case determination of the question, sensitive to the facts of each particular claim. Given the range of conduct that a State might legitimately make criminal, we cannot assume, merely because a law carries criminal sanctions and is generally applicable, that the First Amendment *never* requires the State to grant a limited exemption for religiously motivated conduct.

Moreover, we have not "rejected" or "declined to apply" the compelling interest test in our recent cases. In both *Bowen v. Roy* and *Lyng v. Northwest Indian Cemetery Protective Assn.*, for example, we expressly distinguished *Sherbert* on the ground that the First Amendment does not "require the Government *itself* to behave in ways that the individual believes will further his or her spiritual development. The Free Exercise Clause simply cannot be understood to require the Government to conduct its own internal affairs in ways that comport with the religious beliefs of particular citizens." This distinction makes sense because "the Free Exercise Clause is written in terms of what the government cannot do to the individual, not in terms of what the individual can exact from the government." Because the case *sub judice,* like the other cases in which we have applied *Sherbert,* plainly falls into the former category, I would apply those established precedents to the facts of this case.

Similarly, the other cases cited by the Court for the proposition that we have rejected application of the *Sherbert* test outside the unemployment compensation field, are distinguishable because they arose in the narrow, specialized contexts in which we have not traditionally required the government to justify a burden on religious conduct by articulating a compelling interest. See *Goldman v. Weinberger,* 475 U.S. 503, 507 (1986) ("Our review of military regulations challenged on First Amendment grounds is far more deferential than constitutional review of similar laws or regulations designed for civilian society"). That we did not apply the compelling interest test in these cases says nothing about whether the test should continue to apply in paradigm free exercise cases such as the one presented here.

Finally, the Court today suggests that the disfavoring of minority religions is an "unavoidable consequence" under our system of government and that accommodation of such religions must be left to the political process. In my view, however, the First Amendment was enacted precisely to protect the rights of those whose religious practices are not shared by the majority and may be viewed with hostility. The history of our free exercise doctrine amply demonstrates the harsh impact majoritarian rule has had on unpopular or emerging religious groups such as the Jehovah's Witnesses and the Amish.

JUSTICE BLACKMUN, with whom JUSTICE BRENNAN and JUSTICE MARSHALL join, dissenting. [Opinion omitted.]

Exercise 8:

1. What is *Smith's* holding? What are neutral and/or generally applicable laws?

2. How did *Smith* change the law from before the case?

3. Would *Yoder* come out the same way today, after *Smith*?

4. There was little indication before the Court issued its opinion that *Smith* would be anything other than a doctrinally standard free exercise case. The parties did not argue, in their briefs or oral argument, for or against what became the *Smith* Rule.

What accounts, do you think, for the genesis of the *Smith* Rule *ex nihilio*? Was it sound judicial practice for the *Smith* Court to not request additional briefing on the potential *Smith* Rule?

5. The Court stated that: "It would be true, we think (though no case of ours has involved the point), that a State would be 'prohibiting the free exercise [of religion]' if it sought to ban such acts or abstentions only when they are engaged in for religious reasons, or only because of the religious belief that they display." Why do you think the Court has not faced a case such as this?

6. What arguments did Justice Scalia provide for rejecting the *Sherbert*, strict scrutiny analysis, and adopting the *Smith* Rule in its place? Are you persuaded?

7. Justice Scalia spent much of his majority opinion parsing precedent. Many of the Court's precedents, Justice Scalia was able to argue, supported the *Smith* Rule. However, there were some that did not fit. How did Justice Scalia characterize these precedents?

8. Is Justice Scalia's "hybrid rights" label an accurate characterization of cases such as *Cantwell* and *Yoder*?

9. The *Smith* majority claimed that strict scrutiny was appropriate in the context of unemployment compensation, such as *Sherbert* itself. However, Smith himself was challenging the denial of unemployment compensation. Why did Smith's claim not fall within *Sherbert*, even as limited by Justice Scalia?

10. The *Smith* majority raised the concern that the strict scrutiny analysis of free exercise claims for religious exemptions would place judges in the uncomfortable — and, for the *Smith* majority, unconstitutional — position of evaluating the weight of religious claimants' religious practices. Is it inappropriate for judges to do so? Is there any other alternative?

11. One of the claims upon which the majority spent a significant amount of time was that the *Sherbert* test would threaten the Rule of Law. How would this happen, according to the majority? Is the majority correct in its prediction? Since *Sherbert* was decided in 1963, why had the breakdown of the Rule of Law not occurred prior to *Smith*?

12. Relatedly, Justice Scalia argued that, though requiring the government to establish a compelling governmental interest is common in many doctrinal contexts, it leads to unusual results in the free exercise context. Why is that, according to Justice Scalia? Evaluate Justice Scalia's claim.

13. Another empirical claim made by the Court was that the *Smith* Rule would not lead to significant harm to religious believers because one can generally count on the American political process to afford religious believers adequate protections. Is this true? Is this the kind of judgment that Courts are good at, or should some other branch of government make this type of determination? If so, which branch?

14. Justice Scalia is well known for his public advocacy of originalism. What originalist arguments did Justice Scalia provide to justify the *Smith* Rule? How do you explain this?

15. At a basic level, Justices Scalia and O'Connor sparred over whether neutral and generally applicable laws can infringe "free exercise." Explain their respective positions, and which position is more persuasive.

16. There is an articulate debate over whether the *Smith* Rule is faithful to the Free Exercise Clause's original meaning. The most prominent originalist criticism of the *Smith* Rule is found in Michael W. McConnell, *The Origins and Historical Understanding of Free Exercise of Religion*, 103 Harv. L. Rev. 1409 (1990). The best originalist defense of the *Smith* Rule is Gerard V. Bradley, *Beguiled: Free Exercise Exemptions and the Siren Song of Liberalism*, 20 Hofstra L. Rev. 245 (1991).

17. Justice Scalia was also well known as a social conservative, who was religious. Biskupic, Joan, American Original: The Life and Constitution of Supreme Court Justice Antonin Scalia (2009). If, as most people believe, the *Smith* Rule is relatively less protective of religious liberty than *Sherbert*, how do you account for Justice Scalia's authorship of *Smith*?

18. Justice O'Connor concurred in the Court's judgment because she concluded that it was necessary for Oregon to not exempt people, like Smith, from Oregon's criminal drug prohibition. Is Justice O'Connor's conclusion accurate, or is she doing what Justice Scalia argued the Court had done in the past: reaching correct outcomes by manipulating the legal doctrine?

19. For many proponents of robust religious liberty, *Smith* was perceived as a negative development. One of the few silver linings, from this perspective, was the hybrid rights exception. However, the hybrid rights exception received a decidedly lukewarm reception in the lower courts. Steven H. Aden & Lee J. Strang, *When a "Rule" Doesn't Rule: The Failure of the Oregon Employment Division v. Smith "Hybrid Rights Exception"*, 108 Penn. St. L. Rev. 573 (2003).

20. Subsequent to *Smith*, a number of states, including Oregon, enacted statutory exemptions for religious peyote use. Does this show that Justice Scalia was correct when he argued that the Court should trust the American political process to respect religious liberty? *See* Michael W. McConnell, *The Problem of Singling Out Religion*, 50 DePaul L. Rev. 1, 3–6 (2000) (surveying the significant existing exemptions for religious practices).

2. Note on the Religious Freedom Restoration Act, State "Mini-RFRAs," the Religious Land Use and Institutionalized Persons Act, and State Constitutional Law

There was a tremendous popular reaction against *Smith*. The anti-*Smith* response included critics from across the political and ideological spectrum, and it included legal scholars, politicians, and average Americans. One of the key results of this reaction was the nearly-unanimous passage of the Religious Freedom Restoration Act of 1993, 42 U.S.C. § 2000bb ("RFRA"). The Act purported to restore *Sherbert*'s strict scrutiny analysis to all free exercise claims.

You covered the Supreme Court's partial invalidation of RFRA in *Boerne v. Flores*, 521 U.S. 507 (1997), in Volume 3. After *Boerne*, RFRA applied to the federal government but not to the states. *See, e.g., O'Bryan v. Bureau of Prisons*, 349 F.3d 399, 401 (7th Cir. 2003) (collecting cases); *Burwell v. Hobby Lobby Stores, Inc.*, 573 U.S. 682 (2014) (holding that RFRA protected for-profit, closely-held corporations and that application of the HHS contraceptive mandate to Hobby Lobby violated RFRA). Furthermore, many states have passed their own versions of RFRA, labeled mini-RFRAs. *See* Christopher C. Lund, *Religious Liberty After* Gonzales*: A Look at State RFRAS*, 55 S.D. L. REV. 466, 466–67 (2010) (noting that sixteen states enacted state RFRAs by 2010).

Following *Boerne*, Congress attempted to work within the bounds the Supreme Court described, passing the Religious Land Use and Institutionalized Persons Act of 2000, 42 U.S.C. § 2000cc *et seq.* (2013) ("RLUIPA"). This law had a much narrower focus than RFRA. It required the application of strict scrutiny in only two contexts: land use regulations applied to religious persons and institutions; and prison regulations of prisoners' religious beliefs and practices. The Supreme Court upheld RLUIPA against an Establishment Clause challenge to the State of Ohio's prison regulations in *Cutter v. Wilkinson*, 544 U.S. 709 (2005). However, the Supreme Court has not provided a definitive ruling on the overall constitutionality of RLUIPA.

One last post-*Smith* development is worth noting: many state supreme courts interpreted their state constitutional protections for religious liberty more capaciously than *Smith*. In particular, many of them utilized the *Sherbert* strict scrutiny analysis for all laws that burden religious exercise. Lund, *supra*, at 467. A key point under RFRA, mini-RFRAs, and state constitutions, then, is whether a government action significantly burdens religious exercise. *See, e.g.*, Scott W. Gaylord, *RFRA Rights Revisited: Substantial Burdens, Judicial Competence, and the Religious Nonprofits Cases*, 81 Mo. L. REV. 655 (Summer 2016). Collectively, these developments have blunted some of *Smith*'s impact on religious liberty.

G. Continued Strict Scrutiny in Limited Circumstances

1. When the Preconditions for *Smith* Are Not Met

Smith dramatically altered the free exercise landscape by significantly curtailing the scope of strict scrutiny analysis. A small window of opportunity remained open for free exercise claimants if they could show that the *Smith* rule was inapplicable because the challenged law was not neutral or not generally applicable. The next case exemplifies this option.

Church of the Lukumi Babalu Aye, Inc. v. City of Hialeah

508 U.S. 520 (1993)

JUSTICE KENNEDY delivered the opinion of the Court, except as to Part II-A-2.

The principle that government may not enact laws that suppress religious belief or practice is so well understood that few violations are recorded in our opinions. Concerned that this fundamental nonpersecution principle of the First Amendment was implicated here, however, we granted certiorari.

Our review confirms that the laws in question were enacted by officials who did not understand, failed to perceive, or chose to ignore the fact that their official actions violated the Nation's essential commitment to religious freedom. The challenged laws had an impermissible object; and in all events the principle of general applicability was violated because the secular ends asserted in defense of the laws were pursued only with respect to conduct motivated by religious beliefs.

I

A

This case involves practices of the Santeria religion, which originated in the 19th century. When hundreds of thousands of members of the Yoruba people were brought as slaves to Cuba, their traditional African religion absorbed significant elements of Roman Catholicism. The resulting syncretion is Santeria, "the way of the saints." The Cuban Yoruba express their devotion to spirits, called *orishas*, through the iconography of Catholic saints.

The Santeria faith teaches that every individual has a destiny from God, a destiny fulfilled with the aid and energy of the *orishas*. The basis of the Santeria religion is the nurture of a personal relation with the *orishas*, and one of the principal forms of devotion is an animal sacrifice. The sacrifice of animals as part of religious rituals has ancient roots. Animal sacrifice is mentioned throughout the Old Testament, and it played an important role in the practice of Judaism before destruction of the second Temple in Jerusalem. In modern Islam, there is an annual sacrifice commemorating Abraham's sacrifice of a ram in the stead of his son.

According to Santeria teaching, the *orishas* are powerful but not immortal. They depend for survival on the sacrifice. Sacrifices are performed at birth, marriage, and death rites, for the cure of the sick, for the initiation of new members and priests, and during an annual celebration. Animals sacrificed in Santeria rituals include chickens, pigeons, doves, ducks, guinea pigs, goats, sheep, and turtles. The animals are killed by the cutting of the carotid arteries in the neck. The sacrificed animal is cooked and eaten, except after healing and death rituals.

B

Petitioner Church of the Lukumi Babalu Aye, Inc. (Church), is a not-for-profit corporation organized under Florida law in 1973. The Church and its congregants practice the Santeria religion. In April 1987, the Church leased land in the City of Hialeah, Florida, and announced plans to establish a house of worship as well as a school, cultural center, and museum.

The prospect of a Santeria church in their midst was distressing to many members of the Hialeah community, and the announcement of the plans to open a Santeria church in Hialeah prompted the city council to hold an emergency public session on June 9, 1987.

A summary [of the City's ordinances and resolutions] suffices here, beginning with the enactments passed at the June 9 meeting. First, the city council adopted Resolution 87-66, which noted the "concern" expressed by residents of the city "that certain religions may propose to engage in practices which are inconsistent with public morals, peace or safety," and declared that "[t]he City reiterates its commitment to a prohibition against any and all acts of any and all religious groups which are inconsistent with public morals, peace or safety." Next, the council approved an emergency ordinance, Ordinance 87-40, which incorporated in full, except as to penalty, Florida's animal cruelty laws. Among other things, the incorporated state law subjected to criminal punishment "whoever ... unnecessarily or cruelly ... kills any animal."

[Subsequently, the city council adopted] a hortatory enactment, Resolution 87-90, that noted its residents' "great concern regarding the possibility of public ritualistic animal sacrifices" and the state-law prohibition. The resolution declared the city policy "to oppose the ritual sacrifices of animals" within Hialeah and announced that any person or organization practicing animal sacrifice "will be prosecuted."

In September 1987, the city council adopted three substantive ordinances addressing the issue of religious animal sacrifice. Ordinance 87-52 defined "sacrifice" as "to un-necessarily kill, torment, torture, or mutilate an animal in a public or private ritual or ceremony not for the primary purpose of food consumption," and prohibited own-ing or possessing an animal "intending to use such animal for food purposes." It re-stricted application of this prohibition, however, to any individual or group that "kills, slaughters or sacrifices animals for any type of ritual, regardless of whether or not the flesh or blood of the animal is to be consumed." The ordinance contained an exemption for slaughtering by "licensed establishment[s]" of animals "specifically raised for food purposes." [T]he city council [also] adopted Ordinance 87-71. That ordinance defined sacrifice as had Ordinance 87-52, and then provided that "[i]t shall be unlawful for any person, persons, corporations or associations to sacrifice any an-imal within the corporate limits of the City of Hialeah, Florida." The final Ordinance, 87-72, defined "slaughter" as "the killing of animals for food" and prohibited slaughter outside of areas zoned for slaughterhouse use. The ordinance provided an exemption, however, for the slaughter or processing for sale of "small numbers of hogs and/or cattle per week in accordance with an exemption provided by state law." Violations of each of the four ordinances were punishable by fines not exceeding $500 or im-prisonment not exceeding 60 days, or both.

II

The city does not argue that Santeria is not a "religion" within the meaning of the First Amendment. Nor could it. Although the practice of animal sacrifice may seem abhorrent to some, "religious beliefs need not be acceptable, logical, consistent, or comprehensible to others in order to merit First Amendment protection." Neither the city nor the courts below have questioned the sincerity of petitioners' professed desire to conduct animal sacrifices for religious reasons. We must consider petitioners' First Amendment claim.

In addressing the constitutional protection for free exercise of religion, our cases establish the general proposition that a law that is neutral and of general applicability need not be justified by a compelling governmental interest even if the law has the incidental effect of burdening a particular religious practice. *Employment Div., Dept. of Human Resources of Ore. v. Smith*[, 494 U.S. 872 (1990)]. Neutrality and general applicability are interrelated, and, as becomes apparent in this case, failure to satisfy one requirement is a likely indication that the other has not been satisfied. A law failing to satisfy these requirements must be justified by a compelling governmental interest and must be narrowly tailored to advance that interest. These ordinances fail to satisfy the *Smith* requirements. We begin by discussing neutrality.

A

At a minimum, the protections of the Free Exercise Clause pertain if the law at issue discriminates against some or all religious beliefs or regulates or prohibits conduct because it is undertaken for religious reasons.

1

Although a law targeting religious beliefs as such is never permissible, if the object of a law is to infringe upon or restrict practices because of their religious motivation, the law is not neutral. There are, of course, many ways of demonstrating that the object or purpose of a law is the suppression of religion or religious conduct. To determine the object of a law, we must begin with its text, for the minimum requirement of neutrality is that a law not discriminate on its face. A law lacks facial neutrality if it refers to a religious practice without a secular meaning discernable from the language or context. Petitioners contend that three of the ordinances fail this test of facial neutrality because they use the words "sacrifice" and "ritual," words with strong religious connotations. We agree that these words are consistent with the claim of facial discrimination, but the argument is not conclusive. The words "sacrifice" and "ritual" have a religious origin, but current use admits also of secular meanings. See Webster's Third New International Dictionary 1961, 1996 (1971). The ordinances, furthermore, define "sacrifice" in secular terms, without referring to religious practices.

We reject the contention advanced by the city, that our inquiry must end with the text of the laws at issue. Facial neutrality is not determinative. The Free Exercise Clause, like the Establishment Clause, extends beyond facial discrimination. The Clause "forbids subtle departures from neutrality," and "covert suppression of particular religious beliefs[.]" Official action that targets religious conduct for distinctive treatment cannot be shielded by mere compliance with the requirement of facial neutrality.

The record in this case compels the conclusion that suppression of the central element of the Santeria worship service was the object of the ordinances. First, though use of the words "sacrifice" and "ritual" does not compel a finding of improper targeting of the Santeria religion, the choice of these words is support for our conclusion. There are further respects in which the text of the city council's enactments discloses the improper attempt to target Santeria. Resolution 87-66, adopted June 9, 1987, recited that "residents and citizens of the City of Hialeah have expressed their concern that certain religions may propose to engage in practices which are inconsistent with public morals, peace or safety," and "reiterate[d]" the city's commitment to prohibit "any and all [such] acts of any and all religious groups." No one suggests, and on this record it cannot be maintained, that city officials had in mind a religion other than Santeria.

It becomes evident that these ordinances target Santeria sacrifice when the ordinances' operation is considered. Apart from the text, the effect of a law in its real operation is strong evidence of its object. To be sure, adverse impact will not always lead to a finding of impermissible targeting. The subject at hand does implicate, of course, multiple concerns unrelated to religious animosity, for example, the suffering or mistreatment visited upon the sacrificed animals and health hazards from improper disposal. But the ordinances when considered together disclose an object remote from these legitimate concerns. The design of these laws accomplishes instead a "religious gerrymander," an impermissible attempt to target petitioners and their religious practices.

It is a necessary conclusion that almost the only conduct subject to Ordinances 87-40, 87-52, and 87-71 is the religious exercise of Santeria church members. The texts show that they were drafted in tandem to achieve this result. We begin with Ordinance 87-71. It prohibits the sacrifice of animals, but defines sacrifice as "to unnecessarily kill ... an animal in a public or private ritual or ceremony not for the primary purpose of food consumption." The definition excludes almost all killings of animals except for religious sacrifice, and the primary purpose requirement narrows the proscribed category even further, in particular by exempting kosher slaughter. The net result of the gerrymander is that few if any killings of animals are prohibited other than Santeria sacrifice, which is proscribed because it occurs during a ritual or ceremony and its primary purpose is to make an offering to the *orishas*, not food consumption. Indeed, careful drafting ensured that, although Santeria sacrifice is prohibited, killings that are no more necessary or humane in almost all other circumstances are unpunished.

Operating in similar fashion is Ordinance 87-52, which prohibits the "possess[ion], sacrifice, or slaughter" of an animal with the "inten[t] to use such animal for food purposes." This prohibition, extending to the keeping of an animal as well as the killing itself, applies if the animal is killed in "any type of ritual" and there is an intent to use the animal for food, whether or not it is in fact consumed for food. The ordinance exempts, however, "any licensed [food] establishment" with regard to "any animals which are specifically raised for food purposes," if the activity is permitted by zoning and other laws. This exception, too, seems intended to cover kosher slaughter. Again, the burden of the ordinance, in practical terms, falls on Santeria adherents but almost no others: If the killing is—unlike most Santeria sacrifices—unaccompanied by the intent to use the animal for food, then it is not prohibited by Ordinance 87-52; if the killing is specifically for food but does not occur during the course of "any type of ritual," it again falls outside the prohibition; and if the killing is for food and occurs during the course of a ritual, it is still exempted if it occurs in a properly zoned and licensed establishment and involves animals "specifically raised for food purposes." Each contributes to the gerrymander.

Ordinance 87-40 incorporates the Florida animal cruelty statute. Its prohibition is broad on its face, punishing "[w]hoever ... unnecessarily ... kills any animal." The city claims that this ordinance is the epitome of a neutral prohibition. The problem, however, is ... [that k]illings for religious reasons are deemed unnecessary, whereas most other killings fall outside the prohibition. The city, on what seems to be a *per se* basis, deems hunting, slaughter of animals for food, eradication of insects and pests, and euthanasia as necessary. There is no indication in the record that respondent has concluded that hunting or fishing for sport is unnecessary. Further, because it requires an evaluation of the particular justification for the killing, this ordinance represents a system of "individualized governmental assessment of the reasons for the relevant conduct[.]" As we noted in *Smith*, in circumstances in which individualized exemptions from a general requirement are available, the government "may not refuse to extend that system to cases of 'religious hardship' without compelling reason." Respondent's application of the ordinance's test of necessity devalues religious reasons for killing by judging them to be of lesser import than nonreligious reasons. Thus, religious practice is being singled out for discriminatory treatment.

We also find significant evidence of the ordinances' improper targeting of Santeria sacrifice in the fact that they proscribe more religious conduct than is necessary to achieve their stated ends.... The legitimate governmental interests in protecting the public health and preventing cruelty to animals could be addressed by restrictions stopping far short of a flat prohibition of all Santeria sacrificial practice. If improper disposal, not the sacrifice itself, is the harm to be prevented, the city could have imposed a general regulation on the disposal of organic garbage. It did not do so. Thus, these broad ordinances prohibit Santeria sacrifice even when it does not threaten the city's interest in the public health.

Under similar analysis, narrower regulation would achieve the city's interest in preventing cruelty to animals. With regard to the city's interest in ensuring the adequate care of animals, regulation of conditions and treatment, regardless of why an animal is kept, is the logical response to the city's concern, not a prohibition on possession for the purpose of sacrifice. The same is true for the city's interest in prohibiting cruel methods of killing. Under federal and Florida law and Ordinance 87-40, which incorporates Florida law in this regard, killing an animal by the "simultaneous and instantaneous severance of the carotid arteries with a sharp instrument"—the method used in kosher slaughter—is approved as humane. If the city has a real concern that other methods are less humane, however, the subject of the regulation should be the method of slaughter itself, not a religious classification that is said to bear some general relation to it.

Ordinance 87-72—unlike the three other ordinances—does appear to apply to substantial nonreligious conduct and not to be overbroad. For our purposes here, however, the four substantive ordinances may be treated as a group for neutrality purposes. Ordinance 87-72 was passed the same day as Ordinance 87-71 and was enacted, as were the three others, in direct response to the opening of the Church. It would be implausible to suggest that the three other ordinances, but not Ordinance 87-72, had as their object the suppression of religion.

3

In sum, the neutrality inquiry leads to one conclusion: The ordinances had as their object the suppression of religion. The pattern we have recited discloses animosity to Santeria adherents and their religious practices; the ordinances by their own terms target this religious exercise; the texts of the ordinances were gerrymandered with care to proscribe religious killings of animals but to exclude almost all secular killings; and the ordinances suppress much more religious conduct than is necessary in order to achieve the legitimate ends asserted in their defense. These ordinances are not neutral, and the court below committed clear error in failing to reach this conclusion.

B

We turn next to a second requirement of the Free Exercise Clause, the rule that laws burdening religious practice must be of general applicability. All laws are selective to some extent, but categories of selection are of paramount concern when a law has the incidental effect of burdening religious practice.

The principle that government, in pursuit of legitimate interests, cannot in a selective manner impose burdens only on conduct motivated by religious belief is essential to the protection of the rights guaranteed by the Free Exercise Clause. In this case we need not define with precision the standard used to evaluate whether a prohibition is of general application, for these ordinances fall well below the minimum standard necessary to protect First Amendment rights.

Respondent claims that Ordinances 87-40, 87-52, and 87-71 advance two interests: protecting the public health and preventing cruelty to animals. The ordinances are underinclusive for those ends. They fail to prohibit nonreligious conduct that endangers these interests in a similar or greater degree than Santeria sacrifice does. The underinclusion is substantial, not inconsequential. Despite the city's proffered interest in preventing cruelty to animals, the ordinances are drafted with care to forbid few killings but those occasioned by religious sacrifice. Many types of animal deaths or kills for nonreligious reasons are either not prohibited or approved by express provision. For example, fishing—which occurs in Hialeah—is legal. Extermination of mice and rats within a home is also permitted. Florida law incorporated by Ordinance 87-40 sanctions euthanasia of "stray, neglected, abandoned, or unwanted animals"; destruction of animals judicially removed from their owners "for humanitarian reasons" or when the animal "is of no commercial value"; the infliction of pain or suffering "in the interest of medical science"; the placing of poison in one's yard or enclosure; and the use of a live animal "to pursue or take wildlife or to participate in any hunting," and "to hunt wild hogs[.]"

The ordinances are also underinclusive with regard to the city's interest in public health, which is threatened by the disposal of animal carcasses in open public places and the consumption of uninspected meat. Neither interest is pursued by respondent with regard to conduct that is not motivated by religious conviction. The health risks posed by the improper disposal of animal carcasses are the same whether Santeria sacrifice or some nonreligious killing preceded it. The city does not, however, prohibit hunters from bringing their kill to their houses, nor does it regulate disposal after their activity. Improper disposal is a general problem that causes substantial health risks, but which respondent addresses only when it results from religious exercise.

The ordinances are underinclusive as well with regard to the health risk posed by consumption of uninspected meat. Under the city's ordinances, hunters may eat their kill and fishermen may eat their catch without undergoing governmental inspection. Likewise, state law requires inspection of meat that is sold but exempts meat from animals raised for the use of the owner and "members of his household and nonpaying guests and employees." The asserted interest in inspected meat is not pursued in contexts similar to that of religious animal sacrifice.

Ordinance 87-72, which prohibits the slaughter of animals outside of areas zoned for slaughterhouses, is underinclusive on its face. The ordinance includes an exemption for "any person, group, or organization" that "slaughters or processes for sale, small numbers of hogs and/or cattle per week in accordance with an exemption provided by state law." Respondent has not explained why commercial operations that slaughter "small numbers" of hogs and cattle do not implicate its professed desire to prevent cruelty to animals and preserve the public health....

We conclude, in sum, that each of Hialeah's ordinances pursues the city's governmental interests only against conduct motivated by religious belief. The ordinances "ha[ve] every appearance of a prohibition that society is prepared to impose upon [Santeria worshippers] but not upon itself." This precise evil is what the requirement of general applicability is designed to prevent.

III

A law burdening religious practice that is not neutral or not of general application must undergo the most rigorous of scrutiny. First, even were the governmental interests compelling, the ordinances are not drawn in narrow terms to accomplish those interests. Respondent has not demonstrated, moreover, that, in the context of these ordinances, its governmental interests are compelling.

JUSTICE SCALIA, with whom THE CHIEF JUSTICE joins, concurring in part and concurring in the judgment. [Opinion omitted.]

JUSTICE SOUTER, concurring in part and concurring in the judgment.

This case turns on a principle about which there is no disagreement, that the Free Exercise Clause bars government action aimed at suppressing religious belief or practice. The Court holds that Hialeah's animal-sacrifice laws violate that principle, and I concur in that holding without reservation. I write separately to explain why the *Smith* rule is not germane to this case and to express my view that, in a case presenting the issue, the Court should re-examine the rule *Smith* declared.

JUSTICE BLACKMUN, with whom JUSTICE O'CONNOR joins, concurring in the judgment.

The Court holds today that the city of Hialeah violated the First and Fourteenth Amendments when it passed a set of restrictive ordinances explicitly directed at petitioners' religious practice. With this holding I agree. I continue to believe that *Smith* was wrongly decided, because it ignored the value of religious freedom as an affirmative individual liberty and treated the Free Exercise Clause as no more than an antidiscrimination principle.

Exercise 9:

1. What, according to the Court, triggered application of strict scrutiny in place of the *Smith* rule?

2. What distinguishes a law's neutrality (or lack thereof) from a law's generality (or lack thereof) for purposes of *Smith*?

3. How were the City of Hialeah's ordinances and resolutions not neutral and/or not generally applicable?

4. Does *Lukumi* vindicate the post-*Smith* free exercise approach, or does it show that *Smith* was misbegotten?

5. How broad is the limit on *Smith*, exemplified in *Lukumi*? Will it apply to a few, many, or a lot of situations?

———————

Given that the *Smith* rule does not apply if a law is not neutral or not generally applicable, much depends on the Court's resolution of the question whether a law is not neutral on its face or has been applied against religion in a discriminatory fashion. The line is not altogether clear but frequently may be dispositive given that it determines whether a law will be subject to rational basis (as in *Smith*) or strict scrutiny (as in *Lukumi*). If the government makes a public benefit generally available, can it preclude religious groups from receiving the benefit? Or does withholding such a benefit because of the religious character of the recipient automatically discriminate against religion? The Court considered these questions in the following case.

Trinity Lutheran Church of Columbia, Inc. v. Comer

137 S. Ct. 2012 (2017)

CHIEF JUSTICE ROBERTS delivered the opinion of the Court, except as to footnote 3.

The Missouri Department of Natural Resources offers state grants to help public and private schools, nonprofit daycare centers, and other nonprofit entities purchase rubber playground surfaces made from recycled tires. Trinity Lutheran Church applied for such a grant for its preschool and daycare center and would have received one, but for the fact that Trinity Lutheran is a church. The Department had a policy of categorically disqualifying churches and other religious organizations from receiving grants under its playground resurfacing program. The question presented is whether the Department's policy violated the rights of Trinity Lutheran under the Free Exercise Clause of the First Amendment.

I

A

The Trinity Lutheran Church Child Learning Center is a preschool and daycare center open throughout the year to serve working families in Boone County, Missouri, and the surrounding area. Established as a nonprofit organization in 1980, the Center merged with Trinity Lutheran Church in 1985 and operates under its auspices on church property. The Center admits students of any religion, and enrollment stands at about 90 children ranging from age two to five.

In 2012, the Center sought to replace a large portion of the pea gravel [beneath and surrounding its playground] with a pour-in-place rubber surface by participating in Missouri's Scrap Tire Program. Run by the State's Department of Natural Resources to reduce the number of used tires destined for landfills and dump sites, the program offers reimbursement grants to qualifying nonprofit organizations that purchase playground surfaces made from recycled tires. It is funded through a fee imposed on the sale of new tires in the State.

Due to limited resources, the Department cannot offer grants to all applicants and so awards them on a competitive basis to those scoring highest based on several criteria. When the Center applied, the Department had a strict and express policy of denying grants to any applicant owned or controlled by a church, sect, or other religious entity. That policy, in the Department's view, was compelled by Article I, Section 7 of the Missouri Constitution, which provides:

> "That no money shall ever be taken from the public treasury, directly or indirectly, in aid of any church, sect or denomination of religion, or in aid of any priest, preacher, minister or teacher thereof, as such; and that no preference shall be given to nor any discrimination made against any church, sect or creed of religion, or any form of religious faith or worship." ...

In its application, the Center disclosed its status as a ministry of Trinity Lutheran Church and specified that the Center's mission was "to provide a safe, clean, and attractive school facility in conjunction with an educational program structured to allow a child to grow spiritually, physically, socially, and cognitively." The Center ranked fifth among the 44 applicants in the 2012 Scrap Tire Program. But despite its high score, the Center was deemed categorically ineligible to receive a grant. In a letter rejecting the Center's application, the program director explained that, under Article I, Section 7 of the Missouri Constitution, the Department could not provide financial assistance directly to a church.

The Department ultimately awarded 14 grants as part of the 2012 program. Because the Center was operated by Trinity Lutheran Church, it did not receive a grant.

II

The parties agree that the Establishment Clause of [the First] Amendment does not prevent Missouri from including Trinity Lutheran in the Scrap Tire Program. That does not, however, answer the question under the Free Exercise Clause, because we have recognized that there is "play in the joints" between what the Establishment Clause permits and the Free Exercise Clause compels.

The Free Exercise Clause "protect[s] religious observers against unequal treatment" and subjects to the strictest scrutiny laws that target the religious for "special disabilities" based on their "religious status." Applying that basic principle, this Court has repeatedly confirmed that denying a generally available benefit solely on account of religious identity imposes a penalty on the free exercise of religion that can be justified only by a state interest "of the highest order."

[For example], in *McDaniel v. Paty*, [435 U.S. 618 (1978),] the Court struck down under the Free Exercise Clause a Tennessee statute disqualifying ministers from serving as delegates to the State's constitutional convention.... [Tennessee's] historical tradition did not change the fact that the statute discriminated against McDaniel by denying him a benefit solely because of his "*status* as a 'minister.'" McDaniel could not seek to participate in the convention while also maintaining his role as a minister; to pursue the one, he would have to give up the other. In this way, said Chief Justice Burger, the Tennessee law "effectively penalizes the free exercise of [McDaniel's] constitutional liberties."

In recent years, when this Court has rejected free exercise challenges, the laws in question have been neutral and generally applicable without regard to religion. We have been careful to distinguish such laws from those that single out the religious for disfavored treatment. [I]n *Church of Lukumi Babalu Aye, Inc. v. Hialeah*, the Court recounted the fundamentals of our free exercise jurisprudence. A law, we said, may not discriminate against "some or all religious beliefs." Nor may a law regulate or outlaw conduct because it is religiously motivated. And, citing *McDaniel* and *Smith,* we restated the now-familiar refrain: The Free Exercise Clause protects against laws that "'impose[] special disabilities on the basis of ... religious status.'"

III

A

The Department's policy expressly discriminates against otherwise eligible recipients by disqualifying them from a public benefit solely because of their religious character.

If the cases just described make one thing clear, it is that such a policy imposes a penalty on the free exercise of religion that triggers the most exacting scrutiny.

Like the disqualification statute in *McDaniel,* the Department's policy puts Trinity Lutheran to a choice: It may participate in an otherwise available benefit program or remain a religious institution. Of course, Trinity Lutheran is free to continue operating as a church, just as McDaniel was free to continue being a minister. But that freedom comes at the cost of automatic and absolute exclusion from the benefits of a public program for which the Center is otherwise fully qualified. And when the State conditions a benefit in this way, *McDaniel* says plainly that the State has punished the free exercise of religion: "To condition the availability of benefits ... upon [a recipient's] willingness to ... surrender[] his religiously impelled [status] effectively penalizes the free exercise of his constitutional liberties."

The Department contends that merely declining to extend funds to Trinity Lutheran does not *prohibit* the Church from engaging in any religious conduct or otherwise exercising its religious rights. In this sense, says the Department, its policy is unlike the ordinances struck down in *Lukumi,* which outlawed rituals central to Santeria. Here the Department has simply declined to allocate to Trinity Lutheran a subsidy the State had no obligation to provide in the first place. That decision does not meaningfully burden the Church's free exercise rights. And absent any such burden, the argument continues, the Department is free to heed the State's antiestablishment objection to providing funds directly to a church.

It is true the Department has not criminalized the way Trinity Lutheran worships or told the Church that it cannot subscribe to a certain view of the Gospel. But, as the Department itself acknowledges, the Free Exercise Clause protects against "indirect coercion or penalties on the free exercise of religion, not just outright prohibitions." As the Court put it more than 50 years ago, "[i]t is too late in the day to doubt that the liberties of religion and expression may be infringed by the denial of or placing of conditions upon a benefit or privilege."

Trinity Lutheran is not claiming any entitlement to a subsidy. It instead asserts a right to participate in a government benefit program without having to disavow its religious character. The "imposition of such a condition upon even a gratuitous benefit inevitably deter[s] or discourage[s] the exercise of First Amendment rights." The express discrimination against religious exercise here is not the denial of a grant, but rather the refusal to allow the Church—solely because it is a church—to compete with secular organizations for a grant.

B

The Department attempts to get out from under the weight of our precedents by arguing that the free exercise question in this case is instead controlled by our decision in *Locke v. Davey.* [540 U.S. 712 (2004).] It is not. In *Locke,* the State of Washington created a scholarship program to assist high-achieving students with the costs of postsecondary education. While scholarship recipients were free to use the money at accredited religious and non-religious schools alike, they were not permitted to use the funds to pursue a devotional theology degree—one "devotional in nature or designed to induce religious faith." Davey was selected for a scholarship but was denied the funds when he refused to certify that he would not use them toward a devotional degree. He sued, arguing that the State's refusal to allow its scholarship money to go toward such degrees violated his free exercise rights.

This Court disagreed. Washington's restriction on the use of its scholarship funds was different. According to the Court, the State had "merely chosen not to fund a distinct category of instruction." Davey was not denied a scholarship because of who he *was*; he was denied a scholarship because of what he proposed *to do*—use the funds to prepare for the ministry. Here there is no question that Trinity Lutheran was denied a grant simply because of what it is—a church.

In this case, there is no dispute that Trinity Lutheran *is* put to the choice between being a church and receiving a government benefit. The rule is simple: No churches need apply.[3]

C

Under [strict scrutiny], only a state interest "of the highest order" can justify the Department's discriminatory policy. Yet the Department offers nothing more than Missouri's policy preference for skating as far as possible from religious establishment concerns. In the face of the clear infringement on free exercise before us, that interest cannot qualify as compelling. As we said when considering Missouri's same policy preference on a prior occasion, "the state interest asserted here—in achieving greater separation of church and State than is already ensured under the Establishment Clause of the Federal Constitution—is limited by the Free Exercise Clause."

The State has pursued its preferred policy to the point of expressly denying a qualified religious entity a public benefit solely because of its religious character. Under our precedents, that goes too far. The Department's policy violates the Free Exercise Clause.

And the result of the State's policy is nothing so dramatic as the denial of political office [as in *McDaniel*]. The consequence is, in all likelihood, a few extra scraped knees. But the exclusion of Trinity Lutheran from a public benefit for which it is otherwise qualified, solely because it is a church, is odious to our Constitution all the same, and cannot stand.

JUSTICE THOMAS, with whom JUSTICE GORSUCH joins, concurring in part. [Opinion omitted.]

JUSTICE GORSUCH, with whom JUSTICE THOMAS joins, concurring in part.

[T]he Court leaves open the possibility a useful distinction might be drawn between laws that discriminate on the basis of religious *status* and religious *use*. Respectfully,

---

3. This case involves express discrimination based on religious identity with respect to playground resurfacing. We do not address religious uses of funding or other forms of discrimination.

I harbor doubts about the stability of such a line. Does a religious man say grace before dinner? Or does a man begin his meal in a religious manner? Is it a religious group that built the playground? Or did a group build the playground so it might be used to advance a religious mission? The distinction blurs in much the same way the line between acts and omissions can blur when stared at too long, leaving us to ask (for example) whether the man who drowns by awaiting the incoming tide does so by act (coming upon the sea) or omission (allowing the sea to come upon him).

Generally the government may not force people to choose between participation in a public program and their right to free exercise of religion. I don't see why it should matter whether we describe that benefit, say, as closed to Lutherans (status) or closed to people who do Lutheran things (use). It is free exercise either way.

[F]or similar reasons, I am unable to join the footnoted observation that "[t]his case involves express discrimination based on religious identity with respect to playground resurfacing." Of course the footnote is entirely correct, but I worry that some might mistakenly read it to suggest that only "playground resurfacing" cases, or only those with some association with children's safety or health, or perhaps some other social good we find sufficiently worthy, are governed by the legal rules recounted in and faithfully applied by the Court's opinion. Such a reading would be unreasonable for our cases are "governed by general principles, rather than ad hoc improvisations." And the general principles here do not permit discrimination against religious exercise—whether on the playground or anywhere else.

JUSTICE BREYER, concurring in the judgment. [Opinion omitted.]

JUSTICE SOTOMAYOR, with whom JUSTICE GINSBURG joins, dissenting.

To hear the Court tell it, this is a simple case about recycling tires to resurface a playground. The stakes are higher. This case is about nothing less than the relationship between religious institutions and the civil government—that is, between church and state. The Court today profoundly changes that relationship by holding, for the first time, that the Constitution requires the government to provide public funds directly to a church. Its decision slights both our precedents and our history, and its reasoning weakens this country's longstanding commitment to a separation of church and state beneficial to both.

[Whereas the majority noted and approved of the parties' agreement that the Establishment Clause "does not prevent Missouri from including Trinity Lutheran in the Scrap Tire Program," Justice Sotomayor argued that the Establishment Clause precluded "the Church's funding request because the Church uses the Learning Center, including the playground, in conjunction with its religious mission." Justice Sotomayor then turned to the Free Exercise issue.]

III

A

"[T]here is room for play in the joints productive of a benevolent neutrality which will permit religious exercise to exist without sponsorship and without interference."

This space between the two Clauses gives government some room to recognize the unique status of religious entities and to single them out on that basis for exclusion from otherwise generally applicable laws.

Invoking this principle, this Court has held that the government may sometimes relieve religious entities from the requirements of government programs. A State need not, for example, require nonprofit houses of worship to pay property taxes.... Nor must a State require nonprofit religious entities to abstain from making employment decisions on the basis of religion. It may instead avoid imposing on these institutions a "[f]ear of potential liability [that] might affect the way" it "carried out what it understood to be its religious mission" and on the government the sensitive task of policing compliance. But the government may not invoke the space between the Religion Clauses in a manner that "devolve[s] into an unlawful fostering of religion."

Invoking this same principle, this Court has held that the government may sometimes close off certain government aid programs to religious entities. The State need not, for example, fund the training of a religious group's leaders, those "who will preach their beliefs, teach their faith, and carry out their mission." It may instead avoid the historic "antiestablishment interests" raised by the use of "taxpayer funds to support church leaders."

When reviewing a law that, like this one, singles out religious entities for exclusion from its reach, we thus have not myopically focused on the fact that a law singles out religious entities, but on the reasons that it does so.

B

1

This Court has consistently looked to history for guidance when applying the Constitution's Religion Clauses. Those Clauses guard against a return to the past, and so that past properly informs their meaning. The use of public funds to support core religious institutions can safely be described as a hallmark of the States' early experiences with religious establishment. Every state establishment saw laws passed to raise public funds and direct them toward houses of worship and ministers. And as the States all disestablished, one by one, they all undid those laws....

The course of this history shows that those who lived under the laws and practices that formed religious establishments made a considered decision that civil government should not fund ministers and their houses of worship.

2

As was true in *Locke,* a prophylactic rule against the use of public funds for houses of worship is a permissible accommodation of these weighty interests. The rule has a historical pedigree identical to that of the provision in *Locke.* Almost all of the States that ratified the Religion Clauses operated under this rule. Seven had placed this rule in their State Constitutions. Three enforced it by statute or in practice. Only one had not yet embraced the rule. Today, thirty-eight States have a counterpart to Missouri's Article I, § 7. The provisions, as a general matter, date back to or before these States' original Constitutions. That so many States have for so long drawn a line that prohibits public funding for houses of worship, based on principles rooted in this Nation's understanding of how best to foster religious liberty, supports the conclusion that public funding of houses of worship "is of a different ilk."

3

In the Court's view, none of this matters. It focuses on one aspect of Missouri's Article I, § 7, to the exclusion of all else: that it denies funding to a house of worship, here the Church, "simply because of what it [i]s — a church." The Court describes this as a constitutionally impermissible line based on religious "status" that requires strict scrutiny. Its rule is out of step with our precedents in this area, and wrong on its own terms.

[A] government may act based on a religious entity's "status" as such. It is that very status that implicates the interests protected by the Religion Clauses. Sometimes a religious entity's unique status requires the government to act. Other times, it merely permits the government to act. In all cases, the dispositive issue is not whether religious "status" matters — it does, or the Religion Clauses would not be at issue — but whether the government must, or may, act on that basis.

The Court offers no real reason for rejecting the balancing approach in our precedents in favor of strict scrutiny, beyond its references to discrimination. The Court's desire to avoid what it views as discrimination is understandable. But in this context, the description is particularly inappropriate. A State's decision not to fund houses of worship does not disfavor religion; rather, it represents a valid choice to remain secular in the face of serious establishment and free exercise concerns. That does not make the State "atheistic or antireligious." … The Court's conclusion "that the only alternative to governmental support of religion is governmental hostility to it represents a giant step backward in our Religion Clause jurisprudence."

At bottom, the Court creates the following rule today: The government may draw lines on the basis of religious status to grant a benefit to religious persons or entities but it may not draw lines on that basis when doing so would further the interests the Religion Clauses protect in other ways. Nothing supports this lopsided outcome.

IV

The Court today dismantles a core protection for religious freedom provided in the [Religion] Clauses. It holds not just that a government may support houses of worship with taxpayer funds, but that — at least in this case and perhaps in others — it must do so whenever it decides to create a funding program. History shows that the Religion Clauses separate the public treasury from religious coffers as one measure to secure the kind of freedom of conscience that benefits both religion and government. If this separation means anything, it means that the government cannot, or at the very least need not, tax its citizens and turn that money over to houses of worship. The Court today blinds itself to the outcome this history requires and leads us instead to a place where separation of church and state is a constitutional slogan, not a constitutional commitment.

Exercise 10:

1. According to the Court, why did Article 1, Section 7 of the Missouri Constitution trigger application of strict scrutiny instead of the *Smith* rule?

2. What is the impermissible choice to which the Department of Natural Resources put Trinity Lutheran? Did the Tire Scrap Program infringe Trinity Lutheran's free exercise right simply by imposing such a choice? Does such a choice constitute a substantial obstacle on Trinity Lutheran's ability to freely exercise its religion? Are there any benefits that states can withhold from churches or religious groups without violating this principle? Did *Locke v. Davey* put such a choice to the student who wanted to use the scholarship funds to become a minister?

3. If, as the majority states, the Free Exercise Clause " 'protect[s] religious observers against unequal treatment' and subjects to the strictest scrutiny laws that target the religious for 'special disabilities' based on their 'religious status,' " then why does the majority affirm *Locke v. Davey*, which upheld the "relatively minor" burden imposed on religious observers who wanted to study to become ministers? Is *Trinity Lutheran* consistent with *Locke*? Should the First Amendment tolerate even "mild burdens" on religious exercise absent a state's satisfying strict scrutiny? Or is *Locke* effectively limited to its specific facts in the wake of *Trinity Lutheran*?

4. What is all the fuss about footnote 3 in Chief Justice Roberts's opinion? Why do Justices Thomas and Gorsuch decline to join that footnote? Did the distinction between status and use matter in this case? Might it matter in free exercise cases going forward?

5. According to the majority, why was Article 1, Section 7 of the Missouri Constitution not neutral and/or not generally applicable? Explain the dissent's response to the majority's argument. Does the majority or the dissent have the stronger position? Why?

6. The majority and dissent disagree as to whether the Establishment Clause prevents Missouri from including Trinity Lutheran in the Scrap Tire Program. Based on your study of the Free Exercise Clause in this chapter (and recognizing that the Establishment Clause is not discussed until **Chapter 3**), do you think the Establishment Clause should permit Trinity Lutheran to participate in such programs? Should neutrality concerns govern the Court's Establishment Clause analysis? Something else? Keep these questions in mind as you read the Establishment Clause cases.

7. Suppose the Montana Legislature creates a tuition assistance program for parents who send their children to private schools, whether secular or parochial. Under the program, if a taxpayer donates to specific organizations that award scholarships to selected students attending such private schools, that taxpayer receives a tax credit of up to $150. A single mother seeks to use the scholarships at a religious school but is precluded by a Montana Department of Revenue rule that prohibits families from using such scholarships at religious schools. The parent files suit, and the Montana Supreme Court ultimately strikes down the entire program based on

a "no-aid" provision (which is sometimes referred to as a state Blaine Amendment) in Article X, Section 6 of the Montana Constitution, which states: "The legislature, counties, cities, towns, school districts, and public corporations shall not make any direct or indirect appropriation or payment from any public fund or monies, or any grant of lands or other property for any sectarian purpose or to aid any church, school, academy, seminary, college, university, or other literary or scientific institution, controlled in whole or in part by any church, sect, or denomination." Does Montana's "no-aid" provision violate the Free Exercise Clause of the First Amendment? Is this situation more like *Trinity Lutheran* or *Locke v. Davey*? If the former, can the "no-aid provision" survive strict scrutiny? *See Espinoza v. Montana Dept. of Revenue*, 140 S. Ct. 2246 (2020).

8. During the pandemic of 2020, many states, in an effort to stop the spread of COVID-19, imposed quarantines that (1) closed, what government officials called, "non-essential" businesses and (2) precluded large gatherings of individuals (*e.g.*, groups of ten or more persons) even if the groups met outdoors. At the same time, states permitted "essential" businesses to remain open provided that they followed the CDC's social distancing guidelines. In the wake of these orders, several state and local officials prohibited religious services and gatherings of religious practitioners. As certain states began to allow some retail stores to open and to have more than ten persons in their stores, the limits on churches and religious groups remained in place— even if these religious groups agreed to follow the same social distancing rules that applied to essential and other permitted businesses and activities. If a religious organization challenged these restrictions, should a court be guided by *Smith* or *Lukumi*? Stated differently, are such public health regulations and exemptions neutral and generally applicable (either on their face or as applied)? Are there relevant differences between 100 people gathered for a religious service and 100 people shopping at Home Depot? Do these differences make a constitutional difference? Why or why not? *Compare Soos v. Cuomo*, 1:20-cv-651 (N.D.N.Y. 2020) (finding that New York violated the free exercise rights of religious practitioners), *with Legacy Church, Inc. v. Kunkel*, 2020 WL 1905586 (D.N.M. 2020) (rejecting a free exercise challenge to New Mexico's ban on in-person gatherings of more than five people in a place of worship).

* * *

In *Masterpiece Cakeshop, Ltd. v. Colorado Civil Rights Comm'n*, 138 S. Ct. 1719 (2018), a baker, Jack Phillips ("Phillips") was charged with violating the Colorado Anti-Discrimination Act ("CADA") for refusing to design and make a wedding cake for a same-sex couple. Based on his sincerely held religious beliefs, Phillips declined because "to create a wedding cake for an event that celebrates something that directly goes against the teachings of the Bible, would have been a personal endorsement and participation in the ceremony and relationship that they were entering into." *Id.* at 1724. Phillips explained that he would make birthday cakes for the plaitiffs and sell them other baked goods in the store but would not create a cake for their same-sex wedding. *Id.* An administrative law judge, the Colorado Civil Rights Commission, and the Colorado Court of Appeals concluded that Phillips had violated CADA, which they determined was a neutral law of general applicability. Accordingly, they held that CADA did not violate Phillips's free exercise rights under *Smith*.

The Supreme Court reversed, finding that the proceedings below violated Phillips' right "to the neutral and respectful consideration of his claims in all the circumstances of the case." This violation of Phillips' right to freely exercise his religion stemmed from two sources. First, the Colorado Civil Rights Commission evidenced "some elements of a clear and impermissible hostility toward the sincere religious beliefs that motivated [Phillips'] objection." *Id.* at 1729. Specifically, during two public meetings, certain members of the Commission made disparaging statements about Phillips's religious beliefs. At the second meeting, one of the Commissioners stated: "Freedom of religion and religion has been used to justify all kinds of discrimination throughout history, whether it be slavery, whether it be the holocaust, whether it be—I mean, we—we can list hundreds of situations where freedom of religion has been used to justify discrimination. And to me it is one of the most despicable pieces of rhetoric that people can use to—to use their religion to hurt others." *Id.* Such comments disparaged Phillips's religion "by describing it as despicable, and also by characterizing it as merely rhetorical—something insubstantial and even insincere" and, therefore, "cast doubt on the fairness and impartiality of the Commission's adjudication of Phillips' case." *Id.* at 1729–30.

Second, the Court discerned hostility toward Phillips based on the Commission's treating his case differently from the cases of three "other bakers who objected to a requested cake on the basis of conscience." *Id.* at 1730. In the other cases, the Commission permitted the bakers to refuse to create custom cakes that included religious text and images conveying disapproval of same-sex marriage because (1) the cakes included elements that the bakers deemed "derogatory," "hateful," or "discriminatory," and (2) the bakers were willing to sell other products, including Christian-themed products, to other customers. *Id.* In *Masterpiece Cakeshop*, however, the Commission did not protect Phillips' conscience rights, requiring him to create custom wedding cakes for same-sex couples or to stop making wedding cakes altogether. *Id.* at 1726. In Phillips' case, the Commission indicated "that any message the requested wedding cake would carry would be attributed to the customer, not to the baker," *id.* at 1730, but did not even mention that consideration in the other cases. Moreover, the Commission seemed to completely disregard Phillips' willingness to sell other baked goods to gay and lesbian customers even though that was directly relevant in the other cases: "The Colorado court's attempt to account for the difference in treatment elevates one view of what is offensive over another and itself sends a signal of official disapproval of Phillips' religious beliefs." *Id.* 1731. This the Commission could not do, given that "'no official, high or petty, can prescribe what shall be orthodox in politics, nationalism, religion, or other matters of opinion.'" *Id.* (quoting *West Virginia Bd. of Ed. v. Barnette,* 319 U.S. 624, 642 (1943)).

Drawing directly on *Lukumi*, the Court explained "that the government ... cannot act in a manner that passes judgment upon or presupposes the illegitimacy of religious beliefs and practices. The Free Exercise Clause bars even 'subtle departures from neutrality' on matters of religion." *Id.* at 1731. Under the Free Exercise Clause, the Commission was required to remain "neutral toward and tolerant of Phillips' religious beliefs" such that "'upon even slight suspicion that proposals for state intervention stem from animosity to religion or distrust of its practices, all officials must pause to remember their own high duty to the Constitution and to the rights it secures.'" When assessing government neutrality, courts should consider relevant factors, including "the historical background of the decision under challenge, the specific series of events leading to the enactment or official policy in question, and the legislative or administrative history, including contemporaneous statements made by members of the decisionmaking body." *Id.* (internal punctuation omitted). Applying these factors, the Court concluded that the Commission did not treat Phillips' case in the tolerant and respectful manner that the Free Exercise Clause requires and reversed the orders of the Commission and the Colorado Court of Appeals. *Id.* at 1732.

Based on the Court's analysis, why did *Smith* not apply? And if *Lukumi* provided the guiding principles, why did the Court not apply strict scrutiny? Did the Court create a *per se* rule for situations where the government demonstrates hostility towards one's religious beliefs, *i.e.,* where a practitioner's "religious objection [i]s not considered with the neutrality that the Free Exercise Clause requires"? Or is the Court simply assuming that the government never has a compelling interest in evidencing hostility toward religious beliefs?

2. Another Limit on *Smith*?

Though the *Smith* Court seemed to establish a blanket rule that neutral laws of general applicability are subject to rational basis review, the following case, *Hosanna-Tabor Evangelical Lutheran Church and School v. E.E.O.C.*, 565 U.S. 171 (2012), suggested a second limit on the *Smith* Rule—the ministerial exception. As you read *Hosanna-Tabor*, consider the nature and scope of the ministerial exception. Do the Free Exercise and Establishment Clauses require such an exception to be read narrowly? Broadly? Do you agree with the majority, one of the concurrences, or none of the opinions?

Hosanna-Tabor Evangelical Lutheran Church and School v. E.E.O.C.
565 U.S. 171 (2012)

CHIEF JUSTICE ROBERTS delivered the opinion of the Court.

Certain employment discrimination laws authorize employees who have been wrongfully terminated to sue their employers for reinstatement and damages. The question presented is whether the Establishment and Free Exercise Clauses of the First Amendment bar such an action when the employer is a religious group and the employee is one of the group's ministers.

I

[The Court recounted the facts of the case in some detail. A religious-school teacher, Perich, filed suit under federal employment antidiscrimination law against the Church that operated the school. The Church had fired the school teacher after a prolonged illness, and the teacher argued that the termination violated federal law. The Church defended by claiming that the teacher was a "minister" and, therefore, that the ministerial exception, which is rooted in both the Free Exercise and Establishment Clauses, protected the Church's decision to fire the teacher.]

II

We have said that the [Establishment and Free Exercise] Clauses "often exert conflicting pressures" and that there can be "internal tension ... between the Establishment Clause and the Free Exercise Clause." Not so here. Both Religion Clauses bar the government from interfering with the decision of a religious group to fire one of its ministers.

A

Familiar with life under the established Church of England, the founding generation sought to foreclose the possibility of a national church. By forbidding the "establishment of religion" and guaranteeing the "free exercise thereof," the Religion Clauses ensured that the new Federal Government—unlike the English Crown—would have no role in filling ecclesiastical offices. The Establishment Clause prevents the Government from appointing ministers, and the Free Exercise Clause prevents it from interfering with the freedom of religious groups to select their own.

B

Our decisions in [the context of disputes over church property] confirm that it is impermissible for the government to contradict a church's determination of who can act as its ministers. In *Watson v. Jones,* 13 Wall. [U.S.] 679 (1872), [w]e explained that "whenever the questions of discipline, or of faith, or ecclesiastical rule, custom, or law have been decided by the highest of [the] church judicatories to which the matter has been carried, the legal tribunals must accept such decisions as final, and as binding on them." As we would put it later, our opinion in *Watson* "radiates ... a spirit of freedom for religious organizations, an independence from secular control or manipulation—in short, power to decide for themselves, free from state interference, matters of church government as well as those of faith and doctrine."

[I]n *Serbian Eastern Orthodox Diocese for United States and Canada v. Milivojevich,* 426 U.S. 696 (1976), this Court explained that the First Amendment "permit[s] hierarchical religious organizations to establish their own rules and regulations for internal discipline and government, and to create tribunals for adjudicating disputes over these matters." When ecclesiastical tribunals decide such disputes, we further explained, "the Constitution requires that civil courts accept their decisions as binding upon them." We thus held that by inquiring into whether the Church had followed its own procedures, the State Supreme Court had "unconstitutionally undertaken the resolution of quintessentially religious controversies whose resolution the First Amendment commits exclusively to the highest ecclesiastical tribunals" of the Church.

C

Until today, we have not had occasion to consider whether this freedom of a religious organization to select its ministers is implicated by a suit alleging discrimination in employment. The Courts of Appeals, in contrast, have uniformly recognized the existence of a "ministerial exception," grounded in the First Amendment, that precludes application of such legislation to claims concerning the employment relationship between a religious institution and its ministers.

We agree that there is such a ministerial exception. The members of a religious group put their faith in the hands of their ministers. Requiring a church to accept or retain an unwanted minister, or punishing a church for failing to do so, intrudes upon more than a mere employment decision. Such action interferes with the internal governance of the church, depriving the church of control over the selection of those who will personify its beliefs. By imposing an unwanted minister, the state infringes the Free Exercise Clause, which protects a religious group's right to shape its own faith and mission through its appointments. According the state the power to determine which individuals will minister to the faithful also violates the Establishment Clause, which prohibits government involvement in such ecclesiastical decisions....

The EEOC and Perich contend that our decision in *Employment Div., Dept. of Human Resources of Ore. v. Smith,* 494 U.S. 872 (1990), precludes recognition of a ministerial exception. We held that [the State's denial of unemployment benefits] did not violate the Free Exercise Clause, even though the peyote had been ingested for sacramental purposes, because the "right of free exercise does not relieve an individual of the obligation to comply with a valid and neutral law of general applicability on the ground that the law proscribes (or prescribes) conduct that his religion prescribes (or proscribes)."

It is true that the ADA's prohibition on retaliation, like Oregon's prohibition on peyote use, is a valid and neutral law of general applicability. But a church's selection of its ministers is unlike an individual's ingestion of peyote. *Smith* involved government regulation of only outward physical acts. The present case, in contrast, concerns government interference with an internal church decision that affects the faith and mission of the church itself. The contention that *Smith* forecloses recognition of a ministerial exception rooted in the Religion Clauses has no merit.

III

Having concluded that there is a ministerial exception grounded in the Religion Clauses of the First Amendment, we consider whether the exception applies in this case. We hold that it does.

Every Court of Appeals to have considered the question has concluded that the ministerial exception is not limited to the head of a religious congregation, and we agree. We are reluctant, however, to adopt a rigid formula for deciding when an employee qualifies as a minister. It is enough for us to conclude, in this our first case involving the ministerial exception, that the exception covers Perich, given all the circumstances of her employment.

To begin with, Hosanna-Tabor held Perich out as a minister, with a role distinct from that of most of its members. When Hosanna-Tabor extended her a call, it accord[ed] her the title "Minister of Religion, Commissioned." She was tasked with performing that office "according to the Word of God and the confessional standards of the Evangelical Lutheran Church as drawn from the Sacred Scriptures."

Perich's title as a minister reflected a significant degree of religious training followed by a formal process of commissioning. To be eligible to become a commissioned minister, Perich had to complete eight college-level courses in subjects including biblical interpretation, church doctrine, and the ministry of the Lutheran teacher. She also had to obtain the endorsement of her local Synod district. Finally, she had to pass an oral examination by a faculty committee at a Lutheran college. And when she eventually [met these requirements], she was commissioned as a minister only upon election by the congregation, which recognized God's call to her to teach.

Perich held herself out as a minister of the Church by accepting the formal call to religious service, according to its terms. She did so in other ways as well. For example, she claimed a special housing allowance on her taxes that was available only to employees earning their compensation "'in the exercise of the ministry.'"

Perich's job duties reflected a role in conveying the Church's message and carrying out its mission. Hosanna-Tabor expressly charged her with "lead[ing] others toward Christian maturity" and "teach[ing] faithfully the Word of God, the Sacred Scriptures, in its truth and purity and as set forth in all the symbolical books of the Evangelical Lutheran Church." In fulfilling these responsibilities, Perich taught her students religion four days a week, and led them in prayer three times a day. Once a week, she took her students to a school-wide chapel service, and—about twice a year—she took her turn leading it, choosing the liturgy, selecting the hymns, and delivering a short message based on verses from the Bible. During her last year of teaching, Perich also led her fourth graders in a brief devotional exercise each morning. As a source of religious instruction, Perich performed an important role in transmitting the Lutheran faith to the next generation.

In light of these considerations[,] we conclude that Perich was a minister covered by the ministerial exception.

The EEOC and Perich suggest that Hosanna-Tabor's asserted religious reason for firing Perich—that she violated the Synod's commitment to internal dispute resolution—was pretextual. That suggestion misses the point of the ministerial exception. The purpose of the exception is not to safeguard a church's decision to fire a minister only when it is made for a religious reason. The exception instead ensures that the authority to select and control who will minister to the faithful—a matter "strictly ecclesiastical"—is the church's alone.

* * *

The interest of society in the enforcement of employment discrimination statutes is undoubtedly important. But so too is the interest of religious groups in choosing who will preach their beliefs, teach their faith, and carry out their mission. When a minister who has been fired sues her church alleging that her termination was discriminatory, the First Amendment has struck the balance for us. The church must be free to choose those who will guide it on its way.

JUSTICE THOMAS, concurring.

I join the Court's opinion. I write separately to note that, in my view, the Religion Clauses require civil courts to apply the ministerial exception and to defer to a religious organization's good-faith understanding of who qualifies as its minister. As the Court explains, the Religion Clauses guarantee religious organizations autonomy in matters of internal governance, including the selection of those who will minister the faith. A religious organization's right to choose its ministers would be hollow, however, if secular courts could second-guess the organization's sincere determination that a given employee is a "minister" under the organization's theological tenets. Our country's religious landscape includes organizations with different leadership structures and doctrines that influence their conceptions of ministerial status. The question whether an employee is a minister is itself religious in nature, and the answer will vary widely. Judicial attempts to fashion a civil definition of "minister" through a bright-line test or multi-factor analysis risk disadvantaging those religious groups whose beliefs, practices, and membership are outside of the "mainstream" or unpalatable to some. Moreover, uncertainty about whether its ministerial designation will be rejected, and a corresponding fear of liability, may cause a religious group to conform its beliefs and practices regarding "ministers" to the prevailing secular understanding.

JUSTICE ALITO, with whom JUSTICE KAGAN joins, concurring.

I join the Court's opinion, but I write separately to clarify my understanding of the significance of formal ordination and designation as a "minister" in determining whether an "employee" of a religious group falls within the so-called "ministerial" exception. Because virtually every religion in the world is represented in the population of the United States, it would be a mistake if the term "minister" or the concept of ordination were viewed as central to the important issue of religious autonomy that is presented in cases like this one. Instead, courts should focus on the function performed by persons who work for religious bodies.

The First Amendment protects the freedom of religious groups to engage in certain key religious activities, including the conducting of worship services and other religious ceremonies and rituals, as well as the critical process of communicating the faith. Accordingly, religious groups must be free to choose the personnel who are essential to the performance of these functions.

The "ministerial" exception should be tailored to this purpose. It should apply to any "employee" who leads a religious organization, conducts worship services or important religious ceremonies or rituals, or serves as a messenger or teacher of its faith. If a religious group believes that the ability of such an employee to perform these key functions has been compromised, then the constitutional guarantee of religious freedom protects the group's right to remove the employee from his or her position.

What matters in the present case is that Hosanna-Tabor believes that the religious function that respondent performed made it essential that she abide by the doctrine of internal dispute resolution; and the civil courts are in no position to second-guess that assessment. This conclusion rests not on respondent's ordination status or her formal title, but rather on her functional status as the type of employee that a church must be free to appoint or dismiss in order to exercise the religious liberty that the First Amendment guarantees.

Exercise 11:

1. Given that the Court acknowledges that federal antidiscrimination law is neutral and generally applicable under *Smith*, why does the Court conclude that the *Smith* rule is inapplicable to "government interference with an internal church decision that affects the faith and mission of the church itself"?

2. What are the contours of the ministerial exception under the majority's opinion?

3. Is Justice Thomas' view of the ministerial exception consistent with the majority opinion? How does it differ? Does his view follow from the Court's other decisions holding that courts cannot make religious decisions under the Religion Clauses?

4. How does Justice Alito's concurrence refine or alter the majority's position? With whom do you agree—the majority, Justice Thomas, or Justice Alito? Recall that *Hosanna-Tabor* was a unanimous decision. Is that because of broad agreement on the scope of the ministerial exception or because of the specific facts of *Hosanna-Tabor*?

5. The Supreme Court recently revisited the ministerial exception in *Our Lady of Guadalupe School v. Morrissey-Berru*, ___ S. Ct. ___, 2020 WL 3808420 (2020), which considered whether the ministerial exception precluded a court from hearing the employment discrimination claims of elementary school teachers at two elementary schools in the Archdiocese of Los Angeles. According to the terms of their virtually identical employment agreements, (1) the schools' "mission was 'to develop and promote a Catholic School Faith Community'... [and] '[a]ll [their] duties and responsibilities as [Teachers were to] be performed within this overriding commitment'"; (2) "the school hiring and retention decisions would be guided by its Catholic mission"; and (3) the Teachers were "required to participate in '[s]chool liturgical activities, as requested.'" *Id.* at *4. Both teachers prayed with their students, prepared them for participation in Mass, and instructed them in the tenets of Catholicism. *Id.* at *5–6. Justice Alito, now writing for a seven justice majority, applied "the same rule that dictated our decision in *Hosanna-Tabor*" but emphasized that *Hosanna-Tabor* "did not announce a 'rigid formula' for determining whether an employee falls within this exception." *Id.* at *3. Rather, "[i]n determining whether a particular position falls within the *Hosanna-Tabor* exception, a variety of factors may be important." *Id.* at *9. While *Hosanna-Tabor* relied on Perich's having the title of "minister," her "significant degree of religious training, her holding herself out as a minister to the public, and her role in conveying the Church's message and

teaching the faith," *Our Lady of Guadalupe School* explained that "the recognition of the significance of those factors in Perich's case did not mean that they must be met—or even that they are necessarily important—in all other cases." *Id.* at *9. Thus, contrary to the Ninth Circuit's narrow reading of *Hosanna-Tabor*, the fact that "these teachers were not given the title of 'minister' and have less religious training than [Cheryl] Perish" was not dispositive. *Id.* at *3. In fact, concentrating on religious titles "would risk privileging religious traditions with formal organizational structures over those that are less formal." *Id.* at 10. Instead, "[w]hat matters, at bottom, is what an employee does. And implicit in our decision in *Hosanna-Tabor* was a recognition that educating young people in their faith, inculcating its teachings, and training them to live their faith are responsibilities that lie at the very core of the mission of a private religious school." *Id.* at *10. The record evidence demonstrated both that the teachers performed such "vital religious duties" and that "their schools expressly saw them as playing a vital part in carrying out the mission of the church." *Id.* at 12. In an apparent nod to Justice Thomas' concurrence in *Hosanna-Tabor*, the Court noted the need to rely on the religious institution's understanding of a person's role in the organization:

> In a country with the religious diversity of the United States, judges cannot be expected to have a complete understanding and appreciation of the role played by every person who performs a particular role in every religious tradition. A religious institution's explanation of the role of such employees in the life of the religion in question is important.

Id. at *12. Drawing on "the general principle of church autonomy to which we have already referred: independence in matters of faith and doctrine and in closely linked matters of internal governance," the Court held that the ministerial exception applied to the teachers' employment discrimination claims. *Id.* at *8. As the Court summarized the point at the end of its opinion, "[w]hen a school with a religious mission entrusts a teacher with the responsibility of educating and forming students in the faith, judicial intervention into disputes between the school and the teacher threatens the school's independence in a way that the First Amendment does not allow." *Id.* at *14.

6. For the foreseeable future (*i.e.*, until the Court accepts one of the many petitions for certiorari asking the Court to reconsider *Smith*), the *Smith* Rule will continue to play a central role in the Supreme Court's free exercise jurisprudence. Consequently, plaintiffs will continue to rely primarily on federal and state statutes (such as the Religious Freedom Restoration Act or mini-RFRAs), and state constitutional provisions to ground their religious exercise claims. And the main ferment in the Court's case law will involve the number and scope of exceptions to the *Smith* Rule.

Chapter 3

The Establishment Clause

A. Introduction

The Supreme Court's Establishment Clause doctrine is, to put it charitably, muddled. The Supreme Court first waded into its modern Establishment Clause jurisprudence in the Janus-like case of *Everson v. Board of Education,* 330 U.S. 1 (1947). The Court's subsequent cases have unpredictably oscillated between different tests, historical claims, doctrinal structures, and results. Consequently, **Chapter Three** reviews the case law's initial trajectory following *Everson* and then introduces you to the competing modern tests that the various justices and coalitions of justices have utilized in different contexts in more recent cases.

Exercise 1:

Apply the first four forms of argument to the Establishment Clause.

1. Looking at the Constitution's text, what information do you gather regarding "Congress shall make no law respecting an establishment of religion"?

2. Looking at the Constitution's structure, what do you learn about "Congress shall make no law respecting an establishment of religion"?

3. Reviewing evidence of the Constitution's original meaning, what does it tell you about "Congress shall make no law respecting an establishment of religion"?

4. Do the materials following adoption of the Constitution offer any insight into "Congress shall make no law respecting an establishment of religion"?

As you read the materials below, consider the following issues:

What is an "establishment"? What are its facets or components?

What does it mean for a law to "respect[]" an establishment?

What is the Supreme Court's current definition of "establishment"?

How did the Supreme Court arrive at this definition? Is this definition of "establishment" based on the original meaning, tradition, and/or precedent?

What are the competing "tests" to ascertain whether the Establishment Clause is violated?

Why are there so many competing tests?

Which test is most faithful to the Clause's original meaning, to tradition, and to precedent?

Which tests govern which areas of church-state relations today?

What is the Supreme Court's current definition of "religion"?

How did the Supreme Court arrive at this definition? Is this definition of "religion" based on the original meaning, tradition, and/or precedent?

B. Original Meaning of the Establishment Clause

The Establishment Clause's original meaning has been and remains one of the most focused-on subjects by scholars for nearly seventy years.[1] This constant and strong flow of scholarship is the result of many factors, but most important is the Supreme Court's (contested) historical claims in its seminal case, *Everson v. Board of Education*,[2] discussed in the next section. Both the majority opinion, authored by Justice Black, and Justice Rutledge's dissent, directly tied the Establishment Clause's meaning to historical events, personalities, and documents. Both Justices Black and Rutledge articulated a strict separationist interpretation based on the historical evidence they presented. As Justice Black's opinion put it:

> The "establishment of religion" clause of the First Amendment means at least this: Neither a state nor the Federal Government can set up a church. Neither can pass laws which aid one religion, aid all religions, or prefer one religion over another. Neither can force nor influence a person to go to or to remain away from church against his will or force him to profess a belief or disbelief in any religion. No person can be punished for entertaining or professing religious beliefs or disbeliefs, for church attendance or non-attendance. No tax in any amount, large or small, can be levied to support any religious activities or institutions, whatever they may be called, or whatever form they may adopt to teach or practice religion. Neither a state nor the Federal Government can, openly or secretly, participate in the affairs of any religious organizations or groups and vice versa. In the words of Jefferson, the clause against establishment of religion by law was intended to erect "a wall of separation between [C]hurch and State."[3]

---

1. The best recent book surveying the Establishment Clause's original meaning and the scholarship in this area is DONALD L. DRAKEMAN, CHURCH, STATE, AND ORIGINAL INTENT (2010); *see also* PHILIP HAMBURGER, SEPARATION OF CHURCH AND STATE (2004) (describing the origin and evolution of the concept of separation of church and state). Two other widely-cited sources are ROBERT L. CORD, SEPARATION OF CHURCH AND STATE: HISTORICAL FACT AND CURRENT FICTION (1988); and Leonard W. Levy, THE ESTABLISHMENT CLAUSE: RELIGION AND THE FIRST AMENDMENT (1986). *See also* Vincent Philip Munoz, *The Original Meaning of the Establishment Clause and the Impossibility of its Incorporation*, 8 U. PA. J. CONST. L. 585 (2006) (providing a detailed review of the historical sources that influenced the Clause's original meaning).

2. Everson v. Board of Education, 330 U.S. 1 (1947); *see also* DRAKEMAN, *supra* note 1, at 13–18 (describing the varied scholarly response to *Everson*'s historical claims).

3. *Everson*, 330 U.S. at 15–16 (citations omitted).

Since *Everson*, scholars have advanced three basic interpretations of the Clause's original meaning.[4] The first, strict-separationist interpretation follows *Everson*'s prescriptions. The second interpretation is nonpreferentialism, which states that the federal government may nonpreferentially aid or "prefer" religion over nonreligion, so long as it does so on an equal basis.[5] The third contending school of thought is broadly labeled the "federalism interpretation," and it holds that the Clause affirmed that the federal government did not have authority over the subject of religion, and, in particular, the Clause precluded federal interference with state religious establishments.[6] This Introduction to the Establishment Clause's original meaning will describe some of the key historical events, personages, and documents from which these contending interpretations draw their data.

The American colonies' varied relationships between church and state developed against a background of the United Kingdom's established church, the Church of England.[7] The Church of England, following Henry VIII's Act of Supremacy, and confirmed by the 1689 Toleration Act, held a privileged position in the United Kingdom. The key points to the "relationship" between the British government and the Church of England were: the government selected important Church leaders; governmental regulation of Church doctrine; Church bishops sat in the House of Lords; numerous legal privileges for the Church, such as exclusion of non-Church members from office and higher education; restrictions on non-Church beliefs and practices; Church control of much of primary education; and government control of church structures. To different degrees, many of Britain's American colonies imitated this model, with more and more deviation as the eighteenth century continued.[8]

Most of the colonies maintained a state established church up to the Revolution. In New England, the Congregationalist Church was frequently established, and in

---

4. These categories are generalizations, and do not capture the nuance and variation of the respective arguments that scholars have made.

5. *See* J.M. O'NEIL, RELIGION AND EDUCATION UNDER THE CONSTITUTION (1949) (providing the seminal nonpreferentialist critique of *Everson*).

6. STEVEN D. SMITH, FOREORDAINED FAILURE: THE QUEST FOR A CONSTITUTIONAL PRINCIPLE OF RELIGIOUS FREEDOM (1995); DANIEL L. DREISBACH, REAL THREAT AND MERE SHADOW: RELIGIOUS LIBERTY AND THE FIRST AMENDMENT (1987).

7. *See* THOMAS J. CURRY, THE FIRST FREEDOMS: CHURCH AND STATE IN AMERICA TO THE PASSAGE OF THE FIRST AMENDMENT 192 (1988) ("[T]he image of establishment that continued to dominate the minds of Americans ... was a traditional one modeled on the Anglican establishment in England."); Robert G. Natelson, *The Original Meaning of the Establishment Clause*, 14 WM. & MARY BILL RTS. J. 73, 125 (2005).

8. *See* Natelson, *supra* note 7, at 124 ("[W]hen people referred to an 'establishment of religion,' they generally referred either to a single state church or to some other mechanism whereby one denomination or group of denominations is favored over others."); *see also* DRAKEMAN, *supra* note 1, at 216–17 (arguing that the concept of establishment was broadening during this period to include "the general assessment approach to using taxes to fund churches"); *id.* at 218 n.76 (acknowledging that "'establishment' had a traditional use in describing a Church of England-type of church-state arrangement").

the Southern colonies, the Anglican Church was established. Some of the Middle Colonies, most prominently Pennsylvania, did not erect an established church.

Over the course of the eighteenth century, and accelerating after the Revolution, the American colonies and, later, states, eliminated or reduced the rigor of their establishments. Particularly in the Southern states, the Revolution made it difficult to maintain the Church of England's established role. The most prominent such alteration occurred in Virginia, as we will see below.

Even the stalwart establishment states, such as Massachusetts, modified their establishments in response to accelerating religious pluralism by permitting each town to select to what religious denomination its taxes would go. In theory, this meant that non-Congregationalist denominations could be established in a town. However, both because of demographics and theology, minority religious denominations were infrequent recipients of government support in Massachusetts.

By 1791, seven states maintained established churches.[9] Importantly, many of those state establishments were not exclusive, as was the Church of England. Instead, these states permitted citizens to designate to which church their tax dollars would go and permitted the citizens to attend the church of their choice. Massachusetts' establishment fit this pattern. Its 1780 Constitution stated that "no subordination of any one sect or denomination to another shall ever be established by law."[10]

Even those states that no longer supported, or never supported, established churches frequently continued practices that privileged, not a prior establishment, but Protestant Christianity, Christianity in general, or theism. This generalized support for religion was the product, in part, of the widely-held view of the relationship between religion and civic virtue. Most Americans at the time believed that religious beliefs and practices helped create a virtuous citizenry which, in turn, helped maintain republican institutions.[11] The 1780 Massachusetts Constitution exemplified this view: "As the happiness of a people and the good order and preservation of civil government essentially depend upon piety, religion, and morality[,] the legislature shall ... authorize and require, the several towns, parishes, precincts, and other bodies-politic or religious societies to make suitable provision, at their own expense, for the institution of public worship of God and for the support and maintenance of public Protestant teachers of piety, religion, and morality."[12]

The Establishment Clause itself arose out of the complex ratification process of the original, unamended Constitution. Anti-Federalist opponents of ratification argued that the proposed federal government would threaten the various state relationships with religion.[13] There was also widespread concern that the national gov-

---

9. Levy, *supra* note 1, at xvi.

10. Mass. Const. of 1780, pt. 1, art. III.

11. *See* Natelson, *supra* note 7, at 113 ("There was a very broad consensus that government should foster religion.").

12. Mass. Const. of 1780, pt. 1, art. III.

13. *See* Drakeman, *supra* note 1, at 198–202 (summarizing the evidence).

ernment would establish one of the various Christian sects as a national church, along the lines of the Anglican Church.[14] Others expressed the fear that the national government would become subject to the papacy.[15]

Federalists initially responded to these claims by arguing that the principle of limited and enumerated powers showed that the federal government had no power to establish a national church or to interfere with state establishments. Federalist Edmund Randolph argued in the Virginia Ratification Convention that "I inform those who are of this opinion, that no power is given expressly to Congress over religion."[16] They also argued that Americans' love of liberty would prevent a national establishment. Connecticut Federalist Oliver Wolcott stated that, "[k]nowledge and liberty are so prevalent in this country, that I do not believe that the United States would ever be disposed to establish one religious sect."[17] Federalists also relied on the diversity of religious beliefs in the United States to argue that "there is no cause of fear that any one religion shall be exclusively established."[18]

Anti-Federalists adroitly countered that, even if the federal government did not possess an enumerated power over religion or religious establishments, the threat also came from the federal government's implied powers authorized by the Necessary and Property Clause.[19] Anti-Federalists pointed, for instance, to the federal government's power over federal territories which, coupled with the Necessary and Proper Clause, could imply the power to establish a sect.

When the Federalists' strategy failed to persuade those ratifiers who were on the fence, the Federalists promised to introduce an amendment to affirm the federal government's lack of power to establish a church.[20] As a result, a number of state ratification conventions proposed amendments, including amendments touching on a national establishment. This focus on a national established church revealed the Anti-Federalists' fear. It also preserved the many remaining state establishments, which the Anti-Federalists tended to favor. Four of the states proposed amendments — New York, Virginia, North Carolina, and Rhode Island[21] — that used language suggesting the possibility of nonpreferential assistance to religion. For example, New York's pro-

---

14. *See* 2 E.H. GILLETT, HISTORY OF THE PRESBYTERIAN CHURCH IN THE UNITED STATES OF AMERICA 200 (1864) (stating that the Presbyterian Church was rumored to be a candidate for national establishment).

15. Baptist Minister Henry Abbot, at the North Carolina ratification convention, expressed the concern that, "by the power of making treaties, the [federal government] might make a treaty with foreign powers to adopt the Roman Catholic religion in the United States." Henry Abbot, *in* NEIL H. COGAN, THE COMPLETE BILL OF RIGHTS: THE DRAFTS, DEBATES, SOURCES, AND ORIGINS 62–63 (1997).

16. Edmund Randolph, *in* COGAN, *supra* note 15, at 70.

17. Oliver Wolcott, *in* COGAN, *supra* note 15, at 62.

18. James Iredell, *in* COGAN, *supra* note 15, at 67–68.

19. *See* Natelson, *supra* note 7, at 91–94 (describing this argument).

20. *See id.* at 73 (describing the formation, content, and execution of this agreement).

21. Rhode Island's proposed amendment was not issued until 1790, after Congress passed the Establishment Clause.

posal was "no Religious Sect or Society ought to be favored or established by law in preference to others."[22]

New Hampshire's proposal was arguably broader: "Congress shall make no Laws Touching Religion."[23] It appeared to affirm the lack of federal power over the subject matter of religion.

James Madison took the lead drafting amendments and introduced into the first Congress what was to become the Establishment Clause. In doing so, Madison referred to the reason for the proposed amendment: "Some of the State Conventions, who seemed to entertain an opinion that [Congress could] establish a national religion."[24] The purpose of the Clause, therefore, was to prevent a federal national church and federal interference with state establishments, while, at the same time, not being so broad that the text prevented the federal government from fostering religion (through its implied powers) because Americans believed religion was conducive to republican government.[25]

Madison's initial text stated: "nor shall any national religion be established."[26] This text was tied to the New York-Virginia proposed amendments and to the Anti-Federalists' expressed concern of a national religion, which makes sense, given that Madison only agreed to amend the Constitution to secure ratification and did not want to go beyond that agreement to make any broader pronouncements on church-state relations.[27] Madison summarized his understanding of the text to the House this same way: "[Madison] apprehended the meaning of the words to be, that Congress should not establish a religion, and enforce the legal observation of it by law.... Whether the words are necessary or not he did not mean to say, but they had been required by some of the State Conventions, who seemed to entertain an opinion that [the Necessary and Proper Clause empowered Congress to] establish a national religion."[28] Later, Madison re-stated his goal in offering the proposed Establishment Clause: "He believed that the people feared that one sect might obtain a pre-eminence, or two combine together, and establish a religion to which they would compel others to conform."[29]

The Clause's text went through a number of versions,[30] including the adoption of New Hampshire's broader language,[31] before further developments. The key point to note is that the debated texts originated from Anti-Federalist concerns and texts.[32]

---

22. Ratification of the Constitution by the State of New York (July 26, 1788); *see also* Munoz, *supra* note 1, at 619–23 (discussing the various state proposed amendments).

23. Ratification of the Constitution by the State of New Hampshire (June 21, 1788).

24. James Madison, *in* COGAN, *supra* note 15, at 60.

25. Natelson, *supra* note 7, at 135–36.

26. 1 ANNALS OF CONG. 451 (Joseph Gales ed., 1834).

27. Natelson, *supra* note, at 134–35.

28. 1 ANNALS OF CONG. 730.

29. James Madison, *in* COGAN, *supra* note 15, at 60.

30. *See* DRAKEMAN, *supra* note 1, at 204–14 (describing the Clause's textual evolution along with the sparse debate).

31. 1 ANNALS OF CONG. 759.

32. Munoz, *supra* note 1, at 629.

Some of the debate centered on whether the different versions of the text would protect state establishments. Representative Huntington, for instance, sought clarification that the Clause would protect the Congregational establishments in New England.[33]

One of the key textual facets of the Establishment Clause is "respecting an," which was added to Madison's initial proposal during the debates. Different interpretations of this text have been advanced. One group of scholars has argued that "respecting an" meant that any legislation moving towards, coming close to, or embodying a facet of an establishment violated the Clause.[34] Another school of thought argued that "respecting an" is a capacious term that affirmed the federal government's pre-existing lack of enumerated power over religious subjects.[35]

There was relatively little recorded debate in the state ratification debates, and the records we have suggest that the Establishment Clause was not controversial. If, for instance, the Clause would have banned state denominational preferences or state aid to religion, the state convention delegates would have raised an outcry. The major on-point evidence comes out of the Virginia ratification convention where Anti-Federalists argued that the proposed Establishment Clause "restrain[ed] Congress from passing laws establishing any national religion."[36]

There were many early federal statutes that provided aid to religion, including direct monetary aid for core religious activities. They began early in the Republic. For instance, President Washington signed a bill aiding Christian missionaries "in civilizing and Christianizing … the Indians."[37] This aid continued for over a century.[38]

The First Congress provided for congressional chaplains paid with tax dollars[39] and appointed days of prayer and thanksgiving.[40] Indeed, James Madison served on the House committee that initiated these practices.[41] The First Congress explicitly supported religious practices, despite the criticism raised that doing so violated the Establishment Clause. For example, Congressman Thomas Tucker argued that the proposed national day of prayer and thanksgiving "is a business with which Congress has nothing to do; it is a religious matter, and as such, is proscribed to us."[42] Presidents Washington and Adams issued proclamations of prayer.[43] When the federal capital

---

33. 1 Annals of Cong. 730.

34. Lee v. Weisman, 505 U.S. 577, 614–15 (Souter, J., concurring).

35. Munoz, *supra* note 1, at 629–30.

36. Journal of the Senate of the Commonwealth of Virginia, Begun and Held in the City of Richmond, the 18th of October 1789, at 62 (1828).

37. R. Pierce Beaver, Church, State, and the American Indians 85 (1966) (detailing this episode).

38. *See* Drakeman, *supra* note 1, at 305–14 (detailing the significant federal aid to religion as part of federal Indian policy).

39. Drakeman, *supra* note, at 269–70.

40. 1 Annals of Cong. 914.

41. Later, though, Madison questioned the constitutionality of the practice. *See* Drakeman, *supra* note 1, at 270 (describing Madison's *Detached Memoranda*).

42. 1 Annals of Cong. 914.

43. Drakeman, *supra* note 1, at 268.

moved to the District of Columbia, many federal buildings, including the House of Representatives, hosted worship services.[44] The federal government granted articles of incorporation to churches in the District.[45] The evidence discussed thus far dealt with the federal government; on the state level, establishments of varying degrees of rigor were maintained up to 1832.

Supreme Court Justices and scholars have frequently tried to enlist Thomas Jefferson's and James Madison's writings and actions for their respective position.[46] Jefferson's and Madison's actions and arguments are not easy to pigeonhole. In Virginia, Jefferson and Madison collaborated to enact *A Bill for Establishing Religious Freedom*, which disestablished the Anglican Church.[47] By contrast, they also helped enact Virginia legislation that "punish[ed] disturbers of religious worship and Sabbath breakers."[48]

Jefferson was absent from the United States during the debates over ratification of the Constitution and the debates in Congress over the Establishment Clause.[49] As President, Jefferson signed a treaty with the Kaskaskia Indian tribe the provisions of which obligated the United States to build a church for the tribe and pay for a Catholic priest.[50] Jefferson also wrote "[c]ertainly no power to prescribe any religious exercise, or to assume authority in religious discipline, has been delegated to the general government. It must then rest with the State, as far as it can be in any human authority."[51] As President, Jefferson refused to issue official proclamations of prayer.[52] After his presidency, Jefferson famously founded the University of Virginia. At Jefferson's direction, and with James Madison on the University's board, the University directed that students were "expected to attend religious worship," if the student's denomination created a center for religious instruction near the University.[53]

President Madison vetoed two bills to incorporate churches in the District of Columbia on establishment grounds.[54] Later in life, though it is not clear exactly when, Madison wrote what has become known as his *Detached Memoranda*, where he stated

---

44. *Id.* at 268–69.

45. *Id.* at 273.

46. *Compare* DRAKEMAN, *supra* note 1, at 259 ("Whatever the Congress, the ratifiers, or the people thought the establishment clause meant, there is no evidence that any of those groups believed that it encompassed Madison's Memorial or Jefferson's Statute.").

47. Thomas Jefferson, *A Bill for Establishing Religious Freedom, reprinted in* THE PORTABLE THOMAS JEFFERSON 251, 253 (Merrill D. Peterson ed., 1977).

48. Report of the Committee of Revisors Appointed by the General Assembly of Virginia in MDCCLXXVI 59 (Richmond 1784).

49. *See* David E. Steinberg, *Thomas Jefferson's Establishment Clause Federalism*, 40 HASTINGS CONST. L.Q. 277, 303–06 (2013) (surveying Jefferson's presidency).

50. CHESTER JAMES ANTIEAU, ET AL., FREEDOM FROM FEDERAL ESTABLISHMENT 167 (1965).

51. Thomas Jefferson, *Letter to the Reverend Samuel Miller* (Jan. 23, 1808), *in* 11 THE WRITINGS OF THOMAS JEFFERSON 428–30 (Andrew A. Lipscomb ed., 1905) (1817).

52. *See Lee v. Weisman*, 505 U.S. 577, 623 (1992) (Souter, J., concurring) (noting this).

53. *State ex rel. McCollum v. Bd. of Educ.*, 333 U.S. 203, 246 (1948) (Reed, J., dissenting) (quoting 19 THE WRITINGS OF THOMAS JEFFERSON *supra* note 51, at 449–50).

54. 1 ANNALS OF CONG. 351, 366, 367, 995–98, 1104–06 (collecting Congress' and President Madison's actions); *see also Some of the First Official Meanings Assigned to the Establishment Clause, available at* http://www.constitution.org/jm/jm_estab.htm (same).

that congressional chaplains, for which he had previously voted, were inconsistent with the Establishment Clause.[55]

Justice and Harvard law professor Joseph Story published his *Commentaries on the Constitution of the United States* in 1832, the first major treatise on American constitutional law.[56] Story reflected a nonpreferentialist perspective of the Establishment Clause: "Probably at the time of the adoption of the Constitution, and of the [First] Amendment ... the general if not universal sentiment in America was, that Christianity ought to receive encouragement from the State so far as was not incompatible with the private rights of conscience and the freedom of religious worship."[57] Story's interpretation was bolstered by his civil republican view of the necessary role of religion in public and private life to maintain morality and the government's consequent duty to support religion. Story stated that "the right of a ... government to interfere in matters of religion will hardly be contested by any persons, who believe that piety, religion, and morality are intimately connected with the wellbeing of the state, and indispensable to the administration of civil justice."[58]

One final note before closing this Introduction: the materials covered in this Introduction do not include the evolution of the concept of establishment up to the Fourteenth Amendment's adoption. Some recent scholarship suggests that by 1868 Americans' conception of the bar on establishments had shifted in important ways and that the Privileges or Immunities Clause protected an individual right against establishment.[59] Despite the potential that this evidence holds, the Supreme Court has not utilized it to justify its jurisprudence.

Exercise 2:

1. What is the Establishment Clause's original meaning?

2. What is your degree of confidence in this original meaning? Are there some facets about which you have more confidence than others? What are they and why?

3. Is there anything in the Establishment Clause's history that suggests why the Supreme Court focused on it more than in any other area of the law?

4. As you read the cases and materials describing the modern, competing tests, below, ascertain which one is most faithful to the Establishment Clause's original meaning.

---

55. *See* DRAKEMAN, *supra* note 1, at 160 (discussing this).
56. JOSEPH STORY, COMMENTARIES ON THE CONSTITUTION OF THE UNITED STATES (1833).
57. *Id.* § 1868.
58. *Id.* § 1865.
59. *See* Kurt L. Lash, *The Second Adoption of the Establishment Clause: The Rise of the Nonestablishment Principle*, 27 ARIZ. L.J. 1085 (1996); *but see* Munoz, *supra* note 1, at 633–36 (briefly arguing against a personal right against incorporation).

C. The Seminal Case:
Everson v. Board of Education and the Birth of Strict Separation

1. Introduction

There were only a few Supreme Court cases that involved the Establishment Clause in the nineteenth and early-twentieth centuries. *See Bradfield v. Roberts*, 175 U.S. 291 (1899) (holding that a federal appropriation to a hospital operated by an order of Catholic nuns that served the general public did not violate the Establishment Clause); *Davis v. Beason*, 133 U.S. 333 (1890) (ruling that an Idaho territorial requirement that voters and office holders must swear an oath that they do not believe in polygamous marriage was not an establishment); *Terrett v. Taylor*, 13 U.S. (9 Cranch.) 43 (1815) (ruling that a Virginia statute that had confirmed the Episcopal Church's ownership of church lands following its disestablishment did not constitute an establishment). This situation was similar to that of the Bill of Rights generally, prior to the advent of the Incorporation Doctrine covered in Volume 5.

However, there were additional reasons for the lack of Establishment Clause cases prior to 1947. One was the New Deal. You have seen in various contexts, such as the Commerce Clause and the Tenth Amendment (covered in Volumes 3 and 4 respectively), that the Supreme Court retreated from vigorous judicial review during the New Deal, especially oversight of the federal government. The Supreme Court slowly waded back into significant judicial review, but this occurred primarily in the context of what we today call fundamental rights. You saw this phenomenon, for example, in Volume 5 when you reviewed the history of substantive due process doctrine. Not surprisingly, the Eversonian strict separationist interpretation of the Establishment Clause also blossomed during the height of the Warren Court's fundamental rights jurisprudence.

A second reason was a relaxing of the standing requirements. If you covered standing doctrine in Volume 1, you know that there was and, to a lesser degree, remains a long-standing rule against taxpayer and citizen standing. In the establishment context, this meant that there were few people with standing to challenge allegedly unconstitutional church-state relationships. Beginning with *Flast v. Cohen*, 392 U.S. 83 (1968), however, the Supreme Court carved out an exception to the rule against taxpayer standing for Establishment Clause challenges. This dramatically expanded the universe of potential plaintiffs, and the universe of cognizable harms, to include people who were, for example, emotionally offended by religious displays.

A third cause was the widespread and deeply entrenched set of governmental religious practices. The United States was predominantly a nation of Protestant Christians, so it was natural to most Americans that their legislative sessions opened with prayers, public schools taught the Bible and religion, and public squares hosted religious displays, among many other religious activities. This naturalness made for few aggrieved people and put social pressure on those who were aggrieved to "go along" with the practices. It also made it politically difficult for courts to work against such practices.

Beginning with significant Catholic immigration, followed by non-Christian immigration and ultimately the rise of non-religious Americans, the United States became a nation with significant religious pluralism, which caused these pervasive religious practices to lose their perceived "naturalness" and hence opened them to legal challenge. *See, e.g.,* WILL HERBERG, PROTESTANT-CATHOLIC-JEW: AN ESSAY IN AMERICAN RELIGIOUS SOCIOLOGY (1955) (arguing, famously, that the United States was significantly religiously pluralistic and remained so, despite a rise in superficial religiosity of the early-1950s). This rise of religious pluralism meant that more Americans did not view these traditional religious practices in the same light and that there was less social pressure to "remain quiet" if one was offended by the practices.

2. *Everson v. Board of Education*

As these obstacles waned, the Supreme Court entered into the Establishment Clause fray in a major way in *Everson v. Board of Education*, 330 U.S. 1 (1947), reprinted below. It is difficult to overstate *Everson*'s significance to the evolution of the Supreme Court's Establishment Clause case law, the academic commentary on that Clause, and the political arguments about the proper relationship between religion and government in American life.

Everson v. Board of Education of Ewing Township
330 U.S. 1 (1947)

MR. JUSTICE BLACK delivered the opinion of the Court.

A New Jersey statute authorizes its local school districts to make rules and contracts for the transportation of children to and from schools. The appellee, a township board of education, acting pursuant to this statute authorized reimbursement to parents of money expended by them for the bus transportation of their children on regular busses operated by the public transportation system. Part of this money was for the payment of transportation of some children in the community to Catholic parochial schools. These church schools give their students, in addition to secular education, regular religious instruction conforming to the religious tenets and modes of worship of the Catholic Faith. The superintendent of these schools is a Catholic priest.

The New Jersey statute is challenged as a "law respecting an establishment of religion." The First Amendment ... commands that a state "shall make no law respecting an establishment of religion, or prohibiting the free exercise thereof." These words of the First Amendment reflected in the minds of early Americans a vivid mental picture of conditions and practices which they fervently wished to stamp out in order to preserve liberty for themselves and for their posterity. Doubtless their goal has not been entirely reached; but so far has the Nation moved toward it that the expression "law respecting an establishment of religion," probably does not so vividly remind present-day Americans of the evils, fears, and political problems that caused that expression to be written into our Bill of Rights. Whether this New Jersey law is one respecting the "establishment of religion" requires an understanding of the meaning of that language, particularly with respect to the imposition of taxes. Once again, therefore, it is not inappropriate briefly to review the background and environment of the period in which that constitutional language was fashioned and adopted.

A large proportion of the early settlers of this country came here from Europe to escape the bondage of laws which compelled them to support and attend government favored churches. The centuries immediately before and contemporaneous with the colonization of America had been filled with turmoil, civil strife, and persecutions, generated in large part by established sects determined to maintain their absolute political and religious supremacy. With the power of government supporting them, at various times and places, Catholics had persecuted Protestants, Protestants had persecuted Catholics, Protestant sects had persecuted other Protestant sects, Catholics of one shade of belief had persecuted Catholics of another shade of belief, and all of these had from time to time persecuted Jews. In efforts to force loyalty to whatever religious group happened to be on top and in league with the government of a particular time and place, men and women had been fined, cast in jail, cruelly tortured, and killed. Among the offenses for which these punishments had been inflicted were such things as speaking disrespectfully of the views of ministers of government-established churches, nonattendance at those churches, expressions of non-belief in their doctrines, and failure to pay taxes and tithes to support them.[5]

These practices of the old world were transplanted to and began to thrive in the soil of the new America. The very charters granted by the English Crown to the individuals and companies designated to make the laws which would control the destinies of the colonials authorized these individuals and companies to erect religious establishments which all, whether believers or non-believers, would be required to support and attend. An exercise of this authority was accompanied by a repetition of many of the old world practices and persecutions. Catholics found themselves hounded and proscribed because of their faith; Quakers who followed their conscience went to jail; Baptists were peculiarly obnoxious to certain dominant Protestant sects; men and women of varied faiths who happened to be in a minority in a particular locality were persecuted because they steadfastly persisted in worshipping God only as their own consciences dictated.[7] And all of these dissenters were compelled to pay tithes and taxes to support government-sponsored churches whose ministers preached inflammatory sermons designed to strengthen and consolidate the established faith by generating a burning hatred against dissenters.

---

5. See, e.g., [Charles A.] Beard, [The] Rise of American Civilization (1937) I, 60; [Sanford H.] Cobb, Religious Liberty in America (1902) c. II; [William W.] Sweet, The Story of Religion in America (1939) c. II; [William W.] Sweet, Religion in Colonial America (1942) 320–22.

7. See, e.g., [Robert B.] Semple, Baptists in Virginia (1894); Sweet, Religion in Colonial America, *supra* at 131–52, 322–39.

These practices became so commonplace as to shock the freedom-loving colonials into a feeling of abhorrence.[9] The imposition of taxes to pay ministers' salaries and to build and maintain churches and church property aroused their indignation. It was these feelings which found expression in the First Amendment. No one locality and no one group throughout the Colonies can rightly be given entire credit for having aroused the sentiment that culminated in adoption of the Bill of Rights' provisions embracing religious liberty. But Virginia, where the established church had achieved a dominant influence in political affairs and where many excesses attracted wide public attention, provided a great stimulus and able leadership for the movement. The people there, as elsewhere, reached the conviction that individual religious liberty could be achieved best under a government which was stripped of all power to tax, to support, or otherwise to assist any or all religions, or to interfere with the beliefs of any religious individual or group.

The movement toward this end reached its dramatic climax in Virginia in 1785–86 when the Virginia legislative body was about to renew Virginia's tax levy for the support of the established church. Thomas Jefferson and James Madison led the fight against this tax. Madison wrote his great Memorial and Remonstrance against the law. In it, he eloquently argued that a true religion did not need the support of law; that no person, either believer or non-believer, should be taxed to support a religious institution of any kind; that the best interest of a society required that the minds of men always be wholly free; and that cruel persecutions were the inevitable result of government-established religions. Madison's Remonstrance received strong support throughout Virginia, and the Assembly postponed consideration of the proposed tax measure until its next session. When the proposal came up for consideration at that session, it not only died in committee, but the Assembly enacted the famous "Virginia Bill for Religious Liberty" originally written by Thomas Jefferson.[13] The preamble to that Bill stated among other things that

"Almighty God hath created the mind free; that all attempts to influence it by temporal punishments, or burthens, or by civil incapacitations, tend only to beget habits of hypocrisy and meanness, and are a departure from the plan of the Holy author of our religion who being Lord both of body and mind, yet chose not to propagate it by coercions on either … ; that to compel a man to furnish contributions of money for the propagation of opinions which he disbelieves, is sinful and tyrannical; that even the forcing him to

---

9. Madison wrote to a friend in 1774: "That diabolical, hell-conceived principle of persecution rages among some. * * * This vexes me the worst of anything whatever. There are at this time in the adjacent country not less than five or six well-meaning men in close jail for publishing their religious sentiments, which in the main are very orthodox. I have neither patience to hear, talk, or think of anything relative to this matter; for I have squabbled and scolded, abused and ridiculed, so long about it to little purpose, that I am without common patience. So I must beg you to pity me, and pray for liberty of conscience to all." I Writings of James Madison (1900) 18, 21.

13. For accounts of background and evolution of the Virginia Bill for Religious Liberty see e.g. [Charles F.] James, The Struggle for Religious Liberty in Virginia (1900); [William T.] Thom, The Struggle for Religious Freedom in Virginia; the Baptists (1900).

> support this or that teacher of his own religious persuasion, is depriving him
> of the comfortable liberty of giving his contributions to the particular pastor,
> whose morals he would make his pattern. * * *"

And the statute itself enacted

> "That no man shall be compelled to frequent or support any religious wor-
> ship, place, or ministry whatsoever, nor shall be enforced, restrained, mo-
> lested, or burthened, in his body or goods, nor shall otherwise suffer on
> account of his religious opinions or belief...."

This Court has previously recognized that the provisions of the First Amendment,
in the drafting and adoption of which Madison and Jefferson played such leading roles,
had the same objective and were intended to provide the same protection against governmental intrusion on religious liberty as the Virginia statute. *Reynolds v. United States*,
98 U.S. [145,] 164 [(1878)]. Prior to the adoption of the Fourteenth Amendment, the
First Amendment did not apply as a restraint against the states. Most of them did soon
provide similar constitutional protections for religious liberty. But some states persisted
for about half a century in imposing restraints upon the free exercise of religion and
in discriminating against particular religious groups.[17] In recent years, so far as the provision against the establishment of a religion is concerned, the question has most frequently arisen in connection with proposed state aid to church schools and efforts to
carry on religious teachings in the public schools in accordance with the tenets of a
particular sect. The state courts, in the main, have remained faithful to the language
of their own constitutional provisions designed to protect religious freedom and to
separate religious and governments. Their decisions, however, show the difficulty in
drawing the line between tax legislation which provides funds for the welfare of the
general public and that which is designed to support institutions which teach religion.

The meaning and scope of the First Amendment, preventing establishment of religion or prohibiting the free exercise thereof, in the light of its history and the evils
it was designed forever to suppress, have been several times elaborated by the decisions
of this Court prior to the application of the First Amendment to the states by the
Fourteenth.[21] The broad meaning given the Amendment by these earlier cases has
been accepted by this Court in its decisions concerning an individual's religious freedom
rendered since the Fourteenth Amendment was interpreted to make the prohibitions
of the First applicable to state action abridging religious freedom.[22] There is every
reason to give the same application and broad interpretation to the "establishment of
religion" clause. "The structure of our government has, for the preservation of civil
liberty, rescued the temporal institutions from religious interference. On the other
hand, it has secured religious liberty from the invasions of the civil authority."

---

17. Test provisions forbade office holders to "deny * * * the truth of the Protestant religion," e.g.
Constitution of North Carolina 1776. Maryland permitted taxation for support of the Christian
religion and limited civil office to Christians until 1818.

21. *Reynolds v. United States, supra*, 98 U.S. 162.

22. *Cantwell v. State of Conn.*, 310 U.S. 296 [(1940)]; *West Virginia State Board of Education v.
Barnette*, 319 U.S. 624 [(1943)].

The "establishment of religion" clause of the First Amendment means at least this: Neither a state nor the Federal Government can set up a church. Neither can pass laws which aid one religion, aid all religions, or prefer one religion over another. Neither can force nor influence a person to go to or to remain away from church against his will or force him to profess a belief or disbelief in any religion. No person can be punished for entertaining or professing religious beliefs or disbeliefs, for church attendance or non-attendance. No tax in any amount, large or small, can be levied to support any religious activities or institutions, whatever they may be called, or whatever form they may adopt to teach or practice religion. Neither a state nor the Federal Government can, openly or secretly, participate in the affairs of any religious organizations or groups and vice versa. In the words of Jefferson, the clause against establishment of religion by law was intended to erect "a wall of separation between Church and State." *Reynolds v. United States*, 98 U.S. at page 164.

We must consider the New Jersey statute in accordance with the foregoing limitations imposed by the First Amendment. New Jersey cannot consistently with the "establishment of religion" clause of the First Amendment contribute tax-raised funds to the support of an institution which teaches the tenets and faith of any church. On the other hand, other language of the amendment commands that New Jersey cannot hamper its citizens in the free exercise of their own religion. Consequently, it cannot exclude individual Catholics, Lutherans, Mohammedans, Baptists, Jews, Methodists, Non-believers, Presbyterians, or the members of any other faith, because of their faith, or lack of it, from receiving the benefits of public welfare legislation. While we do not mean to intimate that a state could not provide transportation only to children attending public schools, we must be careful, in protecting the citizens of New Jersey against state-established churches, to be sure that we do not inadvertently prohibit New Jersey from extending its general State law benefits to all its citizens without regard to their religious belief.

Measured by these standards, we cannot say that the First Amendment prohibits New Jersey from spending tax-raised funds to pay the bus fares of parochial school pupils as a part of a general program under which it pays the fares of pupils attending public and other schools. It is undoubtedly true that children are helped to get to church schools. There is even a possibility that some of the children might not be sent to the church schools if the parents were compelled to pay their children's bus fares out of their own pockets when transportation to a public school would have been paid for by the State. Moreover, state-paid policemen, detailed to protect children going to and from church schools from the very real hazards of traffic, would serve much the same purpose and accomplish much the same result as state provisions intended to guarantee free transportation of a kind which the state deems to be best for the school children's welfare. And parents might refuse to risk their children to the serious danger of traffic accidents going to and from parochial schools, the approaches to which were not protected by policemen. Similarly, parents might be reluctant to permit their children to attend schools which the state had cut off from such general government services as ordinary police and fire protection, connections for sewage disposal, public highways and sidewalks. Of course, cutting off church schools from these services, so separate and so indisputably marked off from the religious function, would make it far more difficult for the schools to operate. But such is obviously not the purpose of the First Amendment. That Amendment requires the state to be a neutral in its relations with groups of religious believers and non-believers; it does not require the state to be their adversary. State power is no more to be used so as to handicap religions, than it is to favor them.

This Court has said that parents may, in the discharge of their duty under state compulsory education laws, send their children to a religious rather than a public school if the school meets the secular educational requirements which the state has power to impose. See *Pierce v. Society of Sisters*, 268 U.S. 510 [(1925)]. It appears that these parochial schools meet New Jersey's requirements. The State contributes no money to the schools. It does not support them. Its legislation, as applied, does no more than provide a general program to help parents get their children, regardless of their religion, safely and expeditiously to and from accredited schools.

The First Amendment has erected a wall between church and state. That wall must be kept high and impregnable. We could not approve the slightest breach. New Jersey has not breached it here.

Mr. Justice Jackson, dissenting.

I have a sympathy, though it is not ideological, with Catholic citizens who are compelled by law to pay taxes for public schools, and also feel constrained by conscience and discipline to support other schools for their own children. Such relief to them as this case involves is not in itself a serious burden to taxpayers. The Court's opinion marshals every argument in favor of state aid and puts the case in its most favorable light, but much of its reasoning confirms my conclusions that there are no good grounds upon which to support the present legislation. In fact, the undertones of the opinion, advocating complete and uncompromising separation of Church from State, seem utterly discordant with its conclusion yielding support to their commingling in educational matters.

The Court's holding is that this taxpayer has no grievance because the state has decided to make the reimbursement a public purpose and therefore we are bound to regard it as such. I agree that this Court has left, and always should leave to each state, great latitude in deciding for itself, in the light of its own conditions, what shall be public purposes in its scheme of things. It may socialize utilities and economic enterprises and make taxpayers' business out of what conventionally had been private business. But it cannot make public business of religious worship or instruction, or of attendance at religious institutions of any character. There is no answer to the proposition more fully expounded by Mr. Justice Rutledge that the effect of the religious freedom Amendment to our Constitution was to take every form of propagation of religion out of the realm of things which could directly or indirectly be made public business and thereby be supported in whole or in part at taxpayers' expense. That is a difference which the Constitution sets up between religion and almost every other subject matter of legislation, a difference which goes to the very root of religious freedom and which the Court is overlooking today. This freedom was intended not only to keep the states' hands out of religion, but to keep religion's hands off the state, and above all, to keep bitter religious controversy out of public life by denying to every denomination any advantage from getting control of public policy or the public purse. Those great ends I cannot but think are immeasurably compromised by today's decision.

This policy of our Federal Constitution has never been wholly pleasing to most religious groups. They all are quick to invoke its protections; they all are irked when they feel its restraints. This Court has gone a long way, if not an unreasonable way, to hold that public business of such paramount importance as maintenance of public order, protection of the privacy of the home, and taxation may not be pursued by a state in a way that even indirectly will interfere with religious proselyting.

But we cannot have it both ways. Religious teaching cannot be a private affair when the state seeks to impose regulations which infringe on it indirectly, and a public affair when it comes to taxing citizens of one faith to aid another, or those of no faith to aid all. If these principles seem harsh in prohibiting aid to Catholic education, it must not be forgotten that it is the same Constitution that alone assures Catholics the right to maintain these schools at all when predominant local sentiment would forbid them. *Pierce v. Society of Sisters*, 268 U.S. 510 [(1925)]. Nor should I think that those who have done so well without this aid would want to see this separation between Church and State broken down. If the state may aid these religious schools, it may therefore regulate them. Many groups have sought aid from tax funds only to find that it carried political controls with it.

Mr. Justice Frankfurter joins in this opinion.

Mr. Justice Rutledge, with whom Mr. Justice Frankfurter, Mr. Justice Jackson and Mr. Justice Burton agree, dissenting.

> "Congress shall make no law respecting an establishment of religion, or prohibiting the free exercise thereof. * * *" U.S. Const. Am. Art. I.
>
> "Well aware that Almighty God hath created the mind free; * * * that to compel a man to furnish contributions of money for the propagation of opinions which he disbelieves, is sinful and tyrannical; * * * We, the General Assembly, do enact, That no man shall be compelled to frequent or support any religious worship, place, or ministry whatsoever, nor shall be enforced, restrained, molested, or burthened in his body or goods, nor shall otherwise suffer on account of his religious opinions or belief. * * *"[1]

I cannot believe that the great author of those words, or the men who made them law, could have joined in this decision.

---

1. "A Bill for Establishing Religious Freedom," enacted by the General Assembly of Virginia, January 19, 1786.

I.

Not simply an established church, but any law respecting an establishment of religion is forbidden. The Amendment was broadly but not loosely phrased. It is the compact and exact summation of its author's views formed during his long struggle for religious freedom. Madison could not have confused "church" and "religion," or "an established church" and "an establishment of religion."

The Amendment's purpose was not to strike merely at the official establishment of a single sect, creed or religion, outlawing only a formal relation such as had prevailed in England and some of the colonies. Necessarily it was to uproot all such relationships. But the object was broader than separating church and state in this narrow sense. It was to create a complete and permanent separation of the spheres of religious activity and civil authority by comprehensively forbidding every form of public aid or support for religion. In proof the Amendment's wording and history unite with this Court's consistent utterances whenever attention has been fixed directly upon the question.

II.

No provision of the Constitution is more closely tied to or given content by its generating history than the religious clause of the First Amendment. It is at once the refined product and the terse summation of that history. For Madison, as also for Jefferson, religious freedom was the crux of the struggle for freedom in general. [The Memorial and Remonstrance] is Madison's complete, though not his only, interpretation of religious liberty. It is a broadside attack upon all forms of "establishment" of religion, nondiscriminatory or selective.... [T]he Remonstrance is at once the most concise and the most accurate statement of the views of the First Amendment's author concerning what is "an establishment of religion."

[In 1787,] Madison became a member of the Constitutional Convention. Its work done, he fought valiantly to secure the ratification of its great product in Virginia as elsewhere, and nowhere else more effectively. Madison was certain in his own mind that under the Constitution "there is not a shadow of right in the general government to intermeddle with religion" and that "this subject is, for the honor of America, perfectly free and unshackled. The Government has no jurisdiction over it...." Nevertheless he pledged that he would work for a Bill of Rights, including a specific guaranty of religious freedom, and Virginia, with other states, ratified the Constitution on this assurance.

Ratification thus accomplished, Madison was sent to the first Congress. There he went at once about performing his pledge to establish freedom for the nation as he had done in Virginia. Within a little more than three years from his legislative victory at home he had proposed and secured the submission and ratification of the First Amendment as the first article of our Bill of Rights.

All the great instruments of the Virginia struggle for religious liberty thus became warp and woof of our constitutional tradition, not simply by the course of history, but by the common unifying force of Madison's life, thought and sponsorship. He epitomized the whole of that tradition in the Amendment's compact, but nonetheless comprehensive, phrasing.

As the Remonstrance discloses throughout, Madison opposed every form and degree of official relation between religion and civil authority. For him religion was a wholly private matter beyond the scope of civil power either to restrain or to support. Denial or abridgment of religious freedom was a violation of rights both of conscience and of natural equality. "Establishment" and "free exercise" were correlative and co-extensive ideas, representing only different facets of the single great and fundamental freedom. With Jefferson, Madison believed that to tolerate any fragment of establishment would be by so much to perpetuate restraint upon that freedom. Hence he sought to tear out the institution not partially but root and branch, and to bar its return forever.

In no phase was he more unrelentingly absolute than in opposing state support or aid by taxation. Not even "three pence" contribution was thus to be exacted from any citizen for such a purpose. Tithes had been the life blood of establishment before and after other compulsions disappeared. Madison and his coworkers made no exceptions or abridgments to the complete separation they created. Their objection was not to small tithes. It was to any tithes whatsoever. "If it were lawful to impose a small tax for religion the admission would pave the way for oppressive levies." Not the amount but "the principle of assessment was wrong." And the principle was as much to prevent "the interference of law in religion" as to restrain religious intervention in political matters.

In view of this history no further proof is needed that the Amendment forbids any appropriation, large or small, from public funds to aid or support any and all religious exercises. But if more were called for, the debates in the First Congress and this Court's consistent expressions, whenever it has touched on the matter directly, supply it. By contrast with the Virginia history, the congressional debates on consideration of the Amendment reveal only sparse discussion, reflecting the fact that the essential issues had been settled. Indeed the matter had become so well understood as to have been taken for granted in all but formal phrasing.

III.

[T]oday, apart from efforts to inject religious training or exercises and sectarian issues into the public schools, the only serious surviving threat to maintaining that complete and permanent separation of religion and civil power which the First Amendment commands is through use of the taxing power to support religion, religious establishments, or establishments having a religious foundation whatever their form or special religious function.

Does New Jersey's action furnish support for religion by use of the taxing power? Certainly it does, if the test remains undiluted as Jefferson and Madison made it, that money taken by taxation from one is not to be used or given to support another's religious training or belief, or indeed one's own. Today as then the furnishing of "contributions of money for the propagation of opinions which he disbelieves" is the forbidden exaction; and the prohibition is absolute for whatever measure brings that consequence and whatever amount may be sought or given to that end.

The funds used here were raised by taxation. The Court does not dispute nor could it that their use does in fact give aid and encouragement to religious instruction.... Here parents pay money to send their children to parochial schools and funds raised by taxation are used to reimburse them. This not only helps the children to get to school and the parents to send them. It aids them in a substantial way to get the very thing which they are sent to the particular school to secure, namely, religious training and teaching.

Believers of all faiths, and others who do not express their feeling toward ultimate issues of existence in any creedal form, pay the New Jersey tax. When the money so raised is used to pay for transportation to religious schools, the Catholic taxpayer to the extent of his proportionate share pays for the transportation of Lutheran, Jewish and otherwise religiously affiliated children to receive their non-Catholic religious instruction. Their parents likewise pay proportionately for the transportation of Catholic children to receive Catholic instruction. Each thus contributes to "the propagation of opinions which he disbelieves" in so far as their religions differ, as do others who accept no creed without regard to those differences. Each thus pays taxes also to support the teaching of his own religion, an exaction equally forbidden since it denies "the comfortable liberty" of giving one's contribution to the particular agency of instruction he approves.

New Jersey's action therefore exactly fits the type of exaction and the kind of evil at which Madison and Jefferson struck. Under the test they framed it cannot be said that the cost of transportation is no part of the cost of education or of the religious instruction given. That it is a substantial and a necessary element is shown most plainly by the continuing and increasing demand for the state to assume it. Nor is there pretense that it relates only to the secular instruction given in religious schools or that any attempt is or could be made toward allocating proportional shares as between the secular and the religious instruction. It is precisely because the instruction is religious and relates to a particular faith, whether one or another, that parents send their children to religious schools. And the very purpose of the state's contribution is to defray the cost of conveying the pupil to the place where he will receive not simply secular, but also and primarily religious, teaching and guidance.

An appropriation from the public treasury to pay the cost of transportation to Sunday school, to weekday special classes at the church or parish house, or to the meetings of various young people's religious societies, could not withstand the constitutional attack. This would be true, whether or not secular activities were mixed with the religious. If such an appropriation could not stand, then it is hard to see how one becomes valid for the same thing upon the more extended scale of daily instruction. Surely constitutionality does not turn on where or how often the mixed teaching occurs.

Finally, transportation, where it is needed, is as essential to education as any other element. Its cost is as much a part of the total expense, except at times in amount, as the cost of textbooks, of school lunches, of athletic equipment, of writing and other materials; indeed of all other items composing the total burden. No less essential is [transportation], or the payment of its cost, than the very teaching in the classroom or payment of the teacher's sustenance. Many types of equipment, now considered essential, better could be done without.

For me, therefore, the feat is impossible to select so indispensable an item from the composite of total costs, and characterize it as not aiding, contributing to, promoting or sustaining the propagation of beliefs which it is the very end of all to bring about. Unless this can be maintained, and the Court does not maintain it, the aid thus given is outlawed. Payment of transportation is no more, nor is it any the less essential to education, whether religious or secular, than payment for tuitions, for teachers' salaries, for buildings, equipment and necessary materials. Nor is it any the less directly related, in a school giving religious instruction, to the primary religious objective all those essential items of cost are intended to achieve. No rational line can be drawn between payment for such larger, but not more necessary, items and payment for transportation. The only line that can be so drawn is one between more dollars and less. Certainly in this realm such a line can be no valid constitutional measure.

Exercise 3:

1. Describe the quality and quantity of interactions between the school board and religious institutions. How analogous are those relationships to the established churches in England and some of the states, such as Massachusetts? Do those relationships, even if not fully analogous to an established church, fit some facet(s) of church establishments? Are those relationships a step, or steps, toward a state-established church?

2. What is the Establishment Clause's meaning according to the Court?

3. In many areas of constitutional law, history plays an important role. However, few, if any, areas of American law have been dominated by historical claims as in the Establishment Clause context. For a powerful argument that Justice Black's use of history—along with dissenting Justice Rutledge's—was unprincipled, see DONALD L. DRAKEMAN, CHURCH, STATE, AND ORIGINAL INTENT (2009); *see also* Lee J. Strang, *Introduction: The (Re)Turn to History in Religion Clause Law and Scholarship*, 81 NOTRE DAME L. REV. 1697 (2006) (surveying the ebb and flow of historical research and argumentation on the Establishment Clause).

4. Upon what basis did Justice Rutledge dissent? Did Justice Black and Justice Rutledge disagree on the meaning of the Establishment Clause? Did they disagree on application of the Clause?

5. Did Justice Black's and/or Justice Rutledge's description of the Establishment Clause's history persuade you? If so, does the lack of competing historical narrative by, for instance, dissenting Justices, trouble you? Whose role is it to check the justices' historical claims? One of the key characteristics of subsequent opinions and scholarship critical of *Everson*'s historical narrative was counter-narratives. *See Wallace v. Jaffree*, 472 U.S. 38, 91 (1985) (Rehnquist, J., dissenting) (providing the seminal judicial counter-narrative).

6. If you are inclined to view the history surrounding the Establishment Clause as supporting something other than a strict separationist view, then you have to

explain how the dominant view, represented by a unanimous Supreme Court, came about. For example, scholars have argued that "traditional fears about the anti-Christian character of Catholicism and its union of church and state," coupled with the advent of secularism, during the mid-nineteenth century, caused Americans to adopt the principle of "separation of church and state." PHILIP HAMBURGER, SEPARATION OF CHURCH AND STATE 191–284 (2002).

7. What interpretative tools did Justice Black utilize? Were the tools of equal weight in Justice Black's reasoning? What tools did Justice Rutledge utilize? Does any difference in interpretative approach account for their different outcomes?

8. If the purported object of constitutional interpretation was the federal Establishment Clause, was it appropriate for Justice Black to focus on a couple of individuals, such as Thomas Jefferson and James Madison, and primarily on one state's — Virginia's — legal history? For example, what reason did Justice Black have to privilege Virginia's experience, instead of Massachusetts'? If you argue the focus on Virginia's history was inappropriate, then upon what *should* Justice Black have focused instead?

9. What evidence did Justice Black, along with Justice Rutledge, identify that tied Virginia's experience with the meaning of the federal Establishment Clause? Is that a sufficiently tight relationship?

10. Did the Court's holding follow from Justice Black's reasoning? Or did the Court reach the wrong result, as argued by the dissent?

11. How is the *Everson* Court's holding consistent with this statement in its opinion: "Neither can pass laws which aid one religion, aid all religions, or prefer one religion over another.... No tax in any amount, large or small, can be levied to support any religious activities or institutions, whatever they may be called, or whatever form they may adopt to teach or practice religion"? The plaintiff argued that the tax "aid[ed] ... religion" and "support[ed]" a[] religious activit[y]." How was the plaintiff wrong?

12. The *Everson* majority concluded that the taxpayer-reimbursed bussing was a general welfare policy, like fire and police protection, and therefore was not unconstitutional aid to religion. However, since the district's policy is to *reimburse* parents for expenses already incurred, how are nonreligious aspects, like child transportation safety, being advanced: the parents already procured safe transportation for their children?

13. Would excluding children who attended religious schools from a bussing reimbursement scheme have violated the Free Exercise Clause? If not, then why did the Court raise the subject of free exercise?

14. One of the major challenges to a strong strict-separationist interpretation of *Everson* (and the Establishment Clause) is that such an interpretation would be in tension with many long-standing and deeply-entrenched social, cultural, and legal practices. The weight of these religion-facilitating practices is such that one of the Establishment Clause "tests" that you will cover focuses on these very practices.

15. Each of the opinions referenced the strife caused by religious differences in Europe and, later, in America. Though this claimed potential for inter-religious strife

was not utilized to formally justify the opinions' conclusions, it was an argument used to support the various opinions' claims. (We will return to this strife claim, below, when we review Justice Breyer's revivification of it as an Establishment Clause test.) Is it plausible to argue that prohibiting governmental support of, for example, bussing for religious school children, is necessary "to keep bitter religious controversy out of public life by denying to every denomination any advantage from getting control of public policy or the public purse"?

16. Justice Jackson made two related claims. First, he claimed that religious believers and institutions received protection from the state's interference and, as a corollary, they may not receive governmental aid. Second, Justice Jackson claimed that, if religious institutions receive government monies, then they must also accept government regulation. What is the source of these claims? Are they correct?

17. Is there a principled way to limit Justice Rutledge's reasoning? He argued that tax money for transporting children to religious schools promoted religion, and therefore violated the Establishment Clause. Does the same rationale apply to police and fire protection? How could Justice Rutledge respond?

———

Everson—at least its rhetoric and its analysis—is strictly-separationist. This placed the Court's interpretation of the Establishment Clause in tension with many deeply-entrenched and widely-respected American practices. This became apparent in the Court's very next Establishment Clause case, decided the following year, where the *Everson* dissenters joined with Justice Black to strike down a public school released time religion program. Released time religion programs for public schools were a popular response to two goals: ensure that public education is nonsectarian, and provide the religious education desired by most parents. *McCollum*, reprinted below, cemented the Eversonian strict-separationist interpretation into the Court's case law. This relatively strict-separationist interpretation dominated the Supreme Court until the mid-1970s, at which point cracks began to show.

McCollum v. Board of Education of School Dist. No. 71, Champaign County, Ill
333 U.S. 203 (1948)

MR. JUSTICE BLACK delivered the opinion of the Court.

This case relates to the power of a state to utilize its tax-supported public school system in aid of religious instruction insofar as that power may be restricted by the First and Fourteenth Amendments to the Federal Constitution.

The appellant, Vashti McCollum, began this action for mandamus against the Champaign Board of Education in the Circuit Court of Champaign County, Illinois. Her asserted interest was that of a resident and taxpayer of Champaign and of a parent whose child was then enrolled in the Champaign public schools. Illinois has a compulsory education law which requires parents to send their children, aged seven to sixteen, to its tax-supported public schools where the children are to remain in attendance during the hours when the schools are regularly in session. Parents who violate this law commit a misdemeanor punishable by fine unless the children attend private or parochial schools which meet educational standards fixed by the State.

Appellant's petition for mandamus alleged that religious teachers, employed by private religious groups, were permitted to come weekly into the school buildings during the regular hours set apart for secular teaching, and then and there for a period of thirty minutes substitute their religious teaching for the secular education provided under the compulsory education law.

[T]he following facts are shown by the record without dispute. In 1940 interested members of the Jewish, Roman Catholic, and a few of the Protestant faiths formed a voluntary association called the Champaign Council on Religious Education. They obtained permission from the Board of Education to offer classes in religious instruction to public school pupils in grades four to nine inclusive. Classes were made up of pupils whose parents signed printed cards requesting that their children be permitted to attend; they were held weekly, thirty minutes for the lower grades, forty-five minutes for the higher. The council employed the religious teachers at no expense to the school authorities, but the instructors were subject to the approval and supervision of the superintendent of schools. The classes were taught in three separate religious groups by Protestant teachers, Catholic priests, and a Jewish rabbi. Classes were conducted in the regular classrooms of the school building. Students who did not choose to take the religious instruction were not released from public school duties; they were required to leave their classrooms and go to some other place in the school building for pursuit of their secular studies. On the other hand, students who were released from secular study for the religious instructions were required to be present at the religious classes. Reports of their presence or absence were to be made to their secular teachers.

The foregoing facts show the use of tax-supported property for religious instruction and the close cooperation between the school authorities and the religious council in promoting religious education. The operation of the state's compulsory education system thus assists and is integrated with the program of religious instruction carried on by separate religious sects. Pupils compelled by law to go to school for secular education are released in part from their legal duty upon the condition that they attend the religious classes. This is beyond all question a utilization of the tax-established and tax-supported public school system to aid religious groups to spread their faith. And it falls squarely under the ban of the First Amendment as we interpreted it in *Everson v. Board of Education*, 330 U.S. 1 [(1947)]. The majority in the *Everson* case, and the minority, agreed that the First Amendment's language, properly interpreted, had erected a wall of separation between Church and State. They disagreed as to the facts shown by the record and as to the proper application of the First Amendment's language to those facts.

Recognizing that the Illinois program is barred by the First and Fourteenth Amendments if we adhere to the views expressed both by the majority and the minority in the *Everson* case, counsel for the respondents challenge those views as dicta and urge that we reconsider and repudiate them. They argue that historically the First Amendment was intended to forbid only government preference of one religion over another, not an impartial governmental assistance of all religions. In addition they ask that we distinguish or overrule our holding in the *Everson* case that the Fourteenth Amendment made the "establishment of religion" clause of the First Amendment applicable as a prohibition against the States. After giving full consideration to the arguments presented we are unable to accept either of these contentions.

To hold that a state cannot consistently with the First and Fourteenth Amendments utilize its public school system to aid any or all religious faiths or sects in the dissemination of their doctrines and ideals does not, as counsel urge, manifest a governmental hostility to religion or religious teachings. A manifestation of such hostility would be at war with our national tradition as embodied in the First Amendment's guaranty of the free exercise of religion. For the First Amendment rests upon the premise that both religion and government can best work to achieve their lofty aims if each is left free from the other within its respective sphere. Or, as we said in the *Everson* case, the First Amendment had erected a wall between Church and State which must be kept high and impregnable.

Here not only are the [s]tate's tax supported public school buildings used for the dissemination of religious doctrines. The State also affords sectarian groups an invaluable aid in that it helps to provide pupils for their religious classes through use of the state's compulsory public school machinery. This is not separation of Church and State.

Reversed and remanded.

MR. JUSTICE FRANKFURTER delivered the following opinion, in which MR. JUSTICE JACKSON, MR. JUSTICE RUTLEDGE and MR. JUSTICE BURTON join.

We dissented in *Everson v. Board of Education*, 330 U.S. 1 [(1947)], because in our view the Constitutional principle requiring separation of Church and State compelled invalidation of the ordinance sustained by the majority. Illinois has here authorized the commingling of sectarian with secular instruction in the public schools. The Constitution of the United States forbids this.

MR. JUSTICE JACKSON, concurring. [Opinion omitted.]

MR. JUSTICE REED, dissenting. [Opinion omitted.]

Exercise 4:

1. Describe the quality and quantity of interactions between the school and religious institutions. How analogous are those relationships to the established churches in England and the states early in the nation's history? Do those relationships, even if not fully analogous to an established church, fit some facet(s) of church establishments? Are those relationships a step toward a state established church? Are the relationships between the school and religion here more or less robust than those in *Everson*, and does that account for the different alignment of Justices?

2. What facets of the challenged released-time religion program violated the Establishment Clause according to the Supreme Court?

3. The Court stated that its holding "does not, as counsel urge, manifest a governmental hostility to religion or religious teachings." Is this true? How would the Court respond to the argument that all subjects were permitted in the school, except religion, and that this gap evidenced hostility to religion?

4. The defendant school district argued, in the alternative, that the Supreme Court should reject *Everson*'s strict-separation interpretation of the Establishment Clause. How did the Court respond? Note how, immediately after the Supreme Court has issued a precedent on an issue, the Court follows its precedent, not the reasoning that justified the precedent. What does this tell you about the nature of stare decisis?

5. Is *McCollum* faithful to *Everson*'s holding? Its reasoning?

———————

Four years after *McCollum*, the Supreme Court decided *Zorach v. Clauson*, 343 U.S. 306 (1952). Appearing to reverse course from *McCollum*, the Court upheld a released time religion program in New York that was identical to the one struck down in *McCollum* except that the public schools released the students from class to attend religious instruction off school grounds. The opinion was written by Justice Douglas, who summarized the reasons the Court upheld the practice in frequently-cited language:

> We are a religious people whose institutions presuppose a Supreme Being. We guarantee the freedom to worship as one chooses. We make room for as wide a variety of beliefs and creeds as the spiritual needs of man deem necessary. We sponsor an attitude on the part of government that shows no partiality to any one group and that lets each flourish according to the zeal of its adherents and the appeal of its dogma. When the state encourages religious instruction or cooperates with religious authorities by adjusting the schedule of public events to sectarian needs, it follows the best of our traditions. For it then respects the religious nature of our people and accommodates the public service to their spiritual needs. To hold that it may not would be to find in the Constitution a requirement that the government show a callous indifference to religious groups. That would be preferring those who believe in no religion over those who do believe. Government may not finance religious groups nor undertake religious instruction nor blend secular and sectarian education nor use secular institutions to force one or some religion on any person. But we find no constitutional requirement which makes it necessary for government to be hostile to religion and to throw its weight against efforts to widen the effective scope of religious influence. The government must be neutral when it comes to competition between sects. It may not thrust any sect on any person. It may not make a religious observance compulsory. It may not coerce anyone to attend church, to observe a religious holiday, or to take religious instruction. But

it can close its doors or suspend its operations as to those who want to repair to their religious sanctuary for worship or instruction. No more than that is undertaken here.

Id. at 314–15. The dissenters argued that *Zorach* was unfaithful to both *Everson* and *McCollum.* "I see no significant difference between the invalid Illinois system and that of New York here sustained." *Id.* at 316 (Black, J., dissenting).

Zorach turned out to be a limited exception to the general trend in the Court's post-*Everson* case law. From 1947 up to 1983, the Eversonian strict-separationist paradigmgenerally dominated the Court's jurisprudence, in one form or another. *Everson's* teachings received their ultimate form in the Lemon Test, discussed next.

3. The *Lemon* Test

Over the ensuing two decades, the Supreme Court struggled to articulate the factors that, under the teachings of *Everson,* violated the then-regnant strict-separationist view of the Establishment Clause. This process culminated in *Lemon v. Kurtzman,* where the Court synthesized its prior case law into a famous three-part test.

Lemon v. Kurtzman

403 U.S. 602 (1971)

MR. CHIEF JUSTICE BURGER delivered the opinion of the Court.

These two appeals raise questions as to Pennsylvania and Rhode Island statutes providing state aid to church-related elementary and secondary schools. Both statutes are challenged as violative of the Establishment Clause of the First Amendment and the Due Process Clause of the Fourteenth Amendment.

Pennsylvania has adopted a statutory program that provides financial support to nonpublic elementary and secondary schools by way of reimbursement for the cost of teachers' salaries, textbooks, and instructional materials in specified secular subjects. Rhode Island has adopted a statute under which the State pays directly to teachers in nonpublic elementary schools a supplement of 15% of their annual salary. We hold that both statutes are unconstitutional.

I

The Rhode Island Statute

A three-judge federal court found that Rhode Island's nonpublic elementary schools accommodated approximately 25% of the State's pupils. About 95% of these pupils attended schools affiliated with the Roman Catholic church. To date some 250 teachers have applied for benefits under the Act. All of them are employed by Roman Catholic schools.

The court held a hearing at which extensive evidence was introduced concerning the nature of the secular instruction offered in the Roman Catholic schools whose teachers would be eligible for salary assistance under the Act. Although the court found that concern for religious values does not necessarily affect the content of secular subjects, it also found that the parochial school system was "an integral part of the religious mission of the Catholic Church."

The District Court concluded that the Act violated the Establishment Clause, holding that it fostered "excessive entanglement" between government and religion. In addition two judges thought that the Act had the impermissible effect of giving "significant aid to a religious enterprise." We affirm.

The Pennsylvania Statute

[A three-judge federal] court granted appellees' motion to dismiss the complaint for failure to state a claim for relief. It held that the Act violated neither the Establishment nor the Free Exercise Clause. We reverse.

II

In *Everson v. Board of Education*, 330 U.S. 1 (1947), this Court upheld a state statute that reimbursed the parents of parochial school children for bus transportation expenses. There Mr. Justice Black, writing for the majority, suggested that the decision carried to "the verge" of forbidden territory under the Religion Clauses. Candor compels acknowledgment, moreover, that we can only dimly perceive the lines of demarcation in this extraordinarily sensitive area of constitutional law.

The language of the Religion Clauses of the First Amendment is at best opaque, particularly when compared with other portions of the Amendment. Its authors did not simply prohibit the establishment of a state church or a state religion, an area history shows they regarded as very important and fraught with great dangers. Instead they commanded that there should be "no law respecting an establishment of religion." A law may be one "respecting" the forbidden objective while falling short of its total realization. A law "respecting" the proscribed result, that is, the establishment of religion, is not always easily identifiable as one violative of the Clause. A given law might not establish a state religion but nevertheless be one "respecting" that end in the sense of being a step that could lead to such establishment and hence offend the First Amendment.

In the absence of precisely stated constitutional prohibitions, we must draw lines with reference to the three main evils against which the Establishment Clause was intended to afford protection: "sponsorship, financial support, and active involvement of the sovereign in religious activity."

Every analysis in this area must begin with consideration of the cumulative criteria developed by the Court over many years. Three such tests may be gleaned from our cases. First, the statute must have a secular legislative purpose; second, its principal or primary effect must be one that neither advances nor inhibits religion; finally, the statute must not foster "an excessive government entanglement with religion."

Inquiry into the legislative purposes of the Pennsylvania and Rhode Island statutes affords no basis for a conclusion that the legislative intent was to advance religion. On the contrary, the statutes themselves clearly state that they are intended to enhance

the quality of the secular education in all schools covered by the compulsory attendance laws. There is no reason to believe the legislatures meant anything else. A State
always has a legitimate concern for maintaining minimum standards in all schools
it allows to operate.

The legislatures of Rhode Island and Pennsylvania have concluded that secular
and religious education are identifiable and separable. In the abstract we have no
quarrel with this conclusion. The two legislatures, however, have also recognized that
church-related elementary and secondary schools have a significant religious mission
and that a substantial portion of their activities is religiously oriented. They have
therefore sought to create statutory restrictions designed to guarantee the separation
between secular and religious educational functions and to ensure that State financial
aid supports only the former. We need not decide whether these legislative precautions
restrict the principal or primary effect of the programs to the point where they do
not offend the Religion Clauses, for we conclude that the cumulative impact of the
entire relationship arising under the statutes in each State involves excessive entanglement between government and religion.

III

Our prior holdings do not call for total separation between church and state; total
separation is not possible in an absolute sense. Some relationship between government
and religious organizations is inevitable. *Zorach v. Clauson*, 343 U.S. 306, 312 (1952).
Fire inspections, building and zoning regulations, and state requirements under compulsory school-attendance laws are examples of necessary and permissible contacts.
Judicial caveats against entanglement must recognize that the line of separation, far
from being a "wall," is a blurred, indistinct, and variable barrier depending on all the
circumstances of a particular relationship.

In order to determine whether the government entanglement with religion is excessive, we must examine the character and purposes of the institutions that are benefited, the nature of the aid that the State provides, and the resulting relationship
between the government and the religious authority. Here we find that both statutes
foster an impermissible degree of entanglement.

(a) Rhode Island program

The District Court made extensive findings on the grave potential for excessive
entanglement that inheres in the religious character and purpose of the Roman
Catholic elementary schools of Rhode Island, to date the sole beneficiaries of the
Rhode Island Salary Supplement Act.

The church schools involved in the program are located close to parish churches.
This understandably permits convenient access for religious exercises since instruction
in faith and morals is part of the total educational process. The school buildings contain identifying religious symbols such as crosses on the exterior and crucifixes, and
religious paintings and statues either in the classrooms or hallways. Although only
approximately 30 minutes a day are devoted to direct religious instruction, there are
religiously oriented extracurricular activities. Approximately two-thirds of the teachers

in these schools are nuns of various religious orders. Their dedicated efforts provide an atmosphere in which religious instruction and religious vocations are natural and proper parts of life in such schools.

On the basis of these findings the District Court concluded that the parochial schools constituted "an integral part of the religious mission of the Catholic Church." The various characteristics of the schools make them "a powerful vehicle for transmitting the Catholic faith to the next generation." This process of inculcating religious doctrine is, of course, enhanced by the impressionable age of the pupils, in primary schools particularly. In short, parochial schools involve substantial religious activity and purpose.

The substantial religious character of these church-related schools gives rise to entangling church-state relationships of the kind the Religion Clauses sought to avoid. Although the District Court found that concern for religious values did not inevitably or necessarily intrude into the content of secular subjects, the considerable religious activities of these schools led the legislature to provide for careful governmental controls and surveillance by state authorities in order to ensure that state aid supports only secular education.

The dangers and corresponding entanglements are enhanced by the particular form of aid that the Rhode Island Act provides. Our decisions have permitted the States to provide church-related schools with secular, neutral, or nonideological services, facilities, or materials. Bus transportation, school lunches, public health services, and secular textbooks supplied in common to all students were not thought to offend the Establishment Clause.

We cannot, however, refuse here to recognize that teachers have a substantially different ideological character from books. In terms of potential for involving some aspect of faith or morals in secular subjects, a textbook's content is ascertainable, but a teacher's handling of a subject is not. We cannot ignore the danger that a teacher under religious control and discipline poses to the separation of the religious from the purely secular aspects of precollege education. The conflict of functions inheres in the situation.

In our view the record shows these dangers are present to a substantial degree. The Rhode Island Roman Catholic elementary schools are under the general supervision of the Bishop of Providence and his appointed representative, the Diocesan Superintendent of Schools. In most cases, each individual parish, however, assumes the ultimate financial responsibility for the school, with the parish priest authorizing the allocation of parish funds. With only two exceptions, school principals are nuns. Religious authority necessarily pervades the school system.

The schools are governed by the standards set forth in a "Handbook of School Regulations," which has the force of synodal law in the diocese. It emphasizes the role and importance of the teacher in parochial schools: "The prime factor for the success or the failure of the school is the spirit and personality, as well as the professional competency, of the teacher * * *." The Handbook also states that: "Religious formation is not confined to formal courses; nor is it restricted to a single subject area." Finally, the Handbook advises teachers to stimulate interest in religious vocations and missionary work.

But what has been recounted suggests the potential if not actual hazards of this form of state aid. The teacher is employed by a religious organization, subject to the direction and discipline of religious authorities, and works in a system dedicated to rearing children in a particular faith.

We need not and do not assume that teachers in parochial schools will be guilty of bad faith or any conscious design to evade the limitations imposed by the statute and the First Amendment. We simply recognize that a dedicated religious person, teaching in a school affiliated with his or her faith and operated to inculcate its tenets, will inevitably experience great difficulty in remaining religiously neutral. Doctrines and faith are not inculcated or advanced by neutrals. With the best of intentions such a teacher would find it hard to make a total separation between secular teaching and religious doctrine. What would appear to some to be essential to good citizenship might well for others border on or constitute instruction in religion.

[T]he potential for impermissible fostering of religion is present. The Rhode Island Legislature has not, and could not, provide state aid on the basis of a mere assumption that secular teachers under religious discipline can avoid conflicts. The State must be certain, given the Religion Clauses, that subsidized teachers do not inculcate religion—indeed the State here has undertaken to do so. To ensure that no trespass occurs, the State has therefore carefully conditioned its aid with pervasive restrictions. An eligible recipient must teach only those courses that are offered in the public schools and use only those texts and materials that are found in the public schools. In addition the teacher must not engage in teaching any course in religion.

A comprehensive, discriminating, and continuing state surveillance will inevitably be required to ensure that these restrictions are obeyed and the First Amendment otherwise respected. These prophylactic contacts will involve excessive and enduring entanglement between state and church.

There is another area of entanglement in the Rhode Island program that gives concern. The statute excludes teachers employed by nonpublic schools whose average per-pupil expenditures on secular education equal or exceed the comparable figures for public schools. In the event that the total expenditures of an otherwise eligible school exceed this norm, the program requires the government to examine the school's records in order to determine how much of the total expenditures is attributable to secular education and how much to religious activity. This kind of state inspection and evaluation of the religious content of a religious organization is fraught with the sort of entanglement that the Constitution forbids. It is a relationship pregnant with dangers of excessive government direction of church schools and hence of churches.

(b) Pennsylvania program

The Pennsylvania statute also provides state aid to church-related schools for teachers' salaries. The complaint describes an educational system that is very similar to the one existing in Rhode Island.

As we noted earlier, the very restrictions and surveillance necessary to ensure that teachers play a strictly non-ideological role give rise to entanglements between church and state. The Pennsylvania statute, moreover, has the further defect of providing state financial aid directly to the church-related schools. This factor distinguishes *Everson* [where] the Court was careful to point out that state aid was provided to the student and his parents — not to the church-related school.

The history of government grants of a continuing cash subsidy indicates that such programs have almost always been accompanied by varying measures of control and surveillance. The government cash grants before us now provide no basis for predicting that comprehensive measures of surveillance and controls will not follow. In particular the government's post-audit power to inspect and evaluate a church-related school's financial records and to determine which expenditures are religious and which are secular creates an intimate and continuing relationship between church and state.

IV

A broader base of entanglement of yet a different character is presented by the divisive political potential of these state programs. In a community where such a large number of pupils are served by church-related schools, it can be assumed that state assistance will entail considerable political activity. Partisans of parochial schools, understandably concerned with rising costs and sincerely dedicated to both the religious and secular educational missions of their schools, will inevitably champion this cause and promote political action to achieve their goals. Those who oppose state aid, whether for constitutional, religious, or fiscal reasons, will inevitably respond and employ all of the usual political campaign techniques to prevail. Candidates will be forced to declare and voters to choose. It would be unrealistic to ignore the fact that many people confronted with issues of this kind will find their votes aligned with their faith.

Ordinarily political debate and division, however vigorous or even partisan, are normal and healthy manifestations of our democratic system of government, but political division along religious lines was one of the principal evils against which the First Amendment was intended to protect. The potential divisiveness of such conflict is a threat to the normal political process. To have States or communities divide on the issues presented by state aid to parochial schools would tend to confuse and obscure other issues of great urgency. We have an expanding array of vexing issues, local and national, domestic and international, to debate and divide on. It conflicts with our whole history and tradition to permit questions of the Religion Clauses to assume such importance in our legislatures and in our elections that they could divert attention from the myriad issues and problems that confront every level of government. The highways of church and state relationships are not likely to be one-way streets, and the Constitution's authors sought to protect religious worship from the pervasive power of government. The history of many countries attests to the hazards of religion's intruding into the political arena or of political power intruding into the legitimate and free exercise of religious belief.

Here we are confronted with successive and very likely permanent annual appropriations that benefit relatively few religious groups. Political fragmentation and divisiveness on religious lines are thus likely to be intensified. The potential for political divisiveness related to religious belief and practice is aggravated in these two statutory programs by the need for continuing annual appropriations and the likelihood of larger and larger demands as costs and populations grow.

MR. JUSTICE DOUGLAS, whom MR. JUSTICE BLACK joins, concurring. [Opinion omitted.]

MR. JUSTICE MARSHALL [Opinion omitted.]

Exercise 5:

1. Describe the quality and quantity of interactions between the state and religious institutions. How analogous are those relationships to the established churches in England and the early states? Do those relationships, even if not fully analogous to an established church, fit some facet(s) of church establishments? Are those relationships a step toward a state established church?

2. What is the Lemon Test? Must each of the three prongs be met before the Establishment Clause is violated, or is violation of one prong sufficient (for example, if it is especially egregious)?

3. What is (are) the source(s) of the Lemon Test's three prongs?

4. Which of the prongs of the Lemon Test did Pennsylvania and Rhode Island violate? Explain each argument.

5. On a scale of one to ten, with ten being the most accomodationist and one being the most separationist, where does the Lemon Test fall?

6. In *Lemon* itself, the Court ruled that the challenged statutes had legitimate — secular — purposes and therefore did not fail the Test's first prong. However, the Court still struck down the statutes because of their effect of entangling the state and religion. However, in other contexts, such as the Equal Protection Clause, the Court has ruled that a discriminatory legislative purpose is necessary to make out a constitutional violation. Upon what basis could the Court have justified these different approaches? Are you persuaded?

7. On the one hand, states that wish to provide nonreligious aid to religious institutions must not have a religious purpose or effect. On the other hand, such states may not entangle themselves with religious institutions by creating significant oversight to prevent misuse of such aid for religious purposes. Does the Lemon Test put states in a Catch-22?

8. Following some of the reasoning in *Everson*, Chief Justice Burger discussed the potential for political divisiveness caused by state aid to religious institutions. How likely is it that such divisiveness would/will occur? What evidence supports your judgment in the prior question? Is such divisiveness, if it occurred, worse than divisiveness caused by other sources, such as different political ideologies? Or, is such divisiveness worse than the divisiveness caused by the Lemon Test itself?

9. Is the Lemon Test faithful to the Establishment Clause's original meaning? The Supreme Court's precedent?

———————

The Lemon Test represented the high point of the strict-separationist tide. Beginning in the mid-1970s and gaining steam in the early-1980s, some Justices on the Supreme Court began considering alternative Establishment Clause "tests." A number of factors contributed to this change. First, beginning with President Nixon's appointments to the Supreme Court including, most importantly, William H. Rehnquist, a majority of Supreme Court Justices became open to alternatives to the Eversonian paradigm. Second, a critical mass of scholarship challenging the historical and intellectual underpinnings of the Eversonian strict-separationist interpretation appeared. *See, e.g.,* ROBERT L. CORD, SEPARATION OF CHURCH AND STATE: HISTORICAL FACT AND CURRENT FICTION (1982) (the then-seminal critique of *Everson*'s historical claims). These two factors coalesced, for instance, in then-Justice Rehnquist's dissent in *Wallace v. Jaffree*, 472 U.S. 38, 104 (1985), where he directly challenged *Everson*'s reading of history. Third, there was significant "political" push-back against the Court for its perceived hostility to religion, and this push-back was both symbolized by and effectuated through presidential appointments and critical scholarship.

As the Supreme Court turned to alternative Establishment Clause tests, it also started to recharacterize the Lemon Test in certain important ways. Most prominently, Justice O'Connor pushed the Court to eliminate the Lemon Test's third prong (entanglement). This process culminated in *Agostini v. Felton*, 521 U.S. 203 (1997), where Justice O'Connor, writing for the Court, concluded that "it is simplest to recognize why entanglement is significant and treat it ... as an aspect of the inquiry into a statute's effect." Thereafter, the issue of entanglement between the government and religious entities became a facet of the second prong of the Lemon Test, the primary effect prong.

Furthermore, the Supreme Court began employing an endorsement analysis for the Lemon Test's first and second prongs. For example, in *Santa Fe Indep. Sch. Dist. v. Doe*, 530 U.S. 290, 308 (2000), the Supreme Court evaluated whether a school district had the primary purpose to advance religion by asking whether students would perceive the school as endorsing prayer offered before school sporting events. *See also McCreary County Ky. v. American Civil Liberties Union*, 545 U.S. 844, 860 (2005) (describing *Lemon*'s first prong as ascertaining whether "the government sends ... the message to ... nonadherents that they are outsiders, not full members of the political community") (internal quotations omitted).

Yet in a series of cases starting in the 1980s, the Court either ignored the Lemon Test (and its modification through the endorsement test) or refused to apply it. *See, e.g., Marsh v. Chambers*, 463 U.S. 783 (1983); *Zelman v. Simmons-Harris*, 536 U.S. 639 (2002). Not surprisingly, the proliferation of various Establishment Clause tests, coupled with the lower courts' inconsistent application of *Lemon* and the continued criticism of the Lemon Test by members of the Supreme Court and academics, raised questions about the status of *Lemon* and its continued viability as an Establishment

Clause test. In 2019, the Court addressed these questions in deciding whether a memorial to soldiers who died in World War I, which was in the shape of a Latin cross, violated the Establishment Clause. As you read the following case, consider what the status of *Lemon* is in the wake of this decision and what the Establishment Clause rule going forward is for the government's "established, religiously expressive monuments, symbols, and practices."

American Legion v. American Humanist Association
139 S. Ct. 2067 (2019)

JUSTICE ALITO announced the judgment of the Court and delivered the opinion of the Court with respect to Parts I, II-B, II-C, III, and IV, and an opinion with respect to Parts II-A and II-D, in which THE CHIEF JUSTICE, JUSTICE BREYER, and JUSTICE KAVANAUGH join.

Since 1925, the Bladensburg Peace Cross (Cross) has stood as a tribute to 49 area soldiers who gave their lives in the First World War. Eighty-nine years after the dedication of the Cross, respondents filed this lawsuit, claiming that they are offended by the sight of the memorial on public land and that its presence there and the expenditure of public funds to maintain it violate the Establishment Clause of the First Amendment. To remedy this violation, they asked a federal court to order the relocation or demolition of the Cross or at least the removal of its arms. The Court of Appeals for the Fourth Circuit agreed that the memorial is unconstitutional and remanded for a determination of the proper remedy. We now reverse.

Although the cross has long been a preeminent Christian symbol, its use in the Bladensburg memorial has a special significance. After the First World War, the picture of row after row of plain white crosses marking the overseas graves of soldiers who had lost their lives in that horrible conflict was emblazoned on the minds of Americans at home, and the adoption of the cross as the Bladensburg memorial must be viewed in that historical context. For nearly a century, the Bladensburg Cross has expressed the community's grief at the loss of the young men who perished, its thanks for their sacrifice, and its dedication to the ideals for which they fought. It has become a prominent community landmark, and its removal or radical alteration at this date would be seen by many not as a neutral act but as the manifestation of "a hostility toward religion that has no place in our Establishment Clause traditions." *Van Orden v. Perry*, 545 U.S. 677, 704 (2005) (BREYER, J., concurring in judgment). And contrary to respondents' intimations, there is no evidence of discriminatory intent in the selection of the design of the memorial or the decision of a Maryland commission to maintain it. The Religion Clauses of the Constitution aim to foster a society in which people of all beliefs can live together harmoniously, and the presence of the Bladensburg Cross on the land where it has stood for so many years is fully consistent with that aim.

I

A

The cross came into widespread use as a symbol of Christianity by the fourth century, and it retains that meaning today. But there are many contexts in which the symbol has also taken on a secular meaning. Indeed, there are instances in which its message is now almost entirely secular.

A cross appears as part of many registered trademarks held by businesses and secular organizations, including Blue Cross Blue Shield, the Bayer Group, and some Johnson & Johnson products. Many of these marks relate to health care, and it is likely that the association of the cross with healing had a religious origin. But the current use of these marks is indisputably secular.

The familiar symbol of the Red Cross—a red cross on a white background— shows how the meaning of a symbol that was originally religious can be transformed. The International Committee of the Red Cross (ICRC) selected that symbol in 1863 because it was thought to call to mind the flag of Switzerland, a country widely known for its neutrality. Thus, the ICRC selected this symbol for an essentially secular reason, [b]ut the cross was originally chosen for the Swiss flag for religious reasons. So an image that began as an expression of faith was transformed.

The image used in the Bladensburg memorial—a plain Latin cross—also took on new meaning after World War I. "During and immediately after the war, the army marked soldiers' graves with temporary wooden crosses or Stars of David"—a departure from the prior practice of marking graves in American military cemeteries with uniform rectangular slabs. The vast majority of these grave markers consisted of crosses, and thus when Americans saw photographs of these cemeteries, what struck them were rows and rows of plain white crosses. As a result, the image of a simple white cross "developed into a 'central symbol'" of the conflict. Contemporary literature, poetry, and art reflected this powerful imagery. Perhaps most famously, John McCrae's poem, In Flanders Fields, began with these memorable lines:

"In Flanders fields the poppies blow

Between the crosses, row on row."

The poem was enormously popular. The image of "the crosses, row on row," stuck in people's minds, and even today for those who view World War I cemeteries in Europe, the image is arresting.

After the 1918 armistice, the War Department announced plans to replace the wooden crosses and Stars of David with uniform marble slabs like those previously used in American military cemeteries. But the public outcry against that proposal was swift and fierce. Many organizations, including the American War Mothers, a nonsectarian group founded in 1917, urged the Department to retain the design of the temporary markers. When the American Battle Monuments Commission took over the project of designing the headstones, it responded to this public sentiment by opting to replace the wooden crosses and Stars of David with marble versions of those symbols. This national debate and its outcome confirmed the cross's widespread resonance as a symbol of sacrifice in the war.

B

Recognition of the cross's symbolism extended to local communities across the country. In late 1918, residents of Prince George's County, Maryland, formed a committee for the purpose of erecting a memorial for the county's fallen soldiers. Among the committee's members were the mothers of 10 deceased soldiers. The committee decided that the memorial should be a cross and hired sculptor and architect John Joseph Earley to design it. Although we do not know precisely why the committee chose the cross, it is unsurprising that the committee—and many others commemorating World War I—adopted a symbol so widely associated with that wrenching event.

The Cross was to stand at the terminus of another World War I memorial—the National Defense Highway, which connects Washington to Annapolis. The community gathered for a joint groundbreaking ceremony for both memorials on September 28, 1919; the mother of the first Prince George's County resident killed in France broke ground for the Cross. By 1922, however, the committee had run out of funds, and progress on the Cross had stalled. The local post of the American Legion took over the project, and the monument was finished in 1925.

The completed monument is a 32-foot tall Latin cross that sits on a large pedestal. The American Legion's emblem is displayed at its center, and the words "Valor," "Endurance," "Courage," and "Devotion" are inscribed at its base, one on each of the four faces. The pedestal also features a 9- by 2.5-foot bronze plaque explaining that the monument is "Dedicated to the heroes of Prince George's County, Maryland who lost their lives in the Great War for the liberty of the world." The plaque lists the names of 49 local men, both Black and White, who died in the war. It identifies the dates of American involvement, and quotes President Woodrow Wilson's request for a declaration of war: "The right is more precious than peace. We shall fight for the things we have always carried nearest our hearts. To such a task we dedicate our lives."

Since its dedication, the Cross has served as the site of patriotic events honoring veterans, including gatherings on Veterans Day, Memorial Day, and Independence Day. Like the dedication itself, these events have typically included an invocation, a keynote speaker, and a benediction. Over the years, memorials honoring the veterans of other conflicts have been added to the surrounding area, which is now known as Veterans Memorial Park. These include a World War II Honor Scroll; a Pearl Harbor memorial; a Korea-Vietnam veterans memorial; a September 11 garden; a War of 1812 memorial; and two recently added 38-foot-tall markers depicting British and American soldiers in the Battle of Bladensburg. Because the Cross is located on a traffic island with limited space, the closest of these other monuments is about 200 feet away in a park across the road.

As the area around the Cross developed, the monument came to be at the center of a busy intersection. In 1961, the Maryland-National Capital Park and Planning

Commission (Commission) acquired the Cross and the land on which it sits in order to preserve the monument and address traffic-safety concerns. The American Legion reserved the right to continue using the memorial to host a variety of ceremonies, including events in memory of departed veterans. Over the next five decades, the Commission spent approximately $117,000 to maintain and preserve the monument. In 2008, it budgeted an additional $100,000 for renovations and repairs to the Cross.

C

In 2012, nearly 90 years after the Cross was dedicated and more than 50 years after the Commission acquired it, the American Humanist Association (AHA) lodged a complaint with the Commission. The complaint alleged that the Cross's presence on public land and the Commission's maintenance of the memorial violate the Establishment Clause. The American Legion intervened to defend the Cross.

II

A

The Establishment Clause of the First Amendment provides that "Congress shall make no law respecting an establishment of religion." While the concept of a formally established church is straightforward, pinning down the meaning of a "law respecting an establishment of religion" has proved to be a vexing problem. After *Everson* [*v. Board of Ed. of Ewing*, 330 U.S. 1 (1947),] recognized the incorporation of the Clause, however, the Court faced a steady stream of difficult and controversial Establishment Clause issues, ranging from Bible reading and prayer in the public schools, to Sunday closing laws, to state subsidies for church-related schools or the parents of students attending those schools. After grappling with such cases for more than 20 years, *Lemon* ambitiously attempted to distill from the Court's existing case law a test that would bring order and predictability to Establishment Clause decisionmaking. That test called on courts to examine the purposes and effects of a challenged government action, as well as any entanglement with religion that it might entail. The Court later elaborated that the "effect[s]" of a challenged action should be assessed by asking whether a "reasonable observer" would conclude that the action constituted an "endorsement" of religion.

If the *Lemon* Court thought that its test would provide a framework for all future Establishment Clause decisions, its expectation has not been met. In many cases, this Court has either expressly declined to apply the test or has simply ignored it. [The Court then listed eleven cases supporting this claim.]

This pattern is a testament to the *Lemon* test's shortcomings. As Establishment Clause cases involving a great array of laws and practices came to the Court, it became more and more apparent that the *Lemon* test could not resolve them. It could not "explain the Establishment Clause's tolerance, for example, of the prayers that open legislative meetings, ... certain references to, and invocations of, the Deity in the public words of public officials; the public references to God on coins, decrees, and buildings; or the attention paid to the religious objectives of certain holidays, including Thanksgiving." The test has been harshly criticized by Members of this Court, lamented by lower court judges, and questioned by a diverse roster of scholars.

For at least four reasons, the *Lemon* test presents particularly daunting problems in cases, including the one now before us, that involve the use, for ceremonial, celebratory, or commemorative purposes, of words or symbols with religious associations. Together, these considerations counsel against efforts to evaluate such cases under *Lemon* and toward application of a presumption of constitutionality for longstanding monuments, symbols, and practices.

B

First, these cases often concern monuments, symbols, or practices that were first established long ago, and in such cases, identifying their original purpose or purposes may be especially difficult. In *Salazar v. Buono*, 559 U.S. 700 (2010), for example, we dealt with a cross that a small group of World War I veterans had put up at a remote spot in the Mojave Desert more than seven decades earlier. The record contained virtually no direct evidence regarding the specific motivations of these men. We knew that they had selected a plain white cross, and there was some evidence that the man who looked after the monument for many years was said not to have been "particularly religious."

Without better evidence about the purpose of the monument, different Justices drew different inferences. The truth is that 70 years after the fact, there was no way to be certain about the motivations of the men who were responsible for the creation of the monument. And this is often the case with old monuments, symbols, and practices. Yet it would be inappropriate for courts to compel their removal or termination based on supposition.

Second, as time goes by, the purposes associated with an established monument, symbol, or practice often multiply. Take the example of Ten Commandments monuments, the subject we addressed in *Van Orden* and *McCreary County*. For believing Jews and Christians, the Ten Commandments are the word of God handed down to Moses on Mount Sinai, but the image of the Ten Commandments has also been used to convey other meanings. They have historical significance as one of the foundations of our legal system, and for largely that reason, they are depicted in the marble frieze in our courtroom and in other prominent public buildings in our Nation's capital. In *Van Orden* and *McCreary*, no Member of the Court thought that these depictions are unconstitutional.

The existence of multiple purposes is not exclusive to longstanding monuments, symbols, or practices, but this phenomenon is more likely to occur in such cases. Even if the original purpose of a monument was infused with religion, the passage of time may obscure that sentiment. As our society becomes more and more religiously diverse, a community may preserve such monuments, symbols, and practices for the sake of their historical significance or their place in a common cultural heritage.

Third, just as the purpose for maintaining a monument, symbol, or practice may evolve, "[t]he 'message' conveyed ... may change over time." Consider, for example, the message of the Statue of Liberty, which began as a monument to the solidarity and friendship between France and the United States and only decades later came to be seen "as a beacon welcoming immigrants to a land of freedom."

With sufficient time, religiously expressive monuments, symbols, and practices can become embedded features of a community's landscape and identity. The community may come to value them without necessarily embracing their religious roots. The recent tragic fire at Notre Dame in Paris provides a striking example. Although the French Republic rigorously enforces a secular public square, the cathedral remains a symbol of national importance to the religious and nonreligious alike. Notre Dame is fundamentally a place of worship and retains great religious importance, but its meaning has broadened. For many, it is inextricably linked with the very idea of Paris and France.

In the same way, consider the many cities and towns across the United States that bear religious names. Or take a motto like Arizona's, "*Ditat Deus*" ("God enriches"), which was adopted in 1864, or a flag like Maryland's, which has included two crosses since 1904. Familiarity itself can become a reason for preservation.

Fourth, when time's passage imbues a religiously expressive monument, symbol, or practice with this kind of familiarity and historical significance, removing it may no longer appear neutral, especially to the local community for which it has taken on particular meaning. A government that roams the land, tearing down monuments with religious symbolism and scrubbing away any reference to the divine will strike many as aggressively hostile to religion. Militantly secular regimes have carried out such projects in the past, and for those with a knowledge of history, the image of monuments being taken down will be evocative, disturbing, and divisive. *Van Orden*, 545 U.S. at 704 (opinion of BREYER, J.) ("[D]isputes concerning the removal of longstanding depictions of the Ten Commandments from public buildings across the Nation … could thereby create the very kind of religiously based divisiveness that the Establishment Clause seeks to avoid").

These four considerations show that retaining established, religiously expressive monuments, symbols, and practices is quite different from erecting or adopting new ones. The passage of time gives rise to a strong presumption of constitutionality.

C

The role of the cross in World War I memorials is illustrative of each of the four preceding considerations. Immediately following the war, "[c]ommunities across America built memorials to commemorate those who had served the nation in the struggle to make the world safe for democracy." Although not all of these communities included a cross in their memorials, the cross had become a symbol closely linked to the war. In the wake of the war, the United States adopted the cross as part of its military honors, establishing the Distinguished Service Cross and the Navy Cross in 1918 and 1919, respectively. And as already noted, the fallen soldiers' final resting places abroad were marked by white crosses or Stars of David. The solemn image of endless rows of white crosses became inextricably linked with and symbolic of the ultimate price paid by 116,000 soldiers. And this relationship between the cross and the war undoubtedly influenced the design of the many war memorials that sprang up across the Nation.

This is not to say that the cross's association with the war was the sole or dominant motivation for the inclusion of the symbol in every World War I memorial that features it. But today, it is all but impossible to tell whether that was so. And no matter what the original purposes for the erection of a monument, a community may wish to preserve it for very different reasons, such as the historic preservation and traffic-safety concerns the Commission has pressed here. In addition, the passage of time may have altered the area surrounding a monument in ways that change its meaning and provide new reasons for its preservation. Such changes are relevant here, since the Bladensburg Cross now sits at a busy traffic intersection, and numerous additional monuments are located nearby.

Finally, as World War I monuments have endured through the years and become a familiar part of the physical and cultural landscape, requiring their removal would not be viewed by many as a neutral act. And an alteration like the one entertained by the Fourth Circuit—amputating the arms of the Cross—would be seen by many as profoundly disrespectful. A monument may express many purposes and convey many different messages, both secular and religious. Thus, a campaign to obliterate items with religious associations may evidence hostility to religion even if those religious associations are no longer in the forefront.

D

While the *Lemon* Court ambitiously attempted to find a grand unified theory of the Establishment Clause, in later cases, we have taken a more modest approach that focuses on the particular issue at hand and looks to history for guidance. Our cases involving prayer before a legislative session are an example.

In *Marsh v. Chambers*, the Court upheld the Nebraska Legislature's practice of beginning each session with a prayer by an official chaplain, and in so holding, the Court conspicuously ignored *Lemon*. Instead, the Court found it highly persuasive that Congress for more than 200 years had opened its sessions with a prayer and that many state legislatures had followed suit. We took a similar approach more recently in *Town of Greece* [*v. Galloway*, 572 U.S. 565 (2014)].

We reached these results even though it was clear, as stressed by the *Marsh* dissent, that prayer is by definition religious. As the Court put it in *Town of Greece*: "*Marsh* must not be understood as permitting a practice that would amount to a constitutional violation if not for its historical foundation." "The case teaches instead that the Establishment Clause must be interpreted 'by reference to historical practices and understandings'" and that the decision of the First Congress to "provid[e] for the appointment of chaplains only days after approving language for the First Amendment demonstrates that the Framers considered legislative prayer a benign acknowledgment of religion's role in society."

The prevalence of this philosophy at the time of the founding is reflected in other prominent actions taken by the First Congress. It requested—and President Washington proclaimed—a national day of prayer, and it reenacted the Northwest Territory Ordinance, which provided that "[r]eligion, morality, and knowledge, being necessary to good government and the happiness of mankind, schools and the means of education shall forever be encouraged." President Washington echoed this sentiment in his Farewell Address, calling religion and morality "indispensable supports" to "political prosperity." The First Congress looked to these "supports" when it chose to begin its sessions with a prayer. This practice was designed to solemnize congressional meetings, unifying those in attendance as they pursued a common goal of good governance.

To achieve that purpose, legislative prayer needed to be inclusive rather than divisive, and that required a determined effort even in a society that was much more religiously homogeneous than ours today. Since then, Congress has welcomed guest chaplains from a variety of faiths.

In *Town of Greece,* which concerned prayer before a town council meeting, there was disagreement about the inclusiveness of the town's practice. But there was no disagreement that the Establishment Clause permits a nondiscriminatory practice of prayer at the beginning of a town council session. Of course, the specific practice challenged in *Town of Greece* lacked the very direct connection, via the First Congress, to the thinking of those who were responsible for framing the First Amendment. But what mattered was that the town's practice "fi[t] within the tradition long followed in Congress and the state legislatures."

The practice begun by the First Congress stands out as an example of respect and tolerance for differing views, an honest endeavor to achieve inclusivity and nondiscrimination, and a recognition of the important role that religion plays in the lives of many Americans. Where categories of monuments, symbols, and practices with a longstanding history follow in that tradition, they are likewise constitutional.

III

Applying these principles, we conclude that the Bladensburg Cross does not violate the Establishment Clause.

As we have explained, the Bladensburg Cross carries special significance in commemorating World War I. Not only did the Bladensburg Cross begin with this meaning, but with the passage of time, it has acquired historical importance. As long as it is retained in its original place and form, it speaks as well of the community that erected the monument nearly a century ago and has maintained it ever since. The memorial represents what the relatives, friends, and neighbors of the fallen soldiers felt at the time and how they chose to express their sentiments. And the monument has acquired additional layers of historical meaning in subsequent years. The Cross now stands among memorials to veterans of later wars. It has become part of the community. The monument would not serve that role if its design had deliberately disrespected area soldiers who perished in World War I.

Finally, it is surely relevant that the monument commemorates the death of particular individuals. It is natural and appropriate for those seeking to honor the deceased to invoke the symbols that signify what death meant for those who are memorialized.

IV

The cross is undoubtedly a Christian symbol, but that fact should not blind us to everything else that the Bladensburg Cross has come to represent. For some, that monument is a symbolic resting place for ancestors who never returned home. For others, it is a place for the community to gather and honor all veterans and their sacrifices for our Nation. For others still, it is a historical landmark. For many of these people, destroying or defacing the Cross that has stood undisturbed for nearly a century would not be neutral and would not further the ideals of respect and tolerance embodied in the First Amendment. For all these reasons, the Cross does not offend the Constitution.

JUSTICE BREYER, with whom JUSTICE KAGAN joins, concurring.

I have long maintained that there is no single formula for resolving Establishment Clause challenges. The Court must instead consider each case in light of the basic purposes that the Religion Clauses were meant to serve: assuring religious liberty and tolerance for all, avoiding religiously based social conflict, and maintaining that separation of church and state that allows each to flourish in its "separate spher[e]."

I agree with the Court that allowing the State of Maryland to display and maintain the Peace Cross poses no threat to those ends. The Court's opinion eloquently explains why that is so: The Latin cross is uniquely associated with the fallen soldiers of World War I; the organizers of the Peace Cross acted with the undeniably secular motive of commemorating local soldiers; no evidence suggests that they sought to disparage or exclude any religious group; the secular values inscribed on the Cross and its place among other memorials strengthen its message of patriotism and commemoration; and, finally, the Cross has stood on the same land for 94 years, generating no controversy in the community until this lawsuit was filed. Nothing in the record suggests that the lack of public outcry "was due to a climate of intimidation." ... And, as the Court explains, ordering its removal or alteration at this late date would signal "a hostility toward religion that has no place in our Establishment Clause traditions." The case would be different, in my view, if there were evidence that the organizers had "deliberately disrespected" members of minority faiths or if the Cross had been erected only recently, rather than in the aftermath of World War I.

Nor do I understand the Court's opinion today to adopt a "history and tradition test" that would permit any newly constructed religious memorial on public land. The [plurality of the] Court appropriately "looks to history for guidance," but [the majority] upholds the constitutionality of the Peace Cross only after considering its particular historical context and its long-held place in the community. A newer memorial, erected under different circumstances, would not necessarily be permissible under this approach.

JUSTICE KAVANAUGH, concurring.

I

Consistent with the Court's case law, the Court today applies a history and tradition test in examining and upholding the constitutionality of the Bladensburg Cross [citing

Marsh v. Chambers, Van Orden, and *Town of Greece v. Galloway*]. As this case again demonstrates, this Court no longer applies the old test articulated in *Lemon v. Kurtz-man,* 403 U.S. 602 (1971).

On the contrary, each category of Establishment Clause cases has its own principles based on history, tradition, and precedent. And the cases together lead to an over-arching set of principles: If the challenged government practice is not coercive *and* if it (i) is rooted in history and tradition; or (ii) treats religious people, organizations, speech, or activity equally to comparable secular people, organizations, speech, or activity; or (iii) represents a permissible legislative accommodation or exemption from a generally applicable law, then there ordinarily is no Establishment Clause violation.*

The practice of displaying religious memorials, particularly religious war memorials, on public land is not coercive and is rooted in history and tradition. The Bladensburg Cross does not violate the Establishment Clause.

II

The conclusion that the cross does not violate the Establishment Clause does not necessarily mean that those who object to it have no other recourse. The Court's ruling *allows* the State to maintain the cross on public land. The Court's ruling does not *require* the State to maintain the cross on public land. The Maryland Legislature could enact new laws requiring removal of the cross or transfer of the land. The Maryland Governor or other state or local executive officers may have authority to do so under current Maryland law. And if not, the legislature could enact new laws to authorize such executive action. The Maryland Constitution, as interpreted by the Maryland Court of Appeals, may speak to this question. And if not, the people of Maryland can amend the State Constitution.

JUSTICE KAGAN, concurring in part.

Although I agree that rigid application of the *Lemon* test does not solve every Es-tablishment Clause problem, I think that test's focus on purposes and effects is crucial in evaluating government action in this sphere — as this very suit shows. I therefore do not join Part II-A. I do not join Part II-D out of perhaps an excess of caution. Although I too "look[] to history for guidance," I prefer at least for now to do so case-by-case, rather than to sign on to any broader statements about history's role in Es-tablishment Clause analysis. But I find much to admire in this section of the opinion — particularly, its emphasis on whether longstanding monuments, symbols, and practices reflect "respect and tolerance for differing views, an honest endeavor to achieve in-clusivity and nondiscrimination, and a recognition of the important role that religion plays in the lives of many Americans." Here, as elsewhere, the opinion shows sensitivity

---

* That is not to say that challenged government actions outside that safe harbor are unconstitutional. Any such cases must be analyzed under the relevant Establishment Clause principles and precedents.

to and respect for this Nation's pluralism, and the values of neutrality and inclusion that the First Amendment demands.

JUSTICE THOMAS, concurring in the judgment.

The text and history of th[e Establishment] Clause suggest that it should not be incorporated against the States. Even if the Clause expresses an individual right enforceable against the States, it is limited by its text to "law[s]" enacted by a legislature, so it is unclear whether the Bladensburg Cross would implicate any incorporated right. And even if it did, this religious display does not involve the type of actual legal coercion that was a hallmark of historical establishments of religion. Therefore, the Cross is clearly constitutional.

JUSTICE GORSUCH, with whom JUSTICE THOMAS joins, concurring in the judgment.

[Justice Gorsuch's concurrence focused on whether individuals who are "offended" by an alleged Establishment Clause violation have standing to sue. Standing is covered in **Volume 1** of this casebook series. But Justice Gorsuch also said the following about the Court's Establishment Clause jurisprudence — eds.]

As today's plurality rightly indicates in Part II-A, … *Lemon* was a misadventure. It sought a "grand unified theory" of the Establishment Clause but left us only a mess. How much "purpose" to promote religion is too much (are Sunday closing laws that bear multiple purposes, religious and secular, problematic)? How much "effect" of advancing religion is tolerable (are even incidental effects disallowed)? What does the "entanglement" test add to these inquiries? Even beyond all that, how "reasonable" must our "reasonable observer" be, and what exactly qualifies as impermissible "endorsement" of religion in a country where "In God We Trust" appears on the coinage, the eye of God appears in its Great Seal, and we celebrate Thanksgiving as a national holiday ("to Whom are thanks being given")? Nearly half a century after *Lemon* and, the truth is, no one has any idea about the answers to these questions. As the plurality documents, our "doctrine [is] in such chaos" that lower courts have been "free to reach almost any result in almost any case." Scores of judges have pleaded with us to retire *Lemon*, scholars of all stripes have criticized the doctrine, and a majority of this Court has long done the same. Today, not a single Member of the Court even tries to defend *Lemon* against these criticisms — and they don't because they can't. As Justice Kennedy explained, *Lemon* is "flawed in its fundamentals," has proved "unworkable in practice," and is "inconsistent with our history and our precedents."

In place of *Lemon*, Part II-D relies on a more modest, historically sensitive approach, recognizing that "the Establishment Clause must be interpreted by reference to historical practices and understandings." I agree with all this and don't doubt that the monument before us is constitutional in light of the nation's traditions. But then the plurality continues on to suggest that "longstanding monuments, symbols, and practices" are "presumpt[ively]" constitutional. And about that, it's hard not to wonder: How old must a monument, symbol, or practice be to qualify for this new presumption? It seems 94 years is enough, but what about the Star of David monument erected in South Carolina in 2001 to commemorate victims of the Holocaust, or the cross that marines in California placed in 2004 to honor their comrades who fell during the War on Terror? And where exactly in the Constitution does this presumption come from? The plurality does not say, nor does it even explain what work its presumption does. To the contrary, the plurality proceeds to analyze the "presumptively" constitutional memorial in this case for its consistency with "'historical practices and understandings'" under *Marsh* and *Town of Greece*—exactly the same approach that the plurality, quoting *Town of Greece*, recognizes "'must be'" used *whenever* we interpret the Establishment Clause. Though the plurality does not say so in as many words, the message for our lower court colleagues seems unmistakable: Whether a monument, symbol, or practice is old or new, apply *Town of Greece*, not *Lemon*. But if that's the real message of the plurality's opinion, it seems to me exactly right—because what matters when it comes to assessing a monument, symbol, or practice isn't its age but its compliance with ageless principles. The Constitution's meaning is fixed, not some good-for-this-day-only coupon, and a practice consistent with our nation's traditions is just as permissible whether undertaken today or 94 years ago.

JUSTICE GINSBURG, with whom JUSTICE SOTOMAYOR joins, dissenting.

Decades ago, this Court recognized that the Establishment Clause demands governmental neutrality among religious faiths, and between religion and nonreligion. Numerous times since, the Court has reaffirmed the Constitution's commitment to neutrality. Today the Court erodes that neutrality commitment, diminishing precedent designed to preserve individual liberty and civic harmony in favor of a "presumption of constitutionality for longstanding monuments, symbols, and practices."

The Latin cross is the foremost symbol of the Christian faith, embodying the "central theological claim of Christianity: that the son of God died on the cross, that he rose from the dead, and that his death and resurrection offer the possibility of eternal life." Precisely because the cross symbolizes these sectarian beliefs, it is a common marker for the graves of Christian soldiers. For the same reason, using the cross as a war memorial does not transform it into a secular symbol. Just as a Star of David is not suitable to honor Christians who died serving their country, so a cross is not suitable to honor those of other faiths who died defending their nation. Soldiers of all faiths "are united by their love of country, but they are not united by the cross."

By maintaining the Peace Cross on a public highway, the Commission elevates Christianity over other faiths, and religion over nonreligion. Memorializing the service of American soldiers is an "admirable and unquestionably secular" objective. But the Commission does not serve that objective by displaying a symbol that bears "a starkly sectarian message."

I

In cases challenging the government's display of a religious symbol, the Court has tested fidelity to the principle of neutrality by asking whether the display has the "effect of 'endorsing' religion." The display fails this requirement if it objectively "convey[s] a message that religion or a particular religious belief is favored or preferred."

To make that determination, a court must consider "the pertinent facts and circumstances surrounding the symbol and its placement."

As I see it, when a cross is displayed on public property, the government may be presumed to endorse its religious content. The venue is surely associated with the State; the symbol and its meaning are just as surely associated exclusively with Christianity. "It certainly is not common for property owners to open up their property [to] monuments that convey a message with which they do not wish to be associated." To non-Christians, nearly 30% of the population of the United States, the State's choice to display the cross on public buildings or spaces conveys a message of exclusion: It tells them they "are outsiders, not full members of the political community."

A presumption of endorsement, of course, may be overcome. A display does not run afoul of the neutrality principle if its "setting ... plausibly indicates" that the government has not sought "either to adopt [a] religious message or to urge its acceptance by others." The "typical museum setting," for example, "though not neutralizing the religious content of a religious painting, negates any message of endorsement of that content." Similarly, when a public school history teacher discusses the Protestant Reformation, the setting makes clear that the teacher's purpose is to educate, not to proselytize. The Peace Cross, however, is not of that genre.

II

The Commission urges in defense of its monument that the Latin cross "is not merely a reaffirmation of Christian beliefs"; rather, "when used in the context of a war memorial," the cross becomes "a universal symbol of the sacrifices of those who fought and died."

The Commission's "[a]ttempts to secularize what is unquestionably a sacred [symbol] defy credibility and disserve people of faith." The asserted commemorative meaning of the cross rests on—and is inseparable from—its Christian meaning: "the crucifixion of Jesus Christ and the redeeming benefits of his passion and death," specifically, "the salvation of man."

The cross affirms that, thanks to the soldier's embrace of Christianity, he will be rewarded with eternal life. "To say that the cross honors the Christian war dead does not identify a secular meaning of the cross; it merely identifies a common application of the religious meaning." Scarcely "a universal symbol of sacrifice," the cross is "the symbol of one particular sacrifice."

The Peace Cross is no exception. That was evident from the start. At the dedication ceremony, the keynote speaker analogized the sacrifice of the honored soldiers to that of Jesus Christ, calling the Peace Cross "symbolic of Calvary," where Jesus was crucified. Local reporters variously described the monument as "[a] mammoth cross, a likeness of the Cross of Calvary, as described in the Bible," and "a huge sacrifice cross." The character of the monument has not changed with the passage of time.

The Commission nonetheless urges that the Latin cross is a "well-established" secular symbol commemorating, in particular, "military valor and sacrifice [in] World War I."

Reiterating its argument that the Latin cross is a "universal symbol" of World War I sacrifice, the Commission states that "40 World War I monuments ... built in the United States ... bear the shape of a cross." This figure includes memorials that merely "incorporat[e]" a cross. Moreover, the 40 monuments compose only 4% of the "948 outdoor sculptures commemorating the First World War." The Court lists just seven freestanding cross memorials, less than 1% of the total number of monuments to World War I in the United States. Cross memorials, in short, are outliers. The overwhelming majority of World War I memorials contain no Latin cross.

Holding the Commission's display of the Peace Cross unconstitutional would not, as the Commission fears, "inevitably require the destruction of other cross-shaped memorials throughout the country." When a religious symbol appears in a public cemetery—on a headstone, or as the headstone itself, or perhaps integrated into a larger memorial—the setting counters the inference that the government seeks "either to adopt the religious message or to urge its acceptance by others." In a cemetery, the "privately selected religious symbols on individual graves are best understood as the private speech of each veteran." Such displays are "linked to, and sho[w] respect for, the individual honoree's faith and beliefs." They do not suggest governmental endorsement of those faith and beliefs.

Exercise 6:

1. What is the rule or principle that the majority of the Court adopts in *American Legion*?

2. When do "religiously expressive monuments, symbols, and practices" qualify for the Court's "strong presumption of constitutionality"? We know that the Bladensburg Peace Cross falls within the Court's presumption, but what types of religiously expressive symbols and practices might? Each session of the Supreme Court of the United States begins with "God save the United States and this honorable Court." Is that practice, which Chief Justice Marshall started, entitled to a strong presumption of constitutionality? What about the national motto of the United States, "In God We Trust"? Can it be used in all circumstances or only some? On United States currency? What about "under God" in the Pledge of Allegiance?

3. How old must a religiously expressive monument, symbol, or practice be to fall within the presumption? Why does the majority contend that established religious monuments are entitled to such a presumption?

4. What rule does the Court adopt with respect to new or not well-established monuments? If such newer, religiously expressive monuments, symbols, and practices are not entitled to a strong presumption, are they entitled to any presumption? Should the Court apply a different Establishment Clause test? If so, which one? How would Justice Breyer go about deciding the constitutionality of a new monument?

5. Suppose officials in the small town of Greene in Virginia, after reading about the Bladensburg Peace Cross in *American Legion*, decide to erect an almost identical monument in memory of all of those from the town that lost their lives in service to the United States. The monument will be a 32-foot tall Latin cross sitting on a

large pedestal; the words "Valor," "Endurance," "Courage," and "Devotion" will be inscribed on its base; a bronze plaque will state that the monument is "Dedicated to all of those from Greene, Virginia who lost their lives in service to the United States"; the plaque will list the names of the 128 service members who had died while serving and will have the same quote from Woodrow Wilson's request for a declaration of war. The town officials plan to place the monument in a town park near a busy road. The park is large and has five other monuments commemorating World War II, Nine-Eleven, Vietnam, the Revolutionary War, and the branches of the military. None of the other monuments are visible from the busy road, but all are located in the park. Would this monument violate the Establishment Clause post-*American Legion*? Why or why not?

6. How would Justice Gorsuch analyze a "new" monument, symbol, or practice? Is he correct that "what matters when it comes to assessing a monument, symbol, or practice isn't its age but its compliance with ageless principles"? If a city can draw on the longstanding history of legislative prayer to justify adopting a prayer practice like that found in *Town of Greece*, can the same town erect a religiously themed monument consistent with the tradition of such monuments that the Court discussed in *American Legion*? For Justice Gorsuch? For a majority of the Court?

7. Should a plaintiff ever be able to overcome the "strong presumption" in favor of the constitutionality of longstanding monuments? How might she do that? What might a plaintiff have to show? And if the presumption did not apply, what Establishment Clause analysis should govern?

8. How might religious government speech "deliberately disrespect[]" religious minorities? What types of evidence might establish such deliberate disrespect? What types of arguments did plaintiffs make in *American Legion* to show the alleged disrespect? Why did the Court reject those arguments? If there is such evidence, should it void the presumption of constitutionality? What Establishment Clause test should apply instead? Or should such evidence trigger a presumption of unconstitutionality?

9. Is the Lemon Test dead? How many justices refused to apply *Lemon* in the context of established, religiously expressive monuments, symbols, and practices? What are the four problems that the Court identifies with respect to applying *Lemon* to longstanding monuments, symbols, and practices?

10. What is the test that Justice Thomas articulates in his concurrence? What test does Justice Kavanaugh adopt? How does Justice Kavanaugh's test differ from Justice Thomas' test? How do both differ from the strong presumption that the Court adopts? Which approach most closely accords with the original understanding of the Establishment Clause? With the Court's subsequent Establishment Clause precedents? Are they apt to lead to the same outcomes in many (or most) cases? Keep these questions in mind as you explore the various Establishment Clause tests that the Court employed prior to *American Legion*.

11. Reconstruct the dissent's argument. Do Justice Ginsburg and Justice Sotomayor retain the Lemon Test? Why would they hold that the Bladensburg Peace Cross is unconstitutional? Who has the stronger argument, the majority or the dissent?

One of the consequences of the Supreme Court's altering the Lemon Test was that the Test prohibited a smaller universe of church-state interactions. For example, *Mitchell v. Helms*, 530 U.S. 793 (2000), was a pivotal case that suggested a re-orientation of the *Lemon* line of cases. There, the Court faced an Establishment Clause challenge to federal school-aid money that all schools—public and private, religious and nonreligious—received, in the form of secular educational materials and equipment, based on their student enrollment. A plurality of the Court—Justices Thomas, Scalia, and Kennedy, and Chief Justice Rehnquist—upheld the aid program, reasoning that the money was itself neutral and went to schools based on the neutral criterion of the independent choices of parents, who decided to send their children to particular schools. *Id*. at 809–14. *Mitchell* presaged the last major case in the line of school funding cases, and the most recent use of the Lemon Test in that context:

Zelman v. Simmons-Harris

536 U.S. 639 (2002)

CHIEF JUSTICE REHNQUIST delivered the opinion of the Court.

The State of Ohio has established a pilot program designed to provide educational choices to families with children who reside in the Cleveland City School District. The question presented is whether this program offends the Establishment Clause of the United States Constitution. We hold that it does not.

There are more than 75,000 children enrolled in the Cleveland City School District. The majority of these children are from low-income and minority families. Few of these families enjoy the means to send their children to any school other than an inner-city public school. For more than a generation, however, Cleveland's public schools have been among the worst performing public schools in the Nation. In 1995, a Federal District Court declared a "crisis of magnitude" and placed the entire Cleveland school district under state control. Shortly thereafter, the state auditor found that Cleveland's public schools were in the midst of a "crisis that is perhaps unprecedented in the history of American education." The district had failed to meet any of the 18 state standards for minimal acceptable performance. Only 1 in 10 ninth graders could pass a basic proficiency examination. More than two-thirds of high school students either dropped or failed out before graduation. Of those students who managed to reach their senior year, one of every four still failed to graduate. Of those students who did graduate, few could read, write, or compute at levels comparable to their counterparts in other cities.

It is against this backdrop that Ohio enacted, among other initiatives, its Pilot Project Scholarship Program. The program provides financial assistance to families in any Ohio school district that is or has been "under federal court order requiring

supervision and operational management of the district by the state superintendent."
Cleveland is the only Ohio school district to fall within that category.

The program provides two basic kinds of assistance to parents of children in a
covered district. First, the program provides tuition aid for students in kindergarten
through third grade, expanding each year through eighth grade, to attend a participating public or private school of their parent's choosing. Second, the program provides tutorial aid for students who choose to remain enrolled in public school.

The tuition aid portion of the program is designed to provide educational choices
to parents who reside in a covered district. Any private school, whether religious or
nonreligious, may participate in the program and accept program students so long
as the school is located within the boundaries of a covered district and meets statewide
educational standards. Participating private schools must agree not to discriminate
on the basis of race, religion, or ethnic background, or to "advocate or foster unlawful
behavior or teach hatred of any person or group on the basis of race, ethnicity, national
origin, or religion." Any public school located in a school district adjacent to the covered district may also participate in the program. Adjacent public schools are eligible
to receive a $2,250 tuition grant for each program student accepted in addition to
the full amount of per-pupil state funding attributable to each additional student.

Tuition aid is distributed to parents according to financial need. Families with incomes below 200% of the poverty line are given priority and are eligible to receive
90% of private school tuition up to $2,250. For these lowest income families, par-
ticipating private schools may not charge a parental copayment greater than $250.
For all other families, the program pays 75% of tuition costs, up to $1,875, with no
copayment cap. These families receive tuition aid only if the number of available
scholarships exceeds the number of low-income children who choose to participate.
Where tuition aid is spent depends solely upon where parents who receive tuition
aid choose to enroll their child. If parents choose a private school, checks are made
payable to the parents who then endorse the checks over to the chosen school.

The program has been in operation within the Cleveland City School District since
the 1996–1997 school year. In the 1999–2000 school year, 56 private schools participated in the program, 46 (or 82%) of which had a religious affiliation. None of the
public schools in districts adjacent to Cleveland have elected to participate. More
than 3,700 students participated in the scholarship program, most of whom (96%)
enrolled in religiously affiliated schools. Sixty percent of these students were from
families at or below the poverty line. In the 1998–1999 school year, approximately
1,400 Cleveland public school students received tutorial aid. This number was expected
to double during the 1999–2000 school year.

The program is part of a broader undertaking by the State to enhance the educational
options of Cleveland's schoolchildren in response to the 1995 takeover. That undertaking
includes programs governing community and magnet schools. Community schools
are funded under state law but are run by their own school boards, not by local school
districts.... They can have no religious affiliation and are required to accept students

by lottery. For each child enrolled in a community school, the school receives state funding of $4,518, twice the funding a participating program school may receive.

Magnet schools are public schools operated by a local school board that emphasize a particular subject area, teaching method, or service to students. For each student enrolled in a magnet school, the school district receives $7,746, including state funding of $4,167, the same amount received per student enrolled at a traditional public school.

In July 1999, respondents filed this action in United States District Court, seeking to enjoin the program on the ground that it violated the Establishment Clause. [T]he District Court granted summary judgment for respondents. [A] divided panel of the Court of Appeals affirmed the judgment of the District Court, finding that the program had the "primary effect" of advancing religion in violation of the Establishment Clause. We granted certiorari and now reverse the Court of Appeals.

The Establishment Clause of the First Amendment, applied to the States through the Fourteenth Amendment, prevents a State from enacting laws that have the "purpose" or "effect" of advancing or inhibiting religion. *Agostini v. Felton*, 521 U.S. 203, 222–223 (1997). There is no dispute that the program challenged here was enacted for the valid secular purpose of providing educational assistance to poor children in a demonstrably failing public school system. Thus, the question presented is whether the Ohio program nonetheless has the forbidden "effect" of advancing or inhibiting religion.

To answer that question, our decisions have drawn a consistent distinction between government programs that provide aid directly to religious schools, *Mitchell v. Helms*, 530 U.S. 793, 810–814 (2000) (plurality opinion); *Agostini*, at 225–227, and programs of true private choice, in which government aid reaches religious schools only as a result of the genuine and independent choices of private individuals. While our jurisprudence with respect to the constitutionality of direct aid programs has "changed significantly" over the past two decades, *Agostini, supra*, at 236, our jurisprudence with respect to true private choice programs has remained consistent and unbroken. Three times we have confronted Establishment Clause challenges to neutral government programs that provide aid directly to a broad class of individuals, who, in turn, direct the aid to religious schools or institutions of their own choosing. Three times we have rejected such challenges.

In *Mueller* [*v. Allen*, 463 U.S. 388 (1983)], we rejected an Establishment Clause challenge to a Minnesota program authorizing tax deductions for various educational expenses, including private school tuition costs.... In *Witters* [*v. Washington Dept. of Servs. for the Blind*, 474 U.S. 481 (1986)], we used identical reasoning to reject an Establishment Clause challenge to a vocational scholarship program that provided tuition aid to a student studying at a religious institution to become a pastor.... Finally, in *Zobrest* [*v. Catalina Foothills Sch. Dist.*, 509 U.S. 1 (1993)], we reject[ed] an Establishment Clause challenge to a federal program that permitted sign-language interpreters to assist deaf children enrolled in religious schools.

Mueller, Witters, and *Zobrest* thus make clear that where a government aid program is neutral with respect to religion, and provides assistance directly to a broad class of citizens who, in turn, direct government aid to religious schools wholly as a result of their own genuine and independent private choice, the program is not readily subject to challenge under the Establishment Clause. A program that shares these features permits government aid to reach religious institutions only by way of the deliberate choices of numerous individual recipients. The incidental advancement of a religious mission, or the perceived endorsement of a religious message, is reasonably attributable to the individual recipient, not to the government, whose role ends with the disbursement of benefits.

We believe that the program challenged here is a program of true private choice, consistent with *Mueller, Witters*, and *Zobrest*, and thus constitutional. As was true in those cases, the Ohio program is neutral in all respects toward religion. It is part of a general and multifaceted undertaking by the State of Ohio to provide educational opportunities to the children of a failed school district. It confers educational assistance directly to a broad class of individuals defined without reference to religion, *i.e.*, any parent of a school-age child who resides in the Cleveland City School District. The program permits the participation of *all* schools within the district, religious or nonreligious. Adjacent public schools also may participate and have a financial incentive to do so. Program benefits are available to participating families on neutral terms, with no reference to religion.

Respondents suggest that even without a financial incentive for parents to choose a religious school, the program creates a "public perception that the State is endorsing religious practices and beliefs." But we have repeatedly recognized that no reasonable observer would think a neutral program of private choice, where state aid reaches religious schools solely as a result of the numerous independent decisions of private individuals, carries with it the *imprimatur* of government endorsement. Any objective observer familiar with the full history and context of the Ohio program would reasonably view it as one aspect of a broader undertaking to assist poor children in failed schools, not as an endorsement of religious schooling in general.

There also is no evidence that the program fails to provide genuine opportunities for Cleveland parents to select secular educational options for their school-age children. Cleveland schoolchildren enjoy a range of educational choices: They may remain in public school as before, remain in public school with publicly funded tutoring aid, obtain a scholarship and choose a religious school, obtain a scholarship and choose a nonreligious private school, enroll in a community school, or enroll in a magnet school. That 46 of the 56 private schools now participating in the program are religious schools does not condemn it as a violation of the Establishment Clause. The Establishment Clause question is whether Ohio is coercing parents into sending their children to religious schools, and that question must be answered by evaluating *all* options Ohio provides Cleveland schoolchildren, only one of which is to obtain a program scholarship and then choose a religious school.

JUSTICE SOUTER speculates that because more private religious schools currently participate in the program, the program itself must somehow discourage the participation of private nonreligious schools. But Cleveland's preponderance of religiously affiliated private schools certainly did not arise as a result of the program; it is a phenomenon common to many American cities. Indeed, by all accounts the program has captured a remarkable cross-section of private schools, religious and nonreligious. It is true that 82% of Cleveland's participating private schools are religious schools, but it is also true that 81% of private schools in Ohio are religious schools. To attribute constitutional significance to this figure, moreover, would lead to the absurd result that a neutral school-choice program might be permissible in some parts of Ohio, such as Columbus, where a lower percentage of private schools are religious schools, but not in inner-city Cleveland, where Ohio has deemed such programs most sorely needed, but where the preponderance of religious schools happens to be greater.

Respondents and JUSTICE SOUTER claim that even if we do not focus on the number of participating schools that are religious schools, we should attach constitutional significance to the fact that 96% of scholarship recipients have enrolled in religious schools. They claim that this alone proves parents lack genuine choice, even if no parent has ever said so. We need not consider this argument in detail, since it was flatly rejected in *Mueller*, where we found it irrelevant that 96% of parents taking deductions for tuition expenses paid tuition at religious schools. Indeed, we have recently found it irrelevant even to the constitutionality of a direct aid program that a vast majority of program benefits went to religious schools. *Mitchell* [*v. Helms*, 530 U.S. at] 812 n.6.

This point is aptly illustrated here. The 96% figure upon which respondents and JUSTICE SOUTER rely discounts entirely (1) the more than 1,900 Cleveland children enrolled in alternative community schools, (2) the more than 13,000 children enrolled in alternative magnet schools, and (3) the more than 1,400 children enrolled in traditional public schools with tutorial assistance. Including some or all of these children in the denominator of children enrolled in nontraditional schools during the 1999–2000 school year drops the percentage enrolled in religious schools from 96% to under 20%. The 96% figure also represents but a snapshot of one particular school year. In the 1997–1998 school year, by contrast, only 78% of scholarship recipients attended religious schools.[7]

JUSTICE O'CONNOR, concurring. [Opinion omitted.]

JUSTICE THOMAS, concurring.

Today many of our inner-city public schools deny emancipation to urban minority students. Despite this Court's observation nearly 50 years ago in *Brown v. Board of Education*, 347 U.S. 483, 493 (1954), that "it is doubtful that any child may reasonably be expected to succeed in life if he is denied the opportunity of an education," urban

---

7. JUSTICE BREYER would raise the invisible specters of "divisiveness" and "religious strife" to find the program unconstitutional. It is unclear exactly what sort of principle JUSTICE BREYER has in mind, considering that the program has ignited no "divisiveness" or "strife" other than this litigation. Nor is it clear where JUSTICE BREYER would locate this presumed authority to deprive Cleveland residents of a program that they have chosen but that we subjectively find "divisive."

children have been forced into a system that continually fails them. These cases present an example of such failures.

II

The wisdom of allowing States greater latitude in dealing with matters of religion and education can be easily appreciated in this context. Respondents advocate using the Fourteenth Amendment to handcuff the State's ability to experiment with education. But without education one can hardly exercise the civic, political, and personal freedoms conferred by the Fourteenth Amendment. Faced with a severe educational crisis, the State of Ohio enacted wide-ranging educational reform that allows voluntary participation of private and religious schools in educating poor urban children otherwise condemned to failing public schools. The program does not force any individual to submit to religious indoctrination or education. It simply gives parents a greater choice as to where and in what manner to educate their children. [See, *e.g.*, *Pierce v. Society of Sisters*, 268 U.S. 510, 535 (1925).] This is a choice that those with greater means have routinely exercised.

In addition to expanding the reach of the scholarship program, the inclusion of religious schools makes sense given Ohio's purpose of increasing educational performance and opportunities. Religious schools, like other private schools, achieve far better educational results than their public counterparts.... Of Cleveland eighth graders taking the 1999 Ohio proficiency test, 95 percent in Catholic schools passed the reading test, whereas only 57 percent in public schools passed. And 75 percent of Catholic school students passed the math proficiency test, compared to only 22 percent of public school students.

Today the promise of public school education has failed poor inner-city blacks. While in theory providing education to everyone, the quality of public schools varies significantly across districts. Just as blacks supported public education during Reconstruction, many blacks and other minorities now support school choice programs because they provide the greatest educational opportunities for their children in struggling communities.

While the romanticized ideal of universal public education resonates with the cognoscenti who oppose vouchers, poor urban families just want the best education for their children. The failure to provide education to poor urban children perpetuates a vicious cycle of poverty, dependence, criminality, and alienation that continues for the remainder of their lives. If society cannot end racial discrimination, at least it can arm minorities with the education to defend themselves from some of discrimination's effects.

[Voucher] programs address the root of the problem with failing urban public schools that disproportionately affect minority students. Society's other solution to these educational failures is often to provide racial preferences in higher education. Such preferences, however, run afoul of the Fourteenth Amendment's prohibition against distinctions based on race. See *Plessy* [*v. Ferguson*, 163 U.S. 537,] 555 [(1896)] (Harlan, J., dissenting). By contrast, school choice programs that involve religious schools appear unconstitutional only to those who would twist the Fourteenth Amendment against itself by expansively incorporating the Establishment Clause. Converting the Fourteenth Amendment from a guarantee of opportunity to an obstacle against education reform distorts our constitutional values and disserves those in the greatest need.

As Frederick Douglass poignantly noted, "no greater benefit can be bestowed upon a long benighted people, than giving to them, as we are here earnestly this day endeavoring to do, the means of an education."

JUSTICE STEVENS, dissenting. [Opinion omitted.]

JUSTICE SOUTER, with whom JUSTICE STEVENS, JUSTICE GINSBURG, and JUSTICE BREYER join, dissenting.

The applicability of the Establishment Clause to public funding of benefits to religious schools was settled in *Everson v. Board of Ed. of Ewing*, 330 U.S. 1 (1947). The Court stated: "No tax in any amount, large or small, can be levied to support any religious activities or institutions, whatever they may be called, or whatever form they may adopt to teach or practice religion."

Today, however, the majority holds that the Establishment Clause is not offended by Ohio's Pilot Project Scholarship Program. In the city of Cleveland the overwhelming proportion of large appropriations for voucher money must be spent on religious schools if it is to be spent at all, and will be spent in amounts that cover almost all of tuition. The money will thus pay for eligible students' instruction not only in secular subjects but in religion as well, in schools that can fairly be characterized as founded to teach religious doctrine and to imbue teaching in all subjects with a religious dimension. Public tax money will pay at a systemic level for teaching the covenant with Israel and Mosaic law in Jewish schools, the primacy of the Apostle Peter and the Papacy in Catholic schools, the truth of reformed Christianity in Protestant schools, and the revelation to the Prophet in Muslim schools, to speak only of major religious groupings in the Republic.

How can a Court consistently leave *Everson* on the books and approve the Ohio vouchers? The answer is that it cannot.

II

A

Consider first the criterion of neutrality. Neutrality refers[] to evenhandedness in setting eligibility as between potential religious and secular recipients of public money.... In order to apply the neutrality test, it makes sense to focus on a category of aid that may be directed to religious as well as secular schools, and ask whether the scheme favors a religious direction. Here, one would ask whether the voucher provisions, allowing for as much as $2,250 toward private school tuition (or a grant to a public school in an adjacent district), were written in a way that skewed the scheme toward benefiting religious schools.

This, however, is not what the majority asks. The majority looks not to the provisions for tuition vouchers, but to every provision for educational opportunity. The majority then finds confirmation that "participation of *all* schools" satisfies neutrality by noting that the better part of total state educational expenditure goes to public schools, thus showing there is no favor of religion.

The illogic is patent. If regular, public schools (which can get no voucher payments) "participate" in a voucher scheme with schools that can, and public expenditure is still predominantly on public schools, then the majority's reasoning would find neutrality in a scheme of vouchers available for private tuition in districts with no secular private schools at all.

B

The majority addresses the issue of choice the same way it addresses neutrality, by asking whether recipients or potential recipients of voucher aid have a choice of public schools among secular alternatives to religious schools. Again, however, the majority asks the wrong question. The majority has confused choice in spending scholarships with choice from the entire menu of possible educational placements, most of them open to anyone willing to attend a public school. The majority's view that all educational choices are comparable for purposes of choice ignores the whole point of the choice test: it is a criterion for deciding whether indirect aid to a religious school is legitimate because it passes through private hands that can spend or use the aid in a secular school. The question is whether the private hand is genuinely free to send the money in either a secular direction or a religious one. The majority now has transformed this question about private choice in channeling aid into a question about selecting from examples of state spending (on education) including direct spending on magnet and community public schools that goes through no private hands and could never reach a religious school under any circumstance. When the choice test is transformed from where to spend the money to where to go to school, it is cut loose from its very purpose.

There is, in any case, no way to interpret the 96.6% of current voucher money going to religious schools as reflecting a free and genuine choice by the families that apply for vouchers. The 96.6% reflects, instead, the fact that too few nonreligious school desks are available and few but religious schools can afford to accept more than a handful of voucher students. And contrary to the majority's assertion, public schools in adjacent districts hardly have a financial incentive to participate in the Ohio voucher program, and none has. For the overwhelming number of children in the voucher scheme, the only alternative to the public schools is religious. And it is entirely irrelevant that the State did not deliberately design the network of private schools for the sake of channeling money into religious institutions. The criterion is one of genuinely free choice on the part of the private individuals who choose, and a Hobson's choice is not a choice, whatever the reason for being Hobsonian.

III

A

The scale of the aid to religious schools approved today is unprecedented, both in the number of dollars and in the proportion of systemic school expenditure supported. [T]he sheer quantity of aid, when delivered to a class of religious primary and secondary schools, [i]s suspect on the theory that the greater the aid, the greater its proportion to a religious school's existing expenditures, and the greater the likelihood that public money [i]s supporting religious as well as secular instruction.

The Cleveland voucher program has cost Ohio taxpayers $33 million since its implementation in 1996, and its cost was expected to exceed $8 million in the 2001–2002 school year. These tax-raised funds are on top of the textbooks, reading and math tutors, laboratory equipment, and the like that Ohio provides to private schools, worth roughly $600 per child.

The gross amounts of public money contributed are symptomatic of the scope of what the taxpayers' money buys for a broad class of religious-school students. In paying for practically the full amount of tuition for thousands of qualifying students, the scholarships purchase everything that tuition purchases, be it instruction in math or indoctrination in faith. The majority makes no pretense that substantial amounts of tax money are not systematically underwriting religious practice and indoctrination.

B

It is virtually superfluous to point out that every objective underlying the prohibition of religious establishment is betrayed by this scheme, but something has to be said about the enormity of the violation. [T]he first [objective of the Establishment Clause is] respect for freedom of conscience. Jefferson described it as the idea that no one "shall be compelled to ... support any religious worship, place, or ministry whatsoever," and Madison thought it violated by any "'authority which can force a citizen to contribute three pence ... of his property for the support of any ... establishment.'" Madison's objection to three pence has simply been lost in the majority's formalism.

As for the second objective, to save religion from its own corruption, Madison wrote of the "'experience ... that ecclesiastical establishments, instead of maintaining the purity and efficacy of Religion, have had a contrary operation.'" In Madison's time, the manifestations were "pride and indolence in the Clergy; ignorance and servility in the laity[,] in both, superstition, bigotry and persecution"; in the 21st century, the risk is one of "corrosive secularism" to religious schools, and the specific threat is to the primacy of the schools' mission to educate the children of the faithful according to the unaltered precepts of their faith.

The risk is already being realized. In Ohio, for example, a condition of receiving government money under the program is that participating religious schools may not "discriminate on the basis of ... religion," which means the school may not give admission preferences to children who are members of the patron faith; children of a parish are generally consigned to the same admission lotteries as non-believers. Nor is the State's religious antidiscrimination restriction limited to student admission policies: by its terms, a participating religious school may well be forbidden to choose a member of its own clergy to serve as teacher or principal over a layperson of a different religion claiming equal qualification for the job.

When government aid goes up, so does reliance on it; the only thing likely to go down is independence.... [T]here [is] reason to wonder when dependence will become great enough to give the State of Ohio an effective veto over basic decisions on the content of curriculums? A day will come when religious schools will learn what political leverage can do, just as Ohio's politicians are now getting a lesson in the leverage exercised by religion.

JUSTICE BREYER, with whom JUSTICE STEVENS and JUSTICE SOUTER join, dissenting.

I write separately to emphasize the risk that publicly financed voucher programs pose in terms of religiously based social conflict. I do so because I believe that the Establishment Clause concern for protecting the Nation's social fabric from religious conflict poses an overriding obstacle to the implementation of this well-intentioned school voucher program. And by explaining the nature of the concern, I hope to demonstrate why, in my view, "parental choice" cannot significantly alleviate the constitutional problem.

I

[The Religion] Clauses embody an understanding, reached in the 17th century after decades of religious war, that liberty and social stability demand a religious tolerance that respects the religious views of all citizens, permits those citizens to "worship God in their own way," and allows all families to "teach their children and to form their characters" as they wish. The Clauses reflect the Framers' vision of an American Nation free of the religious strife that had long plagued the nations of Europe.

In part for this reason, the Court's 20th century Establishment Clause cases — both those limiting the practice of religion in public schools and those limiting the public funding of private religious education — focused directly upon social conflict, potentially created when government becomes involved in religious education. In *Engel v. Vitale*, 370 U.S. 421 (1962), the Court held that the Establishment Clause forbids prayer in public elementary and secondary schools because it recognized the "anguish, hardship and bitter strife that could come when zealous religious groups struggl[e] with one another to obtain the Government's stamp of approval...."

When it decided these 20th century Establishment Clause cases, the Court did not deny that an earlier American society might have found a less clear-cut church/state separation compatible with social tranquility. Indeed, historians point out that during the early years of the Republic, American schools — including the first public schools — were Protestant in character. Their students recited Protestant prayers, read the King James version of the Bible, and learned Protestant religious ideals. Those practices may have wrongly discriminated against members of minority religions, but given the small number of such individuals, the teaching of Protestant religions in schools did not threaten serious social conflict.

The 20th century Court was fully aware, however, that immigration and growth had changed American society dramatically since its early years. By 1850, 1.6 million Catholics lived in America, and by 1900 that number rose to 12 million. There were similar percentage increases in the Jewish population. Not surprisingly, with this increase in numbers, members of non-Protestant religions, particularly Catholics, began to resist the Protestant domination of the public schools. Scholars report that by the mid-19th century religious conflict over matters such as Bible reading "grew intense," as Catholics resisted and Protestants fought back to preserve their domination. "Dreading Catholic domination," native Protestants "terrorized Catholics."

The 20th century Court was also aware that political efforts to right the wrong of discrimination against religious minorities in primary education had failed; in fact they had exacerbated religious conflict. Catholics sought equal government support for the education of their children in the form of aid for private Catholic schools. But the "Protestant position" on this matter, scholars report, "was that public schools must be 'nonsectarian' (which was usually understood to allow Bible reading and other Protestant observances) and public money must not support 'sectarian' schools (which in practical terms meant Catholic)." And this sentiment played a significant role in creating a movement that sought to amend several state constitutions (often successfully), and to amend the United States Constitution (unsuccessfully) to make certain that government would not help pay for "sectarian" (*i.e.*, Catholic) schooling for children.

With respect to government aid to private education, did not history show that efforts to obtain equivalent funding for the private education of children whose parents did not hold popular religious beliefs only exacerbated religious strife?

The upshot is the development of constitutional doctrine that reads the Establishment Clause as avoiding religious strife, *not* by providing every religion with an *equal opportunity* (say, to secure state funding or to pray in the public schools), but by drawing fairly clear lines of *separation* between church and state—at least where the heartland of religious belief, such as primary religious education, is at issue.

II

The principle underlying these cases—avoiding religiously based social conflict—remains of great concern. As religiously diverse as America had become when the Court decided its major 20th century Establishment Clause cases, we are exponentially more diverse today. America boasts more than 55 different religious groups and subgroups with a significant number of members. And several of these major religions contain different subsidiary sects with different religious beliefs.

School voucher programs finance the religious education of the young. And, if widely adopted, they may well provide billions of dollars that will do so. Why will different religions not become concerned about, and seek to influence, the criteria used to channel this money to religious schools? Why will they not want to examine the implementation of the programs that provide this money—to determine, for example, whether implementation has biased a program toward or against particular sects, or whether recipient religious schools are adequately fulfilling a program's criteria? If so, just how is the State to resolve the resulting controversies without provoking legitimate fears of the kinds of religious favoritism that, in so religiously diverse a Nation, threaten social dissension?

Consider the voucher program here at issue. That program insists that the religious school accept students of all religions. Does that criterion treat fairly groups whose religion forbids them to do so? The program also insists that no participating school "advocate or foster unlawful behavior or teach hatred of any person or group on the basis of race, ethnicity, national origin, or religion." And it requires the State to "revoke the registration of any school if, after a hearing, the superintendent determines that the school is in violation" of the program's rules. As one *amicus* argues, "it is difficult to imagine a more divisive activity" than the appointment of state officials as referees to determine whether a particular religious doctrine "teaches hatred or advocates lawlessness."

[A]ny major funding program for primary religious education will require criteria. And the selection of those criteria, as well as their application, inevitably pose problems that are divisive. Efforts to respond to these problems not only will seriously entangle church and state, but also will promote division among religious groups, as one group or another fears (often legitimately) that it will receive unfair treatment at the hands of the government.

In a society as religiously diverse as ours, the Court has recognized that we must rely on the Religion Clauses of the First Amendment to protect against religious strife, particularly when what is at issue is an area as central to religious belief as the shaping, through primary education, of the next generation's minds and spirits.

III

I concede that the Establishment Clause currently permits States to channel various forms of assistance to religious schools, for example, transportation costs for students, computers, and secular texts. School voucher programs differ, however, in both *kind* and *degree* from aid programs upheld in the past. They differ in kind because they direct financing to a core function of the church: the teaching of religious truths to young children. For that reason the constitutional demand for "separation" is of particular constitutional concern. Vouchers also differ in *degree*. The aid programs recently upheld by the Court involved limited amounts of aid to religion. But the majority's analysis here appears to permit a considerable shift of taxpayer dollars from public secular schools to private religious schools. That fact, combined with the use to which these dollars will be put, exacerbates the conflict problem.

Exercise 7:

1. Why did the majority opinion spend so much effort detailing the background circumstances of the Cleveland public schools and the challenged voucher program?

2. By the time *Zelman* was decided, what form did the Lemon Test take, as least in the context of school funding?

3. What was Ohio's purpose in enacting the challenged voucher program? What evidence supports your conclusion?

4. Why did Ohio draw its statute—"any Ohio school district that is or has been 'under federal court order requiring supervision and operational management of the district by the state superintendent'"—so oddly?

5. Why, according to the Supreme Court, did the Ohio voucher program not have the "effect" of advancing religion if, in fact, religious schools received a significant amount of state money that, presumably, was beneficial to the schools, and their religious education programs? Under the original Lemon Test, would the Ohio voucher program have the effect of advancing religion?

6. The majority argued that the challenged voucher program did not constitute an endorsement of religion by Ohio. What was the majority's reasoning? Was the majority correct? Or was Justice Souter more persuasive when he argued that the program was not neutral and hence was an endorsement?

7. What role did the presence or absence of "coercion" play in the majority's analysis?

8. Justice Thomas cited to *Brown v. Board of Education.* For what proposition? Was Justice Thomas' use of *Brown* legitimate?

9. Justice Thomas' concurrence articulated his unique position, among the Justices, on the Establishment Clause. What is Justice Thomas' position? What arguments did he marshal in support of that position? What criticisms can you identify of Justice Thomas' position?

10. Are there any other provisions of the Bill of Rights to which Justice Thomas' analysis might apply?

11. Justice Thomas also argued that not incorporating the Establishment Clause would lead to valuable consequences (or avoid bad consequences). What did Justice Thomas have in mind? Why would Justice Thomas, a self-professed originalist, make these "policy" arguments?

12. Justice Stevens' dissent briefly recounted two related reasons for rejecting the Court's holding. What were those reasons? Articulate Justice Stevens' logic supporting his reasons. We will see below, in Section [D][2], that Justice Stevens' reasons have broad resonance with other Justices on the Court.

13. Justice Souter claimed that the Ohio voucher program's size was itself an Establishment Clause problem. Explain his reasoning. Do you agree?

14. Justice Souter argued — quoting Thomas Jefferson and James Madison — that the voucher program would corrupt the religious institutions that received the state money. Describe Justice Souter's argument. How might the majority have responded? Which side's argument is more persuasive?

15. Justice Breyer and the majority engaged over whether the voucher program did, or would, cause "divisiveness." Justice Breyer's argument is complex and nuanced. Explain his claim. What evidence did Justice Breyer provide that the challenged voucher program will cause unacceptable divisiveness? How did the majority respond to Justice Breyer's claims that this and future voucher programs would cause unacceptable divisiveness? Who had the better of the argument? We will see, below, that Justice Breyer has regularly advocated use of divisiveness as a, or the sole, factor to evaluate Establishment Clause challenges.

16. Could one apply Justice Breyer's same concerns to other subjects of great importance to Americans? For example, could one argue that, because Americans have and are engaged in a vigorous debate over abortion, both ethically and legally, the issue is too divisive and the Supreme Court should therefore remove it from governmental debate? Or Americans have always fought over federal and state spending, both how much and to what purposes it would go; does Justice Breyer's reasoning lead to the conclusion that the Supreme Court should limit the divisiveness caused by the subject?

17. Has, or will, the relatively strict-separationist rule proposed by Justice Breyer reduce societal divisiveness over religion, or exacerbate it? One way to test this is to ask whether the Supreme Court's strict-separationist case law has caused more divisiveness than an "equal opportunity" alternative, such as school vouchers.

———————

Following *Zelman*, many expected a rapid proliferation of voucher programs similar to, and broader than, the Ohio program upheld in *Zelman*. That did not happen; indeed, there were prominent failures of voucher initiatives, though there has also been some movement. For instance, after years of advocacy by voucher-proponents, Ohio adopted a broader — though still relatively limited — voucher program, labeled the EdChoice Scholarship Program. Ohio Revised Code Ann. § 3310.01 *et seq.* (West 2013). The key changes in Ohio were to make the program state-wide and to expand the number of eligible scholarship recipients. *Id.* § 3310.02.

———————

Up to this point, we have seen how the strict-separationist conception of the Establishment Clause, first announced in *Everson*, evolved into the Lemon Test. Then, we saw how the Lemon Test itself morphed in the school funding context, ending in *Zelman*. Though, as we will review in Section [D], below, the Lemon Test is not the only (or even the preferred) form of Establishment Clause analysis that the Court utilizes to evaluate government-religion interactions, it remains a possible default approach and, in some contexts, the dominant approach. For example, in the governmental aid to religious schools context, the Lemon Test, though significantly modified, continues to hold sway. In other contexts, however, such as prayer at school events, other tests have supplanted the Lemon Test, as you will see below.

One of the most recent uses of the Lemon Test occurred in the context of what was, at the time, a relatively new public religious display, which likely would fall outside the strong presumption of constitutionality that the Court recently adopted in *American Legion*:

McCreary County, Kentucky v.
American Civil Liberties Union of Kentucky

545 U.S. 844 (2005)

JUSTICE SOUTER delivered the opinion of the Court.

I

In the summer of 1999, petitioners McCreary County and Pulaski County, Kentucky (hereinafter Counties), put up in their respective courthouses large, gold-framed copies of an abridged text of the King James version of the Ten Commandments, including a citation to the Book of Exodus. In McCreary County, the placement of the Commandments responded to an order of the county legislative body requiring "the display [to] be posted in 'a very high traffic area' of the courthouse." In Pulaski County, amidst reported controversy over the propriety of the display, the Commandments were hung in a ceremony presided over by the county Judge-Executive, who called them "good rules to live by" and who recounted the story of an astronaut who became convinced "there must be a divine God" after viewing the Earth from the moon. The Judge-Executive was accompanied by the pastor of his church, who called the Commandments "a creed of ethics" and told the press after the ceremony that displaying the Commandments was "one of the greatest things the judge could have done to close out the millennium."

In November 1999, respondent[] American Civil Liberties Union of Kentucky sued the Counties in Federal District Court and sought a preliminary injunction against maintaining the displays, which the ACLU charged were violations of the prohibition of religious establishment included in the First Amendment of the Constitution. Within a month, and before the District Court had responded to the request for injunction, the legislative body of each County authorized a second, expanded display, by nearly identical resolutions reciting that the Ten Commandments are "the precedent legal code upon which the civil and criminal codes of … Kentucky are founded," and stating several grounds for taking that position: that "the Ten Commandments are codified in Kentucky's civil and criminal laws"; that the Kentucky House of Representatives had in 1993 "voted unanimously … to adjourn …' in remembrance and honor of Jesus Christ, the Prince of Ethics'"; that the "County Judge and … magistrates agree with the arguments set out by Judge [Roy] Moore" in defense of his "display [of] the Ten Commandments in his courtroom"; and that the "Founding Father[s] [had an] explicit understanding of the duty of elected officials to publicly acknowledge God as the source of America's strength and direction."

As directed by the resolutions, the Counties expanded the displays of the Ten Commandments in their locations, presumably along with copies of the resolution, which instructed that it, too, be posted. In addition to the first display's large framed copy of the edited King James version of the Commandments, the second included eight other documents in smaller frames, each either having a religious theme or excerpted to highlight a religious element. The documents were the "endowed by their Creator" passage from the Declaration of Independence; the Preamble to the Constitution of

Kentucky; the national motto, "In God We Trust"; a page from the Congressional Record of February 2, 1983, proclaiming the Year of the Bible and including a statement of the Ten Commandments; a proclamation by President Abraham Lincoln designating April 30, 1863, a National Day of Prayer and Humiliation; an excerpt from President Lincoln's "Reply to Loyal Colored People of Baltimore upon Presentation of a Bible," reading that "[t]he Bible is the best gift God has ever given to man"; a proclamation by President Reagan marking 1983 the Year of the Bible; and the Mayflower Compact.

After argument, the District Court entered a preliminary injunction on May 5, 2000, ordering that the "display ... be removed from [each] County Courthouse IMMEDIATELY" and that no county official "erect or cause to be erected similar displays." The court's analysis of the situation followed the three-part formulation first stated in *Lemon v. Kurtzman*, 403 U.S. 602 (1971). As to governmental purpose, it concluded that the original display "lack[ed] any secular purpose" because the Commandments "are a distinctly religious document." ... The court found that the second version also "clearly lack[ed] a secular purpose" because the "Count[ies] narrowly tailored [their] selection of foundational documents to incorporate only those with specific references to Christianity."

The Counties ... then installed another display in each courthouse, the third within a year. No new resolution authorized this one, nor did the Counties repeal the resolutions that preceded the second. The posting consists of nine framed documents of equal size, one of them setting out the Ten Commandments explicitly identified as the "King James Version" ... and quoted at greater length than before[.]

Assembled with the Commandments are framed copies of the Magna Carta, the Declaration of Independence, the Bill of Rights, the lyrics of the Star Spangled Banner, the Mayflower Compact, the National Motto, the Preamble to the Kentucky Constitution, and a picture of Lady Justice. The collection is entitled "The Foundations of American Law and Government Display" and each document comes with a statement about its historical and legal significance. The comment on the Ten Commandments reads:

> "The Ten Commandments have profoundly influenced the formation of Western legal thought and the formation of our country. That influence is clearly seen in the Declaration of Independence, which declared that 'We hold these truths to be self-evident, that all men are created equal, that they are endowed by their Creator with certain unalienable Rights, that among these are Life, Liberty, and the pursuit of Happiness.' The Ten Commandments provide the moral background of the Declaration of Independence and the foundation of our legal tradition."

The ACLU moved to supplement the preliminary injunction to enjoin the Counties' third display, and the Counties responded with several explanations for the new version, including desires "to demonstrate that the Ten Commandments were part of the foundation of American Law and Government" and "to educate the citizens of the county regarding some of the documents that played a significant role in the foundation of our system of law and government." The court, however, took the objective of proclaiming the Commandments' foundational value as "a religious, rather than secular, purpose" ... and found that the assertion that the Counties' broader educational goals are secular "crumble[s] ... upon an examination of the history of this litigation[.]"

[A] divided panel of the Court of Appeals for the Sixth Circuit affirmed. We now affirm.

II

Twenty-five years ago in a case prompted by posting the Ten Commandments in Kentucky's public schools, this Court recognized that the Commandments "are undeniably a sacred text in the Jewish and Christian faiths" and held that their display in public classrooms violated the First Amendment's bar against establishment of religion. *Stone* [*v. Graham*], 449 U.S. [39], 41 [(1980)]. The Counties ask for a different approach here by arguing that official purpose is unknowable. In the alternative, the Counties would avoid the District Court's conclusion by having us limit the scope of the purpose enquiry so severely that any trivial rationalization would suffice, under a standard oblivious to the history of religious government action like the progression of exhibits in this case.

A

The touchstone for our analysis is the principle that the "First Amendment mandates governmental neutrality between religion and religion, and between religion and non-religion." By showing a purpose to favor religion, the government "sends the ... message to ... nonadherents 'that they are outsiders, not full members of the political community, and an accompanying message to adherents that they are insiders, favored members.'"

B

[T]he Counties ask us to abandon *Lemon's* purpose test, or at least to truncate any enquiry into purpose here. Examination of purpose is a staple of statutory interpretation that makes up the daily fare of every appellate court in the country, and governmental purpose is a key element of a good deal of constitutional doctrine, *e.g.*, *Washington v. Davis*, 426 U.S. 229 (1976) (discriminatory purpose required for Equal Protection violation); *Hunt v. Washington State Apple Advertising Comm'n*, 432 U.S. 333, 352–353 (1977) (discriminatory purpose relevant to dormant Commerce Clause claim); *Church of Lukumi Babalu Aye, Inc. v. Hialeah*, 508 U.S. 520 (1993) (discriminatory purpose raises level of scrutiny required by free exercise claim). With enquiries into purpose this common, if they were nothing but hunts for mares' nests deflecting attention from bare judicial will, the whole notion of purpose in law would have dropped into disrepute long ago.

But scrutinizing purpose does make practical sense, as in Establishment Clause analysis, where an understanding of official objective emerges from readily discoverable fact, without any judicial psychoanalysis of a drafter's heart of hearts. The eyes that look to purpose belong to an "'objective observer,'" one who takes account of the traditional external signs that show up in the "'text, legislative history, and implementation of the statute,'" or comparable official act. There is, then, nothing hinting at an unpredictable or disingenuous exercise when a court enquires into purpose after a claim is raised under the Establishment Clause.

[O]ne consequence of the corollary that Establishment Clause analysis does not look to the veiled psyche of government officers could be that in some of the cases in which establishment complaints failed, savvy officials had disguised their religious intent so cleverly that the objective observer just missed it. But that is no reason for great constitutional concern. If someone in the government hides religious motive so well that the "'objective observer, acquainted with the text, legislative history, and implementation of the statute,'" cannot see it, then without something more the government does not make a divisive announcement that in itself amounts to taking religious sides. A secret motive stirs up no strife and does nothing to make outsiders of nonadherents, and it suffices to wait and see whether such government action turns out to have (as it may even be likely to have) the illegitimate effect of advancing religion.

C

After declining the invitation to abandon concern with purpose wholesale, we also have to avoid the Counties' alternative tack of trivializing the enquiry into it.

1

Lemon said that government action must have "a secular ... purpose[.]" ... [T]he Court often does accept governmental statements of purpose, in keeping with the respect owed in the first instance to such official claims. But in those unusual cases where the claim was an apparent sham, or the secular purpose secondary, the unsurprising results have been findings of no adequate secular object, as against a predominantly religious one.

2

The Counties' second proffered limitation can be dispatched quickly. They argue that purpose in a case like this one should be inferred, if at all, only from the latest news about the last in a series of governmental actions, however close they may all be in time and subject. But the world is not made brand new every morning, and the Counties are simply asking us to ignore perfectly probative evidence; they want an absentminded objective observer, not one presumed to be familiar with the history of the government's actions and competent to learn what history has to show. The Counties' position just bucks common sense: reasonable observers have reasonable memories, and our precedents sensibly forbid an observer "to turn a blind eye to the context in which [the] policy arose."

III

A

The display rejected in *Stone* had two obvious similarities to the first one in the sequence here: both set out a text of the Commandments as distinct from any traditionally symbolic representation, and each stood alone, not part of an arguably secular display. *Stone* stressed the significance of integrating the Commandments into a secular scheme to forestall the broadcast of an otherwise clearly religious message, and for good reason, the Commandments being a central point of reference in the religious and moral history of Jews and Christians. They proclaim the existence of a monotheistic god (no other gods). They regulate details of religious obligation (no graven images, no sabbath breaking, no vain oath swearing). And they unmistakably rest even the universally accepted prohibitions (as against murder, theft, and the like) on the sanction of the divinity proclaimed at the beginning of the text. Displaying that text is thus different from a symbolic depiction, like tablets with 10 roman numerals, which could be seen as alluding to a general notion of law, not a sectarian conception of faith. Where the text is set out, the insistence of the religious message is hard to avoid in the absence of a context plausibly suggesting a message going beyond an excuse to promote the religious point of view. The display in *Stone* had no context that might have indicated an object beyond the religious character of the text, and the Counties' solo exhibit here did nothing more to counter the sectarian implication than the postings at issue in *Stone*. What is more, at the ceremony for posting the framed Commandments in Pulaski County, the county executive was accompanied by his pastor. The reasonable observer could only think that the Counties meant to emphasize and celebrate the Commandments' religious message.

This is not to deny that the Commandments have had influence on civil or secular law; a major text of a majority religion is bound to be felt. The point is simply that the original text viewed in its entirety is an unmistakably religious statement dealing with religious obligations and with morality subject to religious sanction.

B

Once the Counties were sued, they modified the exhibits and invited additional insight into their purpose in a display that hung for about six months.... In this second display, unlike the first, the Commandments were not hung in isolation, merely leaving the Counties' purpose to emerge from the pervasively religious text of the Commandments themselves. Instead, the second version was required to include the statement of the government's purpose expressly set out in the county resolutions, and underscored it by juxtaposing the Commandments to other documents with highlighted references to God as their sole common element. The display's unstinting focus was on religious passages, showing that the Counties were posting the Commandments precisely because of their sectarian content. That demonstration of the government's objective was enhanced by serial religious references and the accompanying resolution's claim about the embodiment of ethics in Christ. Together, the display and resolution presented an indisputable, and undisputed, showing of an impermissible purpose.

C

1

After the Counties changed lawyers, they mounted a third display, without a new resolution or repeal of the old one. The result was the "Foundations of American Law and Government" exhibit. In trying to persuade the District Court to lift the preliminary injunction, the Counties cited several new purposes for the third version, including a desire "to educate the citizens of the county regarding some of the documents that played a significant role in the foundation of our system of law and government."

These new statements of purpose were presented only as a litigating position, there being no further authorizing action by the Counties' governing boards. And although repeal of the earlier county authorizations would not have erased them from the record of evidence bearing on current purpose, the extraordinary resolutions for the second display passed just months earlier were not repealed or otherwise repudiated. Indeed, the sectarian spirit of the common resolution found enhanced expression in the third display, which quoted more of the purely religious language of the Commandments than the first two displays had done. No reasonable observer could swallow the claim that the Counties had cast off the objective so unmistakable in the earlier displays.

Nor did the selection of posted material suggest a clear theme that might prevail over evidence of the continuing religious object. In a collection of documents said to be "foundational" to American government, it is at least odd to include a patriotic anthem, but to omit the Fourteenth Amendment, the most significant structural provision adopted since the original Framing. And it is no less baffling to leave out the original Constitution of 1787 while quoting the 1215 Magna Carta even to the point of its declaration that "fish-weirs shall be removed from the Thames." If an observer found these choices and omissions perplexing in isolation, he would be puzzled for a different reason when he read the Declaration of Independence seeking confirmation for the Counties' posted explanation that the Ten Commandments' "influence is clearly seen in the Declaration"; in fact the observer would find that the Commandments are sanctioned as divine imperatives, while the Declaration of Independence holds that the authority of government to enforce the law derives "from the consent of the governed[.]" If the observer had not thrown up his hands, he would probably suspect that the Counties were simply reaching for any way to keep a religious document on the walls of courthouses constitutionally required to embody religious neutrality.

2

In holding the preliminary injunction adequately supported by evidence that the Counties' purpose had not changed at the third stage, we do not decide that the Counties' past actions forever taint any effort on their part to deal with the subject matter.... Nor do we have occasion here to hold that a sacred text can never be integrated constitutionally into a governmental display on the subject of law, or American history. We do not forget, and in this litigation have frequently been reminded, that our own courtroom frieze was deliberately designed in the exercise of governmental authority so as to include the figure of Moses holding tablets exhibiting a portion of the Hebrew text of the later, secularly phrased Commandments; in the company of 17 other law-givers, most of them secular figures, there is no risk that Moses would strike an observer as evidence that the National Government was violating neutrality in religion.

IV

[T]he principle of neutrality has provided a good sense of direction: the government may not favor one religion over another, or religion over irreligion, religious choice being the prerogative of individuals under the Free Exercise Clause. The principle has been helpful simply because it responds to one of the major concerns that prompted adoption of the Religion Clauses. The Framers and the citizens of their time intended not only to protect the integrity of individual conscience in religious matters, but to guard against the civic divisiveness that follows when the government weighs in on one side of religious debate; nothing does a better job of roiling society, a point that needed no explanation to the descendants of English Puritans and Cavaliers (or Massachusetts Puritans and Baptists).

[T]he dissent's argument for the original understanding is flawed from the outset by its failure to consider the full range of evidence showing what the Framers believed. The dissent is certainly correct in putting forward evidence that some of the Framers thought some endorsement of religion was compatible with the establishment ban. But the fact is that we do have more to go on, for there is also evidence supporting the proposition that the Framers intended the Establishment Clause to require governmental neutrality in matters of religion, including neutrality in statements acknowledging religion.

The historical record, moreover, is complicated beyond the dissent's account by the writings and practices of figures no less influential than Thomas Jefferson and James Madison. Jefferson, for example, refused to issue Thanksgiving Proclamations because he believed that they violated the Constitution. And Madison criticized Virginia's general assessment tax not just because it required people to donate "three pence" to religion, but because "it is itself a signal of persecution. It degrades from the equal rank of Citizens all those whose opinions in Religion do not bend to those of the Legislative authority."

The fair inference is that there was no common understanding about the limits of the establishment prohibition, and the dissent's conclusion that its narrower view was the original understanding, stretches the evidence beyond tensile capacity. What the evidence does show is a group of statesmen, like others before and after them, who proposed a guarantee with contours not wholly worked out, leaving the Establishment Clause with edges still to be determined. And none the worse for that. Indeterminate edges are the kind to have in a constitution meant to endure, and to meet "exigencies which, if foreseen at all, must have been seen dimly, and which can be best provided for as they occur."

Historical evidence thus supports no solid argument for changing course, whereas public discourse at the present time certainly raises no doubt about the value of the interpretative approach invoked for 60 years now. We are centuries away from the St. Bartholomew's Day massacre and the treatment of heretics in early Massachusetts, but the divisiveness of religion in current public life is inescapable. This is no time to deny the prudence of understanding the Establishment Clause to require the Government to stay neutral on religious belief, which is reserved for the conscience of the individual.

Justice O'Connor, concurring. [Opinion omitted.]

Justice Scalia, with whom The Chief Justice and Justice Thomas join, and with whom Justice Kennedy joins as to Parts II and III, dissenting.

I

A

On September 11, 2001, I was attending in Rome, Italy, an international conference of judges and lawyers, principally from Europe and the United States. That night and the next morning virtually all of the participants watched, in their hotel rooms, the address to the Nation by the President of the United States concerning the murderous attacks upon the Twin Towers and the Pentagon, in which thousands of Americans had been killed. The address ended, as Presidential addresses often do, with the prayer "God bless America." The next afternoon I was approached by one of the judges from a European country, who, after extending his profound condolences for my country's loss, sadly observed: "How I wish that the Head of State of my country, at a similar time of national tragedy and distress, could conclude his address 'God bless _____.' It is of course absolutely forbidden."

That is one model of the relationship between church and state—a model spread across Europe by the armies of Napoleon, and reflected in the Constitution of France, which begins, "France is [a] ... secular ... Republic." This is not, and never was, the model adopted by America. George Washington added to the form of Presidential oath prescribed by Art. II, § 1, cl. 8, of the Constitution, the concluding words "so help me God." The Supreme Court under John Marshall opened its sessions with the prayer, "God save the United States and this Honorable Court." The First Congress instituted the practice of beginning its legislative sessions with a prayer. *Marsh v. Chambers*, 463 U.S. 783, 787–788 (1983). The same week that Congress submitted the Establishment Clause as part of the Bill of Rights for ratification by the States, it enacted legislation providing for paid chaplains in the House and Senate. The day after the First Amendment was proposed, the same Congress that had proposed it requested the President to proclaim "a day of public thanksgiving and prayer, to be observed, by acknowledging, with grateful hearts, the many signal favours of Almighty God." President Washington offered the first Thanksgiving Proclamation shortly thereafter, devoting November 26, 1789, on behalf of the American people "'to the service of that great and glorious Being who is the beneficent author of all the good that was, that is, or that will be,'" thus beginning a tradition of offering gratitude to God that continues today. The same Congress also reenacted the Northwest Territory Ordinance of 1787, 1 Stat. 50, Article III of which provided: "Religion, morality, and knowledge, being necessary to good government and the happiness of mankind, schools and the means of education shall forever be encouraged." And of course the First Amendment itself accords religion (and no other manner of belief) special constitutional protection.

These actions of our First President and Congress and the Marshall Court were not idiosyncratic; they reflected the beliefs of the period. Those who wrote the Constitution believed that morality was essential to the well-being of society and that encouragement of religion was the best way to foster morality. President Washington opened his Presidency with a prayer, and reminded his fellow citizens at the conclusion of it that "reason and experience both forbid us to expect that National morality can prevail in exclusion of religious principle[.]" President John Adams wrote to the Massachusetts Militia, "we have no government armed with power capable of contending with human passions unbridled by morality and religion.... Our Constitution was made only for a moral and religious people. It is wholly inadequate to the government of any other." Thomas Jefferson concluded his second inaugural address by inviting his audience to pray.

James Madison, in his first inaugural address, likewise placed his confidence "in the guardianship and guidance of that Almighty Being whose power regulates the destiny of nations, whose blessings have been so conspicuously dispensed to this rising Republic, and to whom we are bound to address our devout gratitude for the past, as well as our fervent supplications and best hopes for the future."

Nor have the views of our people on this matter significantly changed. Presidents continue to conclude the Presidential oath with the words "so help me God." Our legislatures, state and national, continue to open their sessions with prayer led by official chaplains. The sessions of this Court continue to open with the prayer "God save the United States and this Honorable Court." Invocation of the Almighty by our public figures, at all levels of government, remains commonplace. Our coinage bears the motto, "IN GOD WE TRUST." And our Pledge of Allegiance contains the acknowledgment that we are a Nation "under God."

With all of this reality (and much more) staring it in the face, how can the Court *possibly* assert that the "'First Amendment mandates governmental neutrality between ... religion and nonreligion,'" and that "[m]anifesting a purpose to favor ... adherence to religion generally," is unconstitutional? Who says so? Surely not the words of the Constitution. Surely not the history and traditions that reflect our society's constant understanding of those words. Surely not even the current sense of our society, recently reflected in an Act of Congress adopted *unanimously* by the Senate and with only five nays in the House of Representatives criticizing a Court of Appeals opinion that had held "under God" in the Pledge of Allegiance unconstitutional. Nothing stands behind the Court's assertion that governmental affirmation of the society's belief in God is unconstitutional except the Court's own say-so, citing as support only the unsubstantiated say-so of earlier Courts going back no further than the mid-20th century. And it is, moreover, a thoroughly discredited say-so. It is discredited, to begin with, because a majority of the Justices on the current Court (including at least one Member of today's majority) have, in separate opinions, repudiated the brainspun "*Lemon* test" that embodies the supposed principle of neutrality between religion and irreligion. And it is discredited because the Court has not had the courage (or the foolhardiness) to apply the neutrality principle consistently.

What distinguishes the rule of law from the dictatorship of a shifting Supreme Court majority is the absolutely indispensable requirement that judicial opinions be grounded in consistently applied principle. That is what prevents judges from ruling now this way, now that—thumbs up or thumbs down—as their personal preferences dictate. Today's opinion somewhat less than forthrightly admits that it does not rest upon consistently applied principle. In a revealing footnote, the Court acknowledges that the "Establishment Clause doctrine" it purports to be applying "lacks the comfort of categorical absolutes." What the Court means by this lovely euphemism is that sometimes the Court chooses to decide cases on the principle that government cannot favor religion, and sometimes it does not. The footnote goes on to say that "[i]n special instances we have found good reason" to dispense with the principle, but "[n]o such reasons present themselves here." It does not identify all of those "special instances," much less identify the "good reason" for their existence.

Besides appealing to the demonstrably false principle that the government cannot favor religion over irreligion, today's opinion suggests that the posting of the Ten Commandments violates the principle that the government cannot favor one religion over another. That is indeed a valid principle where public aid or assistance to religion is concerned or where the free exercise of religion is at issue, but it necessarily applies in a more limited sense to public acknowledgment of the Creator. If religion in the public forum had to be entirely nondenominational, there could be no religion in the public forum at all. One cannot say the word "God," or "the Almighty," one cannot offer public supplication or thanksgiving, without contradicting the beliefs of some people that there are many gods, or that God or the gods pay no attention to human affairs. With respect to public acknowledgment of religious belief, it is entirely clear from our Nation's historical practices that the Establishment Clause permits this disregard of polytheists and believers in unconcerned deities, just as it permits the disregard of devout atheists. The Thanksgiving Proclamation issued by George Washington at the instance of the First Congress was scrupulously nondenominational—but it was monotheistic.

Historical practices thus demonstrate that there is a distance between the acknowledgment of a single Creator and the establishment of a religion. The former is, as *Marsh v. Chambers* put it, "a tolerable acknowledgment of beliefs widely held among the people of this country." The three most popular religions in the United States, Christianity, Judaism, and Islam—which combined account for 97.7% of all believers—are monotheistic. All of them, moreover (Islam included), believe that the Ten Commandments were given by God to Moses, and are divine prescriptions for a virtuous life. Publicly honoring the Ten Commandments is thus indistinguishable, insofar as discriminating against other religions is concerned, from publicly honoring God. Both practices are recognized across such a broad and diverse range of the population—from Christians to Muslims—that they cannot be reasonably understood as a government endorsement of a particular religious viewpoint.

B

"[R]eliance on early religious proclamations and statements made by the Founders is ... problematic," [JUSTICE STEVENS] says, "because those views were not espoused at the Constitutional Convention in 1787 nor enshrined in the Constitution's text." But I have not relied upon (as he and the Court in this case do) mere "proclamations and statements" of the Founders. I have relied primarily upon official acts and official proclamations of the United States or of the component branches of its Government.

The only mere "proclamations and statements" of the Founders I have relied upon were statements of Founders who occupied federal office, and spoke in at least a quasi-official capacity. The Court and JUSTICE STEVENS, by contrast, appeal to no official or even quasi-official action in support of their view of the Establishment Clause—only James Madison's Memorial and Remonstrance Against Religious Assessments, written before the Federal Constitution had even been proposed, two letters written by Madison long after he was President, and the quasi-official *inaction* of Thomas Jefferson in refusing to issue a Thanksgiving Proclamation. The Madison Memorial and Remonstrance, dealing as it does with enforced contribution to religion rather than public acknowledgment of God, is irrelevant. And as to Jefferson: The notoriously self-contradicting Jefferson did not choose to have his nonauthorship of a Thanksgiving Proclamation inscribed on his tombstone. What he did have inscribed was his authorship of the Virginia Statute for Religious Freedom, a governmental act which begins "Whereas, Almighty God hath created the mind free."

Finally, I must respond to JUSTICE STEVENS' assertion that I would "marginaliz[e] the belief systems of more than 7 million Americans" who adhere to religions that are not monotheistic. Surely that is a gross exaggeration. The beliefs of those citizens are entirely protected by the Free Exercise Clause, and by those aspects of the Establishment Clause that do not relate to government acknowledgment of the Creator. Invocation of God despite their beliefs is permitted not because nonmonotheistic religions cease to be religions recognized by the Religion Clauses of the First Amendment, but because governmental invocation of God is not an establishment. JUSTICE STEVENS fails to recognize that in the context of public acknowledgments of God there are legitimate *competing* interests: On the one hand, the interest of that minority in not feeling "excluded"; but on the other, the interest of the overwhelming majority of religious believers in being able to give God thanks and supplication *as a people*, and with respect to our national endeavors. Our national tradition has resolved that conflict in favor of the majority. It is not for this Court to change a disposition that accounts, many Americans think, for the phenomenon remarked upon in a quotation attributed to various authors, including Bismarck, but which I prefer to associate with Charles de Gaulle: "God watches over little children, drunkards, and the United States of America."

III

Even accepting the Court's *Lemon*-based premises, the displays at issue here were constitutional.

A

To any person who happened to walk down the hallway of the McCreary or Pulaski County Courthouse during the roughly nine months when the Foundations Displays were exhibited, the displays must have seemed unremarkable—if indeed they were noticed at all. The walls of both courthouses were already lined with historical documents and other assorted portraits; each Foundations Display was exhibited in the same format as these other displays and nothing in the record suggests that either County took steps to give it greater prominence.

Entitled "The Foundations of American Law and Government Display," each display consisted of nine equally sized documents. The displays did not emphasize any of the nine documents in any way: The frame holding the Ten Commandments was of the same size and had the same appearance as that which held each of the other documents. Posted with the documents was a plaque, identifying the display, and explaining that it " 'contains documents that played a significant role in the foundation of our system of law and government.' "

B

On its face, the Foundations Displays manifested the purely secular: "to display documents that played a significant role in the foundation of our system of law and government." That the displays included the Ten Commandments did not transform their apparent secular purpose into one of impermissible advocacy for Judeo-Christian beliefs. Even an isolated display of the Decalogue conveys, at worst, "an equivocal message, perhaps of respect for Judaism, for religion in general, or for law." But when the Ten Commandments appear alongside other documents of secular significance in a display devoted to the foundations of American law and government, the context communicates that the Ten Commandments are included, not to teach their binding nature as a religious text, but to show their unique contribution to the development of the legal system. This is doubly true when the display is introduced by a document that informs passersby that it " 'contains documents that played a significant role in the foundation of our system of law and government.' "

The same result follows if the Ten Commandments display is viewed in light of the government practices that this Court has countenanced in the past. The acknowledgment of the contribution that religion in general, and the Ten Commandments in particular, have made to our Nation's legal and governmental heritage is surely no more of a step toward establishment of religion than was the practice of legislative prayer we approved in *Marsh v. Chambers,* and it seems to be on par with the inclusion of a crèche or a menorah in a "Holiday" display that incorporates other secular symbols [as in *Lynch v. Donnelly,* 465 U.S. 668 (1984)].

Acknowledgment of the contribution that religion has made to our Nation's legal and governmental heritage partakes of a centuries-old tradition. Display of the Ten Commandments is well within the mainstream of this practice of acknowledgment. Federal, state, and local governments across the Nation have engaged in such display. The Supreme Court Building itself includes depictions of Moses with the Ten Commandments in the Courtroom and on the east pediment of the building, and symbols of the Ten Commandments "adorn the metal gates lining the north and south sides of the Courtroom as well as the doors leading into the Courtroom." Similar depictions of the Decalogue appear on public buildings and monuments throughout our Nation's Capital. The frequency of these displays testifies to the popular understanding that the Ten Commandments are a foundation of the rule of law, and a symbol of the role that religion played, and continues to play, in our system of government.

C

In any event, the Court's conclusion that the Counties exhibited the Foundations Displays with the purpose of promoting religion is doubtful. In the Court's view, the impermissible motive was apparent from the initial displays of the Ten Commandments all by themselves: When that occurs, the Court says, "a religious object is unmistakable." Surely that cannot be. If, as discussed above, the Commandments have a proper place in our civic history, even placing them by themselves can be civically motivated — especially when they are placed, not in a school (as they were in the *Stone* case upon which the Court places such reliance), but in a courthouse.

The Court has in the past prohibited government actions that "proselytize or advance any one, or ... disparage any other, faith or belief," or that apply some level of coercion. The passive display of the Ten Commandments, even standing alone, does not begin to do either.

Nor is it the case that a solo display of the Ten Commandments advances any one faith. They are assuredly a religious symbol, but they are not so closely associated with a single religious belief that their display can reasonably be understood as preferring one religious sect over another. The Ten Commandments are recognized by Judaism, Christianity, and Islam alike as divinely given.

Turning at last to the displays actually at issue in this case, the Court faults the Counties for not *repealing* the resolution expressing what the Court believes to be an impermissible intent. To begin with, of course, it is unlikely that a reasonable observer *would even have been aware* of the resolutions, so there would be nothing to "cast off." A plaque next to the documents informed all who passed by that each display "contains documents that played a significant role in the foundation of our system of law and government." Additionally, there was no reason for the Counties to repeal or repudiate the resolutions adopted with the hanging of the second displays, since they related *only to the second displays.* After complying with the District Court's order to remove the second displays "immediately," and erecting new displays that in content and by express assertion reflected a *different* purpose from that identified in the resolutions, the Counties had no reason to believe that their previous resolutions would be deemed to be the basis for their actions.

Exercise 8:

1. What facet(s) of the Lemon Test did the majority utilize?

2. Describe the majority's application of the Lemon Test.

3. Did the majority correctly identify the counties' purpose? What was their purpose, according to the majority? What evidence did the majority rely upon to support its conclusion?

4. Why did the posting of the third display not dispel any unconstitutional purpose?

5. What traditions did Justice Scalia identify in dissent? What import did Justice Scalia attribute to those traditions?

6. How did Justice Souter respond to Justice Scalia's invocation of traditional practices? Who had the better of the argument?

7. After *McCreary County* and *American Legion*, may the government post the Ten Commandments? Under what circumstances? Keep your answer in mind when you read *Van Orden v. Perry*, below. What would you advise McCreary County to do if it wanted to post the Ten Commandments, in the wake of this case?

8. Justice Souter engaged in the standard purpose inquiry required by the Lemon Test's first prong. This same type of purpose inquiry is found in many other areas of the law. For instance, in Volume 5, you reviewed the Equal Protection Clause, whose doctrine requires a finding of discriminatory governmental purpose to invoke strict scrutiny. The county and dissenters argued that the Supreme Court should abandon the purpose inquiry. Articulate their argument. How did the majority respond? Which side was correct?

9. What, if anything, does the fact that the majority and dissent disagreed about the challenged display's purpose indicate regarding the efficacy of the purpose inquiry that the Lemon Test required? Does it show that the purpose inquiry is too difficult for the Court to do accurately?

10. The Court in *McCreary* did not defer to the counties' statement of their purpose. Should it have done so? Why or why not?

11. Justice Scouter concluded that the Ten Commandments are an inherently religious object. What did he mean by that? Upon what basis did he conclude that? Is he correct?

12. How could the *McCreary* majority synthesize its ruling with cases upholding legislative prayer? Legislative prayer is clearly religious, as is the Ten Commandments; yet, legislative prayer is permitted while the Ten Commandments are not.

13. Assume that you agree with Justice Scalia's description of the religious practices of Americans in the founding generation up to today. In other words, assume that you agree that public acknowledgements of monotheistic religion occurred and continue to occur. What relevance, if any, should that fact have to your interpretation of our written Constitution? How did Justice Souter respond to Justice Scalia's claim?

D. Varying Approaches to the Establishment Clause

1. Introduction

The history of the Supreme Court's interpretation of the Establishment Clause subsequent to *Everson* is fairly described as tortuous. For that reason, there are a number of plausible ways to describe it. For example, one could review the various common factual contexts in which establishment claims are raised and ascertain the legal rules governing those contexts.

What follows below is a survey of the various Establishment Clause "tests" that the Court and justices have developed since *Everson*. The tests are placed on a spectrum from least to most accepting of government-religion interaction, or most strictly-separationist to most accommodating. The survey builds on what you just covered, in Section [C], with the most separationist test, the Lemon Test and its progeny. In Sections [D][2] and [D][3], we review the moderately separationist, moderately accommodationist tests. Lastly, in Sections [D][4] and [D][5], we cover the most accommodationist tests.

Though the Establishment Clause tests are plotted along an analytical continuum, this continuum also fits, though not perfectly, the gradual evolution of the Supreme Court's case law, away from strict separationism toward greater accommodationism. Also keep in mind that the tests are plotted relative to each other along the continuum, not with any precision of where on the continuum each test falls. Relatedly, be aware that, in the hands of different justices, the same test can take on a more or less separationist/accommodationist hue. For example, the Coercion Test is more accommodationist in Justice Scalia's hands, than Justice Kennedy's.

As you review the various tests, pay attention to the factual contexts in which the tests are employed because, typically, the Court applies the tests fairly consistently in the same contexts. For example, as we saw above, the Supreme Court generally applied the Lemon Test (or its later incarnations) to cases involving financial aid to religious institutions, such as schools.

We will begin this Part by reviewing a case that displays the fracturing that this multitude of establishment tests frequently produces.

County of Allegheny v. American Civil Liberties Union Greater Pittsburgh Chapter
492 U.S. 573 (1989)

JUSTICE BLACKMUN announced the judgment of the Court and delivered the opinion of the Court with respect to Parts III-A, IV, and V, an opinion with respect to Parts I and II, in which JUSTICE STEVENS and JUSTICE O'CONNOR join, an opinion with respect to Part III-B, in which JUSTICE STEVENS joins, an opinion with respect to Part VII, in which JUSTICE O'CONNOR joins, and an opinion with respect to Part VI.

This litigation concerns the constitutionality of two recurring holiday displays located on public property in downtown Pittsburgh. The first is a crèche placed on the Grand Staircase of the Allegheny County Courthouse. The second is a Chanukah menorah placed just outside the City-County Building, next to a Christmas tree and a sign saluting liberty. The Court of Appeals for the Third Circuit ruled that each display violates the Establishment Clause of the First Amendment because each has the impermissible effect of endorsing religion. We agree that the crèche display has that unconstitutional effect but reverse the Court of Appeals' judgment regarding the menorah display.

I

A

The county courthouse is owned by Allegheny County and is its seat of government. Civil and criminal trials are held there. The "main," "most beautiful," and "most public" part of the courthouse is its Grand Staircase, set into one arch and surrounded by others, with arched windows serving as a backdrop.

Since 1981, the county has permitted the Holy Name Society, a Roman Catholic group, to display a crèche in the county courthouse during the Christmas holiday season. Christmas, we note perhaps needlessly, is the holiday when Christians celebrate the birth of Jesus of Nazareth, whom they believe to be the Messiah. As observed in this Nation, Christmas has a secular, as well as a religious, dimension.

The crèche in the county courthouse, like other crèches, is a visual representation of the scene in the manger in Bethlehem shortly after the birth of Jesus, as described in the Gospels of Luke and Matthew. The crèche includes figures of the infant Jesus, Mary, Joseph, farm animals, shepherds, and wise men, all placed in or before a wooden representation of a manger, which has at its crest an angel bearing a banner that proclaims "Gloria in Excelsis Deo!"

During the 1986–1987 holiday season, the crèche was on display on the Grand Staircase from November 26 to January 9. It had a wooden fence on three sides and bore a plaque stating: "This Display Donated by the Holy Name Society." No figures of Santa Claus or other decorations appeared on the Grand Staircase.

The county uses the crèche as the setting for its annual Christmas carol program. During the 1986 season, the county invited high school choirs and other musical groups to perform during weekday lunch hours from December 3 through December 23. The county dedicated this program to world peace and to the families of prisoners-of-war and of persons missing in action in Southeast Asia.

B

The City-County Building is separate and a block removed from the county courthouse and is jointly owned by the city of Pittsburgh and Allegheny County. The city is responsible for the building's Grant Street entrance which has three rounded arches supported by columns.

For a number of years, the city has had a large Christmas tree under the middle arch outside the Grant Street entrance. Following this practice, city employees on November 17, 1986, erected a 45-foot tree under the middle arch and decorated it with lights and ornaments. A few days later, the city placed at the foot of the tree a sign bearing the mayor's name and entitled "Salute to Liberty." Beneath the title, the sign stated: "During this holiday season, the city of Pittsburgh salutes liberty. Let these festive lights remind us that we are the keepers of the flame of liberty and our legacy of freedom."

At least since 1982, the city has expanded its Grant Street holiday display to include a symbolic representation of Chanukah, an 8-day Jewish holiday that begins on the 25th day of the Jewish lunar month of Kislev. The 25th of Kislev usually occurs in

December, and thus Chanukah is the annual Jewish holiday that falls closest to Christmas Day each year. In 1986, Chanukah began at sundown on December 26.

Chanukah, like Christmas, is a cultural event as well as a religious holiday. Indeed, the Chanukah story always has had a political or national, as well as a religious, dimension: it tells of national heroism in addition to divine intervention. Also, [j]ust as some Americans celebrate Christmas without regard to its religious significance, some nonreligious American Jews celebrate Chanukah as an expression of ethnic identity, and "as a cultural or national event, rather than as a specifically religious event."

On December 22 of the 1986 holiday season, the city placed at the Grant Street entrance to the City-County Building an 18-foot Chanukah menorah of an abstract tree-and-branch design. The menorah was placed next to the city's 45-foot Christmas tree, against one of the columns that supports the arch into which the tree was set. The menorah is owned by Chabad, a Jewish group, but is stored, erected, and removed each year by the city. The tree, the sign, and the menorah were all removed on January 13.

II

This litigation began on December 10, 1986, when respondents, the Greater Pittsburgh Chapter of the American Civil Liberties Union and seven local residents, filed suit against the county and the city, seeking permanently to enjoin the county from displaying the crèche in the county courthouse and the city from displaying the menorah. Respondents claim that the displays of the crèche and the menorah each violate the Establishment Clause.

On May 8, 1987, the District Court denied respondents' request for a permanent injunction. Relying on *Lynch v. Donnelly*, 465 U.S. 668 (1984), the court stated that "the crèche was but part of the holiday decoration of the stairwell and a foreground for the high school choirs which entertained each day at noon." Regarding the menorah, the court concluded that "it was but an insignificant part of another holiday display." The court also found that "the displays had a secular purpose" and "did not create an excessive entanglement of government with religion."

Respondents appealed, and a divided panel of the Court of Appeals reversed. We granted all three petitions.

III

A

This Nation is heir to a history and tradition of religious diversity that dates from the settlement of the North American Continent. Sectarian differences among various Christian denominations were central to the origins of our Republic. Since then, adherents of religions too numerous to name have made the United States their home, as have those whose beliefs expressly exclude religion.

Precisely because of the religious diversity that is our national heritage, the Founders added to the Constitution a Bill of Rights, the very first words of which declare: "Congress shall make no law respecting an establishment of religion, or prohibiting the free exercise thereof....." Perhaps in the early days of the Republic these words were understood to protect only the diversity within Christianity, but today they are recognized as guaranteeing religious liberty and equality to "the infidel, the atheist, or the adherent of a non-Christian faith such as Islam or Judaism."

[T]his Court has attempted to encapsulate the essential precepts of the Establishment Clause. In *Lemon v. Kurtzman*, the Court sought to refine these principles by focusing on three "tests" for determining whether a government practice violates the Establishment Clause. Under the *Lemon* analysis, a statute or practice which touches upon religion, if it is to be permissible under the Establishment Clause, must have a secular purpose; it must neither advance nor inhibit religion in its principal or primary effect; and it must not foster an excessive entanglement with religion.

Our subsequent decisions further have refined the definition of governmental action that unconstitutionally advances religion. In recent years, we have paid particularly close attention to whether the challenged governmental practice either has the purpose or effect of "endorsing" religion, a concern that has long had a place in our Establishment Clause jurisprudence. [T]he prohibition against governmental endorsement of religion "preclude[s] government from conveying or attempting to convey a message that religion or a particular religious belief is *favored* or *preferred*."

The Establishment Clause, at the very least, prohibits government from appearing to take a position on questions of religious belief or from "making adherence to a religion relevant in any way to a person's standing in the political community." *Lynch v. Donnelly*, 465 U.S., at 687 (O'CONNOR, J., concurring).[47]

IV

We turn first to the county's crèche display. There is no doubt, of course, that the crèche itself is capable of communicating a religious message. Indeed, the crèche in this lawsuit uses words, as well as the picture of the Nativity scene, to make its religious meaning unmistakably clear. "Glory to God in the Highest!" says the angel in the crèche — Glory to God because of the birth of Jesus. This praise to God in Christian terms is indisputably religious — indeed sectarian.

Under the Court's holding in *Lynch*, the effect of a crèche display turns on its setting. Here, unlike in *Lynch*, nothing in the context of the display detracts from the crèche's religious message. The *Lynch* display composed a series of figures and objects, each group of which had its own focal point. Here, in contrast, the crèche stands alone: it is the single element of the display on the Grand Staircase.

---

47. The county and the city argue that their use of religious symbols does not violate the Establishment Clause unless they are shown to be "coercive." They recognize that this Court repeatedly has stated that "proof of coercion" is "not a necessary element of any claim under the Establishment Clause." But they suggest that the Court reconsider this principle. The Court declines to do so.

Furthermore, the crèche sits on the Grand Staircase, the "main" and "most beautiful part" of the building that is the seat of county government. No viewer could reasonably think that it occupies this location without the support and approval of the government. Thus, by permitting the "display of the crèche in this particular physical setting," the county sends an unmistakable message that it supports and promotes the Christian praise to God that is the crèche's religious message.

The fact that the crèche bears a sign disclosing its ownership by a Roman Catholic organization does not alter this conclusion. On the contrary, the sign simply demonstrates that the government is endorsing the religious message of that organization, rather than communicating a message of its own. But the Establishment Clause does not limit only the religious content of the government's own communications. It also prohibits the government's support and promotion of religious communications by religious organizations. Indeed, the very concept of "endorsement" conveys the sense of promoting someone else's message.

In sum, *Lynch* teaches that government may celebrate Christmas in some manner and form, but not in a way that endorses Christian doctrine. Here, Allegheny County has transgressed this line. It has chosen to celebrate Christmas in a way that has the effect of endorsing a patently Christian message[.]

V

B

Although Justice Kennedy's misreading of *Marsh* is predicated on a failure to recognize the bedrock Establishment Clause principle that, regardless of history, government may not demonstrate a preference for a particular faith, even he is forced to acknowledge that some instances of such favoritism are constitutionally intolerable. He concedes also that the term "endorsement" long has been another way of defining a forbidden "preference" for a particular sect, but he would repudiate the Court's endorsement inquiry as a "jurisprudence of minutiae," because it examines the particular contexts in which the government employs religious symbols.

This label, of course, could be tagged on many areas of constitutional adjudication. It is perhaps unfortunate, but nonetheless inevitable, that the broad language of many clauses within the Bill of Rights must be translated into adjudicatory principles that realize their full meaning only after their application to a series of concrete cases.

Indeed, perhaps the only real distinction between Justice Kennedy's "proselytization" test and the Court's "endorsement" inquiry is a burden of "unmistakable" clarity that Justice Kennedy apparently would require of government favoritism for specific sects in order to hold the favoritism in violation of the Establishment Clause. The question whether a particular practice "would place the government's weight behind an obvious effort to proselytize for a particular religion," is much the same as whether the practice demonstrates the government's support, promotion, or "endorsement" of the particular creed of a particular sect — except to the extent that it requires an "obvious" allegiance between the government and the sect.

Our cases, however, impose no such burden on demonstrating that the government has favored a particular sect or creed. Thus, when all is said and done, Justice Kennedy's effort to abandon the "endorsement" inquiry in favor of his "proselytization" test seems nothing more than an attempt to lower considerably the level of scrutiny in Establishment Clause cases. We choose, however, to adhere to the vigilance the Court has managed to maintain thus far, and to the endorsement inquiry that reflects our vigilance.

VI

The display of the Chanukah menorah in front of the City-County Building may well present a closer constitutional question. The menorah, one must recognize, is a religious symbol: it serves to commemorate the miracle of the oil as described in the Talmud. But the menorah's message is not exclusively religious. The menorah is the primary visual symbol for a holiday that, like Christmas, has both religious and secular dimensions.

Moreover, the menorah here stands next to a Christmas tree and a sign saluting liberty. The necessary result of placing a menorah next to a Christmas tree is to create an "overall holiday setting" that represents both Christmas and Chanukah—two holidays, not one.

The mere fact that Pittsburgh displays symbols of both Christmas and Chanukah does not end the constitutional inquiry. If the city celebrates both Christmas and Chanukah as religious holidays, then it violates the Establishment Clause. The simultaneous endorsement of Judaism and Christianity is no less constitutionally infirm than the endorsement of Christianity alone. Conversely, if the city celebrates both Christmas and Chanukah as secular holidays, then its conduct is beyond the reach of the Establishment Clause. Because government may celebrate Christmas as a secular holiday, it follows that government may also acknowledge Chanukah as a secular holiday.

Accordingly, the relevant question for Establishment Clause purposes is whether the combined display of the tree, the sign, and the menorah has the effect of endorsing both Christian and Jewish faiths, or rather simply recognizes that both Christmas and Chanukah are part of the same winter-holiday season, which has attained a secular status in our society. Of the two interpretations of this particular display, the latter seems far more plausible and is also in line with *Lynch*.

The Christmas tree, unlike the menorah, is not itself a religious symbol. Although Christmas trees once carried religious connotations, today they typify the secular celebration of Christmas. Numerous Americans place Christmas trees in their homes without subscribing to Christian religious beliefs, and when the city's tree stands alone in front of the City-County Building, it is not considered an endorsement of Christian faith. Indeed, a 40-foot Christmas tree was one of the objects that validated the crèche in *Lynch*. The widely accepted view of the Christmas tree as the preeminent secular symbol of the Christmas holiday season serves to emphasize the secular component of the message communicated by other elements of an accompanying holiday display, including the Chanukah menorah.

The tree, moreover, is clearly the predominant element in the city's display. The 45-foot tree occupies the central position beneath the middle archway in front of the Grant Street entrance to the City-County Building; the 18-foot menorah is positioned to one side. Given this configuration, it is much more sensible to interpret the meaning of the menorah in light of the tree, rather than vice versa. In the shadow of the tree, the menorah is readily understood as simply a recognition that Christmas is not the only traditional way of observing the winter-holiday season. In these circumstances, then, the combination of the tree and the menorah communicates, not a simultaneous endorsement of both the Christian and Jewish faiths, but instead, a secular celebration of Christmas coupled with an acknowledgment of Chanukah as a contemporaneous alternative tradition.

Although the city has used a symbol with religious meaning as its representation of Chanukah, this is not a case in which the city has reasonable alternatives that are less religious in nature. It is difficult to imagine a predominantly secular symbol of Chanukah that the city could place next to its Christmas tree. An 18-foot dreidel would look out of place and might be interpreted by some as mocking the celebration of Chanukah. The absence of a more secular alternative symbol is itself part of the context in which the city's actions must be judged in determining the likely effect of its use of the menorah. Where the government's secular message can be conveyed by two symbols, only one of which carries religious meaning, an observer reasonably might infer from the fact that the government has chosen to use the religious symbol that the government means to promote religious faith. But where, as here, no such choice has been made, this inference of endorsement is not present.

The mayor's sign further diminishes the possibility that the tree and the menorah will be interpreted as a dual endorsement of Christianity and Judaism. The sign states that during the holiday season the city salutes liberty. Moreover, the sign draws upon the theme of light, common to both Chanukah and Christmas as winter festivals, and links that theme with this Nation's legacy of freedom, which allows an American to celebrate the holiday season in whatever way he wishes, religiously or otherwise. Here, the mayor's sign serves to confirm what the context already reveals: that the display of the menorah is not an endorsement of religious faith but simply a recognition of cultural diversity.

Given all these considerations, it is not "sufficiently likely" that residents of Pittsburgh will perceive the combined display of the tree, the sign, and the menorah as an "endorsement" or "disapproval ... of their individual religious choices." [T]he constitutionality of its effect must also be judged according to the standard of a "reasonable observer[.]" When measured against this standard, the menorah need not be excluded from this particular display. The Christmas tree alone in the Pittsburgh location does not endorse Christian belief; and, on the facts before us, the addition of the menorah "cannot fairly be understood to" result in the simultaneous endorsement of Christian and Jewish faiths. On the contrary, for purposes of the Establishment Clause, the city's overall display must be understood as conveying the city's secular recognition of different traditions for celebrating the winter-holiday season.

VII

The display of the crèche in the county courthouse has [an] unconstitutional effect. The display of the menorah in front of the City-County Building, however, does not have this effect, given its "particular physical setting."

Justice O'Connor, with whom Justice Brennan and Justice Stevens join as to Part II, concurring in part and concurring in the judgment.

I

Judicial review of government action under the Establishment Clause is a delicate task. The Court has avoided drawing lines which entirely sweep away all government recognition and acknowledgment of the role of religion in the lives of our citizens for to do so would exhibit not neutrality but hostility to religion. Instead the courts have made case-specific examinations of the challenged government action and have attempted to do so with the aid of the standards. Unfortunately, even the development of articulable standards and guidelines has not always resulted in agreement among the Members of this Court on the results in individual cases. And so it is again today.

The constitutionality of the two displays at issue in these cases turns on how we interpret and apply the holding in *Lynch v. Donnelly*, 465 U.S. 668 (1984). In my concurrence in *Lynch*, I suggested a clarification of our Establishment Clause doctrine to reinforce the concept that the Establishment Clause "prohibits government from making adherence to a religion relevant in any way to a person's standing in the political community." The government violates this prohibition if it endorses or disapproves of religion.

For the reasons stated in Part IV of the Court's opinion in these cases, I agree that the crèche displayed on the Grand Staircase of the Allegheny County Courthouse, the seat of county government, conveys a message to nonadherents of Christianity that they are not full members of the political community, and a corresponding message to Christians that they are favored members of the political community. In contrast to the crèche in *Lynch*, this crèche stands alone in the county courthouse. The Court correctly concludes that placement of the central religious symbol of the Christmas holiday season at the Allegheny County Courthouse has the unconstitutional effect of conveying a government endorsement of Christianity.

III

For reasons which differ somewhat from those set forth in Part VI of Justice Blackmun's opinion, I also conclude that the city of Pittsburgh's combined holiday display of a Chanukah menorah, a Christmas tree, and a sign saluting liberty does not have the effect of conveying an endorsement of religion. I agree with Justice Blackmun that the Christmas tree, whatever its origins, is not regarded today as a religious symbol. Although Christmas is a public holiday that has both religious and secular aspects, the Christmas tree is widely viewed as a secular symbol of the holiday, in contrast to the crèche which depicts the holiday's religious dimensions. A Christmas tree displayed in front of city hall, in my view, cannot fairly be understood as conveying government endorsement of Christianity.

In characterizing the message conveyed by this display as either a "double endorsement" or a secular acknowledgment of the winter holiday season, the opinion states that "[i]t is distinctly implausible to view the combined display of the tree, the sign, and the menorah as endorsing Jewish faith alone." That statement, however, seems to suggest that it would be implausible for the city to endorse a faith adhered to by a minority of the citizenry. Regardless of the plausibility of a putative governmental purpose, the more important inquiry here is whether the governmental display of a minority faith's religious symbol could ever reasonably be understood to convey a message of endorsement of that faith. A menorah standing alone at city hall may well send such a message to nonadherents, just as in this case the crèche standing alone at the Allegheny County Courthouse sends a message of governmental endorsement of Christianity, whatever the county's purpose in authorizing the display may have been. Thus, the question here is whether Pittsburgh's holiday display conveys a message of endorsement of Judaism, when the menorah is the only religious symbol in the combined display and when the opinion acknowledges that the tree cannot reasonably be understood to convey an endorsement of Christianity.

In setting up its holiday display, which included the lighted tree and the menorah, the city of Pittsburgh stressed the theme of liberty and pluralism by accompanying the exhibit with a sign bearing the following message: "'During this holiday season, the city of Pittsburgh salutes liberty. Let these festive lights remind us that we are the keepers of the flame of liberty and our legacy of freedom.'" This sign indicates that the city intended to convey its own distinctive message of pluralism and freedom. By accompanying its display of a Christmas tree — a secular symbol of the Christmas holiday season — with a salute to liberty, and by adding a religious symbol from a Jewish holiday also celebrated at roughly the same time of year, I conclude that the city did not endorse Judaism or religion in general, but rather conveyed a message of pluralism and freedom of belief during the holiday season.

A reasonable observer would, in my view, appreciate that the combined display is an effort to acknowledge the cultural diversity of our country and to convey tolerance of different choices in matters of religious belief or nonbelief by recognizing that the winter holiday season is celebrated in diverse ways by our citizens.

JUSTICE BRENNAN, with whom JUSTICE MARSHALL and JUSTICE STEVENS join, concurring in part and dissenting in part.

I continue to believe that the display of an object that "retains a specifically Christian [or other] religious meaning," is incompatible with the separation of church and state demanded by our Constitution. I therefore agree with the Court that Allegheny County's display of a crèche at the county courthouse signals an endorsement of the Christian faith in violation of the Establishment Clause, and join Parts III-A, IV, and V of the Court's opinion. I cannot agree, however, that the city's display of a 45-foot Christmas tree and an 18-foot Chanukah menorah at the entrance to the building housing the mayor's office shows no favoritism towards Christianity, Judaism, or both. Indeed, I should have thought that the answer as to the first display supplied the answer to the second.

The decision as to the menorah rests on three premises: the Christmas tree is a secular symbol; Chanukah is a holiday with secular dimensions, symbolized by the menorah; and the government may promote pluralism by sponsoring or condoning displays having strong religious associations on its property. None of these is sound.

I

[W]hile acknowledging the religious origins of the Christmas tree, JUSTICES BLACKMUN and O'CONNOR dismiss their significance. In my view, this attempt to take the "Christmas" out of the Christmas tree is unconvincing. That the tree may, without controversy, be deemed a secular symbol if found alone, does not mean that it will be so seen when combined with other symbols or objects. Indeed, JUSTICE BLACKMUN admits that "the tree is capable of taking on a religious significance if it is decorated with religious symbols."

II

The second premise on which today's decision rests is the notion that Chanukah is a partly secular holiday, for which the menorah can serve as a secular symbol. It is no surprise and no anomaly that Chanukah has historical and societal roots that range beyond the purely religious. It does not seem to me that the mere fact that Chanukah shares this kind of background makes it a secular holiday in any meaningful sense. The menorah is indisputably a religious symbol, used ritually in a celebration that has deep religious significance. That, in my view, is all that need be said.

III

JUSTICE BLACKMUN, in his acceptance of the city's message of "diversity," and, even more so, Justice O'Connor, in her approval of the "message of pluralism and freedom to choose one's own beliefs," appear to believe that, where seasonal displays are concerned, more is better. Whereas a display might be constitutionally problematic if it showcased the holiday of just one religion, those problems vaporize as soon as more than one religion is included. I know of no principle under the Establishment Clause, however, that permits us to conclude that governmental promotion of religion is acceptable so long as one religion is not favored. We have, on the contrary, interpreted that Clause to require neutrality, not just among religions, but between religion and nonreligion.

JUSTICE STEVENS, with whom JUSTICE BRENNAN and JUSTICE MARSHALL join, concurring in part and dissenting in part.

In my opinion the Establishment Clause should be construed to create a strong presumption against the display of religious symbols on public property. There is always a risk that such symbols will offend nonmembers of the faith being advertised as well as adherents who consider the particular advertisement disrespectful. Some devout Christians believe that the crèche should be placed only in reverential settings, such as a church or perhaps a private home; they do not countenance its use as an aid to commercialization of Christ's birthday. In this very suit, members of the Jewish faith firmly opposed the use to which the menorah was put by the particular sect that sponsored the display at Pittsburgh's City-County Building. Even though "[p]assersby who disagree with the message conveyed by these displays are free to ignore them, or even to turn their backs," displays of this kind inevitably have a greater tendency to emphasize sincere and deeply felt differences among individuals than to achieve an ecumenical goal. The Establishment Clause does not allow public bodies to foment such disagreement.[10]

I concur in the Court's judgment regarding the crèche for substantially the same reasons discussed in JUSTICE BRENNAN's opinion, which I join, as well as Part IV of JUSTICE BLACKMUN's opinion and Part I of JUSTICE O'CONNOR's opinion.

I cannot agree with the Court's conclusion that the display at Pittsburgh's City-County Building was constitutional. Standing alone in front of a governmental headquarters, a lighted, 45-foot evergreen tree might convey holiday greetings linked too tenuously to Christianity to have constitutional moment. Juxtaposition of this tree with an 18-foot menorah does not make the latter secular, as JUSTICE BLACKMUN contends. Rather, the presence of the Chanukah menorah, unquestionably a religious symbol, gives religious significance to the Christmas tree. The overall display thus manifests governmental approval of the Jewish and Christian religions. Although it conceivably might be interpreted as sending "a message of pluralism and freedom to choose one's own beliefs," the message is not sufficiently clear to overcome the strong presumption that the display, respecting two religions to the exclusion of all others, is the very kind of double establishment that the First Amendment was designed to outlaw. I would, therefore, affirm the judgment of the Court of Appeals in its entirety.

JUSTICE KENNEDY, with whom THE CHIEF JUSTICE, JUSTICE WHITE, and JUSTICE SCALIA join, concurring in the judgment in part and dissenting in part.

I

In keeping with the usual fashion of recent years, the majority applies the *Lemon* test to judge the constitutionality of the holiday displays here in question. I am content for present purposes to remain within the *Lemon* framework, but do not wish to be seen as advocating, let alone adopting, that test as our primary guide in this difficult area. The only *Lemon* factor implicated in these cases directs us to inquire whether the "principal or primary effect" of the challenged government practice is "one that neither advances nor inhibits religion." The requirement of neutrality inherent in that formulation has sometimes been stated in categorical terms. For example, in *Everson v. Board of Education of Ewing*, 330 U.S. 1 (1947), Justice Black wrote that the Clause forbids laws "which aid one religion, aid all religions, or prefer one religion over another."

These statements must not give the impression of a formalism that does not exist. Taken to its logical extreme, some of the language quoted above would require a re-

---

10. These cases illustrate the danger that governmental displays of religious symbols may give rise to unintended divisiveness, for the net result of the Court's disposition is to disallow the display of the crèche but to allow the display of the menorah. Laypersons unfamiliar with the intricacies of Establishment Clause jurisprudence may reach the wholly unjustified conclusion that the Court itself is preferring one faith over another.

lentless extirpation of all contact between government and religion. But that is not the history or the purpose of the Establishment Clause. Government policies of accommodation, acknowledgment, and support for religion are an accepted part of our political and cultural heritage.

Rather than requiring government to avoid any action that acknowledges or aids religion, the Establishment Clause permits government some latitude in recognizing and accommodating the central role religion plays in our society. Any approach less sensitive to our heritage would border on latent hostility toward religion, as it would require government in all its multifaceted roles to acknowledge only the secular, to the exclusion and so to the detriment of the religious. A categorical approach would install federal courts as jealous guardians of an absolute "wall of separation," sending a clear message of disapproval.

The ability of the organized community to recognize and accommodate religion in a society with a pervasive public sector requires diligent observance of the border between accommodation and establishment. Our cases disclose two limiting principles: government may not coerce anyone to support or participate in any religion or its exercise; and it may not, in the guise of avoiding hostility or callous indifference, give direct benefits to religion in such a degree that it in fact "establishes a [state] religion or religious faith, or tends to do so." These two principles, while distinct, are not unrelated, for it would be difficult indeed to establish a religion without some measure of more or less subtle coercion, be it in the form of taxation to supply the substantial benefits that would sustain a state-established faith, direct compulsion to observance, or governmental exhortation to religiosity that amounts in fact to proselytizing.

[S]ome of our recent cases reject the view that coercion is the sole touchstone of an Establishment Clause violation. That may be true if by "coercion" is meant *direct* coercion in the classic sense of an establishment of religion that the Framers knew. But coercion need not be a direct tax in aid of religion or a test oath. Symbolic recognition or accommodation of religious faith may violate the Clause in an extreme case. I doubt not, for example, that the Clause forbids a city to permit the permanent erection of a large Latin cross on the roof of city hall. This is not because government speech about religion is *per se* suspect, as the majority would have it, but because such an obtrusive year-round religious display would place the government's weight behind an obvious effort to proselytize on behalf of a particular religion.

This is most evident where the government's act of recognition or accommodation is passive and symbolic, for in that instance any intangible benefit to religion is unlikely to present a realistic risk of establishment. Absent coercion, the risk of infringement of religious liberty by passive or symbolic accommodation is minimal.

In determining whether there exists an establishment, or a tendency toward one, we refer to the other types of church-state contacts that have existed unchallenged throughout our history, or that have been found permissible in our case law. In *Lynch*, for example, we upheld the city of Pawtucket's holiday display of a crèche, despite the fact that "the display advance[d] religion in a sense." And in *Marsh v. Chambers*, we found that Nebraska's practice of employing a legislative chaplain did not violate the Establishment Clause. Noncoercive government action within the realm of flexible accommodation or passive acknowledgment of existing symbols does not violate the Establishment Clause unless it benefits religion in a way more direct and more substantial than practices that are accepted in our national heritage.

II

These principles are not difficult to apply to the facts of the cases before us. In permitting the displays on government property of the menorah and the crèche, the city and county sought to do no more than "celebrate the season," and to acknowledge, along with many of their citizens, the historical background and the religious, as well as secular, nature of the Chanukah and Christmas holidays. This interest falls well within the tradition of government accommodation and acknowledgment of religion that has marked our history from the beginning. It cannot be disputed that government, if it chooses, may participate in sharing with its citizens the joy of the holiday season, by declaring public holidays, installing or permitting festive displays, sponsoring celebrations and parades, and providing holiday vacations for its employees. All levels of our government do precisely that.

If government is to participate in its citizens' celebration of a holiday that contains both a secular and a religious component, enforced recognition of only the secular aspect would signify the callous indifference toward religious faith that our cases and traditions do not require.... Judicial invalidation of government's attempts to recognize the religious underpinnings of the holiday would signal not neutrality but a pervasive intent to insulate government from all things religious. The Religion Clauses do not require government to acknowledge these holidays or their religious component; but our strong tradition of government accommodation and acknowledgment permits government to do so.

There is no suggestion here that the government's power to coerce has been used to further the interests of Christianity or Judaism in any way. No one was compelled to observe or participate in any religious ceremony or activity. Neither the city nor the county contributed significant amounts of tax money to serve the cause of one religious faith. The crèche and the menorah are purely passive symbols of religious holidays. Passersby who disagree with the message conveyed by these displays are free to ignore them, or even to turn their backs, just as they are free to do when they disagree with any other form of government speech.

There is no realistic risk that the crèche and the menorah represent an effort to proselytize or are otherwise the first step down the road to an establishment of religion. Both are the traditional symbols of religious holidays that over time have acquired a secular component. If Congress and the state legislatures do not run afoul of the Establishment Clause when they begin each day with a state-sponsored prayer for divine guidance offered by a chaplain whose salary is paid at government expense, I cannot comprehend how a menorah or a crèche, displayed in the limited context of the holiday season, can be invalid.

Respondents say that the religious displays involved here are distinguishable from the crèche in *Lynch*. Crucial to the Court's conclusion was not the number, prominence, or type of secular items contained in the holiday display but the simple fact that, when displayed by government during the Christmas season, a crèche presents no realistic danger of moving government down the forbidden road toward an establishment of religion.

III

Even if *Lynch* did not control, I would not commit this Court to the test applied by the majority today. The notion that cases arising under the Establishment Clause should be decided by an inquiry into whether a "'reasonable observer'" may "'fairly understand'" government action to "'sen[d] a message to nonadherents that they are outsiders, not full members of the political community,'" is a recent, and in my view most unwelcome, addition to our tangled Establishment Clause jurisprudence.... For the reasons expressed below, I submit that the endorsement test is flawed in its fundamentals and unworkable in practice.

A

I take it as settled law that, whatever standard the Court applies to Establishment Clause claims, it must at least suggest results consistent with our precedents and the historical practices that, by tradition, have informed our First Amendment jurisprudence. Our decision in *Marsh v. Chambers* illustrates this proposition.

If the endorsement test, applied without artificial exceptions for historical practice, reached results consistent with history, my objections to it would have less force. But, as I understand that test, the touchstone of an Establishment Clause violation is whether nonadherents would be made to feel like "outsiders" by government recognition or accommodation of religion. Few of our traditional practices recognizing the part religion plays in our society can withstand scrutiny under a faithful application of this formula.

[Justice Kennedy then argued that such traditional practices as Thanksgiving Proclamations, opening Supreme Court sessions with "God save the United States and this honorable Court," legislative prayer, religious references in the United States Code, the Pledge of Allegiance, and the nation motto "In God we trust" would be unconstitutional under the Endorsement Test — eds.]

Either the endorsement test must invalidate scores of traditional practices recognizing the place religion holds in our culture, or it must be twisted and stretched to avoid inconsistency with practices we know to have been permitted in the past, while condemning similar practices with no greater endorsement effect simply by reason of their lack of historical antecedent. Neither result is acceptable.

B

In addition to disregarding precedent and historical fact, the majority's approach to government use of religious symbolism threatens to trivialize constitutional adjudication. By mischaracterizing the Court's opinion in *Lynch* as an endorsement-in-context test, JUSTICE BLACKMUN embraces a jurisprudence of minutiae. A reviewing court must consider whether the city has included Santas, talking wishing wells, reindeer, or other secular symbols as "a center of attention separate from the crèche." After determining whether these centers of attention are sufficiently "separate" that each "had their specific visual story to tell," the court must then measure their proximity to the crèche. A community that wishes to construct a constitutional display must also take care to avoid floral frames or other devices that might insulate the crèche from the sanitizing effect of the secular portions of the display. The majority also notes the presence of evergreens near the crèche that are identical to two small evergreens placed near official county signs. After today's decision, municipal greenery must be used with care. Another important factor will be the prominence of the setting in which the display is placed. In this case, the Grand Staircase of the county courthouse proved too resplendent.

My description of the majority's test, though perhaps uncharitable, is intended to illustrate the inevitable difficulties with its application. This test could provide workable guidance to the lower courts, if ever, only after this Court has decided a long series of holiday display cases, using little more than intuition and a tape measure. Deciding cases on the basis of such an unguided examination of marginalia is irreconcilable with the imperative of applying neutral principles in constitutional adjudication....

The result the Court reaches in these cases is perhaps the clearest illustration of the unwisdom of the endorsement test. Although JUSTICE O'CONNOR disavows JUSTICE BLACKMUN's suggestion that the minority or majority status of a religion is relevant to the question whether government recognition constitutes a forbidden endorsement, the very nature of the endorsement test, with its emphasis on the feelings of the objective observer, easily lends itself to this type of inquiry. If there be such a person as the "reasonable observer," I am quite certain that he or she will take away a salient message from our holding in these cases: the Supreme Court of the United States has concluded that the First Amendment creates classes of religions based on the relative numbers of their adherents. Those religions enjoying the largest following must be consigned to the status of leastfavored faiths so as to avoid any possible risk of offending members of minority religions.

IV

The suit before us is admittedly a troubling one. It must be conceded that, however neutral the purpose of the city and county, the eager proselytizer may seek to use these symbols for his own ends. The urge to use them to teach or to taunt is always present. It is also true that some devout adherents of Judaism or Christianity may be as offended by the holiday display as are nonbelievers, if not more so.

For these reasons, I might have voted against installation of these particular displays were I a local legislative official. But we have no jurisdiction over matters of taste within the realm of constitutionally permissible discretion. Our role is enforcement of a written Constitution. In my view, the principles of the Establishment Clause and our Nation's historic traditions of diversity and pluralism allow communities to make reasonable judgments respecting the accommodation or acknowledgment of holidays with both cultural and religious aspects. No constitutional violation occurs when they do so by displaying a symbol of the holiday's religious origins.

Exercise 9:

1. What test or analysis did each of the different opinions utilize?

2. Is one of the approaches *clearly* better than the others? Which one? Why?

3. Is one of the approaches better? What standard(s) did you use to make that determination?

4. *County of Allegheny*'s numerous opinions and approaches to the Establishment Clause is not unusual. Why, do you think, do the Justices fracture on the proper way to analyze Establishment Clause cases? Is there something about the Clause itself that accounts for this? Or does the subject matter—government-religion interactions—cause it? Something else?

5. Justice Blackmun utilized the Lemon Test, modified by using the endorsement inquiry for both the purpose and effect prongs of the Lemon Test. How is Justice Blackmun's analysis different from Justice O'Connor's and Justice Brennan's?

6. What is your view on whether a reasonable observer would have perceived either holiday display as an endorsement of Christianity, Judaism, and/or religion in general? Support your answer.

7. One of the frequent criticisms of the Endorsement Test is that it requires judges to delve into the factual minutia of public displays and to draw fine distinctions, as Justice Kennedy argued. Did that occur in this case when Justices Blackmun, O'Connor, and Brennan each evaluated the respective holiday displays? Why or why not?

8. Justice Blackmun concluded that the sign indicating ownership of the nativity scene by a private group did not dispel any governmental endorsement. Is that a correct assumption? Why did the sign not distance the government from the display, like the disclaimers that are common in the media and elsewhere in which the host will say that the views of the participant(s) are not the host's views?

9. Did Justice Blackmun adequately distinguish between the Nativity Scene and the Chanukah display? Are both Nativity Scenes and Chanukah displays religious? If so, how is the governmental approval of the objects' religious messages different for the respective displays?

10. What, if anything, does the fact that Justice O'Connor and Justice Brennan disagree with each other, *and* with Justice Blackmun, on the religious significance of the Chanukah display, show regarding the Endorsement Test?

11. What role did tradition play in the Endorsement Test utilized by the justices?

12. Justice Stevens utilized a presumption against public displays of religious symbols. Is Justice Stevens' presumption faithful to the Establishment Clause's text and history? Is it faithful to American traditions?

13. What role, if any, did tradition play in Justice Stevens' analysis?

14. Justice Kennedy charged the majority with hostility to religion. Explain what Justice Kennedy meant by that claim. How would you defend the majority from that charge?

15. What is the Coercion Test?

16. What counts as sufficient coercion to violate the Test?

17. What are the legal sources of the Coercion Test?

18. Under the Coercion Test, practices by which the government advances religion in a noncoercive manner are permitted. For example, legislative prayer, or public religious monuments, or a tax exemption for all—and only for—religious entities, would not be coercive under even the most lenient version of the Coercion Test. Does this fact undermine the Coercion Test?

19. What is the analysis required by the Coercion Test?

20. What are its purported advantages over the Lemon Test? What, if any, are its costs?

21. Justice Kennedy spent much of his opinion arguing that the Endorsement Test was flawed because it would require the elimination of the numerous public and governmental acknowledgements of God and religion. He also argued that the Coercion Test would not eliminate those traditional practices. Justice Kennedy counted that as a strong fact in the Coercion Test's favor. Is it?

22. On a continuum of one to ten, from the most accomodationist to the most separationist, where do the respective tests utilized by the various justices fall?

2. Divisiveness Test

The claim that government interaction with religion causes civil divisiveness has been a staple on the Supreme Court since *Everson*. Here is how Justice Black described the baleful effect of religious divisiveness that government-religion cooperation causes:

> The centuries immediately before and contemporaneous with the colonization of America had been filled with turmoil, civil strife, and persecutions, generated in large part by established sects determined to maintain their absolute political and religious supremacy. With the power of government supporting them, at various times and places, Catholics had persecuted Protestants, Protestants had persecuted Catholics, Protestant sects had persecuted other Protestant sects, Catholics of one shade of belief had persecuted Catholics of another shade of belief, and all of these had from time to time persecuted Jews. In efforts to force loyalty to whatever religious group happened to be on top and in league with the government of a particular time and place, men and women had been fined, cast in jail, cruelly tortured, and killed. Among the offenses for which these punishments had been inflicted were such things as speaking disrespectfully of the views of ministers of government-established churches, non-attendance at those churches, expressions of non-belief in their doctrines, and failure to pay taxes and tithes to support them.

Everson v. Board of Education, 330 U.S. 1, 8–9 (1947); *see also id.* at 12 (describing one dire effect of religious establishment identified in James Madison's *Memorial and*

Remonstrance as "cruel persecutions were the inevitable result of government-established religions"). The basic point is that government-religion interactions cause strife among citizens, which, in turn, undermines the peace and good will necessary for a functioning democracy.

In the decades since *Everson*, many justices have repeated this same line of argument. Divisiveness, though, has not garnered majority support as a separate and distinct test. Instead, certain justices identify avoidance of religiously-inspired divisiveness as a central purpose of the Establishment Clause and use divisiveness as one factor to take into account when applying another Establishment Clause test, such as the Endorsement Test.

More recently, even justices who have not embraced the Endorsement Test have invoked the Divisiveness Test, particularly Justice Breyer's concurring opinion in the following case. *See, e.g., American Legion v. American Humanist Association,* 139 S. Ct. 2067 (2019) (citing to Justice Breyer's *Van Orden* concurrence six times in the majority opinion, once in the plurality opinion, seven times in Justice Breyer's concurrence, which Justice Kagan joined, and once in Justice Gorsuch's concurrence, which Justice Thomas joined). Justice Breyer has been the most recent and the most consistent advocate for treating divisiveness as a standalone test. You saw Justice Breyer's use of the Divisiveness Test to argue against Ohio's school voucher program above, in *Zelman*, and below, Justice Breyer utilizes the Test to uphold Texas' placement of a Ten Commandments monument on its capital grounds.

Van Orden v. Perry

545 U.S. 677 (2005)

CHIEF JUSTICE REHNQUIST announced the judgment of the Court and delivered an opinion, in which JUSTICE SCALIA, JUSTICE KENNEDY, and JUSTICE THOMAS join.

The question here is whether the Establishment Clause of the First Amendment allows the display of a monument inscribed with the Ten Commandments on the Texas State Capitol grounds. We hold that it does.

The 22 acres surrounding the Texas State Capitol contain 17 monuments and 21 historical markers commemorating the "people, ideals, and events that compose Texan identity." The monolith challenged here stands 6-feet high and 3 1/2-feet wide. It is located to the north of the Capitol building, between the Capitol and the Supreme Court building. Its primary content is the text of the Ten Commandments. An eagle grasping the American flag, an eye inside of a pyramid, and two small tablets with what appears to be an ancient script are carved above the text of the Ten Commandments. Below the text are two Stars of David and the superimposed Greek letters Chi and Rho, which represent Christ. The bottom of the monument bears the inscription "PRESENTED TO THE PEOPLE AND YOUTH OF TEXAS BY THE FRATERNAL ORDER OF EAGLES OF TEXAS 1961."

The legislative record surrounding the State's acceptance of the monument from the Eagles—a national social, civic, and patriotic organization—is limited to legislative journal entries. After the monument was accepted, the State selected a site for the monument based on the recommendation of the state organization responsible for maintaining the Capitol grounds. The Eagles paid the cost of erecting the monument, the dedication of which was presided over by two state legislators.

Petitioner Thomas Van Orden is a native Texan and a resident of Austin. At one time he was a licensed lawyer, having graduated from Southern Methodist Law School. Van Orden testified that, since 1995, he has encountered the Ten Commandments monument during his frequent visits to the Capitol grounds. His visits are typically for the purpose of using the law library in the Supreme Court building, which is located just northwest of the Capitol building.

Forty years after the monument's erection and six years after Van Orden began to encounter the monument frequently, he sued numerous state officials seeking both a declaration that the monument's placement violates the Establishment Clause and an injunction requiring its removal.

Our cases, Januslike, point in two directions in applying the Establishment Clause. One face looks toward the strong role played by religion and religious traditions throughout our Nation's history.... The other face looks toward the principle that governmental intervention in religious matters can itself endanger religious freedom.

This case, like all Establishment Clause challenges, presents us with the difficulty of respecting both faces. Our institutions presuppose a Supreme Being, yet these institutions must not press religious observances upon their citizens. One face looks to the past in acknowledgment of our Nation's heritage, while the other looks to the present in demanding a separation between church and state. Reconciling these two faces requires that we neither abdicate our responsibility to maintain a division between church and state nor evince a hostility to religion by disabling the government from in some ways recognizing our religious heritage.

These two faces are evident in representative cases both upholding and invalidating laws under the Establishment Clause. Over the last 25 years, we have sometimes pointed to *Lemon v. Kurtzman*, 403 U.S. 602 (1971), as providing the governing test in Establishment Clause challenges. Yet, just two years after *Lemon* was decided, we noted that the factors identified in *Lemon* serve as "no more than helpful signposts." Many of our recent cases simply have not applied the *Lemon* test. Others have applied it only after concluding that the challenged practice was invalid under a different Establishment Clause test.

Whatever may be the fate of the *Lemon* test in the larger scheme of Establishment Clause jurisprudence, we think it not useful in dealing with the sort of passive monument that Texas has erected on its Capitol grounds. Instead, our analysis is driven both by the nature of the monument and by our Nation's history.

As we explained in *Lynch v. Donnelly*, 465 U.S. 668 (1984): "There is an unbroken history of official acknowledgment by all three branches of government of the role of religion in American life from at least 1789." For example, both Houses passed resolutions in 1789 asking President George Washington to issue a Thanksgiving Day Proclamation to "recommend to the people of the United States a day of public thanksgiving and prayer, to be observed, by acknowledging, with grateful hearts, the many and signal favors of Almighty God." President Washington's proclamation directly attributed to the Supreme Being the foundations and successes of our young Nation[.] ...

Recognition of the role of God in our Nation's heritage has also been reflected in our decisions. We have acknowledged, for example, that "religion has been closely identified with our history and government," and that "[t]he history of man is inseparable from the history of religion." This recognition has led us to hold that the Establishment Clause permits a state legislature to open its daily sessions with a prayer by a chaplain paid by the State. *Marsh v. Chambers.*

In this case we are faced with a display of the Ten Commandments on government property outside the Texas State Capitol. Such acknowledgments of the role played by the Ten Commandments in our Nation's heritage are common throughout America. We need only look within our own Courtroom. Since 1935, Moses has stood, holding two tablets that reveal portions of the Ten Commandments written in Hebrew, among other lawgivers in the south frieze. Representations of the Ten Commandments adorn the metal gates lining the north and south sides of the Courtroom as well as the doors leading into the Courtroom. Moses also sits on the exterior east facade of the building holding the Ten Commandments tablets.

Similar acknowledgments can be seen throughout a visitor's tour of our Nation's Capital. For example, a large statue of Moses holding the Ten Commandments, alongside a statue of the Apostle Paul, has overlooked the rotunda of the Library of Congress' Jefferson Building since 1897. And the Jefferson Building's Great Reading Room contains a sculpture of a woman beside the Ten Commandments with a quote above her from the Old Testament (Micah 6:8). A medallion with two tablets depicting the Ten Commandments decorates the floor of the National Archives. Inside the Department of Justice, a statue entitled "The Spirit of Law" has two tablets representing the Ten Commandments lying at its feet. In front of the Ronald Reagan Building is another sculpture that includes a depiction of the Ten Commandments. So too a 24-foot-tall sculpture, depicting, among other things, the Ten Commandments and a cross, stands outside the federal courthouse that houses both the Court of Appeals and the District Court for the District of Columbia. Moses is also prominently featured in the Chamber of the United States House of Representatives.[9]

Our opinions, like our building, have recognized the role the Decalogue plays in America's heritage. The Executive and Legislative Branches have also acknowledged the

---

9. Other examples of monuments and buildings reflecting the prominent role of religion abound. For example, the Washington, Jefferson, and Lincoln Memorials all contain explicit invocations of God's importance. The apex of the Washington Monument is inscribed "Laus Deo," which is translated to mean "Praise be to God," and multiple memorial stones in the monument contain Biblical citations. The Jefferson Memorial is engraved with three quotes from Jefferson that make God a central theme. Inscribed on the wall of the Lincoln Memorial are two of Lincoln's most famous speeches, the Gettysburg Address and his Second Inaugural Address. Both inscriptions include those speeches' extensive acknowledgments of God.

historical role of the Ten Commandments. These displays and recognitions of the Ten Commandments bespeak the rich American tradition of religious acknowledgments.

Of course, the Ten Commandments are religious—they were so viewed at their inception and so remain. The monument, therefore, has religious significance. According to Judeo-Christian belief, the Ten Commandments were given to Moses by God on Mt. Sinai. But Moses was a lawgiver as well as a religious leader. And the Ten Commandments have an undeniable historical meaning, as the foregoing examples demonstrate. Simply having religious content or promoting a message consistent with a religious doctrine does not run afoul of the Establishment Clause.

There are, of course, limits to the display of religious messages or symbols. For example, we held unconstitutional a Kentucky statute requiring the posting of the Ten Commandments in every public schoolroom. *Stone v. Graham*, 449 U.S. 39 (1980) (*per curiam*). In the classroom context, we found that the Kentucky statute had an improper and plainly religious purpose. Neither *Stone* itself nor subsequent opinions have indicated that *Stone*'s holding would extend to a legislative chamber or to capitol grounds.

The placement of the Ten Commandments monument on the Texas State Capitol grounds is a far more passive use of those texts than was the case in *Stone*, where the text confronted elementary school students every day. Indeed, Van Orden, the petitioner here, apparently walked by the monument for a number of years before bringing this lawsuit. The monument is therefore also quite different from the prayers involved in *Lee v. Weisman*, [505 U.S. 577 (1992)]. Texas has treated its Capitol grounds monuments as representing the several strands in the State's political and legal history. The inclusion of the Ten Commandments monument in this group has a dual significance, partaking of both religion and government. We cannot say that Texas' display of this monument violates the Establishment Clause of the First Amendment.

JUSTICE SCALIA concurring. [Opinion omitted.]

JUSTICE THOMAS concurring.

This case would be easy if the Court were willing to abandon the inconsistent guideposts it has adopted for addressing Establishment Clause challenges, and return to the original meaning of the Clause.

There is no question that, based on the original meaning of the Establishment Clause, the Ten Commandments display at issue here is constitutional. In no sense does Texas compel petitioner Van Orden to do anything. The only injury to him is that he takes offense at seeing the monument as he passes it on his way to the Texas Supreme Court Library. He need not stop to read it or even to look at it, let alone to express support for it or adopt the Commandments as guides for his life. The mere presence of the monument along his path involves no coercion and thus does not violate the Establishment Clause.

Returning to the original meaning would do more than simplify our task. It also would avoid the pitfalls present in the Court's current approach to such challenges.

First, this Court's precedent permits even the slightest public recognition of religion to constitute an establishment of religion. Second, in a seeming attempt to balance out its willingness to consider almost any acknowledgment of religion an establishment, in other cases Members of this Court have concluded that the term or symbol at issue has no religious meaning by virtue of its ubiquity or rote ceremonial invocation.

Finally, the very "flexibility" of this Court's Establishment Clause precedent leaves it incapable of consistent application. The inconsistency between the decisions the Court reaches today in this case and in *McCreary County v. American Civil Liberties Union of Ky.*, 545 U.S. 844 (2005), only compounds the confusion.

The unintelligibility of this Court's precedent raises the further concern that, either in appearance or in fact, adjudication of Establishment Clause challenges turns on judicial predilections.

JUSTICE BREYER, concurring in the judgment.

[With respect to the Religion Clauses,] there is "no simple and clear measure which by precise application can readily and invariably demark the permissible from the impermissible." One must refer instead to the basic purposes of those Clauses. They seek to "assure the fullest possible scope of religious liberty and tolerance for all." They seek to avoid that divisiveness based upon religion that promotes social conflict, sapping the strength of government and religion alike. *Zelman v. Simmons-Harris*, 536 U.S. 639, 717–729 (2002) (BREYER, J., dissenting). They seek to maintain that "separation of church and state" that has long been critical to the "peaceful dominion that religion exercises in [this] country," where the "spirit of religion" and the "spirit of freedom" are productively "united," "reign[ing] together" but in separate spheres "on the same soil." A[lexis] de Tocqueville, Democracy in America 282–283 (1835) (H. Mansfield & D. Winthrop transls. and eds. 2000).

The Court has made clear that the realization of these goals means that government must "neither engage in nor compel religious practices," that it must "effect no favoritism among sects or between religion and nonreligion," and that it must "work deterrence of no religious belief." But the Establishment Clause does not compel the government to purge from the public sphere all that in any way partakes of the religious. Such absolutism is not only inconsistent with our national traditions but would also tend to promote the kind of social conflict the Establishment Clause seeks to avoid.

Thus, the Court has found no single mechanical formula that can accurately draw the constitutional line in every case. Where the Establishment Clause is at issue, tests designed to measure "neutrality" alone are insufficient, both because it is sometimes difficult to determine when a legal rule is "neutral," and because

> "untutored devotion to the concept of neutrality can lead to invocation or approval of results which partake not simply of that noninterference and noninvolvement with the religious which the Constitution commands, but of a brooding and pervasive devotion to the secular and a passive, or even active, hostility to the religious."

Neither can this Court's other tests readily explain the Establishment Clause's tolerance, for example, of the prayers that open legislative meetings; certain references to, and invocations of, the Deity in the public words of public officials; the public references to God on coins, decrees, and buildings; or the attention paid to the religious objectives of certain holidays, including Thanksgiving.

If the relation between government and religion is one of separation, but not of mutual hostility and suspicion, one will inevitably find difficult borderline cases. And in such cases, I see no test-related substitute for the exercise of legal judgment. That judgment is not a personal judgment. Rather, as in all constitutional cases, it must reflect and remain faithful to the underlying purposes of the Clauses, and it must take account of context and consequences measured in light of those purposes. While the Court's prior tests provide useful guideposts—and might well lead to the same result the Court reaches today—no exact formula can dictate a resolution to such fact-intensive cases.

The case before us is a borderline case. On the one hand, the Commandments' text undeniably has a religious message, invoking, indeed emphasizing, the Deity. On the other hand, focusing on the text of the Commandments alone cannot conclusively resolve this case. Rather, to determine the message that the text here conveys, we must examine how the text is *used*. And that inquiry requires us to consider the context of the display.

In certain contexts, a display of the tablets of the Ten Commandments can convey not simply a religious message but also a secular moral message (about proper standards of social conduct). And in certain contexts, a display of the tablets can also convey a historical message (about a historic relation between those standards and the law).

Here the tablets have been used as part of a display that communicates not simply a religious message, but a secular message as well. The circumstances surrounding the display's placement on the capitol grounds and its physical setting suggest that the State itself intended the latter, nonreligious aspects of the tablets' message to predominate. And the monument's 40-year history on the Texas state grounds indicates that that has been its effect.

The group that donated the monument, the Fraternal Order of Eagles, a private civic (and primarily secular) organization, while interested in the religious aspect of the Ten Commandments, sought to highlight the Commandments' role in shaping civic morality as part of that organization's efforts to combat juvenile delinquency. The Eagles' consultation with a committee composed of members of several faiths in order to find a nonsectarian text underscores the group's ethics-based motives. The tablets, as displayed on the monument, prominently acknowledge that the Eagles donated the display, a factor which, though not sufficient, thereby further distances the State itself from the religious aspect of the Commandments' message.

The physical setting of the monument, moreover, suggests little or nothing of the sacred. The monument sits in a large park containing 17 monuments and 21 historical markers, all designed to illustrate the "ideals" of those who settled in Texas and of those who have lived there since that time. The setting does not readily lend itself to meditation or any other religious activity. But it does provide a context of history and moral ideals. It (together with the display's inscription about its origin) communicates to visitors that the State sought to reflect moral principles, illustrating a relation between ethics and law that the State's citizens, historically speaking, have endorsed. That is to say, the context suggests that the State intended the display's moral message—an illustrative message reflecting the historical "ideals" of Texans—to predominate.

If these factors provide a strong, but not conclusive, indication that the Commandments' text on this monument conveys a predominantly secular message, a further factor is determinative here. As far as I can tell, 40 years passed in which the presence of this monument, legally speaking, went unchallenged (until the single legal objection raised by petitioner). And I am not aware of any evidence suggesting that this was due to a climate of intimidation. Hence, those 40 years suggest more strongly than can any set of formulaic tests that few individuals, whatever their system of beliefs, are likely to have understood the monument as amounting, in any significantly detrimental way, to a government effort to favor a particular religious sect, primarily to promote religion over nonreligion, to "engage in" any "religious practic[e]," to "compel" any "religious practic[e]," or to "work deterrence" of any "religious belief."

This case, moreover, is distinguishable from instances where the Court has found Ten Commandments displays impermissible. The display is not on the grounds of a public school, where, given the impressionability of the young, government must exercise particular care in separating church and state. This case also differs from *McCreary County*, where the short (and stormy) history of the courthouse Commandments' displays demonstrates the substantially religious objectives of those who mounted them, and the effect of this readily apparent objective upon those who view them. That history there indicates a governmental effort substantially to promote religion. And, in today's world, in a Nation of so many different religious and comparable nonreligious fundamental beliefs, a more contemporary state effort to focus attention upon a religious text is certainly likely to prove divisive in a way that this longstanding, pre-existing monument has not.

This display has stood apparently uncontested for nearly two generations. That experience helps us understand that as a practical matter of *degree* this display is unlikely to prove divisive. And this matter of degree is, I believe, critical in a borderline case such as this one.

At the same time, to reach a contrary conclusion here, based primarily on the religious nature of the tablets' text would, I fear, lead the law to exhibit a hostility toward religion that has no place in our Establishment Clause traditions. Such a holding might well encourage disputes concerning the removal of longstanding depictions of the Ten Commandments from public buildings across the Nation. And it could thereby create the very kind of religiously based divisiveness that the Establishment Clause seeks to avoid.

I recognize the danger of the slippery slope. Still, where the Establishment Clause is at issue, we must "distinguish between real threat and mere shadow." Here, we have only the shadow.

JUSTICE STEVENS, with whom JUSTICE GINSBURG joins, dissenting.

The sole function of the monument on the grounds of Texas' State Capitol is to display the full text of one version of the Ten Commandments. The monument is not a work of art and does not refer to any event in the history of the State. It is significant because, and only because, it communicates the following message: "I AM the LORD thy God. Thou shalt have no other gods before me...."

Viewed on its face, Texas' display has no purported connection to God's role in the formation of Texas or the founding of our Nation; nor does it provide the reasonable observer with any basis to guess that it was erected to honor any individual or organization. The message transmitted by Texas' chosen display is quite plain: This State endorses the divine code of the "Judeo-Christian" God.

If any fragment of Jefferson's metaphorical "wall of separation between church and State" is to be preserved—if there remains any meaning to the "wholesome 'neutrality' of which this Court's [Establishment Clause] cases speak"—a negative answer to that question [whether the Texas display is constitutional] is mandatory.

III

The plurality's reliance on early religious statements and proclamations made by the Founders is problematic because those views were not espoused at the Constitutional Convention in 1787 nor enshrined in the Constitution's text. Thus, the presentation of these religious statements as a unified historical narrative is bound to paint a misleading picture. It does so here. In according deference to the statements of George Washington and John Adams, The Chief Justice and Justice Scalia, fail to account for the acts and publicly espoused views of other influential leaders of that time. Notably absent from their historical snapshot is the fact that Thomas Jefferson refused to issue Thanksgiving proclamations based on the argument that to do so would violate the Establishment Clause. The Chief Justice and Justice Scalia disregard the substantial debates that took place regarding the constitutionality of the early proclamations and acts they cite, see, e.g., Letter from James Madison to Edward Livingston (July 10, 1822) (arguing that Congress' appointment of Chaplains to be paid from the National Treasury was "not with my approbation" and was a "deviation" from the principle of "immunity of Religion from civil jurisdiction"), and paper over the fact that Madison more than once repudiated the views attributed to him by many, stating unequivocally that with respect to government's involvement with religion, the " 'tendency to a usurpation on one side, or the other, or to a corrupting coalition or alliance between them, will be best guarded against by an entire abstinence of the Government from interference, in any way whatever, beyond the necessity of preserving public order, & protecting each sect against trespasses on its legal rights by others.' "

These seemingly nonconforming sentiments should come as no surprise. Not insignificant numbers of colonists came to this country with memories of religious persecution by monarchs on the other side of the Atlantic. Others experienced religious intolerance at the hands of colonial Puritans. The Chief Justice and Justice Scalia ignore the separationist impulses—in accord with the principle of "neutrality"— that these individuals brought to the debates surrounding the adoption of the Establishment Clause.[27]

[Moreover, t]he original understanding of the type of "religion" that qualified for constitutional protection under the Establishment Clause likely did not include those followers of Judaism and Islam who are among the preferred "monotheistic" religions JUSTICE SCALIA has embraced in his *McCreary County* opinion. The inclusion of Jews and Muslims inside the category of constitutionally favored religions surely would have shocked Chief Justice Marshall and Justice Story. Indeed, JUSTICE SCALIA is unable to point to any persuasive historical evidence or entrenched traditions in support of his decision to give specially preferred constitutional status to all monotheistic religions. Perhaps this is because the history of the Establishment Clause's original meaning just as strongly supports a preference for Christianity as it does a preference for monotheism. Generic references to "God" hardly constitute evidence that those who spoke the word meant to be inclusive of all monotheistic believers; nor do such references demonstrate that those who heard the word spoken understood it broadly to include all monotheistic faiths.

A reading of the First Amendment dependent on either of the purported original meanings expressed above would eviscerate the heart of the Establishment Clause. It would replace Jefferson's "wall of separation" with a perverse wall of exclusion—Christians inside, non-Christians out. It would permit States to construct walls of their own choosing—Baptists inside, Mormons out; Jewish Orthodox inside, Jewish Reform out. A Clause so understood might be faithful to the expectations of some of our Founders, but it is plainly not worthy of a society whose enviable hallmark over the course of two centuries has been the continuing expansion of religious pluralism and tolerance.

It is our duty, therefore, to interpret the First Amendment's command that "Congress shall make no law respecting an establishment of religion" not by merely asking what those words meant to observers at the time of the founding, but instead by deriving from the Clause's text and history the broad principles that remain valid today. In similar fashion, we have construed the Equal Protection Clause of the Fourteenth Amendment to prohibit segregated schools, see *Brown v. Board of Education*, 349

---

27. The contrary evidence cited by THE CHIEF JUSTICE and JUSTICE SCALIA only underscores the obvious fact that leaders who have drafted and voted for a text are eminently capable of violating their own rules. The first Congress was—just as the present Congress is—capable of passing unconstitutional legislation. Thus, it is no answer to say that the Founders' separationist impulses were "plainly rejected" simply because the first Congress enacted laws that acknowledged God. To adopt such an interpretive approach would misguidedly give authoritative weight to the fact that the Congress that proposed the Fourteenth Amendment also enacted laws that tolerated segregation, and the fact that 10 years after proposing the First Amendment, Congress enacted the Alien and Sedition Act, which indisputably violated our present understanding of the First Amendment.

U.S. 294 (1955), even though those who drafted that Amendment evidently thought that separate was not unequal.

To reason from the broad principles contained in the Constitution does not, as JUSTICE SCALIA suggests, require us to abandon our heritage in favor of unprincipled expressions of personal preference. The task of applying the broad principles that the Framers wrote into the text of the First Amendment is, in any event, no more a matter of personal preference than is one's selection between two (or more) sides in a heated historical debate. We serve our constitutional mandate by expounding the meaning of constitutional provisions with one eye toward our Nation's history and the other fixed on its democratic aspirations. See *McCulloch v. Maryland*, 4 Wheat. 316, 407, 415 (1819) ("[W]e must never forget, that it is *a constitution* we are expounding" that is intended to "endure for ages to come, and, consequently, to be adapted to the various *crises* of human affairs").

The principle that guides my analysis is neutrality. The basis for that principle is firmly rooted in our Nation's history and our Constitution's text. I recognize that the requirement that government must remain neutral between religion and irreligion would have seemed foreign to some of the Framers; so too would a requirement of neutrality between Jews and Christians. Fortunately, we are not bound by the Framers' expectations—we are bound by the legal principles they enshrined in our Constitution. The evil of discriminating today against atheists, "polytheists[,] and believers in unconcerned deities," is in my view a direct descendent of the evil of discriminating among Christian sects. The Establishment Clause thus forbids it and, in turn, prohibits Texas from displaying the Ten Commandments monument the plurality so casually affirms.

JUSTICE O'CONNOR, dissenting. [Opinion omitted.]

JUSTICE SOUTER, with whom JUSTICE STEVENS and JUSTICE GINSBURG join, dissenting. [Opinion omitted.]

Exercise 10:

1. What analysis of the challenged display did Chief Justice Rehnquist utilize?

2. Does the context in which the Ten Commandments monument is set reduce or eliminate any religious message the monument otherwise would have sent?

3. Are you persuaded by the plurality's distinguishing of *Stone v. Graham*? *Lee v. Weisman*?

4. Would the Ten Commandments monument on the Texas Capitol grounds qualify for the strong presumption of constitutionality under *American Legion*? How would one argue that the presumption should apply? Against such a presumption? If the latter, what test(s) should govern the Court's analysis? Would a majority of the Court reach the same result post-*American Legion*?

5. Justice Breyer acknowledged that the Supreme Court's Establishment Clause case law was difficult to synthesize. He then claimed that this was the product of the Establishment Clause's application to a complex world in which there was some interaction between government and religion, but not too much. Is Justice Breyer correct?

6. Justice Breyer then argued that *Van Orden* presented a "borderline case." What made it "borderline" for Justice Breyer?

7. What are the components of, or what is the analysis required by, the Divisiveness Test?

8. From where or what did Justice Breyer draw the Divisiveness Test?

9. What are its purported advantages over the Lemon Test and Endorsement Test? What are its costs?

10. Describe Justice Breyer's application of the Divisiveness Test in *Van Orden*.

11. Justice Breyer argued that the lack of controversy over the monument, especially the absence of litigation, is strong evidence that the monument's message is secular and therefore not divisive. Is Justice Breyer correct?

12. Justice Breyer expressed concern that, if the Supreme Court struck down the monument, that act would itself cause divisiveness. Is he correct? If so, so what? Is it not the case that many correct Supreme Court rulings cause social divisiveness?

13. What did Justice Breyer mean when he stated that many Establishment Clause cases require the "exercise of legal judgment"? Is that consistent with the Rule of Law?

14. Is Justice Breyer's conclusion in *Van Orden* consistent with his position in *Simmons-Harris*, discussed above, and with *McCreary County*?

15. On a scale of one to ten, with ten being the most accommodationist and one being the most separationist, where does the Divisiveness Test fall?

16. Justice Thomas argued that utilizing the Establishment Clause's original meaning would produce a host of benefits. Catalogue those benefits. Justice Stevens, by contrast, claimed that originalism was a flawed approach; what arguments did he make? Who was right?

17. Does this case show why the Supreme Court should narrow or eliminate taxpayer standing? What harm, if any, did the plaintiff, Van Orden, suffer? Should the federal court system be open to redress of that harm?

3. Endorsement Test

The Endorsement Test was the creation of Justice O'Connor in a concurrence in a 1984 case, *Lynch v. Donnelly*, 465 U.S. 668, 687 (1984) (O'Connor, J., concurring). *Lynch* was the Supreme Court's first major pronouncement on governmental holiday displays, followed by *County of Allegheny*, reviewed above.

Justice O'Connor tied the Endorsement Test to earlier Supreme Court statements and reasoning, and offered endorsement as a clarification of earlier case law. She also argued that the Test best fit the Establishment Clause's purposes. The Endorsement Test is one of those relatively rare instances where a concurrence later gained significant prominence in its own right. You saw this in Volume 2, with Justice Jackson's concurrence in *Youngstown Sheet & Tube Co. v. Sawyer (The Steel Seizure Cases)*, 343 U.S. 579 (1952). (Though, here, Justice O'Connor's concurrence has not achieved the canonical status of Justice Jackson's and is under some pressure in the wake of *American Legion*.)

Lynch v. Donnelly

465 U.S. 668 (1984)

THE CHIEF JUSTICE delivered the opinion of the Court.

We granted certiorari to decide whether the Establishment Clause of the First Amendment prohibits a municipality from including a crèche, or Nativity scene, in its annual Christmas display.

I

Each year, in cooperation with the downtown retail merchants' association, the City of Pawtucket, Rhode Island, erects a Christmas display as part of its observance of the Christmas holiday season. The display is situated in a park owned by a nonprofit organization and located in the heart of the shopping district. The display is essentially like those to be found in hundreds of towns or cities across the Nation—often on public grounds—during the Christmas season. The Pawtucket display comprises many of the figures and decorations traditionally associated with Christmas, including, among other things, a Santa Claus house, reindeer pulling Santa's sleigh, candy-striped poles, a Christmas tree, carolers, cutout figures representing such characters as a clown, an elephant, and a teddy bear, hundreds of colored lights, a large banner that reads "SEASONS GREETINGS," and the crèche at issue here. All components of this display are owned by the City.

The crèche, which has been included in the display for 40 or more years, consists of the traditional figures, including the Infant Jesus, Mary and Joseph, angels, shepherds, kings, and animals, all ranging in height from 5" to 5'. In 1973, when the present crèche was acquired, it cost the City $1365; it now is valued at $200. The erection and dismantling of the crèche costs the City about $20 per year; nominal expenses are incurred in lighting the crèche. No money has been expended on its maintenance for the past 10 years.

Respondents, Pawtucket residents and individual members of the Rhode Island affiliate of the American Civil Liberties Union, and the affiliate itself, brought this action in the United States District Court for Rhode Island, challenging the City's inclusion of the crèche in the annual display. The District Court held that the City's inclusion of the crèche in the display violates the Establishment Clause[.] A divided panel of the Court of Appeals for the First Circuit affirmed. We reverse.

II

A

This Court has explained that the purpose of the Establishment and Free Exercise Clauses of the First Amendment is "to prevent, as far as possible, the intrusion of either [the church or the state] into the precincts of the other." *Lemon v. Kurtzman*, 403 U.S. 602, 614 (1971). At the same time, however, the Court has recognized that "total separation is not possible in an absolute sense. Some relationship between government and religious organizations is inevitable." In every Establishment Clause case, we must reconcile the inescapable tension between the objective of preventing unnecessary intrusion of either the church or the state upon the other, and the reality that, as the Court has so often noted, total separation of the two is not possible.

The Court has sometimes described the Religion Clauses as erecting a "wall" between church and state, see, *e.g., Everson v. Board of Education,* 330 U.S. 1, 18 (1947). The concept of a "wall" of separation is a useful figure of speech probably deriving from views of Thomas Jefferson. The metaphor has served as a reminder that the Establishment Clause forbids an established church or anything approaching it. But the metaphor itself is not a wholly accurate description of the practical aspects of the relationship that in fact exists between church and state.

No significant segment of our society and no institution within it can exist in a vacuum or in total or absolute isolation from all the other parts, much less from government.... Nor does the Constitution require complete separation of church and state; it affirmatively mandates accommodation, not merely tolerance, of all religions, and forbids hostility toward any. See, *e.g., Zorach v. Clauson,* 343 U.S. 306, 314, 315 (1952); *McCollum v. Board of Education,* 333 U.S. 203, 211 (1948). Anything less would require the "callous indifference" we have said was never intended by the Establishment Clause.

B

The Court's interpretation of the Establishment Clause has comported with what history reveals was the contemporaneous understanding of its guarantees. A significant example of the contemporaneous understanding of that Clause is found in the events of the first week of the First Session of the First Congress in 1789. In the very week that Congress approved the Establishment Clause as part of the Bill of Rights for submission to the states, it enacted legislation providing for paid chaplains for the House and Senate.

It is clear that neither the seventeen draftsmen of the Constitution who were Members of the First Congress, nor the Congress of 1789, saw any establishment problem in the employment of congressional Chaplains to offer daily prayers in the Congress, a practice that has continued for nearly two centuries.

C

There is an unbroken history of official acknowledgment by all three branches of government of the role of religion in American life from at least 1789. Our history is replete with official references to the value and invocation of Divine guidance in deliberations and pronouncements of the Founding Fathers and contemporary leaders. Beginning in the early colonial period long before Independence, a day of Thanksgiving was celebrated as a religious holiday to give thanks for the bounties of Nature as gifts from God. President Washington and his successors proclaimed Thanksgiving, with all its religious overtones, a day of national celebration and Congress made it a National Holiday more than a century ago. That holiday has not lost its theme of expressing thanks for Divine aid any more than has Christmas lost its religious significance.

Executive Orders and other official announcements of Presidents and of the Congress have proclaimed both Christmas and Thanksgiving National Holidays in religious terms. And, by Acts of Congress, it has long been the practice that federal employees are released from duties on these National Holidays, while being paid from the same public revenues that provide the compensation of the Chaplains of the Senate and the House and the military services. Thus, it is clear that Government has long recognized—indeed it has subsidized—holidays with religious significance.

There are countless other illustrations of the Government's acknowledgment of our religious heritage and governmental sponsorship of graphic manifestations of that heritage.

III

This history may help explain why the Court consistently has declined to take a rigid, absolutist view of the Establishment Clause.... Rather than mechanically invalidating all governmental conduct or statutes that confer benefits or give special recognition to religion in general or to one faith—as an absolutist approach would dictate—the Court has scrutinized challenged legislation or official conduct to determine whether, in reality, it establishes a religion or religious faith, or tends to do so.

In each case, the inquiry calls for line drawing; no fixed, *per se* rule can be framed. The Establishment Clause like the Due Process Clauses is not a precise, detailed provision in a legal code capable of ready application.... In the line-drawing process we have often found it useful to inquire whether the challenged law or conduct has a secular purpose, whether its principal or primary effect is to advance or inhibit religion, and whether it creates an excessive entanglement of government with religion. *Lemon, supra.* But, we have repeatedly emphasized our unwillingness to be confined to any single test or criterion in this sensitive area.

In this case, the focus of our inquiry must be on the crèche in the context of the Christmas season. The District Court plainly erred by focusing almost exclusively on the crèche. When viewed in the proper context of the Christmas Holiday season, it is apparent that, on this record, there is insufficient evidence to establish that the inclusion of the crèche is a purposeful or surreptitious effort to express some kind of subtle governmental advocacy of a particular religious message. In a pluralistic society a variety of motives and purposes are implicated. The City, like the Congresses and Presidents, has principally taken note of a significant historical religious event long celebrated in the Western World. The crèche in the display depicts the historical origins of this traditional event long recognized as a National Holiday.

The narrow question is whether there is a secular purpose for Pawtucket's display of the crèche. The display is sponsored by the City to celebrate the Holiday and to depict the origins of that Holiday. These are legitimate secular purposes. The District Court's inference, drawn from the religious nature of the crèche, that the City has no secular purpose was clearly erroneous.

The District Court found that the primary effect of including the crèche is to confer a substantial and impermissible benefit on religion in general and on the Christian faith in particular. Comparisons of the relative benefits to religion of different forms of governmental support are elusive and difficult to make. We are unable to discern a greater aid to religion deriving from inclusion of the crèche than from these benefits and endorsements previously held not violative of the Establishment Clause.

The dissent asserts some observers may perceive that the City has aligned itself with the Christian faith by including a Christian symbol in its display and that this serves to advance religion. We can assume, *arguendo*, that the display advances religion in a sense; but our precedents plainly contemplate that on occasion some advancement of religion will result from governmental action. The Court has made it abundantly clear, however, that "not every law that confers an 'indirect,' 'remote,' or 'incidental' benefit upon [religion] is, for that reason alone, constitutionally invalid." Here, whatever benefit to one faith or religion or to all religions, is indirect, remote and incidental; display of the crèche is no more an advancement or endorsement of religion than the Congressional and Executive recognition of the origins of the Holiday itself as "Christ's Mass," or the exhibition of literally hundreds of religious paintings in governmentally supported museums.

Entanglement is a question of kind and degree. In this case, however, there is no reason to disturb the District Court's finding on the absence of administrative entanglement.

The Court of Appeals correctly observed that this Court has not held that political divisiveness alone can serve to invalidate otherwise permissible conduct. And we decline to so hold today. This case does not involve a direct subsidy to church-sponsored schools or colleges, or other religious institutions, and hence no inquiry into potential political divisiveness is even called for. In any event, apart from this litigation there is no evidence of political friction or divisiveness over the crèche in the 40-year history of Pawtucket's Christmas celebration. A litigant cannot, by the very act of commencing a lawsuit, however, create the appearance of divisiveness and then exploit it as evidence of entanglement.

We are satisfied that the City has a secular purpose for including the crèche, that the City has not impermissibly advanced religion, and that including the crèche does not create excessive entanglement between religion and government.

IV

JUSTICE BRENNAN describes the crèche as a "re-creation of an event that lies at the heart of Christian faith[.]" The crèche, like a painting, is passive; admittedly it is a reminder of the origins of Christmas. Even the traditional, purely secular displays extant at Christmas, with or without a crèche, would inevitably recall the religious nature of the Holiday. The display engenders a friendly community spirit of good will in keeping with the season. The crèche may well have special meaning to those whose faith includes the celebration of religious masses, but none who sense the origins of the Christmas celebration would fail to be aware of its religious implications. That the display brings people into the central city, and serves commercial interests and benefits merchants and their employees, does not, as the dissent points out, determine the character of the display. That a prayer invoking Divine guidance in Congress is preceded and followed by debate and partisan conflict over taxes, budgets, national defense, and myriad mundane subjects, for example, has never been thought to demean or taint the sacredness of the invocation.

Of course the crèche is identified with one religious faith but no more so than the examples we have set out from prior cases in which we found no conflict with the Establishment Clause. See, *e.g.*, *Marsh, supra*. It would be ironic, however, if the inclusion of a single symbol of a particular historic religious event, as part of a celebration acknowledged in the Western World for 20 centuries, and in this country by the people, by the Executive Branch, by the Congress, and the courts for two centuries, would so "taint" the City's exhibit as to render it violative of the Establishment Clause. To forbid the use of this one passive symbol—the crèche—at the very time people are taking note of the season with Christmas hymns and carols in public schools and other public places, and while the Congress and Legislatures open sessions with prayers by paid chaplains would be a stilted over-reaction contrary to our history and to our holdings. If the presence of the crèche in this display violates the Establishment Clause, a host of other forms of taking official note of Christmas, and of our religious heritage, are equally offensive to the Constitution.

The Court has acknowledged that the "fears and political problems" that gave rise to the Religion Clauses in the 18th century are of far less concern today. *Everson, supra*, 330 U.S., at 8. We are unable to perceive the Archbishop of Canterbury, the Vicar of Rome, or other powerful religious leaders behind every public acknowledgment of the religious heritage long officially recognized by the three constitutional branches of government. Any notion that these symbols pose a real danger of establishment of a state church is far-fetched indeed.

JUSTICE O'CONNOR, concurring.

I concur in the opinion of the Court. I write separately to suggest a clarification of our Establishment Clause doctrine. The suggested approach leads to the same result in this case as that taken by the Court, and the Court's opinion, as I read it, is consistent with my analysis.

I

The Establishment Clause prohibits government from making adherence to a religion relevant in any way to a person's standing in the political community [through] government endorsement or disapproval of religion. Endorsement sends a message to nonadherents that they are outsiders, not full members of the political community, and an accompanying message to adherents that they are insiders, favored members of the political community. Disapproval sends the opposite message.

Our prior cases have used the three-part test articulated in *Lemon v. Kurtzman*, 403 U.S. 602, 612–613 (1970), as a guide to detecting these two forms of unconstitutional government action. It has never been entirely clear, however, how the three parts of the test relate to the principles enshrined in the Establishment Clause. Focusing on institutional entanglement and on endorsement or disapproval of religion clarifies the *Lemon* test as an analytical device.

III

The central issue in this case is whether Pawtucket has endorsed Christianity by its display of the crèche. To answer that question, we must examine both what Pawtucket intended to communicate in displaying the crèche and what message the City's display actually conveyed. The purpose and effect prongs of the *Lemon* test represent these two aspects of the meaning of the City's action. The purpose prong of the *Lemon* test asks whether government's actual purpose is to endorse or disapprove of religion. The effect prong asks whether, irrespective of government's actual purpose, the practice under review in fact conveys a message of endorsement or disapproval. An affirmative answer to either question should render the challenged practice invalid.

A

The purpose prong of the *Lemon* test requires that a government activity have a secular purpose. The proper inquiry under the purpose prong of *Lemon*, I submit, is whether the government intends to convey a message of endorsement or disapproval of religion.

Applying that formulation to this case, I would find that Pawtucket did not intend to convey any message of endorsement of Christianity or disapproval of nonChristian religions. The evident purpose of including the crèche in the larger display was not promotion of the religious content of the crèche but celebration of the public holiday through its traditional symbols. Celebration of public holidays, which have cultural significance even if they also have religious aspects, is a legitimate secular purpose.

B

Focusing on the evil of government endorsement or disapproval of religion makes clear that the effect prong of the *Lemon* test is properly interpreted not to require invalidation of a government practice merely because it in fact causes, even as a primary effect, advancement or inhibition of religion. What is crucial is that a government practice not have the effect of communicating a message of government endorsement or disapproval of religion. It is only practices having that effect, whether intentionally or unintentionally, that make religion relevant, in reality or public perception, to status in the political community.

Pawtucket's display of its crèche, I believe, does not communicate a message that the government intends to endorse the Christian beliefs represented by the crèche. Although the religious and indeed sectarian significance of the crèche, as the district court found, is not neutralized by the setting, the overall holiday setting changes what viewers may fairly understand to be the purpose of the display—as a typical museum setting, though not neutralizing the religious content of a religious painting, negates any message of endorsement of that content. The display celebrates a public holiday, and no one contends that declaration of that holiday is understood to be an endorsement of religion. The holiday itself has very strong secular components and traditions. The crèche is a traditional symbol of the holiday that is very commonly displayed along with purely secular symbols, as it was in Pawtucket.

These features combine to make the government's display of the crèche in this particular physical setting no more an endorsement of religion than such governmental "acknowledgments" of religion as legislative prayers of the type approved in *Marsh v. Chambers*, 463 U.S. 783 (1983), government declaration of Thanksgiving as a public holiday, printing of "In God We Trust" on coins, and opening court sessions with "God save the United States and this [h]onorable [c]ourt." Those government acknowledgments of religion serve, in the only ways reasonably possible in our culture, the legitimate secular purposes of solemnizing public occasions, expressing confidence in the future, and encouraging the recognition of what is worthy of appreciation in society. For that reason, and because of their history and ubiquity, those practices are not understood as conveying government approval of particular religious beliefs. The display of the crèche likewise serves a secular purpose—celebration of a public holiday with traditional symbols. It cannot fairly be understood to convey a message of government endorsement of religion. It is significant in this regard that the crèche display apparently caused no political divisiveness prior to the filing of this lawsuit, although Pawtucket had incorporated the crèche in its annual Christmas display for some years. For these reasons, I conclude that Pawtucket's display of the crèche does not have the effect of communicating endorsement of Christianity.

[W]hether a government activity communicates endorsement of religion is not a question of simple historical fact. Although evidentiary submissions may help answer it, the question is, like the question whether racial or sex-based classifications communicate an invidious message, in large part a legal question to be answered on the basis of judicial interpretation of social facts. The District Court's conclusion concerning the effect of Pawtucket's display of its crèche was in error as a matter of law.

JUSTICE BRENNAN, with whom JUSTICE MARSHALL, JUSTICE BLACKMUN and JUSTICE STEVENS join, dissenting.

As we have sought to meet new problems arising under the Establishment Clause, our decisions, with few exceptions, have demanded that a challenged governmental practice satisfy the following criteria: "First, the [practice] must have a secular legislative purpose; second, its principal or primary effect must be one that neither advances nor inhibits religion; finally, [it] must not foster 'an excessive government entanglement with religion.'" *Lemon v. Kurtzman*, *supra*, 403 U.S., at 612–613.

Applying the three-part test to Pawtucket's crèche, I am persuaded that the City's inclusion of the crèche in its Christmas display simply does not reflect a "clearly secular purpose." First, all of Pawtucket's "valid secular objectives can be readily accomplished by other means." Plainly, the City's interest in celebrating the holiday and in promoting both retail sales and goodwill are fully served by the elaborate display of Santa Claus, reindeer, and wishing wells that are already a part of Pawtucket's annual Christmas display. More importantly, the nativity scene, unlike every other element of the Hodgson Park display, reflects a sectarian exclusivity that the avowed purposes of celebrating the holiday season and promoting retail commerce simply do not encompass. To be found constitutional, Pawtucket's seasonal celebration must at least be non-denominational and not serve to promote religion. The inclusion of a distinctively religious element like the crèche, however, demonstrates that a narrower sectarian purpose lay behind the decision to include a nativity scene. That the crèche retained this religious character for the people and municipal government of Pawtucket is suggested by the Mayor's testimony at trial in which he stated that for him, as well as others in the City, the effort to eliminate the nativity scene from Pawtucket's Christmas celebration "is a step towards establishing another religion, non-religion that it may be."

The "primary effect" of including a nativity scene in the City's display is to place the government's imprimatur of approval on the particular religious beliefs exemplified by the crèche. Those who believe in the message of the nativity receive the unique and exclusive benefit of public recognition and approval of their views. For many, the City's decision to include the crèche as part of its extensive and costly efforts to celebrate Christmas can only mean that the prestige of the government has been conferred on the beliefs associated with the crèche, thereby providing "a significant symbolic benefit to religion...." The effect on minority religious groups, as well as on those who may reject all religion, is to convey the message that their views are not similarly worthy of public recognition nor entitled to public support. It was precisely this sort of religious chauvinism that the Establishment Clause was intended forever to prohibit. Here, Pawtucket itself owns the crèche and instead of extending similar attention to a "broad spectrum" of religious and secular groups, it has singled out Christianity for special treatment.

Finally, it is evident that Pawtucket's inclusion of a crèche as part of its annual Christmas display does pose a significant threat of fostering "excessive entanglement." [I]t is worth noting that after today's decision, administrative entanglements may well develop. Jews and other non-Christian groups, prompted perhaps by the Mayor's remark that he will include a Menorah in future displays, can be expected to press government for inclusion of their symbols, and faced with such requests, government will have to become involved in accommodating the various demands. More importantly, although no political divisiveness was apparent in Pawtucket prior to the filing of respondents' lawsuit, that act, as the District Court found, unleashed powerful emotional reactions which divided the City along religious lines. The fact that calm had prevailed prior to this suit does not immediately suggest the absence of any division on the point for, as the District Court observed, the quiescence of those opposed to the crèche may have reflected nothing more than their sense of futility in opposing the majority.

I dissent.

JUSTICE BLACKMUN, with whom JUSTICE STEVENS joins, dissenting.

Not only does the Court's resolution of this controversy make light of our precedents, but also, ironically, the majority does an injustice to the crèche and the message it manifests. While certain persons, including the Mayor of Pawtucket, undertook a crusade to "keep Christ in Christmas," the Court today has declared that presence virtually irrelevant. The majority urges that the display, "with or without a crèche," "recall[s] the religious nature of the Holiday," and "engenders a friendly community spirit of good will in keeping with the season." Before the District Court, an expert witness for the city made a similar, though perhaps more candid, point, stating that Pawtucket's display invites people "to participate in the Christmas spirit, brotherhood, peace, and let loose with their money." The crèche has been relegated to the role of a neutral harbinger of the holiday season, useful for commercial purposes, but devoid of any inherent meaning and incapable of enhancing the religious tenor of a display of which it is an integral part. The city has its victory—but it is a Pyrrhic one indeed.

Exercise 11:

1. What test did the majority utilize? Did the majority fairly apply it?

2. What are the components of the Endorsement Test?

3. From where or what did Justice O'Connor draw the Endorsement Test?

4. How was Justice O'Connor's analysis of this case different from Chief Justice Burger's?

5. What are the Endorsement Test's purported advantages over the Lemon Test? What are its costs?

6. Why did Justice O'Connor articulate the Endorsement Test? Was it problems with existing analyses? Was it the positive facets of the Endorsement Test?

7. Justice O'Connor claimed that public acknowledgements of religion, such as "government declaration of Thanksgiving as a public holiday, printing of 'in God We Trust' on coins, and opening court sessions with 'God save the United States and this honorable court,'" are "not understood as conveying government approval of particular religious beliefs." Is Justice O'Connor correct?

8. Assume that you are sympathetic with the perspective that wishes to maintain a distinctively religious presence in the public square. For example, you are in favor of Ten Commandments monuments. Does Justice Blackmun's dissent concern you? Describe Justice Blackmun's argument and respond to it from the assumed perspective.

9. On a scale of one to ten, with ten being the most accomodationist and one being the most separationist, where does the Endorsement Test fall?

10. At the end of his opinion, Chief Justice Burger rather flippantly stated: "We are unable to perceive the Archbishop of Canterbury, the Vicar of Rome, or other powerful religious leaders behind every public acknowledgment of the religious heritage long officially recognized by the three constitutional branches of government. Any notion that these symbols pose a real danger of establishment of a state church is far-fetched indeed." How would Justice Breyer respond to Chief Justice Burger's claim?

The Endorsement Test not only shows up frequently in religious display cases like *Lynch*, *County of Allegheny*, and *McCreary County* (above), but it also appears in other contexts, such as school funding cases, like *Zelman*.

4. Coercion Test

The Coercion Test was first distinctly articulated in Justice Kennedy's concurrence in *County of Allegheny*, above. The Coercion Test is more accommodating of religion in the public sphere than the tests we have already covered, which its proponents identify as one of the Test's virtues. (Of course, this is a vice for the Test's opponents!) The Coercion Test respects the deeply-embedded religious practices of the American people and, its proponents claim, hews more closely to the Establishment Clause's original meaning by prohibiting only those government-religion interactions that fit the chief vice of state established churches: coerced religious belief and practices.

Initially, it looked as if there was a solid contingent of justices who would utilize the Coercion Test. However, these justices fractured into two factions, each advocating for a different conception of the Test. Justice Kennedy, who comprises one faction, is more likely to find coercion than the other faction, consisting of Justices Scalia and Thomas.

Lee v. Weisman

505 U.S. 577 (1992)

JUSTICE KENNEDY delivered the opinion of the Court.

School principals in the public school system of the city of Providence, Rhode Island, are permitted to invite members of the clergy to offer invocation and benediction prayers as part of the formal graduation ceremonies for middle schools and for high schools. The question before us is whether including clerical members who offer prayers as part of the official school graduation ceremony is consistent with the Religion Clauses of the First Amendment.

I

A

Deborah Weisman graduated from Nathan Bishop Middle School, a public school in Providence, at a formal ceremony in June 1989. She was about 14 years old. For many years it has been the policy of the Providence School Committee and the Superintendent of Schools to permit principals to invite members of the clergy to give invocations and benedictions at middle school and high school graduations. Many, but not all, of the principals elected to include prayers as part of the graduation ceremonies. Acting for himself and his daughter, Deborah's father, Daniel Weisman, objected to any prayers at Deborah's middle school graduation, but to no avail. The school principal, petitioner Robert E. Lee, invited a rabbi to deliver prayers at the graduation exercises for Deborah's class. Rabbi Leslie Gutterman, of the Temple Beth El in Providence, accepted.

It has been the custom of Providence school officials to provide invited clergy with a pamphlet entitled "Guidelines for Civic Occasions," prepared by the National Conference of Christians and Jews. The Guidelines recommend that public prayers at nonsectarian civic ceremonies be composed with "inclusiveness and sensitivity." The principal gave Rabbi Gutterman the pamphlet before the graduation and advised him the invocation and benediction should be nonsectarian.

Rabbi Gutterman's prayers were as follows:

INVOCATION

God of the Free, Hope of the Brave: For the legacy of America where diversity is celebrated and the rights of minorities are protected, we thank You. May these young men and women grow up to enrich it. For the liberty of America, we thank You. May these new graduates grow up to guard it. For the political process of America in which all its citizens may participate, for its court system where all may seek justice we thank You. May those we honor this morning always turn to it in trust. For the destiny of America we thank You. May the graduates of Nathan Bishop Middle School so live that they might help to share it. May our aspirations for our country and for these young people, who are our hope for the future, be richly fulfilled. AMEN.

BENEDICTION

O God, we are grateful to You for having endowed us with the capacity for learning which we have celebrated on this joyous commencement. Happy families give thanks for seeing their children achieve an important milestone. Send Your blessings upon the teachers and administrators who helped prepare them. The graduates now need strength and guidance for the future, help them to understand that we are not complete with academic knowledge alone. We must each strive to fulfill what You require of us all: To do justly, to love mercy, to walk humbly. We give thanks to You, Lord, for keeping us alive, sustaining us and allowing us to reach this special, happy occasion. AMEN.

The parties stipulate that attendance at graduation ceremonies is voluntary. The graduating students enter as a group in a processional, subject to the direction of teachers and school officials, and sit together, apart from their families. [A]t Deborah's middle school ceremony[,] the students stood for the Pledge of Allegiance and remained standing during the rabbi's prayers. Even on the assumption that there was a respectful moment of silence both before and after the prayers, the rabbi's two presentations must not have extended much beyond a minute each, if that.

The school board (and the United States, which supports it as *amicus curiae*) argued that these short prayers and others like them at graduation exercises are of profound meaning to many students and parents throughout this country who consider that due respect and acknowledgment for divine guidance and for the deepest spiritual aspirations of our people ought to be expressed at an event as important in life as a graduation. We assume this to be so in addressing the difficult case now before us.

II

These dominant facts mark and control the confines of our decision: State officials direct the performance of a formal religious exercise at promotional and graduation ceremonies for secondary schools. Even for those students who object to the religious exercise, their attendance and participation in the state-sponsored religious activity are in a fair and real sense obligatory, though the school district does not require attendance as a condition for receipt of the diploma.

It is beyond dispute that, at a minimum, the Constitution guarantees that government may not coerce anyone to support or participate in religion or its exercise, or otherwise act in a way which "establishes a [state] religion or religious faith, or tends to do so." The State's involvement in the school prayers challenged today violates these central principles.

That involvement is as troubling as it is undenied. A school official, the principal, decided that an invocation and a benediction should be given; this is a choice attributable to the State, and from a constitutional perspective it is as if a state statute decreed that the prayers must occur. The principal chose the religious participant, here a rabbi, and that choice is also attributable to the State. The reason for the choice of a rabbi is not disclosed by the record, but the potential for divisiveness over the choice of a particular member of the clergy to conduct the ceremony is apparent.

The State's role did not end with the decision to include a prayer and with the choice of a clergyman. Principal Lee provided Rabbi Gutterman with a copy of the "Guidelines for Civic Occasions," and advised him that his prayers should be nonsectarian. Through these means the principal directed and controlled the content of the prayers. Even if the only sanction for ignoring the instructions were that the rabbi would not be invited back, we think no religious representative who valued his or her continued reputation and effectiveness in the community would incur the State's displeasure in this regard. It is a cornerstone principle of our Establishment Clause jurisprudence that "it is no part of the business of government to compose official prayers for any group of the American people to recite as a part of a religious program carried on by government," and that is what the school officials attempted to do.

Petitioners argue, and we find nothing in the case to refute it, that the directions for the content of the prayers were a good-faith attempt by the school to ensure that the sectarianism which is so often the flashpoint for religious animosity be removed from the graduation ceremony. The concern is understandable. The question is not the good faith of the school in attempting to make the prayer acceptable to most persons, but the legitimacy of its undertaking that enterprise at all when the object is to produce a prayer to be used in a formal religious exercise which students, for all practical purposes, are obliged to attend.

The First Amendment's Religion Clauses mean that religious beliefs and religious expression are too precious to be either proscribed or prescribed by the State. The design of the Constitution is that preservation and transmission of religious beliefs and worship is a responsibility and a choice committed to the private sphere, which itself is promised freedom to pursue that mission. It must not be forgotten then, that while concern must be given to define the protection granted to an objector or a dissenting nonbeliever, these same Clauses exist to protect religion from government interference. James Madison, the principal author of the Bill of Rights, did not rest his opposition to a religious establishment on the sole ground of its effect on the minority. A principal ground for his view was: "[E]xperience witnesseth that ecclesiastical establishments, instead of maintaining the purity and efficacy of Religion, have had a contrary operation." Memorial and Remonstrance Against Religious Assessments (1785).

The degree of school involvement here made it clear that the graduation prayers bore the imprint of the State and thus put school-age children who objected in an untenable position.

To endure the speech of false ideas or offensive content and then to counter it is part of learning how to live in a pluralistic society, a society which insists upon open discourse towards the end of a tolerant citizenry. By the time they are seniors, high school students no doubt have been required to attend classes and assemblies and to complete assignments exposing them to ideas they find distasteful or immoral or absurd or all of these. Against this background, students may consider it an odd measure of justice to be subjected during the course of their educations to ideas deemed offensive and irreligious, but to be denied a brief, formal prayer ceremony that the school offers in return. This argument cannot prevail, however. It overlooks a fundamental dynamic of the Constitution.

The First Amendment protects speech and religion by quite different mechanisms. Speech is protected by ensuring its full expression even when the government participates, for the very object of some of our most important speech is to persuade the government to adopt an idea as its own. The method for protecting freedom of worship and freedom of conscience in religious matters is quite the reverse. In religious debate or expression the government is not a prime participant, for the Framers deemed religious establishment antithetical to the freedom of all. The Free Exercise Clause embraces a freedom of conscience and worship that has close parallels in the speech provisions of the First Amendment, but the Establishment Clause is a specific prohibition on forms of state intervention in religious affairs with no precise counterpart in the speech provisions. The explanation lies in the lesson of history that was and is the inspiration for the Establishment Clause, the lesson that in the hands of government what might begin as a tolerant expression of religious views may end in a policy to indoctrinate and coerce. A state-created orthodoxy puts at grave risk that freedom of belief and conscience which are the sole assurance that religious faith is real, not imposed.

As we have observed before, there are heightened concerns with protecting freedom of conscience from subtle coercive pressure in the elementary and secondary public schools. Our decisions in *Engel v. Vitale*, 370 U.S. 421 (1962), and *School Dist. of Abington* [*v. Schempp*, 374 U.S. 203 (1963)], recognize that prayer exercises in public schools carry a particular risk of indirect coercion. What to most believers may seem nothing more than a reasonable request that the nonbeliever respect their religious practices, in a school context may appear to the nonbeliever or dissenter to be an attempt to employ the machinery of the State to enforce a religious orthodoxy.

We need not look beyond the circumstances of this case to see the phenomenon at work. The undeniable fact is that the school district's supervision and control of a high school graduation ceremony places public pressure, as well as peer pressure, on attending students to stand as a group or, at least, maintain respectful silence during the invocation and benediction. This pressure, though subtle and indirect, can be as real as any overt compulsion. Of course, in our culture standing or remaining silent can signify adherence to a view or simple respect for the views of others. And no doubt some persons who have no desire to join a prayer have little objection to standing as a sign of respect for those who do. But for the dissenter of high school age, who has a reasonable perception that she is being forced by the State to pray in a manner her conscience will not allow, the injury is no less real. There can be no doubt that for many, if not most, of the students at the graduation, the act of standing or remaining silent was an expression of participation in the rabbi's prayer. That was the very point of the religious exercise. It is of little comfort to a dissenter, then, to be told that for her the act of standing or remaining in silence signifies mere respect, rather than participation. What matters is that, given our social conventions, a reasonable dissenter in this milieu could believe that the group exercise signified her own participation or approval of it.

Finding no violation under these circumstances would place objectors in the dilemma of participating, with all that implies, or protesting. We do not address whether that choice is acceptable if the affected citizens are mature adults, but we think the State may not, consistent with the Establishment Clause, place primary and secondary school children in this position. Research in psychology supports the common assumption that adolescents are often susceptible to pressure from their peers towards conformity, and that the influence is strongest in matters of social convention. To recognize that the choice imposed by the State constitutes an unacceptable constraint only acknowledges that the government may no more use social pressure to enforce orthodoxy than it may use more direct means.

There was a stipulation in the District Court that attendance at graduation and promotional ceremonies is voluntary. Petitioners and the United States, as *amicus*, made this a center point of the case, arguing that the option of not attending the graduation excuses any inducement or coercion in the ceremony itself. The argument lacks all persuasion. Law reaches past formalism. And to say a teenage student has a real choice not to attend her high school graduation is formalistic in the extreme. True, Deborah could elect not to attend commencement without renouncing her diploma; but we shall not allow the case to turn on this point. Everyone knows that in our society and in our culture high school graduation is one of life's most significant occasions. A school rule which excuses attendance is beside the point. Attendance may not be required by official decree, yet it is apparent that a student is not free to absent herself from the graduation exercise in any real sense of the term "voluntary," for absence would require forfeiture of those intangible benefits which have motivated the student through youth and all her high school years. Graduation is a time for family and those closest to the student to celebrate success and express mutual wishes of gratitude and respect, all to the end of impressing upon the young person the role that it is his or her right and duty to assume in the community and all of its diverse parts.

[According to the school district and the United States,] the prayers are an essential part of these ceremonies because for many persons an occasion of this significance lacks meaning if there is no recognition, however brief, that human achievements cannot be understood apart from their spiritual essence. We think the Government's position that this interest suffices to force students to choose between compliance or forfeiture demonstrates fundamental inconsistency in its argumentation. It fails to acknowledge that what for many of Deborah's classmates and their parents was a spiritual imperative was for Daniel and Deborah Weisman religious conformance compelled by the State. While in some societies the wishes of the majority might prevail, the Establishment Clause of the First Amendment is addressed to this contingency and rejects the balance urged upon us. The Constitution forbids the State to exact religious conformity from a student as the price of attending her own high school graduation. This is the calculus the Constitution commands.

Inherent differences between the public school system and a session of a state legislature distinguish this case from *Marsh v. Chambers*. The atmosphere at the opening of a session of a state legislature where adults are free to enter and leave with little comment and for any number of reasons cannot compare with the constraining potential of the one school event most important for the student to attend. The influence and force of a formal exercise in a school graduation are far greater than the prayer exercise we condoned in *Marsh*. At a high school graduation, teachers and principals must and do retain a high degree of control over the precise contents of the program, the speeches, the timing, the movements, the dress, and the decorum of the students. In this atmosphere the state-imposed character of an invocation and benediction by clergy selected by the school combine to make the prayer a state-sanctioned religious exercise in which the student was left with no alternative but to submit. This is different from *Marsh* and suffices to make the religious exercise a First Amendment violation.

We do not hold that every state action implicating religion is invalid if one or a few citizens find it offensive. People may take offense at all manner of religious as well as nonreligious messages, but offense alone does not in every case show a violation. We know too that sometimes to endure social isolation or even anger may be the price of conscience or nonconformity. But, the conformity required of the student in this case was too high an exaction to withstand the test of the Establishment Clause. The prayer exercises in this case are especially improper because the State has in every practical sense compelled attendance and participation in an explicit religious exercise at an event of singular importance to every student, one the objecting student had no real alternative to avoid.

JUSTICE BLACKMUN, with whom JUSTICE STEVENS and JUSTICE O'CONNOR join, concurring. [Opinion omitted.]

JUSTICE SOUTER, with whom JUSTICE STEVENS and JUSTICE O'CONNOR join, concurring. [Opinion omitted.]

JUSTICE SCALIA, with whom THE CHIEF JUSTICE, JUSTICE WHITE, and JUSTICE THOMAS join, dissenting.

In holding that the Establishment Clause prohibits invocations and benedictions at public-school graduation ceremonies, the Court lays waste a tradition that is as old as public-school graduation ceremonies themselves, and that is a component of an even more longstanding American tradition of nonsectarian prayer to God at public celebrations generally. As its instrument of destruction, the bulldozer of its social engineering, the Court invents a boundless, and boundlessly manipulable, test of psychological coercion. Today's opinion shows more forcefully than volumes of argumentation why our Nation's protection, that fortress which is our Constitution, cannot possibly rest upon the changeable philosophical predilections of the Justices of this Court, but must have deep foundations in the historic practices of our people.

I

Justice Holmes' aphorism that "a page of history is worth a volume of logic" applies with particular force to our Establishment Clause jurisprudence. As we have recognized, our interpretation of the Establishment Clause should "compor[t] with what history reveals was the contemporaneous understanding of its guarantees." The history and tradition of our Nation are replete with public ceremonies featuring prayers of thanksgiving and petition. Illustrations of this point have been amply provided in our prior opinions, but since the Court is so oblivious to our history as to suggest that the Constitution restricts "preservation and transmission of religious beliefs ... to the private sphere," it appears necessary to provide another brief account.

[Justice Scalia then recounted some of the history of prayers at government ceremonies, including religious references in the Declaration of Independence, President Washington's inaugural address, the inaugural addresses of Presidents Jefferson, Madison, and Bush, Thanksgiving Proclamations, prayers at the start of congressional sessions, and invocations before court sessions. — ed.]

In addition to this general tradition of prayer at public ceremonies, there exists a more specific tradition of invocations and benedictions at public school graduation exercises. By one account, the first public high school graduation ceremony took place in Connecticut in July 1868 — the very month, as it happens, that the Fourteenth Amendment was ratified — when "15 seniors from the Norwich Free Academy marched in their best Sunday suits and dresses into a church hall and waited through majestic music and long prayers." [T]he invocation and benediction have long been recognized to be "as traditional as any other parts of the [school] graduation program and are widely established."

II

The Court presumably would separate graduation invocations and benedictions from other instances of public "preservation and transmission of religious beliefs" on the ground that they involve "psychological coercion." I find it a sufficient embarrassment that our Establishment Clause jurisprudence regarding holiday displays has come to "requir[e] scrutiny more commonly associated with interior decorators than with the judiciary." But interior decorating is a rock-hard science compared to psychology practiced by amateurs. A few citations of "[r]esearch in psychology" that have no particular bearing upon the precise issue here cannot disguise the fact that the Court has gone beyond the realm where judges know what they are doing. The Court's argument that state officials have "coerced" students to take part in the invocation and benediction at graduation ceremonies is, not to put too fine a point on it, incoherent....

A

The Court declares that students' "attendance and participation in the [invocation and benediction] are in a fair and real sense obligatory." But what exactly is this "fair and real sense"? According to the Court, students at graduation who want "to avoid the fact or appearance of participation" in the invocation and benediction are *psychologically* obligated by "public pressure, as well as peer pressure, ... to stand as a group or, at least, maintain respectful silence" during those prayers. This assertion— *the very linchpin of the Court's opinion*—is almost as intriguing for what it does not say as for what it says. It does not say, for example, that students are psychologically coerced to bow their heads, place their hands in a Dürer-like prayer position, pay attention to the prayers, utter "Amen," or in fact pray. (Perhaps further intensive psychological research remains to be done on these matters.) It claims only that students are psychologically coerced "to stand ... *or*, at least, maintain respectful silence." (emphasis added). Both halves of this disjunctive merit particular attention.

To begin with the latter: The Court's notion that a student who simply *sits* in "respectful silence" during the invocation and benediction (when all others are standing) has somehow joined—or would somehow be perceived as having joined—in the prayers is nothing short of ludicrous. We indeed live in a vulgar age. But surely "our social conventions," have not coarsened to the point that anyone who does not stand on his chair and shout obscenities can reasonably be deemed to have assented to everything said in his presence. Since the Court does not dispute that students exposed to prayer at graduation ceremonies retain the free will to sit, there is absolutely no basis for the Court's decision. It is fanciful enough to say that "a reasonable dissenter," standing head erect in a class of bowed heads, "could believe that the group exercise signified her own participation or approval of it[.]" It is beyond the absurd to say that she could entertain such a belief while pointedly declining to rise.

But let us assume the very worst, that the nonparticipating graduate is "subtly coerced" ... to stand! Even that half of the disjunctive does not remotely establish a "participation" in a religious exercise. The Court acknowledges that "in our culture standing ... can signify adherence to a view or simple respect for the views of others." But if it is a permissible inference that one who is standing is doing so simply out of respect for the prayers of others that are in progress, then how can it possibly be said that a "reasonable dissenter ... could believe that the group exercise signified her own participation or approval"? Quite obviously, it cannot. I may add, moreover, that maintaining respect for the religious observances of others is a fundamental civic virtue that government can and should cultivate.

The opinion manifests that the Court itself has not given careful consideration to its test of psychological coercion. For if it had, how could it observe, with no hint of concern or disapproval, that students stood for the Pledge of Allegiance, which immediately preceded Rabbi Gutterman's invocation? The government can, of course, no more coerce political orthodoxy than religious orthodoxy. If students were psychologically coerced to remain standing during the invocation, they must also have been psychologically coerced, moments before, to stand for (and thereby, in the Court's view, take part in or appear to take part in) the Pledge. Must the Pledge therefore be barred from the public schools (both from graduation ceremonies and from the classroom)? In *Barnette*, we held that a public school student could not be compelled to *recite* the Pledge; we did not even hint that she could not be compelled to observe respectful silence—indeed, even to *stand* in respectful silence—when those who wished to recite it did so. Logically, that ought to be the next project for the Court's bulldozer.

I also find it odd that the Court concludes that high school graduates may not be subjected to this supposed psychological coercion. I had thought that the reason graduation from high school is regarded as so significant an event is that it is generally associated with transition from adolescence to young adulthood. Many graduating seniors, of course, are old enough to vote. Why, then, does the Court treat them as though they were first-graders? Will we soon have a jurisprudence that distinguishes between mature and immature adults?

B

The other "dominant fac[t]" identified by the Court is that "[s]tate officials direct the performance of a formal religious exercise" at school graduation ceremonies. "Direct[ing] the performance of a formal religious exercise" has a sound of liturgy to it, summoning up images of the principal directing acolytes where to carry the cross, or showing the rabbi where to unroll the Torah. All the record shows is that principals of the Providence public schools have invited clergy to deliver invocations and benedictions at graduations; and that Principal Lee invited Rabbi Gutterman, provided him a two-page pamphlet, prepared by the National Conference of Christians and Jews, giving general advice on inclusive prayer for civic occasions, and advised him that his prayers at graduation should be nonsectarian. How these facts can fairly be transformed into the charges that Principal Lee "directed and controlled the content of [Rabbi Gutterman's] prayer," that school officials "monitor prayer," and attempted to "'compose official prayers,'" and that the "government involvement with religious activity in this case is pervasive," is difficult to fathom. The Court identifies nothing in the record remotely suggesting that school officials have ever drafted, edited, screened, or censored graduation prayers, or that Rabbi Gutterman was a mouthpiece of the school officials.

III

The deeper flaw in the Court's opinion lies in the Court's making violation of the Establishment Clause hinge on such a precious question. The coercion that was a hallmark of historical establishments of religion was coercion of religious orthodoxy and of financial support *by force of law and threat of penalty*. Typically, attendance at the state church was required; only clergy of the official church could lawfully perform sacraments; and dissenters, if tolerated, faced an array of civil disabilities. Thus, for example, in the Colony of Virginia, where the Church of England had been established, ministers were required by law to conform to the doctrine and rites of the Church of England; and all persons were required to attend church and observe the Sabbath, were tithed for the public support of Anglican ministers, and were taxed for the costs of building and repairing churches.

The Establishment Clause was adopted to prohibit such an establishment of religion at the federal level (and to protect state establishments of religion from federal interference). I will further acknowledge for the sake of argument that, as some scholars have argued, by 1790 the term "establishment" had acquired an additional meaning—"financial support of religion generally, by public taxation"—that reflected the development of "general or multiple" establishments, not limited to a single church. But that would still be an establishment coerced *by force of law*. And I will further concede that our constitutional tradition, from the Declaration of Independence and the first inaugural address of Washington, quoted earlier, down to the present day, has, with a few aberrations, ruled out of order government-sponsored endorsement of religion—even when no legal coercion is present, and indeed even when no ersatz, "peer-pressure" psycho-coercion is present—where the endorsement is sectarian, in the sense of specifying details upon which men and women who believe in a benevolent, omnipotent Creator and Ruler of the world are known to differ (for example, the divinity of Christ). But there is simply no support for the proposition that the officially sponsored nondenominational invocation and benediction read by Rabbi Gutterman—with no one legally coerced to recite them—violated the Constitution of the United States. To the contrary, they are so characteristically American they could have come from the pen of George Washington or Abraham Lincoln himself.

Thus, while I have no quarrel with the Court's general proposition that the Establishment Clause "guarantees that government may not coerce anyone to support or participate in religion or its exercise," I see no warrant for expanding the concept of coercion beyond acts backed by threat of penalty—a brand of coercion that, happily, is readily discernible to those of us who have made a career of reading the disciples of Blackstone rather than of Freud. The Framers were indeed opposed to coercion of religious worship by the National Government; but, as their own sponsorship of nonsectarian prayer in public events demonstrates, they understood that "[s]peech is not coercive; the listener may do as he likes."

The Court relies on our "school prayer" cases, *Engel v. Vitale*, 370 U.S. 421 (1962), and *School Dist. of Abington v. Schempp*, 374 U.S. 203 (1963). But whatever the merit of those cases, they do not support, much less compel, the Court's psycho-journey. [W]e have made clear our understanding that school prayer occurs within a framework in which legal coercion to attend school (*i.e.*, coercion under threat of penalty) provides the ultimate backdrop.

* * *

The reader has been told much in this case about the personal interest of Mr. Weisman and his daughter, and very little about the personal interests on the other side. They are not inconsequential. Church and state would not be such a difficult subject if religion were, as the Court apparently thinks it to be, some purely personal avocation that can be indulged entirely in secret, like pornography, in the privacy of one's room. For most believers it is *not* that, and has never been. Religious men and women of almost all denominations have felt it necessary to acknowledge and beseech the blessing of God as a people, and not just as individuals, because they believe in the "protection of divine Providence," as the Declaration of Independence put it, not just for individuals but for societies; because they believe God to be, as Washington's first Thanksgiving Proclamation put it, the "Great Lord and Ruler of Nations." One can believe in the effectiveness of such public worship, or one can deprecate and deride it. But the longstanding American tradition of prayer at official ceremonies displays with unmistakable clarity that the Establishment Clause does not forbid the government to accommodate it.

I must add one final observation: The Founders of our Republic knew the fearsome potential of sectarian religious belief to generate civil dissension and civil strife. And they also knew that nothing, absolutely nothing, is so inclined to foster among religious believers of various faiths a toleration—no, an affection—for one another than voluntarily joining in prayer together, to the God whom they all worship and seek. Needless to say, no one should be compelled to do that, but it is a shame to deprive our public culture of the opportunity, and indeed the encouragement, for people to do it voluntarily. The Baptist or Catholic who heard and joined in the simple and inspiring prayers of Rabbi Gutterman on this official and patriotic occasion was inoculated from religious bigotry and prejudice in a manner that cannot be replicated. To deprive our society of that important unifying mechanism, in order to spare the nonbeliever what seems to me the minimal inconvenience of standing or even sitting in respectful nonparticipation, is as senseless in policy as it is unsupported in law.

Exercise 12:

1. What are the two versions of the Coercion Test offered by the various justices?

2. Why did the justices, who had initially agreed on the Coercion Test in *Allegheny County*, divide?

3. Review Justice Kennedy's opinion in *Allegheny County*, where he argued that no one was coerced by the challenged holiday displays. Which version is more faithful to the Test as first articulated by Justice Kennedy in *Allegheny County*? Which is more faithful to the Court's precedent generally? To the Clause's original meaning?

4. Are you persuaded by Justice Kennedy that Deborah Weisman was coerced into praying? Or are you persuaded by the dissent's argument that, even under Justice Kennedy's version of the Test, no coercion occurred?

5. What evidence did Justice Kennedy offer to support his conclusion? What evidence would be sufficient to support that claim? How did or would Justice Kennedy garner such evidence?

6. Justice Kennedy emphasized the potential for divisiveness caused by the school district's practice. What role did this claim play in Justice Kennedy's analysis?

7. What evidence did Justice Kennedy offer to support that claim? What evidence would be sufficient to support that claim? How did or would Justice Kennedy garner such evidence?

8. Justice Kennedy also emphasized that one of the purposes of the Establishment Clause was to protect religion from corruption by the government. How, if at all, is that purpose served in this case by the Court's ruling?

9. If you believe that Justice Scalia's version of the Coercion Test is better than Justice Kennedy's, then where do you draw the line? What counts as coercion sufficient to violate the Test? Is drawing the line there consistent with precedent? Original meaning?

10. Justice Scalia here, as in other Establishment Clause contexts generally—and in other contexts, such as substantive due process, for that matter—put significant weight on the widespread and deeply entrenched practice of public prayer and thanksgiving. What role does this tradition play in Justice Scalia's analysis? Does he put too much weight on tradition?

11. Is Justice Scalia right that Justice Kennedy's version of the Coercion Test is manipulable and that it is unsuited to the skills and knowledge of federal judges? If so, what follows?

12. Justice Scalia called for the final interment of the Lemon Test. What arguments did he make in favor of this move by the Court? Are you persuaded? Did *American Legion* do that in all Establishment Clause cases or only in the context of longstanding religion monuments, symbols, and practices?

13. Justice Scalia argued that a cause of the tension between the Supreme Court's relatively-strict separationist jurisprudence and the relatively accommodationist practices of the American people is that Supreme Court justices fail to understand that religion is both an individual and communal belief system. Therefore, rulings like those in *Lee*, based on a misunderstanding of religion, perpetuate this tension. Is Justice Scalia correct that religion is (nearly) always a communal activity? Is he right that cases like *Lee* cause a tension?

14. Justice Scalia proposed, at the end of his dissent, that public prayers—like the ones that *Lee* struck down—actually *limit* religious divisiveness, contrary the claim of others like Justice Breyer. Is he correct? If so, what, if anything, follows?

———————

Following *Lee*, the Coercion Test garnered a majority in *Santa Fe Indep. Sch. Dist. v. Doe*, 530 U.S. 290 (2000), where the Supreme Court faced a challenge to a school district policy allowing the school's students to vote whether an invocation would be delivered at football games and providing for a second election to determine which student would deliver the invocation. The Court, through Justice Stevens, concluded that, as in *Lee*, students were coerced to attend and participate in the prayers. *Id.* at 311–13. Furthermore, the existence or lack of coercion—broadly or narrowly understood—is a factor in other later cases' analyses. For instance, in *Good News Club v. Milford Central Sch.*, 533 U.S. 98, 115–16 (2001), the Court held that neither students nor their parents were coerced to participate in an after-school Bible club.

5. History and Tradition Test

The most accommodationist test the Supreme Court has articulated is the History and Tradition Test. It is a minimal check on church-state interaction because its standard is the body of past church-state interactions, which have been fairly robust. Therefore, under the History and Tradition Test, only novel church-state interactions are suspect. However, even when analyzing novel situations, one can analogize the new church-state interaction to an extant tradition, arguing that the current interaction should be subsumed under the pre-existing tradition.

The first post-*Lemon* case articulating the History and Tradition Test was *Marsh v. Chambers*, 463 U.S. 783 (1983), which upheld the Nebraska Legislature's practice of opening legislative sessions with a prayer that a state-paid chaplain delivered. *Marsh* marked a significant development in the Court's Establishment Clause jurisprudence for at least two reasons. First, the majority did not mention, let alone apply, *Lemon* or the endorsement test. Second, the Court invoked the longstanding American practice of beginning legislative sessions with prayer: "In light of the unambiguous and unbroken history of more than 200 years, there can be no doubt that the practice of opening legislative sessions with prayer has become part of the fabric of our society. To invoke Divine guidance on a public body entrusted with making the laws is not, in these circumstances, an 'establishment' of religion or a step toward establishment; it is simply a tolerable acknowledgment of beliefs widely held among the people of this country." *Id.* at 792. According to the Court, "historical evidence sheds light not only on what the draftsmen intended the Establishment Clause to mean, but also on how they thought that Clause applied to the practice authorized by the First Congress.... An act 'passed by the first Congress assembled under the Constitution, many of whose members had taken part in framing that instrument, ... is contemporaneous and weighty evidence of its true meaning.'" *Id.* at 790. Moreover, drawing on the nation's historical practice, *Marsh* indicated that courts generally should not consider the specific wording of such prayers: "The content of the prayer is not of concern to judges where, as here, there is no indication that the prayer opportunity has been exploited to proselytize or advance any one, or to disparage any other, faith or belief. That being so, it is not for us to embark on a sensitive evaluation or to parse the content of a particular prayer." *Id.* at 794–95.

In *Van Orden v. Perry*, 545 U.S. 677 (2005), reviewed earlier, a plurality of the Court invoked the same History and Tradition Test to explain why the Ten Commandments monument on the grounds of the Texas State Capitol was constitutional. *Id.* at 686 (explaining that "our analysis is driven both by the nature of the monument and by our Nation's history"). Most recently, in the following case, a majority of the Court once again applied the History and Tradition Test in the context of legislative prayer—this time prayer at the start of board meetings in the Town of Greece, New York. As you read through this opinion, consider (1) how the prayers in *Marsh* and *Town of Greece* are similar and how they differ, and (2) whether America's history of legislative prayer supports either or both of the prayer practices in these cases.

Town of Greece, New York v. Galloway

572 U.S. 565 (2014)

Justice Kennedy delivered the opinion of the Court, except as to Part II-B[, which Justice Scalia and Justice Thomas did not join—eds.].

I

Greece, a town with a population of 94,000, is in upstate New York. For some years, it began its monthly town board meetings with a moment of silence. In 1999, the newly elected town supervisor, John Auberger, decided to replicate the prayer practice he had found meaningful while serving in the county legislature. Following the roll call and recitation of the Pledge of Allegiance, Auberger would invite a local clergyman to the front of the room to deliver an invocation. After the prayer, Auberger would thank the minister for serving as the board's "chaplain for the month" and present him with a commemorative plaque. The prayer was intended to place town board members in a solemn and deliberative frame of mind, invoke divine guidance in town affairs, and follow a tradition practiced by Congress and dozens of state legislatures.

The town followed an informal method for selecting prayer givers, all of whom were unpaid volunteers. A town employee would call the congregations listed in a local directory until she found a minister available for that month's meeting. The town eventually compiled a list of willing "board chaplains" who had accepted invitations and agreed to return in the future. The town at no point excluded or denied an opportunity to a would-be prayer giver. Its leaders maintained that a minister or layperson of any persuasion, including an atheist, could give the invocation. But nearly all of the congregations in town were Christian; and from 1999 to 2007, all of the participating ministers were too.

Greece neither reviewed the prayers in advance of the meetings nor provided guidance as to their tone or content, in the belief that exercising any degree of control over the prayers would infringe both the free exercise and speech rights of the ministers. The town instead left the guest clergy free to compose their own devotions. The resulting prayers often sounded both civic and religious themes. Typical were invocations that asked the divinity to abide at the meeting and bestow blessings on the community.

Some of the ministers spoke in a distinctly Christian idiom; and a minority invoked religious holidays, scripture, or doctrine, [which in one prayer included:] "We acknowledge the saving sacrifice of Jesus Christ on the cross. We draw strength, vitality, and confidence from his resurrection at Easter...."

Respondents Susan Galloway and Linda Stephens attended town board meetings to speak about issues of local concern, and they objected that the prayers violated their religious or philosophical views. At one meeting, Galloway admonished board members that she found the prayers "offensive," "intolerable," and an affront to a "diverse community." After respondents complained that Christian themes pervaded the prayers, to the exclusion of citizens who did not share those beliefs, the town invited a Jewish layman and the chairman of the local Baha'i temple to deliver prayers. A Wiccan priestess who had read press reports about the prayer controversy requested, and was granted, an opportunity to give the invocation.

Galloway and Stephens brought suit alleg[ing] that the town violated the First Amendment's Establishment Clause by preferring Christians over other prayer givers and by sponsoring sectarian prayers, such as those given "in Jesus' name." They did not seek an end to the prayer practice, but rather requested an injunction that would limit the town to "inclusive and ecumenical" prayers that referred only to a "generic God" and would not associate the government with any one faith or belief.

II

In *Marsh v. Chambers*, 463 U.S. 783 [1983], the Court found no First Amendment violation in the Nebraska Legislature's practice of opening its sessions with a prayer delivered by a chaplain paid from state funds. The decision concluded that legislative prayer, while religious in nature, has long been understood as compatible with the Establishment Clause. As practiced by Congress since the framing of the Constitution, legislative prayer lends gravity to public business, reminds lawmakers to transcend petty differences in pursuit of a higher purpose, and expresses a common aspiration to a just and peaceful society. The Court has considered this symbolic expression to be a "tolerable acknowledgement of beliefs widely held," rather than a first, treacherous step towards establishment of a state church.

Marsh is sometimes described as "carving out an exception" to the Court's Establishment Clause jurisprudence, because it sustained legislative prayer without subjecting the practice to "any of the formal 'tests' that have traditionally structured" this inquiry. The Court in *Marsh* found those tests unnecessary because history supported the conclusion that legislative invocations are compatible with the Establishment Clause.

Yet *Marsh* must not be understood as permitting a practice that would amount to a constitutional violation if not for its historical foundation. The case teaches instead that the Establishment Clause must be interpreted "by reference to historical practices and understandings." That the First Congress provided for the appointment of chaplains only days after approving language for the First Amendment demonstrates that the Framers considered legislative prayer a benign acknowledgment of religion's role in society. In the 1850's, the judiciary committees in both the House and Senate reevaluated the practice of official chaplaincies after receiving petitions to abolish the office. The committees concluded that the office posed no threat of an establishment because lawmakers were not compelled to attend the daily prayer; no faith was excluded by law, nor any favored; and the cost of the chaplain's salary imposed a vanishingly small burden on taxpayers. *Marsh* stands for the proposition that it is not necessary to define the precise boundary of the Establishment Clause where history shows that the specific practice is permitted. Any test the Court adopts must acknowledge a practice that was accepted by the Framers and has withstood the critical scrutiny of time and political change. A test that would sweep away what has so long been settled would create new controversy and begin anew the very divisions along religious lines that the Establishment Clause seeks to prevent.

The Court's inquiry, then, must be to determine whether the prayer practice in the town of Greece fits within the tradition long followed in Congress and the state legislatures.

A

Respondents maintain that prayer must be nonsectarian, or not identifiable with any one religion; and they fault the town for permitting guest chaplains to deliver prayers that "use overtly Christian terms" or "invoke specifics of Christian theology."

An insistence on nonsectarian or ecumenical prayer as a single, fixed standard is not consistent with the tradition of legislative prayer outlined in the Court's cases. The Court found the prayers in *Marsh* consistent with the First Amendment not because they espoused only a generic theism but because our history and tradition have shown that prayer in this limited context could "coexis[t] with the principles of disestablishment and religious freedom." The Congress that drafted the First Amendment would have been accustomed to invocations containing explicitly religious themes of the sort respondents find objectionable. One of the Senate's first chaplains, the Rev. William White, gave prayers in a series that included the Lord's Prayer, the Collect for Ash Wednesday, prayers for peace and grace, a general thanksgiving, St. Chrysostom's Prayer, and a prayer seeking "the grace of our Lord Jesus Christ, &c." The decidedly Christian nature of these prayers must not be dismissed as the relic of a time when our Nation was less pluralistic than it is today. Congress continues to permit its appointed and visiting chaplains to express themselves in a religious idiom. It acknowledges our growing diversity not by proscribing sectarian content but by welcoming ministers of many creeds.

To hold that invocations must be nonsectarian would force the legislatures that sponsor prayers and the courts that are asked to decide these cases to act as supervisors and censors of religious speech, a rule that would involve government in religious matters to a far greater degree than is the case under the town's current practice of neither editing or approving prayers in advance nor criticizing their content after the fact. Our Government is prohibited from prescribing prayers to be recited in our public institutions in order to promote a preferred system of belief or code of moral behavior. It would be but a few steps removed from that prohibition for legislatures to require chaplains to redact the religious content from their message in order to make it acceptable for the public sphere. Government may not mandate a civic religion that stifles any but the most generic reference to the sacred any more than it may prescribe a religious orthodoxy.

Respondents argue, in effect, that legislative prayer may be addressed only to a generic God. There is doubt, in any event, that consensus might be reached as to what qualifies as generic or nonsectarian. Honorifics like "Lord of Lords" or "King of Kings" might strike a Christian audience as ecumenical, yet these titles may have no place in the vocabulary of other faith traditions. The difficulty, indeed the futility, of sifting sectarian from nonsectarian speech is illustrated by a letter that a lawyer for the respondents sent the town in the early stages of this litigation. The letter opined that references to "Father, God, Lord God, and the Almighty" would be acceptable in public prayer, but that references to "Jesus Christ, the Holy Spirit, and the Holy Trinity" would not. Perhaps the writer believed the former grouping would be acceptable to monotheists. Yet even seemingly general references to God or the Father might alienate nonbelievers or polytheists.

In rejecting the suggestion that legislative prayer must be nonsectarian, the Court does not imply that no constraints remain on its content. The tradition reflected in *Marsh* permits chaplains to ask their own God for blessings of peace, justice, and freedom that find appreciation among people of all faiths. That a prayer is given in the name of Jesus, Allah, or Jehovah, or that it makes passing reference to religious doctrines, does not remove it from that tradition. These religious themes provide particular means to universal ends. Prayer that reflects beliefs specific to only some creeds can still serve to solemnize the occasion, so long as the practice over time is not "exploited to proselytize or advance any one, or to disparage any other, faith or belief."

From the earliest days of the Nation, these invocations have been addressed to assemblies comprising many different creeds. These ceremonial prayers strive for the idea that people of many faiths may be united in a community of tolerance and devotion. Even those who disagree as to religious doctrine may find common ground in the desire to show respect for the divine in all aspects of their lives and being. Our tradition assumes that adult citizens, firm in their own beliefs, can tolerate and perhaps appreciate a ceremonial prayer delivered by a person of a different faith.

The prayers delivered in the town of Greece do not fall outside the tradition this Court has recognized. A number of the prayers did invoke the name of Jesus, the Heavenly Father, or the Holy Spirit, but they also invoked universal themes, as by celebrating the changing of the seasons or calling for a "spirit of cooperation" among town leaders.

Respondents point to other invocations that disparaged those who did not accept the town's prayer practice. One guest minister characterized objectors as a "minority" who are "ignorant of the history of our country," while another lamented that other towns did not have "God-fearing" leaders. Although these two remarks strayed from the rationale set out in *Marsh*, they do not despoil a practice that on the whole reflects and embraces our tradition. Absent a pattern of prayers that over time denigrate, proselytize, or betray an impermissible government purpose, a challenge based solely on the content of a prayer will not likely establish a constitutional violation. *Marsh*, indeed, requires an inquiry into the prayer opportunity as a whole, rather than into the contents of a single prayer.

Finally, the Court disagrees with the view taken by the Court of Appeals that the town of Greece contravened the Establishment Clause by inviting a predominantly Christian set of ministers to lead the prayer. The town made reasonable efforts to identify all of the congregations located within its borders and represented that it would welcome a prayer by any minister or layman who wished to give one. That nearly all of the congregations in town turned out to be Christian does not reflect an aversion or bias on the part of town leaders against minority faiths. So long as the town maintains a policy of nondiscrimination, the Constitution does not require it to search beyond its borders for non-Christian prayer givers in an effort to achieve religious balancing.

B

Respondents further seek to distinguish the town's prayer practice from the tradition upheld in *Marsh* on the ground that it coerces participation by nonadherents. They and some *amici* contend that prayer conducted in the intimate setting of a town board meeting differs in fundamental ways from the invocations delivered in Congress and state legislatures, where the public remains segregated from legislative activity and may not address the body except by occasional invitation. Citizens attend town meetings, on the other hand, to accept awards; speak on matters of local importance; and petition the board for action that may affect their economic interests, such as the granting of permits, business licenses, and zoning variances. Respondents argue that the public may feel subtle pressure to participate in prayers that violate their beliefs in order to please the board members from whom they are about to seek a favorable ruling. In their view the fact that board members in small towns know many of their constituents by name only increases the pressure to conform.

It is an elemental First Amendment principle that government may not coerce its citizens "to support or participate in any religion or its exercise." On the record in this case the Court is not persuaded that the town of Greece, through the act of offering a brief, solemn, and respectful prayer to open its monthly meetings, compelled its citizens to engage in a religious observance. The inquiry remains a fact-sensitive one that considers both the setting in which the prayer arises and the audience to whom it is directed.

The prayer opportunity in this case must be evaluated against the backdrop of historical practice. As a practice that has long endured, legislative prayer has become part of our heritage and tradition, part of our expressive idiom, similar to the Pledge of Allegiance, inaugural prayer, or the recitation of "God save the United States and this honorable Court" at the opening of this Court's sessions. It is presumed that the reasonable observer is acquainted with this tradition and understands that its purposes are to lend gravity to public proceedings and to acknowledge the place religion holds in the lives of many private citizens, not to afford government an opportunity to proselytize or force truant constituents into the pews. That many appreciate these acknowledgments of the divine in our public institutions does not suggest that those who disagree are compelled to join the expression or approve its content.

The principal audience for these invocations is not, indeed, the public but lawmakers themselves, who may find that a moment of prayer or quiet reflection sets the mind to a higher purpose and thereby eases the task of governing. The District Court in *Marsh* described the prayer exercise as "an internal act" directed at the Nebraska Legislature's "own members," rather than an effort to promote religious observance among the public. To be sure, many members of the public find these prayers meaningful and wish to join them. But their purpose is largely to accommodate the spiritual needs of lawmakers and connect them to a tradition dating to the time of the Framers. For members of town boards and commissions, who often serve part-time and as volunteers, ceremonial prayer may also reflect the values they hold as private citizens. The prayer is an opportunity for them to show who and what they are without denying the right to dissent by those who disagree.

The analysis would be different if town board members directed the public to participate in the prayers, singled out dissidents for opprobrium, or indicated that their decisions might be influenced by a person's acquiescence in the prayer opportunity. No such thing occurred in the town of Greece. Although board members themselves stood, bowed their heads, or made the sign of the cross during the prayer, they at no point solicited similar gestures by the public. Respondents suggest that constituents might feel pressure to join the prayers to avoid irritating the officials who would be ruling on their petitions, but this argument has no evidentiary support. Nothing in the record indicates that town leaders allocated benefits and burdens based on participation in the prayer, or that citizens were received differently depending on whether they joined the invocation or quietly declined. In no instance did town leaders signal disfavor toward nonparticipants or suggest that their stature in the community was in any way diminished. A practice that classified citizens based on their religious views would violate the Constitution, but that is not the case before this Court.

In their declarations in the trial court, respondents stated that the prayers gave them offense and made them feel excluded and disrespected. Offense, however, does not equate to coercion. Adults often encounter speech they find disagreeable; and an Establishment Clause violation is not made out any time a person experiences a sense of affront from the expression of contrary religious views in a legislative forum, especially where, as here, any member of the public is welcome in turn to offer an invocation reflecting his or her own convictions. If circumstances arise in which the pattern and practice of ceremonial, legislative prayer is alleged to be a means to coerce or intimidate others, the objection can be addressed in the regular course.

This case can be distinguished from the conclusions and holding of *Lee v. Weisman*, 505 U.S. 577 [1992]. There the Court found that, in the context of a graduation where school authorities maintained close supervision over the conduct of the students and the substance of the ceremony, a religious invocation was coercive as to an objecting student. [B]ut the circumstances the Court confronted there are not present in this case and do not control its outcome. Nothing in the record suggests that members of the public are dissuaded from leaving the meeting room during the prayer, arriving late, or even, as happened here, making a later protest. In this case, as in *Marsh*, board members and constituents are "free to enter and leave with little comment and for any number of reasons." Should nonbelievers choose to exit the room during a prayer they find distasteful, their absence will not stand out as disrespectful or even noteworthy. And should they remain, their quiet acquiescence will not, in light of our traditions, be interpreted as an agreement with the words or ideas expressed. Neither choice represents an unconstitutional imposition as to mature adults, who "presumably" are "not readily susceptible to religious indoctrination or peer pressure."

JUSTICE ALITO, with whom JUSTICE SCALIA joins, concurring.

[A]ny argument that nonsectarian prayer is constitutionally required runs headlong into a long history of contrary congressional practice. Not only is there no historical support for the proposition that only generic prayer is allowed, but as our country has become more diverse, composing a prayer that is acceptable to all members of the community who hold religious beliefs has become harder and harder. It was one thing to compose a prayer that is acceptable to both Christians and Jews; it is much harder to compose a prayer that is also acceptable to followers of Eastern religions that are now well represented in this country. Many local clergy may find the project daunting, if not impossible, and some may feel that they cannot in good faith deliver such a vague prayer.

In addition, if a town attempts to go beyond simply *recommending* that a guest chaplain deliver a prayer that is broadly acceptable to all members of a particular community (and the groups represented in different communities will vary), the town will inevitably encounter sensitive problems. Must a town screen and, if necessary, edit prayers before they are given? If prescreening is not required, must the town review prayers after they are delivered in order to determine if they were sufficiently generic? And if a guest chaplain crosses the line, what must the town do? Must the chaplain be corrected on the spot? Must the town strike this chaplain (and perhaps his or her house of worship) from the approved list?

JUSTICE THOMAS, with whom JUSTICE SCALIA joins as to Part II, concurring in part and concurring in the judgment.

II

[T]he municipal prayers at issue in this case bear no resemblance to the coercive state establishments that existed at the founding. "The coercion that was a hallmark of historical establishments of religion was coercion of religious orthodoxy and of financial support *by force of law and threat of penalty.*" In a typical case, attendance at the established church was mandatory, and taxes were levied to generate church revenue. Dissenting ministers were barred from preaching, and political participation was limited to members of the established church.

None of these founding-era state establishments remained at the time of Reconstruction. But even assuming that the framers of the Fourteenth Amendment reconceived the nature of the Establishment Clause as a constraint on the States, nothing in the history of the intervening period suggests a fundamental transformation in their understanding of *what constituted an establishment.* At a minimum, there is no support for the proposition that the framers of the Fourteenth Amendment embraced wholly modern notions that the Establishment Clause is violated whenever the "reasonable observer" feels "subtle pressure" or perceives governmental "endors[ement]." For example, of the 37 States in existence when the Fourteenth Amendment was ratified, 27 State Constitutions "contained an explicit reference to God in their preambles." In addition to the preamble references, 30 State Constitutions contained other references to the divine. These provisions strongly suggest that, whatever nonestablishment principles existed in 1868, they included no concern for the finer sensibilities of the "reasonable observer."

Thus, to the extent coercion is relevant to the Establishment Clause analysis, it is actual legal coercion that counts — not the "subtle coercive pressures" allegedly felt by respondents in this case.

JUSTICE BREYER, dissenting.

As both the Court and Justice Kagan point out, we are a Nation of many religions. And the Constitution's Religion Clauses seek to "protec[t] the Nation's social fabric from religious conflict." The question in this case is whether the prayer practice of the town of Greece, by doing too little to reflect the religious diversity of its citizens, did too much, even if unintentionally, to promote the "political division along religious lines" that "was one of the principal evils against which the First Amendment was intended to protect."

In seeking an answer to that fact-sensitive question, "I see no test-related substitute for the exercise of legal judgment." Having applied my legal judgment to the relevant facts, I conclude, like Justice Kagan, that the town of Greece failed to make reasonable efforts to include prayer givers of minority faiths, with the result that, although it is a community of several faiths, its prayer givers were almost exclusively persons of a single faith. Under these circumstances, Greece's prayer practice violated the Establishment Clause.

JUSTICE KAGAN, with whom JUSTICE GINSBURG, JUSTICE BREYER, and JUSTICE SOTOMAYOR join, dissenting.

I respectfully dissent from the Court's opinion because I think the Town of Greece's prayer practices violate th[e] norm of religious equality — the breathtakingly generous constitutional idea that our public institutions belong no less to the Buddhist or Hindu than to the Methodist or Episcopalian. I do not contend that principle translates here into a bright separationist line. To the contrary, I agree with the Court's decision in *Marsh v. Chambers*, upholding the Nebraska Legislature's tradition of beginning each session with a chaplain's prayer. And I believe that pluralism and inclusion in a town hall can satisfy the constitutional requirement of neutrality; such a forum need not become a religion-free zone. But still, the Town of Greece should lose this case. The practice at issue here differs from the one sustained in *Marsh* because Greece's town meetings involve participation by ordinary citizens, and the invocations given—directly to those citizens—were predominantly sectarian in content. Still more, Greece's Board did nothing to recognize religious diversity: In arranging for clergy members to open each meeting, the Town never sought (except briefly when this suit was filed) to involve, accommodate, or in any way reach out to adherents of non-Christian religions. So month in and month out for over a decade, prayers steeped in only one faith, addressed toward members of the public, commenced meetings to discuss local affairs and distribute government benefits. In my view, that practice does not square with the First Amendment's promise that every citizen, irrespective of her religion, owns an equal share in her government.

Exercise 13:

1. The majority in *Town of Greece* explains that *Marsh* did not "carv[e] out an exception" to the Establishment Clause; rather, *Marsh* taught that "the Establishment Clause must be interpreted 'by reference to historical practices and understandings.'" What is the History and Tradition Test?

2. From where did the Court draw the History and Tradition Test?

3. Is the History and Tradition Test consistent with the Court's other Establishment Clause tests? All of them? Some of them? How should the Court decide when to use the History and Tradition Test as opposed to one of its other Establishment Clause tests?

4. In *American Legion v. American Humanist Association*, 139 S. Ct. 2067, 2087 (2019), a majority of the Court rejected the application of the Lemon Test to "established, religiously expressive monuments, symbols, and practices." In his concurrence, Justice Gorsuch argued that *American Legion* sent lower courts the message that "[w]hether a monument, symbol, or practice is old or new, apply *Town of Greece*, not *Lemon*." Is Justice Gorsuch correct?

5. If the Court had applied the Lemon Test, what would have been the result?

6. At the beginning of this section, we read *County of Allegheny*, which was decided after *Marsh* and before *Town of Greece*. Are these three cases consistent?

7. Earlier, we also read *Lee*; is *Lee* consistent with *Town of Greece*?

8. One of the most frequent criticisms of the History and Tradition Test is that it permits too much church-state interaction. What limits are there to the History and Tradition Test? What interactions will it not permit?

9. On a scale of one to ten, with ten being the most accommodationist and one being the most separationist, where does the History and Tradition Test fall?

10. Is the History and Tradition Test faithful to the Establishment Clause's original meaning? Supreme Court precedent?

11. What factors or standards guide Justice Breyer's "exercise of legal judgment"? Is this a separate Establishment Clause test?

12. Justice Kagan, in dissent, contends that the majority and Justice Alito read the relevant history too broadly, that *Marsh* identified a narrower historical practice. Justice Alito disagrees, arguing that the Constitution requires neither nonsectarian prayers nor a "rotating system" of clergy from different faiths. Should the factual differences between *Marsh* and *Town of Greece* make a constitutional difference under the Establishment Clause? Does the majority (and Justice Alito) or Justice Kagan have the stronger argument on this point?

13. Justice Kagan's dissent contrasts the sectarian prayers in *Town of Greece* with the "[c]eremonial references to the divine [that] surely abound," such as "the Pledge of Allegiance, inaugural prayer, or the recitation of 'God save the United States and this honorable Court.'" In the wake of *Town of Greece* and *American Legion*, would the Court unanimously uphold such "ceremonial deism"? Should the Court use the History and Tradition Test? Would certain justices use one or more other tests? Which ones?

14. What is the status of Justice Breyer's "divisiveness" test, which he articulated in his concurrence in *Van Orden* and to which the majority and the principal dissent cite in *Town of Greece* (see 572 U.S. 565, 577 (2014); *id.* at 636)? Has a majority of the Court adopted that test? Or do different justices incorporate the underlying principles into other tests? How does the Divisiveness Test relate to the History and Tradition Test?

Following *Marsh*, the History and Tradition Test has influenced many of the justices' perspective on the Establishment Clause's meaning. This has happened in a couple of ways. First, many justices utilize traditional government-religion relationships as a standard by which to judge application of other Establishment Clause tests. We saw this earlier, when Justice Kennedy justified the Coercion Test in his *Allegheny County* dissent. He argued that the Coercion Test was better than the Endorsement Test because it respected the deeply entrenched and widespread American tradition of public displays of religion.

Second, some justices utilize tradition to evaluate results in a particular case. For instance, Chief Justice Burger spent many pages of the *United States Reports* in *Lynch* describing the tradition of public displays and recognition of religion.

The justice who most frequently relied on tradition to determine the bounds of the Establishment Clause was Justice Scalia. We saw him do so, for instance, in his *Lee* dissent. We earlier saw Justice Scalia's use of the History and Tradition Test in his *McCreary County v. ACLU*, 545 U.S. 844, 885 (2005) (Scalia, J., dissenting), dissent, where he catalogued the long tradition of public acknowledgments of religion. If Justice Gorsuch is correct in his *American Legion* concurrence, then lower courts and a majorty of the Supreme Court should use this test going forward when analyzing religious monuments, symbols, and practices.

E. The Relationship between Free Speech and Establishment: Religion's Proper Place in the Public Forum

In **Chapter 1**, you covered the Free Speech Clause. One area of free speech law involves speech in a public forum. In a series of cases stretching back to the 1980s, the Supreme Court faced the question of the extent to which religious speech is permitted within, or may be excluded from, public fora. One reason why this question arose was that some government officials argued—plausibly, given the Court's relatively strict-separationist precedents at the time—that they must exclude religious speech from the fora to avoid an Establishment Clause violation.

The typical factual scenario where this occurred was when religious groups sought to utilize a public school's facilities after hours for religious activities, such as a Bible study. The school, in this scenario, would prohibit the group from using its facilities for such religious purposes. Then, the religious group would sue claiming that the school's content discrimination against its religious speech violated the Free Speech Clause.

The seminal case, in this line, was *Widmar v. Vincent*, 454 U.S. 263 (1981). There, the University of Missouri-Kansas City prohibited a registered religious student group, Cornerstone, from utilizing University buildings. *Id.* at 265. Cornerstone meetings included religious activities such as "prayer, hymns, Bible commentary, and discussion of religious views and experiences." *Id.* at 265 n.2. The University relied on a regulation that prohibited use of University facilities "for purposes of religious worship or religious teaching." *Id.* at 265.

Relying on its public forum analysis, the Supreme Court ruled that the University had created a limited public forum and violated the Free Speech Clause by excluding Cornerstone from that forum. First, the Court found a limited public forum, because the University had opened its facilities to use by registered student groups. *Id.* at 267–74. Second, the Court held that the University's exclusion of religious groups, such as Cornerstone, was a content-based exclusion predicated on the groups' religious speech. *Id.*

Third, the *Widmar* Court held that that the University did not have a compelling state interest to justify its exclusion of Cornerstone's religious speech. *Id.* at 275–78. In particular, the Court ruled that avoiding an Establishment Clause violation did not justify the University's discrimination, because permitting religious speech into a public forum on a nondiscriminatory basis would not constitute an establishment. *Id.*

Applying the Lemon Test, Justice Powell found that the University's primary secular legislative purpose was the creation of a forum for the exchange of ideas; the Court found that the forum did not excessively entangle the University with religion; and the majority concluded that the forum's inclusion of religious speech would not have the primary effect of advancing religion because the University did not endorse the religious speech in the forum and because of the existence of both religious and non-religious speech in the forum. *Id.* at 271–75.

The Supreme Court, in subsequent cases, expanded on *Widmar's* reasoning. In *Board of Educ. of Westside Comm. Schs. v. Mergens*, 496 U.S. 226 (1990), the Court ruled that the federal Equal Access Act, which required secondary public schools (that received federal funding) to permit religious speech into their limited public fora, was consistent with the Establishment Clause. *See also Lamb's Chapel v. Center Moriches Union Free School Dist.*, 508 U.S. 384 (1993) (coming to the same conclusion in the primary and secondary school context under the Free Speech and Establishment Clauses); *Good News Club v. Milford Central Sch.*, 533 U.S. 98 (2001) (ruling that a grade school violated the Free Speech Clause when it excluded a religious student group from its limited public forum and that the grade school's exclusion was not justified by the Establishment Clause).

As discussed in **Chapter 1**, the Supreme Court articulated the rule that the Free Speech Clause required that governments admit religious speech into public fora on the same terms as other speech. In other words, the rules governing public fora are the same for all types of speech, including religious speech.

In the case below, the Court considered an interconnected question, which we had put on hold in **Chapter 1**: Does the government violate the Establishment Clause by allowing religious speech into public fora? And, relatedly, does the government violate the Establishment Clause by providing financial and other support to religious speech on the same terms as other speech, in a public forum? As you will see in the following case, the Court definitively answered these questions in the negative.

Rosenberger v.
Rector and Visitors of the University of Virginia
515 U.S. 819 (1995)

Justice Kennedy delivered the opinion of the Court.

The University of Virginia authorizes the payment of outside contractors for the printing costs of a variety of student publications. It withheld any authorization for payments on behalf of petitioners for the sole reason that their student paper "primarily promotes or manifests a particular belie[f] in or about a deity or an ultimate reality." That the paper did promote or manifest views within the defined exclusion seems plain enough. The challenge is to the University's regulation and its denial of authorization, the case raising issues under the Speech and Establishment Clauses of the First Amendment.

II

Based on the principles we have discussed, we hold that the regulation invoked to deny SAF [Student Activity Fund] support, both in its terms and in its application to these petitioners, is a denial of their right of free speech guaranteed by the First Amendment. It remains to be considered whether the violation following from the

University's action is excused by the necessity of complying with the Constitution's prohibition against state establishment of religion. We turn to that question.

III

Before its brief on the merits in this Court, the University had argued at all stages of the litigation that inclusion of WAP's contractors in SAF funding authorization would violate the Establishment Clause. Indeed, that is the ground on which the University prevailed in the Court of Appeals.

A central lesson of our decisions is that a significant factor in upholding governmental programs in the face of Establishment Clause attack is their neutrality towards religion. We have decided a series of cases addressing the receipt of government benefits where religion or religious views are implicated in some degree. The first case in our modern Establishment Clause jurisprudence was *Everson v. Board of Ed. of Ewing*, 330 U.S. 1 (1947). We have held that the guarantee of neutrality is respected, not offended, when the government, following neutral criteria and evenhanded policies, extends benefits to recipients whose ideologies and viewpoints, including religious ones, are broad and diverse. More than once have we rejected the position that the Establishment Clause even justifies, much less requires, a refusal to extend free speech rights to religious speakers who participate in broad-reaching government programs neutral in design.

The governmental program here is neutral toward religion. There is no suggestion that the University created it to advance religion or adopted some ingenious device with the purpose of aiding a religious cause. The object of the SAF is to open a forum for speech and to support various student enterprises, including the publication of newspapers, in recognition of the diversity and creativity of student life.... The category of support here is for "student news, information, opinion, entertainment, or academic communications media groups," of which Wide Awake was 1 of 15 in the 1990 school year. WAP did not seek a subsidy because of its Christian editorial viewpoint; it sought funding as a student journal, which it was.

The neutrality of the program distinguishes the student fees from a tax levied for the direct support of a church or group of churches. A tax of that sort, of course, would run contrary to Establishment Clause concerns dating from the earliest days of the Republic. The apprehensions of our predecessors involved the levying of taxes upon the public for the sole and exclusive purpose of establishing and supporting specific sects. The exaction here, by contrast, is a student activity fee designed to reflect the reality that student life in its many dimensions includes the necessity of wide-ranging speech and inquiry and that student expression is an integral part of the University's educational mission. The fee is mandatory, [b]ut the $14 paid each semester by the students is not a general tax designed to raise revenue for the University. The SAF cannot be used for unlimited purposes, much less the illegitimate purpose of supporting one religion. Much like the arrangement in *Widmar*, the money goes to a special fund from which any group of students with CIO status can draw for purposes consistent with the University's educational mission; and to the extent the student is interested in speech, withdrawal is permitted to cover the whole spectrum of speech, whether it manifests a religious view, an antireligious view, or neither. Our decision, then, cannot be read as addressing an expenditure from a general tax fund. Here, the disbursements from the fund go to private contractors for the cost of printing that which is protected under the Speech Clause of the First Amendment. This is a far cry from a general public assessment designed and effected to provide financial support for a church.

Government neutrality is apparent in the State's overall scheme in a further meaningful respect. The program respects the critical difference "between *government* speech endorsing religion, which the Establishment Clause forbids, and *private* speech endorsing religion, which the Free Speech and Free Exercise Clauses protect." In this case, "the government has not fostered or encouraged" any mistaken impression that the student newspapers speak for the University. The University has taken pains to disassociate itself from the private speech involved in this case[,] and there is no real likelihood that the speech in question is being either endorsed or coerced by the State.

It does not violate the Establishment Clause for a public university to grant access to its facilities on a religion-neutral basis to a wide spectrum of student groups, including groups that use meeting rooms for sectarian activities, accompanied by some devotional exercises. This is so even where the upkeep, maintenance, and repair of the facilities attributed to those uses are paid from a student activities fund to which students are required to contribute. The government usually acts by spending money. Even the provision of a meeting room, as in *Mergens* and *Widmar*, involved governmental expenditure, if only in the form of electricity and heating or cooling costs. The error made by the Court of Appeals, as well as by the dissent, lies in focusing on the money that is undoubtedly expended by the government, rather than on the nature of the benefit received by the recipient. If the expenditure of governmental funds is prohibited whenever those funds pay for a service that is, pursuant to a religion-neutral program, used by a group for sectarian purposes, then *Widmar*, *Mergens*, and *Lamb's Chapel* would have to be overruled. Given our holdings in these cases, it follows that a public university may maintain its own computer facility and give student groups access to that facility, including the use of the printers, on a religion neutral, say first-come-first-served, basis. If a religious student organization obtained access on that religion-neutral basis and used a computer to compose or a printer or copy machine to print speech with a religious content or viewpoint, the State's action in providing the group with access would no more violate the Establishment Clause than would giving those groups access to an assembly hall. There is no difference in logic or principle, and no difference of constitutional significance, between a school using its funds to operate a facility to which students have access, and a school paying a third-party contractor to operate the facility on its behalf. The latter occurs here. The University provides printing services to a broad spectrum of student newspapers qualified as CIO's by reason of their officers and membership. Any benefit to religion is incidental to the government's provision of secular services for secular purposes on a religion-neutral basis. Printing is a routine, secular, and recurring attribute of student life.

By paying outside printers, the University in fact attains a further degree of separation from the student publication, for it avoids the duties of supervision, escapes the costs of upkeep, repair, and replacement attributable to student use, and has a clear record of costs. As a result, and as in *Widmar*, the University can charge the SAF, and not the taxpayers as a whole, for the discrete activity in question. It would be formalistic for us to say that the University must forfeit these advantages and provide the services itself in order to comply with the Establishment Amendment Clause. It is, of course, true that if the State pays a church's bills it is subsidizing it, and we must guard against this abuse. That is not a danger here, based on the considerations we have advanced and for the additional reason that the student publication is not a religious institution, at least in the usual sense of that term as used in our case law, and it is not a religious organization as used in the University's own regulations. It is instead a publication involved in a pure forum for the expression of ideas, ideas that would be both incomplete and chilled were the Constitution to be interpreted to require that state officials and courts scan the publication to ferret out views that principally manifest a belief in a divine being.

Were the dissent's view to become law, it would require the University, in order to avoid a constitutional violation, to scrutinize the content of student speech, lest the expression in question—speech otherwise protected by the Constitution—contain too great a religious content. The dissent, in fact, anticipates such censorship as "crucial" in distinguishing between "works characterized by the evangelism of Wide Awake and writing that merely happens to express views that a given religion might approve." That eventuality raises the specter of governmental censorship, to ensure that all student writings and publications meet some baseline standard of secular orthodoxy. To impose that standard on student speech at a university is to imperil the very sources of free speech and expression. As we recognized in *Widmar*, official censorship would be far more inconsistent with the Establishment Clause's dictates than would governmental provision of secular printing services on a religion-blind basis.

> "[E]ven if the distinction drew an arguably principled line, it is highly doubtful that it would lie within the judicial competence to administer. Merely to draw the distinction would require the university—and ultimately the courts—to inquire into the significance of words and practices to different religious faiths, and in varying circumstances by the same faith. Such inquiries would tend inevitably to entangle the State with religion in a manner forbidden by our cases."

To obey the Establishment Clause, it was not necessary for the University to deny eligibility to student publications because of their viewpoint. The neutrality commanded of the State by the separate Clauses of the First Amendment was compromised by the University's course of action. The viewpoint discrimination inherent in the University's regulation required public officials to scan and interpret student publications to discern their underlying philosophic assumptions respecting religious theory and belief. That course of action was a denial of the right of free speech and would risk fostering a pervasive bias or hostility to religion, which could undermine the very neutrality the Establishment Clause requires. There is no Establishment Clause violation in the University's honoring its duties under the Free Speech Clause.

JUSTICE O'CONNOR, concurring.

This case lies at the intersection of the principle of government neutrality and the prohibition on state funding of religious activities. When two bedrock principles so conflict, understandably neither can provide the definitive answer. Resolution depends on the hard task of judging—sifting through the details and determining whether the challenged program offends the Establishment Clause.

[C]ertain considerations specific to the program at issue lead me to conclude that by providing the same assistance to Wide Awake that it does to other publications, the University would not be endorsing the magazine's religious perspective. First, the student organizations, at the University's insistence, remain strictly independent of the University. Second, financial assistance is distributed in a manner that ensures its use only for permissible purposes. Third, assistance is provided to the religious publication in a context that makes improbable any perception of government endorsement of the religious message. Finally, although the question is not presented here, I note the possibility that the student fee is susceptible to a Free Speech Clause challenge by an objecting student that she should not be compelled to pay for speech with which she disagrees.

JUSTICE THOMAS, concurring.

Stripped of its flawed historical premise, the dissent's argument is reduced to the claim that our Establishment Clause jurisprudence permits neutrality in the context of access to government *facilities* but requires discrimination in access to government *funds*. The dissent purports to locate the prohibition against "direct public funding" at the "heart" of the Establishment Clause, but this conclusion fails to confront historical examples of funding that date back to the time of the founding. To take but one famous example, both Houses of the First Congress elected chaplains, and that Congress enacted legislation providing for an annual salary of $500 to be paid out of the Treasury. Madison himself was a member of the committee that recommended the chaplain system in the House.

The historical evidence of government support for religious entities through property tax exemptions is also overwhelming. In my view, the dissent's acceptance of this tradition puts to rest the notion that the Establishment Clause bars monetary aid to religious groups even when the aid is equally available to other groups. A tax exemption in many cases is economically and functionally indistinguishable from a direct monetary subsidy Whether the benefit is provided at the front or back end of the taxation process, the financial aid to religious groups is undeniable.

Consistent application of the dissent's "no-aid" principle would require that "'a church could not be protected by the police and fire departments, or have its public sidewalk kept in repair.'" The dissent admits that "evenhandedness may become important to ensuring that religious interests are not inhibited." Surely the dissent must concede, however, that the same result should obtain whether the government provides the populace with fire protection by reimbursing the costs of smoke detectors and overhead sprinkler systems or by establishing a public fire department. If churches may benefit on equal terms with other groups in the latter program—that is, if a public fire department may extinguish fires at churches—then they may also benefit on equal terms in the former program.

Our Nation's tradition of allowing religious adherents to participate in evenhanded government programs is hardly limited to the class of "essential public benefits" identified by the dissent. A broader tradition can be traced at least as far back as the First Congress, which ratified the Northwest Ordinance of 1787. Article III of that famous enactment of the Confederation Congress had provided: "Religion, morality, and knowledge ... being necessary to good government and the happiness of mankind, schools and the means of education shall forever be encouraged." Congress subsequently set aside federal lands in the Northwest Territory and other territories for the use of schools. Many of the schools that enjoyed the benefits of these land grants undoubtedly were church-affiliated sectarian institutions as there was no requirement that the schools be "public."

Thus, history provides an answer for the constitutional question posed by this case, but it is not the one given by the dissent. The dissent identifies no evidence that the Framers intended to disable religious entities from participating on neutral terms in evenhanded government programs. The evidence that does exist points in the opposite direction and provides ample support for today's decision.

JUSTICE SOUTER, with whom JUSTICE STEVENS, JUSTICE GINSBURG, and JUSTICE BREYER join, dissenting.

I

A

The Court's difficulties [become] all the more clear after a closer look at Wide Awake than the majority opinion affords. The character of the magazine is candidly disclosed on the opening page of the first issue, where the editor-in-chief announces Wide Awake's mission in a letter to the readership signed, "Love in Christ": it is "to challenge Christians to live, in word and deed, according to the faith they proclaim and to encourage students to consider what a personal relationship with Jesus Christ means." The masthead of every issue bears St. Paul's exhortation, that "[t]he hour has come for you to awake from your slumber, because our salvation is nearer now than when we first believed. Romans 13:11." Each issue of Wide Awake contained in the record makes good on the editor's promise and echoes the Apostle's call to accept salvation.

This writing is no merely descriptive examination of religious doctrine or even of ideal Christian practice in confronting life's social and personal problems. Nor is it merely the expression of editorial opinion that incidentally coincides with Christian ethics and reflects a Christian view of human obligation. It is straightforward exhortation to enter into a relationship with God as revealed in Jesus Christ, and to satisfy a series of moral obligations derived from the teachings of Jesus Christ. These are not the words of "student news, information, opinion, entertainment, or academic communicatio[n]" (in the language of the University's funding criterion).

Using public funds for the direct subsidization of preaching the word is categorically forbidden under the Establishment Clause, and if the Clause was meant to accomplish nothing else, it was meant to bar this use of public money. Evidence on the subject antedates even the Bill of Rights itself, as may be seen in the writings of Madison, whose authority on questions about the meaning of the Establishment Clause is well settled. Four years before the First Congress proposed the First Amendment, Madison gave his opinion on the legitimacy of using public funds for religious purposes, in the Memorial and Remonstrance Against Religious Assessments, which played the central role in ensuring the defeat of the Virginia tax assessment bill in 1786 and framed the debate upon which the Religion Clauses stand: "Who does not see that ... the same authority which can force a citizen to contribute three pence only of his property for the support of any one establishment, may force him to conform to any other establishment in all cases whatsoever?"

Madison wrote against a background in which nearly every Colony had exacted a tax for church support. Madison's Remonstrance captured the colonists' "conviction that individual religious liberty could be achieved best under a government which was stripped of all power to tax, to support, or otherwise to assist any or all religions, or to interfere with the beliefs of any religious individual or group." Their sentiment, as expressed by Madison in Virginia, led not only to the defeat of Virginia's tax assessment bill, but also directly to passage of the Virginia Bill for Establishing Religious Freedom, written by Thomas Jefferson. That bill's preamble declared that "to compel a man to furnish contributions of money for the propagation of opinions which he disbelieves, is sinful and tyrannical," and its text provided "[t]hat no man shall be compelled to frequent or support any religious worship, place, or ministry whatsoever." We have "previously recognized that the provisions of the First Amendment, in the drafting and adoption of which Madison and Jefferson played such leading roles, had the same objective and were intended to provide the same protection against governmental intrusion on religious liberty as the Virginia statute."

The principle against direct funding with public money is patently violated by the contested use of today's student activity fee. Like today's taxes generally, the fee is Madison's three pence. The University exercises the power of the State to compel a student to pay it, and the use of any part of it for the direct support of religious activity thus strikes at what we have repeatedly held to be the heart of the prohibition on establishment. *Everson*, 330 U.S., at 15–16 ("The 'establishment of religion' clause ... means at least this.... No tax in any amount, large or small, can be levied to support any religious activities or institutions, whatever they may be called, or whatever form they may adopt to teach or practice religion").

The Court, accordingly, has never before upheld direct state funding of the sort of proselytizing published in Wide Awake and, in fact, has categorically condemned state programs directly aiding religious activity.

B

Nevertheless, even without the encumbrance of detail from Wide Awake's actual pages, the Court finds something sufficiently religious about the magazine to require examination under the Establishment Clause, and one may therefore ask why the unequivocal prohibition on direct funding does not lead the Court to conclude that funding would be unconstitutional. The answer is that the Court focuses on a subsidiary body of law, which it correctly states but ultimately misapplies. That subsidiary body of law accounts for the Court's substantial attention to the fact that the University's funding scheme is "neutral," in the formal sense that it makes funds available on an evenhanded basis to secular and sectarian applicants alike. While this is indeed true and relevant under our cases, it does not alone satisfy the requirements of the Establishment Clause. This recognition reflects the Court's appreciation of two general rules: that whenever affirmative government aid ultimately benefits religion, the Establishment Clause requires some justification beyond evenhandedness on the government's part; and that direct public funding of core sectarian activities, even if accomplished pursuant to an evenhanded program, would be entirely inconsistent with the Establishment Clause and would strike at the very heart of the Clause's protection.

At the heart of the Establishment Clause stands the prohibition against direct public funding, but that prohibition does not answer the questions that occur at the margins of the Clause's application. Is any government activity that provides any incidental benefit to religion likewise unconstitutional? Would it be wrong to put out fires in burning churches, wrong to pay the bus fares of students on the way to parochial schools, wrong to allow a grantee of special education funds to spend them at a religious college? These are the questions that call for drawing lines, and it is in drawing them that evenhandedness becomes important. However the Court may in the past have phrased its line-drawing test, the question whether such benefits are provided on an evenhanded basis has been relevant, for the question addresses one aspect of the issue whether a law is truly neutral with respect to religion (that is, whether the law either "advance[s] [or] inhibit[s] religion)." In the doubtful cases (those not involving direct public funding), where there is initially room for argument about a law's effect, evenhandedness serves to weed out those laws that impermissibly advance religion by channelling aid to it exclusively. Evenhandedness is therefore a prerequisite to further enquiry into the constitutionality of a doubtful law, but evenhandedness goes no further. It does not guarantee success under Establishment Clause scrutiny.

Evenhandedness as one element of a permissibly attenuated benefit is, of course, a far cry from evenhandedness as a sufficient condition of constitutionality for direct financial support of religious proselytization, and our cases have unsurprisingly repudiated any such attempt to cut the Establishment Clause down to a mere prohibition against unequal direct aid.

C

1

If the Court's suggestion is that this feature of the funding program [that under the University's Guidelines, funds are sent to the printer chosen by Wide Awake, rather than to Wide Awake itself] brings this case into line with *Witters*, *Mueller*, and *Zobrest*, the Court has misread those cases, which turned on the fact that the choice to benefit religion was made by a nonreligious third party standing between the government and a religious institution. Here there is no third party standing between the government and the ultimate religious beneficiary to break the circuit by its independent discretion to put state money to religious use. The printer, of course, has no option to take the money and use it to print a secular journal instead of Wide Awake. It only gets the money because of its contract to print a message of religious evangelism at the direction of Wide Awake, and it will receive payment only for doing precisely that. The formalism of distinguishing between payment to Wide Awake so it can pay an approved bill and payment of the approved bill itself cannot be the basis of a decision of constitutional law. If this indeed were a critical distinction, the Constitution would permit a State to pay all the bills of any religious institution; in fact, despite the Court's purported adherence to the no-direct-funding principle, the State could simply hand out credit cards to religious institutions and honor the monthly statements (so long as someone could devise an evenhanded umbrella to cover the whole scheme).

2

It is more probable, however, that the Court's reference to the printer goes to a different attempt to justify the payment. On this purported justification, the payment to the printer is significant only as the last step in an argument resting on the assumption that a public university may give a religious group the use of any of its equipment or facilities so long as secular groups are likewise eligible. The Court starts with the cases of *Widmar*, *Mergens*, and *Lamb's Chapel*, in which religious groups were held to be entitled to access for speaking in government buildings open generally for that purpose. The Court reasons that the availability of a forum has economic value; and that economically there is no difference between the University's provision of the value of the room and the value, say, of the University's printing equipment; and that therefore the University must be able to provide the use of the latter. Since it may do that, the argument goes, it would be unduly formalistic to draw the line at paying for an outside printer, who simply does what the magazine's publishers could have done with the University's own printing equipment.

The argument is as unsound as it is simple, and the first of its troubles emerges from an examination of the cases relied upon to support it. The common factual thread running through *Widmar*, *Mergens*, and *Lamb's Chapel*, is that a governmental institution created a limited forum for the use of students in a school or college, or for the public at large, but sought to exclude speakers with religious messages. But each case drew ultimately on unexceptionable Speech Clause doctrine treating the evangelist, the Salvation Army, the millennialist, or the Hare Krishna like any other speaker in a public forum. It was the preservation of free speech on the model of the street corner that supplied the justification going beyond the requirement of evenhandedness.

The Court's claim of support from these forum-access cases is ruled out by the very scope of their holdings. While they do indeed allow a limited benefit to religious speakers, they rest on the recognition that all speakers are entitled to use the street corner (even though the State paves the roads and provides police protection to everyone on the street) and on the analogy between the public street corner and open classroom space. Thus, the Court found it significant that the classroom speakers would engage in traditional speech activities in these forums, too, even though the rooms (like street corners) require some incidental state spending to maintain them. The analogy breaks down entirely, however, if the cases are read more broadly than the Court wrote them, to cover more than forums for literal speaking. There is no traditional street corner printing provided by the government on equal terms to all comers, and the forum cases cannot be lifted to a higher plane of generalization without admitting that new economic benefits are being extended directly to religion in clear violation of the principle barring direct aid. The argument from economic equivalence thus breaks down on recognizing that the direct state aid it would support is not mitigated by the street corner analogy in the service of free speech. Absent that, the rule against direct aid stands as a bar to printing services as well as printers.

3

It must, indeed, be a recognition of just this point that leads the Court to take a third tack, not in coming up with yet a third attempt at justification within the rules of existing case law, but in recasting the scope of the Establishment Clause in ways that make further affirmative justification unnecessary. The opinion of the Court concludes that the activity fee is not a tax, and then proceeds to find the aid permissible on the legal assumption that the bar against direct aid applies only to aid derived from tax revenue.

Although it was a taxation scheme that moved Madison to write in the first instance, the Court has never held that government resources obtained without taxation could be used for direct religious support, and our cases on direct government aid have frequently spoken in terms in no way limited to tax revenues.

Allowing nontax funds to be spent on religion would, in fact, fly in the face of clear principle. [A]ny such use of them would ignore one the dual objectives of the Establishment Clause, which was meant not only to protect individuals and their republics from the destructive consequences of mixing government and religion, but to protect religion from a corrupting dependence on support from the Government. Since the corrupting effect of government support does not turn on whether the Government's own money comes from taxation or gift or the sale of public lands, the Establishment Clause could hardly relax its vigilance simply because tax revenue was not implicated. Accordingly, in the absence of a forthright disavowal, one can only assume that the Court does not mean to eliminate one half of the Establishment Clause's justification.

Exercise 14:

1. What was UVA's argument for why it could not provide funds to WAP? Articulate UVA's argument in terms of the Lemon Test.

2. Describe the majority's analysis of UVA's claim. Why did funding WAP not violate the Establishment Clause?

3. How did the majority cabin the scope of its authorization of government money flowing to religious organizations? Why, after this decision, could the government not directly distribute tax revenues, in a neutral manner, to religious groups?

4. Justice O'Connor's endorsement analysis concluded that a reasonable person would not perceive that UVA was endorsing WAP and its Christian message. Is that true? What facts would a reasonable observer observe: that WAP was a Christian message, and WAP was a UVA student group that received UVA money? Is that all, or would the observer know other facts? How do you know what the observer would know?

5. How did the dissent counter Justice Thomas' historical examples of governmental financial contributions to religious organizations, both through direct land and monetary grants, and indirectly through tax breaks? Was Justice Souter's response persuasive?

6. Relatedly, Justices Thomas and Souter disagreed about how to characterize the import of governmental provision of services, such as fire and police protection, to religious organizations. Describe the Justices' respective positions, and which Justice's position the practice supported. Is there a reasonable way Justice Souter can distinguish those services from UVA's provision of funds to WAP?

7. What limit, if any, was there to Justice Thomas' reasoning? Why, on Justice Thomas' reasoning, could the government not distribute tax revenues, in a neutral manner, to religious groups?

8. Justice Souter laid a lot of emphasis on the fact that the governmental benefit at issue was money. Should that fact have played such a significant role?

9. What alternative outcome did Justice Souter propose? That religious student groups should be excluded from university fora like this?

10. Justice Souter argued that WAP was a religious institution. How would Justice Souter distinguish between student groups that fit in the forum and those that do not, because they are too religious?

11. Justice Scouter distinguished the Court's earlier public forum case law from UVA's student funding program. Upon what basis did Justice Scouter do so? Was the majority or Justice Souter correct on application of this precedent to UVA's program?

12. How would this case have come out under (both versions of) the Coercion Test? The Tradition Test? The Divisiveness Test?

13. *Rosenberger* was decided in 1995. Earlier, we covered *Zelman v. Simmons-Harris*, a 2002 decision. In what ways did *Rosenberger* prepare the ground for *Zelman*? In what ways is *Zelman* a move beyond *Rosenberger*?

In 2001, the Supreme Court decided *Good News Bible Club v. Milford Central School*, 533 U.S. 98 (2001). The Good News Bible Club, a school group, requested and was denied permission by the school to utilize a classroom after school for the Club's activities, which included singing songs, learning Bible lessons, memorizing Scripture, and prayer. The School justified its decision on the basis of the Establishment Clause. The Court, in a six-three decision authored by Justice Thomas, followed *Rosenberger's* teaching, and ruled in favor of the Club. The Court found that permitting a religious student group to utilize the school facilities after school, on a neutral basis like other student groups, would not coerce participation in religion or endorse religion. *Id.* at 114–20.

———————

At this point in your legal education, you have learned a wide variety of areas of law, including constitutional law. The Establishment Clause material you have just finished, has to rank as one of the least coherent bodies of law you have encountered. Assuming you agree with this description, how do you account for it? Why has this body of law become tangled when other, equally controversial areas of law, such as substantive due process, remain relatively more coherent?

Table of Cases

Index

[References are to sections.]